ORGANIZATIONAL BEHAVIOR AND MANAGEMENT IN LAW ENFORCEMENT

FOURTH EDITION

Gennaro F. Vito, PH.D.

Professor,
Department of Criminal Justice and Southern Police Institute,
University of Louisville

John C. Reed, PH.D.

Associate Director,
Southern Police Institute,
University of Louisville

Harry W. More, PH.D.

Late Professor Emeritus,
Department of Justice Studies,
San Jose State University

 Pearson

Vice President, Portfolio Management: Andrew Gilfillan
Portfolio Manager: Gary Bauer
Editorial Assistant: Lynda Cramer
Vice President, Product Marketing: Brad Parkins
Product Marketing Manager: Heather Taylor
Product Marketing Assistant: Liz Bennett
Director, Digital Studio and Content Production: Brian Hyland
Managing Producer: Jennifer Sargunar
Content Producer: Rinki Kaur
Manager, Rights Management: Johanna Burke

Manufacturing Buyer: Deidra Headlee
Creative Digital Lead: Mary Siener
Full-Service Management and Composition: Integra Software Services Pvt. Ltd.
Full-Service Project Manager: Yohalakshmi Segar
Cover Design: Studio Montage
Cover Photos: Sergey Novikov/Shutterstock
Printer/Binder: LSC Communications, Inc.
Text Font: 11/13 Times LT Pro-Roman
Cover Printer: LSC Communications

Library of Congress Cataloging-in-Publication Data

Names: Vito, Gennaro F., author. | Reed, John C., author. | More, Harry W., author.
Title: Organizational behavior and management in law enforcement / Gennaro F. Vito, PH.D., Professor, Department of Criminal Justice and Southern Police Institute, University of Louisville, John C. Reed, PH.D., Associate Director, Southern Police Institute, University of Louisville, Harry W. More, PH.D., Late Professor Emeritus, Department of Justice Studies, San Jose State University.
Description: Fourth edition. | Upper Saddle River, New Jersey: Pearson Education, Inc., [2020] | Earliest edition entered under title; third edition entered under: More, Harry W.
Identifiers: LCCN 2018046348| ISBN 9780135186206 | ISBN 013518620X
Subjects: LCSH: Police administration. | Organizational behavior.
Classification: LCC HV7935 .O74 2020 | DDC 363.2068—dc23
   LC record available at https://lccn.loc.gov/2018046348

6 2020

ISBN-13: 978-0-13-518620-6
ISBN-10:   0-13-518620-X

Dedication

This text is dedicated to two individuals who made significant contributions to criminal justice education and exemplified a true spirit of professionalism in the preparation of students. They coauthored previous editions of this textbook.

WILLIAM F. WALSH, PH.D.

William F. Walsh is the former Director of the Southern Police Institute and Professor Emeritus in the Department of Criminal Justice. He holds a BA in Behavioral Science, an MA in Criminal Justice from John Jay College of Criminal Justice, and a Ph.D. in Sociology from Fordham University. A former Lieutenant with the New York City Police Department with 21 years of service, he has researched police and security issues and authored several articles in scholarly journals, monographs, book chapters and books on police administration, supervision, and management.

Before joining the University of Louisville, he served on the administration of justice faculty at The Pennsylvania State University, where he received the National Continuing Education Association Faculty Service Award in 1988. He has been a consultant to numerous United States law enforcement agencies and the national police forces of Hungary and Romania. The Academy of Criminal Justices Sciences awarded him the O.W. Wilson Award for his outstanding contributions to police education, research, and practice in 1999. In 2003, he received the Governor's Award for his contributions to Kentucky law enforcement. He was awarded the Melvin Shein Award by the Kentucky Law Enforcement Council in 2004 for Distinguished Service to the Kentucky Police Community. In 2006, he was named the first recipient of the James J. Fyfe Award for a lifetime of service and scholarship to the law enforcement profession by the Police Partnership of New York City. In 2008, Mayor Jerry E. Abramson of the city of Louisville, Kentucky, presented him with the Community Partnership Award for his services to the Louisville Metro Police Department.

Bill Walsh is our valued friend, mentor, colleague and collaborator. His knowledge guided our development and education as scholars of policing. His contributions to the Southern Police Institute influenced the careers of a generation of police administrators and impacted policing in our world. His influence on the fourth edition of this textbook is notable.

HARRY W. MORE, PH.D.

Harry W. More was Professor Emeritus at San Jose University where he served as chair of the Administration of Justice program. He held a B.S. in Criminology from the University of California at Berkeley, an M.S. in Public Administration from American University, and a Ph.D. in Political Science from the University of Idaho. His first teaching position was at Washington State University. Also, he was the founder and chairman of the Department of Criminology at Indiana University of Pennsylvania. He served as a juvenile probation officer and a Special Agent in the U.S. Secret Service.

Active in professional organizations, Dr. More served as President of the Western Society of Criminology and received its Fellows Award in 1978. He was elected President of the Academy of Criminal Justice Sciences in 1980.

Harry More was an acclaimed scholar, publishing numerous articles in professional journals. His textbooks influenced the development of American police management—*Effective Police Management* (co-authored with Terry L. More) and *Effective Police Supervision* (co-authored with Larry Miller and Michael Braswell). The scholarship and contributions of the late Professor Harry More bolster the creation of the fourth edition of this textbook.

Contents

4

5

6

10

11

12

Foreword

Gennaro F. Vito, Ph.D.
Professor
University of Louisville

This text is the third revision of the original text. I found the first edition as I sought to find an organizational behavior textbook for a course offered in the Administrative Officer's Course in the Southern Police Institute at the University of Louisville. Then known as *Police Behavioral Management*, it filled the bill – a text covering organizational behavior from a law enforcement point of view. I was new to the AOC faculty but familiar with the subject due to my education in public administration and courses offered at The Ohio State University by Orlando Behling. The original text covered all the major topical areas and offered the bonus of case studies for classroom analysis and discussion. The use of case studies was a key feature of my education and provides students the opportunity to apply their knowledge to real-world situations.

Throughout the revision, we maintained these features and updated theoretical and research findings. Professors More and Walsh drew upon their professional experience as law enforcement administrators as well as university educators. Thus, they were a part of a distinguished group of distinguished police educators, including August Vollmer and his protégés – V.A. Leonard, O.W. Wilson and John P. Kenney as well as contemporaries such as Bruce Smith. My instruction also benefitted from studying the works of professors who contributed police administration and management – Gary Cordner. James Fyfe, Thomas Barker, Robert W. Taylor, Larry Gaines, and Paul Whisenand.

I have been involved in the education of in-service police students from the very start of my career. It began with a research methods seminar, certified under the California Peace Officers' Standards and Training program as a faculty member of the criminal justice department at California State University Long Beach. At Temple University, the department offered classes that were a part of the Philadelphia police academy training for rookies. I quickly learned in-service police students were quite different from my typical undergraduate students. They had little patience for material that was not relevant to their day-to-day work life. However, they were keenly interested, involved, and willing to share their experiences in the classroom.

We prepared this edition with these desires in mind. It represents our review of the state of the art in law enforcement management and organizational issues. We hope our audience will continue to find it useful as they deal with problems in their everyday work lives.

Preface

Management in contemporary police departments is constantly in flux. Police management has a rich history that is, for the most part, an integration of knowledge developed originally in the private sector. Most law enforcement agencies have evolved from a highly political style of policing to a more professional model and are currently developing a style based upon community and strategic policing. Within this context, police managers have become increasingly aware of social and individual behavior in the organization. When the quality of working life within the organization is good, it is easier to attain organizational goals and accommodate individual needs. The creation of positive relationships between line officers, between groups within the organization, and between police managers at every level is critical to the success of any police department. Police managers must recognize the ecology of the organization, accepting it as a dynamic social system. We focus on organizational behavior as a means of understanding both the complexity of the criminal justice organization and the interaction between officers and managers as they work to resolve community problems.

New to This Edition

This revision was intended to integrate new research into an organizational behavioral approach to police management and demonstrate the relationship between research in this dynamic and changing field and its application to the discipline. The text focuses on the discussion of problems and issues confronting contemporary police leaders. Also, it considers the interaction of police officers with the organization and the community. The substantial content revision includes:

- A reorganization of chapters as a result of comments rendered by reviewers. References and readings are current. The text contains new learning objectives with key terms listed at the front of each chapter and rendered as bold throughout the text to guide the student.
- Chapters feature classic and recent materials on organizational behavior. The issues examined are vital to the successful development of law enforcement agencies. New materials from on private sector management scholarship focus on leadership, decision making, and change.
- The text features 38 case studies based on law enforcement issues from the field. They provide instructors with materials to foster class discussion and analysis.

Today's police managers have to develop behavioral and social skills to deal effectively with a rapidly changing community and with the new generation of police officers. The modern police executive must integrate each member of the organization into the managerial process so that the organization can improve both its internal and external adaptive capabilities. Chapter 1 is the core to understanding the historical and managerial development of police organizations. The instructor should make every effort to emphasize the complexity of organizational development and managerial responsibility. Chapter 2 covers the integrative variable in a behavioral text namely –leadership. The second group of chapters (3–10) deals with the organizational processes. To deal with truly changing an organization, the student should understand the relationship between personality, beliefs, values, attitudes, motivation, and stress to individual and organizational behavior. The final chapter (12) emphasizes the interactive process in the organization – change. Regardless of the way the instructor decides to use the text and this manual, it should be used to maximize student learning. An effort is made in these chapters to present information that provides a real understanding of behavior in the organization.

We are also concerned with social behavior and organizational processes. Chapters consider key elements such as decision making (Chapter 8), power (Chapter 9), communications (Chapter 10), groups and the group process (Chapter 11), and the aspects of organizational change Chapter 12). The text presents behavioral theories and applies them to law enforcement organizations and the problems they face. We intend to help current and potential police managers understand the different beliefs and assumptions they hold about themselves, others, the organization, and the community.

Our goal is to emphasize the importance of human behavior and its relationship to organizational processes. The transition from theoretical to practical has been accomplished by providing numerous realistic examples throughout the text and by the inclusion of current organizational behavior research. Also, we offer real case studies to stimulate class discussion and active learning. Tables and figures amplify and reinforce important points discussed in each chapter. In addition to a Summary, each chapter has sections entitled: Learning Objectives, Key Terms, Discussion Topics and Questions, and For Further Reading. Each of these features makes the text user-friendly and provides a range of activities to maximize instructor and student interaction. Lastly, the text has been written using an informal writing style. The experience of the authors is that students respond to it with a great deal of enthusiasm.

Organizational Behavior and Management in Law Enforcement is also the product of our instruction in the Administrative Officers' Course (AOC) in the Southern Police Institute at the University of Louisville. The discussion and issues raised by our law enforcement manager students illuminate our scholarship.

Instructor Supplements

Instructor's Manual with Test Bank. Includes content outlines for classroom discussion, teaching suggestions, and answers to selected end-of-chapter questions from the text. This also contains a Word document version of the test bank.

TestGen. This computerized test generation system gives you maximum flexibility in creating and administering tests on paper, electronically, or online. It provides state-of-the-art features for viewing and editing test bank questions, dragging a selected question into a test you are creating, and printing sleek, formatted tests in a variety of layouts. Select test items from test banks included with TestGen for quick test creation, or write your own questions from scratch. TestGen's random generator provides the option to display different text or calculated number values each time questions are used.

PowerPoint Presentations. Our presentations offer clear, straightforward outlines and notes to use for class lectures or study materials. Photos, illustrations, charts, and tables from the book are included in the presentations when applicable. To access supplementary materials online, instructors need to request an instructor access code. Go to **www.pearsonhighered.com/irc**, where you can register for an instructor access code. Within 48 hours after registering, you will receive a confirming email, including an instructor access code. Once you have received your code, go to the site and log on for full instructions on downloading the materials you wish to use.

Alternate Versions

eBooks. This text is also available in multiple eBook formats. These are an exciting new choice for students looking to save money. As an alternative to purchasing the printed textbook students can purchase an electronic version of the same content. With an eTextbook, students can search the text, make notes online, print out reading assignments that incorporate lecture notes, and bookmark important passages for later review. For more information, visit your favorite online eBook reseller or visit **www.mypearsonstore.com**.

Acknowledgments

Numerous individuals and organizations contributed to the completion of this textbook by either providing material or granting permission to reproduce material contained in other publications. We want to thank the following people, who provided the information utilized in the preparation of *Organizational Behavior and Management in Law Enforcement*:

James Beeks, Sr., Kennewaw State University; Phoenix University; Andrew Gulcher, El Camino College; Patrick Webb, St. Augustine's University; Donald R. Burr, Retired Councilman, Campbell, CA; James D. Sewell (retired), State Department of Law Enforcement, FL; Gary Leonard, Chief (retired), Sandy City, UT; William J. Winters, Chief (retired), Chula Vista, CA; Joseph McNamara, Hoover Institute, Stanford, CA; O. Ray Shipley, Chief (retired) Medford, OR; Director, U.S. Secret Service, Washington, DC; Louis A. Mayo, Police Association; William Nay (retired), U.S. Department of Energy, Washington, DC; and Charlotte Police Department, Charlotte, NC.

We extend a special thanks to our many law enforcement officer students in the Administrative Officers' Course classes in the Southern Police Institute at the University of Louisville for their comments on previous versions of this textbook. Our three anonymous reviews provided very thoughtful and helpful analysis of the third edition of the text. Their comments and suggestions guided our revision of the manuscript.

Finally, we acknowledge the contributions of our fellow faculty members and the University of Louisville Department of Criminal Justice and Southern Police Institute for their thoughtful and sometimes informal discussions about organizational behavior and theory.

GFV
JCR
HWM

1

DYNAMICS OF MANAGEMENT

Managers and Organizational Behavior

Learning Objectives

1. Define *management*.
2. Identify and describe the management functions.
3. Identify and describe the three levels of organizational management.
4. Describe the skills managers use to achieve their objectives.
5. Identify the new emerging police manager's role.
6. Define what is meant by organizational behavior.
7. Identify the four types of behavior with which a police manager should be concerned.

Key Terms

controlling
control function
executive/strategic level
four primary functions of group behavior
individual behavior
interpersonal behavior
leading
learning organizations
line and staff managers
management
management functions

manager
managerial levels
managerial skills
middle management/administrative level
operational manager expectations
organizational behavior
organizing
planning
supervisory/technical level
technical/operational level

Police departments are government organizations that are created to provide public safety for defined jurisdictional areas such as towns, boroughs, cities, counties, or states. The Justice Department's Bureau of Justice Statistics reports there were 750,340 full-time sworn law enforcement officers, serving in a total of 17,398 state and local police departments in the United States.[1] Police officers are responsible for safeguarding lives and property, maintaining the quality of community life, and protecting the constitutional rights of everyone, regardless of political or social persuasion. They fulfill this mission by providing a variety of services that include responding to emergency calls for service, preventing crime, rendering first-responder aid, enforcing laws and ordinances, resolving disputes, regulating traffic, investigating criminal events, and arresting violators. A police department's chief executive and his or her management team are expected to provide organizational direction and performance oversight to achieve the department's mission effectively and efficiently. Police managers are responsible for the achievement of organizational goals and objectives through the management of their employees' performance. The **direction** and oversight of employees are accomplished through a process that involves the following activities:

CASE STUDY   Lieutenants Smits and Miles

In a large metropolitan police department, two sergeants were promoted to lieutenant at the same time, and both were assigned to the patrol division. Within six months, Lt. Marge Smits proved to be a very competent and effective manager. Unfortunately, Lt. Roger Miles was less than successful. Upper management is becoming genuinely concerned about Lt. Miles's inability to function as a manager. Capt. William Proctor is completing six-month reviews for each of the lieutenants and is truly perplexed about this situation. Both officers had performed outstandingly in their former positions, but Smits has risen to the challenge of her new position, while Miles demonstrates an inability to adjust to his.

Lt. Smits finds that the demands of her new position contrast sharply with what was expected of her when she was a sergeant. When she was a first-line supervisor, she was expected to function as an operational expert, focusing on the performance of her officers and leaving command or managerial decisions to upper management. Smits views her role as something entirely different than anything she has ever done; she relishes the interaction with the personnel she manages and the challenge of accomplishing goals and objectives through others. On assuming her new job, she immediately reviewed the personnel files for each of the supervisors and officers in her unit and became familiar with their knowledge, skills, and abilities. Utilizing this information, she has little difficulty in attaining unit objectives, starting to identify individual weaknesses and working with her supervisors to improve employee performance. When officers accomplish organizational objectives, she has her supervisors give them immediate feedback. She works diligently to improve her coaching skills and provide positive leadership.

Roger Miles, who had an exceptional record in his previous position, is clearly lost as a lieutenant. His primary concern is to scrutinize every officer's performance to such an extent that he can always find an error or omission. In each instance, the supervisor and the officer is made aware of inadequate performance. Lt. Miles intensifies his managerial control by paying careful attention to every incident and report. Nothing is too small to correct. As a result, he undermines the role of his supervisors, and unit objectives fall by the wayside.

His intensive supervision dominates the relationship between Lt. Miles, his supervisors, and the officers in the unit. Miles does not tolerate errors because he believes they reflect poorly on his leadership skills. Lt. Miles personifies the "See Me" syndrome where subordinates find their mailboxes filled with memos asking for further information or clarification. The officers have reached the point where it seems to be more important to respond to memos than to perform police work.

Lt. Smits is functioning as a manager. Lt. Miles is performing as an organizational enforcer. Capt. Proctor prefers the former. Management is a unique activity requiring the application of distinct skills. Lt. Miles feels comfortable performing tasks best done by first-line supervisors. The situation in which Lt. Miles finds himself is typical. It continually challenges managers such as Capt. Proctor. This dilemma demands a solution.

Capt. Proctor expects Lt. Miles to accomplish departmental goals through the supervisors and officers he is managing and to refrain from performing nonmanagerial tasks. What should Capt. Proctor do to get Lt. Miles to perform as a manager? Some managers feel this is "Who Wants to Be a Millionaire?" question—one that is easy to ask but difficult to resolve. Our purpose here is to help you understand why such leadership problems arise, how they can be analyzed, and what techniques are available to resolve the problems.

To understand why an employee does not perform at their assignment level (or performs inadequately) will probably require a manager not only to view the employee as an individual but also to examine his or her relationship to the group and the organization.

What is the responsibility of Capt. Proctor in this case? How should he begin to analyze the performance of Lt. Miles? Does Lt. Miles need training? Does he need additional mentoring or resources to accomplish his job? These questions illustrate the complex problems managers encounter.

This case focuses on the reality of how and what occurs in an organization. Employees adapt to their position differently. Police managers must learn to analyze their employee's performance problems and develop a plan to correct existing problems.

---

1. Developing a departmental mission, vision, goals, and operational objectives
2. Creating strategic, operational, procedural, tactical, and budgetary plans
3. Creation of an organizational structure focused on ensuring fulfillment of mission and performance objectives
4. Employment of a leadership direction and style that, while focused on mission fulfillment, will also achieve willing compliance and support from employees of the department and members of the community
5. Controlling and assessing departmental activities through measurement, evaluation, and—when necessary—redirection
6. Ensuring that all members of the department are competent and adhere to the highest standards of integrity and ethics

The importance of this managerial process is vital. It is hard to imagine any department operating effectively without it.

Police departments are characterized by authority relationships and a division of labor that, depending on their size, can be simple or complex. Research has consistently found that police work influences the behavior of those who perform it.[2] Through their daily work, officers can develop a sense of pride, belonging, and accomplishment or they can experience hostility, anger, stress, and frustration. Organizational design and management styles can enhance, limit, or inhibit employee coordination, cooperation, and mission fulfillment.[3] However, managers must understand the effects of individual behavior on their organization as well as the impact of the organization on individual and group behavior. The more managers understand their role and the impact of human behavior in the work setting, the more effective they will be in achieving organizational objectives.

Police managers are becoming increasingly aware of the need to understand human behavior in the workplace. Through the study of organizational behavior, they can begin to understand not only why organizations are such complex entities but also how their behavior as managers and their interaction with their officers can affect the organization.

Management Defined

A **manager** is a person who plans, organizes, leads, and controls the work of others so that the organization achieves its goals.[4] The manager serves the critical function of linking the organization's mission, its desired goals, and its operational accomplishment. In this text, we define *management* as *a continuing process that includes all activities focusing on the identification, improvement, and attainment of objectives by the application of organizational resources.* Management is also a behavioral relationship between managers and their employees.

This definition is dynamic, and based on the fundamental concept, positive management of a police organization is the only way of maximizing the effectiveness of resources, both human and technical, to achieve departmental goals. It defines the concept of managing regarding what managers *do* and their relationship with those they manage.

Management Functions

Our definition of management can be accepted and understood much more readily through an understanding of the responsibilities of a manager. The primary purpose of all managers is to achieve results effectively and efficiently through the individuals under their command. In addition to achieving performance results, the police manager is also responsible for the achievement of results. The sensitivity of the police role, in a democratic society with its legal constraints on police use of authority, means that the method used is as important as the ends achieved. Accountability for the conduct of subordinates is such an important managerial function that it is usually clearly defined in department manuals and guidelines.

Four primary functions represent the types of activities managers engage in to fulfill the responsibilities of their positions. These basic functions include planning, organizing, leading, and controlling, which are similar to those identified by Henri Fayol in the early 20th century. The time spent on each activity will vary, depending on the managerial level within the organization. However, these functions are part of all managerial levels, and they must be performed to some degree on a continuing basis if the department is to function effectively.

1. **Planning**. A plan is the careful development of activities to achieve desired goals or control projected conditions.[5] Planning involves the translation of mission, vision, and unit goals into specific operational objectives and the identification of the resources needed to achieve these objectives. It is a problem-prevention as well as problem-solving activity that prepares the department for the future. Police departments operate in demanding and changing environments. They cannot function effectively if they consistently maintain the status quo. They should not be required to continually respond to one crisis after another due to a lack of planning. Police managers must be aware of and evaluate external and internal environmental forces affecting their departments. Managers plan to develop strategies and methods for addressing the demands these environmental

forces place on their organizations. For example, negative economic indicators may forecast future budgetary reductions by the municipality. Police executives aware of these indicators will plan to adjust their budgets to maintain operational services. Executives must continually evaluate plans and alter them to meet changing conditions.

One plan will not accomplish all things. Police departments develop a variety of plans that address issues associated with operational control, procedural requirements, tactical strategies, fiscal accountability, personnel allocation, and managerial projects. Planning is an organizational necessity that must be strongly supported by the police executive if it is to be effectively supported throughout the department. It allows the manager to answer the following questions:

1. What should be done?
2. When should it be done?
3. How should it be done?
4. Who should do it?

2. **Organizing**. The organizing and coordinating function of management involve the structuring of an organization and the deployment of resources designed to achieve the organization's goals and objectives. Management organizes to achieve the alignment of strategy, structure, process, information systems, reward systems, employees, and operational service delivery.[6] Organizing is necessary to establish accountability, distribute the department's workload and resources logically, and create a mission-focused, unified organizational effort.

In policing, the decision to group-related activities usually takes into consideration such variables as the major purpose of the activity or function, the services demanded, the process or method to be utilized to achieve objectives, the nature of the clientele, the geographical distribution, and time. Most of these factors operate simultaneously. A well-organized department acts as a unified team, with each unit focused on mission accomplishment and service to the community. Organizational structure should support the department's strategy. The organization's mission should guide how the department is organized to achieve maximum effectiveness.

Police departments depict their organization structurally with a chart. The chart shows the organization's line of authority known as the chain of command. The department's chain of command displays each managerial position and the units under that position's authority. It depicts what each managerial position is accountable for and to whom each unit is responsible.

3. **Leading**. Managerial leadership is the ability to influence others to perform their duties willingly. It is the essential function for the achievement of a department's mission, goals, and objectives. Managers must provide leadership at all levels of the police agency. Managers are ultimately judged by the quality of their leadership as reflected in the performance of their subordinates. The complexity of relationships between managers and police officers requires unique insight and a special awareness of individuals, groups, and the needs of the department. Leaders must have an understanding of their department's driving forces, resources, and positive motivational factors (not fear). Leadership is a social contract predicated equally on the leader's desire to lead and on the consent of those led.[7]

Police managers must work with and through people to establish a positive organizational culture focused on mission accomplishment. All managers must maintain a serious and continuing effort to direct the creation of a results-oriented working environment. However, they will fail without employee support and commitment. The manager who strives on a daily basis to provide leadership and build a relationship of trust and respect with his or her employees will find that it is contagious and that the officers will respond to their positive direction. Successful leaders, by their daily actions, convince their subordinates that the interests of leader and subordinates are the same. Given the right leadership, people can achieve remarkable results.

4. **Controlling**. Controlling involves establishing goals and objectives, fixing accountability, creating policy and procedures, setting performance standards, comparing actual behavior with objectives, procedures and standards, and then taking corrective

action where needed.[8] All police managers are accountable for the competency and commitment of the people they command. It is the managers' responsibility to know what is happening with the resources, both technical and human, entrusted to them by the organization. Managers must check on progress to determine if previously agreed-upon objectives have been attained. The **control function** involves the following activities:

1. Identifying goals and objectives
2. Establishing accountability for their accomplishment
3. Developing and maintaining performance standards
4. Monitoring performance
5. Evaluating personnel
6. Rewarding when appropriate
7. Disciplining when necessary

Control begins at the level of monitoring the performance of the subordinates who are accountable for accomplishing the tasks. However, the manager must ensure that those subordinates clearly understand what they are to accomplish and that they have the knowledge, skills, and ability to perform their duties. To achieve control, managers must properly inform, train, and make their subordinates aware of the level of performance expected. Managers must communicate their expectations and provide training when necessary. Monitoring performance is essential to control. Effective managers obtain, and share with superiors and subordinates, the hard data needed to review operational progress. Data-based management uses fact, not a subjective opinion, in the evaluation of individual performance and results. When conditions change, or when specific deviations from previously agreed-upon standards are identified and measured, managers must take corrective action. Data-based management is a core foundation element of strategic management and the operational strategies of CompStat and Intelligence-led policing.

One example of the control function is the follow-up and assessment of operational tactics and their results. During CompStat's department-wide crime-control strategy meetings, executives review what operational managers have achieved with their crime-control strategies. These meetings are designed to identify what a successful tactic or strategy is and what is not. By knowing how well a particular tactic worked on a specific crime or quality-of-life problem and by knowing which specific elements of the tactical response worked, managers are better able to construct and implement effective responses for similar problems in the future. This control process also allows for the redeployment of departmental resources to meet newly identified problems.[9] The four managerial functions discussed earlier are not mutually exclusive, but they are highly interrelated. They do not necessarily occur in the sequence we listed but can happen at the same time. Managers must be aware of the following factors affecting the performance of these functions:

1. Changing environmental demands
2. Managerial knowledge and competence
3. Organizational level
4. Nature and type of activity
5. Knowledge, competence, and commitment of employees

In response to a federal consent decree, the New Orleans Police Department (NOPD) developed an automated data management system (MAX—Management Analytics for Excellence) to monitor compliance with the decree's requirements. Audits were conducted monthly to hold NOPD leadership accountable for reforms. NOPD officials collected data on such issues as body camera use, custodial interrogation compliance, appropriate use of force, and police–citizen interactions. The MAX system established compliance checks by developing electronic forms, tracking systems, and management meetings to review the results.10

Domonske (2006, p. 326) defines police management as "the study of the management of discretion in the regulation of community conflict."[11] Discretion is a significant component because line police officers must attempt to control the behaviors of persons violating the criminal law under the constraints of rapid response—including deciding to make an arrest including the possible use of physical force. Line officers need direction in making these decisions via training in departmental policy.

Managerial Levels

Police organizations vary in size and complexity, from micro-departments with fewer than 25 officers to multilevel macro-departments employing a thousand or more people. The number of managerial levels increases when organizations are large and complex. In a very small police agency, the chief of police and one sergeant will often be the only managers; in a very large agency, there can be 15 or more managers at the executive level alone. In general, all organizations have three distinct but overlapping **managerial levels**: the executive/strategic level, the middle management/administrative level, and the **supervisory/technical level** (see Figure 1–1).

Police managers at the **executive/strategic level** have a variety of titles, such as commissioner, director, chief, colonel, or superintendent. They are assisted by other top-level managers who have titles such as assistant chief, deputy chief, assistant director, deputy commissioner, colonel, or lieutenant colonel. These senior administrators deal with strategic issues, on the order of how the goals and objectives of the department interrelate with the needs of government and community. Police chiefs are increasingly expected to conceptualize and define the role of their departments in the communities they serve. The police executive's role is inherently political because he or she is appointed by the controlling governmental authority and represents the department to that authority and the community.[12] In many departments, the chief executive occupies a demanding, high-profile position and must be available 24 hours a day, seven days a week.

Managers at this level are primarily responsible for organizational effectiveness and efficiency. They accomplish these objectives by planning, setting direction, maintaining organizational integrity, creating goals, developing policies, ensuring fiscal accountability, and responding to political and community inquiries. A key requirement for police executives is leadership: The organizational direction they develop must effectively meet current organizational and community needs while simultaneously preparing to meet future needs.[13] Police executives must be willing to challenge their organization's status quo while at the same time establishing a direction that will lead to present and future effectiveness to accomplish their

Figure 1–1
Relationship of Level of Management to Functions Performed.

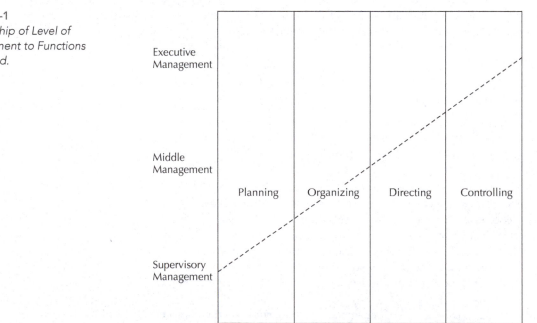

leadership role. An assistant chief, second in command, normally functions as the alter ego of a police chief executive and is a key figure in the management team, with in-line administrative responsibilities. Generally, deputy chiefs are responsible for supervising major functions such as line operations, technical services, investigations, or staff services. They may recommend goals and objectives; assist in the development and administration of policies and procedures; manage, direct, and organize operational services; and conduct internal investigations as directed by the chief executive.

Managers at the ***middle management/administrative level*** in policing are captains, lieutenants, or civilian managers in administrative positions. They manage divisions or units carrying such titles as patrol, traffic, records, communications, personnel, or research and development. Managers at this level are responsible for interpreting policies and procedures and for creating programs that translate departmental goals into the day-to-day tasks of operational units. They are responsible for converting the chief executive's vision into operational reality. These managers organize, coordinate, and control departmental resources and personnel. In the exercise of their control function, they evaluate supervisory accountability and unit performance.[14]

In their analysis of the administrative problems associated with the implementation of community policing, George L. Kelling and William J. Bratton contend that captains and lieutenants gained control of the practice, knowledge, and skill base of the police occupation during the development of the professional reform model of policing in the early 20th century. During this reform period, middle managers became the main proponents of centralizing control over the police organization's internal environment and operations.[15] Their success in establishing central control and their continuing role in exercising it make them the critical actors in the implementation of the organizational change required for the adoption of community policing and strategic management. Failure to win middle management's support was a primary contributor to the demise of team policing in the 1970s.[16] Malcolm K. Sparrow, Mark Moore, and David Kennedy identified six ways that police middle managers influence their organizations. First, middle managers operate at the boundary between knowledge and power in the department. Because of their positional authority, they translate the executive's vision and direction into operational strategies. Second, middle managers largely control the nature of the department's professional environment. The procedures they develop and the actions they take in dealing with subordinates define and reinforce the core cultural values of the department. These core values let the officers know what is and what is not acceptable operational behavior. Third, middle managers are the ones who can determine how employees view the department's procedural manual—as a means to justify command-and-control discipline or as a source of knowledge, guidance, and inspiration. Fourth, middle managers have the power to quash new ideas (and they have been routinely accused of doing so, especially ideas that they believe challenge their authority). Fifth, middle managers have the ability to define work in a way that encourages their officers to tackle harder, broader problems: They can empower their officers by letting them know that the organization values their knowledge and expertise. Finally, middle managers control the extent to which discretion can be built explicitly into the department's value system.[17] In summary, the middle managers' organizational position gives them the power to choose what they will do: passively resist, tolerate, or lend their support and lead in the reengineering of their organizations.

Kelling and Bratton suggest resolving the problem of mid-managers' resistance requires ensuring these managers become the department's leading edge for creativity and innovation. The chief executive officer can accomplish this by clearly articulating a strong vision of the business of the organization, its values and strategy. They must also involve the mid-managers in planning that direction, giving them space and freedom to innovate within their context. A new organizational direction requires support through resource allocation, administrative action, and emergent policies and procedures. Identify early successes and reward them. Failure must be acknowledged and resolved. By setting a clear direction with input and effort from the mid-managers in creating it, they become the organization's leading edge of innovation and creativity. As the chief executive of both New York City and Los Angeles police departments, William J. Bratton used this formula to great effect.[18]

The managers who operate at the **technical/operational level** of the department are the supervisors. Sergeant is the principal rank held, except for integrated police–fire organizations, where the title is lieutenant. They constitute the first level of management in the department. These first-line supervisors are generally held responsible for accomplishing short-term goals and exercising oversight of day-to-day operational activities.

Supervision of police personnel is the critical factor in achieving departmental performance objectives and officer compliance with procedures, policy, and law. It is each supervisor's responsibility to make certain that the individuals under his or her command perform their duties and accomplish organizational objectives according to law, departmental procedures, and ethical values. In the daily performance of their duties, supervisors make important decisions that affect the quality and manner of police operations—both the type of service provided to a community and the commitment and competence of the employees who provide that service. They also serve as the model of appropriate behavior and professionalism for their officers. Supervisors are the department's principal quality-control agents and significantly impact the effectiveness and financial liability of the law enforcement organization.[19]

Supervisors are accountable and responsible not only for their performance but also for that of their units: Their subordinates' accomplishments reflect their ability. However, a work unit's outcomes cannot simply be understood as the sum of individual performances. Work groups develop their dynamics, problem-solving processes, and cultures, which have an impact on their performance. The supervisor's success will depend on how effectively he or she can build a positive relationship of mutual respect and trust with his or her work unit.[20] In addition to managing their team of employees, supervisors are also part of the department's management team. Being promoted to a position on this team calls for a radical change in operational philosophy and outlook. Supervisors are required to develop skills and abilities that will allow them to manage the variety of people and performance challenges that occur daily in policing. Thus, becoming a supervisor requires that the new manager commence a personal and intellectual transformation that will change his or her organizational perspective, basic concepts of work, and relationships with others in the department. This adjustment takes time and effort. The supervisor is often required to exert authority over individuals who are his or her social and professional colleagues. In many departments, new supervisors find themselves supervising officers with whom they have closely worked with for years. Directing the performance of a former close colleague from patrol days is not an easy task.

The supervisors' organizational position places them in a unique and somewhat conflicting role. They are caught between two organizational worlds: management and operations, bosses and cops, and the office and the street. In some departments, these two worlds view each other with great hostility; in others, there is mutual respect and cooperation. Where the organizational climate is negative, this in-between position can be a source of conflict for the supervisor. The differing expectations of the two sides, if not understood and responded to correctly, can develop into contradictory pressures that create conflict and role ambiguity for supervisors.[21] Of the three managerial levels in police departments, the operational/technical (supervisory) level is the largest.

Part of this supervisory process is knowing when to assign blame. Baldwin identifies five important rules for placing blame:

1. Know when to blame and when not to.
2. Blame in private and praise in public.
3. Realize that the absence of blame can be far worse than its presence.
4. Manage misguided blame.
5. Be aware that confidence is the first casualty of blame.

Blame can be a powerful constructive force, teaching people to avoid repeating their mistakes, inspiring them to put forth their best effort, and maintaining their confidence.[22] Bad habits must be corrected to ensure effective organizational performance.

Line and Staff

Another way of viewing managers and the functions they perform is to distinguish between *line* and *staff*. **Line managers** have the authority to give orders to achieve organizational goals. **Staff managers** assist and advise line managers in accomplishing these goals. Recognizing the line/staff distinction is the initial step to take when a department arranges related functions under unified supervision and command. Once this step is accomplished, it becomes readily apparent how to allocate effort between the department's two principal functions: preparation for the delivery of police services and the actual delivery of those services.

The accepted classification of staff functions and line operations in police departments can be seen in Figure 1–2, which depicts the structure of a medium-sized department. Staff functions deal exclusively with supporting activities. In some larger agencies, they have been broken down into various administrative and technical services, but in all cases, the key is that they function to support line operations and the attainment of organizational goals. Line operations translate policy into action. Ultimately, the delivery of police services to the community is the responsibility of the line, but it is staff elements that provide the personnel, technical expertise, records, material support, and other services that enable the line to accomplish its job.

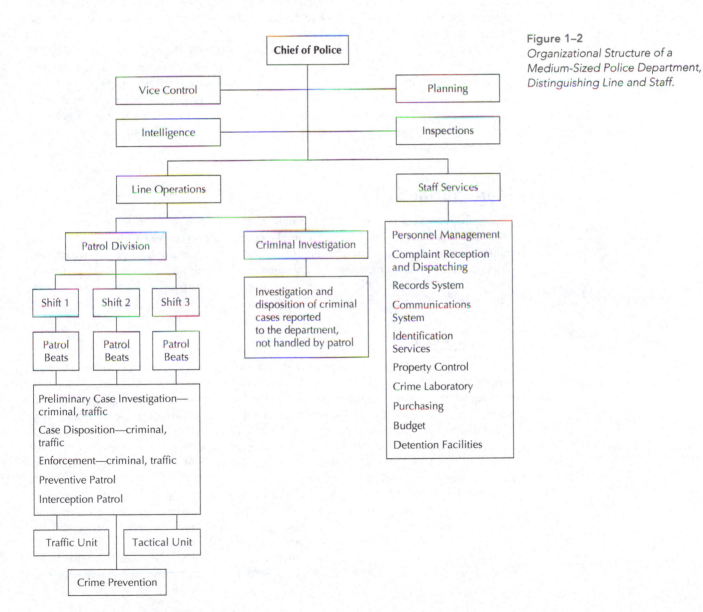

Figure 1–2

Organizational Structure of a Medium-Sized Police Department, Distinguishing Line and Staff.

The following list documents the variety of activities and functions of staff services:

1. Administrative Services
   Personnel
   Training
   Budget
   Community Outreach
   Research and Planning
   Crime Analysis
2. Technical Services Records
   Communications/Dispatch
   Property
   Crime Laboratory/CSI Units
   Prisoner-Holding Facility

The distinction between line and staff services allows for the orderly arrangement of elements within the structure of the police organization. Such an arrangement provides for clarification of lines of authority and the chain of command, and it facilitates the distribution of power and accountability within the organization. A clear distinction between the two allows each service to devote total energies to the accomplishment of its functional objectives.

The effectiveness of a police organization generally depends on the quality of working life within it. In the short run, managers can attain objectives by threatening employees (ordering them to do something or suffer the consequences), but experience has shown that in today's working environment, officers do not readily accept authoritarian management that uses coercion or executive fiat. Effective organizations have a positive working environment reflecting mutual respect, trust, and ethical relationships between managers and officers.

Managerial Skills

Successful managers not only have the right ability to know what they are supposed to do, but they also have the skills to accomplish their objectives. A *skill* is the capacity to translate knowledge into action leading to successful task accomplishment.[23] To achieve objectives and goals, which is what management is all about, managers need to have three essential kinds of skills—technical, human, and conceptual—and to exercise them effectively.[24]

Technical Skills

All managers must be technically proficient. This skill ensures the correct performance of specific duties. Craft experience, training, knowledge, operational procedures, laws, and techniques of policing are the bases of technical skills. Every police manager must be current on the changes in the law, policy, procedures, and standards of performance that affect themselves and their subordinates. All managers should also know how to create a plan, organize, lead, and control. Additionally, they must be skilled communicators because of the diverse groups and individuals they interact with on a daily basis during the performance of their official functions.

Every managerial position has technical skills directly related to its responsibilities. For example, the manager of an investigative unit has to be knowledgeable in such areas as case management, legal aspects of interviewing and interrogation techniques, proper utilization of informants, legal rights of suspects, and surveillance techniques.[25] CompStat and Intelligence-led policing require that operational commanders and managers have the technical knowledge to ensure that crime data are gathered constantly and analyzed quickly and accurately.[26]

Human Skills

This skill set involves working with people both within and without of the department. It includes understanding employee behavior being familiar with what motivates employees and how to utilize group processes to influence employee performance. Good human skills enable a police manager to provide necessary leadership and direction to his or her organizational unit and ensure timely completion of tasks with the least expenditure of resources. The interpersonal skills managers need include knowledge of human behavior and group dynamics, understanding of attitudes and motives of employees, and the ability to communicate clearly and persuasively.[27] Managers should know when to be diplomatic and tactful and when to hold fast to their position in dealing with people. Managers must know how to build positive interpersonal relationships with their employees, peers, superior managers, and stakeholders outside the organization. All of this requires the managers not only to possess knowledge and understanding of human behavior but also to employ this skill on a daily basis.

Conceptual Skills

Effective managers have more cognitive ability than less effective ones, and they are perceived as more intelligent by their subordinates.[28] Conceptual skills can help a manager take a system's view of his or her department's mission and goals. They help managers to understand the organization as a whole and assess the working relationships of its parts. When the interrelatedness of units and tasks is clearly understood, actions truly beneficial to the organization result. Coordination is enhanced, and effectiveness is the result.

Today's managers require advanced analytical and problem-solving skills to respond to the complex real-world problems they face. At the heart of this conceptual ability is an understanding and knowledge of cause-and-effect relationships. This skill permits the manager to move beyond the mere execution of tasks to confront and solve larger and more complex problems. The ultimate expression of this conceptual skill is the development of a highly trained intuition that allows the manager to know when to do the right thing at the right time.

Figure 1–3 lists the three skills required in varying degrees at each of the managerial levels. As we move up in the hierarchy, conceptual skills become more important and technical skills less so, but the common denominator for all levels of management is human skills. Supervisory managers, in particular, will find that human skills are a dominant factor in their working environment since for the most part they will be required to manage the work of others rather than perform technical tasks themselves. Executive managers will find themselves using conceptual skills extensively as they plan and make decisions affecting the entire organization and its future, but they too will be only as successful as their ability to attain goals and objectives through the efforts of others. The importance of human skills is strongly significant.

Managerial Role Expectations

A *role* is a set of behavior patterns expected of the person occupying a given position in a social unit such as an organization.[29] No matter what level of the organization they occupy, managers usually find themselves dealing with conflicting role expectations.

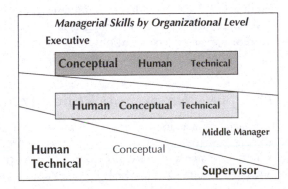

Figure 1–3
Managerial Skills by Organizational Level.

The police organization expects that the manager will act and make decisions on its behalf, but employees—who have their desires for fair treatment and their rights in the workplace—also expect the manager to act on their behalf.

More specifically, on the organizational side, every police manager is expected to be competent, loyal to his or her department and its mission, and committed to the department's goals and objectives. The manager is expected to be in command of his or her organizational unit, to be accountable for the employees assigned to the unit, and to achieve results. This means that the manager must have a clear understanding of the department's mission, vision, policy, procedures, and objectives.

On the employee side, police officers expect support, respect, and fair treatment from their managers. They expect their managers to understand them and treat them in a rational, consistent manner. The interrelationship between managers and employees forms the foundation for mutual trust and respect. Management based on mutual trust and respect is the most effective way to deal with people. How managers act toward their employees, while responding to the needs and demands of the organization and display competence as a manager, is critical to their success. The potentially competing expectations listed later can be sources of uncertainty and stress for the manager, but it is important to understand that between them, these two lists present all the essential elements of good leadership.

Police organizations expect managers to do the following:

1. Manage day-to-day operations.
2. Work for the attainment of organizational objectives.
3. Maintain a well-trained, motivated work unit.
4. Use authority responsibly.
5. Adhere to and administer the department's policies and procedures.
6. Keep superiors, employees, and peers informed.
7. Identify and prevent problems as well as solve them.
8. Be creative and flexible.
9. Provide leadership and use initiative.
10. Be accountable.

Police employees expect their manager to do the following:

1. Make them aware of performance expectations.
2. Give them timely and accurate feedback about their performance.
3. Recognize and reward good performance.
4. Listen to them.
5. Provide them with the opportunity to grow and develop in their positions.
6. Treat them equitably and fairly.
7. Use authority appropriately.
8. Provide support, resources, knowledge, and understanding.[30]

Managers at different levels in the organization handle each set of expectations differently and to different degrees of intensity. Lower-level managers spend a great deal of time concerned with employee needs and expectations, whereas police chief executives are more apt to concentrate on the organizational expectations. In every instance, the manager's personality may affect *how* a role is performed but not *whether* it should done.

The New Emerging Police Management Role

In police organizations during the professional reform era of the early 20th century, the primary function of the manager was to control operations and personnel. Managers sought guidance and direction from their department's policy and procedures manual. Whenever an employee asked for direction in a situation, the standard response was,

"Do as the policy and procedures manual directs you to do." If a situation does not co-incide with a rule or procedure, create a new one to prevent future problems. The prime directives of the police manager aimed at maintaining the status quo through oversight and control.

However, substantial societal change has challenged earlier methods of police ad-ministration and management. Police departments are restructuring and experimenting with strategic management processes to respond more effectively to the forces of change. The emergence of community problem-solving policing, CompStat and Intelligence-led policing, has resulted in the development of a new set of roles for police managers. Today, the primary role of the police manager is to be effective and achieve results. Managers are expected to be more analytical in managing organizational problems. They are expected to have positive people skills. However, managers must also know and accomplish the tasks necessary to meet organizational objectives.[31]

Effective organizations are ones in which people work to their full potential to achieve the mission. Peter Senge[32] identifies effective organizations as those that are skilled at creating, acquiring, and transferring knowledge and at modifying their behavior to reflect new knowledge and insights. He calls organizations that do this and develop the intellectual capabilities of their people "double-loop **learning organizations.**" Double-loop learning involves questioning basic operating assumptions, entertain-ing different approaches, and experimenting with different arrangements. Managers in these organizations are creative and open to new information; they are system thinkers and self-confident learners. In contrast, adaptive or "single-loop" learners focus on solving problems in the present, without examining how these problems may affect the entire police department or its future.[33] Senge's theoretical construct appropriately describes the managerial processes that are developing in policing as a result of the emergence of the new strategic policing era.[34] A variety of organi-zational adaptations of CompStat and Intelligence-led policing are currently taking place throughout the United States, Canada, and Europe. Each adaptation is a system that first identifies and focuses on emerging crime trends or quality-of-life issues and then attempts to effectively and efficiently use operational resources to control these trends. CompStat reinforces the long-held managerial value of maximizing every asset of the organization, including each employee.[35] Intelligence-led policing uses data analysis to enhance the decision-making process, shift resources as needed, and ensure that law enforcement resources are best utilized to (a) target specific crimi-nals and criminal operations that promise the greatest results in crime reduction and (b) create more opportunities to prevent and disrupt crime before it occurs.[36]

Strategic management uses organizational strategy to unite the decisions and ac-tions of executives, operational commanders, and frontline officers into a coordinated and compatible pattern. In this process, the crafting, implementing, and execution of operational strategies become critical managerial functions. Another critical management function in this type of organization is the capacity to manage human intellect and to apply it to useful organizational activities.[37]

Strategy is the means by which an organization responds to environmental condi-tions such as crime, disorder, citizen demand, and public safety. Strategy development must consider the critical managerial issue of how to achieve performance objectives, given an organization's capabilities and resources. Objectives are the ends, and strategy is the means of achieving these ends. An organization's strategy should be both pro-active (intended) and reactive (adaptive)—a combination of planned actions and on-the-spot reactions to unanticipated changes in conditions. An organizational strategy is something that is shaped and reshaped as events take place and operational demands change.

For CompStat and Intelligence-led policing to be successful and for police de-partments to become effective **learning organizations,** operational managers must be empowered with authority to develop clear, effective tactics to address crime and quality-of-life conditions in their operational areas. Managers must be flexible and ready to change their plans when crime conditions change. Intelligence-led policing aims to ensure that a department's resources are targeting specific crimes and individuals who are contribut-ing to community disorder. Like CompStat, it is a department management strategy that supports managerial decision-making based upon data collection and intelligence analysis to improve crime-control strategies. Intelligence-led policing and CompStat require that all operational managers be accountable for the following:

- The quality of their plans
- The quality of their efforts toward crime reduction
- Their managerial oversight of operations (including evaluation and feedback) and results obtained

For these strategic processes to be successful, a department's management must develop an ongoing process of rigorous follow-up to assess the achievement of performance results. Executives, as well as operational managers, must constantly follow up on and evaluate results. Evaluation makes it possible to assess the viability of particular strategic responses and to incorporate the knowledge gained into subsequent strategy development efforts. By knowing how well a particular strategy worked on a problem, and by knowing which specific elements of the strategy worked most effectively, departments will be better able to construct and implement effective responses for similar problems in the future. The follow-up and assessment process also permits the redeployment of resources to meet newly identified challenges once a problem has abated. **Operational managers** are expected to follow up on tactics and deployment by the following means:

- Getting out of their offices and seeing what conditions and operations are really like in their areas of responsibility
- Asking the operational personnel questions about current cases of interest, crime patterns, or situations requiring attention
- Reviewing crime reports daily
- Paying special attention to daily reports of serious crime
- Reviewing crime analysis materials (daily or weekly, depending on production schedules)
- Communicating daily with operational personnel about crime conditions
- Frequently discussing specific cases and crime conditions with their subunit managers and key personnel

Eli B. Silverman[38] has identified CompStat as an agent of organizational change that generates key reform processes such as new strategies, reengineering, and reorganization. In his view, CompStat serves as the glue that binds all these changes together because it involves double-loop learning. CompStat Crime Strategy meetings are forums where creative problem solving takes place and turned into action. Crime Strategy meetings lead to the discovery of difficulties and obstacles, clarification of positions, ownership and responsibility demanded, problems diagnosed, alternative strategies designed, and solutions defined and delivered. CompStat lets agency managers at all levels see their results every week and permit them to change tactics and deployment based on what they see and know. Because of this double-loop learning process, a deeper organizational transformation takes place. CompStat differs from Intelligence-led policing because it is a total management process that forces police managers at all levels of the organization to be concerned with how they and their units are contributing to the department's mission. Intelligence-led policing has a broader problem range and more specific offender focus than CompStat. Both strategies required a managerial skill set that involves utilization of information management, planning, strategy development, measurement, and ongoing communication. The department's executive team must be able to help operational managers develop strategies and tactics to meet objectives. Both of these levels of management must be able to accept failure and, rather than punishing staff for it, use it to modify or replace tactics. The ability and willingness to reallocate resources, support creative solutions to problems, track progress, and integrate functions within the agency require a strategic management orientation similar to that found in successful business organizations.

Organizational Behavior

It is clear from the preceding discussion that management is a people-related function. Organizations are made up of people; they are not collections of interrelated mechanical parts. Managerial success and organizational effectiveness depend on how well managers understand human behavior in the workplace. If police managers are to be effective, they must pay increasing attention to the interpersonal aspects of their managerial roles. More and more police agencies expect managers to develop operational strategies and strategic management practices that depend on other individuals to be effective.

Work is a fundamental and natural aspect of everyday life in our society; it is central to our social, economic, and psychological existence. An adequately paying job provides not only the necessities of life but also a sense of personal identity and accomplishment. Most people describe themselves regarding a work group or organization. Police officers are no different. They define their identities through their work. Achieving work-related goals is just as important to most officers as material rewards.

Personal interaction in organizations gives members a sense of belonging. In the case of police departments, the result is a social bond unique to the police culture. The sharing of duties and responsibilities heightened by the presence of danger generally results in officers becoming strongly committed to police work, which for them is more than just a job. Properly accomplished tasks provide a feeling of well-being and fulfillment.

Police managers have great success when managing highly motivated employees. However, not all officers fit into this category. There is no simple explanation of why some employees are highly productive, and others are not, any more than there is of other aspects of human behavior. Why employees do what they do and why the same situation can provoke different responses are relevant questions. Some theorists argue that participation in the decision-making process is the answer to the problem of motivating employees.[39] Unfortunately, some previously highly motivated individuals prefer to follow instructions and not be involved. Other experts recommend continuous communication from top management. They posit that effective communication tends to encourage better performance and leads to job satisfaction.[40] Some employees respond positively to this technique and want to know what is going on. Others seem to care less and only want to hear from the top when the message has to do with compensation or perks. Human behavior is a complex phenomenon.

Police managers are increasingly aware of the need to understand human behavior in the workplace. They generally have a definite view (usually based on personal experience and observation) of how officers behave within the organization. Views based on myth or misinformation lead to less productive and less efficient employee relations. Such misunderstanding causes managers waste time and effort on personnel performance issues.

Through the study of organizational behavior, we can begin to understand not only the complexities of organizations but also something about managerial behavior and the interactions between officers, managers, and the organization. Such study will also help us develop a better work-related understanding of ourselves and other people.[41]

To effectively deal with critical aspects of organizational behavior, police managers must develop and utilize motivational skills while enhancing their conceptual skills. Such skills have little to do with technical and operational expertise. They require a different level of attention by the manager.

Organizational Behavior Defined

Organizational behavior is the systematic study of the behavior and attitudes of individuals and groups in organizations.[42] The behavioral sciences, such as sociology, psychology, and anthropology, provide a basis for understanding human behavior at both the individual and group levels. Police managers utilize knowledge of human behavior to manage individual and group behavior.

To understand behavior in an organization is difficult because it involves understanding not only individual but also impact of group behavior. The organization is a social system conditioned and reconditioned by its environment. According to this perspective, police organizations are not isolated entities but are part of a large societal environment. Thus, it is becoming increasingly apparent that law enforcement agencies cannot function in isolation.

Police managers face many challenges, including understanding individual differences (in such areas as skills, motivation, and learning abilities). When concerned with individuals in groups, managers must also consider factors like communication, decision-making, power,

Table 1–1
TYPES OF BEHAVIOR IN THE ORGANIZATION
Individual
Interpersonal
Group
Organizational

and leadership. With this understanding as a basis, the manager can focus on work itself and can consider such variables as attitudes toward work, conflict, stress, and work design.

When tasks, individuals, and groups are interrelated, organizational design becomes a means of maximizing performance. The more successful a manager is in dealing with human behavior, the more successful the unit and the organization will be.[43] To understand organizational behavior, police managers should concern themselves with the following behaviors: individual, interpersonal, group, and organizational (see Table 1–1).

Individual

Individual behavior in the work setting has a highly significant impact on the effectiveness of an organization. People are different from each other; their behavior influences the behavior of other individuals, the attitudes of the small groups of which they are members, and the performance of the organization as a whole. Individuals have different perceptions of organizational reality, and they react accordingly. Therefore, it is important to understand how individuals develop their beliefs, attitudes, and values (see Chapter 4). It is also a continuing challenge for a manager to understand what motivates an individual (see Chapter 5). Another factor is that the values, attitudes, and perceptions officers bring to the job or those they acquire after employment become exceedingly significant when managers strive to achieve agency goals.[44]

Another aspect of individual behavior is the personality of each officer. Other individuals, groups, and the organization impact the personality of the officer (see Chapter 3). A law enforcement agency exerts considerable influence on each officer, and this process of occupational socialization continues throughout the officer's career. Everyone makes assumptions about his or her peers, supervisors, and managers, and these assumptions influence individual behavior toward others. It is essential that managers become truly aware of individual differences as they attempt to understand individual and organizational needs. Finally, individuals and especially police officers who work in high-service demand areas can suffer from stress created by organizational life (see Chapter 6).

Interpersonal

The **interpersonal behavior** that arises when two people interact can be of considerable concern to managers. This interaction may occur between two police officers, a superior and a subordinate, or two managers. In most instances, it involves such factors as leadership style, power, influence, and communication (see Chapters 2, 9, and 10).

Interpersonal communication is a critical factor affecting both behavior and performance in police organizations. Effective communication is essential, and it seldom just occurs—it must be cultivated. Poor communication can lead to poor decisions. Power, leadership style, and influence effect communication. Power is a natural phenomenon in organizational life, the thing that makes it possible to influence people's behavior to achieve objectives and goals. In some police departments, power serves as a positive feature, allowing people to control their destinies while accomplishing the mission. However, power inevitably modifies interpersonal relationships within the organization. When individuals compete for it, conflict can occur, and it is difficult to imagine an organization where power is not a key variable in the relationships among members. Leadership is the catalyst that makes an organization effective. The interpersonal skills that police managers possess directly affect individuals and groups as well as the total organization. Finally, managers need to reduce and manage interpersonal conflict to achieve departmental objectives and goals.

Group

Even though most police officers perform their duties singularly or in pairs, group behavior is becoming increasingly important to police managers. SWAT teams, task forces, and unions are examples of formal groups found in policing. Chapter 12 discusses in detail the dynamics of the group and the group process. Groups, both formal and informal, are powerful forces working for the attainment of goals and assisting in the adaptation to change (see Chapter 12).

Groups exert influence over the attitudes and behavior of each officer. As members of a work group, officers often feel or act differently than they would alone. The group can foster teamwork that results in the attainment of objectives, or its members can sabotage innovative programs. A manager can be more effective in understanding how groups form, what types of groups are there, and how groups found in the work environment operate. Groups have a strong influence on individual behavior. The manager who does not understand the role they play within the organization will be less successful than the manager who directs group behavior in such a way that there is a positive contribution to the organization.

Organizational

The structure of the organization itself is significant because faulty organizational design can limit or inhibit coordination and cooperation among employees. Organizational design brings together like functions and provides for formal internal communication. In some instances, police departments become fragmented, and individual units within a department function with total disregard for other units. In the early part of the 20th century, detective units operated independently. In some instances, the heads of detective units were political appointments.

The complexity of the organizational work to be performed also influences behavior: Managers have to be especially concerned with how individuals and groups adjust to their assignments, and all managers should be aware of the need to deal with job stress, conflict, turnover, and absenteeism.

It is increasingly apparent that police organizations continually react to the external environment and that the nature of this ongoing reaction modifies the internal environment of the organization. It is the task of the police manager to enhance the working relationship between the external and internal environments and effectively manage resultant behavior. This is not an easy task, so managers must utilize every resource at their command to identify, understand, assess, and resolve organizational problems. The current trend toward strategic policing places an exceptional demand for all police personnel, as the department focuses on attaining the crime control goals outlined in departmental vision statements.

Historical Foundations of Organizational Behavior

The growth of organizations and their increasing importance within society resulted in greater attention being given by researchers to employees and their needs in the workplace. Probably the most lasting of the early research products are Abraham H. Maslow's motivation studies. Maslow studied what he called the "self-actualized individual," a superior character whose personality was harmonious and whose perceptions were less distorted than those of other people by desires, anxieties, fears, hopes, false optimism, or pessimism.[45]

From his analysis of the self-actualized individual, Maslow created a theory of human behavior. He identified five levels of human needs within a motivational hierarchy. With the basic needs (physiological well-being and safety) fulfilled, the growth need comes into play, influencing the individual to seek belongingness, esteem, and self-actualization (see Chapter 6).

Another researcher, Douglas McGregor believed all management acts are based on specific assumptions, generalizations, and hypotheses about employee behavior. He suggested that if a manager holds workers in relatively low esteem, he or she will see the majority of workers as somewhat limited in their commitment to the organization (in contrast with managers, an elite group whose focus is the organizational needs).

Such a manager assumes that most employees are inherently lazy, want to have someone take care of them, and work best when subjected to firm control and positive direction.[46] This managerial perspective is known as "Theory X." In contrast to this is the "Theory Y" perspective that sees workers as committed, intelligent, responsible, and honest.

A manager functioning under a positive set of assumptions about worker behavior is concerned about relationships and the creation of an environment emphasizing the development of initiative and self-direction. Theory Y assumptions challenged the fundamental tenets postulated in the "ideal bureaucracy" and "scientific management" theories. However, its basic assumptions support the premises of community policing and strategic management.

Frederick Herzberg postulated a two-factor theory of worker motivation and focused on job satisfaction. In other words, what do employees want from their work? When subjects of his investigation reported feeling unhappy with their jobs, he found that they identified conditions external to task accomplishment.[47] The factors sponsoring employee motivation include work itself, advancement, achievement, and recognition. Herzberg also listed "hygiene" factors such as administration, supervision, salaries, and working conditions. Herzberg encouraged managers to create a working environment emphasizing "satisfiers" rather than "dissatisfiers" (see Chapter 5).

Other researchers directed their attention to leadership. In what has become known as the Ohio State leadership studies, Rensis Likert identified management styles in organizations as lying along a continuum from authoritarian to participative.[48] He found that, with few exceptions, the highest-producing units within an organization were those in which the management style was participative.[49] According to Likert, human resources are a significant organizational asset.

During the same period, the 1950s, Robert Blake and Jane Mouton developed the highly popular "managerial grid." The grid identified five different styles of leadership: "impoverished," "task," "country club," "middle-of-the-road," and "team." The relationship between concern for production and concern for employees defined the style. The most desirable style was found to be team management.[50] (See Chapter 11.)

As behavioral researchers reviewed the numerous studies on leadership and motivation, they found them to be highly prescriptive and, in many instances, mutually contradictory. These researchers declared an end to efforts to identify universal principles, the best leadership style, or optimal motivational factors, and the "contingency approach" was born.

Fred Fiedler, Martin Chemers, and Linda Maher's discussion of leadership suggested the adoption of a contingency approach, which would recognize that different situations and conditions require different management approaches.[51] They identified three dimensions determining the situational control of a job:

1. *The relationship between the leader and followers.* Do they get along together?
2. *Nature of the task structure.* Are the procedures, goals, and job evaluation techniques clearly defined?
3. *Amount of position power.* How much actual authority does the leader possess to hire, fire, and discipline?

Chris Argyris set forth (in a series of articles and texts) his theories concerning the difficulty of adjusting the individual to the organization. Argyris's view is that an organization that emphasizes task specialization, chain of command, unity of direction, and limited span of control is fostering "immaturity" among its employees and that the leadership style of such organizations tends to create conflict and frustration by pressuring "maturity-directed" employees to behave immaturely. Argyris viewed an effective organization as one requiring employees to be self-responsible, self-directed, and self-motivated. The pursuit of goals and experiences of psychological growth and independence maximizes motivation.[52]

The contingency approach came into existence as a consequence of the frustration that behavioral scientists and consultants experienced in implementing ideas set forth by the traditional theories. For the most part, the business world has been more receptive to evolving managerial theories than has the world of public administration.

Seeking ideal management concepts is something like the search for the Holy Grail that, in ancient times, proved to be so difficult. Many of us are still looking for the "one best way" to do things, but those who accept the contingency approach believe that differing situations require different management approaches. Contingency supporters reject the concept of "one best way" to accomplish something and prefer an eclectic approach. For example, in one situation work, simplification might prove highly successful, whereas in another, changing the relationships within a work group could be the best solution.

The approach taken by this book is to include contributions from most of the major theories of management, with a primary focus on organizational behavior. Our review of the history of management theories makes it clear that the traditional assumption that there was only one best way to manage people in organizations has received less and less support through the years. The foundation for a new approach to management was laid by later theorists who began to emphasize the necessity of understanding organizational behavior.

As previously indicated, law enforcement managers for the most part still emphasize traditional management approaches, but progressive police organizations are turning to managerial approaches that are currently more widely accepted by organizations outside the law enforcement world.

CASE STUDY   Chief Cindy Miller

Cindy Miller was appointed to the position of chief six months ago, after serving in a neighboring police department for 12 years. The last rank she held there was lieutenant. Miller's predecessor as chief had served for many years. His managerial style was "Don't do anything that rocks the boat."

Soon after assuming the position, Chief Miller instituted a program of personally reviewing the daily reports of officers by randomly selecting them from different shifts. This new program went over like a lead balloon. Shock waves permeated the whole organization. The typical reaction was that the chief was treating everyone like children. The chief's position is that while some officers might find it demeaning to be made accountable in detail for their activities, in her judgment daily reports should be a managerial tool, not a meaningless form.

The chief's review program created such dissent that several officers complained to members of the city council. The media soon picked up on the issue. The chief became very defensive and pointed out that it was an in-house matter and officers had no business taking it outside the department.

What might the chief have done to prevent this conflict? Is it a question of organizational behavior that is a function of interpersonal relations or group dynamics? Did the officers have a right to challenge the chief? If you agree, explain why.

Police managers should be fully aware of both the advantages and the disadvantages of different managerial theories. Although the pragmatic police executive might feel somewhat uncomfortable with how many competing theories there are, there is a definite need for managers to be aware of new theories and ideas when implementing new programs. Change is always with us, and rapid change places urgent demands on the organization's ability to respond. What worked yesterday might not work as well today. The eclectic approach we have chosen provides the law enforcement manager with tools benefiting not only the organization but also the employees and the public.

CASE STUDY   Chief Max D. Kenney

Max D. Kenney had previously served as a chief in two other communities before being appointed chief of Websterville, a city with a population of 110,000. The department has 120 sworn personnel and 21 civilians. Websterville is a bedroom suburb in a large metropolitan area.

Chief Kenney, when initially employed, was known as a visionary, and the officials who hired him expected him to make the department the most professional in the area. Kenney has a master's degree in public administration, has been a police officer for 14 years, and is considered by most to be an excellent selection.

As chief, Kenney spends the majority of his time externally, networking with community organizations, the business community, professional organizations and as spokesperson for the department. The assistant chief supervises operations. Chief Kenney's internal supervision is limited to issues that might threaten the integrity or reputation of the department.

Chief Kenney holds numerous press conferences and does everything possible to maximize positive press relations. As a matter of policy, reporters are required to deal directly with the chief on any case of significance. The chief is also deeply involved in three major police professional organizations and spends a great deal of his time attending meetings and serving on committees. Also, he attends every city council meeting plus neighborhood association meetings and every cultural or social event his busy schedule allows.

From the preceding description, it is apparent the chief believes the chief executive should spend most of his time engaging in activities external to the department. Do you think the chief is truly performing the roles required, or should he be more concerned with the internal aspects of the department? Roles?

SUMMARY

Police managers are becoming increasingly aware of the need to understand human behavior in the workplace. Through a study of organizational behavior, we can begin not only to understand why organizations are such complex entities but also to learn something about managerial behavior and the interactions among officers, managers, and the organization. It is essential to become aware of behavior at the individual, interpersonal, and group levels. As a field of study, organizational behavior is a product of evolution. Its historical antecedents included ideal bureaucracy theories, scientific management research, and the human relations movement.

To perform effectively, a manager must develop three areas of skills: technical, human, and conceptual. The common denominator for all levels of management is human skills—they are of the utmost importance. It is evident that managers are most effective when goals and objectives are attained through the efforts of others.

Management is a continuing process that focuses on the identification, refinement, and attainment of objectives by the effective application of resources. Operationally, a police manager accomplishes this by articulating value statements that guide the department in its effort to attain defined goals.

DISCUSSION TOPICS AND QUESTIONS

1. Generally, what behaviors must be considered to fully understand the concept of organizational behavior?

2. Why is it important to understand the concept of organizational behavior?

3. Differentiate between the managerial skills needed by a manager at the supervisory level and those needed by middle managers.

4. Describe what a manager should do to understand his or her subordinates.

5. Why does a police chief spend a great amount of time on the interpersonal role?

6. What are the responsibilities of the new strategic manager?

FOR FURTHER READING

Gary Dessler, *Management: Principles and Practices for Tomorrow's Leaders* (Upper Saddle River, NJ: Prentice Hall, 2013).

Dessler provides an in-depth analysis of the role of the manager in today's organizational environment.

David H. Freedman, *Corps Business: The 30 Management Principles of the U.S. Marines* (New York: HarperCollins, 2000).

Excellent analysis of a winning leadership and organizational management process.

Malcolm K. Sparrow, Mark Moore, and David Kennedy, *Beyond 911: A New Era for Policing* (New York: Basic Books, 1992).

Good basic analysis of traditional and innovative management in the operational world of policing.

ENDNOTES

1. Bureau of Justice Statistics, *National Sources of Law Enforcement Employment Data* (Washington, D.C.: U.S. Department of Justice, April 2016).

2. Michael E. Cavanagh, *Policing within a Professional Framework* (Upper Saddle River, NJ: Prentice Hall, 2004), pp. 73–104.

3. Richard M. Ayres, *Preventing Law Enforcement Stress: The Organization's Role* (Washington, D.C.: Bureau of Justice Assistance, 1990).

4. Gary Dessler, *Management: Principles and Practices for Tomorrow's Leaders* (Upper Saddle River, NJ: Prentice Hall, 2004), p. 3.

5. James J. Fyfe, Jack R. Greene, William F. Walsh, O. W. Wilson, and Roy C. McLaren, *Police Administration* (New York: McGraw-Hill, 1997), p. 212.

6. Jay R. Galbraith, Edward E. Lawler, and Associates, *Organizing for the Future: The New Logic for Managing Complex Organizations* (San Francisco: Jossey-Bass, 1993), p. 2.

7. David H. Freedman, *Corps Business: The 30 Management Principles of the U.S. Marines* (New York: HarperCollins, 2000), pp. xii–xiii.

8. Dessler, *Management*, p. 3.

9. William Bratton with Peter Knobler, *Turnaround* (New York: Random House, 1998) and Jack Maple with Chris Mitchell, *The Crime Fighter: Putting the Bad Guys Out of Business* (New York: Doubleday, 1999).

10. Susie Morgan, Danny Murphy, and Benjamin Horwitz, "Police Reform through Data-Driven Management," *Police Quarterly*, Vol. 20, No. 3 (2017), pp. 275–294.

11. C. Domonske, "Towards an Integrative Theory of Police Management," *International Journal of Police Science & Management*, Vol. 8, No. 4 (2006), pp. 326–341.

12. G. Cordner, *Police Administration* (New York: Routledge, 2016), pp. 180–208.

13. Albert J. Reiss, "Shaping and Serving the Community: The Role of the Police Chief Executive," in William A. Geller ed., *Police Leadership in America: Crisis and Opportunity* (New York: Praeger, 1985), pp. 61–69.

14. Malcolm K. Sparrow, Mark Moore, and David Kennedy, *Beyond 911: A New Era for Policing* (New York: Basic Books, 1992), pp. 213–214.

15. George L. Kelling and William J. Bratton, *Implementing Community Policing: The Administrative Problem* (Washington, D.C.: National Institute of Justice, 1993).

16. Lawrence W. Sherman, Catherine H. Milton, and Thomas V. Kelly, *Team Policing: Seven Case Studies* (Washington, D.C.: Police Foundation, 1973).

17. Sparrow, Moore, and Kennedy, *Beyond 911*, pp. 213–214.

18. Kelling and Bratton, *Implementing Community Policing*, pp. 10–11.

19. L. S. Miller, H. W. More, and M. C. Braswell, *Effective Police Supervision* (New York: Routledge, 2017), pp. 30–43.

20. Cordner, *Police Administration*, p. 188.

21. Miller, More, and Braswell, *Effective Police Supervision*, pp. 40–42.

22. D. Baldwin, "How to Win the Blame Game," *Harvard Business Review* (July–August 2001), p. 4.

23. Robert L. Katz, "Skills of an Effective Administrator," *Harvard Business Review*, Vol. 52 (1974), pp. 90–110.

24. Dessler, *Management*, p. 10.

25. Charles R. Swanson, Neil C. Chamelin, Leonard Territo, and Robert W. Taylor, *Criminal Investigation* (New York: McGraw-Hill, 2008).

26. Vincent E. Henry, *The Compstat Paradigm: Management Accountability in Policing, Business and the Public Sector* (Flushing, NY: Looseleaf Law Publications, 2002).

27. Gary Yukl, *Leadership in Organizations* (Upper Saddle River, NJ: Prentice Hall, 2013), p. 152.

28. Ibid., p. 148.

29. S. P. Robbins and M. Coulter, *Management* (Upper Saddle River, NJ: Pearson Education, 2018), p. 17.

30. The two sets of role expectations have been developed by William F. Walsh through the use of interactive training exercises during 30 years of training police managers throughout the United States.

31. Peter F. Drucker, "What Makes an Effective Executive?" *Harvard Business Review*, Vol. 82, No. 6 (2004), pp. 58–62.

32. Peter M. Senge, *The Fifth Discipline: The Art & Practice of the Learning Organization* (New York: Doubleday, 1990), p. 13.

33. Ibid.

34. William F. Walsh, "CompStat: An Analysis of an Emerging Police Managerial Paradigm," *Policing: An International Journal of Police Strategies & Management*, Vol. 24 (2001), pp. 347–362.

35. Walter Schick, "CompStat in the Los Angeles Police Department," *The Police Chief*, Vol. LXXI (January 2004), pp. 17–23.

36. Jerry Ratcliffe, *Intelligence-Led Policing* (New York: Routledge, 2016).

37. William F. Walsh, "Policing at the Crossroads: Changing Directions for the New Millennium," *Policing: An International Journal of Police Science and Management*, Vol. 1 (1998), pp. 17–25.

38. Eli B. Silverman, *NYPD Battles Crime: Innovative Strategies in Policing* (New York: Northeastern University Press, 1998), p. 190.

39. Susan E. Jackson, "Participation in Decision Making as a Strategy for Reducing Job-Related Strain," *Journal of Applied Psychology*, Vol. 68 (1983), pp. 3–19.

40. J. David Pincus, "Communication Satisfaction, Job Satisfaction, and Job Performance," *Human Communication Research*, Vol. 12 (1986), pp. 395–419.

41. John R. Schermerhorn, James G. Hunt, and Richard N. Osborn, *Organizational Behavior* (New York: John Wiley & Sons, 2012), p. 3.

42. Ibid.

43. Gary Dessler, *A Framework for Human Resource Management* (Upper Saddle River, NJ: Prentice Hall, 2013), p. 15.

44. Robert E. Worden, "Police Officer Belief Systems: A Framework for Analysis," *American Journal of Policing*, Vol. 14 (1995), pp. 49–81.

45. Abraham H. Maslow, *Towards a Psychology of Being* (New York: Van Nostrand, 1962).

46. Douglas McGregor, *The Human Side of Enterprise* (New York: McGraw-Hill, 1960).

47. Frederick Herzberg, Bernard Mausner, and Barbara Snyderman, *The Motivation to Work* (New York: Wiley, 1959).

48. Rensis Likert, *New Patterns in Management* (New York: McGraw-Hill, 1961).

49. Rensis Likert, *The Human Organization Patterns* (New York: McGraw-Hill, 1967).

50. Robert R. Blake and Jane S. Mouton, *The Managerial Grid* (Houston, TX: Gulf, 1964).

51. Fred E. Fiedler, Martin M. Chemers, and Linda Mahar, *Improving Leadership Effectiveness: The Leader Match Concept* (New York: Wiley, 1976).

52. Chris Argyris, *Personality and Organization* (New York: Harper & Row, 1957).

2
LEADERSHIP
The Integrative Variable

Learning Objectives

1. Identify the key aspects of management leadership and theories of leadership.
2. Compare theories of leadership.
3. Describe participatory management.
4. Compare the managerial grid, leadership quadrants, and path-goal leadership.
5. Identify the key components of "Good to Great."
6. Differentiate between transformational and transactional leadership styles.

Key Terms

adaptive

authority

autocratic

conceptual

contingency

democratic

initiating structure

least preferred co-worker

managerial grid

participatory

path-goal

situational

trait

transactional

transformational

universal

Law enforcement is a fluid working environment that is conditioned and reconditioned by **situational** factors that influence our perspective of what constituted viable leadership. Through the years, it has become readily apparent that if there is a singular purpose of leadership it is to mobilize others to serve a purpose.[1] By itself, a law enforcement agency is a lifeless, inanimate entity until positive leadership becomes an actuality. While leadership is intangible, it has proven to be the catalyst that enervates the organization. When positive leadership becomes a dynamic force within a law enforcement agency, things happen. Inspirational leadership is extremely contagious and provides a sense of organizational purpose. It can be a synergistic reality that maximizes efforts that result in mission attainment. At the same time, it is an elusive quality that must be present if an organization is to fulfill its purpose. Officers readily respond to the fire-like quality of enthusiastic leadership. It is contagious and can reverberate throughout an agency. A leader influences employees and possesses the character and competence needed to achieve individual and organizational excellence. In the search for police executives, announcements vary considerably when listing characteristics and necessary skills for appointment to a police executive position. Some of these are displayed in Table 2–1.

Table 2–1
POLICE CHIEF EXECUTIVE OFFICER—MULTIDIMENSIONAL LEADERSHIP

Core Traits	Descriptive Characteristics of High Scores
Conscientiousness	Dependable, hardworking, organized, self-disciplined, persistent, responsible
Emotional stability	Calm, secure, happy, unworried
Agreeableness	Cooperative, warm, caring, good-natured, courteous, trusting
Extraversion	Sociable, outgoing, talkative, assertive, gregarious
Openness to experience	Curious, intellectual, creative, cultured, artistically sensitive, flexible, imaginative

These attributes emphasize distinct yet interrelated aspects of police administration. Top executives are expected to have outstanding leadership and administrative skills. They must lead employees as they strive to accomplish the organization's mission, goals, and objectives. They must demonstrate interpersonal and communication skills and be committed to community service. They must have problem-solving skills and the capacity to lead. Like the proverbial horse and carriage, interpersonal skills, management, and leadership form a natural unit, or gestalt. Under ideal circumstances, "You can't have one without the other."

The term *motivation* is derived from a Latin word meaning "to move." It involves the use of incentives to encourage or reinforce member behavior that is consistent with and contributes to the organization's purpose. It is incumbent on management to create a hospitable milieu within which police officers are able to satisfy personal as well as organizational needs. Motivation is the key to personal productivity. According to Michael LeBoeuf, good leaders have the ability to turn subordinates on and convert collective efforts into productive work.[2] *Things that are rewarded get done!* There is a very direct and inextricable link between motivation and productivity in law enforcement organizations.

CASE STUDY   Captain Bill Jackson

Bill Jackson, formerly the officer in charge of the police department's Special Weapons and Tactics (SWAT) unit, was recently promoted to captain. Departmental policy required that he be transferred to another departmental unit inasmuch as the SWAT team did not call for the rank of captain. Bill had served in SWAT for seven years and prior to that he had been a patrol sergeant. And he had 14 years of experience in the City of Possible and placed in charge of a medium-sized district station. While the captain gets along with most of his subordinates, in his current assignment, they see him as a no-nonsense cop who exemplified the mind-set of command and control. It was immediately apparent that his leadership style was to make decisions and tell the officers in his district what to do. His power orientation focused on autocratic leadership. He exemplified structure and going by the books and gave little consideration to other variables. His subordinates were not allowed to make meaningful independent decisions. He felt he had the answers, so why consult or listen to anyone else below him in the chain of command. Prior to entering the department, he had spent four years in the Marine Corp and had served in combat for one year. This background proved to be useful and as head of the SWAT team, he was a health nut and physically fit. He ran the SWAT team with an iron fist, and everyone knew he was the leader and operationally ran the show. No one questioned his authority. In his position at SWAT, he always received ratings of *outstanding*, and those under him responded positively to his leadership style.

Bill had been trained when he received his last two promotions, but when elevated to captain, he was left to fend for himself. His natural instinct was to utilize the leadership methods he had used successfully as a SWAT commander.

Captain Jackson's commitment was to a (9-1) task-oriented management leadership style—in what could be considered a textbook example of bureaucratic leadership. He never sought input from his immediate subordinates because it was not needed. He could best be described as the proverbial taskmaster. He issued orders and expected a positive response.

He was at his best when he was in the field and "hands-on management" was what he liked best. When he arrived at any scene, he immediately took command. While he did not exploit personnel, he felt his focus on results was what counted. After nine months as the district captain, he began to hear through the grapevine regarding some low-key dissent from the lieutenants under his command who felt that he was usurping their authority. At first he was shocked that anyone would question his leadership style. The four lieutenants did not want to go out of the chain of command, so they asked for a meeting in order to discuss their working relationship with the captain. Bill's initial reaction was to not meet with them, but then he decided to authorize the meeting as a means of clearing the air and forging a team. He had hopes that his immediate subordinates would see the necessity of forging an alliance to meet head-on the many problems confronting the district. He entered the meeting with a positive frame of mind, but was astounded at what he heard. No one had ever questioned his leadership abilities. At first, he was defensive, but as the give and take took place, he had a slight glimmer that he had a problem that he did not fully understand. It began to dawn on Bill that most of those under him had more formal education and looked at the work environment entirely differently.

If you were the captain, what would you do to conclude the meeting? Would you wait and see if time would smooth things out? Why or why not? Based on the information you have, what do you think happened in this situation? How much place does a 9-1 leadership style have in law enforcement? List five situations where a 9-1 style would be appropriate. As the captain, would you consult with your immediate superior? Explain. What can be done to help ensure that it does not happen again? Explain in detail.

Management is the art of getting things done in conjunction with and through others in formally organized task-oriented groups. Truly effective leaders use legitimate authority and real power to create a work environment in which police personnel perform individually, yet cooperate with others to form synergistic groups or teams to achieve a common purpose. Such leaders devise strategies and use various techniques designed to remove obstacles to productivity. Experienced leaders rely on their knowledge of behavioral sciences to motivate employees and to enhance the efficiency, effectiveness, and the productivity of human resources.

Police executives plan, direct, and control police operations. An organization is inert until it is infused with leadership. Then it becomes a dynamic force with a compelling thrust toward the achievement of its overall mission.[3] Proactive leadership is a behavioral transaction that involves the art of influencing, guiding, instructing, directing, and controlling human beings in an effort to gain their willing obedience, cooperation, confidence, support, and respect.[4] Effective management is built on a foundation of trust. Managerial leaders have the ability to elicit productive work that is considerably beyond the minimum required of employees in a particular job. Police leaders are expected to generate a sense of purpose, to motivate and direct the workforce, and to lead subordinates so that individual police officers voluntarily make meaningful contributions to the department.

Perspectives on Leadership

Empirical evidence and common sense suggest that an organization's performance is closely related to the quality of its leadership. While leadership may not be the only important variable in the success or failure of a collective effort, it is an essential one. There is no doubt that inept leaders lower employee morale and hamper police operations. Law enforcement cannot afford leaders who fail to lead. A strong and resourceful leader, on the other hand, can—in the right environment and with proper resources—transform a disparate collection of individuals into an interrelated, aggressive, and successful organization.[5] The leader is the person who energizes the group. He or she knows how to elicit initiative and to draw from employees what they have to give.[6] V. A. Leonard and Harry More contend that leadership is the critical catalyst in this nation's law enforcement agencies.[7] They note that the fundamental basis for success in any police enterprise is found in the energy, effort, and expertise of the leader.

Leadership Defined

Leadership is a very difficult term to define. While most people are able to recognize leaders, few can satisfactorily explain exactly what makes a leader different from a nonleader. Defining leadership is even harder since there is no direct relationship between the ability to lead and those who are chosen to provide leadership in any given situation. Scholars have expended considerable time and effort trying to explain the phenomenon of leadership and yet—after more than 55 years of theory construction and research—there are still no provable generalizations.[8] Genuine leadership appears to be something internal to a given individual and is nurtured by the situation. Real leadership (as opposed to formal **authority**) is not a commodity that can be dispensed by those in positions of power.

The word *leadership* is a recent addition to the English language, in use for only a little over 200 years. It describes the traits, behavior, and/or style of those persons who—either formally or informally—assume responsibility for the activities of a goal-oriented group.

In simple terms, leadership is the knack of getting others to follow and to do willingly those things the leader wants them to do.[9] Leadership is a group phenomenon involving interaction between two or more persons. It also involves an influence process whereby the leader exerts intentional influence over followers. The concept of leadership implies that the follower acknowledges that the focal leader is a source of guidance and inspiration.[10]

Requisite Qualifications

Trust

While many desirable attributes have been espoused for leadership, trust is one of the most important. It is one of the most principled elements in fostering relationships. In law enforcement, it is the foundation of effectiveness, innovation, and employee retention, morale, and dedication. To the contrary, mistrust nurtures skepticism, aggravation, low productivity and turnover.[11] Clear values and subsequent behaviors that reflect truthfulness demonstrate commitment that bolsters trust.

Leaders often believe others trust them due to the sanction of their title. Trust is not accepted solely based on a person's rank or position. When subordinates have confidence in a leader's capabilities, dependability, dedication, integrity, and perseverance to deliver both tangibles and intangibles, they begin to trust. But that is not all…trust begets trust. In other words, being trustworthy builds trust.

Building trust takes commitment, effort, and character. It is not a task, nor is it immediate, but rather, it is a cumulative process. It takes determination and, if you are not careful, it can be lost overnight. Trust is built over time, no matter whether it is internal or external to the organization. Trust is realized by building and maintaining certain strengths. These common leadership qualities include:[12]

1. *Transparency.* Transparency is about being open, honest and communicating effectively. This is crucial during good and bad times. Being open nurtures relationships (see #6 below). Be precise and uncomplicated when discussing your expectations and purpose. This is especially the case when conveying information about your vision, the mission and values of the agency, and even issues such as everyday undertakings. Being direct and clear helps to ensure your expectations are met. And remember, the most important component to effective communication is listening.

2. *Empathy.* Think about others, not just yourself. While tasks matter, people are the most important part of the organization. Emotionally intelligent leaders build trust by relating to thoughts, beliefs, emotions, and experiences of others. They consider the effects of decision-making and behaviors on employees' feelings and understand and appreciate what they are experiencing. Be empathetic, show concern for others, and treat them as you wish to be treated.

3. *Integrity.* Be honorable in what you do. Always be highly ethical, forthright, and reliable. Do the right thing no matter how difficult it may seem to you. Treat people fairly, irrespective of their position or status in the organization. Leaders build trust by doing the right thing, even when no one is looking.

4. *Participation.* Results build trust. Be involved to assist in achieving results. Not by micromanaging, but rather by being engaged with your employees. Remember, it is your job to get your people the resources they need to accomplish the task and achieve results. Get to know your employees. Participating also means being approachable and available, not only during "open door" times, but whenever needed. By participating, you will help to establish trust.

5. *Proficiency.* People tend to be more certain and ultimately, more trusting of leaders who are proficient. Leaders are always learning and looking for ways to improve their competencies and proactively work to stay relevant in the profession. But, it doesn't stop there. Great leaders are always interested in the capabilities of their employees and the organization and recognize and demonstrate a commitment to employee growth through skill development and their career path(s). While leaders may be proficient, they are humble and know they can learn from anyone and at every available opportunity.

6. *Relationships.* Trust is nurtured through relationships. Relationships are derived by authentic bonds. Show sincerity and interest when conversing with others, especially when listening. Always be appreciative of others, their experiences, and what they have to offer. In building relationships, gifted leaders meet people where they are in their level of development. This not only refers to their career level, but also considers levels of maturity, emotion, competence, and commitment.

7. *Dedication.* Be dedicated and loyal to the profession and to the people who work with and for you. Great leaders persevere in times of hardship. They are trusted because they are dedicated. They see well beyond themselves and are willing to yield in order to achieve the common good.

8. *Reliability.* Let your values guide your behavior. Be consistent in your actions. To be reliable, you must be dependable. You must follow through and do what you say you are going to do. A good leader does not offer excuses or place blame on others. He/she pays attention to the little things and does them consistently. This will enhance trust and reap better results.

9. *Accountability.* Trust is an outcome of initiating accountability. Accountability must be created in a constructive and ethical manner. Most importantly, accountability starts at the top of the organization and must be exemplified. Leaders must hold themselves accountable for their mistakes. They also must be willing to confront others while encouraging transparency which allows people to acknowledge their mistakes and learn from them.

Leaders who utilize these attributes can attain success and allow those who they lead to excel. These attributes are not mutually exclusive. They work collectively to build trust. Leaders should trust in their employees and support their decisions. They must remain open-minded to new ideas, skills, and talents of their peers, subordinates, and superiors. Mistakes will occur, however, they can be overcome by a straightforward, transparent and caring approach.

Integrity

The relationship between trust and integrity cannot be overstated in the relationships involving the leader and his/her subordinates. Most leaders are evaluated by their employees on their vision, performance, communication, and intelligence. Even more important, people assess leaders on their character and character includes integrity.

Dwight D. Eisenhower once stated, "The supreme quality for leadership is unquestionably integrity. Without it, no real success is possible...." While the world has changed since Eisenhower made this declaration, time has not devalued the significance of integrity as a requisite quality of leadership.

Integrity and leadership are inseparably associated. Integrity is a concept and culmination of consistency related to values, principles, procedures, activities, expectations of actions, methods, measures, opportunities, and conclusions. It purports a profound obligation and dedication to doing not only the appropriate thing, but doing it for the right reason, irrespective of the situation. Leaders who have integrity are principled. They keep their word, are not judgmental, make fair decisions, and communicate honestly. They are incapable of breaking a trust. Selecting the right thing to do irrespective of the outcome, or the receptivity to it, is a distinguishing attribute of a leader with integrity.

Leaders at every level of the organization should model integrity, and they need to espouse and emphasize it at every possible moment. This promotes and helps create an organization's values and culture of not only integrity, but also compliance, accountability, and ethical behavior.

Ethical Behavior

Leaders establish the culture and direction for ethical behavior in their particular organizations. They are the ones who set the tone for the organization. Leaders who are properly prepared and motivated are a crucial factor for realizing high standards across the agency.

One of the problems highlighted in research is perplexing nature of what embodies ethical behavior and the awareness of it.[13] Corrupt behavior can be expressed in small ways which usually lead to more serious transgressions. Leaders who recognize warning signs often can prevent incidents through the use of proper training and intervention.

However, the pervasiveness of ethics violations in an organization often is relational to the quality of its leadership. Some researchers have proposed a "trickle down" model where the effects of ethical leadership are reproduced by workers throughout the ranks and are eventually copied by employees at all levels of the organizational structure.[14] In a survey administered to employees and leaders in corporations in southeastern United States, researchers determined the following:

1. Top management has an effect on employee behavior indirectly through supervisory leadership.
2. Employees imitate the behavior of leaders.
3. Employees will behave in a manner consistent with what they believe are the values of the employer.
4. It is likely that leaders who demonstrate ethical behavior influence middle managers who influence all employees.[15]

Law enforcement agencies must develop, hire, and promote strong ethical leaders to reduce unethical behavior among officers.[16] Leaders must consistently exhibit strong moral character and not accept anything less than ethical conduct.

Related Concepts

There is a symbiotic relationship between leaders and followers. They are best viewed as two different sides of the same coin. One view is that leaders—based on their position or power—exert influence on and motivate followers to act in certain ways. Other researchers feel that leadership is not determined by positions of **authority** but by an individual's capacity to influence peers.[17] At the same time, some experts express the belief that without follower consent, an inspiring leader cannot lead.[18] Followers, on the other hand, have a self-imposed zone of acceptance within which they willingly allow themselves to be activated, directed, and controlled by a leader. They establish psychological parameters and permit leaders to influence personal choices within limits.[19]

Once a leader–follower relationship develops, leaders are thrust into a group maintenance role. Effective leaders focus the group's energy and help members function in such a way that the police department is able to accomplish its mission, goals, and objectives. A leader creates a vision for his or her followers and guides them toward achieving that vision.[20]

The term *leadership* means different things to different people. Our definition evolved from a chain or series of related definitions:

1. *Influence.* To cause some behavior in another human being without the use of authority or physical force; influence is manifest in one's ability to affect the character and actions of others. Influence is the major process, function, or activity involved in the leadership role.[21] The behavior of the leader is also influenced by its consequences. A major consequence of leader behavior is predictable follower behavior. Follower behavior tends to reinforce, diminish, or extinguish leadership.
2. *Power.* The ability of a leader to influence other human beings in such a way as to produce a particular behavior. Whether it is formal (authority) or informal (influence), power carries with it the means necessary to ensure that subordinates respond positively to suggestions, instructions, and orders. According to Richard Plunkett, power is the capacity to command and to get others to do what the leader wants done, when and how the leader wants it done.[22] Leader power comes from different sources (e.g., reward power, coercive power, legitimate power, referent power, and expert power). Power is not a static condition; it changes over time.[23] Real power may or may not coincide with the theoretical distribution of formal authority depicted on an organizational chart.
3. *Authority.* Legitimate power vested in some person for a specific purpose. This is institutionalized power inherent in the position rather than the individual.

Authority is the right to act or cause others to act in an effort to accomplish the organization's mission. Ultimate **authority** rests with the police chief executive, who delegates appropriate authority down through the formal chain of command to all personnel within the department. Laws, policies, procedures, rules, and regulations control the delegation of **authority**. Management personnel and supervisors are granted formal authority to determine, direct, control, and regulate the behavior of subordinates. While they are often treated as synonyms, authority and power should be viewed as distinct yet related concepts. There are police administrators who occupy positions with a great deal of formal **authority** but who have no real power to influence the behavior of the men and women who work for them. Others have no formal **authority** per se yet exercise a great deal of influence over the people with whom they work. Effective leaders have the **authority** and power to fulfill their role in law enforcement agencies.[24]

4. *Reciprocal response.* Mutual influence between parties to a behavioral transaction. Leadership simply cannot exist in a social vacuum. There is a functional relationship between leaders and followers. Mary Parker Follett, a well-known management theorist, noted that a stimulus is always influenced to some degree by the resulting response.[25] Each party to the transaction reacts not just to the other person but to the total situation that he or she helped create. The result is a situation that neither person could have produced alone. Leadership—much like life in general—is reflected in a series of social situations orchestrated by synergistic relationships. Each situation is dynamic.

5. *Zone of acceptance.* The parameters within which followers are inclined to do willingly what is asked of them by their leaders. This zone or area reflects the exercise of power and formal authority that subordinates voluntarily accept as legitimate (Figure 2–1).

The zone of acceptance, which Chester Barnard calls the zone of indifference, is to be found in the mind and behavior of the follower, not in a position or a leader. It represents follower-imposed limitations on the power and **authority** of superiors.[26] People's zones of acceptance are getting smaller. People do not blindly follow orders today even if they are in religious or military organizations.[27] This makes the job of the police leader more complex and difficult.

Figure 2–1
Zone of Acceptance.

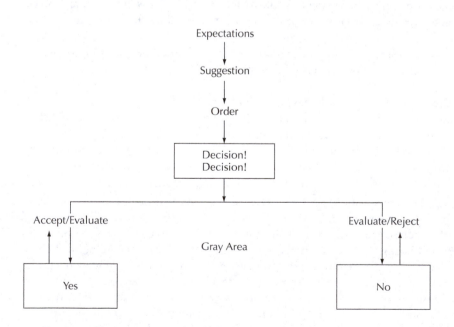

Expectations, suggestions, and orders that fall within the zone of acceptance are adopted with a minimum of analysis. Those that fall outside of the zone of acceptance are not easily converted into voluntary or willing behavior; they may become insurmountable obstacles to human productivity.

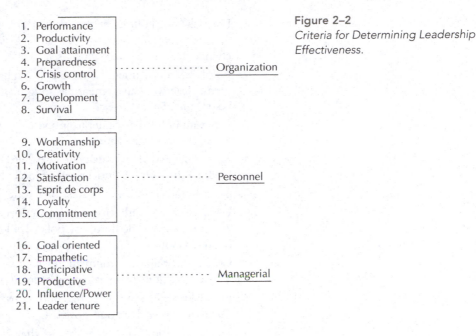

Figure 2–2
Criteria for Determining Leadership Effectiveness.

Leadership is slowly but surely displacing **autocratic** control in police departments throughout the nation. This is especially true in smaller and medium-sized departments, while some larger agencies retain vestiges of leadership based on power and authority.

Functional Leadership

Emphasis has shifted away from charismatic and autocratic leadership models to a new form of leadership based on function. The evidence is clear. A subordinate's zone of acceptance is flexible. It expands and contracts based on the police administrator's formal **authority**, real power, managerial know-how, competence, credibility, leadership style, and interpersonal skills.

The origin of the word *leadership* can be traced to early Greek and Latin. It is derived from an archaic term meaning "to act" and/or "to carry out."[28] Every act of leadership consists of two elements: (1) *initiation by a leader* and (2) *execution by followers*. Based on this concept, leadership theorists have developed an almost endless array of definitions. Since leadership is a very complex, multifaceted phenomenon, there is no real agreement on what the term means. For our purpose, leadership can be defined as follows:

> An interactive goal-oriented process through which individual human beings are (for a variety of reasons) induced to follow someone and to receive psychosocial satisfaction from willingly doing what that person wants them to do.

Leader effectiveness is measured by diverse criteria ranging from the group's performance to the leader's tenure (see Figure 2–2). Two commonly used measures of leader effectiveness in law enforcement are the degree to which police officers work and how well they accomplish the department's mission, goals, and objectives.

Police Administrators as Leaders

Police administrators are responsible for providing competent managerial leadership and are expected to provide it. In fulfilling this role expectation, they initiate goal-oriented action by others and manage those assigned to do the work. Police executives and other upper-level managers perform the specialized task of maintaining the organization in operation.[29] As managerial leaders, police administrators carry out the following:

1. Formulate and refine the department's mission, goals, and objectives. This should be done periodically rather than after a significant event has occurred forcing a change that meets societal needs.
2. Fulfill the department's mission through goal-oriented and proactive management. Reactive management has long plagued the police field and has proven to be detrimental.
3. Motivate police personnel to invest time, energy, effort, and expertise when engaged in job-related activities.
4. Make police work a fundamentally rewarding and productive profession. This can be done through job enrichment or job enlargement.
5. Set a moral, ethical, and professional tone for the organization.
6. Use power and authority to help employees to become more efficient, effective, and productive. The power of police leaders is extraordinary and should be exercised judiciously.
7. Create a working environment in which police officers willingly accomplish tasks. This can be done by utilizing followership tenets.
8. Reward people as a matter of continuous and constant practice. Go out of your way to acknowledge good works.
9. Maximize input from every level of the organization.
10. Above all communicate constantly and with effectiveness.

According to Sam Souryal, the essence of management leadership is for administrators to identify the needs of people in work groups and to meet work-related needs in ways designed to produce optimal productivity.[30]

This is sage advice, from an expert, and should be followed by current leaders and those who aspire to be leaders.

Managerial Leadership

Managerial leaders make an effort to identify and understand the needs of subordinates and to mesh them with those of the organization.[31] While these needs vary from person to person, from one organization to the next, and over time, they are normally separated into two distinct categories:

1. *Task-oriented needs* are work centered and directly related to defining goals, making policy, building programs, establishing process, and creating organizations based on the efficient division of labor. Management organizes the elements of productive enterprise (money, material, equipment, and human resources) to accomplish its stated goals and objectives.
2. *People-oriented needs* are employee centered and related to improving interpersonal relations, facilitating communication, motivating personnel, providing support, generating morale through meaningful participation, and resolving destructive conflict. The task of management is to create conditions that allow people to achieve their own goals by directing their productive effort toward organizational objectives.[32]

The "task" and "people" dimensions of management leadership are not, and never have been, mutually exclusive. They are interdependent. Effective managers exhibit both orientations simultaneously. They seek to create work environments that are productive as well as satisfying for human beings. People-oriented leadership—interactive behavior based on mutual trust, friendship, support, and respect—is directly related to job performance and employee satisfaction in a wide range of organizations. Those leaders who are more considerate of others usually have the most-satisfied subordinates.[33]

Modern police work is labor intensive. Somewhere between 70 and 85 percent of a typical budget is earmarked for recruiting, screening, training, nurturing, and retaining personnel. Under these conditions, managerial leaders must possess the knowledge and skills required to maximize the efficiency, effectiveness, and productivity of the organization's human resources. Researchers have identified the following major knowledge areas and leadership skills associated with good management:

Knowledge Areas or Areas of Understanding	Leadership Skills
1. Organization theory (workflow or structure/achievements)	1. Conceptual skills
2. Industrial engineering (job or tasks)	2. Human skills
3. Behavioral science (attitudes or viewpoint)	3. Technical skills

We now explore these knowledge areas (areas of understanding) and leadership skills to provide you with a foundation for a more detailed discussion of managerial leadership in law enforcement. Frederick Herzberg refers to organization theory (workflow or structure/achievement), industrial engineering (job or tasks), and behavioral science (attitudes or viewpoint) as the *eternal triangle*.[34] Contemporary managerial leaders utilize organizational theory to structure work in a logical and sequential manner and ensure coordinated efforts by all personnel in order to achieve a work unit's goals and objectives. They function as industrial engineers in the sense that it is their task to create and/or modify individual jobs so that each employee is productive and makes a substantive contribution to the organization. As applied social scientists, managerial leaders use their knowledge of human behavior to motivate employees, nurture positive attitudes toward work, and cultivate appropriate norms, values, and ethical orientations (see Figure 2–3). Good police managers bring the disparate elements of the *eternal triangle* into dynamic equilibrium in order to preserve and strengthen the organization as a consciously coordinated and goal-oriented system of human interaction.[35]

Managerial leaders understand human nature. They know that subordinates learn, participate, and produce best when they are allowed to set some of their own goals, choose activities related to achievement of those goals, and exercise freedom of choice in other important areas of life within the organization. An effective leader acts as a catalyst, a consultant, and a resource person for the work group. The leader's job is to help the group emerge as a collective entity, grow in terms of solidarity, and become less dependent on external direction or outside control. Managers serve the interests of the group best when, as leaders, they are spontaneous, empathetic, direct, open, and honest in dealing with their subordinates. They have a unique ability to apply knowledge readily and effectively in any given situation. In addition to their knowledge, police managers draw on and exhibit a dynamic mix of leadership skills. In this particular context, management leadership requires **conceptual** skills, human skills, and technical skills.[36] *Conceptual skills* are used to organize and integrate experience. They involve the ability to comprehend and ascribe meaning to bits and pieces of information (data) as they are converted into comprehensive thought. This is not merely an intellectual exercise. It is a part of a process that allows the manager to translate knowledge into action.

Police administrators with well-developed **conceptual** skills are able to perceive themselves in relation to the department and learn to appreciate how their behavior affects interpersonal transactions and functional relationships within the organization. Effective managers evaluate their own personal worth in terms of their leadership role in the police department, the criminal justice system, and the government itself. While

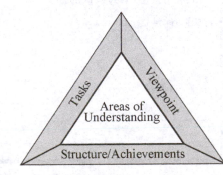

Figure 2–3
Modified from Herzberg's "Eternal Triangle."
Adapted from Fredrick Herzberg, "One More Time: How Do You Motivate Employees?" *Harvard Business Review* (January–February 1968). Also released as a *Harvard Business School Review Classic* in 2008.

conceptual skills are required at every level in police work, the standards for handling different kinds of information become less clear, and the level of abstraction rises when one moves up in the hierarchy of **authority**.[37]

Human skills involve those aspects of behavior and/or personality that influence the individual's ability to interact in a positive way with other persons in the organization. They include, but are certainly not limited to, tolerance for ambiguity, empathetic understanding, and interpersonal communication skills. Tolerance for ambiguity refers to the managerial leader's capacity to deal effectively with problems, even though the lack of information might preclude making a totally informed choice from among the available alternatives. Empathy is the ability to position oneself to see a situation or series of situations from the perspective of others. Empathy is a prerequisite for understanding human behavior. Communication represents an "idea transplant" from the mind of one person to the mind of another. Effective communication is a critical variable in the success or failure of any cooperative effort. Tolerance for ambiguity, empathetic understanding, and goal-oriented communication help transform idiosyncratic behavior into coordinated human effort designed to accomplish the police department's mission, goals, and objectives. Managerial leaders have a unique ability to function as members of an organization while fostering a cooperative spirit and guiding its activities (Table 2–2).

The *technical skills* utilized by police personnel vary depending on the level they have attained within the organization. According to Robert Katz, technical skill represents specialized knowledge, analytical ability related to the specialty, and competence in the use of those tools and techniques associated with police work.[38] The technical skills needed in law enforcement are diverse and normally acquired through job experience or job-related training programs. These skills are more operational than managerial. The techniques and mechanics of arrest, for example, have little or nothing to do with the use of preventive detention to protect the community from potentially dangerous criminals. The ability to shoot a revolver accurately is unrelated to the manager's decision to control the use of deadly force through the imposition of policies, procedures, rules, and regulations.

As police officers attain rank and move up the chain of command, the leadership mix they need in order to function properly changes to reflect the task-oriented and people-oriented demands placed on managerial leaders at higher levels in the hierarchy. Without attempting to split hairs about what constitutes a **conceptual**, human, or technical skill. Figure 2–4 demonstrates the relative mix of leadership skills needed by line supervisors (corporals/sergeants), middle-level managers (lieutenants/captains), and top managers (division chiefs/deputy chiefs/chief executive officers). As one moves up the chain of command, conceptual skills become increasingly important and the need for technical skills lessens. At the same time, it should be acknowledged that the intensity of the combination of skills varies from department to department.

Table 2–2
ORGANIZATION LEVELS AND REQUIRED SKILLS

Level	Combination of Skills
Top management	Amplified conceptual skills
	Lesser emphasis on technical skills
Human skills always necessary	
Middle management	Increasing use of conceptual skills
	Technical skills become less important
	Human skills always necessary
Supervisors	Notable emphasis on technical skills
	Limited use of conceptual skills
	Human skills are an essential component

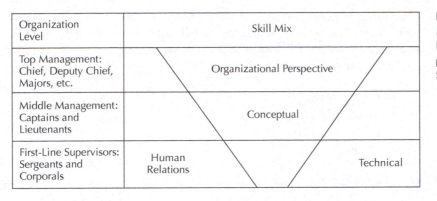

Figure 2–4
Rank-Specific Leadership Skill Mix.
Police administration: structures,
processes, and behavior, Charles R.
Swanson (New York: Macmillan, 1988).

In assessing whether the right leaders are being selected, Sorcher and Brant question the overvaluing of six sought-after management skills associated with leadership. One skill, that of being a team player, is often overvalued as consensus managers usually cannot make decisions on their own. The groups they assemble are much like themselves. Most exceptional leaders are independent thinkers and most often assemble diverse teams. They tend to embrace others who are more experienced and intelligent on a particular subject matter. Another overrated skill is hands-on coaching. Foregone are the days of close mentoring. Excellent leaders choose sound, effective people and delegate to them completely. Great leaders influence the thoughts and beliefs of others instead of prescribing their proposals and observe their own priorities come to life through the inspired achievements of others.[39] They allow people to flourish through experience and their own mistakes. Operation proficiency is the third skill that is often glorified. Leaders possessing this skill are often guided primarily by policies and procedures often repressing innovation. Good leaders prosper in indistinct, multifarious situations and see opportunities in uncertainty. Dynamic public speaking is another overemphasized skill. While public-speaking skills have been believed to be vital, more importantly, today, strong one-on-one skills are needed to inspire others to act. Raw ambition has always been seen as a positive attribute for leaders. Foote, Eisenstat, and Fredberg even describe a "new breed" of leader, the higher-ambition leader, who attempts to produce high performance by creating long-term economic value, generating significant advantages for the wider community, and building strong social capital in their organization.[40] However, the most successful leaders are humble and display great modesty while being intrinsically motivated and competitive. Finally, similarity and familiarity are overvalued in that many believe leaders too different from others in the organization won't fit into the agency. Leaders of diverse backgrounds, that is, race, ethnicity, gender, or socioeconomic status, make brilliant leaders and provide different views from mainstream organizations.[41]

Only those officers with leadership skills or the ability to acquire them through education, training, and supervised practical experience should be promoted to higher rank in the police department. Once promoted, they should be judged on their performance as managerial leaders. Performance-based management (PBM) is discussed in detail in Chapter 14.

Theories of Leadership

Many theories have been developed to explain those factors thought to produce leaders and sustain leadership in complex organizations. The **conceptual** approaches used to study leadership are ordinarily grouped into two basic categories: (1) *universal theories* and (2) *situational theories*. **Universal** theories search for an explanation of leadership unrelated to follower behavior or the social environment within which it develops. To the extent that these theories are truly universal in nature, they fail to shed much light on managerial leadership in very specific situations.[42] **Situational** theories, on the other hand, tend to place undue emphasis on **contingency** variables in an effort to explain the emergence of leaders (and leadership) in particular sets of circumstances. While neither approach has proven to be satisfactory per se, both of them provide us with starting points for further discussion.

Great leaders of the past came to the fore in several different ways. Their personal traits, their leadership styles, and the overall situation came together in such a way as to guarantee them a place in history. Experts in management leadership agree. Gary Dessler contends that there are at least four components in effective management leadership:[43]

1. Congruent leader style
2. Meaningful participation
3. People-oriented approach
4. Positive personal traits

We discuss these factors here in order to describe the ideal type of police administration.

Trait Theory

Trait theory, one of the earliest approaches used to study leadership, was very popular until the mid-1950s and is still viable in one form or another. Trait theories were formulated by luminaries such as Thomas Carlyle, George Friedrich Hegel, and Francis Galton and are based on the assumption that some people are born leaders. Carlyle saw leaders as unusually endowed and talented people who made history. Hegel took a different approach. He argued that events brought out the latent leadership potential in great men and women. Francis Galton believed that leadership skills were simply inherited biologically.[44]

Trait theory is based on the concept that good leaders always have certain physical, mental, and character traits that poor leaders do not possess. There is an implicit assumption that one's ability to lead develops concurrently with the personality during the formative years of childhood.[45] According to **trait** theory, leaders differ from followers with respect to several specific key traits that do not change much over time.[46] Persons with these special traits are virtually predestined to exercise informal as well as formal leadership in a variety of situations. Those who worked to refine **trait** theory and apply it to police administration were confident that adequate leadership could be obtained through a simple two-step process. First, researchers would study good leaders and compare them to nonleaders in order to determine special traits that only the leaders possess. Second, police departments would identify officers with these special traits and promote them to managerial positions.

Researchers have been trying to identify the special traits that set effective managerial leaders apart from poor managers for over 50 years. Different researchers—depending on their philosophy and/or academic training—have reached radically different conclusions concerning exactly what constitutes an essential leadership trait. A review of selected research data helps to illustrate this problem.

Based on extensive survey data regarding the qualifications of an executive, Ralph C. Davis found 56 different characteristics or traits that he considered important. While admitting it was unlikely that any manager would exhibit all, he claimed that the following 10 were required for executive success:[47]

1. Intelligence
2. Experience
3. Originality
4. Receptiveness
5. Teaching ability
6. Personality
7. Knowledge of human behavior
8. Courage
9. Tenacity
10. Sense of justice and fair play

Davis did not attempt to rate these factors in terms of their relative importance in determining effective management leadership.

Cecil Goode's research determined that the following traits were essential for successful leadership in complex organizations:[48]

1. Leaders are more intelligent than the *average* follower.
2. Leaders are well-rounded persons in terms of knowledge, interests, and aptitudes.
3. Leaders have an unusual flair for language. They speak and write intelligently, persuasively, understandably, and simply.
4. Leaders are physically, mentally, and emotionally mature.
5. Leaders have a powerful inner drive that compels them to strive for accomplishment.
6. Leaders are fully aware of the need for cooperative effort in order to accomplish tasks and get things done. They practice effective human skills.
7. Leaders rely on their conceptual skills more than on their technical skills.

Goode's list of traits tends to emphasize the people-oriented aspect of managerial leadership.

Typical of later leadership studies is one carried out by Edwin Ghiselli at the University of California, which looked at 306 managers employed by 90 different companies. Several characteristics were found to have a significant relationship to managerial performance: supervisory ability, achievement orientation, intelligence, self-assurance, decisiveness, and the need for self-actualization.[49] In a comprehensive analysis of more than 280 trait studies conducted over 64 years, Ralph M. Stogdill described a managerial leader as someone who acquires status through purposeful social interaction and a demonstrated ability to facilitate efforts of the work group in goal attainment. The traits most often associated with the assumption and performance of this role were intelligence, sensitivity to the needs of others, understanding of the task, initiative and persistence in handling problems, and a desire to accept responsibility and to occupy a position of dominance and control. Based on this research, Stogdill developed a trait profile designed to describe successful managerial leaders. According to the profile, effective leaders exhibit these traits:[50]

1. Strong need to assume responsibility and complete tasks
2. Vitality and perseverance in pursuit of goals
3. Inventiveness in problem solving
4. Drive to exercise initiative in social situations
5. Self-assurance and sense of personal individuality
6. Willingness to accept consequences for their actions
7. Skills in coping with interpersonal stress
8. Patience when dealing with uncertainty and aggravation
9. Skills to influence the behavior of other people
10. Ability to organize a cohesive group

In a thorough review of the literature on **trait** theory, Joe Kelly produced what he considered a definitive list of those traits most often identified in research as having a positive correlation with managerial leadership. This list of leader traits included intelligence, initiative, extroversion, sense of humor, enthusiasm, fairness, sympathy, and self-confidence.[51] While these traits seem to be important, there is simply no way to prove whether they are or are not essential elements in effective managerial leadership. There has been and will continue to be an avid interest in those physical, social, and psychological traits that separate leaders from nonleaders and good managers from poor managers. There is, however, no quick and easy test to assess leadership potential. In fact, most management theorists now agree that there are no **universal** leader traits.[52] Applied research has failed to discover a definite, consistent correlation between genetically determined traits and truly effective leadership.

There are inherent methodological problems in defining, identifying, and measuring leader traits. Consequently, no particular set of traits has emerged to differentiate effective leaders from nonleaders in any theoretically meaningful sense.[53] Based on the analysis of available data, the opposite appears to be true. It is clear that **situational** factors and pressures, rather than innate traits, are critical variables in determining who becomes an effective police manager. Robert Baron argues that different situations require managers with different personal characteristics, leader styles, and leadership skills. In some situations, direct and forceful action by the leader is necessary. It enhances productivity and morale.[54] In others, this type of behavior creates resentment and becomes counterproductive. A flexible, unstructured approach works best. In some circumstances, an autocratic style of decision-making, in which the designated leader gathers information and then acts unilaterally, may be effective. In other circumstances, a participative approach, involving consultation and collaboration with one's subordinates, might be necessary to ensure that important decisions are acceptable to various members of the work group. In short, there is no evidence to support the contention that one particular set of traits produces effective leadership in all situations.

The age-old assumption that leaders are born and develop their **conceptual**, human, and technical skills independent of **situational** variables has been completely discredited. The notion that effective managers possess specific leader traits and leadership skills has not been confirmed by research. Consequently, we have been developing a more reasonable and balanced paradigm concerning the importance of traits. It is now believed that certain traits and functional skills increase the likelihood that a given person will be an effective manager. There are no guarantees, however. According to Gary Yukl, the relative importance of the police administrator's personal traits and skills will be determined by the leadership situation.[55]

Leader Behavior Approach

Behavioral scientists abandoned **trait** theory because it provided few clues as to exactly what caused effective leadership. Researchers wanted to identify those proactive leadership strategies that elicited superior performance by human resources and were consistently effective. As a result, they shifted their attention to the study of actual leader behavior. This shift in paradigms had important implications. First, to focus on what leaders do and how they do it (as opposed to who they are) is to make a tacit assumption that there is some best way to lead. Second, in contrast to personal traits (which remain stable over time), leader behavior can be learned.[56] Most management theorists reject the notion that leaders are born and accept the idea that they are created in an interactive social milieu.

Researchers began to study how leader behavior affected follower performance and job-related satisfaction. As a result, leadership came to be viewed as a process of maintaining supportive social relationships in an organized work unit while getting members of that unit to perform assigned tasks at some acceptable level. Although this inquiry did not uncover a list of behaviors that always distinguish leaders from nonleaders, it served to identify major patterns or styles of leader behavior. It also demonstrated that management style has a significant influence on the productivity and morale of personnel within any type of complex criminal justice organization.

Leadership Styles

Early studies, using the methodological approach pioneered by Kurt Lewin, Ronald Lippit, and Ralph White, viewed leadership style as an interaction continuum ranging from people-centered to task-centered managerial behavior.[57] The focus of style theory is to determine which leadership style produces the greatest increase in productivity. Three basic styles (**autocratic**, **democratic**, and laissez-faire) have been identified:[58]

1. *Autocratic leadership* is power oriented. **Autocratic** leaders prefer to make decisions and give orders rather than to invite group participation. Loyalty, acquiescence, and obedience are rewarded. This style is useful when there is a genuine need for strict control and quick decision-making. This can occur during SWAT operations or other team efforts where execution is imperative. It is a question of just doing it, and a leader controls the entire operation. Review or consultation can occur later. When evidence can be destroyed or dangerous conditions are involved,

control is the only answer. Without question, obedience is essential during unusual occurrences. While the autocratic approach might be effective in the short run, the organization simply may be unable to function properly when the leader is absent. There would seem to be little justification for high-handed leadership during routine police operations. This type of police management stifles the development of leadership ability in subordinates because they are rarely allowed to make meaningful independent decisions.

2. *Democratic leadership* is people oriented. There is an emphasis on participation and collaboration. Leaders work with subordinates to help them achieve the organization's goals and objectives and their personal objectives. These managers strive to establish positive relationships based on mutual respect and trust. **Democratic** leaders create administrative environments in which they consult with and draw ideas from their personnel. This can be a very positive and fruitful process because involvement can generate unquestionable commitment to goal attainment and accomplishment of the organizational mission. Insurance of success in this situation depends upon delegating sufficient authority to accomplish tasks. In crises requiring a highly structured response, a **democratic** leadership style might prove to be too time consuming or awkward to be effective. While participative management has merit in police work, it also has its downside. So much time can be taken evaluating or considering a problem that requires subordinate participation that little or nothing gets accomplished. Excessive officer participation can require reacting to every utterance in an effort to maximize involvement, and the result can stifle the decision-making process and interfere with accomplishment of tasks. Even though this style of leadership is people oriented, research indicates that as leaders ascend through the ranks and extend their power base, their ability to perceive and maintain personal connections tends to suffer.[59]

3. *Laissez-faire leadership* represents a hands-off approach to management in complex organizations. In this style, the leader is actually a nonleader who acts as an information center and exercises almost no control. The organization runs itself with little or no input from management. This places the entire organization in jeopardy. Many theorists no longer consider this a true style. The laissez-faire approach is now viewed as a form of administrative abdication.[60] It is easy to see why an administrator who is in the twilight of his or her career does not want to rock the boat or make any decision that can impede a pending retirement. This is especially true when a situation or event is considered to be unnecessary work or, simply put, just rocks in the roadway. In other words, the incumbent takes the stand that he or she had been there and done that, so let someone else deal with it. In other instances, some have taken the position of just waiting for the situation to clear out by itself or to no longer require an urgent decision.

In a somewhat sophisticated approach, Robert Tannenbaum and Warren Schmidt identified four basic leadership styles that they described as "tell," "sell," "consult," and "join."[61] The most prevalent style used in law enforcement for many years for someone in command was to render a decision and then tell the troops what to do. It was a clear-cut example of autocratic leadership. Over time there has been a shift to other styles of leadership wherein authoritarian leadership gave ways to differing styles leading up to joining together wherein a skillful manager allowed for democratic participation. In this example, the leader delegated circumscribed authority. Phillip Applewhite identified a somewhat different set of four managerial leadership categories, which he named "authoritarian," "democratic laissez-faire," "bureaucratic," and "charismatic."[62] Bureaucratic management is based on the process model of leadership, whereas charismatic management is completely idiosyncratic and fueled by personal magnetism.

One of the problems associated with the leadership style approach is that it does not permit management personnel to rate high at both ends of the continuum. It implies that leaders are one-dimensional players who are unable to exhibit people-oriented and task-oriented behavior at the same time. Most leadership theorists now feel that the people and task dimensions of leader behavior are not mutually exclusive. They are, in fact, independent variables that can be exhibited simultaneously.[63] A large body of applied research data suggests that the either/or view of leadership is out of sync with reality. In more recent years, other leadership terms have entered the lexicon of police leadership to include such terms as shared, driven, dispersed, **transformational**, followership, co-leaders, and collaborative. All of these demonstrate a continuing search for the essence of leadership.

Much of our knowledge about leadership in police agencies is rooted in studies conducted by Ohio State University and the University of Michigan in the late 1940s. While the researchers used different methodologies and focused their attention on different aspects of leadership, they reached very similar conclusions. They cast doubt on the validity of viewing leader behavior as a single continuum; instead, they developed a two-dimensional independent-factor approach to management. The factors identified in the Ohio State University studies were "consideration" and "initiating structure." The University of Michigan researchers defined them as "people-oriented" and "production-oriented" aspects of leadership. Regardless of the terminology used, these factors are now considered the two most important dimensions of managerial leadership.[64]

Leadership Quadrants

Based on an analysis of extensive survey data, E. A. Fleishman and his colleagues at Ohio State University discovered that subordinates tend to think of leadership in terms of the *consideration* and *initiating structure* provided for them by those in positions of **authority**.[65] *Consideration* was measured by behavior items such as openness, communication, consultation, friendship, supportiveness, appreciation, respect, and empathetic understanding. These human relations–oriented behaviors help leaders establish and maintain positive relationships with their subordinates. **Initiating structure** was measured by behavioral items such as planning, coordinating, monitoring, evaluating, directing, and problem solving. These task-related behaviors promote the efficient utilization of personnel and resources in achieving the organization's mission, goals, and objectives. Effective police administrators are not one-dimensional. They have learned to emphasize both *consideration* and **initiating structure** in a concerted effort to influence, motivate, coordinate, and control their subordinates.[66]

The patterns of management leadership described in the Ohio State studies form a composite model with four quadrants plotted along two separate axes. One axis measures a leader's *consideration* for employees, and the other measures his or her emphasis on **initiating structure**. It is clear, based on an analysis of the research data, that police managers can and often do exhibit concern for their subordinates as well as the task. The underlying assumption is that truly effective managers rank high in both areas.[67] Because leader behavior and leadership skills are learned, police managers might benefit from exposure to leader-effectiveness training. Altering one aspect of their style could lead to an appreciable increase in the productivity of work groups they manage.

Numerous research projects have been conducted to determine what effects consideration and initiating structure have on the performance, productivity, and morale of subordinates. The assumption that managers who adopt leadership styles high in both consideration and **initiating structure** will be effective in all situations has simply not been proven. Many studies have concluded that no single leadership style is best in all situations. One review of 24 studies related to leadership behavior revealed that 13 found a significant positive correlation between showing consideration and **initiating structure** for subordinates, 9 found no correlation, and 2 studies found a negative correlation.[68]

Researchers began to realize that what sounds good in theory may not prove so in practice. There is no consistent pattern of research results to demonstrate that one leader style is superior to another.[69]

Even Ralph Stogdill, one of the originators of the Ohio State leadership studies, believes it may be overly simplistic to claim that an effective manager merely needs to behave in a considerate and structuring manner.[70] As stated earlier, an adequate analysis of leadership must take into consideration the leader, the followers, and the situation.

While the Ohio State leadership studies do not provide the aspiring police administrator with a comprehensive "how-to-do-it" explanation of proactive leadership in law

CASE STUDY   Lieutenant Charles Wainwright

Lt. Wainwright is a watch commander in the Sea Breeze municipal police department. The department serves a community with a population just under 200,000. There are 286 sworn positions, and the department is at full strength. Sixty percent of the officers are assigned to patrol, which is divided into three shifts. The lieutenant works the midnight shift, and the majority of officers that he supervises have had more than seven years' experience and have volunteered to work this shift. The department has 25 female officers, and 9 percent of the officers are African American, and 17 percent are Hispanic. The educational entry requirement is a high school diploma or its equivalent, and officers receive educational incentive pay and tuition reimbursement. Additionally, they receive shift differential pay, which has proven to be attractive to many officers. The department has 10 officers assigned primarily to the swing shift that work narcotics, and two officers are assigned to a multiagency drug task force. All recruits receive community-policing training, and there are seven neighborhood substations.

During the last year, there were 49 homicides, 69 sexual assaults, 956 robberies, and 2,569 aggravated assaults. In addition, there were 918 burglaries, 4,529 larceny/thefts, 1,297 auto thefts, and 91 incidents of arson. Major problems for the midnight shift occur when bars and night clubs close at 2:00 A.M., requiring a police response. The dominant offenses include sexual assaults, DWIs, public drunkenness, and aggravated assaults. In recent years, the number of auto thefts has increased, and on this shift, there never seems to be a lack of activity requiring police attention.

Lt. Wainwright is an idealist, and he believes that everyone in law enforcement has chosen this career because of the challenges involved—as if it were a calling. His persona suggests a concern for getting things done as well as possible for people. In actuality, he reflects an intermediate level of interest in productivity and a modest concern for subordinates. Lt. Wainwright assumes that there will be conflict between organizational goals and personal needs. What he tries to do is strike a balance between the two. He is laid-back and easy going and has a good sense of humor. He gets along with just about everyone, and it is seldom that he pulls rank on subordinates. He is convinced that if you treat people right, they will return the favor. He firmly believes that the people under him are pragmatic and will, in most instances, put forth some effort based on self-interest. He views himself as a middle-of-the-roader in terms of his managerial leadership style, and he strives diligently to strike a balance between getting things done and the needs of officers.

Deputy Chief Harry Brighter, head of the uniformed division and Lt. Wainwright's immediate superior, has reviewed the personnel rating submitted by Lt. Wainwright, and he has found that everyone is rated as satisfactory. The deputy chief firmly believes that a team management approach will provide greater benefits to the organization as well as the individual. He has found that Lt. Foster is the only one under his command who does not operate with a strong emphasis on team management. From the feedback he has received, the deputy chief believes that Wainwright does not allow meaningful participation and he decides the conditions of work. The deputy chief believes there should not be any conflict between the goals of the uniformed division and the needs of each officer. He urged the lieutenant to become more open, honest, empathetic, and trusting in his relations with subordinates. Deputy Chief Bright discussed the value of collaboration, mutual goal setting, and joint decision-making. He stressed the manager's role as a motivator, teacher, and team builder. Chief Bright also encouraged the lieutenant to become familiar with various leadership theories and to begin to assess his own strengths and weaknesses in terms of those theories. He placed a great deal of emphasis on the importance of developing supportive relationships throughout the entire organization. What started out as a mere exchange of information quickly became a seminar in the human relations approach to management in complex criminal justice organizations.

Which of the two approaches just discussed—middle-of-the-road or team management—do you feel would work for you if you were Lt. Wainwright? Explain in detail. Compare the two leadership styles' pros and cons. What would you have done differently if you were in the lieutenant's shoes? Has Deputy Chief Bright taken the best-possible approach in this situation? Why? What steps would you take as the deputy chief to insure that Lt. Wainwright adequately rates the officers under his supervision?

enforcement departments, their importance should not be underestimated. The Ohio State research stimulated interest in a systematic study of leaders, leader behaviors, and leadership. The Ohio State studies set the stage for further inquiry and provided a **conceptual** framework for the well-known **managerial grid** and the **situational** leadership theories proposed by Paul Hersey and Kenneth Blanchard.

The University of Michigan launched its own program of research on leadership behavior at about the same time as Ohio State began its program. The focus of the research was to identify relationships between leadership behavior, group processes, and group performance. A major objective of the project was to determine what pattern or style of leadership behavior most often leads to efficient, effective, and productive work by subordinates. Researchers used field studies and survey data in an effort to discover what differences there were between effective managers and ineffective managers. They came up with a two-dimensional leadership profile. Employee-oriented behavior included taking an interest in individual employees and their needs, encouraging two-way communication, developing supportive interpersonal relations, and dealing with conflict. Production-oriented behavior, on the other hand, dealt with planning, establishing goals, giving instructions, monitoring performance, stressing productivity, and assigning people to specific tasks.[71]

The University of Michigan researchers also found that effective managerial leaders do not spend most of their time and effort doing the same kind of work as their subordinates. Effective leaders concentrate on supervisory functions such as planning, scheduling work, coordinating worker activities, and distributing resources (supplies, equipment, and technical assistance). This production-oriented behavior did not detract from them concern for human relations. Effective managers were more considerate, supportive, and helpful with their subordinates than less effective ones. They were likely to use general supervision rather than close supervision. After establishing goals and general guidelines, effective leaders allowed their subordinates some freedom in deciding how to do the work and how to pace themselves while doing the work.[72] While the University of Michigan studies unearthed a great deal of information about leadership, they tell only part of the story. These studies are vulnerable to the same criticisms as were leveled at the Ohio State leadership studies. Leaders are but one element in the mosaic of human interaction.

The Managerial Grid

Robert Blake and Jane Srygley Mouton have also dealt with the task and people dimensions of managerial leadership. They proposed a framework in which leader style is plotted on a two-dimensional grid. The managerial grid—a charting technique developed independently of the Ohio State studies—identifies five normative leadership styles based on the relationship between concern for production and concern for people.

Leadership style is determined according to how a particular manager ranks in both of these areas. The **managerial grid** is used as a diagnostic to help individual managers assess their own leadership style.[73] The **Grid** is a 9 by 9 matrix. The horizontal axis indicates graduated concern for production. A rating of nine reflects maximum concern for production. The vertical axis, on the other hand, shows regard for subordinates as human beings. The higher the rating is, the greater the concern is. A nine on this axis is indicative of maximum concern for people.[74] Because the grid is a 9 by 9 matrix, there are 81 possible combinations, or styles of managerial leadership. Only the five basic styles are discussed in the following sections. This is sufficient to understand the concepts behind grid theory, however.

The five basic managerial leadership styles identified by Blake and Mouton are (1) impoverished, (2) task-oriented, (3) country club, (4) middle-of-the-road, and (5) team.

(1,1) Impoverished Management. People are hired, placed in a job, and left alone. Managers exert minimum effort. They sense little or no conflict between production goals and needs of subordinates. Very little is expected from these managers. They are out of it and seem to be lost among their people rather than actively managing them. A 1,1 style, sometimes referred to as laissez-faire management, represents an abdication of professional responsibility.

(9,1) Task-Oriented Management. The leader exhibits a very strong interest in productivity and almost no concern for employee needs or morale. The manager is a proverbial taskmaster. Human considerations are not allowed to interfere with productivity and/or efficiency. The 9,1 position represents an **autocratic** management style in which the end justifies the means and the exploitation of personnel becomes the rule, rather than the exception.

(1,9) Country Club Management. Leaders are overly concerned with creating and maintaining a friendly atmosphere. They spend much of their time placating employees in an effort to meet human needs. The attitudes and feelings of subordinates are their only real concern. People always come first. Managers in the 1,9 positions exhibit a low functional concern for productivity. Work becomes a ritualistic exercise, designed to sustain the employees' personal lifestyles.

(5,5) Middle-of-the-Road Management. Leaders exhibit basic concern for production and people. Their managerial behavior reflects an intermediate level of interest in productivity and a modest concern for subordinates. While they assume that there will be a conflict between organizational goals and personal needs, they seek to strike a balance between the two. The manager's survival often depends on creating and maintaining a state of equilibrium. The 5,5 manager believes that most people are practical and will normally put forth some effort based on self-interest. The middle-of-the-road approach to managerial leadership is very common in modern police work.

(9,9) Team Management. Managers in the 9,9 position rate high in terms of their concern for both productivity and personnel. They assume there is no conflict between the goals of the organization and the needs of their subordinates. There is an emphasis on meaningful participation. Integration of organizational goals and employee needs is achieved by involving all personnel in determining the goals, methods, and conditions of work.

Blake and Mouton argue that the 9,9 position on the grid represents an ideal leadership style that all managers should try to adopt. They contend that the 9,9 leadership style is the one most positively associated with efficiency, effectiveness, productivity, and employee satisfaction. According to Richard Plunkett, 9,9 managers succeed because they motivate others to join with them in accomplishing the work of the organization. They cultivate a sense of commitment and interdependence by providing their employees with a common stake in the organization. Effective managerial leaders develop goal-oriented relationships with subordinates based on influence, trust, and mutual respect.[75]

Managers ordinarily adopt and retain a dominant mode or style of management that can be described in terms of the grid. Their actions are normally consistent with this grid style unless it fails to work, in which case they may shift into a backup style keyed to the situation. Consequently, where individual managers fit on the grid at any given point in time is not entirely up to them. A variety of factors must be taken into consideration. The demands of the situation as well as the manager's personality, managerial philosophy, administrative acumen, and interaction patterns influence the placement. While police administrators should strive to achieve the 9,9 position on the grid, they must be flexible enough to adapt to changing situations and changes in their personnel when necessary. Truly effective leaders know and have an appreciation for those forces that affect their managerial behavior. They understand themselves, the interpersonal dynamics of the work group, and the **situational** context within which they function.[76] Due to the paramilitary structure of most police departments, there has not been much of an emphasis on team management in law enforcement. As a result, the grid approach has been used infrequently. In a recent study of 76 police administrators, however, nearly 70 percent of the respondents reported that the team management approach was their dominant leadership style.[77] They identified middle-of-the-road management as their primary backup style. In a study of 25 managers from a large police department, it was discovered that 45 percent of them had 9,9 leadership styles. While these studies are certainly encouraging, they should not be used to make far-reaching generalizations.

In related research, Jack Kuykendall and Peter Unsinger found that police managers either tended to have no dominant leadership style or used the "sell" approach to accomplish the organization's goals and objectives.[78] They were most effective when using leadership styles placing an emphasis on the task and least effective in styles requiring delegation of authority and/or work-group participation. According to Roy Roberg and Jack Kuykendall, there is simply no proof to support the assertion by some management theorists that the team management style of leadership is superior to other styles in all situations.[79] While concern for both production and people is important, concern alone cannot ensure effective managerial leadership in police organizations.

All behavioral approaches to leadership are based on similar concepts, even though they may be couched in different terms and generate different sets of labels. The notion that effective managerial leaders seek to influence both work output and social factors is a fundamental assumption inherent in all behavior theories. Even though their basic approach was different, Blake and Mouton came to the same conclusions as the Ohio State researchers. Ohio State used a behavioral model to examine leader actions as perceived by subordinates in the workforce. The managerial grid, on the other hand, is an attitudinal model that has been designed to measure the predispositions of effective managers. Both discovered a positive relationship between the production-oriented and people-oriented dimensions of proactive managerial leadership. The work of these leader behavior theorists provided the foundation for further study of managerial leadership, because it strongly suggested that the most effective way to lead is a dynamic and versatile process that adapts itself—by way of dominant and backup styles—to unique situations.[80]

Supporters of the **managerial grid** concept believe the 9,9 leadership style is the best way to lead and manage. They view leadership as the interaction between two interdependent variables (e.g., concern for production and concern for people). Emphasis is placed on using all available resources to determine the optimum course of action. The 9,9 police leader seeks to achieve coordinated direction through multiloop open communication designed to find the best alternative or course of action congruent with the logic inherent in a given situation. Even in crises, 9,9 managers continue—to the extent possible—to rely on superordinate goals and the processes of participation, conflict resolution, and group problem solving. Their behavior remains consistent with humanistic principles of openness, involvement, and **participatory** management. The 9,9 leader seeks input, contributions, recommendations, reservations, and doubts from those involved and acts quickly to define problems and devise solutions. Proponents of participation view it as an interaction procedure predicated on the following:[81]

1. Candor
2. Conflict resolution
3. Delegation
4. Effective advocacy
5. Openness
6. Strong initiative
7. Team work
8. Systematic inquiry
9. Two-way evaluation

If the 9,9 approaches fail, police managers may be compelled to shift into a backup style keyed to the needs of the situation. Once the crisis is over, the 9,9 orientation tends to reemerge as the dominant style of management. This is known as 9,9 versatility.

Some situation theorists discount the importance of philosophical and behavioral continuity in the managerial process. They regard effective leadership as a very complex multidimensional social phenomenon, which can only be understood from an interactionist perspective that emphasizes **contingency** factors. Managerial leadership is thought to be the product of an interaction/influence system in which leaders exert influence on other people in a concrete situation and in turn are influenced by them.[82] The key variables in the **situational** approach to leadership are the leaders themselves, the followers, and unique **situational** factors.

Situational Leadership Approach

Situational leadership theories attempt to explain effective managerial leadership in terms of the *interaction/influence* system just discussed. The situational approach is based on the implicit assumption that leadership is always exercised in specific situations that involve real people in a given physical environment.[83] It utilizes **contingency** variables to explain leader behavior. Contingency variables are those factors within situations or followers that determine the style of management leadership most likely to be effective in a given set of circumstances. In other words, different situations call forth and reinforce different kinds of leadership.

While **situational** theories cannot explain exactly what causes a human being to become an effective leader, they do provide an analytical frame of reference for thinking about it. Situational theory says, in effect, that managerial leadership is linked to adaptability. Success is contingent on the individual manager's ability to sense, interpret, and deal with various issues shaped by situational forces and unfolding events. According to Robert

Fulmer, the situational approach to leadership is expressed symbolically as L = f (LP, GP, S): leadership (L) is a function (f) of the leader's personality (LP), the work group's personality (GP), and the dynamic situation (S).[84]

Situational approaches are **conceptual** tools that leaders use to assess circumstances in which their leadership may become an important factor. A careful analysis of each potential leadership situation is of critical importance and is part of the process used by effective managers as they contemplate the most appropriate leadership style. Effective management is dependent on the degree to which the leader's style fits a given situation.

One of the most important aspects of the managerial role is to diagnose and evaluate the disparate factors that could have positive or negative effects on leadership. An accurate assessment of the situation involves identifying and understanding the influences of factors such as individual differences, group dynamics, and organizational policies, procedures, rules, and regulations. As Paul Whisenand pointed out, an accurate diagnosis in a given situation requires police administrators to examine four extremely important areas: (1) managerial characteristics, (2) subordinate characteristics, (3) work-group structure and the nature of the task, and (4) organizational factors.[85]

1. *Managerial characteristics.* Leader behavior in a given situation depends on the forces or personal characteristics of the individual manager. The most important factors seem to be maturity, personality, needs, motives, past experience, and reinforcement.

2. *Subordinate characteristics.* Before managers adopt a particular leadership style, they assess intuitively the personal characteristics and behavioral patterns of others within the work group. Police officers, like their managers, have many internal forces that affect them and that shape their behavior in a given set of circumstances. These factors include maturity, personality, needs, motives, past experience, and reinforcement.

3. *Work-group structure.* Groups are an omnipresent feature in modern society and represent a keystone in the structure of all complex criminal justice organizations. The characteristics of the work group usually have a direct impact on a manager's ability to exercise effective leadership. The significance of the group's influence depends on factors such as its proficiency, cohesiveness, structure, maturity, and work ethic. Work groups that are engaged in ambiguous activities, for example, are much more likely to require a very different kind of leadership than those performing routine tasks. As a rule, the truly effective managerial leader is flexible when it comes to dealing with the collective needs of the group.

4. *Organizational factors.* One of the most crucial yet least understood aspects of a leadership situation is the organization itself. Some of the more important considerations relate to the assigned mission; the influence base (power and legitimate authority) utilized by leaders; the department policies, procedures, rules, and regulations; the skill and professional competence needed to do the job; and the time allotted to make decisions and/or to achieve the goals and objectives of the work group. The complexity of the task, the size of the organization, the work group's interaction pattern, and the reward system help determine the most appropriate leadership style.

Managerial leadership is an art, not a science. Effective managers have the unique ability to create and maintain an *interaction/influence* system based on a dynamic equilibrium between themselves, their followers, and the leadership situation. They derive inner satisfaction from achieving the organization's goals and meeting the psychosocial needs of their subordinates.

It has—after decades of theory construction and research—become apparent that there are no **universal** leadership traits and no one best way to manage complex goal-oriented organizations. In reality, the effective police manager is one who is able to call on and integrate all of the available leader styles in order to adapt to the demands of a given situation. Good management requires **adaptive** leadership. In essence, police managers who are able to adjust their styles according to the demands of the situation and the needs of their subordinates are those who will be most effective in achieving personal as well as organizational objectives.[86] Paul Whisenand contends that adaptive leaders are much more likely to be successful than those who remain inflexible in the face of change.[87] Being flexible enough to shift into and out of various leadership styles creates a complete manager. Flexibility is the element in dynamic leadership that permits managers to adjust their style to fit the situation.

Contingency Management

The **contingency** approach to understanding leadership effectiveness attempts to combine elements of both trait theory and **situational** theory in a single model. It is based on the fundamental assumption that elements in the leadership situation influence the effectiveness of the manager's leadership style. According to the **contingency** model developed by Fiedler and his associates, the most important **situational** factors are (1) leader–member relations, (2) task structure, (3) position power of the leader, and (4) favorableness of the situation.[88] Since a leader's personality is set and not easy to change, the way for him or her to be an effective manager is to alter the elements of a particular leadership situation in order to effect a proper fit between leader style and the unique demands of that situation.

According to **contingency** theory, the effectiveness of groups in achieving organizational goals and objectives ultimately depends on the personalities of their leaders as manifest in their leadership styles and the dynamics of the situations in which they and their subordinates find themselves. The leader's personality, leadership style, and **situational** control—based on real power and the legitimate authority to reward or punish subordinates—determine exactly what can be achieved through the efforts of others.

Contingency theorists contend that managerial leaders are primarily motivated by either tasks or interpersonal relationships with their subordinates. Task-oriented leaders seek accomplishments in order to reinforce their sense of self-esteem and competence. In general, these leaders are no-nonsense people, who are at their best when they can follow detailed guidelines. If guidelines are nonexistent, this type of leader will develop the guidelines that identify assignments that can be given to subordinates—what counts is to go by the book. To a task-oriented individual, in any highly controlled situation, attention can be given to being considerate, warm, and supportive. Relationship-oriented leaders, on the other hand, seek admiration and respect from subordinates in order to meet their social and esteem needs. Interpersonal relations are extremely important to this type of leader, and tasks can be ignored. If work is not accomplished, it is of no consequence. On the other hand, in a peaceful and well-controlled situation, greater attention can be given by such a leader to actual task awareness.

Another consideration is the orientation of the leader, and this can be applied by utilizing Fiedler's **Least Preferred Co-worker** (LPC) scale. The LPC classifies leadership orientation by measuring the manager's perceived psychological distance from the least preferred co-worker.

Fiedler's LPC scale, which measures certain attributes or factors of co-workers, requires you to reflect about a person with which you least enjoyed working. You then rate this person for each attribute/factor and compile the scores. If the total score is high (64 or above), it is probable you are a relationship-orientated leader. If your total score is low (57 or below), you are more likely to be task-orientated leader.

When a score falls between 58 and 63, each leader has to decide for himself or herself the category that best describes his or her leadership style. The 8-point LPC scale—which rates leadership attitudes using a set of bipolar adjectives such as rejecting/accepting and quarrelsome/harmonious—assumes that if managers are inclined to describe in positive terms those persons with whom they work least well, they are motivated by interpersonal relationships. If they describe these people in clearly negative terms, they are task motivated.[89] The LPC measures leader attitudes and values. Low-LPC leaders emphasize the task. High-LPC leaders are more concerned with establishing and maintaining good relationships in the workplace. They are more cognitively complex than low-LPC leaders and are much more adaptable to changes in the situation.[90]

Whether a task or relationship orientation is more appropriate depends on the nature of the leadership situation. **Situational** factors determine the power and influence the manager has at any given time. **Contingency** theory is built on an assumption that all managerial leaders are likely to find themselves in one of three leadership situations: high-control, moderate-control, or low-control situations.

1. *High-control situations.* Leaders are allowed by their subordinates—based on positive relationships, task structure, and position power—to exercise a great deal of influence and control. This creates a predictable organizational environment in which to direct the work of their employees.

2. *Moderate-control situations.* Leaders are faced with a number of different problems but tend to deal with them all in the same manner. They have either good relationships (with low position power and little emphasis on task structure) or poor relationships (with high position power and high emphasis on task structure).

3. *Low-control situations.* Leaders are not permitted to exercise much influence or control because members of the work group do not support them. Neither task structure nor position power gives managers much influence or control. Low-control situations breed chaos.

V. A. Leonard and Harry More emphasize that leader–member relationships, task structure, and position power determine whether a manager has **situational** control of the job.[91] These three factors are critical and may be described as follows:

1. *Leadership–member relationships* measure how well leaders and members of the work group get along. Close leader–follower relationships are normally favorable to the leader. Well-liked and respected leaders can influence a work group far beyond what their legitimate reward and coercive power would suggest.

2. *Task structure* measures how clearly goals, procedures, and performance expectations are defined. Well-defined tasks with minimal ambiguity provide the most favorable situation for a leader. There are four characteristics of structured tasks:

   • The goal is clearly understood by members of the group.
   • There are relatively few correct solutions to a problem.
   • There are only a few ways to accomplish a specific task.
   • Decisions about work tasks can be evaluated objectively.

3. *Position power* measures how much **authority** leaders have to hire, reward, discipline, and fire subordinates. Managerial leaders who have the real power and formal authority to direct, reward, and punish their employees find themselves in a very favorable leadership situation. Interaction between these factors determines the favorableness of the situation for the leader. When matching leadership styles to appropriate situations, Fiedler and his co-researchers determined that *relationship-motivated* leaders seemed to perform best when they found themselves in moderate control situations. Furthermore, it was determined that task-motivated leaders performed best in either high- or low-control situations.

Contingency theory's criterion for organizational effectiveness is productivity. In very favorable situations, those in which the manager has real power, group support, and a well-structured task to accomplish, members of the workforce volunteer to be led, and they do willingly all that is expected of them. In relatively unfavorable situations, however, the work group tends to disintegrate unless there is active intervention and control by the leader. Consequently, it appears that a more **autocratic** and task-oriented leadership style is best when **situational** factors are very favorable or very unfavorable for the leader.[92] A substantial body of research utilizing Fiedler's contingency model has shown a positive correlation between high-LPC (human relations) leadership and productivity in intermediate to moderately difficult situations. Under these conditions, effective leaders seek to create a nonthreatening and much more **democratic** atmosphere in which subordinates are encouraged to participate in solving the problems faced by the work group. In other words, high-LPC leadership style seems to work well in average leadership situations but not in very favorable (good) or very unfavorable (bad) situations.[93]

Contingency theorists argue that it is often necessary for a leader to change his or her normal style in order to meet the challenges presented by a given situation. They contend that both types of leaders should be able to shift gears and play both kinds of roles. Task-oriented leaders may, under certain circumstances, be required to adopt a human relations approach to motivate their subordinates. On the other hand, a relationship-oriented manager might have to emphasize getting the job done during a crisis or when time constraints demand it but will revert to the high-LPC approach when the situation returns to normal. Richard Plunkett points out that nearly all effective managers are actually situationalists; this flexibility is the hallmark of a true leader.[94] Unfortunately, not everyone has this flexibility. According to Leonard and More, police managers can modify the situation if they find that their leadership style is disharmonious with the demands of the situation in which they are working.[95] Leaders can reengineer their jobs by adjusting the three factors involved in **situational** control (human relations, task structure, and position power). A number of research studies suggest that the **contingency** approach has practical implications for the training of leaders. Recent research shows, for example, that we can improve organizational performance by teaching managers how to diagnose and modify **situational** control; this allows them to achieve an optimal match between leadership style and the situation as it unfolds in a constantly changing organizational environment.

While there have been criticisms of the LPC scale and other aspects of Fred Fiedler's **contingency** model of leadership, it still represents one of the major thrusts in leadership theory.[96] It is a valuable frame of reference that emphasizes the interaction between the manager (based on a consideration of traits), followers, and the leadership situation. The model is antithetical to the notion that there is one best way to manage complex interaction/influence systems like a police department. Successful police administrators learn to adapt their managerial styles to the requirements, constraints, and opportunities presented in the leadership situation (see Figure 2–5).

Figure 2–5
Contingency Leadership Model.

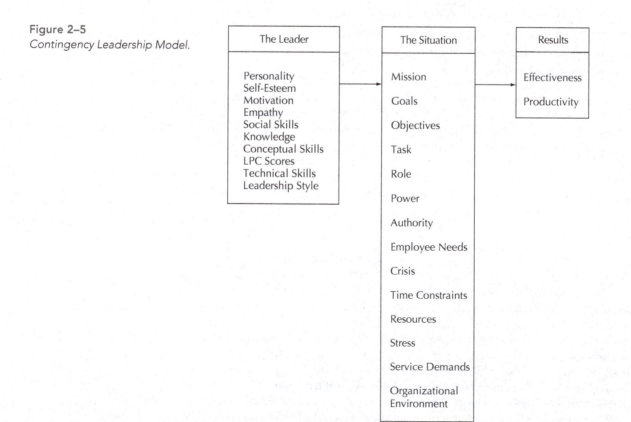

The Leader	The Situation	Results
Personality Self-Esteem Motivation Empathy Social Skills Knowledge Conceptual Skills LPC Scores Technical Skills Leadership Style	Mission Goals Objectives Task Role Power Authority Employee Needs Crisis Time Constraints Resources Stress Service Demands Organizational Environment	Effectiveness Productivity

Path-Goal Leadership Model

The **path-goal** theory of leadership explains how the behavior of the manager influences the motivation and satisfaction of subordinates.[97] The managerial leader's motivational function consists of increasing the personal payoffs associated with work-goal attainment and making the path to these payoffs easier to follow; he clarifies the path, removes roadblocks, and increases the opportunities for the personal satisfaction of employees while en route. In other words, leaders set goals for their subordinates and clear the path they must take to reach them. The basic assumption underlying **path-goal** theory is that certain leadership approaches will be much more effective in situations where leader behavior contributes to achievement of the employee's work-related goals. Managers play a supplemental role in the sense that they provide their subordinates with coaching, guidance, and performance incentives that are otherwise not provided by either the organization or the work group.

The **path-goal** model views leadership as being potentially the most important factor in determining what is to be accomplished (goals) and exactly how it is to be done (job behavior) within the parameters of the situation. Leaders engage in activities designed to identify proper methods (paths) by which their subordinates are allowed to accomplish organizational goals. The key to **path-goal** leadership is that effective managers create, nurture, and reinforce a meaningful connection between organizational goals and worker goals.[98] These managers affect the relationship between legitimate goals and appropriate means in the following manner:[99]

1. Delegating sufficient authority and assigning tasks
2. Supporting the efforts of subordinates as they strive to accomplish work goals
3. Determining the amount and kind of extrinsic rewards to be provided
4. Recognizing, reinforcing, and rewarding goal attainment
5. Enhancing subordinate satisfaction, reducing stress in the workplace, and removing the barriers that frustrate goal achievement

Path-goal theorists have identified four very basic leader behavior systems, or styles, commonly found in complex organizations: (1) achievement-oriented leadership, (2) instrumental leadership, (3) supportive leadership, and (4) participative leadership.

1. *Achievement-oriented leadership.* Managers set challenging goals, expect subordinates to perform at the highest level, and constantly seek improvements in job performance. Achievement-oriented managers emphasize excellence and are confident that their subordinates will meet the high standards set for them.
2. *Instrumental leadership.* This type of directive leadership is similar to the **initiating structure** discussed earlier; it emphasizes planning, organizing, controlling, and coordinating by the manager. The manager lets subordinates know what they are expected to do and controls their job behavior through formal policies, procedures, rules, and regulations.
3. *Supportive leadership.* Supportive leadership is similar to the concept of consideration used in the original Ohio State studies. Supportive managers pay attention to the people dimension of leadership. They are concerned with the social needs of subordinates and exhibit a sincere interest in their well-being.
4. *Participative leadership.* Participative managers share information with subordinates and seek input from them in order to reach group consensus. They consult with their employees and permit them to have meaningful roles in the decision-making process.

The manager's leadership style is an important factor in determining the kinds of rewards that will be used in a given situation. A relationship-oriented manager uses praise, emotional support, encouragement, and various sociopsychological strokes to supplement standard rewards such as pay raises and promotions. They value individual differences and are inclined to tailor reward packages to meet the needs of their employees. Task-oriented managers, on the other hand, use a narrower set of rewards that is normally unrelated to individual psychological needs. They tend to stress pay and job security. In order to be effective managers, police administrators must exercise leadership styles that coincide with the rewards being sought by their subordinates.

There are two very important **situational** or contingency variables in the **path-goal** approach. The first one relates to the personal characteristics of subordinates: their individual needs (for achievement, affiliation, and autonomy), their abilities (job skills, knowledge, and experience), and their personalities (emotional stability, self-esteem, and self-confidence). The second variable relates to the nature of the task and the environment in which it is performed. Some tasks are certainly much more demanding and stressful than others. Robert Albanese suggests that three aspects of the organizational environment have a significant impact on leader behavior: (1) the nature and complexity of the task, (2) the formal authority system, and (3) primary group relations.[100] Both the personal characteristics of subordinates and the nature of the task and environment influence the manager's leadership style as it relates to motivating subordinates. Motivation, in turn, is presumed to influence employee satisfaction and job performance. Subordinates perceive leaders' behavior as legitimate and accept it when it is an immediate source of satisfaction or when they anticipate that it will lead to future satisfaction.[101]

Path-goal theory assumes that subordinates respond differently to different leadership styles. **Situational** factors help determine their preference for certain types of leader behavior. For example, when subordinates are involved in a task that is stressful, tedious, boring, frustrating, time-consuming, dangerous, or otherwise unpleasant, effective managers make the work more tolerable by acting in an empathetic, caring, and supportive manner designed to minimize (moderate) the negative aspects of the job. Supportive relationships tend to increase the intrinsic value (valence) of the task. Increased satisfaction, at least in theory, leads to more effort on the part of most employees.

Directive leadership increases subordinate satisfaction and effort where there is role ambiguity. This condition occurs when the task is relatively unstructured, there is little or no formalization, and employees are inexperienced in relation to the task. Role ambiguity causes subordinates to have a low expectation of success in performing a complex task even if they plan to exert maximum effort. The path-goal model assumes that role ambiguity is dysfunctional, dissatisfying, and counterproductive. Under these circumstances, directive leader behavior will increase employee satisfaction with work and the leader. Increased satisfaction may lead to an overall increase in productivity.

Directive leader behavior is best at motivating subordinates who have a need for autonomy, responsibility, and self-actualization but who find themselves in very complex and ambiguous situations. They want to know what is expected of them. They need to know the parameters within which they are expected to operate.

In situations where organizational goals and the paths for achieving them are unambiguous, competent workers who have a strong self-image seek autonomy and want to work for a supportive relationship-oriented manager. Less skilled, more passive employees are much more amenable to task-oriented leaders. The trick, of course, is for police managers to make sure that their leadership styles are in harmony with the needs of subordinates and the demands of the situation.

The **path-goal** model just discussed (see Figure 2–6) is a complex view of leadership. It is designed to deal with the interaction between leader behavior and **situational** factors. In essence, it views the manager's role as that of motivating employees who are not motivated sufficiently by intrinsic satisfaction or extrinsic rewards. The goal is to increase productivity. The ability of managers to satisfy employee needs and generate increased productivity will be contingent on their leadership style, the moderating effect of subordinate characteristics, and various environmental factors.

As principal actors in the motivation process, managerial leaders are expected to establish legitimate and realistic goals, to identify and clear the most direct path to follow in achieving those goals, and to reward appropriate goal-oriented behavior. A leader style (achievement-oriented, instrumental, supportive, or participatory) that corresponds with employee needs and situational variables will, at least in theory, satisfy subordinates and

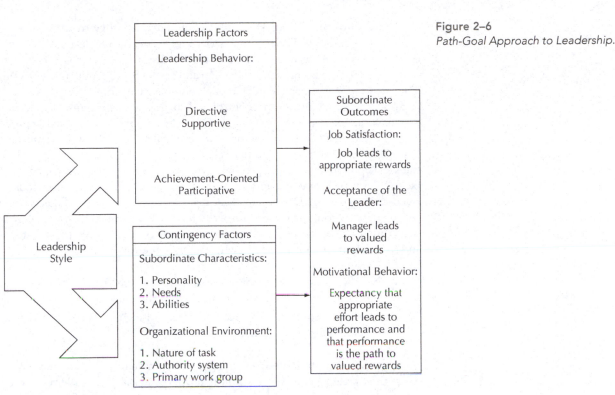

Figure 2–6
Path-Goal Approach to Leadership.

lead to increased productivity on the part of individual employees and the work group as a whole.

Research on **path-goal** theory has produced mixed results. Some studies support the concept; others do not. Most support is found for the notion that leader behavior has a direct effect on subordinate satisfaction. In one recent study (of 110 bank employees and 205 manufacturing employees), investigators found that task structure moderated the effects of leader behavior on subordinate satisfaction. When tasks were varied, provided little or no feedback, and offered few opportunities for meaningful social interaction, directive leader behavior (**initiating structure**) increased employee satisfaction. When tasks were routine, provided feedback, and offered opportunities for social interaction, **initiating structure** became dysfunctional and dissatisfying. It has been much more difficult to demonstrate the link between satisfaction and increased productivity.

Participatory Leadership

As noted earlier in this chapter, several leadership studies link managerial style to group performance and have developed classification systems to depict this relationship. These classifications (or ideal types) are usually viewed as elements on a **conceptual** continuum ranging from completely **autocratic** to completely **democratic** leadership. A popular way to illustrate this range of leadership styles is one that identifies and differentiates among styles based on the degree of managerial **authority** and group involvement. Given the fact that one style is not necessarily superior to another, the most appropriate leadership style will depend on the situation and the criteria used to judge what is considered appropriate. If productivity is the criterion, any leader style could be effective. If quick, unambiguous decision-making is the criterion, a leadership style at the leader-centered end of the continuum might be the best one. If, on the other hand, optimizing group participation is the objective, group-centered styles are much more effective than those emphasizing the unilateral exercise of **authority** by managers in positions of power. Robert Albanese points out that the value of a particular leader's style must be assessed in terms of the desired outcomes.[102]

Group-oriented leadership—known as **participatory** management—involves the "consults," "joins," and "delegates" styles and is specifically designed to involve employees in the leadership process. **Participatory** leaders make a sincere effort to get their subordinates involved in the task of creating and maintaining productive work environments. The **participatory** management model assumes that employees prefer some form of self-governance to **autocratic** control and that, as achievement-oriented human beings, they have an absolute need to be included in the group decision-making process.

Management by participation is an essential concept for the organizational humanists and an extension of the human relations school of thought. It implicitly assumes that full participation in the management process meets employee needs, enhances the satisfaction derived from work, and increases organizational as well as individual productivity. According to the late Douglas M. McGregor, decentralization and delegation are ways of freeing people from the close control of traditional bureaucratic organizations. They give subordinates a degree of freedom to direct their own activities, to assume responsibility, and to satisfy their egoistic needs, which include the following:[103]

1. Needs related to employee's self-esteem such as knowledge, attainment, self-confidence, competence, and self-sufficiency.
2. Needs related to the employee's reputation, such as recognition, appreciation, status, and the respect of peers.

In the right circumstances, **participatory** management encourages employees to direct their creative energies toward organizational goals, gives them a voice in decisions that affect them, and produces significant opportunities for satisfaction of both social and egoistic needs.

The concept of **participatory** managerial leadership is rooted in the humanistic theories developed by people such as Mary Parker Follett ("power with" versus "power over" in industrial democracy), Elton Mayo (the Hawthorne effect), Abraham Maslow (the hierarchy of needs), Frederick Herzberg (motivation-hygiene theory), and Douglas McGregor (Theory X and Theory Y). These theories are built on the assumption that an increase in participation will usually have a favorable effect on subordinates who have relatively high needs for independence, are ready to assume responsibility, have the necessary knowledge and expertise to deal with problems, and identify with organizational goals.

Participatory management is often touted as the one best way to develop organizational conditions and operational procedures that will motivate individual employees to attain their (social and psychological) goals as they direct their efforts toward achievement of organizational goals and objectives. In fact, some humanist ideologues argue that **participatory** leadership is the only way to enhance employee satisfaction, performance, and morale in complex organizations. They contend that most people will voluntarily commit to and accept those decisions they helped to make.

The human relations approach to managerial leadership is consistent with the American ideals of equity, democracy, and individual dignity. In one study, J. M. Roscow found that just over one-half of all Americans feel they have a right to participate in making decisions that affect their job. Among younger workers, the proportion was close to two-thirds. There is every reason to believe that the demand for worker participation in organizational decision-making will continue to grow.[104]

Organizational humanists have advanced a number of guidelines for enhancing meaningful employee participation. Some of those explanations have been synopsized here:[105]

1. Create an environment in which employees feel they can express their concerns.
2. Propose tentative solutions, and encourage officers to improve on them.
3. Make notes in order to ensure that ideas are recorded.
4. Look for positive aspects of suggestions.
5. If concerned about some aspects of a suggestion, work at making them less objectionable.

6. Do not be defensive when listening to a dissenting opinion.
7. Utilize suggestions and deal with expressed concerns.
8. Give people credit for their suggestions and ideas.

Humanist police managers attempt to deal with the people-oriented problems of bureaucracy through an emphasis on management by participation or team management. They try to create organizational environments in which subordinates are kept fully informed and given meaningful roles in the decision-making process. These administrators spend much of their time counseling, training, and developing personnel. Humanists embrace change and stress the human relations approach in which subordinates are treated in an empathetic and supportive manner to enhance morale. Morale is seen as a pathway to efficiency, effectiveness, and productivity.

Once again, the results of the research on participative management have been mixed. While participation is important, some believe that the ideological air of organizational humanism has distorted the true relationship between participation and motivation. Some research indicates that **participatory** leader behavior is most effective when the tasks being performed are ego involving, ambiguous, and nonroutine. Other studies have concluded that participatory management is most effective when subordinates have enough knowledge and competence to make a meaningful contribution to the organization's decision-making process. According to Robert Albanese, the effects of participation on employee satisfaction and performance will depend on the characteristics of the actors, task variables, and situational factors.[106] Consequently, participation should not be considered as a panacea for creating congruence between employee needs and organizational needs. In some situations and for certain types of personnel, participatory leadership techniques might be very effective. In other situations, however, they are definitely inappropriate.

Management Systems Model

Participative leadership, as espoused by the human relationists and organizational humanists, is predicated on the fundamental assumption that there is a genuine need for power equalization in the management of complex organizations. They argue that it is essential to reduce the power and status differential between superiors and subordinates in order to facilitate meaningful participation. The goal is to deemphasize hierarchical **authority**, to give workers a collective voice in the decision-making process, to encourage creative responses to change, and to overcome apathy by morale-building approaches in which employees become involved with the organization's mission, goals, and objectives and committed to achieving them.[107]

The late Rensis Likert was a leading advocate of **participatory** management. Likert's management systems model represents a continuum of styles ranging from **autocratic** to participatory. The model contrasts traditional management (Theory X) with **democratic** managerial leadership (Theory Y).

Using the well-known Likert scale to measure attitudes and values, he identified four basic management styles or climates:

1. Exploitive authoritarian   System 1
2. Benevolent authoritative   System 2
3. Consultative   System 3
4. Participative group   System 4

Each of these management systems reflects a different approach to handling major organizational processes like motivation, communication, decision-making, goal setting, coordination, and control. Ronald Lynch, in a book on police management, explored Likert's climate concept. A synopsis of his findings is presented here.[108]

System 1—Exploitive Authoritative

Management is seen as having no confidence or trust in its personnel and seldom involves them in any aspect of organizational decision-making. Top management makes virtually all decisions, sets goals, and issues policies, procedures, rules, and regulations through the chain of command. Employees are kept in line through intimidation and manipulation of the reward system. The emphasis is on meeting what Maslow called basic and security needs. Managerial contacts with subordinates often take the form of disciplinary action aimed at correcting employee mistakes or misconduct. The trend in police work (notwithstanding some pockets of resistance) is to move away from System 1 and toward the other end of the continuum.

System 2—Benevolent Authoritative

Management places some degree of confidence and trust in lower-level police personnel, but the organization retains its rigid paramilitary structure. Most decision-making and goal setting take place at the top and are filtered down through the chain of command. System 2 managers accept some input from lower levels and permit personnel in lower-level positions to make some of the less important decisions. Rewards, punishments, and threats of punishment are used to motivate employees. Managers still instill fear and caution in their employees. While there is some delegation and decentralization, rank-and-file police officers continue to be distrustful of their superiors.

System 3—Consultative

Management exhibits substantial but not total trust between leaders and subordinates. Under this arrangement, most decisions are made at lower levels. Effective leaders tend to manage by exception. Policy making and high-level decisions remain in the hands of top administrators. Communication flows upward and downward. Rewards and occasional punishments are used to motivate personnel. Since there is more and more interaction between leaders and followers, mutual trust and confidence replace fear and suspicion. Both the higher and lower levels feel a responsibility for increasing productivity and maintaining quality. A System 3 managerial style places emphasis on what Maslow called the belongingness and self-esteem needs of working police officers.

System 4—Participative Group

Leader behavior and managerial practices demonstrate the total trust and confidence that mid-level and executive-level managers have in their subordinates. Decision-making is widely dispersed and promoted throughout the organization. Communication flows not only up and down within the organization but also horizontally among peers as well. Lower-level employees get involved in (1) establishing organizational goals, (2) improving techniques, procedures, and operations, and (3) evaluating the overall success of the organization in accomplishing its mission, goals, and objectives. System 4 managers create a warm and friendly atmosphere in which all levels are fully involved in decision-making and the control process flows from lower units to the top. System 4 leadership is based on empathetic understanding, mutual trust, meaningful participation, and teamwork in very complex interaction/influence structures.

The variables are labeled: causal, intervening, and end-result. In System 4, stress is placed on group decision-making, and trust and peer group loyalties are clearly evident. On the other hand, System 1 is more reflective of tight work standards and poor communications.

According to Daniel Wren, System 4 management style is built on three basic principles:[109]

1. Supportive relationships
2. Group decision-making and supervision
3. High performance goals

The principle of supportive relationships means leaders must ensure that each member of the work group recognizes a sense of personal worth and self-esteem created and maintained for him or her by the group. The principle of group decision-making and supervision involves an overlapping group structure in which individual work groups are linked to the rest of the organization through persons ("linking pins") who are members of more than one group. The principle of high-performance goals encourages members of the organization to commit themselves to efficiency, effectiveness, and productivity. These high goals should be keyed to the employee's personal needs as well as to the needs of others within the work group. System 4 management allows personnel at all levels of the organization to move toward what Abraham Maslow described as self-actualization.

Organizational humanists contend that a System 4 management style improves employee morale and that good morale is the harbinger of increased productivity. They are convinced that leadership styles at the System 1 end of the continuum lead to frustration, dissatisfaction, apathy, and decreased productivity. Likert believed that System 2 management styles are the most common.

CASE STUDY   Sheriff Ron Hamlin

Hamlin is the sheriff in Monroe County that has a population of 295,321, and there are three communities within the county boundary, the largest of which has a population of 43,451 and is located in the eastern part of the county. He was elected on the consideration of being a change agent and had campaigned vigorously, given a mandate for reform and bringing the department into the 21st century. As the potential replacement for the retiring sheriff, who had been in office for 20 years, if elected, he was going to inherit a department that was viewed as out of touch with the population of the county. Morale in the organization was low, and segments of the local community had lost faith in the retiring sheriff and others in the command structure. It could safely be said that the department was less than efficient. Prior to winning the election, Hamlin was a captain in the department of a large city in the adjoining county, and he had resided in Monroe County for the past 20 years.

Hamlin, in his previous employment, was seen as a competent, emotionally secure, goal-oriented, and very decisive manager. In his campaign, he repeatedly took the position that he had the training to deal effectively with any chaotic situation, and his goal was to professionalize the department. He stressed that he would put all employees on notice that they had to pull their weight or suffer the consequences. It became obvious to the voters and members of the department that he was a man with a mission and that he planned to upgrade his department by whatever means necessary. Hamlin believed strongly in participative management. His principal opponent, who was endorsed by the outgoing sheriff, had the support of the majority of the County Board of Supervisors and the Deputy Sheriffs Association. Hamlin received strong support from the business community and many of the rural residents. Hamlin waged a strong campaign and spent considerable time giving talks before community groups throughout the county. The overwhelming theme was Time or a Change. After the smoke cleared, the results reflected that he won the office by a landslide, it was readily apparent that a new "top gun" was in office, and he would determine the rules and develop policies by which the game would be played.

After the initial flurry of incumbent activities, the sheriff appointed an assistant sheriff and promoted two other members of the department to the positions of captain. These three were strong supports of community policing and participative management.

The first six months were spent in training programs as a means of giving personnel the tools needed to implement community policing and problem solving. The sheriff convened a series of meetings designed to incorporate all of the remaining personnel into the decision-making process. The meetings were held on a regular basis and were designed to reestablish trust through open and honest dialogue. The sheriff encouraged participation and acted more as a teacher and group facilitator than as a dictator. The deputies were given an opportunity to help formulate short-term goals and devise strategies for achieving them. Chief Strock made every attempt to strike an appropriate balance between the needs of the department (for efficiency, effectiveness, and productivity) and the physical, psychological, and social needs of his subordinates. He was convinced that his brand of organizational humanism would lead to more efficiency, effectiveness, and productivity.

Many things were not a bed of roses. Some deputies rejected the sheriff's efforts to draw them into the decision-making process. They were content to sit back and complain about things as they waited for the revolutionary type of management style to fail. They were used to being spectators, not participants, in the management process. The officers were mistrustful and saw participative management as just a political ploy. They did not want to become guinea pigs and knuckle under to the new administration.

The County Board of Supervisors decided to wait and see what would happen. They were fully aware that the new sheriff had been elected by a landslide, and the voters had approved a clean sweep of the department. The board was also aware that the new sheriff was gaining a great deal of political clout. Sheriff Hamlin never anticipated the resistance to his managerial style, but he decided to just charge ahead and let happen what would happen.

Under the circumstances of the described situation, did he make any mistakes in what he did? If any, what were they and what could he have done differently? Is participative management relevant to law enforcement? Why or why not? Defend the decision to implement community policing and problem solving. Outline a paper in support of this decision. Should he have considered a different style of management to start with? If so, what style of management? What would you—as an aspiring police administrator—have done differently in this particular situation? Specify.

If we can assume that the actual situation in police organizations reflects prevailing management theories, we would expect to find that most police employees find themselves in a System 2 climate. In one recent study of 18 local police departments of various sizes in 15 different states, Charles R. Swanson, Leonard Territo, and Robert W. Taylor asked 629 uniformed police officers assigned to field duties to describe their department's management climate. The results were interesting and tended to confirm Likert's *management systems model*. Some 16.6 percent of the officers assessed their climate as System 1, 42.9 percent reported living under System 2, 35.9 percent identified with System 3, and a mere 4.6 percent thought their departments used the System 4 approach to management.[110]

Research on the participation factor has found that it—much like the other theories discussed in this chapter—produces mixed results. There is no reason to believe that **participatory** leadership is the one best way to manage law enforcement agencies.

Transformational and Transactional Leadership Styles

A somewhat newer model of leadership that is receiving increased attention is best described as **transformational**/transactional. *Transformational leadership* alters employee relationships with, and views of, the organization. It is a process that focuses on building commitment and creating working relationships that allow task accomplishment. Organizational goals and needs become paramount. Self-indulgence and the satisfaction of personal needs become secondary. Subordinate employees are empowered, and in accepting that empowerment, they consciously seek higher levels of morality and motivation. Abstract concepts such as equality, justice, liberty, and humanitarianism supersede their baser instincts.[111] The process is two pronged: At the same time as employees are taking on responsibility for organizational enhancement, their leaders are taking on responsibility to provide for the employees' personal and professional growth. This motivates followers to do more than anticipated—more, in many instances, than they thought possible.[112]

Expectations set so high that they challenge, empower, and stimulate clearly result in improved performance.[113]

The strategy of empowerment is best implemented by emphasizing a range of managerial leadership activities including communication, goal setting, and feedback. Through empowerment, it is believed that there will be a commitment to organizational goals and objectives. When the empowerment process is implemented properly, officers are encouraged to think for themselves and utilize their talents and expertise when dealing with law enforcement problems. When leadership addresses the self-worth of subordinates, it provides for commitment that is foundational to the organization. The result is a total and ceaseless process of leader–follower interchange that invokes response from subordinates and modifies their behavior. Conflict is mediated, and motivational techniques are paramount.[114] **Transformational** leadership makes the skills and knowledge of subordinates a means of goal attainment; employee recommendations become a vehicle that enhances transition and realization. Throughout the process, leadership communicates the reasons for decisions and actions. The greater understanding this gives subordinates not only allows them to operate more efficiently, but it also empowers them to exercise initiative—which is the keystone to operational effectiveness. This type of leadership focuses on the positive treatment of officers and fosters the development of idealized influence and the positive motivation of employees. It is viewed as a social process that emphasizes the vision of the organization.[115]

Transformational leadership utilizes the following indicators of leadership: intellectual inspiration, inspiring leadership, idealized stimulus, and individualized consideration that enhance commitment.

The leader influences organizational members by stressing the vision he or she has for the organization as a means of providing direction to the organization and motivating personnel. The goal is to get all members to support organizational improvement and function as change agents and to become involved. Another key is to challenge the traditional way of doing things by encouraging the consideration of innovative ideas.[116]

Transformational leadership strives to achieve superior results by following these precepts:[117]

1. Present charismatic role models.
2. Motivate and inspire.
3. Stimulate innovation and creativity.
4. Stress individual needs for achievement and growth.

Leadership becomes charismatic when officers strive to identify with the superior and imitate him or her. However, research indicates that while having at least a moderate level of charisma is important, having too much may hinder a leader's effectiveness.[118] The true leader is one who is trusted and demonstrates extraordinary capabilities. Because of inspired motivation, the officers respond with enthusiasm and optimism and become committed to such an extent that team spirit is aroused. Transformational leadership encourages innovation and readily allows for the questioning of assumptions without recrimination. Additionally, special attention is given to individual needs, and growth is provided for through coaching and mentoring.[119] The great leaders mentor on a range of topics, but their most crucial teachings relate to professionalism (doing the right thing), elements of the job (extensive knowledge and experience related to the basics of the profession), and life lessons (insight about life).[120]

A considerably different approach, taken by some leaders, is the *transactional leadership* style. The specific techniques used by this style range from rewarding officers to disciplining. Notable achievements are acknowledged through contingency rewards. Tasks are assigned or agreed to, and rewards are given upon successful task achievement. Tasks are assigned in writing and include detailed listings of all rules, regulations, and other guidance that may be relevant. The benefits associated with task achievement and the negative consequences of failure are clearly identified. *Management by exception* is practiced, meaning that leaders focus all their attention on monitoring employee work and looking for errors and mistakes. Monitoring is the byword of the day, and deviance from standards is anticipated.

The leader who relies exclusively on a **transactional** style takes on a lot of baggage. Subordinate commitment is usually short term, and such things as creativity and innovation become a thing of the past—if they ever existed. Other negative aspects of this style include the absence of room for individual growth and the negative sanctions that can result even from an honest mistake. **Transactional** leadership can work in some situations, but the leaders who have used it most effectively have selectively used its techniques together with transformational techniques, in combinations tailored to particular situations.[121]

Lifelong learning is becoming a reality of the day if a police leader is to keep abreast of demanding change. It has been pointed out by two leading experts (Jim Kouzes and Barry Posner) that leadership development is first and foremost self-development. It is suggested that effective leaders inherently know the value of constantly seeking self-improvement and keeping up with the latest thoughts and ideas. Positive growth can result in self-improvement and organizational mission achievement.[122] Unfortunately, the promised land of leadership has been and will continue to be an elusive destination, but self-improvement can narrow the gap between the past and the future. Tremendous progress has been made during the last few decades, and it is hoped that quantum leaps will occur in the near future.

Good to Great

The Good-to-Great concept is a refreshing and unique outlook on managerial leadership. This view has begun to have considerable impact on the field of law enforcement. It has been strongly supported by the Community Oriented Policing Services (COPS), U.S. Department of Justice, and the Police Executive Research Forum (PERF).[123] It is the most recent effort to apply business management principles to the public sector.

James Collins and his colleagues examined 11 great companies and compared them to 11 companies that did not achieve greatness. A key element of this approach is initially striving to identify highly competent individuals and incorporating them into a viable team. These should be people who are truly committed and have a real enthusiasm for accomplishment. With the right people, motivation becomes less important as everyone strives to create an unbelievable and dynamic organization. The internal drive of each member of the team provides the impetus needed to move from a good organization to a great organization. The key as expressed by James Collin is that the right people are central to organizational achievement.[124]

Another key element is for managerial leadership to set the tone that calls for becoming the very best at what it does and does it in such a way that the core purposes are fulfilled and members of the community are given the best possible law enforcement services. Collins describes this as the *Hedgehog Concept* and sees great managers as those who act like a hedgehog and ploddingly sift through data and the organizational maze and have an ability to determine what is really important coming up with an underlying organizational strategy that provides for the application of the mission as well as the implementation of a unified vision and a devotion to the agency's core values. When this is coupled with one's passion about what needs to be achieved, things begin to happen wherein the organization becomes the very best at what it does.[125] Additionally, the great companies have a *Culture of Discipline* and employees have self-discipline, and consequently, they can be given greater freedom and increasing amounts of responsibility. Collin's caution that in a social agency such as the police what is important is the output of the organization and that the transformation to a really great police agency can be a slow process over a period of time before an actual conversion occurs. This is known as the *Flywheel*, and the best companies found that the transformation was incremental rather than the result of some single dramatic action. On the other hand, the less-successful companies followed the *Doom Loop*, reacting to managerial fads and demonstrating a real lack of consistency.[126] Another characteristic of a great organization is that people who are hired have a definite capacity for self-discipline, and this allows leaders with the task of managing the system, not the people in the organization.[127]

From this research, it was determined that the highest level in a hierarchal arrangement was a Level 5 leader. An individual in this position was found to be at the highest level of executive capabilities. It was especially interesting to determine that individuals functioning at this level were self-effacing, quiet, reserved, and even shy. Also leaders at this level possessed qualities of humility and strong professional drive. Level 5 leaders had the capacity to channel their ambitions into the building of a great company, and personal ego needs were subordinated to any consideration of self-interest.[128] Table 2–3 sets forth the characteristics of Level 5 leadership. An important characteristic is that leaders in

Table 2–3
LEVEL 5 LEADERSHIP CHARACTERISTICS

Personal humility	Professional will
Self-effacing	Quiet
Reserved	Organizational success viewed as imperative
Reticent	Successfulness based on some luck
Mild mannered	Understanding
Ego-supported organizational attainment	Unpretentious

Sources: Jim Collins, *Good to Great: Why Some Companies Make the Leap and Others Don't* (New York: HarperCollins Publishers, 2001), pp. 12–13, 40; Chuck Wexler, Mary Ann Wycoff, and Craig Fischer, "*Good to Great*" *Policing: Application of Business Management Principles in the Public Sector* (Washington, D.C.: Police Executive Research Forum, 2007), pp. 1–51.

this category support subordinates so that they are in a position to assume positions of leadership.

Level 5 leaders are described by Jim Collins as people who display a workman-like diligence and always attribute success to others in the organization, and if things go poorly, they look in the mirror and assume blame. Another quality for this type of leader is to get the right people on the bus and work diligently at creating a superior executive team. Jim Collins rejects the old adage—that people are the real asset of the organization—and re-phrases this adage into the "right people." This research found that the really great or-ganizations had a "culture of discipline" and employees could be given a great deal of freedom and responsibility—bureaucratic rules, for the purpose of control, are rejected out of hand.[129] These are very interesting leadership characteristics, and at initial blush, some of the features seem to be incongruent to law enforcement. It is difficult for some to see how a police executive can be reticent, quiet, or mild-mannered or just be lucky to have organizational attainment occur. One might ask how luck can have anything to do with Level 5 leadership. Traditionalists have taken the view that everyone knows that clear, concise decision-making is what counts; all together it seems to be shades of a new ap-proach to the previously discarded **trait** theory, but if you are lucky who can argue with it. Over the years, it has been conventional to view many police executives as forceful, deci-sive, and possessing a strong personal persona—significant attributes in any crisis situation. The public environment is different than the business arena, but at the same time, there is food for thought in Level 5 leadership, and it should give us pause as to what is relevant and important.

There is great value in the concept Good to Great, and at the very least, it can give current and potential leaders a frame of reference for evaluating their own view of lead-ership. The PERF notes that achieving greatest in many instances is about "overcoming obstacles," and this has direct application to the field of law enforcement. The PERF view might be summed as "Collins has given us the dots and the challenge is to connect the dots in the context of organizational puzzles."[130]

SUMMARY

There is absolutely no doubt that leadership plays a pivotal role in organizational dynam-ics. Police administrators are expected to be leaders as well as managers. Management leadership, as we have called it, is a behavioral transaction that involves influencing, mo-tivating, guiding, and controlling human resources in cooperative efforts to accomplish an organization's mission, goals, and objectives. It is an interactive achievement-oriented process through which individual members of the work group are induced to follow a leader; in so doing, they receive psychosocial satisfaction from willingly behaving the way the leader wants them to behave. Part of the task of the leader is to get subordinates to participate in the leadership process.

Many types of people make good leaders. No one leadership style has proven to be effective in all situations. Consequently, management theorists tend to define leadership in terms of their own perspective and/or those aspects of the phenomenon that interest them the most. As we have seen, the concept of leadership has been explored in terms of traits, behavior, style, influence, roles, interaction, and situational variables. Five major explanatory paradigms have emerged and dominated the study of leadership in general and managerial leadership in particular. They are (1) the trait approach, (2) the leader be-havior approach, (3) the situational approach, (4) the interaction/influence approach, and (5) the human relations approach. After more than 50 years of contemplation and applied research, theoretical pragmatists have concluded that there is no one best way to manage complex organizations.

Rensis Likert used the well-known Likert scale to measure attitudes and values to identify four basic management styles or climates:

1. Exploitive authoritative	System 1
2. Benevolent authoritative	System 2
3. Consultative	System 3
4. Participative group	System 4

Each of these approaches reflects a different way of handling major organizational processes like motivation, communication, decision-making, goal setting, coordination, and control.

While **participatory** leadership is often touted as the ultimate form of management, the situational approach is much closer to reality. When the chips are down, the most appropriate leadership style will depend on the synergistic interactions among the actors, the task, and the environmental factors that coalesced to create the particular leadership situation. A relatively recent theme is the potential application of transformational and transactional leadership styles to law enforcement agencies.

A considerably different approach, taken by some leaders, is the *transactional leadership* style. The specific techniques used by this style range from rewarding officers to disciplining. Transformational leadership encourages innovation and readily allows for the questioning of assumptions without recrimination. Additionally, special attention is given to individual needs, and growth is provided for through coaching and mentoring.

Lifelong learning is becoming a reality of the day if a police leader is to keep abreast of demanding change. It has been pointed out by two leading experts (Jim Kouzes and Barry Posner) that leadership development is first and foremost self-development. It is suggested that effective leaders inherently know the value of constantly seeking self-improvement and keeping up with the latest thoughts and ideas.

Under the concept from "Good to Great," Level 5 leadership business executives of highly successful enterprises exhibited a number of characteristics such as self-effacing, humble, reserved, mild-mannered, and quiet. In addition, it is interesting to note they had a strong professional will and were driven by the need to attain sustainable results. Other qualities included being unpretentious, and interestingly enough, they acknowledged that luck plays an important part of their achievement. Of additional importance are such variables as the Hedgehog concept, a culture of discipline and the defining of success.

Many management theorists now believe that adaptive leaders—those who are able to change their style of leadership based on the situation and the needs of their subordinates—will be the most effective when it comes to achieving both personal and organizational objectives. They see adaptive management as a pathway to effective police administration in the 21st century.

DISCUSSION TOPICS AND QUESTIONS

1. Distinguish between knowledge areas and leadership skills. Explain their relationship to effective police management.

2. What place does trait theory have in the scheme of preparing to be an effective police manager?

3. Based on the managerial grid, what is 5-5 management, and how does it relate to Rensis Likert's System 3 approach?

4. Describe Fred Fiedler's contingency model of leadership.

5. Discuss the importance of managerial leadership in terms of the interactive/influence system.

6. Identify the four basic leader behavior styles as proposed by path-goal theorists.

7. Why do most police officers find themselves working in a System 2 organizational environment?

8. What are the implications of Good to Great? What is Level 5 leadership?

9. Discuss the concept of the eternal triangle. Why is it essential for leaders to understand human behavior?

10. Discuss the attributes of the transactional style of leadership.

FOR FURTHER READING

H. R. Haberfeld, *Police Leadership* (Upper Saddle River, NJ: Pearson Prentice Hall, 2006).

A well-written text that conceives of leadership in terms of a broad range of organizational leadership theories including a consideration of transformational theory and other organizational leadership theories such as team theory, leader–member exchange theory, and style theory. It also includes a consideration of situational theory, contingency theory, and path-goal theory. Consideration is given to parameters for empowerment and trust theory. Of special interest is its focus on the leadership of ethics and integrity. The author also touches on the future by a consideration of big hairy audacious goals as set forth by James Collins. Additional attention is given to community-oriented policing as well as leadership in a critical incident.

Donald Griner, "People-Oriented Leadership," *The Police Chief*, Vol. LXX (2003), pp. 10, 30–34.

The author recommends that police leaders focus on work processes much less than they do on the people who work within the processes. People-oriented managers know their employees' strengths and talents, and they place people in positions that take advantage of those positive characteristics. The author suggests that great managers know the mission of the police department and how to accomplish that mission. He stresses that a leader unlocks the potential in each employee to achieve organizational goals. He also discusses the importance of communication and problem-solving models.

Robert Adlam and Peter Villiers, eds., *Police Leadership in the 21st Century* (London: Waterside Press Company, 2004).

This is a collection of works on the concept of policing leadership that are authoritative and innovative. The articles are approached from three views: philosophy, doctrine, and developmental. Leadership is viewed as something that is not as much of a mystery as some believe. Their position is that leadership in the police field can turn to mainstream leadership theory. It is their position that the qualities of leadership can be acquired by education and training. This book addresses the challenges of leadership at all levels of the police service.

Ronald W. Serpas and Matthew Morley, "The Next Step in Accountability—Driven Leadership: 'CompStating' the CompStat Data," *The Police Chief*, Vol. LXXV, No. 5 (2008), pp. 60–70.

The author discusses the importance of accountability driven leadership that moves beyond the initial use of CompStat. It is viewed as a critical step in the continual professionalization of law enforcement. Accountability is viewed as the key to improving departmental efficiency and effectiveness. Consideration is given to a wide range of activities when conducting quantitative and qualitative analysis of internal and external data. A description is provided of the importance of analysis of original and supplemental reports and computer-aided dispatch data. There is a description of virtual audit teams that focus their attention on the auditing of units and commands. There is also a brief discussion of the use of polling services to assess the perceptions and observations of the public at large.

ENDNOTES

1. James M. Kouzes and Barry Z. Posner, *A Leader's Legacy* (San Francisco, CA: Jossey-Bass, 2006), p. 17.
2. Michael LeBoeuf, *GMP: The Greatest Management Principle in the World* (New York: Berkley Books, 1985), pp. 12–18.
3. Vivian A. Leonard and Harry W. More, *Police Organization and Management*, 9th ed. (New York: Foundation Press, 2000), pp. 256–258.
4. Nathan F. Iannone, M. D. Iannone, and Jeff Bernstein, *Supervision of Police Personnel*, 7th ed. (Upper Saddle River, NJ: Prentice Hall, 2009), pp. 83–86.
5. Keith D. Bushey, "The Unproductive Executive," *The Police Chief*, Vol. LXVI, No. 3 (1999), pp. 69–73.
6. Mary Parker Follett, "Leader and Expert," in E. M. Fox and L. Urwick, eds. *Dynamic Administration* (New York: Hippocrene Books, 1978).
7. Leonard and More, *Police Organization and Management*, p. 280.
8. Warren G. Bennis, *The Unconscious Conspiracy: Why Can't Leaders Lead* (New York: AMACOM, 1976).
9. Lester R. Bittel, *What Every Supervisor Should Know: The Complete Guide to Supervisory Management*, 6th ed. (New York: McGraw-Hill, 1992), pp. 275–276.
10. Gary A. Yukl, *Leadership in Organization*, 6th ed. (Upper Saddle River, NJ: Prentice Hall, 2005), p. 6.
11. Horsager, D. You Can't be a Great Leader without Trust-Here's How You Build It. *Forbes Leadership Forum*, 2012. Retrieved from https://www.forbes.com/sites/forbesleadershipforum/2012/10/24/you-cant-be-a-great-leader-without-trust-heres-how-you-build-it/#192c39854ef7.
12. Ibid.
13. "Ethical Breakdowns," *Harvard Business Review*, April 2011.
14. D. M. Mayer, M. Kuenzi, R. Greenbaum, M. Bardes, and R. Salvador, "How Low Does Ethical Leadership Flow?" *Test of a Trickle-Down Model, Organizational Behavior and Human Decisions Processes*, Vol. 108 (2009), pp. 1–13.
15. Ibid.

16. B. V. Zuidema and H. W. Duff, Jr., "Organizational Ethics through Effective Leadership," *FBI Law Enforcement Bulletin*, March 2009, 8–11, Retrieved from http://leb.fbi.gov/2009-pdfs/leb-march-2009 (accessed June 30, 2018).

17. Craig L. Pearce and Jay A. Conger, eds., *Shared Leadership: Reframing the Hows and Whys of Leadership* (Thousand Oaks, CA: Sage, 2003), p. xi.

18. Jean Lipman-Blumen, *Connective Leadership: Managing in a Changing World* (Oxford: Oxford University Press, 1999), p. 32.

19. Herbert A. Simon, *Administrative Behavior* (New York: Free Press, 1976).

20. Andrew J. Dubrin, *The Complete Idiot's Guide to Leadership* (New York: Alpha Book, A Simon & Schuster Macmillan Company, 1998), p. 5.

21. Ronald G. Lynch, *The Police Manager*, 5th ed. (Cincinnati, OH: Anderson, 1998).

22. Richard Plunkett, *Supervision: The Direction of People at Work*, 9th ed. (Dubuque, IA: William C. Brown, 2000).

23. Yukl, *Leadership in Organization*, p. 189.

24. John R. Schermerhorn, James G. Hunt, and Richard N. Osborne, *Organizational Behavior*, 9th ed. (New York: Wiley, 2002), pp. 71–76.

25. Schermerhorn, *Organizational Behavior*.

26. Richard Holden, *Modern Police Management*, 2nd ed. (Englewood Cliffs, NJ: Prentice Hall, 2000), pp. 37–38.

27. David A. Tansik, Richard B. Chase, and Nicholas J. Aquilano, *Management: A Life Cycle Approach* (Homewood, IL: Richard D. Irwin, 1980), pp. 85–90.

28. Hannah Arendt and Margaret Canovan, *The Human Condition* (Chicago, IL: University of Chicago Press, 1998), p. 127.

29. Chester I. Barnard and Kenneth Richard Andrews, *The Functions of the Executive* (Cambridge, MA: Harvard University Press, 2007), pp. 216–134.

30. Sam S. Souryal, *Police Administration and Management* (St. Paul, MN: West, 1977), pp. 39–61.

31. Douglas M. McGregor, *The Human Side of Enterprise* (New York: McGraw-Hill, 1960), pp. 23–49.

32. Gary Dessler, *A Framework for Management*, 2nd ed. (Upper Saddle River, NJ: Pearson, 2001), pp. 420–424.

33. Frederick Herzberg, "One More Time: How Do You Motivate Employees?," *Harvard Business Press* (January 2003), pp. 35–40.

34. Barnard and Andrews, *The Functions of the Executive*.

35. Robert L. Katz, "Skills of an Effective Administrator," *Harvard Business Review*, Vol. 52, No. 5 (1974), pp. 6–12.

36. Edward A. Thibault, Lawrence M. Lynch, and R. Bruce McBride, *Proactive Police Management*, 7th ed. (Upper Saddle River, NJ: Prentice Hall, 2006).

37. Robert M. Fulmer, *The New Management* (New York: Macmillan, 1983), pp. 339–340.

38. Katz, "Skills of an Effective Administrator," p. 39.

39. Jesse Sostrin, "To Be a Great Leader, You Have to Learn How to Delegate Well," *Harvard Business Review* (2017). Retrieved from https://hbr.org/2017/10/to-be-a-great-leader-you-have-to-learn-how-to-delegate-well.

40. Nathaniel Foote, Russell Eisenstat, and Tobias Fredberg, "The Higher-Ambition Leader," *Harvard Business Review* (2011). Retrieved from https://hbr.org/2011/09/the-higher-ambition-leader.

41. Melvin Sorcher and James Brant, "Are You Picking the Right Leaders," *Harvard Business Review* (2002). Retrieved from https://hbr.org/2002/02/are-you-picking-the-right-leaders.

42. Robert Albanese, Geralyn McClure Franklin, and Peter Wright, *Management*, 2nd ed. (New York: Notre Dame Publishing, 1999), pp. 231–287.

43. Dessler, *A Framework for Management*.

44. Charles R. Swanson, Leonard Territo, and Robert W. Taylor, *Police Administration: Structures, Processes and Behavior*, 7th ed. (Upper Saddle River, NJ: Prentice Hall, 2007), pp. 45–83.

45. Holden, *Modern Police Management*.

46. Robert A. Baron, *Behavior in Organizations: Understanding and Managing the Human Side of Work* (Boston, MA: Allyn & Bacon, 1983).

47. Ralph C. Davis, *Industrial Organization and Management*, 3rd ed. (New York: Harper and Brothers, 1957).

48. Cecil E. Goode, "Significant Research on Leadership," *Personnel*, Vol. 18, No. 3 (1976), pp. 25–29.

49. E. E. Ghiselli, *Explorations in Management Talent* (Pacific Palisades, CA: Goodyear, 1971), p. 139.

50. Ralph M. Stogdill, *Handbook of Leadership* (New York: Free Press, 1999), pp. 8–132.

51. Joe Kelly, *Organizational Behavior: An Existential Systems Approach* (Homewood, IL: Richard D. Irwin, 1974), pp. 12–89.

52. Albanese, Franklin, and Wright, *Management*.

53. Schermerhorn, Hunt, and Osborne, *Organizational Behavior*.

54. Baron, *Behavior in Organizations*.

55. Yukl, *Leadership in Organization*, pp. 29–32.

56. Tansik, Chase, and Aquilano, *Management*.

57. Philip V. Lewis, Ronald Lippit, and Ralph K. White, "Patterns of Aggressive Behavior in Experimentally Created 'Social Climates,'" *Journal of Social Psychology*, Vol. 10 (1939), pp. 271–301.

58. Philip V. Lewis, *Managing Human Relations* (Boston, MA: Kent, 1983).

59. Daniel Galeman, "The Focused Leader," *Harvard Business Review* (2013). Retrieved from https://hbr.org/2013/12/the-focused-leader.

60. Holden, *Modern Police Management*.

61. Robert Tannenbaum and Warren H. Schmidt, "How to Choose a Leadership Pattern," *Harvard Business Review Classic*, Vol. 51, No. 3 (2008), pp. 5–9.

62. Phillip B. Applewhite, *Organizational Behavior* (Englewood Cliffs, NJ: Prentice Hall, 1965), pp. 130–132.

63. Dessler, *A Framework for Management*.

64. Leonard and More, *Police Organization and Management*, pp. 259–261.

65. Fulmer, *The New Management*, pp. 15–32.

66. Yukl, *Leadership in Organization*, pp. 46–47; Albanese, Franklin, and Wright, *Management*.

67. H. Joe Reitz, *Behavior in Organizations* (Homewood, IL: Richard D. Irwin, 1981).

68. Justin G. Longenecker and Charles D. Pringle, *Principles of Management and Organizational Behavior* (Columbus, OH: Charles E. Merrill, 1984), p. 214.

69. Stogdill, *Handbook of Leadership*.

70. Reitz, *Behavior in Organizations*.

71. Yukl, *Leadership in Organization*, pp. 133–136.

72. Robert R. Blake and Jane Srygley Mouton, *The Managerial Grid III: The Key to Leadership Excellence* (Houston, TX: Gulf, 1985), p. 29.

73. Ibid.

74. Plunkett, *Supervision*.

75. Blake and Mouton, *The Managerial Grid III*, p. 12.

76. Leonard and More, *Police Organization and Management*, p. 263.

77. Jack L. Kuykendall and Peter Unsinger, "The Leadership Style of Police Managers," *Journal of Criminal Justice*, Vol. 9 (1982), pp. 182–189.

78. Ibid.

79. Roy R. Roberg and Jack L. Kuykendall, *Police Organization and Management: Behavior, Theory and Practice*, 2nd ed. (Pacific Grove, CA: Brooks/Cole, 1996).

80. Jack L. Kuykendall, "Police Leadership: An Analysis of Executive Style," *Criminal Justice Review*, Vol. 2, No. 1 (1977), pp. 7–9.

81. Blake and Mouton, *The Managerial Grid III*, pp. 98–103.

82. Fred Luthans, *Organizational Behavior*, 11th ed. (New York: McGraw-Hill, 2006).

83. Longenecker and Pringle, *Principles of Management and Organizational Behavior*; Albanese, Franklin, and Wright, *Management*.

84. Fulmer, *The New Management*.

85. Paul M. Whisenand, *The Effective Police Manager* (Englewood Cliffs, NJ: Prentice Hall, 1981).

86. Lynch, *The Police Manager*.

87. Paul Whisenand, *The Managing of Police Organizations*, 7th ed. (Upper Saddle River, NJ: Prentice Hall, 2008), pp. 221–232.

88. Fred Fiedler, "A Contingency Model of Leadership Effectiveness," in L. Berkowitz, ed. *Advances in Experimental Social Psychology* (New York: Academic Press, 1964).

89. Plunkett, *Supervision*.

90. Reitz, *Behavior in Organizations*.

91. Leonard and More, *Police Organization and Management*, pp. 264–265.

92. Tansik, Chase, and Aquilano, *Management*.

93. Longenecker and Pringle, *Principles of Management and Organizational Behavior*.

94. Plunkett, *Supervision*.

95. Leonard and More, *Police Organization and Management*, p. 265.

96. Fiedler, *Managerial Control and Organizational Democracy*.

97. Robert J. House, "A Path-Goal Theory of Leadership Effectiveness," *Administrative Science Quarterly*, Vol. XVI (1971), p. 321.

98. Gary Johns, *Organizational Behavior* (Dallas, TX: Foresman, 1988).

99. Reitz, *Behavior in Organizations*.

100. Albanese, Franklin, and Wright, *Management*, pp. 237–291.

101. Dessler, *A Framework for Management*.

102. Albanese, Franklin, and Wright, *Management*.

103. McGregor, *The Human Side of Enterprise*.

104. J. M. Roscow, "Quality of Work Life Issues for the 1980s," in C. Kerr and J. M. Roscow, eds. *Work in America: The Decade Ahead* (New York: Van Nostrand, 1979).

105. Daniel Wren, *The Evolution of Management Thought* (New York: Wiley, 1987).

106. Albanese, Franklin, and Wright, *Management*.

107. Wren, *The Evolution of Management Thought*.

108. Lynch, *The Police Manager*.

109. Wren, *The Evolution of Management Thought*.

110. Swanson, Territo, and Taylor, *Police Administration*.

111. Yukl, *Leadership in Organization,* p. 324.

112. Bernard M. Bass, *A New Paradigm of Leadership: An Inquiry into Transformational Leadership* (Alexandria, VA: U.S. Army Research Institute for the Behavioral and Social Sciences, 1996), p. 4.

113. Tracey G. Gove, "Empowerment and Accountability—Tools for Law Enforcement Leaders," *FBI Law Enforcement Bulletin*, Vol. 75, No. 9 (2007), pp. 8–12.

114. Ray Bynum, "Transformational Leadership and Staff Training in the Law Enforcement Profession," *The Police Chief*, Vol. LXXV, No. 2 (2008), pp. 72–81.

115. Yukl, *Leadership in Organization*, pp. 325–326.

116. Steven Murphy and Edward Drodge, "The Four I's of Police Leadership: A Case Study of Heuristic," *International Journal of Police Science & Administration*, Vol. 6, No. 1 (2003), pp. 1–15.

117. Bass, *A New Paradigm of Leadership*, pp. 5–6.

118. Jasmine Vergauwe, Bart Wille, Joeri Hofmans, Robert B. Kaiser, and Filip De Fruyt, "Too Much Charisma Can Make Leaders Look Less Effective," *Harvard Business Review* (2017). Retrieved from https://hbr.org/2017/09/too-much-charisma-can-make-leaders-look-less-effective.

119. Bernard M. Bass, *Transformational Leadership: Industrial, Military, and Educational Impact* (Mahwah, NJ: Lawrence Erlbaum Associates, 1998), pp. 4–6.

120. Sydney Finkelstein, "The Best Leaders Are Great Teachers," *Harvard Business Review* (2018). Retrieved from https://hbr.org/2018/01/the-best-leaders-are-great-teachers.

121. Department of the Army, *Army Leadership: Be, Know, Do*, FM 22–100 (Washington, D.C.: Headquarters, Department of the Army, August 1999), pp. 1-3–1-18.

122. Jeffrey C. Lindsey, "Eagles Flock Together," *FBI Law Enforcement Bulletin*, Vol. 76, No. 5 (2007), p. 9.

123. Chuck Wexler, Mary Ann Wycoff, and Craig Fischer, "*Good to Great*" *Policing: Application of Business Management Principles in the Public Sector* (Washington, D.C.: Police Executive Research Forum, 2007), pp. 1–52.

124. James C. Collins, *Good to Great: Why Some Companies Make the Leap and Others Don't* (New York: HarperCollins, 2001), pp. 12–13.

125. Ibid., pp. 41–43.

126. Ibid.

127. Ibid., pp. 90–100.

128. Ibid., pp. 112, 165.

129. Ibid., pp. 113, 120–140.

130. Wexler, Wycoff, and Fisher, "*Good to Great*" *Policing*, pp. 51–52.

3
PERSONALITY

Understanding the Complexity of Human Behavior in the Organization

Learning Objectives

1. Define *personality*.
2. Identify personality determinants.
3. List the various personality theories.
4. Describe the relationship of personality to work.

Key Terms

avoidance
culture
defense mechanisms
ego
emotional intelligence
"Five-Factor" Model
heredity
High-Machs
humanistic theory
id
interactional psychology
locus of control
Machiavellianism

personality
personality determinants
police personality
projection
psychoanalytical theory
screening process
situational factors
socialization
superego
trait theory
traits
Type A behavior
Type B behavior

A police department is a group of people joined together in order to achieve organizational goals and satisfy their personal needs. The methods used to achieve these goals, and the presence or absence of competition among the goals, depend in part on the personalities of the managers and employees involved. People are the organization, and they represent the most important departmental asset. The nature of the police role with its power and authority requires that police departments not only hire qualified individuals but also manage their behavior as they perform their duties. Police departments are expected to put hiring and management systems in place that protect the community from unstable or incompetent officers. Personality is often seen as the determinate of the way people react to situations. Police managers are expected to know and understand their employees as well as continually monitor and analyze their performance. This is a difficult but necessary task that is vital to both the effectiveness of the department and the safety of the community. Unfortunately, there has not been universal agreement on the exact meaning and creation of personality. This is because psychologists disagree as to how personality is acquired and what causes it to change.[1] Nevertheless, managers must deal with the reality of the situations they encounter and the different personalities of the employees involved.

Linda Willard is a member of the Sea View Police Department and is in her ninth year of service. She is married and has two children, three and six years old. She is a graduate of the local community college, with a degree in law enforcement. As a college student, she interned in three different local law enforcement agencies. She was an explorer scout, and, as a youth, she spent weekends riding a dirt bike, which influenced her career goal to become a motorcycle officer.

The Sea View Police Department has 642 sworn positions, including 14 motorcycle officers who make up the traffic unit. Officer Willard had been on a waiting list for six years before passing a series of rigid coordination and safety tests and receiving the appointment to the motorcycle unit.

As a patrol officer, she enforces the law aggressively, and her orientation is extremely legalistic. In her view, the law is "absolute," and a violation is a violation. There is no room for consideration of the spirit of the law. A transgressor of the law should always be arrested or cited, she feels; social consideration should be left up to social workers.

Officer Willard really enjoys her work and riding her bike in the countryside. She refused to take a promotional examination prior to her assignment to traffic, because it was more important to her to become a motor officer than to receive a promotion. Within the department, the motor officers are looked upon as a different breed. They are viewed as highly aggressive and always in the thick of things, with a real love of facing danger. The unit members consider themselves the real elite unit in the department. All members have a

great deal of pride not only in the work they perform but also in their uniform and physical appearance, which set them apart from other members of the department.

Officer Willard has been involved in three accidents since her appointment to the motorcycle unit. In every instance, she was fortunate enough not to be seriously injured, but the motorcycles were totaled. Top management in the police department is becoming increasingly concerned about the aggressive behavior of the members of the motorcycle unit—not only in their contact with the public but also in the increasing number of accidents and injuries to officers. During the last calendar year, motorcycle officers have been involved in nine accidents. As a result of injuries, one officer has been retired on disability, and three officers have been on sick leave for a total of 61 days. Unfortunately, during the same period, the number of citizen complaints against motor officers has doubled as compared to the average for the previous five calendar years.

The officer in charge of the traffic unit, Captain Roger Miles, has been asked to devise a program for reducing motorcycle accidents and citizen complaints. The chief questions Miles's selection of Linda Willard because of her aggressive nature, the number of accidents she has been involved in recently, and the fact that she has received four citizen complaints during the last year. If you were Captain Miles, how would you handle this problem? Do you think motor officers should be selected because they are aggressive? After reaching a conclusion, keep it in mind, and then after reading this chapter, review this case and see if your solution changes.

Personality

Personality Defined

The term **personality** refers to the unique combination of ways of thinking and behaving that make an individual who he or she is. It embodies amalgamation of the complete combination of characteristics that encapsulate the distinctive nature of a person as that individual responds to and interacts with others.[2] Many people make loose use of psychological terms like "introvert" and "extrovert" to describe the personalities of others. Such labels convey a brief impressionistic description of the person being referred to.[3]

Although attempts to categorize personalities have pitfalls, the process can be useful to managers because there is evidence to show that personality can influence behavior. A realistic awareness of personality can be helpful to managers because it can allow them to predict the behavior of employees, peers, and superiors. Here is one formal definition of personality:

> Personality is a stable set of characteristics and tendencies that determine the commonalities and differences in the psychological behavior (thoughts, feelings, and actions) of people, having continuity in time, and that may not be easily understood as the sole result of the social and biological pressures of the moment.[4]

This definition expresses a general theory of human behavior. It applies to everyone, not just to one individual or a class of individuals in a given situation. Personality, so defined, describes a person's total behavior under varying circumstances and at different times. Some feel personality is so important that it describes the very essence of what it means to be a *Homo sapiens.*

Another feature of this definition is it addresses both commonalities and differences. Our personalities include some features that we have in common with everyone else and some that are exclusive to us, not seen in others. Managers must look for and understand the features that all employees share as well as the ones that make each individual employee unique. This combination of similarities and differences is what makes humans unique and what makes managing the human resources of an organization so challenging.

Admittedly, personality is relatively stable. Although it can change, this usually happens gradually over a period of time. At the same time, **situational factors** can have a definite influence on personality, as is clearly apparent from studies of individuals who have completed police academy training. These studies discovered how much the graduates were influenced by the peer-socializing process of the organization once they spent time in the work setting with other officers.[5] Many officers have commented on the difference between what they were taught in the academy and what was expected of them by officers with greater field experience. In this field-training stage, the new officer learns to conform to the informal socialization process of peer values rather than to the organizational values taught in the academy.[6] Thus, police officers' working personality is shaped by their experiences once they begin performing their police duties.

Personality Determinants

How does one's personality develop? There are a number of theories describing the process. The following four basic assumptions about human behavior are drawn from **interactional psychology**:

1. Behavior is a function of a continuous, multidirectional interaction between the person and the situation.
2. The person is active in this process, both changing the situation and being changed by it.
3. People differ from each other in many characteristics, including cognition, affect (emotion), motivation, and ability.
4. Both the objective situation and the person's subjective view of the situation are important.[7]

Interactional psychology attributes human behavior jointly to the personality of the individual, the nature of the situation, and the continual interaction between the two. This makes personality a very important consideration for managers within an organization because it influences how employees react to and evaluate the demands of their work setting. For example, an officer who is achievement oriented will, in all probability, evaluate each working situation in terms of its potential to aid his or her career advancement. Such an individual is more apt to volunteer for assignments, pursue special training or higher education, and develop an expertise needed by others, all with the intent of achieving the highest possible recognition or advancement in the shortest possible time. However, officers who are strongly influenced by the patrol officer's peer group culture will seek recognition from the group and adjust their behavior to conform to the work group's norms of behavior and view of the world.[8]

Heredity

Heredity refers to factors present at birth, such as physical stature, gender, energy level, muscular composition, reflexes, and temperament. Beth Azar concluded after a review of 20 years of research with twins and adopted children that there is a genetic component to just about every human trait and behavior, including personality, general intelligence, and behavioral disorders.[9] This perspective views heredity as the final arbiter of how one acquires a personality.

Research that is more recent suggests that while heredity is one of the major determinants of behavior, it is not the final arbitrator of who we are. The brain—which we still know relatively little about—may or may not hold more answers for personality than does heredity. In fact, it is currently believed that only a limited part of behavior can be definitely attributed to heredity. Current research in the field of genetic engineering may eventually answer many of the questions regarding the part heredity plays in determining personality, but as of today, those questions have not been answered. Up to now, we are still seeking to understand the basis for the development of consciousness and personality and the mechanism of learning and memory. We do know that the brain receives information from the world around us through our senses. Thus, personality is not static; it is constantly acted upon, energized, coerced, or repelled by various sights, sounds, and visuals we experience through senses. These are deeply embedded in the brain, and depend upon the individual's receptivity, which is affected by their emotions and state of mind.

Managers should consider that, based on our current knowledge, nonhereditary factors probably exert more influence on personality development and the subsequent behavior of employees than do hereditary factors. If all personality characteristics were fixed at birth and solely the result of heredity, then one could not be influenced by experience, environment, or the variety situations encountered during one's lifetime. In summary, heredity is a limited explanation of personality and cannot fully explain why individuals behave the way they do.

Culture

Another determinant of personality is culture. **Culture** is a system of shared beliefs, values, attitudes, and meanings that guide individual behavior. This system is acquired by individuals through their interactions with significant others such as parents, teachers, and peers in a process called *socialization*. Over time, cultural socialization conditions and reconditions individuals, providing them with an accepted system of norms that structures their day-to-day behavior. Culture provides the individual with a socially constructed set of meanings upon which rest evaluations of people and situations. Thus, for the manager to understand behavior, he or she must also understand the meaning attached to that behavior by the individual involved.

Organizational theorists believe that culture is the hidden meaning behind behavior and that it must be observed and understood by managers, if they wish to change behavior.[10] In a strong culture, the organization's values, attitudes, and definitions of the world are intensely held and widely shared. The more members believe in and accept these socially constructed meanings, the greater will be the organization's commitment to those values and the stronger will be its culture. A strong culture will have greater influence on the behavior of its members by creating a climate of intense internal behavioral control and group commitment. For example, World War II Japanese soldiers killed themselves rather than surrender and admit defeat, which meant failure and disgrace in their culture. An increasing body of research indicates that a strong culture is associated with successful organizational performance.[11]

Organizational culture theorists claim that formal rules, authority, and procedures designed to govern behavior do not restrain the personal preferences of employees, but cultural norms, values, beliefs, and assumptions do.[12] For example, the veteran police officer who tells the rookie, "Never mind what the manual says, this is the way we do it in the real world," is instructing the new officer in the accepted pragmatic way of getting the day-to-day job of policing done in that department. In order to understand or predict how an organization member will behave under different circumstances, one must know what the patterns of basic beliefs and values are that form the employee's *organizational culture* (see Chapter 5).

In an organization, culture serves four basic functions:

1. It provides a sense of identity to members and increases their commitment to the organization or their work group (a sense of belonging or esprit de corps).

2. It provides a way for members to interpret the meaning of organizational events and the organization's external environment (a way to structure and make sense of what they can't control).

3. It reinforces the values of the organization (everybody knows what counts and what is the right way to do things).

4. It serves as a behavioral control mechanism for organizational members (if you don't conform to the accepted ways of acting, you are an outsider or outcast).[13]

People's concepts of what actions should or should not be exercised in a given situation are strongly influenced by the culture in which they were socialized. Cultural influences are especially noticeable in employee motivation.

For example, many young men and women currently entering the police service are less oriented to authority and less competitive than their predecessors; their lives can be complete without relying heavily on job satisfaction. These changing employee expectations may require managers to consider assigning work in different ways.[14]

Situation

Learning to recognize how the traits we are born with and the beliefs and attitudes we acquire through socialization influence us will add to our understanding of the human personality. The person–situation interaction is another factor influencing personality. As we noted, personality is usually relatively stable, but that stability can be altered by situations. Unfortunately, our knowledge is somewhat limited in this area, and there is not a system for categorizing specific situations and how they impact personality. Each situation is different. Differences may seem very small, but when filtered by a person's cognitive mediating processes (such as perception), they can lead to quite large subjective differences and diverse behavioral outcomes.[15]

What we do know is that under certain circumstances, an individual can react in ways seemingly almost foreign to his or her personality. In numerous instances, officers have performed heroically, placing their lives in jeopardy, when if they had considered the event logically and rationally, they may never have reacted as they did. Conversely, in other instances, officers fully aware of what is right, and of the potential outcome of doing wrong, have acted unethically or engaged in illegal behavior for personal gain.[16]

Managers should be careful when generalizing about the way employees behave unless they take into account the nature of each situation. They must understand the strengths and weaknesses of each of their employees. It is important for managers to encourage and build upon their employees strengths. It is the responsibility of each manager to analyze and correct employee weaknesses. Managers usually address performance weaknesses through on-the-job training and mentoring. However, in cases of serious performance deficiencies, a formal training program may be needed to help the employee. More study remains to be done of situational factors and their influence on personality. What we do know is that people are not static, acting the same way in all situations, but instead are changing and flexible. Figure 3–1 illustrates how the three determinants work together to create personality.

Personality Theories

It is important that managers thoroughly understand the various theories of personality in order to assess the way people behave in their organizations. Numerous theories have been proposed during the last two centuries. Most prominent among them are the **psychoanalytical theory**, **trait theory**, and *humanistic theory* (Figure 3–2). Each presents a different view of personality, and each has both supporters and detractors. No one theory of personality development totally explains all variation in behavior, but a manager who understands various theories has taken the first step in dealing with the complexity of human behavior—individual, interpersonal, group, or organizational.

Figure 3–1
Personality Determinants.

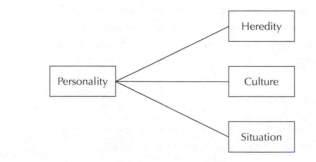

Psychoanalytical Theory

Sigmund Freud (1856–1939) developed the first comprehensive theory of personality. He believed that the human mind is dominated by the unconscious and claimed that to truly understand a person's behavior, it is necessary to analyze the unconscious motivations that underlie many of his or her thoughts, wishes, feelings, and memories.[17] According to this perspective, personality results from a dynamic process that involves a constant state of tension and conflict between the conscious and the unconscious.

Freud theorized, based on observing and listening to his patients, that personality results from the interaction between three parts of the mind: the **id**, the **ego**, and the **superego**. Each of these performs a different function and develops at a different time.[18] Freud viewed these three components as constructs, not physical entities. The basic component of personality is the **id**, which is present at birth and is the source of impulses that operate in an uncensored manner. The id strives to fulfill such basic needs as hunger, thirst, and sex. It operates on the pleasure principle and demands immediate and complete gratification. The individual is not aware of the id because it is not expressed consciously. The id is primitive, uninhibited, and not subject to rational control. At birth, the id is the total personality of each person.

The second component that develops is the *ego*. It begins to develop shortly after birth, when the child realizes that not everything wanted is immediately available. The task of this construct is to mediate between the needs expressed by the id and the real world. It is the only personality component that, in Freud's theory, has access to and a relationship with the actual environment.[19]

The ego distinguishes between what exists in the subjective mind and what exists in the reality of the external world. It may be described as the rational cognitive process that decides one's course of action. It serves as the manager of an individual's personality structure and has the capacity of recognizing, evaluating, and testing reality. It reasons and learns from experience. Like the id, the ego generally functions at the unconscious level; Freud believed that none of the three components of personality operates solely at the level of consciousness.[20]

The ego functions as the problem-solving element of personality as it deals with the real world and copes with life. This process becomes increasingly complex as the third component of personality, the *superego*, begins to develop.

Up to this point, the ego need only check with reality to see whether the demands of the id can be met, but the superego adds a new dimension. The superego is shaped by society's concepts of what is right and what is wrong, what conduct is acceptable and what is unacceptable. These ideals and values are acquired by everyone (either through being taught or through learning from example) during childhood. Over the years, each person develops his or her own norms and standards of behavior, which are reflected in the superego.[21]

Thus, the superego is concerned with morality, with what is right and what is wrong. It is formed early during childhood and influences reality via the ego. It is like a conscience that contains values and a control system telling us what we should and should not do. The superego permits the fulfillment of id impulses only when they are found to be moral, regardless of whether the ego determines that such fulfillment would be safe and reasonable.[22]

Generally speaking, when the id is in control, an individual tends to act in a selfish manner, is easily angered, and can be impulsive. If one's superego is overdeveloped, an individual will tend to feel guilty and unworthy. When the ego dominates an individual's personality, there is a more realistic behavior pattern, the person tends to react logically, and life is generally more satisfying.[23]

Freud's psychoanalytical explanation of personality is based on the idea of conflict; it involves constant interplay between the id and the superego, moderated by the ego. The behavior patterns of individuals are viewed as the result of defense mechanisms that respond to the anxiety created by the conflict.

Managers may encounter various defense mechanisms as they deal with employees and other managers. **Defense mechanisms** are one way people distance themselves from a full awareness of unpleasant thoughts, feelings, and behaviors. Each mechanism is designed to reduce the anxiety created in an individual by conflict among the three components of his or her personality.[24] Most defense mechanisms are unconscious, and the person does not realize that he or she is using it.

One of the most common defense mechanisms is ***projection***. Individuals using this mechanism tend to see in others the traits or characteristics they have themselves. For example, an officer might project his or her own personal feelings, emotions, anxieties, and motives when judging other officers or supervisors. A supervisor who is highly judgmental and critical of everything done by subordinates will, in many cases, view his or her own immediate manager as too strict and demanding in never allowing freedom to perform assigned tasks. Projection also occurs when managers assume all employees being supervised are like themselves, hardworking, industrious, goal oriented, and totally devoted to work. It can be a shock when a manager realizes that some employees have a greater orientation to their family or to personal activities than to work.[25]

Avoidance is another defense mechanism. Managers who consistently withdraw from conflict situations involving their subordinates are using this mechanism. This can be costly not only to the officers involved but also to the organization. Patrol officers who practice this form of behavior have been known to respond too slowly to calls for service involving potential physical confrontations or danger. It is also common to find an officer who is harboring a deep feeling of resentment toward his or her peers to handle this feeling by avoiding social interaction with other officers. Such officers may at times resort to e-mail as their only means of communication with others. Still others will use all their available sick leave (but not to the point of jeopardizing their job) as a means of avoiding organizational conflict and reducing anxiety.[26]

Additional defense mechanisms include the following:

- Rationalization—the individual validates his or her behavior by offering a different explanation in the face of changing reality. For example, the officer who claims that the reason he acted the way he did was because he was not trained properly.
- Reaction Formation—the individual converts unwanted and nonacceptable thoughts, feelings, or impulses into the opposites. For example, the officer who is inwardly fearful while on patrol acts aggressively when dealing with people.
- Sublimation—it is the channeling of unacceptable impulses, thoughts, and emotions into acceptable ones. For example, the officer who seeks to relieve his or her stress by following a physical workout program designed to reduce job-related tension.
- Denial—it is the refusal to accept reality or fact of a situation. For example, officers who in reality are poor performers but describe themselves as tough street cops.

For police officers in the performance of their duties to exhibit anger, hostility, or aggression is considered unprofessional conduct. However, anger is a very powerful feeling, and many officers have trouble dealing with either their own anger or that of others. It should be kept in mind that anger, like any other feeling, is not good or bad in and of itself, but police officers are expected to repress or deny any anger they may feel when dealing with others.

The fact is that almost all people become angry from time to time, and some act on this feeling by becoming aggressive. The improper use of force by an officer is often a reaction to deeply repressed feelings of anger and fear. There is no one correct way to respond to anger. Police managers must be constantly aware of the psychological well-being of their officers. Line supervisors are the closest to their subordinates and are usually the first to sense problems in their officers' behavior reactions.

Police managers should receive training in counseling. It is their responsibility to investigate incidents in which their officers' behavior has violated department regulations or the law. However, through training and counseling they may be able to act in a positive manner through early intervention to prevent this type of incident from occurring. Generally speaking, the first sign of a problem of this nature is not physical but verbal aggression.

Freud's psychoanalytical explanation of personality is not accepted by all behavioral scientists, but his early works have had a strong influence on others who have investigated the concept of personality. At the very least, the theory points out the complexity of human behavior and provides managers with a way of understanding how subconscious conflicts can lead to anxieties that affect the behavior of their officers.

Trait Theory

Another approach to analyzing human personality, called trait theory, focuses on specific attributes peculiar to individuals. Each individual's personality is viewed as growing out of a particular collection of traits, such as ambition, loyalty, and aggression, which remains consistent from situation to situation. Some of the trait approaches identify distinct personality categories against which individuals are matched. Other approaches see personality differences more as a matter of degree than of the distinct presence or absence of certain traits.[27]

In contrast to Freud's emphasis on the unconscious, Gordon Allport and H. S. Odbert believed that conscious determinants of behavior were what really counted. They theorized that each person's unique behavior could be accounted for or predicted based on the lasting, stable presence of certain major and minor traits by which a single life is known. A personality trait is a biological, psychological, and social mixture that disposes a person toward specific kinds of behavior under certain circumstances.[28] These **traits** are basic descriptive terms for how each individual interacts within both society and organizations. They include such attributes as being quick tempered, aggressive, or social.

Allport and Odbert identified three modes in which traits influence behavior: *cardinal*, *central*, and *secondary*. They described a *cardinal* trait as a single trait dominating the behavior of an individual; they believed such individuals to be rare. A possible example of an individual with a cardinal trait would be a police executive who displays a calm, secure, and unworried demeanor in all situations, no matter how out of control his or her words or actions may seem to others involved.

CASE STUDY   John Powell

John Powell has been a patrol officer for seven years in the Metropolitan Police Department. He is a graduate of the local university, where he majored in political science. During his college years, he was an outstanding football player and could favorably be described as a big man on campus. After graduation, he served in the Army for six years and was discharged with the rank of Captain.

In the police academy, he was considered by his instructors to be one of the best cadets to ever graduate from the program. Powell passed the field-training and probationary periods with flying colors, and each of his supervisors anticipated that he would move rapidly through the ranks. After his second year in patrol, he served successfully as a member of the department's SWAT team and then as a member of a special task force that monitored the activities of paroled offenders with extensive criminal records.

Officer Powell has taken the sergeants examination twice but failed the written portion both times. He reacted by continually criticizing the promotion examination, pointing out that it is not actually a true measure of the skills an individual needs in order to be an effective supervisor. Over the last two years, he has slowly but surely become disgruntled with the police department's management. He criticizes many of the department's policies and constantly questions the promotional process.

He has begun to function at a minimum level and only does what is necessary to keep out of trouble. He arrives late for roll call but not late enough to be disciplined. He takes coffee and meal breaks exceeding the time set forth by departmental policy. His general negative attitude is rubbing off on younger officers, and some of the older officers refuse to work with him. During this same time, he has become very active in the local police union, and he uses his membership as a platform for criticizing department management. He constantly finds fault with every immediate supervisor, saying that they are exceedingly strict and refuse to give officers the freedom needed to perform effectively. Officer Powell is increasingly viewed as a thorn in management's side and a real problem employee.

His immediate supervisor has become stricter in her supervision and is documenting the times he is late for roll call or takes too much time for meal and coffee breaks. Every arrest Officer Powell makes is reviewed with careful scrutiny, and the reports he prepares are rejected with increasing frequency. Officer Powell filed a grievance against his immediate supervisor, charging that he has been singled out for punishment because he is active in the police union.

If you were Officer Powell's supervisor, how would you deal with him? Is there something in Officer Powell's conduct that suggests he has a personality problem? If so, what is it? How should a manager work with an employee who is constantly negative? Can something be done to change the negative traits that Officer Powell exhibits?

More typically, according to Allport, an individual's behavior will be the expression of a larger group of *central* traits. Allport felt that an evaluator could form an accurate understanding of an individual's personality by knowing as few as 5–10 of his or her traits.

The third level Allport identified consisted of *secondary* traits, which are sometimes displayed by individuals but which fluctuate and change from time to time. These "surplus" traits are not strong enough to influence individual behavior successfully. In general, Allport's efforts were directed toward finding a way to describe or identify personalities rather than trying to explain what causes them.[29]

Police Personality

Trait theory implicitly has been applied to the manifestations of the **"police personality."** Police officers, in the performance of their duties, face a range of potentially stressful situations and events. These have the capacity to have significant personal impact on the officers, leading to short-term changes in mood and psychological functioning. Skolnick claims that the working personality of police officers is shaped by their need to establish their authority over others, the ever-present threat of danger, and the need for efficiency.[30] It is argued that over the course of their police careers officers develop a number of traits, such as cynicism, aloofness, suspiciousness, and alienation, which help them cope with the stresses of their jobs. As the years pass in their careers, officers often experience social isolation for everyone but other police officers. Positive attitudes are replaced with negative worldviews, personal relationships can become strained, and early career enthusiasm is replaced with cynicism and pessimism.[31] The personality of the veteran officer with 20 or more years of service no longer resembles the positive, committed, and motivated individual they were in their first year with the department. It is believed that as this police working personality becomes internalized, it has a direct effect on the behavioral responses of officers.

There emerges in this literature a description of the police officer as alienated labor. Police departments with their discipline, elaborate procedures, and rules are punishment-centered bureaucratic systems. They attempt to address this problem by employing a complex **multiple hurdle screening process** in the attempt to hire qualified candidates who are better able to adjust to the demands of police work. This process consists of a variety of steps that include the following:

1. Application
2. Written examination
3. Oral interview
4. Physical ability test
5. Polygraph
6. Psychological testing (Traits)
7. Character and background investigation
8. Financial record review
9. Medical examination
10. Police academy training
11. Field-training program
12. Probationary period

Departments using this selection process employ a variety of psychological screening procedures that involve the use of validated personality assessment instruments such as the Minnesota Multiphasic Personality Inventory-2 (MMPI-2), California Personality Inventory (CPI), the Inwald Personality Inventory (IPI), the Edwards Personal Preference Schedule (EPPS), and projective tests such as the House, Tree and Person, and Roschach.[32] This selection process unfortunately does not always choose the best applicants but rather weeds out the most unqualified candidates.[33] Part of the difficulty in tying psychological traits to job performance is the lack of consensus surrounding the identification of desirable traits of police officer. Defining what a good police officer is can be difficult and is often described as a list of desirable traits unsubstantiated by empirical research.[34]

Table 3–1
THE "FIVE-FACTOR" PERSONALITY TRAITS

Core Traits	Descriptive Characteristics of High Scores
Conscientiousness	Dependable, hardworking, organized, self-disciplined, persistent, responsible
Emotional stability	Calm, secure, happy, unworried
Agreeableness	Cooperative, warm, caring, good-natured, courteous, trusting
Extraversion	Sociable, outgoing, talkative, assertive, gregarious
Openness to experience	Curious, intellectual, creative, cultured, artistically sensitive, flexible, imaginative

Recently, the **"Five-Factor" Model**, a different personality theory also based on predispositional traits, has been found valuable in understanding personality and work behavior.[35] Table 3–1 identifies the five personality elements used in this model and their major characteristics. There is now considerable agreement on which personality trait predispositions lie at the core of personality, and there is also accumulated research that these five best predict performance in the workplace.[36] Although the five traits are largely independent factors of a personality, like primary colors, they can be mixed in countless proportions and with other characteristics to yield a unique personality whole. However, also like colors, one may dominate in describing an individual's personality.[37]

Of the five factors, *conscientiousness* has been identified as the one with the strongest positive relationship to job performance. It indicates the individual's degree of organization, persistence, and motivation in goal-directed behavior. Individuals who are dependable, persistent, goal directed, and organized tend to be higher performers, especially in police work.[38] Conscientious police officers and managers set higher achievement goals for themselves, hold higher performance expectations, and respond well to empowerment. They are also less likely to be absent from work.[39]

Although conscientiousness has received the most attention because of its impact on employee performance, the remaining traits are also important. Equally important, especially for managers, is *emotional stability*. Police officers and managers who maintain a calm, secure disposition in emotionally charged situations are highly valued. Their behavior serves as a model to the officers they supervise.[40] Recently, it was found that the five factors might also be predictive of team performance. Higher-performance teams were found to have better than average scores on traits of conscientiousness, agreeableness, extraversion, and emotional stability.[41] Sanders found in a recent study of 96 police officers from eight nonurban police departments that age and attitude were better predictors of job performance than personality traits. Nevertheless, a cynical work attitude was negatively related to job performance ratings.[42] In conclusion, depending on the situation, personality traits warrant attention when analyzing organizational behavior.

While we have listed factors that are indicative of work performance, there are also "dark side" traits that, when obsessively taken, bear a resemblance to the most common personality disorders.[43] Research indicates most people display at least three of these traits. And, nearly 40 percent score in a range that put them at risk for discord in their careers.[44] These "dark side" traits are clustered under three groupings. Cluster one are the Distancing Traits; these are apparent traits that cause displeasure to others and drive other people away. They include being excitable (moody, easily annoyed, hard to please, and emotionally unstable), skeptical (distrustful, cynical, sensitive to criticism, and focused on the negative), cautious (unassertive, resistant to change, and slow to make decisions), reserved (aloof and indifferent to others' feelings), and leisurely (overly cooperative but privately irritable, stubborn, and uncooperative).[45] Cluster two, the Seductive Traits, are those traits that attract people. While appealing to many, these traits can have negative outcomes since they can lead people to overvalue their own worth. The traits in this cluster include being bold (overly self-confident, entitled, and having an inflated sense of self-worth), mischievous (risk-taking, limit-testing, and excitement seeking), colorful (dramatic, attention-seeking, and tends to interrupt rather than listen), and imaginative (thinks and acts in unusual or eccentric ways).[46] Cluster three are the Ingratiating Traits. These traits can have a positive inference for followers, but seldom when depicting leaders. Traits in this cluster encompass being diligent (meticulous, precise, and detail oriented) and dutiful (eager to please, reluctant to act independently, or express disagreement).[47]

While many leaders have several of the "dark side" traits, absence of them can also be harmful. Fundamentally, the solution is to manage and augment your weakness to formulate positive operational function.

Humanistic Theory

Humanistic theory is a positive approach that views each individual as important in determining his or her own growth. It is represented by psychologist Carl Rogers, who had a very optimistic view of human strength and who believed self-concept was the core of personality. Rogers believed that all people have a basic drive toward self-actualization, that is, toward being all they can be. Self-concept includes the attitudes, values, thoughts, and beliefs that individuals have developed during a lifetime of experience. Rogers viewed the workings of the unconscious mind as a positive motivator for individual behavior. He said that the concept of self evolves from one's early experience in dealing with the environment, from the regard shown by others, and ultimately from reaching a point where the ideal self and the real self are congruent.[48]

The *congruent* individual functions at the very highest level. Such a person is open, does not react defensively, gets along well with others, and possesses high self-esteem. Rogers suggests this individual is one whose fundamental desire is to become everything he or she is capable of being. This means that for each individual, self-actualization is something unique, specific, and totally individualized.[49]

Other individuals may have an *incongruent* personal view, may become tense or anxious, and may react defensively as a means of protecting and preserving the view they have of themselves. From a managerial perspective, humanistic theory would suggest that such employees need to be treated positively, that is, understood and respected as individuals. In the humanistic view, employees are positive assets of the organization; if it becomes necessary to discipline or criticize them, the focus should be on the unacceptable or inadequate behavior and not on the individual. Under no circumstances should an employee be rejected as an individual. Feedback should emphasize tasks to be performed, with the aim of helping employees improve their job performance. The key is not to attack an employee's self-esteem, because that will result in many undesirable effects.[50]

Humanistic theory, like other personality theories, has both supporters and detractors, but its value is that it focuses on the positive aspects of human nature, acknowledging that the human organism seeks growth, self-actualization, and pleasant, productive relationships with others.

Personality is exceedingly complex, as is evident from the personality theories discussed earlier. Each of these theories makes a significant contribution to the understanding of personality. Depending on his or her education, preparation, training, and background, a manager may feel most comfortable with the explanations offered by one of the theories and find that that theory meets his or her specific needs. It is essential for managers to choose one or more of the theories to use as a means of gaining insight into organizational behavior (see Table 3–2 for a comparative chart of the theories). A manager might use the psychoanalytical approach by working to identify the nature and extent of conflict exhibited by employees and the defense mechanisms they employ. Some managers might feel comfortable in evaluating personality by utilizing observable traits such as self-sufficiency, control, or conscientiousness. Another manager might find that the most satisfactory approach is to assist employees in achieving goals and enhancing their self-esteem. Each of these approaches can be used to provide insight into an individual's total personality—including the actual character, behavior, and temperament of the employee.

Table 3–2 PERSONALITY THEORIES		
Theory Type	**Motivation for Behavior**	**Primary Interest**
Psychoanalytical	Unconscious	General behavior
Trait	Conscious	The individual
Humanistic	Conscious or unconscious	The individual

Dimensions of Personality

Researchers have identified a number of personality dimensions that have special relevance in the work environment. The significance of these dimensions varies from organization to organization and from situation to situation. Each is related to the overall concept of personality rather than to any specific personality theory. The dimensions we discuss here are locus of control, Type A/Type B behavior, emotional intelligence, **Machiavellianism**, and adapting to bureaucratic orientation.

Locus of Control

Locus of control refers to a person's belief about the control he or she has over the good and bad events that affect one's life. According to this concept, people can be broadly divided into those ("internals") who believe that they themselves are responsible for what happens to them and those ("externals") who believe that what happens to them is determined by situations or other people (Figure 3–3).[51] These expectations are the result of social learning and represent the ends of a continuum, not an either/or typology. Internals believe they control their own fate; externals believe luck and chance control their fate.

For example, a police officer with a strong *internal* locus of control may believe that his or her position on a promotion list reflects his or her own abilities and efforts. However, officers with a strong *external* locus of control may believe that their position on the list has more to do with luck or favoritism of the executive command. As a result, they have little faith that their effort will result in a favorable listing and are less likely to work hard for a higher position. Officers who are externals often become highly cynical and develop a sense of pessimism about the results of their work. As a result, their performance will suffer, which will require attention by their supervisor (see Table 3–3).

Locus of control is a continuous personality dimension, and employees actually are arranged somewhere on a continuum ranging from high external to high internal. Research on locus of control has strong implications for organizations. There is some evidence that internals have greater control over how they behave in any given situation, are more social, and actively search out information needed to accomplish a task. Internals

Table 3–3 CHARACTERISTICS OF EMPLOYEES WHO HAVE AN INTERNAL LOCUS OF CONTROL	
Information seeking	Involvement in decision-making
Goal oriented	Self-control
Social	Limited risk taker
Extroverted	Achievement oriented
Responsive to motivation programs	Persuasive

have been found to have higher job satisfaction, to be more willing to accept managerial responsibility, and to prefer participative management.[52]

Internal locus of control has additional implications for police managers. Internals have been shown to display higher work motivation and to believe more strongly that effort leads to accomplishment. They are more likely to want some control over their jobs and will generally exhibit a strong desire to assume some responsibility for decision-making. They want to be part of the organization and control as much of their working environment as possible.[53]

Internals enjoy work over which they have some control and usually gain satisfaction from the work itself. They exhibit a great deal of self-control, conform to reasonable guidelines, and limit risk taking. Internals, as a group, are more extroverted in interpersonal relations and more apt to relate to fellow employees as well as to the public. They are responsive to motivation techniques and programs, and their careers advance more rapidly than those of individuals with an external orientation.

Locus of control has serious implications for police managers. Internals want to be involved, so each manager should strive to create an inclusive working environment that seeks officer input. The working environment should foster individuality and reduce employee dependency. It should also be kept in mind that people's expectations can change; they are not set in concrete. Managers can make a difference, and this is best done when the organization continually acknowledges and rewards outstanding performance.

An effective manager can change the expectations of employees, thereby improving morale and making a positive impact on employee performance. As employees become aware that hard work and the attainment of objectives are adequately rewarded, they are persuaded that what they do and how they do it can make a significant difference. The goal of the manager is to affect performance positively by demonstrating that each individual has the potential to influence outcomes. Subordinates must be made to feel that the things they do are significant.[54]

Type A and Type B Behavior

Another personality dimension of interest to police managers is one that distinguishes what is called **Type A behavior** from **Type B behavior**. Both of these types intrigue behavioral scientists because of their impact on the organization and its employees. (Figure 3–4).

The Type A personality is characterized by a competitive striving for achievement, an exaggerated sense of time urgency, and a tendency toward aggressiveness and hostility. Individuals who exhibit Type A traits are more than three times as likely to experience serious heart disease.[55] Type A individuals tend to work rapidly on assigned tasks, and their working relationships with others are often uncomfortable, impatient, irritating, and even aggressive. Police managers described as "Type A" typically set high performance standards, are hard driving and detail oriented, and thrive on routine (see Table 3–4).

Type A individuals work fast even when there is no need to do so. When this tendency is carried to the extreme, their concern for details can become more important than the results they are trying to achieve. In addition, Type A individuals dislike being interrupted and show outward signs of annoyance and impatience such as frowns and

Table 3–4
TYPE A PERSONALITY

Competitive	Hard driving
Achievement oriented	Impatient
Tendency toward aggressiveness	Easily irritated
Tendency toward hostility	Detail oriented

grimaces when it happens.[56] When work becomes all-important, this type of person will resist change, tightly control the activities of subordinates, and behave in a way that has a negative impact on interpersonal relations.[57]

The impatient nature of Type A personalities causes them to perform poorly when the task requires a delayed response. Current research suggests individuals of Type A perform better when they function under the pressure of a deadline, when they are required to respond to multiple demands, or when they are performing solitary work. On the other hand, they function below par when they have to perform tasks requiring complex judgment and when required to work as a member of a team.[58]

The Type B personality can be described as easygoing and not especially competitive. Current evidence suggests that about 40 percent of the general population is Type A and 60 percent Type B.[59] Obviously, the two types have different impacts on a police organization and have to be handled differently. Type B personalities are more easygoing, relaxed, unhurried, deferential, and satisfied. They are easier to manage because their behavior is predictable. Because they are noncompetitive and prefer to work with others, they are good candidates for team assignments or for working in two-officer patrol vehicles. When they assume supervisory and managerial positions, they prove to be people oriented and interact well with peers and with those they supervise.

Some Type B personalities have refused promotions because moving to higher ranks would force them to function as administrators rather than as managers continually interacting with subordinates. Type B managers are more apt to delegate authority, let employees work at their own pace, and provide detailed supervision. The ability to get along with others and the desire to work as a team are significant characteristics of Type B managers. On the other hand, the Type B personality needs closer supervision to ensure that deadlines are met and organizational objectives achieved.

Machiavellianism

Naturally, the personalities of police managers vary considerably. Occasionally a supervisor or manager exhibits the characteristics attributed to Niccolo Machiavelli (1469–1527), who more than 400 years ago wrote a book entitled *The Prince*, which outlined a strategy for obtaining and keeping power.[60] This book is still required reading in several business schools.

Machiavelli's book advocates a strong leadership style, including manipulation of others as a way to attain goals. He admonishes readers: "It is better to be feared than loved," and "Humility not only is of no service, but is actually harmful."[61] Clearly, Machiavelli believed that ends always justify means. A true Machiavellian manager is pragmatic, maintains emotional distance, and manipulates others for personal gain.[62] Making friends, being loyal, and expressing anything resembling ethics or morality are viewed as inhibitors of true success.

Two psychologists, Richard Christie and Florence Geis, developed a short questionnaire termed the *Mach Scale*. Those who score high on the test are termed **High-Machs** and behave in ways consistent with the principles espoused by Machiavelli.[63] High-Mach managers are not the least bit concerned about whether they lie or not and will use deceit in their relationships to achieve their desires. In their view, morality can be ignored if necessary to achieve desired objectives. Their goal is to achieve their objectives and win at any cost. What counts is winning, nothing else matters. High-Machs are usually convincing liars and are adept at identifying weaknesses in others. In general, others are viewed as being gullible and not aware of what is best for them. Thus, High-Machs will likely justify their behavior as ethical because they were acting in the best interest of others[64] (see Table 3–5 and Figure 3–5).

Managers with a High-Mach personality orientation approach tasks logically and thoughtfully, do not respond to persuasion, and have little regard for the opinions of others. They consider their problems with cool detachment and never allow emotions to enter into the equation. High-Machs function best when they control the situation.[65]

Table 3–5
HIGH-MACH PERSONALITY

Power hungry	Deceitful
Manipulative	Logical
Pragmatic	Adept at identifying weaknesses in others
Emotionally distant	Influential
Not concerned with morality	Detached

Interestingly enough, High-Machs feel no guilt as they manipulate others for personal gain. It is a game, and the winner takes all. They perform at their zenith when dealing with others face to face, when emotions cloud the judgment of others, and when the situation is loosely structured.[66]

Managers of this type are quickly identified by patrol officers, who see through their deceit and manipulations and respond with passive resistance and minimum work output. The officers know that the High-Mach manager is only concerned for his or her own personal objectives, and they resist through small actions, such as working strictly according to rules and regulations, refusing to perform work outside their job title, and generating just enough citations and arrests to meet minimum productivity standards.[67]

Emotional Intelligence

Police officers are confronted with dangerous incidents as well as with periods filled with boring routine tasks during their average workday. They are expected to control their emotions and separate these from the incidents they respond to. The suppression of human emotions can lead to serious psychological consequences for the officer. To address issues associated with the effects of police work on the officers, a number of police training programs have developed courses on emotional intelligence. For example, the U.S. Department of Justice COPS Office has funded curricula development for a series of training courses with emotional intelligence components for the Regional Community Policing Institutes.

Emotional intelligence (EQ) is the ability to recognize and understand one's own and others' feelings and emotions, to discriminate among them, and to use this awareness to manage the self and relationships with others.[68] It relates to how we manage behavior, social complexities, and make decisions to achieve desired results. The ability to be self-aware and then regulate one's own emotions in a healthy and positive way is an important competency for police officers to develop. Research conducted in the early 1990s by Mayer, DiPaolo, and Salovey confirmed that emotional intelligence is a major indicator of achievement and explains why two people of the same intelligence could attain different levels of success in their work and personal lives.[69] Personality influences how emotional intelligence takes form, but this does not occur in predictable way. A person's emotional intelligence, IQ, and personality are independent of one another.

It is suggested that emotional intelligence is more critical than IQ in determining successful performance.[70] An individual's moods or emotions, and the way that they self-manage them influence interpersonal relations and the effectiveness of decision-making.[71] Emotional intelligence consists of four unique skills that identify how to recognize and understand emotions, that is, how you manage self-behavior and relationships. They are as follows: self-awareness, self-management, social awareness, and relationship management.

Self-Awareness: The cognitive ability to accurately appraise one's own emotions, feelings, and behaviors. It also pertains to expressing one's feelings. This dimension relates to an individual's ability to self-reflect and understand his or her emotions. Reflection facilitates the use of emotional information for making judgments and decisions. The level of understanding of feelings will impact the accuracy of communicating emotions, which in turn should enhance communication with others in terms of facilitating the understanding of other's needs, goals, and objectives.

Self-Management: The ability to use awareness of self-emotions to stay flexible and positively directed. This means managing emotional reactions and behaviors according to their situational appropriateness. This requires cognitive reflection on the potential way in which an emotional behavior will affect and be affected within a specific situation. Policing often involves situations that engender emotions that may lead to explosive episodes. The ability to manage these emotions appropriately would lead to more positive relations.

Social Awareness: The ability to accurately pick up on emotions in other people and understand what is really going on. It consists of "taking the role of the other" and experiencing as well as understanding another's emotions from his or her perspective as well as your own. This interpersonal skill is critical to a manager's ability to establish positive interpersonal relationships with his or her subordinates. It is also an excellent problem-diagnosing skill. Managers who lack this skill will likely be seen as indifferent and uncaring.

Relationship Management: The ability to use awareness of your emotions and the emotions of others to manage interactions successfully. This ensures clear communication and the effective handling of conflict.

Taking each of these factors together, emotional intelligence may lead to more successful outcomes within the law enforcement environment than intellectual or technical (IQ) prowess. The social skill component of emotional intelligence appears to be the core factor affecting successful outcomes.

Bureaucratic Orientation

Police departments, for the most part, are bureaucratic organizations that foster top-down management control systems. Many agencies hold sacred the concepts of rationality, hierarchy, specialization, and positional authority. Rules and regulations dominate daily operations. It is the view of many that a bureaucracy thwarts communication and stifles innovation and creativity. Many people also feel that such an organization demands conformity and group thinking but limits personal growth.[72]

Is there such a thing as a bureaucratic personality? That is, are there certain personality features that best describe those who achieve rank in bureaucratic organizations? Bureaucracies are very demanding in their own special way, and it appears that individuals who exhibit the following attitudes and behaviors seem to be the best-adjusted individuals within such organizations:

1. They exhibit absolute conformity and adherence to rules and regulations. Individualization is minimal; abstract rules dominate operations.
2. Their social interactions are impersonal and are not allowed to interfere with their decisions and other organizational processes.
3. They accept higher authority without question. The chain of command dominates and must never be violated, so acquiescence to authority is essential.
4. They are traditionalists and supporters of the status quo: Members are expected to identify with the department and accept the traditions developed over the years.
5. They operate deep within the box of rules, focusing on what was and is, not on what could be.[73]

Those who are out of step with the demands of a bureaucratic organization are more apt to seek employment elsewhere. It is also quite apparent that some personalities

Philip Mulhall has been a member of the Continental Police Department for eight years. He is currently assigned to the chief's office and is responsible for supervising the investigation of complaints against sworn personnel. He has been a lieutenant for two years, having assumed his current position after serving as a watch commander in the patrol division. Lt. Mulhall graduated from the local university where he majored in public administration. Within the department, there are a number of officers and supervisors who feel Mulhall achieved his current rank because of his skill at manipulating people and his total disregard for the feelings of others.

Lt. Mulhall is viewed as someone who clawed his way to the top in a relatively short period of time, and the general consensus is that he is power hungry, using deceit without any thought of the moral consequences. He is very pragmatic in his approach to decision-making and goes out of his way to meet the needs and demands of the executive staff whenever he can. Many officers feel he is preparing for an early promotion to captain.

Mulhall goes by the book and is a stickler for the application of each and every rule or regulation. He may be described as a real micromanager that is totally devoted to maintaining his control and the organizational status quo. Whatever comes down from the top is viewed as gospel and is never questioned. There is considerable anxiety about whether Mulhall will use his new position in such a way as to ensure his next promotion.

Mulhall is aware of how he is viewed by some of the members of the department. He says he believes some of it is sour grapes, but he is still concerned about the potential negative influence on his career.

How would you describe Lt. Mulhall's personality? Does he have a strong bureaucratic orientation? Would you describe him as a Type A or as possessing a High-Mach personality? If you were Mulhall, how would you deal with those who object to the way you operate? Would it be counterproductive for you to try to change your behavior in your new position? If you were Mulhall's immediate supervisor, how would you relate to him?

have no difficulty in accepting bureaucratic standards and adjusting well to such an organization. Many individuals find bureaucracies meet their personal needs because rules dominate, positional authority is viewed as important, and the organization is looked on as more important than the individual.

SUMMARY

Police managers must continually analyze personality and its impact on employee behavior. There are a number of theories describing how personality develops. Each of these makes the following assumptions about human behavior: (1) Every individual possesses specific personality characteristics; (2) life experiences influence personality characteristics; and (3) each individual develops a distinct personality as a result of life experiences.

Early research into personality postulated heredity as the final arbiter of how one acquires personality, but it is currently believed that heredity plays a limited part in determining behavior. Culture is another factor influencing personality development. Culture exposes everyone to certain norms, attitudes, and values that are passed from parents to children. Culturally based factors exert a great deal of influence on organizational behavior, and police managers must respond not only to cultural variance but also to the different ways culture influences each person.

Another factor influencing personality is the situation. A situation may alter the behavior of an individual, causing a manager a great deal of difficulty when trying to supervise an employee. Unfortunately, much research remains to be done on situational factors and their influence on personality.

There are numerous theories of personality development. The most prominent are psychoanalytical, trait, and humanistic. Each theory can provide a manager with useful insights into the complexities of human individual, interpersonal, group, and organizational behavior.

Researchers have identified a number of personality dimensions that may have special relevance in the work environment. These dimensions include locus of control, Type A/Type B behavior, emotional intelligence, Machiavellianism, and bureaucratic orientation.

DISCUSSION TOPICS AND QUESTIONS

1. How does personality develop?

2. How important is culture in the development of the individual?

3. Why do individuals who have a bureaucratic orientation seem to perform effectively in police organizations?

4. Differentiate between individuals who have an external and an internal locus of control.

5. How would you deal with a manager who uses avoidance as a defensive technique?

6. In what ways do situational factors determine personality?

7. Differentiate between psychoanalytical and trait theories.

8. Describe three kinds of traits.

9. What are the characteristics of employees who have an internal locus of control?

10. Describe the personality orientation of a High-Mach employee.

FOR FURTHER READING

Elizabeth Reuss-Ianni, *Two Cultures of Policing: Street Cops and Management Cops* (New Brunswick, CT: Transaction Books, 1983).

Classic study of the distinctly different organizational cultures that exist between line and management cops in the same department.

John P. Crank, *Understanding Police Culture*, 2nd ed. (Cincinnati, OH: Anderson, 2003).

A thought-provoking analysis of police culture that raises serious questions about management operations and ethical issues.

ENDNOTES

1. Fred Luthans, *Organizational Behavior*, 9th ed. (New York: McGraw-Hill, 2002), p. 215.

2. John R. Schermerhorn, Jr., James G. Hunt, Richard N. Osborn, and Mary Uhl-Bien, *Organizational Behavior*, 11th ed. (Hoboken, NJ: John Wiley & Sons, 2010), p. 31.

3. John R. Schermerhorn, Jr., James G. Hunt, and Richard N. Osborn, *Organizational Behavior* (New York: John Wiley & Sons, 2002), p. 51.

4. Salvatore R. Maddi, *Personality Theories: A Comparative Analysis* (Homewood, IL: Dorsey, 1980), p. 32.

5. Larry K. Gaines, Victor E. Kappler, and Joseph B. Vaughn, *Police in America* (Cincinnati, OH: Anderson, 1994), pp. 241–242.

6. Roy Roberg, John Crank, and Jack Kuykendall, *Police & Society* (Los Angeles, CA: Roxbury, 2000), pp. 129–131.

7. James R. Terborg, "Interactional Psychology and Research on Human Behavior in Organizations," *Academy of Management Review*, Vol. 6 (1981), pp. 561–576.

8. Elizabeth Reuss-Ianni, *Two Cultures of Policing: Street Cops and Management Cops* (New Brunswick, CT: Transaction Books, 1983).

9. Beth Azar, "Nature, Nurture: Not Mutually Exclusive," *American Psychological Association Monitor* (May 1997), p. 1.

10. J. Steven Ott, *The Organizational Culture Perspective* (Pacific Grove, CA: Brooks/Cole, 1989), pp. 1–12.

11. Terrence E. Deal and A. Kennedy, *Corporate Cultures* (Reading, MA: Addison-Wesley, 1982).

12. Yoash Weiner and Yoav Vardi, "Relationships between Organizational Culture and Individual Motivation: A Conceptual Integration," *Psychological Reports*, Vol. 67 (1990), pp. 295–306.

13. Debra L. Nelson and James Campbell Quick, *Organizational Behavior: Foundations, Realities, and Challenges* (St. Paul, MN: West, 1995), pp. 494–497.

14. Ron Zemke, Clair Raines, and Bob Filipizak, *Generations at Work: Managing the Clash of Veterans, Boomers, Xers and Nexters in Your Workplace* (New York: AMACOM, 2000).

15. Luthans, *Organizational Behavior*, p. 218.

16. Victor E. Kappler, Richard D. Sluder, and Geoffrey P. Alpert, *Forces of Deviance: Understanding the Dark Side of Policing* (Prospect Heights, IL: Waveland Press, 1998).

17. David G. Myers, *Psychology* (New York: Worth, 1986).

18. Peter Gay, *The Freud Reader* (New York: W. W. Norton, 1995).

19. Samuel E. Wood and Ellen G. Wood, *The World of Psychology* (Boston, MA: Pearson Allyn and Bacon, 2001).

20. D. Nelson and J. C. Quick, *Organizational Behavior: Science, The Real World, and You*, 8th ed., (Boston, MA: Cengage Learning, 2013).

21. Alan O. Ross, *Personality: The Scientific Study of Complex Human Behavior* (New York: International Thomson Publishing, 1987).

22. Jerald Greenberg and Robert A. Baron, *Behavior in Organizations: Understanding the Human Side of Work* (Upper Saddle River, NJ: Prentice Hall, 2002).

23. Donald A. Laird, Eleanor C. Laird, and Rosemary T. Fruehling, *Psychology: Human Relations and Work Adjustment* (New York: McGraw-Hill, 1993).

24. Duane Schultz and Sydney Ellen Schultz, *Psychology and Work Today: Introduction to Industrial and Organizational Psychology* (Upper Saddle River, NJ: Prentice Hall, 2001).

25. Donald D. White and David D. Bednar, *Organizational Behavior: Understanding and Managing People at Work* (Boston, MA: Pearson Allyn and Bacon, 1986).

26. Schermerhorn, Hunt, and Osborn, *Organizational Behavior*, p. 387.

27. Stephen P. Robbins, *Managing Today* (Upper Saddle River, NJ: Prentice Hall, 1997), pp. 354–360.

28. Gordon W. Allport, *Personality: A Psychological Interpretation* (New York: Henry Holt 1937); R. Richard Bootzin, Gordon H. Bower, Robert B. Zajonic, and Elizabeth Hall, *Psychology Today* (New York: Random House, 1986); C. F. Monte, *Beneath the Mask: An Introduction to Theories of Personality*, 6th ed. (New York: Harcourt Brace, 1999).

29. Gordon W. Allport and H. S. Odbert, "Trait Names: A Psychological Study," *Psychological Monographs*, Vol. 4 (1936), pp. 211–214.

30. Jerome H. Skolnick, *Justice Without Trial* (New York: John Wiley & Sons, 1966).

31. Arthur Niederhoffer, *Behind the Shield: The Police in Urban Society* (Garden City, NJ: Doubleday 1967); Kevin M. Gilmartin, *Emotional Survival for Law Enforcement* (Tucson, AZ: E-S Press, 2002).

32. P. A. Weiss, "Potential Uses of the Rorschach in the Selection of Police Officers," *Journal of Police and Criminal Psychology*, Vol. 17, No. 2 (2002), pp. 63–70.

33. Larry K. Gaines and Steven Falkenberg, "An Evaluation of the Written Selection Test: Effectiveness and Alternatives," *Journal of Criminal Justice*, Vol. 26, No. 3, pp. 175–183.

34. J. J. Fyfe, "Good Policing," in S. Stojkovic, S. Klofas, and D. Kalinich, eds. *The Administration and Management of Criminal Justice*, 3rd ed. (Prospect Heights, IL: Waveland Press, 1999), pp. 113–133.

35. J. M. Digman, "Personality Structure: Emergence of the Five-Factor Model," *Annual Review of Psychology*, Vol. 41 (1990), pp. 417–440; J. Black, "Personality Testing and Police Selection, Utility of the 'Big Five'," *New Zealand Journal of Psychology*, Vol. 29, No. 1, pp. 1–9; J. M. Cortina, M. L. Doherty, N. Schmitt, G. Kaufman, and R. G. Smith, "The 'Big Five' Personality Factors in the IPI and MMPI: Predictors of Police Performance," *Personnel Psychology*, Vol. 45, No. 1 (1992), pp. 119–140.

36. Robert J. House, Scott A. Shane, and David M. Herold, "Rumors of the Death of Dispositional Research Are Vastly Exaggerated," *Academy of Management Review*, Vol. 21 (January 1996), p. 203.

37. Luthans, *Organizational Behavior*, pp. 220–222.

38. Michael K. Mount and Murray R. Barrick, "Five Reasons Why the Big Five Article Has Been Frequently Cited," *Personnel Psychology*, Vol. 5 (1998), pp. 849–857.

39. T. A. Judge, J. J. Martocchio, and C. J. Thoresen, "Five-Factor Model of Personality and Employee Absence," *Journal of Applied Psychology*, Vol. 82 (1998), pp. 745–755.

40. Paul M. Whisenand and R. Fred Ferguson, *The Managing of Police Organizations* (Upper Saddle River, NJ: Prentice Hall, 2002).

41. Murray R. Barrick, G.L. Stewart, M.J. Neubert, and M.K. Mount, "Relating Member Ability and Personality to Work-Team Processes and Team Effectiveness," *Journal of Applied Psychology*, Vol. 83 (1998), pp. 377–391.

42. Beth A. Sanders, "Using Personality Traits to Predict Police Officer Performance," *Policing: An International Journal of Police Strategies & Management*, Vol. 31, No. 1 (2008) pp. 129–147.

43. Thomas Chamorro-Premuzic, "Could Your Personality Derail Your Career," *Harvard Business Review* (September–October 2017). Retrieved from https://hbr.org/2017/09/could-your-personality-derail-your-career.

44. Ibid.

45. Ibid.

46. Ibid.

47. Ibid.

48. Carl Rogers, *On Becoming a Person: A Therapist View of Psychotherapy* (Boston, MA: Houghton Mifflin, 1970).

49. Bootzin, Bower, Zajonic, and Hall, *Psychology Today*.

50. Whisenand and Ferguson, *Managing Police Organizations*, pp. 288–308.

51. Nelson and Quick, *Organizational Behavior*, p. 80.

52. T. R. Mitchell, C. M. Smyser, and S. E. Weed, "Locus of Control: Supervision and Work Satisfaction," *Academy of Management Journal*, Vol. 57 (1975), pp. 623–631.

53. Paul E. Spector, "Behavior in Organizations as a Function of Locus of Control," *Psychological Bulletin*, Vol. 93 (1982), pp. 482–497.

54. Ronald G. Lynch, *The Police Manager* (Cincinnati, OH: Anderson, 1998), pp. 27–42.

55. Myer Friedman and Ray H. Rosenman, *Type A Behavior and Your Heart* (New York: Knopf, 1974).

56. Robert E. Franken, *Human Motivation* (Pacific Grove, CA: Brooks/Cole, 1988).

57. Schermerhorn, Hunt, and Osborn, *Organizational Behavior*, p. 236.

58. C. Lee, L. F. Jamison, and P. C. Earley, "Beliefs and Fears and Type A Behavior: Implications for Academic Performance and Psychiatric Health Disorder Symptoms," *Journal of Organizational Behavior*, Vol. 17 (1996), pp. 151–177.

59. Greenberg and Baron, *Behavior in Organizations*.

60. Niccolo Machiavelli, *The Prince* (New York: Simon & Schuster, 1970).

61. Ibid., pp. 71–75.

62. James Bowditch and Anthony Buono, *A Primer on Organizational Behavior* (New York: Wiley, 1994), p. 115.

63. Richard Christie and Florence L. Geis, *Studies in Machiavellianism* (New York: Academic Press, 1970).

64. R.A. Giacalone and S.B. Knouse, "Justifying Wrongful Employee Behavior: The Role of Personality in Organizational Sabotage," *Journal of Business Ethics*, Vol. 9 (1990), pp. 55–56.

65. Schermerhorn, Hunt, and Osborn, *Organizational Behavior*, pp. 54–55.

66. Robbins, *Managing Today*, p. 356.

67. See William F. Walsh, "Patrol Officer Arrest Rates: A Study in the Social Organization of Police Work," *Justice Quarterly*, Vol. 3 (1986), pp. 271–290.

68. T. Bradberry and J. Greaves, *Emotional Intelligence 2.0* (San Francisco, CA: Group West, 2009).

69. J. D. Mayer, M. T. DiPaolo, and P. Salovey, "Perceiving Affective Content in Ambiguous Visual Stimuli: A Component of Emotional Intelligence," *Journal of Personality Assessment*, Vol. 54 (1990), pp. 772–781.

70. D. Goleman, *Emotional Intelligence* (New York: Bantam Books, 1995).

71. N. Scutte, J. Malouff, C. Coston, and D. Tracie, "Emotional Intelligence and Interpersonal Relations," *Journal of Social Psychology*, Vol. 144, No. 4 (2001), pp. 523–536.

72. Mark H. Moore and Darrel W. Stephens, *Beyond Command and Control: The Strategic Management of Police Departments* (Washington, D.C.: Police Executive Research Forum, 1991), pp. 1–6.

73. David Osborne and Ted Gaebler, *Reinventing Government: How the Entrepreneurial Spirit Is Transforming the Public Sector* (New York: Penguin Group, 1993), pp. 212–214.

4

BELIEFS, VALUES, AND ATTITUDES

Determinants of Human Behavior

Learning Objectives

1. Define *behavior*.
2. Define *culture*, and identify the steps involved in the socialization process.
3. Compare and contrast ideas, beliefs, values, attitudes, opinions, and motives.
4. Define *perception*.
5. List and describe the steps involved in perception formation.
6. Describe the sources of perceptual distortion.
7. Describe the manager's role in creating and changing organization culture.

Key Terms

attitudes
behavior
$B = F(P \times E)$
beliefs
change agent
culture
ideas
introspection
job satisfaction
morale
motivation
motives

operant behavior
opinion
paradigm
paradigm shift
perception
perceptual distortion
perceptual organization
significant others
social relationship
socialization
value system
values

Police departments are dynamic, organic organizational settings created by and composed of human beings. They are microcosms of the society at large and provide a sociocultural setting in which people interact with, react to, and influence one another as they pursue common goals and objectives. However, it is common for many officers to refer to their organization as a distinct separate thing—"the department." This practice implies they consider the department as an objective force distinct from themselves. They fail to recognize that they and their activities *are* the organization.

The individual is the fundamental subsystem upon which organizations are built. Individuals consist of interdependent physiological and psychosocial systems that work in concert with environmental factors to produce distinctive behavior. The dynamic interdependence between human (internal) and environmental (external) factors helps to account for the complexity of human behavior.[1]

CASE STUDY   Captain Steve Stivers

Steve Stivers is a lieutenant in charge of the midnight patrol shift in a large urban police department located in the Midwest. He is 57 years old and has been a police officer for nearly 30 years. Once considered progressive and a good leader, he has been having great difficulty dealing with many of the social changes taking place in society. Stivers is, in fact, being investigated by the State Human Relations Commission. He has been charged with sexual discrimination against a female police officer.

Officer Jo Andleman, 26 years old, has been with the department for two years. She is the only female officer on Stivers' shift. Andleman has been working the midnight shift for about eight months. A strong advocate for women's rights, she "marches to her own drummer." Andleman is outspoken in her support of equal rights and comparable pay for women. Officer Andleman is also a pro-choice activist.

When Lt. Stivers heard rumors that Andleman was living with a male police officer assigned to the same shift, he called her into his office and ordered her to sever the "immoral" relationship immediately. Even though she had a good performance record, he gave her a written reprimand for "conduct unbecoming an officer." When she objected, he criticized her for "living in sin" and subjecting the police department to ridicule. Stivers told Andleman that if she had to "shack up" with a police officer that she should "make it legal" and become his "little mama." Stivers told her that

he would do all he could to get her fired if she failed to heed his "advice."

Officer Andleman filed a grievance to have the written reprimand removed from her folder because the department's rules regarding conduct do not specifically prohibit fraternization or cohabitation with other police personnel. She also filed a sexual discrimination charge with the Human Relations Commission. Lt. Stivers is upset by the incident and has put in for retirement. He told the chief he could no longer stand to work in the same department with "morally bankrupt people."

The Human Relations Commission investigation revealed that Steve Stivers was raised in a traditional and very religious family. As a fundamentalist, he interprets the Bible in literal terms. Stivers was taught that women are subservient to men and should function as homemakers. He feels that women have no place in a "man's job" like police work. Thus Lt. Stivers has a very negative attitude toward female police officers. He belittles them and expresses his opinions in overtly sexist terms.

Is Capt. Stivers a dinosaur and out of step with society? Or is his feelings representative of other male officers who believe women have no place in policing? Prepare a written analysis of this case. Indicate whether or not you feel that the lieutenant should undergo sensitivity training or that his resignation was in the best interest of the police department.

Human Behavior

Humans are social beings who exhibit recurrent, regular, and recognizable patterns of behavior. In a general sense, **behavior** can be defined as anything an individual does that involves self-initiated action and/or reaction to a given stimulus. From an organizational point of view, behavior consists of adaptive adjustments people make as they cope with one another, with problems, with opportunities, and with synergistic aspects of specific situations.[2] All human behavior involves the conscious or subconscious selection of particular actions from among those that are possible and over which a person exercises some influence, control, or authority. At times, the selection of alternatives is almost automatic and is made without very much thought. For example, a police sergeant who responds to the scene of a traffic accident will quickly direct his officers to set out cones or place their vehicles in a manner that will enhance the safety of the people at the scene. In other cases, behavior is the product of a complex chain of activities that involves planning and designated operational activities by specific officers.[3] A police officer learning to qualify with her department's weapon, for example, engages in a series of behavioral adaptations during firing practices that are keyed to internal as well as external factors designed to achieve a successful outcome.

Normal human beings exhibit two basic types of behavior simultaneously and are able to integrate them into a stable persona. These are (1) inherited behavior and (2) learned behavior.[4]

1. *Inherited behavior.* Inherited, or innate, behavior refers to any behavioral response or reflex exhibited by people due to their genetic endowment or the process of natural selection. The survival of the species is contingent on behaviors like breathing, ingesting food, voiding wastes, mating, and defending oneself. These behaviors are modified through adaptation as the environment acts on the individual.

2. *Learned behavior.* Learned, or operant, behavior involves cognitive adaptations that enhance a human being's ability to cope with changes in the environment and

to manipulate the environment in ways that improve the chances for survival. Learned behaviors (such as verbal communication, logical problem-solving techniques, and job skills) give people more control over their lives. The importance of learned behavior lies in its consequences for the person and the organization.

It is learned (self-initiated and goal-oriented) social behavior that sets human beings apart from other animals. Abstract thinking leads to vicarious learning and activates the adaptive process.

Social Relationships

Human beings live and work in groups. Throughout their existence, humans have learned that by forming groups they can accomplish more than they can by working alone. A group is a collection of individuals who derive satisfaction from interacting with each other in some consistent and coordinated way as they strive to achieve a common goal or objective. Groups are held together by a variety of social relationships (see Figure 4–1). A **social relationship** exists when people have reciprocal expectations about one another so that they act in relatively patterned ways. This concept is important because almost all human behavior is oriented toward others. Not only do people live and work together, they share common beliefs, values, attitudes, and normative understandings. They continuously interact with and respond to significant others. **Significant others** are individuals who have great importance for an individual such as a police officer's immediate supervisor, family member, or partner. People shape their (conscious and unconscious) behavior in relation to the behavioral expectations of significant others within groups.[5]

Groups, like the societies they belong to, develop distinctive ways of interacting with their internal and external environments. Recurring patterns of behavior evolve into group cultures that define appropriate ways of feeling, behaving, and thinking for group members. **Culture** reflects the shared language, events, symbols, rituals, values, and norms indigenous to a particular group. It is developed by groups to help them survive and create meaning for their behavior as they cope with the demands of their environments. While culture is derived from past behavior, it is perpetually reconstituted in

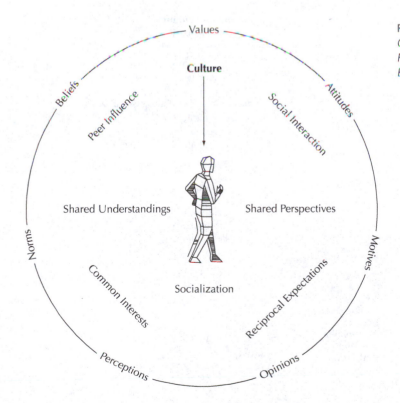

Figure 4–1
Group Dynamics, Social Relationships, and Learned Behavior.

current members via the socialization process. From a pragmatic point of view, culture embodies shared beliefs (how things work) and values (what is important) that are internalized by members of a group to produce behavioral norms (the way things "ought to be done").[6] It is a term that explains how employees identify with the characteristics of an organization. Culture must be learned before it can be internalized (see Figure 4–2). In this context, learning is defined as a dynamic process that manifests itself in behavior that is based on prior experience.[7] People possess few—if any—instinctive skills and no instinctive knowledge that will enable them to survive. They survive only by virtue of what they have learned. The central idea is that culture is learned from other human beings in group settings, shared with them, and modified through interaction with them. It gives meaning to the world and explains why things are done or not done in a certain way.

As groups mature, they develop their own ways of behaving, which cannot be identified solely with the characteristics of any specific group member. In fact, individual characteristics are usually overshadowed by those of the group itself. A police work group such as a patrol shift that has worked together for several years, for example, will usually exhibit characteristics apart from and beyond the mere sum of the characteristics of its members. However, people cannot be directed to work as a productive group. People have to want to work together and have to develop, through their daily interactions, closeness to each other and to what they are doing. This is the basis for teamwork. It is the role of every manager to create an environment in which teamwork will develop. However, to have a successful team, each member must place the team's objectives first, ahead of his or her individual objectives.

The performance of a work group is, or should be, more than the simple sum of the individual efforts of its members. By coordination across individuals, activities, or functions, it becomes possible to create a high-performance group whose performance as a whole is greater than the sum of its parts. This is known as the "synergistic effect."[8]

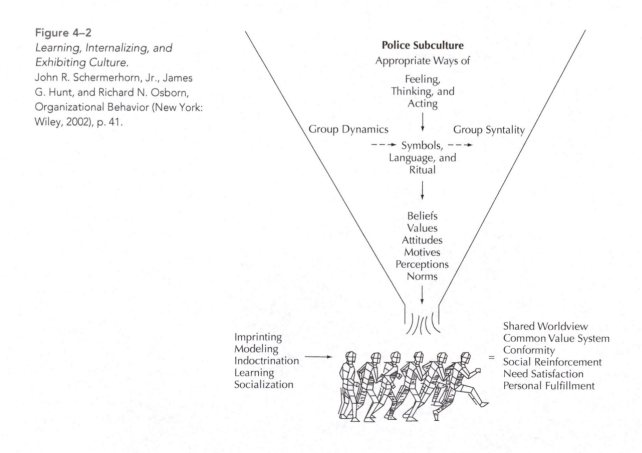

Figure 4–2
Learning, Internalizing, and Exhibiting Culture.
John R. Schermerhorn, Jr., James G. Hunt, and Richard N. Osborn, Organizational Behavior (New York: Wiley, 2002), p. 41.

Police Subculture
Appropriate Ways of
Feeling,
Thinking, and
Acting

Group Dynamics   Group Syntality

Symbols,
Language, and
Ritual

Beliefs
Values
Attitudes
Motives
Perceptions
Norms

Imprinting
Modeling
Indoctrination
Learning
Socialization

Shared Worldview
Common Value System
Conformity
Social Reinforcement
Need Satisfaction
Personal Fulfillment

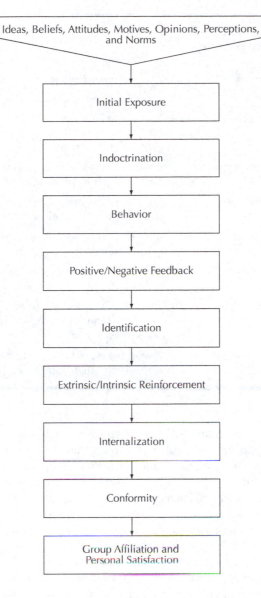

Figure 4–3
The Human Socialization Process.

Every group attempts to socialize its members as they move through the cycle from initiation to full participation. **Socialization** is the process by which group-shared beliefs, values, attitudes, and norms are inculcated into each member's psyche (see Figure 4–3). Once these beliefs, values, attitudes, and norms have been internalized, they serve as prescriptive guides to appropriate behavior (see Table 4–1 for a definition of these terms). Consistent beliefs, values, attitudes, and norms produce conformity with group-shared expectations. Inconsistency creates ambivalence and conflict. Conflict and ambivalence about norms of behavior can result in anomie, a sense of normlessness that frequently leads to deviant behavior.[9]

An organization's values, beliefs, and accepted ways of behaving make up its culture. Stories, rituals, and myths transmit this culture from one generation of employees to another. An organization's history and traditions are the source of these stories, rituals, and myths. They form the basis of the organization's culture and belief system. The importance of an organization's culture is that it provides a sense of meaning and purpose to the behavior of its members. The reasons police officers act in a specific manner can be found in their values and the meaning they attach to their behavior. These beliefs, values, and acceptable modes of behavior are learned through the process of organizational socialization and are often expressed as rationalizations for behavior.

Table 4–1
GLOSSARY

Ideas	Abstract mental images of something imagined, seen, or known.
Beliefs	Ideas accepted as true and acted on as an article of faith.
Values	Strong and enduring beliefs about appropriate conduct and/or end states of existence (e.g., goals), which are preferable to opposite or inverse conduct or end states.
Value system	Enduring values arranged hierarchically in terms of relative importance to a particular individual.
Attitudes	Predispositions, based on one's beliefs and values, to react either positively or negatively to various ideas, persons, events, or things.
Motives	Cognitive variables that activate, direct, sustain, or inhibit a person's goal-oriented behavior.
Opinions	Judgments about ideas, persons, events, and things translated into words that reflect one's ideas, beliefs, values, attitudes, and motives.
Perception	Filtering processes through which individuals transform, attach meaning to, and structure information coming from their experience or memory.
Norms	Shared beliefs, values, attitudes, expectations, and rules—spoken or understood—that guide human behavior in specific situations.

A thriving culture consists of two defining characteristics. The first is a unique personality and atmosphere based on shared values and heritage.[10] While law enforcement agencies have many similarities, they also have many differences. For example, the culture of state police agencies is much different than those of municipal policing agencies. The second characteristic is the norms and behaviors that interpret the organization's distinctive personality and atmosphere into a focus on client or community actions and organizational outcomes. To accomplish these two characteristics can be complex, and to accomplish them, it requires leaders to modify employees' thought processes about the organization and revise habitual behaviors.[11]

Seven main characteristics seem to encapsulate the fundamental nature of an organization's culture.[12] The focus of intensity regarding these characteristics ranges from one end of the spectrum to the other, and assessing them comprehensively can provide a multifaceted representation of a law enforcement agency's organizational culture.[13]

- *Innovation and risk taking*: The extent to which employees are inspired to be risk-takers and be innovative
- *Attention to detail*: The level of expectation for employees to exhibit precision, analysis, and attention to detail
- *Outcome orientation*: The measure to which management places on or emphasizes results or outcomes rather than on the methods and practices used to attain them
- *People orientation*: The extent management decisions take into account the influences have upon employees in the organization
- *Team orientation*: The degree to which work behaviors structured focusing on teams rather than individuals
- *Aggressiveness*: The level of aggressiveness and competitiveness among employees
- *Stability*: The level of prominence in activities to preserve the existing state of affairs in relation to growth

Managers who understand the importance of organization culture appreciate the power of vision, rituals, ceremonies, and stories. They use these to create a set of shared values that help shape their organization's self-image. Many police organizations have developed strong organizational cultures based on meaningful rituals, traditions, and visions of what is their actual function.

Organizational symbols can also be used to camouflage or distort. The certified police officer may be incompetent because of a lack of training after the certification was originally achieved. The training officer may give out test questions and answers during mandatory training sessions. The organization that states "People Come First" in their value statement might treat their workers terribly. There may be one set of rules for managers and one for workers. The "mission statement" on the wall may mean nothing at all. All of these can create a culture of distrust and conflict in an organization.

People who study organizational culture claim that all organizations have two stages, one in front and one in the back. The front stage projects the image the organization wants outsiders to see and believe. They want outsiders to believe this is the real organization. Only insiders, the organization's employees, get to see and know the back stage—what the organization truly is and how it operates behind the front stage. In well-managed ethical organizations, there is little difference between these two stages, but in organizations that lack integrity and ethical accountability, there is a vast difference between the two.[14]

For change to take place in an organization, managers must understand the true culture (core values) of their organization and how this culture impacts organizational behavior. However, this can be difficult for insiders to do because their organization's cultural system is very much a part of their psychological makeup. At the same time, for any leadership intervention to succeed, the **change agent** must be able to stand outside of the cultural value system of the organization, understand it, and change it, if that is necessary. Remember from a cultural perspective, what is real is real, whether in fact it is real or not.

By the time young men and women become police officers, most of them have developed a stable worldview and fixed personality structure. They have a repertoire of beliefs, values, attitudes, and norms that they bring with them into the workplace.[15] As these individuals become police recruits and participate in their department's entry-level training program, they begin to acquire new ideas, beliefs, values, attitudes, motives, and norms and to incorporate these into their preexisting frame of reference. They learn the police organization's definition of the world. When they leave the training academy and commence their field training, they begin to interact with the day-to-day experiences of police patrol work. These experiences add to the officers' common sense methodologies and rationalizations for dealing with the demands of their job.

Police Cultural Learning Process

- Police organizational culture is learned
- In a process of interaction with significant others
- During police academy training and experiences on the job
- It consists of accepted techniques of doing the job and
- Beliefs, core values, attitudes, rationalizations, and norms of behavior
- Individuals are accepted or not accepted based on peer evaluation of their behavior

Consequently, a police officer is a dynamic composite of past learning and experience as modified by current events. Research has consistently found that the police operational experience and how individuals adjust to it are the most important factors in the development of good or bad individual police officer behavior.[16]

People-Oriented Management

It is also clear that the beliefs, values, and attitudes of individual police managers help to determine their capacity to work effectively with subordinates. Modern police management became more people oriented in the later part of the 20th century.

Managers who subscribe to this style of management are "organizational humanists." They believe in achieving productivity through people and seek to instill in all employees awareness that their best efforts are essential for the success of the enterprise.

Thomas J. Peters and Robert H. Waterman, Jr., became the leading proponents of organizational humanism in America with the publication of their book *In Search of Excellence* (Warner, NY, 1982). Based on their research, Peters and Waterman conclude that there is hardly a more pervasive theme in excellent organizations than respect for the individual. Such organizations, they found, use an abundance of structural devices, systems, styles, and values interacting to reinforce one another, which enable them to "achieve extraordinary results through ordinary people."

Peters and Waterman believe that workers should be permitted control over their own destinies, but they do not advocate mollycoddling people. They are talking about tough-minded respect for individual workers and a willingness to develop their ability to set clear and reasonable expectations for themselves. These authors hold that employees should be given genuine autonomy to step out and make a meaningful contribution to the organization. Peters and Waterman contend that managers in excellent organizations are quite different from their counterparts in less healthy organizations. They are more open and trusting. They treat people as partners in the collective enterprise. They respect their subordinates and see them as the wellspring of productivity. They make people feel like winners, and they celebrate winning ways with a variety of nonmonetary psychosocial rewards. Organizational humanists seek to unleash the power in their people and focus that power on the achievement of positive outcomes for the organization.

In a sense, all intentional behavior is the product of intrinsic motivation. People, based on psychosocial needs and/or environmental stimuli, set their own goals and expend the amount of effort necessary to demonstrate to themselves that they can reach, or nearly reach, these goals. There is an implicit question of values in all goal setting. Setting personal goals and activating goal-oriented behavior are inextricably linked to one's judgment of good and evil, right and wrong, and desirable and undesirable. These judgments are rooted in each person's cultural heritage, ethical perspective, and normative orientation. The heterogeneous nature of modern American society helps to reinforce ethical relativity and anomie. Since police managers perceive reality in terms of their own values, attitudes, and expectations, they must learn a great deal more about themselves in order to minimize distortion and prevent interpersonal conflict.

In order to become truly effective managers who have the ability to get things done through others, police managers must understand themselves as well as their subordinates. **Introspection** is the process of looking inward through the process of self-examination of one's inner thoughts, feelings, and beliefs. It is the key to self-understanding and leadership, the first step in what Peter Senge calls "personal mastery."[17] The individual who achieves personal mastery has developed an understanding and control of his or her emotions, strengths, weaknesses, needs, and drives. Managers can achieve high levels of personal mastery by continually clarifying what is important to themselves and their organizations. In this manner, they can develop a clear understanding of how they and their individual units fit into the overall mission and strategy of the organizations to which they belong. This knowledge provides them with a special sense of direction that enables them to clarify their visions and goals.

Effective managers understand that who they are (in terms of background, experience, beliefs, values) usually determines what they do with the organization's human resources. Self-awareness allows them, when necessary, to reevaluate their style and to adjust their behavior accordingly. Self-awareness is one of the four skills of emotional intelligence identified in Chapter 4.

Being comfortable with their role as a manager in a complex organization is much easier when they do the following:

1. Be aware of and have the ability to accept their own strengths and weaknesses.
2. Develop realistic expectations so as not to demand perfection from themselves or subordinate personnel.
3. Have the capacity to recognize and deal effectively with negative attitudes and less-than-acceptable behavior exhibited by some others within the organization.
4. Come to realize that their own and their subordinate's self-esteem is dynamic and subject to change.

Successful police managers know that their own personal beliefs, values, attitudes, and expectations have a substantive influence on perceptions, interpersonal relations, and work-group dynamics. Thus good managers exhibit the following characteristics:

1. Understand that they are a "walking system" of conscious and unconscious values, which are so much a part of their personality that they are scarcely aware of their existence or influence.
2. Use all means at their disposal to identify personal biases that reduce their own objectivity in assessing the on-the-job behavior of others.
3. Strive to evaluate themselves and their personal values in a rational and objective manner.
4. Endeavor to change any of their own values (and related behaviors) that, based on serious self-evaluation, need to be changed.

Ideas, Beliefs, and Values

Human beings use the power of reason to draw conclusions, make judgments, and guide their goal-oriented behavior. A healthy mind produces a continuous stream of ideas. **Ideas** are generated during the thought process and can be described as relatively abstract mental images of something imagined, seen, or known. They are cognitive representations of what is or what could be. Ideas are untested concepts that may or may not reflect reality. Creative people have the ability to translate good ideas into positive action.

Ideas, once formed, are cycled through the mind for (conscious or subconscious) evaluation. Some seem implausible and are discarded outright. The rest are arranged along a continuum of support ranging from *some* to *complete*. **Beliefs** are ideas accepted as good or true (whether they are or not) and acted on as an article of faith. Since the person involved makes an emotional commitment, beliefs take on an existence of their own. Selective perception is used to confirm and reinforce them. Consequently, they can withstand virtually any challenge. Facts become irrelevant! Logic becomes irrelevant! A Theory X police manager, for example, who believes that his or her officers lack ambition, dislike responsibility, and prefer to be led will reject Peters and Waterman's assertion that giving employees respect and autonomy will help police departments achieve extraordinary results through ordinary people. Theory X administrators find it difficult or impossible to share power with, rather than exercise power over, their employees. As human beings, we learn and share the values by which we live. **Values** represent the ideas and beliefs through which we define our personal goals, choose particular courses of action, and judge our own behavior in relation to that of others. Values are not specifically defined rules for action but general precepts to which people are expected to give their allegiance and about which they are likely to have strong sentiments. Values are very important in that they have a direct influence on our perceptions, preferences, aspirations, and choices. In addition, personal fulfillment depends in large measure on how well our values find expression in our daily life.[18]

Values are the foundation of one's character, personality, management style, and on-the-job behavior. Values echo a person's sense of right and wrong. Past values help determine who we are and what we want out of life. Current values give substance to our personal and professional being. Future values will influence our behavior at some point down the road. Values are mental constructs representing behaviors and end states of existence (goals) that are important to us as individuals.[19]

Psychologist Milton Rokeach advanced a set of values categorized into two general categories: terminal and instrumental values.[20] Terminal values signal a person's preferences concerning the realized objective. These are the goals of the individual to be achieved over their lifespan. Rokeach further distributes these values into 18 terminal values and 18 instrumental values as synopsized in Table 4–2.[21]

Instrumental values reflect the method or means for achieving desired objectives. This method is dependent upon the importance an individual assigns to the instrumental values. Research implies both terminal and instrumental values differ by group or rank.

Table 4–2
ROKEACH TERMINAL AND INSTRUMENTAL VALUES

Terminal Values	Instrumental Values
A comfortable life (and prosperous)	Ambitious (hardworking)
An exciting life (stimulating)	Broad-minded (open-minded)
A sense of accomplishment (lasting contribution)	Capable (competent, effective)
A world at peace (free of war and conflict)	Cheerful (lighthearted, joyful)
A world of beauty (beauty of nature and the arts)	Clean (neat, tidy)
Equality (brotherhood, equal opportunity)	Courageous (standing up for beliefs)
Family security (taking care of loved ones)	Forgiving (willing to pardon)
Freedom (independence, free choice)	Helpful (working for others' welfare)
Happiness (contentedness)	Honest (sincere, truthful)
Inner harmony (freedom from inner conflict)	Imaginative (creative, daring)
Mature love (sexual and spiritual intimacy)	Independent (self-sufficient, self-reliant)
National security (attack protection)	Intellectual (intelligent, reflective)
Pleasure (leisurely, enjoyable life)	Logical (rational, consistent)
Salvation (saved, eternal life)	Loving (affectionate, tender)
Self-respect (self-esteem)	Obedient (dutiful, respectful)
Social recognition (admiration, respect)	Polite (courteous, well-mannered)
True friendship (close companionship)	Responsible (reliable, dependable)
Wisdom (mature understanding of life)	Self-controlled (self-disciplined)

These reference differences can encourage conflict or agreement when different groups have to deal with each other.[22]

From a practical point of view, a value is a strong and persistent belief that certain behaviors and/or end states of existence are preferable to other behaviors or end states. A **value system** is an enduring set of beliefs, ranged in order of importance, about preferred conduct (instrumental values) and end states of existence (terminal values). Because all people possess more than one value, managers need to adopt a broader perspective and think in terms of value systems. Those managers who value honesty and openness in human relationships will do everything in their power not to manipulate or appear to be manipulating their subordinates.

Values are enduring yet changeable beliefs about appropriate ends (goals) and acceptable goal-oriented behaviors (means). Basic values are acquired through imprinting, modeling, and socialization in a group setting (see Chapter 8). These values influence virtually every aspect of life. There is evidence to support the following general propositions concerning human values:

1. The actual number of values that people possess is relatively small (typically between 30 and 60).
2. Values are organized into value systems.
3. Each person's values can be traced back to his or her formative years; to the culture, institutions, and society he or she belongs to; and, to some extent, to his or her unique genetic makeup.

4. The consequences of our values will be manifested in virtually all that we think, feel, and do.

5. A large part of a police manager's effectiveness or lack of it results from his or her value system.

6. Enhanced or continued leadership is linked to our awareness of our values and the values of our co-workers.[23]

Individual values and value systems are critically important variables in that they automatically filter the way people perceive the world around them. They serve as ethical as well as moral standards. Values and value systems help resolve internal conflicts and facilitate the decision-making process. They encourage analytical thinking about legitimate goals and the socially acceptable means for achieving those goals. Values and value systems also motivate people to get off dead center and move toward the accomplishment of important organizational goals and objectives.

In many police departments, bureaucratic values shape organizational goals and set performance standards. Utilitarian values like efficiency, effectiveness, productivity, and accountability stress the rational aspects of work and virtually ignore what Douglas M. McGregor called "the human side of enterprise." Police managers who are preoccupied with control values are badly cast to play the exceedingly complex managerial roles assigned to them today. Their ineptitude in dealing with human resources leads to internal strife and a demonstrable reduction in the problem-solving capacity of the complex organizations they administer.

Humanistic Values

While mechanistic values like efficiency, effectiveness, productivity, and accountability are still very important, in many organizations much more emphasis is now being placed on the quality of work life. This shift in values is based on profound dissatisfaction with the traditional bureaucracy and its emphasis on the principles of scientific management. The shift is also related to the rising influence of humanism in contemporary American society. Humanists place a great deal of emphasis on goal-oriented communication, interaction, and collaboration. Effective managers are viewed as pragmatists who understand they must temper bureaucratic values with genuine empathy (for employees and clients) if they are to accomplish the mission, goals, and objectives of the police department.[24]

As police managers adapt to a more existential/humanist philosophy of work, more and more of them are questioning and moving away from traditional bureaucratic values. They are constructing new multidimensional value systems that stress service, efficiency, effectiveness, productivity, and accountability while addressing employee needs for personal growth, self-esteem, competence, and autonomy.[25]

Since management is often defined as "the art of getting things done with and through the efforts of other people," all credible management theories have a humanistic component. They are based—to one degree or another—on the value-laden assumption that organizations should be designed to meet the legitimate needs of people (including employees) as they seek to accomplish their missions, goals, and objectives. Even the infamous "paramilitary mentality" of traditional police administrators is not impervious to humanistic values. Most mainstream police managers know that the effectiveness of their organizations depends upon the effective use of human resources. They understand the importance of autonomy, empowerment, shared decision-making, and team management. Little by little, their values are shifting away from the typical Theory X belief system.

Today, police managers have abandoned the overly simplistic view of man embodied in bureaucratic theory. They have replaced it with human resource management concepts that envision the manager's primary responsibility as creating an organizational environment in which employees can grow, develop, and perform effectively. In the organizations led by such managers, power is based on competence, collaboration, and teamwork. Such managers believe that most police officers want to be good at their job and have a need to exercise self-direction and self-control. Under the right set of circumstances, they encourage their officers to seek out and accept responsibility. They mentor their officers in order to develop the knowledge, imagination, creativity, ingenuity, and practical skills necessary to help the police department accomplish its mission, goals, and objectives, today and in the future. A police manager's primary job is to get things done through others. In order to do this, he or she is expected to motivate personnel, supervise employees, set the ethical tone, and perform all of the other specialized work required to keep the organization in operation.

Attitudes and Opinions

As noted earlier, the term *culture* refers to the characteristic values, traditions, and behaviors a particular group shares. Police officers are members of a unique occupational group and share a distinctive cultural orientation.[26] Beliefs are major components of that culture. *Beliefs* are ideas that people in a group share about themselves and the physical, biological, and social world in which they live. Beliefs, regardless of their accuracy or merit, influence perception and regulate our relations with other human beings, society, and nature itself. *Values* are very strong beliefs about what is good and/or what is bad. A *personal value system* is a relatively permanent perceptual framework that influences and shapes our attitudes, opinions, motives, and behavior.[27]

Values and attitudes are similar in that both are beliefs about appropriate ways of feeling, thinking, and behaving. Values are much broader, however, and cut across specific situations to which personal attitudes are tied. Values are also more enduring than attitudes. They transcend attitudes and serve as a guide to our attitudes, judgments, choices, and behavior.[28]

An attitude is a general point of view that is a composite of our beliefs concerning a particular person, object, event, or situation. It represents a way of looking at someone or something and is coupled with a predisposition to react to that person, object, event, or situation in a predetermined manner. An attitude can also be described as a state of mind in which one's likes and dislikes are translated into a judgment about the intrinsic worth of a certain person, event, or thing. An **opinion** is the verbal expression of this judgment and reflects the personal beliefs, values, and attitudes of the person doing the expressing. Human behavior is thus understandable in terms of the meaning people attach to their actions. Police managers can learn a great deal about the beliefs, values, and attitudes of the people who work for them if they take the time to analyze their behavior, language, and opinions. This is true because *values* (general principles) generate *attitudes* (favorable or unfavorable feelings) that are translated into our *opinions* (personal judgments) and lead to specific *behavior* (cognitive response to stimuli).

This process is illustrated in Figure 4–4. Table 4–3 gives examples and demonstrates the dynamic interaction between these variables.

Paul Whisenand and R. Fred Ferguson[29] have analyzed the relationship between values and attitudes. They point out the following distinctions between the two:

1. A value is a single belief; an attitude grows out of several related beliefs concerning a single object or situation.
2. A value ranks objects and situations; an attitude focuses on a specific object or situation.
3. A value is a standard; an attitude may or may not function as a standard.
4. Values are enduring beliefs, few in number; attitudes are multiple and tend to change as new objects or situations are encountered.
5. Values are central to the personality and the cognitive makeup; attitudes are less so.
6. Values are very broad, whereas attitudes are more overtly linked to particular objects or situations.
7. Values reflect adjustive, ego-defensive, and knowledge functions explicitly, whereas attitudes do so implicitly. Attitudes are identifiable predispositions to react in a favorable or unfavorable way to a particular person, event, or object in the environment.

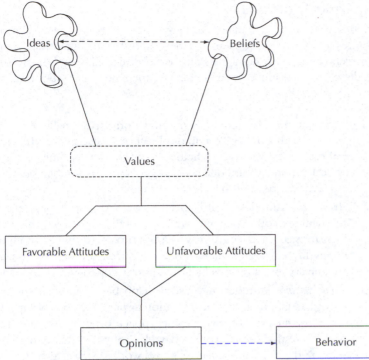

Figure 4–4
Values in Action.

Table 4–3
BEHAVIOR FORMATION

	Example 1	Example 2	Example 3
Value	Belief in the ethical use of police power to protect and serve the community.	Belief in and respect for people regardless of their station in life.	Belief in the legitimate use of authority to accomplish management goals and objectives.
Attitude	Feeling that criminal activity by police officers violates the Law Enforcement Code of Ethics and should not be tolerated.	Feeling that empathetic understanding and support will help others to achieve their full potential.	Feeling that police officers are to carry out all legitimate orders given to them by their superiors.
Opinion	"Blue coat crime" should be rooted out, and police officers who violate the criminal code ought to be prosecuted to the full extent of the law.	Police officers should have an opportunity to be involved in making those decisions that directly affect them.	Insubordination should not be tolerated and must be dealt with in a forthright manner.
Behavior	A police officer reports his partner for stealing jewelry from the body of an accident victim.	The police chief forms a task force to recommend ways to improve the overall quality of work life in the police department.	An acting lieutenant suspends a senior patrol officer for failure to follow a direct order.

Acquiring Attitudes

Attitudes are learned, not inherited. People acquire positive as well as negative attitudes as the result of their personal experiences, and they maintain them if there is sufficient reinforcement to justify doing so. Police officers, like all other human beings, acquire their attitudes in three distinct ways: (1) direct experience, (2) association, and (3) the social learning process.[30]

1. *Direct experience.* Attitudes can develop from a personally rewarding or painful experience with a person, event, or object. A rookie police officer who has lost several criminal cases may—whether he or she was at fault or not—develop a very cynical attitude toward due process and argue that public safety is in jeopardy because the courts are too lenient on criminals.

2. *Association.* Attitudes toward a person, event, or object may develop from associating them with other persons, events, or objects about which attitudes have already been formed. A detective may be predisposed to think that all patrol officers are sloppy investigators because he has received several case assignments in which preliminary investigations had been poorly conducted by the reporting officers.

3. *Social learning.* Attitudes may also develop based on what someone is told about some person, event, or object by another person. A patrol supervisor may employ very close supervision over women police officers because his peers have convinced him that "most women have less physical ability than males" and cannot perform the physical aspects of patrol work as well as their male counterparts.

Attitudes that are value specific and have been acquired through personal experience are usually more resistant to change than those learned through association or from other people. When attitudes that are formed as the result of association and/or the vicarious learning process are integrated into a mutually reinforcing cluster of values and attitudes, they become much more stable and resistant to change.

Functions and Characteristics

Attitudes are personal and reflect an individual's beliefs, feelings, and behavioral predispositions. They serve four very distinct functions for the individual:

1. *Knowledge function.* An attitude can help people organize and make some sense out of their knowledge, experiences, and beliefs. As such, an attitude serves as a standard or frame of reference. A stereotype, for example, is an attitude that ascribes certain traits or characteristics to all members of a particular group regardless of their individual differences. Accuracy is irrelevant.

2. *Instrumental function.* An attitude may develop because it (the attitude) or its object (person, event, or thing) is instrumental in obtaining rewards or avoiding punishments. Attitudes serve as means to an end. A lieutenant's positive attitude toward police work and co-workers could be instrumental in achieving a more productive work unit (reward) or in helping to avoid rejection and being labeled as a poor manager by executive command personnel (punishment). In other cases, the object itself becomes a means to an end, and attitudes develop from associating the object with its outcome. For example, a sergeant may develop a very favorable attitude toward police officers who are easily controlled and a negative attitude toward subordinates who question the need for so much control. The sergeant clearly associates "success" with the ability to exert control and "failure" with the lack of control.

3. *Value-expressive function.* Attitudes may serve as a concrete expression of one's basic values or self-image. A police officer who places great value on social order, for example, may display a negative attitude toward ambiguity, individuality, and the so-called excesses caused by too much freedom. While on the other hand, a captain who considers himself a firm, fair, and unbiased manager may exhibit a very positive, unbiased attitude in all his interactions with his officers, regardless

of their sex or ethnicity. A person's real values can be inferred through the analysis of personal attitudes only if the attitudes displayed are, in fact, genuine. Any type of game playing is detrimental in that it distorts the process and reduces the accuracy of the analysis.

4. *Ego-defensive function.* Attitudes also serve to protect people's egos from unpleasant or threatening knowledge about themselves and their psychosocial environment. Accepting this kind of negative data induces stress and emotional anxiety. Consequently, we develop and deploy defense mechanisms. Rationalizations are used to (1) block or (2) alter these negative data in an effort to control physical stress and emotional anxiety. Under these circumstances, rationalizations function as a device to control cognitive dissonance (e.g., tension that arises when a person holds cognitions—ideas, beliefs, values, attitudes, motives—which are psychologically inconsistent) and create a dynamic equilibrium between different yet interrelated elements of the thought process. Thus, the tension within the individual that is causing the opposing attitudes is controlled. A police chief who views himself or herself as a natural leader yet treats uniformed police patrol officers harshly, without regard for their personal feelings or professional competence, may adopt an ego-defensive attitude. He or she may rationalize that this manner of treatment reflects the strong leadership that officers expect. This particular rationalization makes it unnecessary for the chief to come to grips with the fact that as an autocratic person there is a compulsive need to control subordinates. It tends to justify the chief's innate, psychologically well-camouflaged need for superiority based on differential psychosocial status. Police officers who develop ritualistic attitudes about their work may be trying to protect themselves against deep-seated feelings of inadequacy, insecurity, and inequity.

An **attitude** is a psychological mind-set that influences our opinions, perception, and behavior. Attitudes are the positive and negative predispositions that people interject into virtually everything they do. An individual's attitude has a number of identifiable characteristics. They are ordinarily discussed in terms of their valence, multiplicity, relation to need, centrality, and determinance:

1. *Valence.* The valence, or magnitude, of a particular attitude is indicative of the degree to which it is positive or negative toward a particular attitude object. For the purpose of this discussion, an attitude object is an idea, person, place, or thing. Most attitude research involves the empirical measurement of valence. We want to know the intensity of feeling. Valence is easy to quantify.

2. *Multiplicity.* Multiplicity refers to the total number of factors incorporated into one's attitude. Police officers might have a very positive attitude toward the department (because it takes care of its own) yet feel free to criticize it when their sense of fair play is violated by the arbitrary actions of some administrators. Other officers in the department may feel loyal, respectful, and totally dependent. Criticizing the department would be equivalent to a mortal sin. Because of the dynamics involved in formulating and maintaining attitudes, it is nearly impossible to find a one-dimensional attitude. The more factors we incorporate into and use to support a particular attitude, the less susceptible it will be to substantive change.

3. *Relation to need.* Attitudes differ widely in terms of their relation to individual needs. As we indicated, attitudes are keyed to and reflect our level of existence. A humanist police manager's attitude about sharing power with instead of exercising power over subordinates is the manifestation of his or her personal needs for social interaction, collaboration, achievement, and self-actualization. Other attitudes are more peripheral in nature and cluster around aesthetic, intellectual, occupational, and recreational interests.

4. *Centrality.* Some attitudes are, for various reasons, more central or salient than others. They cluster around high-priority values. They are fully integrated into our personality. Central attitudes become **motives** or cognitive variables that activate, direct, sustain, or stop goal-oriented behavior. They are easily reinforced

and usually resistant to change. Racial prejudice is an attitude built on our predisposition to react very negatively toward other human beings due to their race or ethnicity. Discrimination, on the other hand, involves prejudicial action or treatment. While a particular attitude may change, our central attitudes are almost never changed with reason alone.

5. *Determinance.* Determinance measures the degree to which our attitudes directly influence our personal behavior. A police officer's negative attitude toward procedural due process could lead to apathy, mechanistic performance, and absenteeism. Countervailing factors may be more influential, however. The fear of being fired may act as a constraint. Under these circumstances, fear keeps the negative attitude in check. Male police administrators with a negative attitude about women may bend over backward not to discriminate against female police officers because the administrators have developed strong feelings about equity, equal employment opportunity, and affirmative action. The stronger the attitude, the more likely it is to evolve into a motive for goal-oriented behavior.[31]

Attitudes are important variables in the psychosocial landscape of collective behavior. They influence perception and serve as guides for human conduct. Police administrators must learn how to identify and analyze their own attitudes vis-à-vis those of superiors, subordinates, and society. This knowledge will help individual managers to understand themselves and should provide them with a vehicle to identify their own values, understand their own motives, explain the behavior of others, develop healthy (empathetic) relationships, and avoid interpersonal conflicts caused by the misinterpretation of someone else's motives (see Table 4–4).

Attitudes and Work

Work plays a dominant role in our life. It occupies most of our time and consumes more energy than any other single activity. It is a critical factor in development of the self-concept. Most people learn to define themselves, in part, by their occupation, profession, or career. Job performance is influenced by factors such as (1) individual levels of aspiration, (2) pride in one's work group, and (3) interest in the job itself.[32] While there is no clear-cut scientific evidence to show that job satisfaction and job performance are directly related, there is no doubt that a police officer's attitude toward work can have a positive or a negative effect on how well the job gets done.

In simple terms, **job satisfaction** is an attitude. It is a reflection of our general attitude toward work (composed of beliefs, feelings, and a predisposition to act) and a set

---

Table 4–4
THE BENEFITS OF ATTITUDE ANALYSIS

Introspection and attitude analysis help police managers to:

1.   Identify their basic beliefs.

2.   Clarify their personal values.

3.   Explore their attitudes.

4.   Understand their motives.

5.   Accept individual differences.

6.   Understand behavior of others.

7.   Develop healthy relationships.

8.   Avoid interpersonal conflict.

9.   Manage personnel effectively.

of relatively specific attitudes concerning certain aspects of a particular job. From a conceptual point of view, job satisfaction and dissatisfaction are a function of the perceived relationship between what employees expect from their job and what they actually get.[33] **Morale** (job satisfaction) is the degree to which the needs of individuals are satisfied and the extent to which they attribute that satisfaction to the job.[34] The main components of job satisfaction are as follows:

1. Relevant and meaningful work
2. Acceptable working conditions
3. Positive work-group dynamics
4. Satisfaction with the agency
5. Adequate general supervision
6. Accessible and fair rewards
7. Intrinsic satisfactions

While these components may not be applicable to all work environments, they appear to be significant aspects of job satisfaction in complex criminal justice organizations.

Poor morale (job dissatisfaction), like any other bad attitude, is contagious. It can spread throughout a police department just like a virus. Poor morale tends to lower the efficiency, effectiveness, and productivity of human resources. It often manifests itself in forms such as (1) apathy, (2) disruptive behavior, (3) interpersonal conflict, (4) absenteeism, and (5) employee turnover. It is the police manager's job to counteract the job dissatisfaction that leads to these behaviors. In order to carry out this responsibility, managers use a variety of techniques:

1. Job analysis
2. Job redesign
3. Job enlargement
4. Job enrichment
5. Participation
6. Job rotation
7. Organization development

These techniques are normally incorporated into a motivation strategy.

Paradigms, Perception, Motives, and Human Behavior

Human beings are rational animals who have the ability to convert raw data into conceptual representations of reality. Beliefs, values, attitudes, and opinions help shape a person's understanding of the physical, social, and psychological world. People do not react to each event in their lives as something unique. They construct a perceptual frame of reference, a paradigm that establishes a sense of order and gives meaning to their experiences.

Paradigms

Decision-making is intimately related to the individual's perceptual frame of reference. The futurist Joel A. Barker defines this cognitive frame of reference a *paradigm*. He defines a paradigm as "a cognitive set of rules and regulations that does two things: (1) establishes or defines boundaries, and (2) tells a person how to behave inside the boundaries in order to be successful." Barker claims that we evaluate and organize information based upon the rules of our internal paradigms that we have acquired through a lifetime of experiential learning.[35]

Thomas Kuhn, an American physicist and philosopher, defined a paradigm shift as an essential change in the concepts and investigational practices of a scientific discipline. Kuhn, in his work, *The Structure of Scientific Revolutions*,[36] developed a cycle depicting how

Figure 4–5
The Kuhn Cycle.

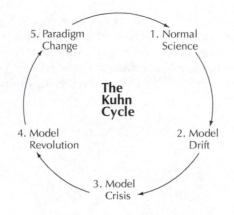

paradigms change. This cycle is preceded by a Pre-science step which indicated the discipline has no workable paradigm to successfully guide its work. The Pre-science step is followed by five steps as shown in Figure 4–5 beginning with Normal Science. Normal Science is where the discipline has a paradigm that currently works. The Model Drift step occurs when there are a number of anomalies which occur that the model or paradigm cannot explain. A Model Crisis occurs when the drift becomes so extreme, the model is not working and is no longer reliable, nor feasible to utilize for solving problems. During this stage, there may be attempts to salvage the current model/paradigm, but they are ineffective. At this point, the discipline is in distress. The fourth step, the Model Revolution occurs when a meaningful, radically different model is developed and accepted by those in the discipline. At this point, a new paradigm materializes and the discipline shifts to it. Hence, the new paradigm becomes the Paradigm Change, the fifth stage, and the cycle is complete.

One example in law enforcement utilizing Kuhn's cycle is that of police/community relations. Over the past few years, the media has shown numerous accounts of police misconduct/abuse. While the majority of officers are dedicated to serving the public, a minimal number of ill-intended officers can create the impression that abuse and lack of integrity are out of control. Lack of prudence and ineptitude can corrupt the hard work of those who are dedicated to the profession and can even affect an honest mistake by an officer.

As a result of these incidents, the Normal Science step of what has been successful in police/community relations has moved into the Model Drift stage. In the past, departments have utilized community policing to enhance police/community relations. While programs associated with community policing have mostly been beneficial to public safety and community relations, they are often programmatic, incident specific, and inconsistently applied.[37]

With more and more of these events occurring (i.e., a police officer shooting and killing a fleeing motorist in South Carolina, a young black man shot in his grandmother's backyard in Sacramento, the choking death of a man in New York, etc.) the model has moved into the Model Crisis stage. At this point, the community policing initiatives once used to patch and repair police/community relations are failing to reap fruitful results.

Many professionals are suggesting a "paradigm shift" in the law enforcement culture and shift to a police/community collaboration model. Academics are also analyzing legitimacy issues and how police should create and/or reestablish it. These ideas are all part of the Model Revolution stage of Kuhn's cycle. At this particular point in time, the profession is still searching for a widely accepted model for the Paradigm Change stage.

Organizationally, perceptions and decisions are shaped by established paradigms, which limit individual ability to recognize and develop new ways of doing things. It is easier to acknowledge the success of existing rules and methods (*the status quo*) that have been successful in the past instead of venturing into the unknown with a new method.

During the life span of an organization, problems are encountered and solved. As more and more problems are resolved, the organization's leadership enjoys a period of success. The success convinces organizational members that their way of "doing things" is correct, and a mind-set can develop whereby managers are no longer able or allowed to solve new problems in any way other than what has worked in the past. When unsolved problems are not dealt with and start accumulating within an organization, a paradigm shift is likely to occur. Someone sees the unresolved problems and goes about seeking new ways (new paradigm) to address the unresolved problems. The status quo will become challenged. A **paradigm shift** occurs when there is a change to a new paradigm having new rules, boundaries, and behaviors. This is what happened when policing began to shift from the traditional operational methods to community problem-solving policing. It is happening now as departments seek to be more effective through CompStat and Intelligence-led policing.

Our paradigms or cognitive pictures of the world around us are synthesized and constructed out of information derived from the five senses. The process by which people organize and interpret sensory input is known as **perception**.[38] Because of the subjective nature of this process, reality exists only in the eye of the beholder. Truth becomes relative and is merely a reflection of an individual's point of view.[39]

A paradigm is a mental screen or cognitive filter through which information must pass before it can be integrated into human thought processes and behaviors. People use this perceptual apparatus to help them do the following:

1. Relate their past experiences to current situations.
2. Choose the various stimuli to which they will react.
3. Group stimuli into a manageable number of categories.
4. Fill in missing data about persons, places, or things.
5. Defend themselves against serious threats to the ego.

It is through the manipulation of our perceptual paradigms that we create and maintain a sense of consistency and order in a complex world where rapid change is the rule rather than the exception. Perception is used to process environmental stimuli. This process of selecting from a number of available stimuli is called *accommodation*. Accommodation is one of several processes that determine what stimuli will be converted into useful information, perform the conversion, and then link the resulting information to an appropriate behavioral response. In this context, perception helps to protect the human mind from systemic overload.[40]

Perceptions

Every perceptual event has three components. Perceptions are formed based on interaction between (1) the perceiver, (2) the target, and (3) the situation in which the perceptions take place. These factors influence the perceiver's interpretation of all sensory data related to an idea, event, person, place, or thing:

1. *Perceiver.* While there is some disagreement, most social scientists contend that there is no such thing as objective reality. They operate on the assumption that what is perceived as "reality" depends largely on the personal characteristics and background of the perceiver. Research in organizational behavior (OB) indicates that emotions, beliefs, values, attitudes, motives, interests, experiences, and expectations skew perception. They also help to determine the actual behavioral response in any given situation.[41]

2. *Target.* In addition to the factors just noted, perception is affected by the characteristics of the target itself. Two of the most important characteristics are the degree of ambiguity of the target and the target's social status. Since perception involves the attribution of meaning as well as interpretation, ambiguous targets are particularly susceptible to **perceptual distortion**. Research clearly indicates that in the perception of persons, the social status of the target influences the perceiver's perception of the person as much as the target's words and actions do. Status and perceptual distortion go hand in hand. Because targets are not looked at in isolation, the relationship of a target to its background (or perceptual field) also influences perception.[42] People have a natural inclination to group close things and similar things together. Proximity is frequently translated into cause and effect. Stereotypical thinking may be the rule rather than the exception.[43]

3. *Situation.* There are a number of situational variables with the potential to influence an individual's perception of people, places, and things. The physical surroundings, social setting, emotional atmosphere, and time frame are important factors

in perception formation.[44] While the perceiver and the target might remain unchanged, the perceiver's *perception* of the target is anchored to the situation and changes with it. Perception is an inherently complex psychosocial process by which human beings attach meaning to those things they experience through the senses. There are forces in each of us (perceivers), in the stimuli (targets), and in the environment (situations) that cause perceptions to differ. It is no wonder that sincere people adopt opposing points of view and exhibit radically different behaviors.

The Perception Process

Behavior can most simply be viewed as an individual's response to a stimulus in a given situation. This view is known as the stimulus–response (S-R) model and is often used to explain reflex actions. In more complicated behaviors, however, there is a chain of discrete events between the stimulus and the operant (intentional) response. The chain includes three intervening subprocesses—*reception, organization,* and *interpretation*—that work to convert information input into decisions or behavioral outputs.[45] The perception process is illustrated in Figure 4–6.

Sensing is the first step in the perception formation process. In other words, a stimulus is encountered by one of the five senses: touching, tasting, seeing, hearing, or smelling.

Since people simply cannot deal with all of the stimuli in the physical, social, and psychological environment, they become selective in picking out those stimuli they feel are important and tuning out the others. This is known as *selective perception,* which is the psychological predisposition to see and evaluate raw data (about people, places, and things) in light of our own ideas, beliefs, values, attitudes, opinions, motives, and past experiences. People sort through the data related to sensory stimuli and consciously or, more likely, unconsciously select information that is supportive and satisfying. They tend to ignore information that is painful and/or disturbing.[46] Whether a particular stimulus captures our attention and elicits a behavioral response will depend on the following:

1. The properties of the stimulus itself (size, intensity, contrast, repetition, motion, and so forth)
2. Past experience with the given stimulus and other competing stimuli within the environment
3. Our inclination (based on our personality, values, motives, and paradigms) to see certain things and not others, regardless of the properties of the target itself

Figure 4–6
The Perception Process.

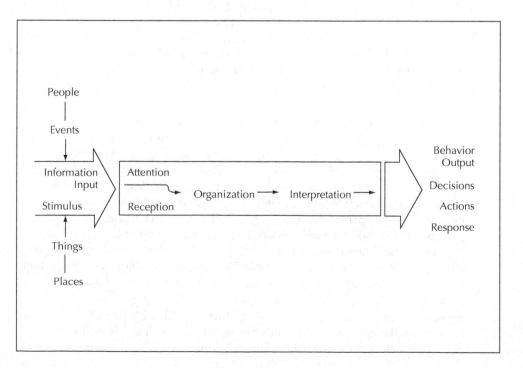

Selective attention leads to selective perception and serves as the springboard for all purposeful human behavior.

Once attention has been focused, the bits and pieces of information derived from both the target and the situation must be organized in such a way that they can be incorporated into one of the perceiver's cognitive systems. (A cognitive system is a set of interrelated perceptions and cognitions about people, places, and things.) Our perceptual mechanisms operate to organize the information into patterns and categories that make some sense. This process is known as perceptual organization.

Perceptual organization is the psychological predisposition to avoid the discomfort normally associated with unorganized information by reconfiguring and attributing meaning to it based on each person's beliefs, values, attitudes, interests, motives, experiences, and expectations. Our mind automatically sorts all sensory information into patterns or categories in an effort to avoid systemic overload. Consequently, there is a natural tendency to do the following:

1. Distinguish a *central object* (person, event, place, or thing) from its surroundings. Leaders tend to stand out more than support players do in crises.

2. Respond to people, things, and situations based on *anticipated rather than actual* information input. A mind-set is a compulsive proclivity to think and act without rational analysis.

3. Combine bits and pieces of information into wholes by creating *groupings* based on proximity, similarity, closure, and continuity (see Figure 4–7).

4. Perceive the characteristics of a target (person, place, or thing) as remaining relatively *constant* despite variations in the stimuli that produced the original information. This helps people deal with the instability caused by change.[47]

5. Predict behavior and *ascribe meaning* to the motives of others. This process, called attribution, is designed to make the behavior of others more understandable.

These perceptual organizers are beneficial most of the time. There is a downside, however. They add to and distort reality. When it comes to the perception of persons, several other perceptual tendencies influence how people organize their perceptions and convert them into cognitive systems. Following is a discussion of these further perception organizers.

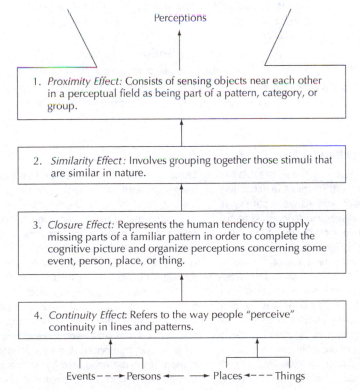

Perceptions

1. *Proximity Effect:* Consists of sensing objects near each other in a perceptual field as being part of a pattern, category, or group.

2. *Similarity Effect:* Involves grouping together those stimuli that are similar in nature.

3. *Closure Effect:* Represents the human tendency to supply missing parts of a familiar pattern in order to complete the cognitive picture and organize perceptions concerning some event, person, place, or thing.

4. *Continuity Effect:* Refers to the way people "perceive" continuity in lines and patterns.

Events - - -► Persons ◄— —► Places ◄- - - Things

Figure 4–7
Perceptual Organization through Grouping.

1. *Frame of reference.* A frame of reference is a perspective, or vantage point, from which people view people, events, and things. Frames of reference are both windows on the world and lenses that bring the world into focus. Perception is dependent on the context in which it occurs and on the frame of reference used by the perceiver. Managers, consultants, and policy makers draw upon a variety of frames of reference, or paradigms, in their efforts to change and improve organizations.[48]

2. *Stereotyping.* Since it is impossible for one person to know everyone else in terms of their distinctive traits, people develop and use stereotypes. One way to simplify the management and organize sensory data about other people is just to assume that they all have the same characteristics because of some category (or group or pigeonhole) they fall into. For example, one could put police officers into mental categories based on their ethnicity and respond the same way to everyone in the same category. This might conserve cognitive energy but is likely to result in a loss of information and the spread of misinformation. Stereotypes based on race, gender, and age skew perception if they predispose the perceiver to ignore specific information concerning the individual and rely on preexisting stereotypical images.[49]

3. *Halo effect.* This occurs when one personal trait or attribute is used to develop an overall impression of another person. It involves generalizing from one characteristic to the total person. The halo effect, like stereotyping, tends to obscure individual differences. People are perceived as being either good or bad. Once they have been assigned to a particular category, we tend to ascribe only good qualities to those labeled as being good and all bad qualities to those labeled as bad. Selective perception is used to confirm our expectations.[50]

4. *Projection.* In this mode of organizing perception, the perceiver ascribes his or her own characteristics to other people and uses himself or herself as the norm for judging others. It is much easier to comprehend the behavior of others if we assume that they are similar to us. Consequently, our own characteristics influence what we are likely to see in others. A classic projection error is for managers to assume they and their subordinates have the same unmet needs or motives.

5. *Expectancy.* Expectancy is the tendency for people to find or create in another person what they expected in the first place. This is also known as the *Pygmalion effect* and is similar to selective perception in some respects. People often see what they want to see in order to validate their original expectations.

Once sensory stimuli garner attention and are organized in a way to facilitate their integration into the thought process, normal people use the power of reason to interpret the already-processed data, generate further useful information, and select appropriate operant responses. Perceptions are interpretations of sensory data.[51]

CASE STUDY   Officer Mike Fredrick

Mike Fredrick was, at age 29, the youngest detective sergeant in the history of the Milesburg Police Department. Fredrick's meteoric rise in the police hierarchy began three years ago. As we might say, it was "in the cards." Fredrick was a relatively undistinguished patrol officer in this industrial city of 38,000. After five years on the street as a patrol officer, he was temporarily assigned to the five-member detective bureau to fill in for another officer who was on sick leave. As duty officer on the midnight shift, he was dispatched to investigate the abduction of a 3-year-old boy who had been taken from the home of his mother's boyfriend. The child's body was found a week later. It had been dismembered and discarded in a landfill in another county. After an extensive investigation, the police came up with the name of a prime suspect and put out a bulletin on local radio stations. A confidential informant contacted Officer Fredrick and told him where the suspect could be found. Fredrick and his partner,

Leonard Smitts, went to the suspect's hideout. After several gunshots were exchanged, the suspect surrendered. Because he captured the suspect, Fredrick became the darling of the media.

The trial itself became a media spectacular. Officer Fredrick seized the opportunity and used the media to his advantage. He made local news almost every night for two weeks. The suspect was convicted, and after an emotional episode in which he admitted he had killed the boy, he was sentenced to death by electrocution.

The trial took place in an election year. The leading candidate for mayor liked Fredrick and, sensing his popularity, announced publicly that if elected he would promote Fredrick to the rank of detective sergeant. The candidate won the election. The incumbent detective sergeant was transferred to a new assignment, and since all command officers are appointed by and serve at the pleasure of the mayor, Mike Fredrick was promoted to the exempt rank of detective sergeant. The other detectives resented the mayor's action. They saw Fredrick as an opportunistic individual with little experience to fill the rank he was now given. There was an informal work slowdown and an escalation in the level of interpersonal conflict, and productivity declined drastically. Fredrick was like a fish out of water. He was not a manager or a leader. He did not know how to handle the rebellion, and things became intolerable. After 10 months of continuous rancor,

Mike Fredrick was reduced in rank and quietly reassigned to the patrol division. He resigned from the department after three years. He now owns a private security company.

What happened here? Was a perceptual distortion involved in this case? What is the lesson to be learned? How would you as the police chief executive deal with the mayor in this type of situation?

Interpretation is the psychological process by which people evaluate information input concerning a particular stimulus and choose an operant behavioral response. The cognitive context for interpretation is in the mind and consists of the concepts, theories, and cause–effect models we use to construct our own versions of reality. How police officers interpret sensory stimuli will depend in large measure on their past experience, their value system, and their attitudinal propensity to think or act in certain ways. This helps to explain why different people "see" different things even when they are looking at the same person, event, or object. In a sense, as we noted before, there is no such thing as objective reality. Sensory inputs are transformed through perception into interpretive or "normative" reality and complete the perception formation process.[52]

It attaches meaning to our experiences in relation to other people, events, and things. Figure 4–8 illustrates the dynamics involved in perception formation.

In order to survive and thrive in a complex sociocultural milieu, we must be prepared to receive, organize, interpret, and react to all kinds of environmental stimuli. The

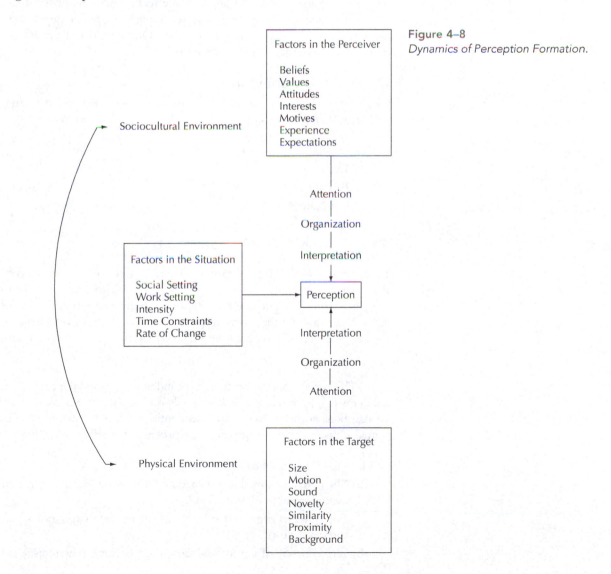

Figure 4–8
Dynamics of Perception Formation.

accuracy of our perception is a critically important factor in the struggle for physical as well as psychosocial survival. The inability to interpret cues correctly and cope with dangerous situations can lead to tragedy in police work. Overestimation of danger cues in some situations can lead to the unnecessary use of force, while in other instances, officers can suffer serious injury or death as a result of underestimating danger cues.

Successful police managers understand the psychosocial dynamics involved in perception formation and are aware of the inherent potential for perceptual distortion. They have learned that personal beliefs, values, motives, experiences, and expectations put subjective constraints on perception. Truly perceptive managers

1. Have a relatively high level of self-awareness and know how to avoid most of the perceptual pitfalls that we discussed earlier in this chapter.
2. Seek information from a variety of sources to confirm or disconfirm their personal impressions of a given person, event, or thing.
3. Tend to form empathetic relationships and are often able to see situations as they are perceived by others.
4. Know when to intervene and how to influence the perceptions of significant others who are drawing incorrect impressions about people, events, or things in the work setting.
5. Appreciate individual differences and seek to avoid those perceptual distortions that bias performance evaluations.[53]

There is no doubt that perception has an effect on managerial decision-making, and these decisions affect work unit efforts to accomplish the police department's mission, goals, and objectives. It is also clear that values and value-based perceptions are motivators. They trigger and shape operant behavior.

On-the-Job Behavior

Behavior refers to the conduct of human beings as they react to environmental stimuli and includes the actions people take or things they say with regard to

1. Objects
2. Events
3. People
4. Problems
5. Opportunities
6. Situations

Based on knowledge derived from the behavioral sciences, there is every reason to believe that behavior is (1) caused, (2) motivated, and (3) goal oriented. In other words, most human behavior is purposeful.[54] **Operant behavior** is intentional behavior involving some choice among alternative responses. In very simple terms, behavior is a function of the interaction between people and their environment. The basic equation is as follows:

$$B = F(P \times E)$$

This means that factors within the individual (P) and the environment (E) determine behavior (B), both directly and indirectly due to their effect on each other.[55] Purposeful human behavior is produced by a sequential process involving a feedback loop. The essential steps in the behavior formation process are outlined as follows:

1. There is an implicit or explicit goal to be achieved.
2. The behavior aimed at goal accomplishment is caused by reaction to an environmental stimulus of some kind.
3. The stimulus is generated by needs (or wants) that, if not satisfied, cause tension and discomfort.
4. The reduction of tension and discomfort becomes a hedonistic imperative, or goal.[56]

While the behavior formation process is the same for all human beings, actual behaviors vary substantially. Because people are unique (with different backgrounds, value systems, perceptions, and motives), they react idiosyncratically to environmental stimuli. This is compounded by the fact that an individual's needs, wants, and expectations are subject to change. Consequently, a person's response to the same stimuli will ordinarily deviate from time to time. A patrol captain, for example, may give a subordinate a verbal warning for a minor infraction one day (depending on the captain's needs, wants, and expectations), whereas he or she might write up the subordinate for the same behavior in a different situation or at a different time. Good managers know that because of individual and situational differences with respect to needs, wants, tension, and discomfort, human behavior—even under similar circumstances—is difficult to predict.

Management's Role in Changing Attitudes and Behavior

As noted earlier, attitudes are the product of related beliefs and values. They are incorporated into our motives, opinions, and behaviors. Positive attitudes toward work in general, one's job, and the department (as a whole) are indicative of high morale. High morale produces an esprit de corps that is conducive to cooperation and collaboration.[57] Negative attitudes, on the other hand, often lead to interpersonal conflict and have been linked, at least indirectly, to poor on-the-job performance. It is the police manager's job to accentuate the positive and minimize the influence of negative attitudes.

Police managers have three basic options for dealing with employees who exhibit negative attitudes:

1. *Do nothing.* They attempt to contain negative attitudes through benign neglect. This "let the sleeping dog lie" strategy seldom works and usually makes the situation worse. Doing nothing allows the employee to think that the administrator approves or condones his or her behavior.
2. *Intervene.* They seek to transform negative attitudes into neutral or positive attitudes. The success of any attempted intervention will depend on the strength of the negative attitude and the skill of the manager.
3. *Discipline.* They try to punish the employee. Police departments have some of the strongest civil service unions in the country. In a unionized and litigious environment, the use of discipline against someone for having a bad attitude is a very difficult task. Managers are required to make a good-faith effort to change the person's unacceptable behavior through counseling and training before they are permitted to use discipline.

In order to do their job properly, police managers must be able to understand and change the meanings their employees ascribe to their behavior. This is not an easy task. Since attitudes are anchored to beliefs and values, they are always resistant to change. Two principal barriers tend to limit the extent to which employees are likely to change their attitudes. These are (1) insufficient justification and (2) previous commitments. In the absence of a compelling need to change, people prefer to maintain the status quo. This inertia is very difficult to overcome. The second barrier encompasses past successes and strongly held values. A person's link to the past may be powerful enough to block a change in attitude and accompanying behavior. People are prone to take a position and defend it. They invest their ego, reputation, resources, and sometimes their job maintaining their position.[58]

Organizational Culture and the Manager

Managers play an important role in shaping and reinforcing organizational values and employee attitudes. This requires positive leadership and maintaining support for appropriate organizational values on a daily basis by all members of the management team. Managers should understand they play an important role in shaping and maintaining organizational value systems. Every organization has a set of core values that are the standards by which organizational members judge each other's behavior and accomplishments.

Value-based management is a critical tool for creating and maintaining organizational integrity and ethical conduct. All organizational managers should be held responsible for value-based management. How well employee attitudes and behavior work to support the organization's performance objectives and maintain its integrity and value to the community will depend upon the strength of the department's core values and the manager's role in maintaining them. However, in some organizations, individual manager's behavior may contradict these stated values. When the stated values of the organization or individual manager are not consistent value conflict, distrust and unethical behavior will result. Managerial behavior supported by organizational reward systems should always support a positive organizational culture.

Example of Organizational Core Values

Community Service	Continuous Improvement
Customer Focus	Professional Pride
Integrity	Honor
Ethical Behavior	Teamwork
Personal Responsibility	Quality
Organizational Respect	Leadership
Truth	Honesty
Loyalty	Effectiveness
Professional Development	Reliability

Shared positive values promote loyalty, feelings of personal effectiveness, consensus on goals, and sense of ownership for the organization and its people. They form the foundation for mobilization of commitment to the organization's vision and mission. Thus, it is critical that all managers maintain a positive culture within their work units.

Developing a strong ethical organizational culture is the primary responsibility of every manager. However, managers must always model what they expect in what they say and do. In addition to making clear the existence of a set of positive core values, managers must continue to sustain these values through communication and positive reinforcement on a daily basis. It is through culture maintenance that managers keep their units focused on the mission and protect both the organization and the individual officer from liability.

Five ways managers can create and sustain a positive organizational culture in their daily interactions with their subordinates are as follows:

1. Model what you expect in others.
2. Pay attention to important things.
3. Reward when appropriate.
4. Discipline when necessary.
5. React calmly in stressful situations.

How the Manager Behaves (Modeling)

The police chief executive and other members of the management team are in an excellent position to change attitudes by setting an example for their employees. Managers should be aware that their employees are constantly evaluating what they do and how they do it. They must model the way they want their officers to behave at all times. This means that through behavior, actions, communication, teaching, mentoring, and coaching managers should reinforce the core ethical and organizational values of their department. Employees often emulate managers' behavior and look to them for cues to appropriate behavior. Managers must be concerned with the levels of *competence and commitment* they display on a daily basis. Officers will respect and emulate the working values of their manager if they are positive in nature. However, they will come to disrespect the manager who fails to model what he or she expects from their personnel.

What the Manager Pays Attention to (Communication)

Managers should always be engaged in honest and open communications with their employees. Communication is an important managerial tool of building a positive culture. Verbally and behaviorally, managers communicate their priorities, values, and beliefs in the events they pay attention to in the workplace. These emerge out of what the manager notices, comments on, measures, and controls. If managers are consistent in what they notice, measure, and control, employees receive clear signals about what is important in the organization. The opposite is true when managers are inconsistent. What we suggest here is that managers play a crucial role in establishing the concept of "meaning" in the workplace. Employees want to be part of an organization that has a clear sense of purpose. They want to feel that their work is contributing to something worthwhile.

How the Manager Allocates Rewards (Positive Reinforcement)

Managerial reward systems must support the organization's core value system. Rewards should serve to reinforce positive behavior and accomplishments. They can range from a simple verbal recognition of an employee's effort to a medal for valor. A simple form of reward often overlooked by many managers is a letter of recognition placed in the employee's personnel file. To ensure that values are accepted managers should reward behavior that is consistent with the values they are trying to uphold. Rewarding any other form of behavior sends a confusing and inconsistent message. Managers should let their people know when they are doing the right thing. A simple act of recognition for a job well done is a powerful motivator for some individuals. However, a reward too easily obtained or too freely given will have the potential to become a demotivator.

How the Manager Disciplines (Training/Negative Reinforcement)

The way managers discipline employees and the rationale behind their action also communicate culture. There are times managers must act in a decisive way when confronted with an accountability or performance failure. Managers who fail to do so are often viewed as weak and ineffective by their employees. When the situation warrants and discipline is called for, managers should use it. Managers should hold people accountable to the highest ethical and performance standards because their reputation as well as that of the department depends upon it. Being a leader can often be lonely especially when an unpopular action is demanded. However, the decision to take disciplinary action should never be because of personal bias but always for a just cause.

How the Manager Behaves under Stress (Emotional Intelligence)

The way a manager performs during times of stress and crises communicates a powerful message. Emotions are heightened during these incidents, and managers are perceived as showing their true feelings during such events. How a manager reacts under stress can damage employee relations for years to come in an organization. Crises are challenges that are often neither foreseen nor planned for. Managers must remain emotionally under control during such a situation and perform their duties in a calm and reassuring manner. This type of behavior will set an example for others to follow during times of stress and crises.

Whether or not police managers succeed in changing the attitudes (and behavior) of employees will depend largely on their credibility and believability as *communicators*. We see others as credible and believable when we perceive them as knowledgeable, unbiased, and likable.

Initiating Change

Managers can usually bring about a change in their subordinates' attitudes (and accompanying behavior) if they use the following five-step process. Once managers observe improper behavior or hear improper attitudes expressed, they should (1) identify the improper attitude, (2) determine its root causes, (3) weaken the root causes, (4) offer a practical substitute, and (5) reward all those employees who exhibit the new attitude or behavior:

1. *Identifying the improper attitude.* Once managers determine that a subordinate's behavior is improper, they must look for the attitude behind it. The attitude should be defined in specific terms. By investigating an improper attitude, showing genuine concern, and making constructive comments, managers are frequently able to resolve the problem without further intervention. Employees may come to the realization that their behavior is unacceptable and change it to conform to the general expectations of the manager.

2. *Determining the root causes.* The manager should collect and analyze relevant information in an effort to determine the roots (or primary causes) that support and feed the attitude in the employee's mind. The best way to accomplish this objective is to get employees talking about their beliefs, feelings, attitudes, motives, and expectations. Some of the root causes that nurture and support improper attitudes are listed here:

   • Group pressures
   • Faulty logic
   • Ambiguous standards
   • Prior experiences
   • Selective perception

3. *Weakening the root causes.* Once the root causes have been identified, they can be analyzed in terms of strength and vulnerability. A program of action should be developed to attack these causes systematically, using reason. One way to attack an improper attitude (and the accompanying behavior) is to point out flaws in the employee's assumptions or draw attention to the changes that have taken place to weaken those assumptions since they were originally formed.

4. *Offering a substitute.* While managers may be able to change an employee's attitude by constant harping and the use of criticism, this approach takes too long and leaves some noticeable scars. It will also lead to the employee fixating on the manager's behavior instead of his or her own. As a rule, people will change only when they determine that the attitudes they hold are no longer worth keeping. Orders and threats tend to suppress natural and observable behavior and drive it underground. Employees become wary and do what managers want only when management personnel are present. When managers are absent, old attitudes and behaviors will resurface. Permanent change comes about when employees begin to question their own beliefs, values, attitudes, and motives.

5. *Rewarding proper attitudes.* Change is normally reinforced by positive social sanctions. Managers should remember that *"Things that get rewarded, get done."*

While these five steps sound simple enough, good managers know it takes a great deal of time, energy, skill, and expertise to bring about substantive attitudinal change on the part of personnel in any complex police organization.

The traditional view held by most police management theorists is that changed beliefs and/or values produce new attitudes that lead to changes in on-the-job behavior. Some management theorists contend that, on the contrary, it is more sensible to change a person's behavior first. This is based on research indicating that people realign their attitudes in support of their behavior. A few management theorists argue that people should be taught specific behaviors that they can apply on the job and that correspond to the desired attitude change. When the trainees learn that they will be rewarded for their behavior, their attitudes will change to agree with the newly learned behaviors. In order to teach these appropriate behaviors, trainers use modeling techniques, role playing, and social reinforcement.

CASE STUDY   Chief Barry Green

Corona is a small yet relatively prosperous city located in the corridor between New York City and Washington, D.C. The police department has an authorized strength of 113. Virtually all of the officers on the force have taken college courses, and a large percentage of the younger officers hold BA degrees. Some of them are working toward an MS in criminal justice. Sworn police personnel are covered by civil service. All members of the department except the chief and commanders in exempt positions (with the rank of captain or above) are represented by the same labor union. Commanders have formed a team to serve as their bargaining agent.

The former chief of police was a politically astute autocrat who maintained power through tight administrative control and manipulation of the reward system. He was, in terms of his values system, anything but an organizational humanist. He found it impossible, regardless of the composition of the workforce, to share power with others rather than exercise power over them. The chief used selective perception to protect his ego and vilify those with the audacity to question his authority and/or style of management. Everything "hit the fan" when a study conducted by the State Department of Community Affairs concluded that the police department was "plagued by labor/management conflict, bad attitudes, low morale, and disruptive infighting." As a result, the city manager asked for and received the chief's resignation.

Larry Green, an administrative lieutenant with 22 years of experience, was promoted to chief. He was given a mandate from the mayor to "clean up the mess." Chief Green is a pragmatist. He is convinced that the only way to increase the efficiency, effectiveness, and productivity of the police department is to improve officer attitudes and morale.

If you were Chief Green, how would you go about transforming this organization? Outline the change strategies you would use to change the negative attitudes of the work force.

SUMMARY

Human behavior involves the conscious or subconscious selection of actions over which the person exercises some degree of influence, control, or authority. People are social animals that live in groups and engage in purposeful (self-initiated and goal-oriented) behavior. Each group develops a unique way of interacting or culture. **Culture** is the cement that holds a group together and defines appropriate ways of feeling, thinking, and acting. Beliefs, values, attitudes, motives, and expectations are passed from one generation to the next through the socialization process. Values are the linchpin in one's personality, character, management style, and goal-directed behavior.

Police managers who have a humanistic orientation are moving away from traditional bureaucratic values. They adopt multidimensional value systems that stress efficiency, effectiveness, and productivity while responding to each employee's need for personal growth, self-esteem, competence, and autonomy. Good managers try to cultivate positive attitudes in their subordinates because employee attitudes are critical variables in the success or failure of any goal-oriented enterprise. Attitudes reflect values, express feelings, and indicate a predisposition to act in a certain way with regard to a given stimulus.

Human beings are rational animals with the unique ability to convert sensory data into cognitive representations of reality. Attitudes (which are based on values and past experiences) influence perceptions and are factored into the motives that produce operant behavior. **Motivation** is the inner state that causes a person to behave in ways designed to satisfy a need. Perceived needs that are linked to basic values become potent motives and are always accompanied by powerful drives. Good managers understand the links between values, attitudes, perception, and on-the-job behavior. Positive attitudes toward work, the job, and the organization are indicative of good morale and may lead to increased productivity. Negative attitudes, on the other hand, can lead to interpersonal conflict and have been linked, indirectly, to poor job performance. Good managers work to transform negative attitudes into positive attitudes. Some use the traditional five-step process in which they identify improper attitudes, determine root causes, weaken the root causes, offer substitutes, and reward those who exhibit appropriate new attitudes and concomitant behaviors. Other managers reverse the process. They seek to change behavior first, on the assumption that people will realign their ideas, beliefs, values, attitudes, motives, opinions, and expectations to support the new behavior. They emphasize the importance of modeling, focus on what is important, reward and discipline when necessary, and control their emotions in times of stress.

DISCUSSION TOPICS AND QUESTIONS

1. How do organization/management theorists define behavior and differentiate between inherited and operant behaviors?

2. Where do our beliefs, values, attitudes, and motives come from, and how are they transmitted from one generation to the next?

3. What is introspection? Explain why an officer needs to do it in order to become a truly effective police administrator.

4. Define ideas, beliefs, values, attitudes, motives, and opinions. How are these psychological concepts related to one another?

5. What does it mean to say that attitudes are cognitive, affective, and conative?

6. What is an attitude? Explain its functions.

7. Define perception. Explain the impact perception has on our decision-making.

8. What are motives? How are they formed? How do they influence our expectations, perceptions, and behavior?

9. Discuss the six strategies police administrators use to modify the attitudes of their subordinates.

10. How does the behavior modification/attitude change approach differ from the traditional five-step attitude/behavior change process?

FOR FURTHER READING

John Crank and Michael Caldero, *Police Ethics: The Corruption of a Noble Cause*, 2nd ed. (Cincinnati, OH: Anderson, 2004).

Crank and Caldero succinctly hit the nature of police corruption—the ends justifying the means—the traditional "Dirty Harry" problem.

Peter M. Senge, *The Fifth Discipline: The Art & Practice of the Learning Organization* (New York: Doubleday, 1994).

Senge introduces the concept of a "learning organization" that adapts to its changing environment in order to achieve a competitive advantage. This concept which uses strategic thinking is at the heart of the CompStat process.

ENDNOTES

1. Gary W. Cordner, Kathryn E. Scarborough, and Robert Sheehan, *Police Administration*, 6th ed. (Cincinnati, OH: Anderson, 2007), pp. 215–241.

2. Gary Dessler, *Management: Principles and Practices for Tomorrow's Leaders* (Upper Saddle River, NJ: Prentice Hall, 2004), pp. 213–282.

3. Herbert A. Simon, *Administrative Behavior* (New York: The Free Press, 1997), pp. 77–78.

4. Joseph H. Reitz, *Behavior in Organizations* (Homewood, IL: Richard D. Irwin, 1981).

5. Paul Hersey and Kenneth H. Blanchard, *Management of Organizational Behavior: Utilizing Human Resources* (Upper Saddle River, NJ: Prentice Hall, 1993), pp. 19–52.

6. Stephen P. Robbins, *Essentials of Organizational Behavior* (Upper Saddle River, NJ: Prentice Hall, 2000), pp. 241–246.

7. Linda K. Stroh, Gregory B. Northcraft, and Margaret A. Neale, *Organizational Behavior: A Management Challenge* (Mahwah, NJ: Lawrence Erlbaum, 2000), pp. 74–75.

8. Stephen R. Covey, *The Seven Habits of Highly Effective People* (New York: Simon & Schuster, 1990), pp. 262–270.

9. Robert K. Merton, *Social Theory and Social Structure* (New York: The Free Press, 1957), pp. 131–195.

10. Paul Meehan, Darrell Rigby, and Paul Rogers, "Creating and Sustaining a Winning Culture," *Harvard Management Update*,

Harvard Business School (2007). Retrieved from https://hbr.org/2008/02/creating-and-sustaining-a-winn-1.

11. Ibid., p. 1.

12. C. A. O'Reilly III, J. Chatman, and D. F. Caldwell, "People and Organizational Culture: A Profile Comparison Approach to Assessing Person-Organization Fit," *Academy of Management Journal*, Vol. 34, No. 3 (September 1991), pp. 487–516; J. A. Chatman and K. A. Jehn, "Assessing the Relationship between Industry Characteristics and Organizational Culture: How Different Can You Be?" *Academy of Management Journal*, Vol. 37, No. 3 (June 1994), pp. 522–553.

13. Stephen P. Robbins and Timothy A. Judge, *Organizational Behavior*, 15th ed. (Boston: Pearson Publishing, 2013).

14. Erving Goffman, *The Presentation of Self in Everyday Life* (New York: Anchor Books, 1959).

15. John Crank and Michael Caldero, *Police Ethics: The Corruption of a Noble Cause* (Cincinnati, OH: Anderson, 1999).

16. Roy Roberg, Kenneth Novak, and Gary Cordner, *Police & Society* (Los Angeles, CA: Roxbury, 2005), p. 272.

17. Peter M. Senge, *The Fifth Discipline: The Art & Practice of the Learning Organization* (New York: Doubleday, 1990), pp. 7–8.

18. Ramon J. Aldag and Loren W. Kuzuhara, *Organizational Behavior and Management: An Integrated Skills Approach* (Mason, OH: South-Western, 2002), pp. 346–347.

19. Paul M. Whisenand and R. Fred Ferguson, *The Managing of Police Organizations* (Upper Saddle River, NJ: Prentice Hall, 2002), pp. 3–22.

20. John R. Schermerhorn, James G. Hunt, Richard N. Osborn, and M. Uhl-Bien, *Organizational Behavior*, 11th ed. (Hoboken, NJ: John Wiley & Sons, 2010), p. 31; John R. Schermerhorn, Jr., James G. Hunt, and Richard N. Osborn, *Organizational Behavior* (New York: Wiley, 2002), p. 41.

21. Ibid., p. 41.

22. Ibid., p. 42.

23. Ibid., p. 13.

24. Warren Bennis and Bert Manus, *Leaders: The Strategies for Taking Charge* (New York: Harper & Row, 1985).

25. Ronald G. Lynch, *The Police Manager* (Cincinnati, OH: Anderson, 1998).

26. John P. Crank, *Understanding Police Culture* (Cincinnati, OH: Anderson, 1998).

27. Joel A. Barker, *Future Edge: Discovering the New Paradigms of Success* (New York: William Morrow, 1992).

28. Dessler, *Management*, p. 38.

29. Whisenand and Ferguson, *The Managing of Police Organizations*, p. 9.

30. Aldag and Kuzuhara, *Organizational Behavior and Management*, p. 115.

31. Dessler, *Management*, p. 287.

32. Fred Luthans, *Organizational Behavior*, 9th ed. (New York: McGraw-Hill, 2002), pp. 126–139.

33. Craig Pinder, *Work Motivation in Organizational Behavior* (Upper Saddle River, NJ: Prentice Hall, 1998), p. 245.

34. Roy R. Roberg, Jack Kuykendall, and Kenneth Novak, *Police Management* (Los Angeles, CA: Roxbury, 2002), pp. 185–211.

35. Jole A. Barker, *Paradigms: The Business of Discovering the Future* (New York: HarperCollins, 1993).

36. Thomas S. Kuhn, *The Structure of Scientific Revolutions* (Chicago, IL: University of Chicago Press, 1970).

37. D. Vialpando (2016). "Criminal Justice in Crisis: A Paradigm Shift in Law Enforcement," Retrieved from https://www.linkedin.com/pulse/paradigm-shift-law-enforcement-david-vialpando on August 16, 2018.

38. Luthans, *Organizational Behavior*, p. 183.

39. Kuhn, *The Structure of Scientific Revolutions*.

40. Stroh, Northcraft, and Neale, *Organizational Behavior*, p. 33.

41. Luthans, *Organizational Behavior*, pp. 195–197.

42. Robbins, *Essentials of Organizational Behavior*, pp. 23–25.

43. Robert P. Vecchio, *Organizational Behavior: Core Concepts* (Mason, OH: Thompson, 2003), p. 39.

44. Aldag and Kuzuhara, *Organizational Behavior and Management*, pp. 96–100.

45. Luthans, *Organizational Behavior*, pp. 183–195.

46. M. J. Waller, G. P. Huber, and W. H. Glick, "Functional Background as a Determinant of Executives Selective Perception," *Academy of Management Journal*, Vol. 38 (1995), pp. 218–235.

47. Alvin Toffler, *Future Shock* (New York: Bantam Books, 1972).

48. Lee Bolman and Terrence E. Deal, *Reframing Organizations: Artistry, Choice and Leadership* (San Francisco, CA: John Wiley, 2003), p. 11.

49. Claude M. Steele, "A Threat in the Air: How Stereotypes Shape Intellectual Identity and Performance," *American Psychologist*, Vol. 52 (1997), p. 617.

50. Kevin R. Murphy, Robert A. Jacko, and Rebecca L. Anhalt, "Nature and Consequences of Halo Error: A Critical Analysis," *Journal of Applied Psychology*, Vol. 78 (April 1993), pp. 218–225.

51. Cordner, Scarborough, and Sheehan, *Police Administration*, pp. 233–235.

52. Richard M. Hodgetts and Fred Luthans, *International Management: Culture, Strategy, and Behavior with World Map* (New York: McGraw-Hill/Irwin, 2002).

53. John R. Schermerhorn, Jr., James G. Hunt, and Richard N. Osborn, *Organizational Behavior* (New York: John Wiley & Sons, 1997).

54. R. R. Roberg, J. P. Crank, and J. Kuykendall, *Police & Society* (Los Angeles, CA: Roxbury, 2000), pp. 265–267.

55. Luthans, *Organizational Behavior*, pp. 25–27.

56. Harold J. Leavitt and Homa Bahrami, *Managerial Psychology: Managing Behavior in Organizations* (Chicago, IL: University of Chicago Press, 1988).

57. Dan Carrison and Rod Walsh, *Business Leadership: The Marine Corps Way* (New York: Barnes & Noble, 1999).

58. Harry W. More, W. Fred Wegener, and Larry S. Miller, *Effective Police Supervision* (Cincinnati, OH: Anderson, 2003), pp. 305–313.

5
MOTIVATION
The Force behind Behavior

Learning Objectives

1. Discuss the etiology of goal-oriented human behavior in the workplace.
2. Define *motivation* and terms associated with the motivation process.
3. Describe the interplay between individual, social, and situational factors related to human motivation.
4. Explain needs and the adaptive behavior elicited in the motivation process.
5. Differentiate between content theory and process theory as they relate to the human motivation to work.
6. Discuss the differences between job enlargement and job enrichment.

Key Terms

content theories	job satisfaction
drives	motivation
equity theory	motivation-hygiene
E.R.G. theory	motivation process
expectancy	operant conditioning theory
expectancy theory	participative
hierarchy of needs	performance
job design	process theories
job enlargement	psychosocial
job enrichment	social entities
job rotation	Theory X and Theory Y

It has been said that motives are the "why" of human behavior, and it is well known that motives guide people when making decisions. Without question police leaders must be skilled at motivating others, and there is general consensus that this is something that can be learned. Within organizations, motives are what cause things to happen and provide a frame of reference for engaging in the proactive process of getting things done with and through other people. Individual efforts must be guided toward the accomplishment of common goals and objectives resulting in mission attainment. In order to achieve this, there must be an energization of relevant behavior. While police administrators are expected to allocate and manage time, equipment, material, and money, the most significant aspect of their job is the management of people. Human beings are far different from any other type of resource they are asked to deal with. This is because each person is truly unique and brings various attitudes, values, sentiments, motives, behaviors, and skills with him or her into the workplace. According to Paul Whisenand,[1] a police supervisor is responsible for first releasing and then directing an employee's **motivation** to accomplish the mission of the department.

George Curtis has been the chief of police for two years in a community that has a population of 83,751 in the southern part of the state. The department has an authorized strength of 105 full-time sworn police officers.

Chief Curtis is anxious to fill a new position that calls for a lieutenant, and the incumbent of the position will function as the home defense expert for the department and liaison with other agencies. For three years, federal funding will be used for this new position, and then it will become a regular budget position. The city has a nearby nuclear power plant that could be a prime target. The new lieutenant would work out of the chief's office. This position is not covered by civil service, and the chief had the authority to promote whoever he chose, subject only to the advice and consent of the mayor. But rather than doing this, the chief wants to promote someone off of the lieutenants list.

After a very careful review of the situation, Chief Curtis concluded that Raymond Charles, a 12-year veteran, was the best person for the job. Sergeant Charles was an amiable, energetic, and capable man with excellent investigative skills. He is a natural leader with a strong commitment to the department. Charles was always a go-getter and respected by departmental members. He was number one on the eligibility list that had been in place for two years. As far as the chief was concerned, he really had no alternative but to offer the position to Sergeant Charles. All the time that Charles had been with the department, he remained in the local National Guard Unit, assigned to a military intelligence unit located in a nearby metropolitan area. He currently holds the rank of Major. The chief felt that he and Charles were simpatico and would complement one another.

After securing the mayor's authorization to fill the vacant position, Chief Curtis asked Sergeant Charles to stop by his office. They exchanged pleasantries and then the chief told Officer Charles he would be promoted to the rank of lieutenant effective the first of the month. Much to the chief's surprise, Charles declined the promotion.

The chief did everything he could to get Sergeant Charles to change his mind, but the sergeant maintained he was simply not interested in functioning as a staff person and wanted to remain in his position as a field operations sergeant, supervising 15 evidence technicians. Charles enjoyed responding to various crime sconces involving homicides, sexual assaults, officer-involved shootings, and armed robberies. He said he would rather be operational and not work in an office. Additionally, he pointed out that he was heavily involved in his National Guard assignment. He thanked the chief, left the office, and returned to work.

Chief Curtis was surprised—actually shocked. He felt Sergeant Charles was not being loyal to the department. He felt that Sergeant Charles should "stand up and be counted" and decided where his loyalties were. Although he was unhappy with the situation, Chief Curtis promoted another officer on the promotion list.

The chief's unhappiness with Sergeant Charles led to him being transferred to a less desirable position in field operations. Over a period of time, Sergeant Charles became increasingly dissatisfied with his job. He became a chronic complainer. Poor morale reduced his performance and led to increased absenteeism and an increased effort for his National Guard assignment. Charles found himself in a box and never worked at a level above average.

Describe the motivations that are present in this case. What actually happened in this particular situation? What assumptions did Chief Curtis make, and why did he become so upset with Sergeant Charles? If you were the chief of police, how would you deal with an officer who does not seek promotion per se as the preferred path to job satisfaction and/or career advancement? What position would you take when officers want to remain in a National Guard or Reserve position? If you could, would you support a policy that would prohibit police officers from serving in military units? Why or why not?

Pursuing Excellence

Leading others as they pursue an organization's mission, vision, core values, and goals is the essence of police management. Leadership does not exist in a vacuum, however. There is a symbiotic relationship between leadership, **motivation**, and **performance** in complex goal-oriented police departments. Most management theorists believe that highly motivated individuals, working smarter, are more productive and produce a better quality product or service than their less motivated co-workers.[2]

Human **motivation** is a fascinating topic. Motivating people to work has become one of the most pervasive concerns in contemporary management theory—a buzzword in industry and an "in" term in the lexicon of police management. Increasingly, it is adopted as the goal of staff development. There is probably no other topic in which police administrators express more interest. The **motivation** of police personnel is viewed as an antidote for poor **performance**, a magic key to productivity, and the answer to all sorts of organizational problems—even the external constraints, like funding limitations, under which police agencies operate.[3] However, the application of simplistic solutions to very complex social problems rivals baseball as America's favorite pastime.

The **motivation** perspective just discussed is not the panacea it was made out to be by the theorists and practitioners who argued that it had ushered in a new era of enlightened human resources management. After nearly a half-century of rigorous scientific inquiry, we still do not know, beyond a general way, what motivates a human being to act in a certain way. It is very difficult to tell why some police officers are self-starters and seem to be high achievers in almost everything they do, whereas other police officers need prodding and external incentives to do anything productive. It is hard to explain why activities that generate enthusiasm and energy in one person might well trigger boredom and apathy in someone else. Research suggests that there are several types of **motivation**. Some officers are best described as achievement motivated. Moderate challenges and risks are acceptable to them, and they seem to be attracted to fairly difficult tasks. These officers are best described as strivers and work diligently at improving themselves and honing skills resulting in task accomplishment. Other officers are best described as competence oriented, based on their own belief that they can master confronting and confounding problems. It is a process of self-efficacy and striving for excellence. In the latter case, the officers really believe in themselves and the impetus that causes them to accept a challenge can be either intrinsic or extrinsic.[4]

Motivation to Work

Motivating human beings to work, produce more, and seek excellence is one of the simplest yet most complex tasks in management. It is simple in the sense that people are hedonistic. They have been programmed socially as well as genetically to minimize pain and to maximize pleasure. Consequently, motivating them should be easy. It is up to management to determine what a person wants and to use it as a reward or incentive. Whenever people act in any way, good or bad, it is because they have been motivated to act.[5] In earlier days, extrinsic rewards such as pay, specialized assignments, or promotion motivated officers, but in more recent years, intrinsic rewards have assumed a prominent place and officers find themselves developing self-management skills. Intrinsic rewards as they become more viable are the satisfaction of a job well done, such as making a significant arrest, successfully completing a complex case, saving a child, or performing some other action that emanates from actual work. With this type of intrinsic reward, officers become more energized and goal oriented, and they readily see that the work they do is making a difference not only to themselves but also to others.[6] Reward people for appropriate behavior, and you usually get desired results. Fail to reward the right kind of behavior, and you will most likely get the wrong results. Things are not as simple as they may appear at first glance, however; different people have different desires and needs. Rewards one police officer considers important may be viewed by others as undesirable or merely superfluous. In some cases, the needs of employees are not the same as those of the organization; if the differences are irreconcilable, they can lead to dysfunctional conflict, disorganization, and deterioration in **performance**. Even an enticing reward is not a surefire motivator. Rewards, in themselves, do not ordinarily motivate people unless there is a belief that an effort on their part will lead to a payoff. Police personnel, like all other human beings, differ from one another in how they size up their chances of earning meaningful rewards or achieving their own personal goals.[7]

Police administrators have a managerial responsibility to recruit, screen, select, and develop human resources with the potential to be efficient, effective, and productive employees. Unless these individuals are motivated to draw on this potential, however, they are not likely to achieve the level of performance that is desired from them. Managers at all levels are faced with the problem of motivating subordinates to unleash their potential so that the mission, goals, and objectives of the organization can be accomplished. One way to deal with the so-called motivation problem is to create conditions in which people satisfy personal needs and achieve their own goals and act in such a way that the work desired by the organization gets done as well.[8] Police managers must learn to recognize symptoms of flagging motivation and to design jobs and reward systems to alleviate the problem. Failure to act will only compound the motivation problem and could eventually harm the organization.

Job Satisfaction

Job satisfaction is one of the most widely investigated job attitudes, as well as one of the most extensively researched subjects in industrial/organizational psychology.[9] Research on job satisfaction among criminal justice personnel is relatively new compared to similar research conducted among employees of other occupations; however, some does exist.[10] Job satisfaction is noteworthy because a person's attitude and beliefs may affect his or her behavior in the workplace. Job satisfaction has been linked to a multitude of behaviors and attitudes. This includes, but is not limited to productivity, motivation, absenteeism/tardiness, accidents, mental/physical health, general life satisfaction, and even commitment to the organization.[11]

According to some studies, satisfied employees tend to be more committed to their employers.[12] Other researchers assert job satisfaction is so important, its absence often leads to reduced organizational commitment.[13] For example, there is a relationship between job satisfaction and affective organizational commitment. Affective commitment refers to the degree to which an employee becomes emotionally attached, associates with, and trusts in the organization.[14] There is also an inverse relationship between affective commitment and intent to leave a position and stress in that position.[15] In light of recruiting issues in law enforcement today, one can see how important job satisfaction is to employees in the profession and the organization as a whole.

The breadth to which the needs and values of employees are sustained by the working environment and the individual's reaction to that environment constitute job satisfaction.[16] When assessing the level of employee satisfaction with his or her job, consideration of numerous factors is necessary to determine which are most important to each individual employee. Job satisfaction is conditional and particular to every employee and every situation being appraised.

Mueller and Kim characterize two types of job satisfaction: (1) global job satisfaction and (2) job facet satisfaction.[17] They further delineate global satisfaction as an employee's overall satisfaction with their job while describing job facet satisfaction as addressing specific aspects of the job such as salary, benefits, etc. When assessing job facet satisfaction, each employee evaluates job aspects differently. In law enforcement, satisfaction can be considered differently by individual officers depending upon factors such as assignment, rank, seniority, gender, and age.

For example, a key factor in job satisfaction for millennials is to find fulfilling work. They want work to provide them the opportunity to make new friends, learn new skills, and bond to a larger purpose.[18] This feeling of purpose is a primary factor in a millennial's satisfaction with their job. Another example of job satisfaction relates to supervision. Research indicates that job satisfaction is increased when supervisors impart a supportive environment where employees are reassured to interact and voice issues related to the workplace.[19] Improving management can be as effective as reforming the work of officers.[20] Similarly, job satisfaction is increased when there is a progressive environment both vertically between supervisors and employees and horizontally between personnel.[21] There is also a positive relationship between employee's job satisfaction and commitment and a participative management style utilized by managers.[22]

With limited resources in terms of fiscal funding, equipment, and most importantly, human capital, much of the focus of reform in law enforcement organizations has been efficiency and effectiveness. These reforms, for the most part, have been positive. However, organizational effectiveness is primarily determined by employees' level of job commitment.[23] If leaders and managers in law enforcement endeavor to make their agencies more effective, they will be prudent to address issues which negate employee commitment and strive to increase job satisfaction.

Organizations as Social Entities

Organizations are unique social entities that are created by human beings in order to accomplish certain goals that require cooperative effort. A formal organization is a social unit that has been designed to achieve a common objective or set of objectives. As instruments created for a specific purpose, all formal organizations have similar structural characteristics, including (1) a fairly distinct division of labor; (2) built-in mechanisms to regulate, coordinate, and control the activities of members; and (3) the capacity to replenish depleted human resources. Healthy organizations have the ability to adapt to changes in the environment, alter internal processes, reconfigure job assignments, and withstand the influx of replacement personnel. Consequently, a typical formal organization acquires an identity independent of its members, a distinctive persona of its own that—while it will change based on situational factors—tends to perpetuate itself from one generation to the next.[24] An unhealthy organization, like an unhealthy animal, is very likely to wither away and risks death. In order for a police department to survive and thrive, management personnel must learn to deal effectively with the behavioral requirements of every officer and civilian employee.

In order to become effective managers, police administrators must learn to understand and appreciate the importance of their role in the **motivation process**. They must also develop a repertoire of motivational techniques that will encourage qualified people not only to join and remain in the police department but also to perform their duties in an enthusiastic, competent, consistent, and professional manner. **Motivation** is the pin that connects employee needs and job performance within organizations. It is the key to a productive and satisfying life. In particular, highly motivated, productive, and satisfied employees are the mainstay of quality police service. As Whisenand notes, "The supervisor-as-leader is in a pivotal position to recruit, get the best out of, and retain police employees."[25]

Organizations should be viewed as living organisms rather than inanimate things. Police departments, for example, are deliberately constructed social systems, with structures and processes designed to coordinate the activities of workers as they seek to accomplish group-shared goals and objectives. An organization is a coalition of many participants with diverse needs, values, attitudes, and behaviors.[26]

Organizations are **social entities** in which members take part and to which they react.[27] An organization consists of people with formally assigned roles who work together to achieve stated goals.[28] For the purpose of our discussion, **motivation** is the energizing force that brings people together and that serves as the springboard to individual effort as well as goal-oriented group interaction.

Motivation and the Motivation Process

The study of **motivation** and the **motivation process** can be traced back to antiquity. There have always been attempts to describe, explain, and predict goal-oriented human behavior. The ongoing interest in **motivation** is based on the assumption that those in authority need to know what turns people on or off about their work. Until quite recently, the emphasis was on the use of coercive power to increase individual productivity and/or organizational output. Things began to change several decades ago. Most police administrators now subscribe to the old adage, "You can lead a horse to water, but you can't make it drink."

Defining Motivation

"Motivation" is not a particularly easy term to define. While just about everyone agrees that it has something to do with human behavior, no one has been able to formulate a single definition that is acceptable to all of the behavioral scientists and management personnel with an interest in this topic. Some writers avoid definitions altogether. They are content to focus their attention on the consequences of human behavior. Others, in the classical tradition of Frederick W. Taylor (see Chapter 1), explain **motivation** in terms of economic rationality. As years have gone by, the vice-like grip of the rational–economic paradigm has slowly eroded as its weaknesses have become more apparent and its assumptions have not been able to provide an adequate explanation of human behavior.[29] They see human beings as goal-oriented individuals who have been programmed to avoid pain (punishment) and to seek pleasure (rewards). Still other organization/management theorists reject utilitarian views and contend that **motivation** is a subconscious psychological process that evolves in people as the result of personality, background, environment, and cultural factors.

Motivation is defined as *the intensity of a person's desire to engage in some activity*.[30] The process of **motivation** is often described in terms of a simple stimulus–response model.[31] But the process is not that simple: Between the stimulus and the response are a number of mediating factors that differ with each individual worker. There are a number of mediating factors that intercede between the stimulus and the response, resulting in a highly variable situation. It can readily be seen from Table 5–1 that these elements call for a variance from individual to individual.

Table 5–1
MEDIATING FACTORS THAT INTERCEDE BETWEEN A STIMULUS AND A RESPONSE THAT VARY FROM INDIVIDUAL TO INDIVIDUAL

Personality

Abilities

Self-concept

Perception

Attitudes

Personality (as presented in Chapter 4). The characteristic and distinctive traits of each individual. It is also viewed as the unique combination of the way of thinking and acting that makes someone the distinctive individual that he or she is.

Abilities. The set of work-related knowledge and skills that employees bring to the job. These interact with **motivation** to create technical and contextual **performance**.

Self-concept. The perceptions people have of themselves and their relationships to people in other aspects of their life such as their view of the environment and their interaction with the community. It includes an interpretation of their strengths and weaknesses.

Perception. The way our personalities and experiences cause us to decipher stimuli. Meaning and structure are given to information as filtered by one's experience or memory.

Attitudes. Predisposition, based on a person's beliefs and values, to respond to objects, people, ideas, or events in either a positive or negative way. Job satisfaction is one example of an attitude.

Again, it must be emphasized that these factors differ with each individual. The law of individual differences states that people differ in their personalities, abilities, self-concept, perception, values, and needs.[32] Still others are convinced that **motivation** is a conscious and continuous process in which individuals make choices about what they will or will not do in given situations.[33]

There are conflicting definitions of **motivation** based on etiological considerations. In much simpler times, **motivation** was thought of as the means, methods, and techniques used by management to stimulate workers to engage in activities designed to achieve the organization's mission, goals, and objectives. Over the years, managerial leaders and other authority figures were expected to use extrinsic motivators (motivators external to the person) such as pay, promotion, fringe benefits, and camaraderie as carrots to induce employees to increase their output and to upgrade overall quality of their service. On the other side of the coin, the famous Hawthorne experiments conducted during the mid-1920s clearly demonstrated that intrinsic factors also motivated people to behave in certain ways. Intrinsic innovators like instinct, **drives**, desires, values, feelings, emotions, and needs are internal to the individual and, as such, are largely unaffected by environmental stimuli. An intrinsically focused officer strives to achieve, to be competent, to contribute, and to derive real satisfaction from work. The theorists, researchers, and practitioners who subscribe to this human relations school of thought place most of their emphasis on internal, as opposed to external, variables. The primary function of management is to create a situation in which worker needs and organization needs are not only congruent but mutually reinforcing.[34]

Police officers, like all other human beings, are motivated in reality by a combination of intrinsic and extrinsic factors. Both are necessary. According to Stephen P. Robbins,[35] the motivation to work is caused by a set of energetic forces, originating within and beyond the individual, which initiates work-related behavior and determines its form, direction, intensity, and duration.

Motivated employees are in a state of tension created by an unsatisfied need. This tension leads to creation of **drives** until the need is satisfied and tension is reduced. Motivated behavior is aimed at reducing these tensions. Thus, motivation to work can be described as dynamic forces within an individual that account for the strength, direction, and relative persistence of the energy expended at work.[36] Researchers have found a direct link between **motivation** and effort. In fact, motivation is a predictor of overall effort. In the long run, effort, individual ability, and organizational support determine the level of an officer's job **performance**.

Motivation is the drive within people to alleviate the discomfort caused by internal tensions. Thus, a drive is an energetic force fueled by human needs. These needs become a motivator for action. Mental and physical actions are conscious and unconscious efforts to achieve goals. Goals are desired outcomes an individual feels will lead to a reduction in internal tension. Once their needs, desires, and wants are fulfilled, people experience a measure of individual satisfaction.

Related Terminology

Before proceeding with a discussion of the **motivation process** itself, let us review some basic terminology, one more time. A precise vocabulary is very important because ambiguity leads to confusion and helps perpetuate misunderstanding.

1. *Needs.* Something within people that moves them to engage in work-related behavior in an effort to accomplish personal goals.
2. *Drives.* Dynamic inner forces created and energized by needs.
3. *Tension.* The frustration or discomfort caused by unfulfilled needs.
4. *Motives.* Inner impulses, **drives**, needs, and abstract values that energize, activate, move, and direct behavior that is designed to achieve specific goals.
5. *Goals.* Objects, conditions, or activities toward which a particular motive is directed.
6. *Incentives.* Internal and external stimuli, such as anticipated satisfaction (positive as well as negative), social reinforcement, and financial rewards, that bring about goal-oriented behavior designed to reduce the tension caused by unfulfilled human needs.
7. *Performance.* The purposeful activity that results from an individual's goal-oriented behavior and that is normally evaluated in terms of specific outcomes.
8. *Motivation.* A psychosocial process that produces an attitude that results in an action leading to a particular result.
9. *Internal motivation.* **Motivation** that comes from within a person (based on needs, **drives**, feelings, desires, and values) and that activates certain conscious and unconscious behaviors designed to produce satisfaction.
10. *External motivation.* Motivation resulting from the application of incentives to encourage patterns of behavior that will contribute to accomplishment of an organization's mission, goals, and objectives.

While there is no simple answer to the question of what "turns on" human beings or motivates them to act as they do in a given situation, police administrators will be ahead of the game if they learn to view **motivation** as a dynamic interactive process rather than as a collage of marginally related managerial tasks. It is through knowledge and the skillful use of **motivation** that modern police leaders endeavor to mold their people into productive units capable of achieving new and much higher levels of **performance**.[37]

Motivation Cycle

According to Calvin Swank and James Cosner,[38] the **motivation** cycle or process consists of needs setting up **drives** to accomplish goals. They argue that the intensity of the **drive** toward a goal is always proportional to the severity of the need. A police officer's absolute need for peer acceptance, for example, could supersede his or her desire to be considered a professional, leading him or her to elect to conform to the "code of silence" rather than testify against a fellow officer involved in a brutality case.

Figure 5–1
Basic Motivation Process.
Stephen P. Robbins, Essentials of Organizational Behavior (Upper
Saddle River, NJ: Prentice Hall, 2007), p. 44.

Unsatisfied → Tension → Drives → Search   → Satisfied → Reduction
Need   Behavior   Need   of
                                                          Tension

Again, Stephen Robbins[39] describes the **motivation process** in terms of unsatisfied needs (see Figure 5–1). He sees unsatisfied needs as a motivator that prompts people
to engage in work-related behaviors that are directed toward the attainment of goals they
feel are capable of satisfying their needs. Thus, the **motivation process** consists of six
sequential steps: (1) unsatisfied need, (2) tension, (3) drives, (4) search behavior, (5) a satisfied need, and (6) reduction of tension.

The simplicity of the diagram is somewhat deceptive, however. Behavioral scientists
and experienced police administrators know that human behavior is "multi-motivated,"
in that any number of conscious, subconscious, and at times conflicting needs demand
satisfaction simultaneously. It is the intensity of a need or the relative mix of needs that
determines behavior in a given set of circumstances. We will never know, for example,
exactly what motivates an otherwise passive police officer to become a supercharged hero
in a dangerous or life-threatening situation involving very young children; it is always difficult to isolate a single causal factor in relation to job-related behavior in complex law
enforcement organizations.

While many police administrators still believe that **motivation** is something they do
to their subordinates, they are wrong. **Motivation** is a dynamic and goal-oriented *internal*
process. It is—in essence—what individual officers feel and do in relation to their particular needs. Seen from this standpoint, the only true form of motivation is self-motivation.[40]
Almost all successful police managers have the unique ability to elicit self-motivation in
their employees and reinforce it. They do this by creating environments in which police
personnel are able to satisfy needs through affiliation, competence, recognition, and productive police work itself.[41]

Motivating Yourself and Others

Motivated people continuously set new goals because their needs, desires, and wants are
nearly insatiable. It is only human nature to want more, to strive to progress. People want
to improve themselves and their condition, to acquire new things, and to improve their
position vis-à-vis others within their organizations. Robert B. Denhardt and his colleagues
have raised the issue of motivating public-sector workers. **Motivation** in the public sector, they say, is *aimed at the achievement of public purposes*, and it is critical if public workers
are to fulfill their responsibilities to the citizens and communities they serve.[42] The "conventional wisdom," however, is that public-sector workers are fundamentally lazy and unmotivated. Denhardt and colleagues suggest three basic reasons for this popular belief:[43]

1. Rewards and incentives available for use by public-sector managers, particularly in
   terms of pay and promotion, might be limited.
2. People who pursue public-sector careers may be less achievement oriented than
   people in the private sector, that is, they may by their very nature be a not very
   highly motivated group, primarily attracted to public service by job security.
3. Motivation in public organizations may be complex because of ambiguous goals
   (unlike the private sector, where the clear and fundamental goal is profit).

Of course, these authors do not adhere to such beliefs; in their view, public employees are
clearly the equals of their private-sector counterparts.

Whisenand squarely puts the job of **motivation** in the lap of police managers: "When I encounter unmotivated police employees, inevitably I see an unmotivated

supervisor."[44] He defines worker motivation as the psychological forces within a person that determine the following:

- The direction of a person's behavior in an organization
- A person's level of effort
- A person's level of persistence in the face of obstacles

Additionally, it would seem appropriate to add conscientiousness, dependability, and hard-working as other elements in this equation. If these forces are present in an employee, then it is the job of supervision to facilitate and sponsor employee **motivation**.

Even though **motivation** is something inside each person, police administrators activate and guide the **motivation process** as they seek to improve the **performance** of a department's human resources. Performance—the results of workers' positive behavior—is the bottom line in management. **Motivation** is only one of the factors that contribute to that results.[45]

Based on the preceding discussion, it is evident that there is no satisfactory simple answer to the question, "What motivates people to act as they do in a given set of circumstances?" Behavioral scientists have developed an array of different theories to explain the dynamics involved in human motivation. Fortunately, most of these theories tend to reinforce each other to some degree. We devote the remainder of this chapter to categorizing and describing some of the major theories. Our purpose is to provide information, not to say a particular theory is right or wrong. It is, in the final analysis, up to each police administrator to abstract, synthesize, and reconfigure this information in such a manner that it will work in a given environment with a specific clientele. Broad generalizations usually lack substance and are of little or no real value in motivating personnel to work in law enforcement organizations.

Approaches to Motivation Theory

As noted earlier, the **motivation** to work has been the subject of serious scientific inquiry for more than a half century. Behavioral scientists normally approach the study of human motivation from two general perspectives—**content theory** and **process theory**:

1. *Content theories.* Content theories endeavor to explain *what* motives (needs, desires, and wants) are and how they influence human behavior. In addition, these theories provide ways to profile and analyze people in order to identify their motives. They have little or nothing to say about the process by which needs arise and are manifested in actual behavior. As seen by these theories, understanding **motivation** is primarily a matter of recognizing basic needs and the process by which they are satisfied.

The centerpiece of **content theory** is that unmet needs motivate people to act. People seek to reduce inner tension by fulfilling these needs. Satisfied needs do not motivate. While content theory does not explain how people are motivated to do some particular thing, it does provide some insight into individual needs and may help police administrators understand what their subordinates will or will not value as work incentives. Content theory helps us understand what people want.[46]

2. *Process theories.* **Process theories** explain *how* people are motivated. These theories examine goal-oriented behavior based on the degree of satisfaction associated with particular rewards used to initiate it. **Process theories** focus on the **motivation process** rather than on motives per se. They strive to shed light on the cognitive (mental) processes by which human beings choose to engage in certain behaviors designed to satisfy their own needs. While content theories emphasize needs themselves, process theories zero in on decision-making as it relates to job **performance**. **Process theories** are built on the assumption that people make conscious and subconscious evaluations of contemplated behavior and assess the consequences of their actions. These personal expectations are critical in determining how a person is motivated to perform in any given situation.[47]

These theoretical approaches are not mutually exclusive. In fact, most content and process theories reinforce one another and provide police administrators with an information base which can be transformed into action designed to help subordinates become more efficient, effective, and productive workers. The theories provide clues about people, explain why people (do or do not) work, and examine how the **psychosocial** environment influences job **performance**. Job **performance** is the bottom line in management and is the key factor in determining the long-term health of any complex law enforcement organization.

Content and process theories represent a radical departure from the classical concept of motivation advocated by Frederick W. Taylor in the early 1900s, as discussed in Chapter 1. Taylor was a utilitarian looking for practical ways to increase the productivity of available human resources. He believed identifying the one best way to do each particular job and segmenting each task into a series of simple operations or steps that could achieve maximum organizational efficiency. Each worker would be trained to perform a few task-related operations. The combined efforts of all workers would then maximize efficiency and productivity. Taylor also believed that workers were not capable of self-motivation. They had to be motivated by external forces (managers) in order to overcome their natural inclination for "soldiering" (his word for doing just enough to get by). Increased productivity would be achieved by creating incentives (in the form of financial rewards) to work harder during a specific period of time. Taylor devised a bonus system to reward and reinforce the behavior of those who exceeded the minimum expectations set for them. In a Pavlovian sense, improved **performance** and increased productivity reflect a conditioned response activated by external reward systems.[48]

Content Theories

Interest in **content theory** can be traced back to the Hawthorne studies conducted in Chicago during the mid-1920s. The researchers wanted to know how productivity is affected by negative environmental factors, but they found fewer negative effects than they expected. They concluded that unanticipated "psychological factors" had somehow influenced the productivity of the experimental group. While the researchers were unable to find a direct relationship between physical working conditions and worker outputs, it became clear that organizations do not exist for production alone. They are organic social settings in which people seek to satisfy their own intrinsic psychological and social needs. The experiment itself became a motivator. The assembly workers felt they were being treated as people rather than machines. Management's interest in their situation made them feel special. It was a recognition of their worth as human beings. The researchers concluded that when human needs are met, workers develop a very positive attitude toward work, management, and their organization. The need for achievement often leads to greater job satisfaction, improved **performance**, increased productivity, and commitment to the goals and objectives of the organization.[49]

Content theories attempt to explain what motivates people to behave as they do in relation to their work. While most of the theories are consistent with one another, there are some important differences. The theories presented here are representative of this genre.

Hierarchy of Needs Theory

Abraham Maslow's "progression" theory of employee needs is one of the best-known content theories. As a positive humanistic theory of motivation, it stresses the importance of both biological drives and **psychosocial** needs. According to Maslow,[50] five basic human needs activate, fuel, and shape the internal drive to overcome inertia affiliated with the status quo. He classes them as physiological (survival) needs, safety (security) needs, belonging (social) needs, self-esteem (ego) needs, and self-actualization (fulfillment) needs. These terms are ordinarily defined as follows:

1. *Survival needs.* The most basic of all human needs is to sustain life. Biological maintenance requires food, water, air, shelter, sex, and so on. Due to the nature of the life cycle, the satisfaction of physiological needs is of limited duration. As soon as

one need is satisfied, another replaces it. When police managers concentrate on meeting survival needs to motivate personnel, they are operating on the assumption that most people work based on economic incentives (the rational–economic assumptions discussed earlier). This model created reward systems (extrinsic) that served as an attainment platform that created the desired behavior. This was done by emphasizing such things as pay increases, improved working conditions, and better fringe benefits as the best way to motivate their personnel.[51]

2. *Security needs.* Security needs emerge once basic survival needs have been met. People have an intrinsic need to be relatively free from fear, to feel safe, and to have some stability in both the physical and interpersonal events involved in day-to-day living. According to Frank Goble,[52] these needs can be grouped into two categories: (1) the need for order and stability and (2) the need for freedom from anxiety and insecurity related to personal safety, job security, financial survival, and the capricious actions of others. Police administrators who place primary emphasis on meeting the security needs of their personnel rely on policies, procedures, rules, and regulations to produce order, promote safety, improve **performance**, and increase productivity.

3. *Social needs.* Once physiological and security needs have been satisfied, social needs emerge as a very important source of **motivation**. Human beings have an inherent need to interact with significant others. People derive personal satisfaction from group membership. Groups fulfill their need for human companionship, love, affection, and a sense of belonging. Police administrators who understand and appreciate the importance of the social needs of subordinates know that employees have a strong tendency to identify with and internalize the norms and values of the work group. Effective managers facilitate communication, promote purposeful interaction, and encourage meaningful participation in order to improve job **performance** and the individual productivity of their human resources.[53]

4. *Ego needs.* Ego-esteem needs have two dimensions. First, people have a need to be respected by important *others* for who they are and what they can contribute to the work group. They have a desire to be competent, and they look to the work group as a source of recognition, acceptance, prestige, and status. Second, people have an absolute need for self-esteem. In other words, they need to feel they are worth something to themselves as well as to others. Self-esteem is manifested in feelings of adequacy, worthiness, fulfillment, and self-confidence. Managers who understand the importance of ego-esteem needs do everything they possibly can to ensure that their employees become competent and exhibit self-confidence, harbor few self-doubts, and have a good self-image. Effective police administrators help their subordinates to realize that "public service offers distinct opportunities for motivating people to do excellent and often extraordinary work."[54]

5. *Self-actualization needs.* The need for self-actualization is triggered when people have to some extent satisfied their physiological, security, social, and ego needs. The need for self-actualization is the need to grow, to be creative, and to fulfill one's potential. While this need varies from one person to another, in all cases it causes people to pursue interests and knowledge for their own sake and for the joy of becoming the persons they feel they have the potential to become.[55] Self-actualized people have successfully met a need to become increasingly competent and to gain mastery over their own life. All of their talents and potential are put to use. At this stage, motivation has become an internal process. External stimulation is unnecessary. Management's job is to provide resources and to create an environment in which self-actualizing people are given the freedom to make truly significant contributions to the organization.

The order in which Maslow listed his five human needs, shown earlier, amounts to a hierarchy ranging from the most basic instinctive **drives** to the most abstract **psychosocial** motives (see Figure 5–2). Maslow divided this hierarchy into lower-order (survival, security, and social) needs and higher-order (ego and self-actualization) needs.

Figure 5–2
Maslow's Hierarchy of Needs.

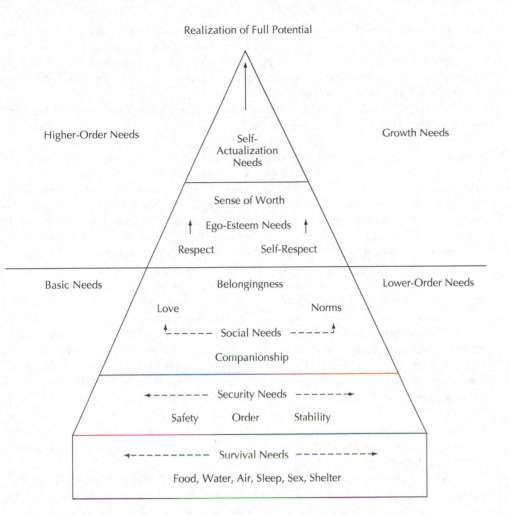

According to Maslow's **hierarchy of needs** theory, the effect of human needs on job **performance** is governed by three basic principles: (1) countervailing needs, (2) satisfaction deficit, and (3) progressive fulfillment.

1. *Countervailing needs.* Human beings are viewed as multidimensional social animals that sort through, prioritize, and strive to satisfy a variety of competing (lower- and higher-level) needs on a simultaneous basis.
2. *Satisfaction deficit.* Unsatisfied human needs create a state of tension, a perception of deprivation, and an impetus to act in a way to satisfy those needs.
3. *Progressive fulfillment.* The five-level **hierarchy of needs** determines the order in which needs will serve as motivators: Needs at any given level can affect behavior only after needs at the lower level below have been satisfied.

An unmet need creates a satisfaction deficit that commands individual attention and determines goal-oriented behavior. When deficits at one level are reasonably well satisfied, they cease to act as motivators, allowing people to focus more attention on the next higher level of needs. As needs are satisfied, people move up the hierarchy, and this movement is known as "satisfaction progression."[56] The key to understanding the dynamics of this process lies in accepting the progression principle, the idea that people are motivated by the lowest level of unsatisfied needs. If all of a person's four lower levels are reasonably well satisfied (in terms of that person's expectations, personality, and past experience), he or she will move on to seek self-actualization. It should also be noted that once a need is satisfied, there is a natural tendency to reevaluate the definition of what is reasonable and to upgrade expectations. Consequently, people cycle back to lower-level needs when the reasonable level of satisfaction is defined upward or when the status of a previously satisfied need is jeopardized.[57] A police officer who accepted a low starting salary to launch a career, for example, will likely redefine what is reasonable pay as he or she becomes more competent and moves up the career ladder. A new definition of what is reasonable may create a satisfaction deficit and motivate one to seek a promotion or look for another, higher-paying, position.

According to Maslow's **hierarchy of needs**, police administrators should identify the unfulfilled needs of their subordinates. This will give them a better understanding of why police officers may or may not perform as expected. Management must find incentives that will stimulate and reinforce desired work-related behavior. In practical terms, police departments should provide employees with sufficient financial compensation to meet their basic needs, a reasonably safe environment in which to work, and a nonmonetary reward system that reinforces individual self-esteem. Enlightened police administrators recognize the need for the personal growth of their subordinates and support it by providing opportunities for career advancement, encouraging self-development, and creating environments in which police officers are allowed to explore their own talents and dreams.[58]

While very few people (probably less than 10 percent of the general population) achieve self-actualization, most professional police officers are acutely aware of their higher-order needs. As they have moved in the direction of self-actualization, their need structure has changed. Growth needs (for competence, fulfillment, and respect) have displaced survival needs as primary motivators. Consequently, modern police administrators must be willing to de-emphasize their short-term goals and pay more attention to developing human resources. Failure to meet the growth needs of professional employees is certain to have a negative effect on the efficiency, effectiveness, and productivity of the police department. As Thomas Peters and Robert Waterman pointed out in their book, *In Search of Excellence*,[59] outstanding companies go to great lengths to meet the higher-order human needs of professional employees. This type of proactive management strategy is designed to counteract the dysfunctional influence of stress, absenteeism, shoddy workmanship, interpersonal conflict, and poor morale.

While there has been little or no scientific validation of Maslow's theory, it is still accepted as an article of faith by organizational humanists and theoreticians who subscribe to the human relations school of management. Maslow's concepts have been repackaged in many ways, and they serve as a foundation for most content theories.

E.R.G. Theory

While Maslow's theory has a great deal of humanistic appeal, there is simply no consistent evidence to prove his contention that satisfying a human need at one level actually decreases the motivational importance of that need so that the satisfaction of a person's needs is a process that becomes less and less concrete as time goes on.[60] Consequently, some motivation theorists have attempted to modify the **hierarchy of needs** concept to make it more realistic in terms of its application to goal-oriented behavior. Clayton Alderfer's "E.R.G." (existence/relatedness/growth) theory has become one of the better-known content theories. Alderfer developed his **E.R.G. theory** in an effort to simplify Maslow's hierarchical model. E.R.G. collapses Maslow's five human need categories into just three and contends they are active in all human beings:

1. *Existence needs.* These include all of the **drives**, desires, and wants related to a person's physiological and material well-being. Maslow's survival and security needs are combined into a single category focusing on the need for food, water, shelter, safety, pay, fringe benefits, working conditions, and so on.
2. *Relatedness needs.* These involve the innate sociability of human animals as they search for meaningful and mutually satisfying relationships with significant others, individually, or in groups. The satisfaction of social (interaction) and ego (esteem) needs grows out of the process of sharing.
3. *Growth needs.* These are directly related to the **psychosocial** processes that produce a sense of self-esteem (personal worth) and/or self-actualization (personal fulfillment). When growth needs are reasonably well satisfied, people exhibit confidence in themselves and engage in tasks that not only require the full use of their existing capabilities but may also require the development of new skills.[61]

People are very complex social animals; they exhibit a myriad of behaviors as they consciously or subconsciously strive to satisfy a variety of competing (even, at times, conflicting) needs.

E.R.G. theory has no hierarchical progression component. There is absolutely no assumption that lower-level human needs must be satisfied before higher-level needs can be activated. In fact, any need may be activated regardless of whether or not any other needs are satisfied.[62] As a result, people may be motivated at any given time. This makes it very difficult to tell exactly what motivates people to behave as they do in a particular situation.[63]

Alderfer's E.R.G. theory is straightforward and simple to understand. It is built on three basic principles: the need–escalation principle, the satisfaction–progression principle, and the frustration–regression principle.

1. *Need–escalation principle.* The less any level of need has been satisfied, the more the individual will desire satisfaction at that level.

2. *Satisfaction–progression principle.* The more that lower-level needs have been satisfied, the stronger will be an individual's desire for satisfaction of higher-level needs.

3. *Frustration–regression principle.* The less those higher-level needs have been satisfied, the more likely will be a renewed emphasis on previously satisfied lower-level needs.

E.R.G. theory is based on dynamic interaction between perceived needs. The combination of satisfaction–progression and frustration–regression can result in cycling as a person focuses on one need, then another, and then back again.[64]

Acquired Needs Theory

David McClelland, a psychologist, used the Thematic Apperception Test (TAT) to identify and measure basic human needs. The TAT asks people to look at pictures and write about what they see. Based on extensive data, McClelland and his colleagues identified three basic human **drives**: (1) need for achievement, (2) need for affiliation, and (3) need for power. He defined these needs in the following way:

1. *Need for achievement (nAch).* Human beings have a basic need for achievement. This relates to each person's desire to be competent, to solve problems, to accomplish complex tasks, and to make a meaningful contribution to the organization. People with this need will want to do well no matter what goal they pursue. Individuals with this drive strive to excel and surpass others. When applied properly, it increases self-regard by the successful exercise of talent. It is the most widely investigated motivational trait and was initially addressed by H. A. Murray and his colleagues in 1938.[65]

2. *Need for affiliation (nAff).* The human need for interpersonal contact and group affiliation is insatiable. It is reflected in a person's desire to establish and maintain meaningful social relationships with significant others. People rated high on nAff welcome tasks that require interaction with others; those rated less high prefer to work alone. This need will have important consequences for an individual with respect to team work or groups and impact on how one develops competence and creates value to a team.[66]

3. *Need for power (nPower).* People strive to acquire power in order to influence or control the behavior of others. People rated high on nPower might be overly concerned with personal power. Those with less of a need for power might not take the necessary actions if they could offend the group.[67]

These three needs (nAch, nAff, and nPower) exist in all people all of the time. One need is predominant in each person, however. It motivates people to act and shapes their job behavior.

McClelland's theory is based on the fundamental assumption that the needs for achievement, affiliation, and power are acquired over time and because of various life experiences. They are learned motives that are given substance by an individual's personality, background, and values. People are normally motivated by their dominant need. This dominant need is usually translated into a person's work preferences. People with a high nPower usually become much better managers than the high achievers. They have a sincere desire to influence others in an effort to accomplish the organization's mission, goals, and objectives. They thrive on ambiguity, seek responsibility, and feel comfortable being involved in the executive decision-making process. McClelland's theory encourages managers to learn how to recognize dominant needs in themselves and others and how to create work environments that are responsive to the personal need profile of each employee; managers are also encouraged to learn how to help identify the characteristics of people who may be best suited for particular kinds of jobs in the organization.[68]

McClelland's nAch, nAff, and nPower are needs very similar to those identified by Maslow and Alderfer. They can help police administrators understand why people act the way they do and what determines their work preferences (see Table 5–2). Identifying an

---

Table 5–2

WORK PREFERENCES BASED ON A HIGH NEED FOR ACHIEVEMENT, AFFILIATION, AND POWER

Individual Need	Work Preferences	Exemplar
High need for achievement	Skill	A rookie police officer with a dominant need to master his/her craft and be a true professional.
	Competence	
	Responsibility	
	Autonomy	
	Challenging goals	
	Feedback	
	Competitiveness	
High need for affiliation	Interaction	A community relations specialist assigned to help ease the conflict between the police and inner-city minority community.
	Relationships	
	Communication	
	Participation	
	Camaraderie	
	Sharing	
	Group orientation	
High need for power	Manage	A newly promoted major with the will to manage human resources in order to achieve a police department's goals and objectives.
	Influence	
	Control	
	Direct	
	Decide	
	Instruct	
	Motivate	

employee's dominant need could give managers a unique opportunity to match the right person with the right job in the right set of circumstances—ideally taking much of the guesswork out of the **motivation process** and increasing the likelihood that management will achieve a harmonious balance between the **psychosocial** needs of the individual and the needs of the organization.[69] Finding the right balance is critical in determining the productivity of a law enforcement agency.

Taking his cue from Maslow and other content theorists, Douglas McGregor developed a different humanistic theory of management. It is based on two distinct sets of assumptions about human nature (he called them **Theory X** and **Theory Y**) and the idea that managers tend to fall into one of two groups depending on which of the two assumptions they make about their employees. **Theory X** (the traditional approach to direction, control, and management) is based on a negative view of people. **Theory Y** (a more modern humanistic view) sees people as innately motivated and improvable. According to McGregor, managers organize, control, and attempt to motivate employees based on one or the other of these assumptions.

Theory X, the framework for much of traditional management thinking, includes the following negative assumptions. This theory stresses control and direction. Rules and regulations abound, and micro-management is viewed as the only way to accomplish department's mission. The workers are viewed as drowns, and managers view themselves as the gifted. Officers are seen as possessing limited abilities and in need of constant supervision.

CASE STUDY   Chief Sam Avery

Avery is the chief of police in a middle-class suburban community of 92,000 located just outside a large Midwestern industrial city. Avery was the fourth officer to be employed in a community that was incorporated with a population of 10,250 some 27 years ago. He was appointed chief 21 years ago, and he watched the community grow to its present population. The community has a substantial residential area and has considerable commercial and light industry. Many of its residents commute and work in the industrial city that is 24 miles north of the community. Over the years, the chief has been responsible for approving the hiring of everyone in the department and he looks upon the department as a big family. Currently, there are 108 sworn positions in the department, and 32 of those officers have been in the department long enough to assume positions in supervision, management, or specialized assignments. All of the investigators in the department (16 percent of the sworn strength) assumed their positions some 10 years ago. Fourteen percent of the officers are female, and most of them have been hired in the last eight years. The majority of the officers are Caucasian, and the next largest group is Hispanics.

The chief is a very powerful man in the community with an institutionalized political base that has been built up over the years. He has outstayed numerous members of the city council, and he attends every meeting of the council. He has always developed a positive relationship with the last four city managers, and once he served as an acting manager. Additionally, numerous business owners are his personal friends, and he belongs to three different civic groups.

Chief Avery is a laissez-faire leader in that he accepts reasonable judgment of his subordinates with whom he has worked for many years and at the same time makes virtually every decision that affects the police department; but each decision is paternalistic in the sense that he takes care of those officers who are trusted friends, especially those who have been in the department for more than 15 years. The older officers (who refer to themselves as "family") are content to let the "old man" run the show. They are very protective of each other and view many of the newer officers as interlopers. Historically, the uniformed officers conduct a preliminary investigation, and the investigators conduct all follow-up investigations. Supervision in the Investigative Bureau is very lax, and many of the follow-up investigations receive only cursory examination. Some of the investigators have retired intellectually and avoid responsibility like the plague. They have absolutely no desire to jeopardize their lucrative pensions by making "decisions." Some of the more senior investigators are ritualistically counting the days until they can "hang 'em up."

Younger officers—who are ordinarily better educated, more participative minded, and often risk oriented—have been challenging the status quo. They feel left out. They want more involvement. This is especially true for a number of the line personnel who want to do more than just conduct preliminary investigations. The chief has 18 months to go until he reaches mandatory retirement age, and many of the younger officers, both men and women, can hardly wait until that date arrives. They hope that the powers to be in the city will hire someone from outside to run the department, and the police association is calling for a nationwide search for a replacement for the current chief. Even after the chief retires, there will still be a significant split between those who remain and are comfortable in working under a system where internal motivation is stagnate and Theory X is acceptable. On the other hand, there are an increasing number of newer officers who are chomping at the bit for a new chief who has a Theory Y orientation.

What is the real issue? Is it motivation? Why or why not? How would Abraham Maslow and Douglas McGregor describe the dynamics of the situation? If you were the new chief of police, how would you make effective use of expectancy theory? Explain in detail. What would you do to resolve this problem? What part could job enrichment play in this case?

1. The typical human being has a normal dislike for work and will take avoiding action whenever possible.

2. Because employees really have an aversion to work, the majority of people must be coerced, directed, controlled, and threatened with punishment in order to get them to work productively and achieve organizational goals and objectives.

3. Nearly everyone lacks ambition, avoids responsibility, and needs constant direction. Their paramount concerns are survival and job security. Consequently, employees are viewed as expendable resources (a necessary evil) with little or no value in and of themselves. They simply become a means to an end.

The tragedy of **Theory X** is that it is a self-fulfilling prophecy. **Theory X** police administrators treat their subordinates in a suspicious and authoritarian manner. They threaten them, exploit them, and look down on them. The belief is that if an officer does not acquiesce to authority, they can be replaced or transferred to an undesirable assignment. New employees soon learn that their drive, ideas, initiative, and commitment are neither respected nor rewarded. They learn to behave the way they are expected to behave. Police officers who find themselves in **Theory X** environments adapt quickly. They adopt a nonproductive, "What's the use?" attitude. As poor morale robs an organization of vitality, the organization becomes progressively more dysfunctional.

Theory Y represents the other end of the continuum and is based, in large measure, on Maslow's **hierarchy of needs. Theory Y** assumes that once people's lower-level needs (for survival, security, and belongingness) have been reasonably well satisfied, they are motivated by higher-order needs for self-esteem and self-actualization. If they are deprived of the opportunity to satisfy these higher-level needs at work, they become frustrated. They often react to this frustration by becoming indolent, passive, resistant to change, nonproductive, and unhappy. Poor morale creates a dilemma for proactive managers, and its resolution calls for a totally different set of assumptions about what motivates people to work. Douglas McGregor offered **Theory Y** as a "modest beginning for a new theory" with respect to the day-to-day management of human resources.[70] **Theory Y** is built on the following set of assumptions:

1. The typical individual is not someone who inherently dislikes work. In fact, the expenditure of physical and mental effort is viewed as normal.

2. External control and the threat of punishment are not the only means by which to elicit individual effort. Employees are capable of exercising self-direction and self-control in order to achieve goals to which they are committed.

3. Motivation, the potential for development, the capacity to assume responsibility, and the readiness to direct one's behavior toward organizational goals are present in every person.

4. Commitment to goals is a function of the rewards that are associated with their achievement. The most important rewards are to be found in intrinsic rewards such as ego satisfaction, self-management, and the self-fulfillment aspects of commitment.

5. The most important function of management is to create an organizational environment so people can achieve their own goals by directing individualized efforts toward objective attainment. The manager's job is to create opportunities, release potential, encourage growth, and provide guidance.

6. The capacity to exercise a relatively high degree of imagination, ingenuity, and creativity in seeking solutions to organizational problems is widespread throughout the population.[71]

Intrinsic **motivation** is viewed as the key to improved **performance** and increased productivity. **Theory Y**, in sharp contrast to **Theory X**, emphasizes managerial leadership through motivation by objectives—that is, by permitting subordinate personnel to experience need satisfaction as they contribute to the achievement of the organization's mission, goals, and objectives. If workers are not motivated, it is because of poor management practices that do not allow employees' natural positive attitudes toward work to emerge.[72]

Theory Y managers respect their personnel and use rewards to enhance **performance**. They also seek to motivate their people through allowing them meaningful participation in the organization's decision-making process. Police officers who feel like part of the team and who receive **psychosocial** satisfaction from their job are much more likely to invest time, talent, energy, and expertise in the organization.[73]

As with Theory X, **Theory Y** may have a Pygmalion effect. Assuming the best about people often results in their giving their best. All other things being equal, people learn to give what they are expected to give. By treating subordinates as mature, fully functional human beings who are capable of making a significant contribution to the police department, **Theory Y** administrators frequently motivate police personnel to achieve extraordinarily high levels of **performance**.[74] **Theory X** and **Theory Y** are not mutually exclusive managerial strategies; they represent the assumptions on which managerial strategies are built. While McGregor did not argue that either **Theory X** or Y is always correct, he did suggest that managers tend to adopt Theory X assumptions more often than can be justified by the characteristics of their employees. He argued that where and whenever appropriate, management practices that are consistent with **Theory Y** would produce much greater personal and organizational benefits. His typology suggests that police administrators should tailor their managerial approach to meet the profile (X or Y) exhibited by police personnel. Perhaps the optimal theory would encourage the police administrator to employ either of the approaches at one time or another, depending on the behavior patterns of his or her personnel and the demands of the situation.[75] Figure 5–3 explores the relationship between McGregor's concepts and other content theories.

Motivation-Hygiene Theory

Frederick Herzberg developed another view of human needs. His **"motivation-hygiene,"** or "two-factor," theory was originally derived from an analysis of critical incidents reported by 200 engineers and accountants. They were asked to describe the times when they felt exceptionally good and exceptionally bad about their jobs. Based on the different things respondents identified as sources of satisfaction and dissatisfaction in their work, Herzberg identified two themes characteristic of all jobs: (1) "maintenance" or "hygiene" factors and (2) "motivational" factors. He explained these terms as follows:

1. *Maintenance factors.* Maintenance or hygiene factors are those things in the work environment that meet an employee's hedonistic need to avoid pain. They include the necessities of any job (e.g., adequate pay, fringe benefits, job security, appropriate working conditions, supervision, interpersonal relations, managerial practices, and realistic policies, procedures, rules, and regulations). Hygiene factors do not satisfy (or motivate); they set the stage for motivation. On the other hand, they are the major source of job dissatisfaction when they are perceived to be inadequate.

Figure 5–3
McGregor's Theory X and Theory Y.

2. *Motivational factors.* Motivators are those **psychosocial** factors in work that provide intrinsic satisfaction and serve as an incentive for people to invest more of their time, talent, energy, and expertise in productive goal-oriented behavior. The primary human motivators are (1) achievement, (2) recognition, (3) advancement, (4) the work itself, (5) the potential for growth, and (6) responsibility. The absence of motivators does not necessarily produce job dissatisfaction.[76]

While these concepts are obviously related, they represent completely different dimensions of satisfaction.

In terms of **motivation**, hygiene factors provide the milieu within which motivators (or satisfiers) function. They create a neutral state by meeting lower-level human needs and preventing negative or dysfunctional behavior. Actions designed to improve hygiene factors can prevent or help to eliminate job dissatisfaction but cannot increase job satisfaction per se. Whisenand offers the following suggestions based on needs theory:

- Do not assume that all police employees are motivated by the same needs or values.
- To determine what will motivate any given worker, determine what needs that individual is trying to satisfy on the job.
- Make sure that you have the authority and power to administer or withhold consequences that will satisfy a person's need.
- Design job situations so that the officers and civilians can satisfy their needs by engaging in behaviors that enable the department to achieve its mission.[77]

The least-desirable situation from a management point of view is to have police officers experiencing low satisfaction (of higher-level human needs) and high dissatisfaction (with the organization's efforts to meet lower-level survival, security, and social needs). The best mix involves high satisfaction and low dissatisfaction (see Figure 5–4). The police administrator's goal under the two-factor theory is to minimize job dissatisfaction and to maximize job satisfaction. Once improved hygiene factors reduce job dissatisfaction, managers must be prepared to shift their attention to motivational factors if they are to create more job satisfaction.

The best way to motivate workers (to be more efficient, effective, and productive) is to give them a bigger stake in the job itself. In fact, upgrading the job itself is the core component of Herzberg's theory. According to Herzberg, managers motivate their subordinates by eliciting their input, encouraging participation, involving people in the decision-making process, and enlarging or enriching the job.[78]

Figure 5–4
Satisfaction/Dissatisfaction and Adaptive Behavior.

Job Satisfaction* (Satisfiers)	Job Dissatisfaction* (Hygiene)	Adaptive Behavior
High ←--------→	High	Competition Conflict Normlessness Wheel spinning Individualism
High ←--------→	Low	Cooperation Self-direction Self-control Responsibility Productivity
Low ←--------→	High	Stress Low morale Poor workmanship Absenteeism Turnover
Low ←--------→	Low	Ritualism Apathy Status quo Soldiering Resists change

* Motivational factors interact with hygiene factors to produce adaptive behavior.

Frederick Herzberg's **motivation-hygiene** theory draws heavily on Maslow, Alderfer, and McGregor. It emphasizes the importance of dynamic interaction between maintenance needs (hygiene) and motivation needs (satisfiers). Like all other content theories, it has been criticized for its methodological imprecision. A major debate concerns Herzberg's contention that hygiene factors function only as dissatisfiers, not as satisfiers. Researchers have found little or no support for this position. Nevertheless, there does seem to be some substance to the rest of Herzberg's theory. According to Lyman Porter and Raymond E. Miles,[79] much of the evidence supports the conclusion that job content factors are considered to be critically important to those workers who are asked to report their most highly satisfying job experiences.

Content Theory Revisited

While it is virtually impossible to tell exactly what motivates people to act as they do in a given situation, theorists such as Maslow, Alderfer, McGregor, and Herzberg have made important contributions to our knowledge of the **psychosocial** processes that produce goal-oriented human behavior. They have provided us with food for thought and a springboard to further inquiry. In sum, the content theories address the following "bottom-line" requirements for managing employee motivation:[80]

- Assess employee needs.
- Identify the most active needs of employees.
- Develop specific strategies to satisfy active employee needs.
- Implement strategies.
- Evaluate the plan.

Process Theories

Many behavioral scientists have been frustrated by the seeming subjectivity and introspectiveness of the **content theories**.[81] They are much more interested in how people are motivated to engage in goal-oriented behavior. Some of them subscribe to behavior modification approaches based on classic reinforcement theory. With Pavlovian zeal and Skinnerian logic, they believe workers can be trained to be more efficient, effective, and productive through the use of stimulus–response techniques, with money as the primary reward. Some behaviorists recommend the use of what they call "operant conditioning" to make people operate in a certain way to receive a certain reward. They contend that people are what they are and do what they do because of environmental factors rather than internal **drives**, needs, or abstract intellectual calculations.[82] **Operant conditioning theory** is based on the assumption that when an operant response (the desired behavior) is followed by a pleasant incident (a reward), it causes people to associate that pleasant outcome with the desired behavior. What is needed is to target specific variable that rewards significant behaviors. Since human beings are hedonistic animals who prefer pleasure to pain, people usually behave in a way that brings them pleasure. **Operant conditioning** theorists encourage managers to avoid the use of punishment as the primary means of **motivation**; more effective, they say, is the following approach:

1. Specify the desired behavior in clear operational terms.
2. Use positive reinforcements (rewards) whenever possible.
3. Minimize the time lag between desired behavior and reinforcement.
4. Use a variable-ratio schedule as opposed to continuous reinforcement.
5. Determine the response level, and use shaping techniques to obtain appropriate behavior.
6. Manipulate environmental factors so that they will all reinforce the desired behavior.
7. Keep the positive reinforcement at the lowest level needed to maintain **performance**.[83]

While the operant conditioning process has been recognized for some time, there are issues that challenge its use. Managers within law enforcement agencies frequently utilize formal and informal rewards (and punishments) to motivate police officers. To encourage an explicit behavior, rewards are utilized to influence the likelihood the behavior will take place. A reward is what an individual perceives as desirable. In order for these rewards to motivate employees, they must be valued by the recipient. Not all employees view rewards (or punishments) equally. In fact, a reward by one employee might be viewed as such by another.[84]

Richard Johnson conducted research on police officer perceptions of agency rewards and punishments. While there are some limitations to the study in applying the results to all police agencies, there are some interesting findings of which leaders and managers should take note. The most notable finding of Johnson's research was that officers viewed rewards (and punishment) in a hierarchal arrangement.[85] Another interesting finding is that the standing of rewards is associated with how they impact the officer's off duty quality of life. For example, promotion or transfer was minimally ranked in value by officers. Finally, differences in rewards were determined depending upon gender, tenure, and education.[86]

Leaders and managers should be cognizant of rewards and punishments, and how they can differ from employee to employee. By doing so, rewards and punishments can be interrelated to officer work behaviors leaders and managers seek to motivate and amend.[87]

The operant conditioning process became the centerpiece of Frederick W. Taylor's scientific management and is still popular in some management circles. Most new **process theories** stress the decision-making dimension of work **performance**. Newer **process theories** represent a dynamic alternative to the more descriptive content theories discussed in the last section. They have been designed to help police administrators understand the cognitive (thought) processes by which individual workers choose to engage in specific behaviors in order to satisfy their personal needs. Two of the most popular process theories are **expectancy theory** and **equity theory**. Both are based on the assumption that people make conscious and subconscious assessments of contemplated actions and the consequences of those actions. Personal expectations of the outcomes associated with goal-oriented behavior are critical variables in determining how people are motivated to perform at work. Let us take a closer look at these two theories.

Expectancy Theory

Expectancy theory assumes not only that people are driven by intrinsic needs but that they also make subjective decisions about what they will or will not do based on what they think will result from their effort. The **motivation** to work is determined, in large measure, by what the individual believes about effort-to-performance relationships and about the desirability of the work outcomes (rewards) associated with different potential levels of **performance**. In other words, police officers will evaluate behavioral alternatives and choose the one they believe will lead to the best ratio of reward to effort.

The greater the expectation that a given behavior will pay off (in terms of an anticipated reward), the more likely people are to invest their time, talent, and expertise in order to do it well. Victor Vroom's **expectancy theory** is designed to explain the dynamics involved in this type of choice behavior.[88] Vroom, a well-known management consultant, introduced his **expectancy theory** in the early 1960s. He identified five critically important variables: (1) expectancies (beliefs about **performance** capabilities), (2) valences (beliefs about outcome desirabilities), (3) outcomes, (4) instrumentalities (beliefs about outcome contingencies), and (5) choices. Vroom discussed these variables as follows:

1. *Expectancy.* **Expectancy** is a probability estimate made by a person concerning the likelihood that a particular behavior will be followed by a particular outcome. The degree of **expectancy** ranges from zero (none) to one (absolute certainty). There are two levels of **expectancy**: Expectancy 1 (E → P) is a person's perception of the chances that a certain level of effort (E) will lead to first-level outcomes that result in adequate job performance (P). Expectancy 2 (P → O) is a person's perception of the chances that performance (P) will lead to desired second-level outcomes (O).

2. *Valences.* A valence is the strength of one's preference for a particular outcome. Unlike expectancies, valences can be positive or negative and are measured on a scale from −1 (very undesirable) to +1 (very desirable). The level of motivation will depend on how much someone wants the ends (goals) of work effort as well as the means (or tools) needed to achieve these ends.

3. *Outcomes.* An outcome or reward is any need-related consequence of a behavior. First-level outcomes are the outcomes of successful job **performance** (a sense of accomplishment, feelings of competence, goal achievement, and so forth). Second-level outcomes are the consequences to which first-level outcomes are expected to lead (a pay increase, promotion, professional status, and so forth). Some outcomes are intrinsic to the person; others are extrinsic.

4. *Instrumentality.* An instrumentality is the belief that if the necessary level of **performance** is achieved, the anticipated outcome (reward) will be forthcoming. The overall strength of an instrumentality ranges from zero (none) to one (certainty).

5. *Choice.* A choice concerns the selection of a particular pattern of behavior. People weigh the potential value and consequence of each action they contemplate in order to estimate the probability that certain outcomes can be attained by choosing a particular behavior.

These variables interact with each other to affect motivation. The interactions of three of them in particular—expectancy (E), instrumentalities (I), and valence (V)—determine the extent of the **motivation** to perform (M). All three must have high positive values to produce goal-oriented choices. If the value of any one of these three variables for a person approaches zero, the probability that he or she will be motivated to perform well also approaches zero. Vroom contends these factors are interrelated multiplicatively, as expressed in the equation $M = E \times I \times V$. When people believe they have the ability to accomplish a certain task if they perform at a particular level, their self-confidence may produce a high level of expectation (**expectancy**).[89] This belief will not, in and of itself, motivate goal-oriented behavior, however. They must also have a high level of confidence that if they put forth the necessary effort and perform at a high level, they will be rewarded (instrumentality), and they must place high value on the reward or other anticipated outcomes (valence). A patrol officer, for example, may have the skill, steady **performance**, and the intradepartmental support for appointment to the SWAT team but may turn the opportunity down because this special assignment is far less important to him than maximizing the amount of time he can spend with his terminally ill wife.

Managers play a key role in operationalizing **expectancy theory** in the workplace. The multiplier effect (just discussed) requires police administrators to attempt to maximize *expectancy*, instrumentality, and valence when they seek to use work-based rewards to create high levels of work **motivation** among their subordinates. In order to make effective use of expectancy **theory** in motivating their personnel, police administrators should perform the following:

1. Establish reasonably high expectations and a climate of police professionalism that encompasses high ethical standards.

2. Recruit, screen, select, and retain well-qualified personnel.

3. Create an incentive system based on equal access to meaningful rewards.

4. Supervise subordinates in such a way that they are always learning, developing, and expanding their horizons.

5. Implement an effective in-service training program keyed to the concept of employee development.

6. Forge a direct linking pen between job performance and positive reinforcement.

7. Analyze the total situation for conflicting expectancies, and take appropriate action to minimize conflict that is injurious to the organization.

8. Check to make sure there is an equitable distribution of rewards based on actual **performance**.

9. Keep the motivation system in a state of dynamic equilibrium.

From an **expectancy** perspective, *the things that get rewarded get done!* Establishing the proper link between job **performance** and meaningful rewards is the single most effective way to improve organizational efficiency, effectiveness, and productivity.[90]

Expectancy theory has evolved into a very complex explanation of **motivation**, which is built around the assumption that human beings are rational animals who voluntarily choose to engage in those behaviors that their expectancy calculation tells them will consistently produce anticipated rewards (see Figure 5–5). The complexity of the **expectancy** model has made it very difficult to validate it through applied research. The lack of supportive data does not invalidate the concept, however. Common sense tells us that motivation depends on the dynamic interaction between our expectations, opportunities, desired outcomes, and the intensity of our desire for particular rewards. While they may not be able to explain it in technical terms, most effective police administrators have incorporated **expectancy** theory into their overall philosophy of management.

Equity Theory

One of the most sensitive issues confronting modern management is achieving equity in rewarding individual workers for their job **performance**. Equity means fairness. From a **motivation** standpoint, equity refers to the perceived fairness of rewards and of the reward system itself. J. Stacy Adams[91] formulated one of the best-known equity theories. He contends that a feeling of inequity is a motivating state of mind. In other words, when people feel that there is an inequity in the way they are being treated, they will be moved psychologically to eliminate the discomfort and to restore a sense of equity to the situation. Inequities are perceived when people believe the rewards or incentives they receive for their work output are unequal to the rewards other workers appear to be getting for comparable output. This violates the widely accepted norm that people should be treated equitably (not equally). Workers expect meaningful rewards that commensurate with their job **performance**. In law enforcement, equity is still a critical issue in some agencies. This is especially true in rural areas where monetary rewards are considerably less than those in urban areas, and in numerous instances, a rural deputy will have minimal health insurance for himself and members of his or her family. Equity theory is based on the idea that people want to maintain a sense of balance. They are especially interested in maintaining *distributive fairness*. This exists when employees think people are getting what they deserve—not more, not less.[92]

According to Adams's **equity theory**, a key element in determining the fairness of a particular relationship lies in this type of social comparison. A perceived inequity involves the comparison of an existing state or condition with a given standard. Employees instinctively compare themselves and their particular situations with others in the workplace. It is common for officers to compare the work their jobs require of them with the work of other employees—for example, sergeants assigned to what are often perceived as "rubber gun squad," details requiring little or no real police work. Comparisons of this

Figure 5–5
Simplified Version of Expectancy Theory.

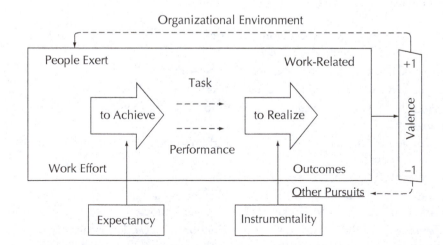

Human beings are rational animals who voluntarily choose those behaviors their expectancy calculation tells them will consistently produce anticipated rewards.

type tend to lower morale. It is often impossible for management to justify the allocation of work. It does not matter what managers believe is fair and equitable, because pay and equity are in the minds of those affected. Even if police officers and sergeants were rewarded in exactly the same way, inequities would still be found. Inequity exists when unequals are treated as equals as well as when equals are treated as unequals. The bottom line is that perceived inequities are inevitable whenever large numbers of people interact with one another in complex law enforcement organizations. They are caused by factors such as the following:

1. Pay differentials and discretionary incentives
2. Racial, religious, sexual, and social discrimination (actual or perceived)
3. Unpredictable access to organizational resources
4. Political as opposed to merit-based promotion
5. Favoritism
6. Selective communication
7. Preferential assignment based on seniority
8. Differential status and the distribution of perquisites

Equity theory is based on the assumption that all workers have been socially programmed to compare themselves and other employees in terms of what they get out of their job (outcomes) and what they invest in their job (inputs). Outcomes include pay, fringe benefits, prestige, feelings of achievement, a sense of personal satisfaction, and so on. Inputs are factors such as special skills, training, ingenuity, perseverance, and hard work. These comparisons are then translated into ratios that reflect their inputs and outcomes vis-à-vis those of others within the workforce. A negative inequity exists when a police officer feels that he or she is receiving relatively less of a valued outcome than other officers in proportion to work inputs. A positive inequity, on the other hand, exists when an officer feels that he or she is receiving relatively more of a valued outcome than others doing the same type of work. If an individual's input/outcome ratio is equal to that of the others, the person will experience a sense of equity. Both negative and positive inequities are motivators.[93]

When the reward for **performance** equals or exceeds what is considered fair, the satisfaction will produce repeat behavior.[94] If a reward falls short of perceived equity, dissatisfaction will reduce the motivation to continue the effort. Adams noted that when employees perceive either positive (overpayment) or negative (underpayment) inequity, they will suffer cognitive dissonance and disequilibrium; to reduce these **psychosocial** discomforts, they will consciously or subconsciously engage in one or more of the following behaviors:

1. Increase performance, workload, and other kinds of inputs to justify higher rewards when they perceive a positive inequity.
2. Decrease performance, workload, and other kinds of inputs when they perceive a negative inequity.
3. Change outcomes (or rewards) through personal persuasion, collective bargaining, legal action, or dysfunctional behavior such as misappropriation, employee theft, and outright corruption.
4. Change comparisons by persuading low performers with equal pay to increase their efforts and by discouraging high performers from being rate busters.

Ramon J. Aldag and Loren W. Kuzuhara[95] contend that managers can maintain control of the equity dynamic in their work unit if they follow these rules:

1. Assess employee perceptions of equity in their work situations.
2. Identify employees who perceive inequities.
3. Identify the basis for employee perceptions of inequity. Openness is critical because it tends to reduce suspicion and helps defuse the perception of inequity.

4. Evaluate management policies and practices to determine the validity of employee perceptions.

5. Identify specific changes that can be made to address employee equity concerns. Work with human resource experts, unions, and community administrators to resolve concerns.

6. Implement changes and communicate them to employees. This is a very important step, and it has been found that there are few instances of overcommunication.

While these relatively simple rules will not cure all of the very complex problems associated with **psychosocial** equity comparisons, they should help to make the process more objective. Since most Americans equate objectivity with fairness, there could be a genuine reduction in labor–management conflict.

Even though recent research has consistently demonstrated that the perception of inequity leads to reduced output, more absenteeism, and higher employee turnover, some motivation theorists feel that equity theory is of limited value because it is a special-purpose theory rather than a general theory of motivation.[96] They argue that **equity theory** does not explain how people select a person to compare themselves with or how they arrive at the value placed on inputs and outcomes. Nevertheless, equity theory provides police administrators with an intellectual framework for thinking about issues such as equity, fairness, and justice in the allocation of rewards. In fact, feelings of inequity and injustice have served to motivate human beings throughout all of recorded history.

Implications for Police Management

Police administrators today must come to grips with one simple fact of life—they are dealing with a new breed of employee. Modern police personnel are more sophisticated than their predecessors. They are better educated, more **participative**, and much less resistant to change. They demand respect and expect to be treated as professionals. While money is still a magical word in the police subculture, it has a much different meaning than it did a generation ago. Salaries and fringe benefits have been improved to the point where more money, in and of itself, no longer serves as the primary motivator in many agencies, while other agencies lag behind in salaries and benefits. Police officers demand more than just money. Most of them want to do meaningful work that meets their conscious and subconscious higher-order needs for growth, self-esteem, and a sense of fulfillment.[97]

Police managers, who are expected to get things done through others, are in a position to help satisfy the higher-order needs of their subordinates. Their job is to translate individual effort into collaborative action. Effective managers tend to be people developers who subscribe to the **Theory Y** assumptions of Douglas McGregor. They emphasize the importance of (1) participation, (2) **job design**, (3) **job enlargement**, (4) **job enrichment**, and (5) **job rotation**.

1. *Participation.* As police officers move up the professional ladder, they have an increased need to become involved in charting the course of an enterprise. They experience a strong desire to help shape its mission, set its goals, and determine its objectives. Meaningful participation in the organization's decision-making process gives them a sense of ownership in, and a strong commitment to, the decisions it produces. Since collective decisions are often superior to those made by a single individual, managers should solicit input from their personnel and employ strategies designed to facilitate full participation. A police department will be much stronger when management is comfortable sharing power with, rather than exercising power over, its professional employees.[98]

2. *Job design.* A job consists of a task or series of tasks a person performs in support of the organization's mission (purpose). **Job design** involves deliberate and purposeful planning in order to bring both the structural and **psychosocial** aspects of the activity together in one basic process. It is the police administrator's responsibility to design the task and the work setting so that employees will have intrinsic motivation to perform and will derive satisfaction from a job well done. Properly designed jobs are interesting, challenging, achievable, and rewarding. Managers usually prepare job descriptions that

spell out the duties, processes, authority, responsibility, and accountability inherent in a given job.[99] Police managers can sometimes address morale and motivation problems by designing jobs to make them more meaningful. This is especially true for the area of discretion.

3. *Job enlargement.* One of the first modern methods of motivating employees through **job design** was **job enlargement**.[100] This involved injecting some variety into a fairly repetitive, boring job by introducing different, yet related, kinds of tasks. Instead of doing just the same repetitive task for eight hours, police patrol personnel might do three or four different, but related, tasks requiring the same level of skill. The "police agent" concept in law enforcement represents another practical application of this idea. Police agents are patrol personnel who have responsibility of performing many of the routine duties usually assigned to detectives. Patrol officers are often allowed to conduct preliminary investigations in misdemeanor and lower-level felony cases. These job enlargement strategies are built on the assumption that variety is the spice of life. **Job enlargement** motivates employees to improve job **performance** and increase their productivity.

4. *Job enrichment.* **Job enrichment** is a different **job design** strategy, which aims to counteract the negative aspects of specialization by building motivating factors into job content. Frederick Herzberg called this "vertical loading"; it is calculated to meet higher-order human needs for autonomy, growth, and self-actualization. Both **job enrichment** and **job enlargement** add variety to a job by introducing new tasks, but enlargement adds them "horizontally," at the same skill or decision-making level, whereas enrichment adds them "vertically," requiring higher levels of skill or decision-making ability. According to Herzberg,[101] the purpose of **job enrichment** is to motivate people by the following ways:

1. Removing some controls while maintaining overall accountability
2. Increasing the accountability of each person for his or her own work
3. Assigning responsibility to employees for performing a natural and complete unit of work
4. Granting additional authority to people in their area of responsibility
5. Encouraging autonomy in decision-making as it relates to the task being performed
6. Introducing new and more difficult tasks not previously handled by employees at a particular level
7. Assigning individual police officers to enhanced or highly specialized tasks to help them become experts

Because of the rigid bureaucratic structure of most American police departments, **job enrichment** programs have not been widespread. Where such programs have been implemented, they have produced encouraging results. They motivate police personnel by targeting their higher-order needs for achievement, responsibility, recognition, advancement, and personal growth. As police departments' personnel become more and more sophisticated, it will take innovative strategies like **job enrichment** to motivate them to become team players whose personal goals coincide with those of the organization.

5. *Job rotation.* **Job rotation** is a motivation strategy in which people are moved into different jobs, usually on a temporary basis, in order to give them additional experiences, understandings, and challenges. It is most often used to cross-train employees so that they gain a better appreciation for the importance of different jobs and the relationships between jobs in an organization. Employees who become involved in **job rotation** programs are usually more valuable to themselves and their employers because they develop the ability to perform more than one limited function.[102] **Job rotation** tends to give employees more self-confidence and helps prepare them for promotions and transfers. While many police departments have experimented with **job rotation** programs, they have not been as effective as originally envisioned. The enemies are bureaucracy and the lack of good management. Bureaucracy prevents police administrators from becoming leaders by turning them into paper shufflers rather than people developers.

Almost all of the available evidence suggests that these **motivation** strategies work if managers are careful about when, how, and with whom they are used. Their success in improving efficiency, effectiveness, productivity, and morale will depend on the composition of the workforce, the managerial skill of the police administrator, and the dynamics of the situation. These motivational strategies will probably have more influence on quality than on quantity.

CASE STUDY   Captain Shirley Carr

Captain Carr is the commander of a Field Operations Division in the City of Rogersville that has a population of 101,603, and the community covers 65.4 square miles. Captain Carr has worked her way up through the ranks achieving the position of captain after 18 years of service. She is the first woman to hold this high of a position in the department. Prior to this she served as Lieutenant of Administrative Services. The preponderance of her service has been in patrol, where she served as a sergeant and then a watch commander.

Within the department, 65 percent of the officers are white, and the next largest ethnic group is Hispanic, at 27 percent. Seven percent of the force is women. Based on tradition and operational policy, the department has a definitive chain of command and is keyed to job specialization. Patrol officers are assigned to a specific beat and respond to calls, conduct preliminary investigations (when minor crimes are involved), and engage in preventive patrol when time allows. The Bureau of Criminal Investigations conducts all other investigations. Job descriptions are definitive, and everyone follows them religiously. Deviation from a job description results in immediate supervisory action that usually calls for being written-up. The Division handles 62 percent of the police department's measurable workload and has 58 percent of the manpower.

Within the Division, there is a lieutenant who serves as an adjutant, three lieutenants who serve as watch commanders, a traffic sergeant who supervises six officers, a sergeant who supervises the Neighborhood Police unit that has a complement of 10 officers, three school resource officers, and 71 patrol officers. Officers in the specialized assignment have higher morale and seem well satisfied with their assignments. They have an opportunity to interact with each other and create meaningful and satisfying relationships. Almost all patrol officers feel that their workload is excessive and complain that all they do is go from one incident to the next and spend an inordinate amount of time creating police reports. In fact, they feel that they are unable to complete their preliminary investigations and, in many instances, have to cut corners in order to complete a shift. Except for backup in certain cases, they never get to interact with fellow officers apart from coming and going to roll-call sessions. Every patrol officer in the department works solo, and departmental police prohibits more than two officers eating meals or taking coffee breaks at the same time in the same restaurant.

The dehumanizing aspect of an excessive workload has taken its toll on the personnel assigned to the patrol division. A survey conducted by a member of the chief's staff indicates that patrol officers feel in the following ways:

1. The job is viewed as dissatisfying.
2. Morale is low.
3. Response time is long.
4. The number of citizen-initiated complaints is up.
5. More officers are filing disability claims.
6. Employee turnover is exceeding projections.

The situation has become critical and imperils the division's ability to function efficiently, effectively, and productively and has to be dealt with as soon as possible.

The solution is to design a program that meets the needs of both the department and the employees.

What philosophical approach do you believe Captain Carr should take in carrying out this project? What specific motivational strategies would you recommend that she consider? Would E.R.G. theory be applicable in this instance? Why or why not? Give several concrete examples. Would job enlargement or job enrichment be applicable in this case? Explain.

SUMMARY

Management can be defined as getting things done with and through the efforts of others. Thus, it is the police administrator's job to create an environment within which professional employees motivate themselves. This can be done by establishing a concrete link between appropriate job behavior and meaningful rewards. Motivation is a **psychosocial** process. It produces an attitude that generates actions that lead to anticipated results. All other things being equal, well-motivated police officers are more efficient, effective, productive, and satisfied than unmotivated ones.

Most motivation theories are based on the assumption that psychosocial tensions caused by intrinsic and/or extrinsic factors are translated into human needs. Needs elicit instrumental behaviors and these are designed to reduce the tension. Of course, different needs generate different and unique adaptive responses. The intensity of a felt need (or needs) activates and energizes people as they interact with one another in the workplace.

Abraham Maslow's "progression" theory of employee needs is one of the best-known content theories. As a positive humanistic theory of **motivation**, it stresses the importance of both biological drives and psychosocial needs. According to Maslow, five basic human needs activate, fuel, and shape the internal drive to overcome inertia affiliated with the status quo. He classes them as physiological (survival) needs, safety (security) needs, belonging (social) needs, self-esteem (ego) needs, and self-actualization (fulfillment) needs.

While Maslow's theory has a great deal of humanistic appeal, there is simply no consistent evidence to prove his contention that satisfying a human need at one level actually decreases the motivational importance of that need so that the satisfaction of a person's needs is a process that becomes less and less concrete as time goes on. Consequently, some motivation theorists have attempted to modify the hierarchy of needs concept to make it more realistic in terms of its application to goal-oriented behavior. Clayton Alderfer's "E.R.G." (existence/relatedness/growth) theory has become one of the better-known content theories. Alderfer developed his **E.R.G. theory** in an effort to simplify Maslow's hierarchical model. E.R.G. collapses Maslow's five human need categories into just three and contends they are active in all human beings.

Taking his cue from Maslow and other content theorists, Douglas McGregor developed a different humanistic theory of management. It is based on two distinct sets of assumptions about human nature (he called them Theory X and Theory Y) and the idea that managers tend to fall into one of two groups depending on which of the two assumptions they make about their employees. Theory X (the traditional approach to direction, control, and management) is based on a negative view of people. Theory Y (a more modern humanistic view) sees people as innately motivated and improvable. According to McGregor, managers organize, control, and attempt to motivate employees based on one or the other of these assumptions.

Frederick Herzberg developed another view of human needs. His "motivation-hygiene," or "two-factor," theory was originally derived from an analysis of critical incidents reported by 200 engineers and accountants. They were asked to describe the times when they felt exceptionally good and exceptionally bad about their jobs. Based on the different things respondents identified as sources of satisfaction and dissatisfaction in their work, Herzberg identified two themes characteristic of all jobs: (1) "maintenance" or "hygiene" factors and (2) "motivational" factors.

We all covet meaningful work. Victor Frankl, a philosopher, asserted that the pursuit for meaning is so great in human nature, people search for their purpose in life, even under the most extreme conditions.[103]

Currently, researchers have exhibited the significance of meaningfulness to be crucial to employees even more so than any other factor relating to employment, to include pay and rewards, promotion, or environmental conditions at work.[104] Byproducts of meaningful work include motivation, job satisfaction, commitment, and enhanced performance.

To the contrary, meaningless work can devastate employees and ultimately the organization. Most times, according to research, work that is meaningless is a consequence of treatment from managers and leaders toward employees.[105]

Bailey and Madden conducted a study of 135 people who worked in 10 different occupations. Interviews were conducted and, as a result, those interviewed noted several things that leaders did to generate a feeling of meaninglessness.[106] These items are ranked from most to least serious.

1. *Take your employees for granted.* Not recognizing employees for the work they do. Not acknowledged by managers or leaders for contributions.

2. *Treat people unfairly.* Being unfair or unequal treatment. Procedural injustices.

3. *Give people pointless work to do.* Required to do tasks that did not fit with job duties. This included bureaucratic tasks and completing forms not directly related to their primary job purpose.

4. *Over-ride people's better judgment.* Disempowerment or disenfranchisement over an employee's work and how it was done. In other words, where people believed their opinions and experience did not count, or that they could not have a voice in their work, they were more likely to feel work to be meaningless.

5. *Put people at risk of physical or emotional harm.* Unnecessary exposure to physical or emotional risk.

6. *Disconnect people from supportive relationships.* Feelings of isolation or marginalization at work through deliberate ostracism on the part of managers or through feeling disconnected from co-workers and teams. Camaraderie and relations with co-workers were viewed as important.

7. *Disconnect people from their values.* Disconnect between employees' personal values and those of their employer or work group. Tension between an organizational focus on the bottom line and the employee's focus on the quality or professionalism of work.[107]

The aforementioned items affect employees and their feeling of meaningful work. One should be aware that these items may appear and work individually or in combination and, where present, meaningfulness can be assumed to be significantly lower in the organization.[108]

The **motivation** theories discussed in this chapter fall into two very distinct categories: (1) content theories and (2) process theories. Content theories attempt to explain exactly *what* motivates people to act as they do in a given set of circumstances. **Process theories**, on the other hand, deal with *how* people are motivated. While none of these theories provides a complete explanation of motivation or the motivation process, they tend to supplement one another and provide the police administrator with a comprehensive perspective on this very complex **psychosocial** phenomenon.

Police administrators today must come to grips with one simple fact of life—they are dealing with a new breed of employee. Modern police personnel are more sophisticated than their predecessors. They are better educated, more participative, and much less resistant to change. They demand respect and expect to be treated as professionals. While money is still a magical word in the police subculture, it has a much different meaning than it did a generation ago. Salaries and fringe benefits have been improved to the point where more money, in and of itself, no longer serves as the primary motivator in many agencies while other agencies lag behind in salaries and benefits. Police officers demand more than just money. Most of them want to do meaningful work that meets their conscious and subconscious higher-order needs for growth, self-esteem, and a sense of fulfillment.

DISCUSSION TOPICS AND QUESTIONS

1. What do social scientists mean when they say that all human behavior is caused? Why is this important to the study of motivation?

2. Define the term *motive*. What are the basic steps in the motivation process, and what role do motives play in this process?

3. Explain the difference between content theory and process theory. Why is this distinction important? Are these theories mutually exclusive?

4. Explain Maslow's hierarchy of needs, and show how this theory has been factored into other major content theories. What contribution did the Hawthorne experiments make to Maslow's thinking?

5. What, from Herzberg's perspective, is the difference between a hygiene factor and a motivator? Give an example, and explain why poor hygiene leads to dissatisfaction but good hygiene does not serve as a motivator.

6. Discuss the basic assumptions on which the Theory X and Theory Y continuum is built. How does the theory's self-fulfilling prophecy influence job performance? Is Theory Y always superior to Theory X? Explain your answer.

7. What are the five elements in expectancy theory? What do expectancy theorists mean when they say that the three key elements interact multiplicatively to determine the intensity of motivation? Give an example.

8. How do people ordinarily adapt their job behavior to compensate for a perceived inequity in the way they are being treated vis-à-vis others in the workforce? What can police administrators do to control the equity dynamic in their work unit?

9. Identify the major strategies—beyond "more money"—that have developed for motivating police officers. What do you feel would be best for motivating police personnel? Why?

FOR FURTHER READING

Andrew J. Elliot and Carol S. Dweck, eds., *Handbook of Competence and Motivation* **(New York: The Guilford Press, 2007).**

This handbook is a comprehensive resource for researchers and theoreticians on the broad topic of achievement motivation. Its primary focus is on the concept of competence. There are 35 chapters in the text, and they consider a wide range of features from contextual influences to the self-regulatory processes. They view competence as an innate, pancultural, and psychological need from a number of disciplines to include social-psychological psychology, industrial-organizational psychology, and developmental perspectives. With its focus on competence, a foundation is laid for a rapprochement between the cognitive, rational world of the individual and one's self-protective, defensive tendencies. It is generally conceded that the handbook represents a signal contribution to the field of achievement motivation. The text takes the position that it is readily apparent that the role of competence is playing an influential role in achievement motivation.

Kenneth W. Thomas, *Intrinsic Motivation at Work— Building Energy and Commitment* **(San Francisco, CA: Berrett-Koehler Publishers, 2002).**

The author presents a broad conceptual framework for understanding intrinsic motivation and discusses why it is an essential component in today's working environment. Consideration is given to the need for intrinsic rewards as well as the need to move away from the rational–economic ways of the past. The writer lays a foundation for this new model of viewing rewards and introduces the concept of self-management in pursuit of purposes and clearly identifies the steps needed to become involved in self-management. The text reviews the four intrinsic rewards that come from and energize the self-management steps: a sense of meaningfulness, choice, competence, and progress. There is also a discussion of the leadership role needed to energize individuals on a work team as well as a presentation on how to enhance one's intrinsic rewards.

Stewart Liff, *Managing Government Employees* **(New York: AMACOM, 2007).**

The author believes that the overwhelming majority of individuals want to do a good job. At the same time, an organization needed a solid system and control if the agency is to be successful. This approach uses control variables positively, not punitively. With this perspective of employees, a manager can maintain a consistent set of core values. The author believes that the more you treat employees as valued, the more they will do a good job. It is also suggested that employees want to be part of a winning organization, but they must be given freedom not controlled, included not excluded, and provided with a meaningful role so they can contribute to the organization. The author also believes that a manager should always treat employees with respect, and this can be done by sending positive messages to people to include treating people ethically.

Charles B. Handy, *Understanding Organizations,* **4th ed. (East Rutherford, NJ: Penguin Global, 2005).**

In its 4th edition, this text has been tested and found to be an excellent addition to the literature on organizations. Charles Handy discusses numerous key concepts to include the following: culture, motivation, leadership, power, role playing, and groups. He believes that organizations are not simple charts, but in reality they can best be described as micro-societies. He reviews the tools needed to analyze and improves these micro-societies, which in turn would be useful to law enforcement administrators. The chapter on motivation is comprehensive and leaves the reader with a great deal of food for thought. Of additional usefulness are the chapters on power and leadership, and he does an excellent job of linking them to organizations in terms of their impact. The cultural concepts he reviews are useful in organizational analysis, and he very adequately describes their relationship to the organization during times of change.

ENDNOTES

1. Paul Whisenand, *Supervising Police Personnel: The Fifteen Responsibilities*, 6th ed. (Upper Saddle River, NJ: Prentice Hall, 2006), p. 134.
2. Ibid., p. 135.
3. Ibid.
4. Robert J. Sternberg, "Intelligence, Competence and Expertise," in Andrew J. Elliot and Carol S. Dweck, eds. *Handbook of Competence and Motivation* (New York: The Guilford Press, 2007), p. 19.
5. Michael L. Vasu, Debra W. Stewart, and G. David Carson, *Organizational Behavior and Public Management* (New York: Marcel Dekker, 1998), p. 61.
6. Gary Dressler, *Management: Principles and Practices for Tomorrow's Leaders* (Upper Saddle River, NJ: Prentice Hall, 1999), p. 284.
7. Kenneth W. Thomas, *Intrinsic Motivation at Work—Building Energy & Commitment* (San Francisco, CA: Berrett-Koehler, 2002), pp. 6–9.
8. Vasu, Stewart, and Carson, *Organizational Behavior and Public Management*, p. 57.
9. T. A. Judge and A. H. Church, "Job Satisfaction: Research and Practice," in C. L. Cooper and E. A. Locke, eds. *Industrial and Organizational Psychology: Linking Theory with Practice* (Oxford, UK: Blackwell, 2000), pp. 166–198.
10. Paula Brough and Rachael Frame, "Predicting Police Job Satisfaction and Turnover Intentions: The Role of Social Support and Police Organizational Variables," *New Zealand Journal of Psychology*, Vol. 33, No. 1 (2004), pp. 8–16.

11. Frank J. Landy, "An Opponent Process Theory of Job Satisfaction," *Journal of Applied Psychology*, Vol. 63, No. 5 (1978), pp. 533–547. Retrieved from http://dx.doi.org/10.1037/0021-9010.63.5.533.

12. J. Michael Syptak, David W. Marsland, and Deborah Ulmer, "Job Satisfaction: Putting Theory into Practice," *Family Practice Management*, Vol. 6, No. 9 (1999 October), pp. 26–30; Yvonne Brunetto and Rod Farr-Wharton, "The Commitment and Satisfaction of Lower-Ranked Police Officers: Lessons for Management," *Policing: An International Journal of Police Strategies & Management*, Vol. 26, No. 1 (2003), pp. 43–63. Retrieved from https://doi.org/10.1108/13639510310460297.

13. K. Moser, "Commitment in Organizations," *Psychologies*, Vol. 41, No. 4 (1997), pp. 160–170.

14. John E. Mathieu and Dennis M. Zajac, "A Review and Meta-Analysis of the Antecedents, Correlates and Consequences of Organizational Commitment," *Psychological Bulletin*, Vol. 108, No. 2 (1990), pp. 171–194.

15. Ibid.

16. Seble Getahun, Barbara Sims, and Don Hummer, "Job Satisfaction and Organizational Commitment among Probation and Parole Officers: A Case Study," *Professional Issues in Criminal Justice*, Vol. 3, No. 1 (2008), pp. 1–16; Richard Tewksbury and George E. Higgins, "Prison Staff and Work Stress: The Role of Organizational and Emotional Influences," *American Journal of Criminal Justice*, Vol. 30 (2006), pp. 247–266.

17. Charles W. Mueller and Sang-Wook Kim, "The Contented Female Worker: Still a Paradox?" *Advances in Group Processes*, Vol. 25, No. 1 (2008), pp. 17–49.

18. Yvonne Brunetto and Rod Farr-Wharton, "The Commitment and Satisfaction of Lower-Ranked Police Officers: Lessons for Management," *Policing: An International Journal of Police Strategies & Management*, Vol. 26, No. 1 (2003), pp. 43–63.

19. Ibid.

20. Yumin R. Wang, "Does Community Policing Motivate Officers at Work and How?," *International Journal of Police Science and Management*, Vol. 8, No. 1 (2005), pp. 67–77.

21. Mark A. Emmert and Walled A. Taher, "Public Sector Professionals: The Effects of Public Sector Jobs on Motivation, Job Satisfaction and Work Involvement," *American Review of Public Administration*, Vol. 22, No. 1 (1992), pp. 37–48.

22. Soonhee Kim, "Participative Management and Job Satisfaction: Lessons for Management Leadership," *Public Administration Review*, Vol. 62 (2002), pp. 231–241.

23. Kuo-Tsai Liou and Ronald C. Nyhan, "Dimensions of Organizational Commitment in the Public Sector: An Empirical Assessment," *Public Administration Quarterly*, Vol. 18, No. 1 (1994), pp. 99–118. Retrieved from http://www.jstor.org/stable/40861613.

24. Robert P. Vecchio, *Organizational Behavior: Core Concepts*, 4th ed. (Mason, OH: Thompson, 2003), p. 332.

25. Whisenand, *Supervising Police Personnel*, p. 153.

26. James L. Bowditch and Anthony F. Buono, *A Primer on Organizational Behavior*, 2nd ed. (New York: John Wiley & Sons, 2007), p. 69.

27. Lyman W. Porter, Edward E. Lawler, and J. Richard Hackman, *Behavior in Organizations*, 2nd ed. (New York: McGraw-Hill, 1986).

28. Dressler, *Management*, pp. 2–3.

29. Thomas, *Intrinsic Motivation at Work—Building Energy & Commitment*, p. 11.

30. Dressler, *Management*, p. 283.

31. Vasu, Stewart, and Carson, *Organizational Behavior and Public Management*, p. 59.

32. Dressler, *Management*, pp. 284–287.

33. F. M. Levine, ed., *Theoretical Readings in Motivation* (Chicago, IL: Rand McNally, 1975).

34. Paul M. Whisenand, *The Effective Police Manager* (Englewood Cliffs, NJ: Prentice Hall, 1981).

35. Stephen P. Robbins, *Essentials of Organizational Behavior*, 9th ed. (Upper Saddle River, NJ: Prentice Hall, 2007), p. 44.

36. Ibid.

37. Ronald G. Lynch, *The Police Manager* (Cincinnati, OH: Anderson, 1998), pp. 63–65.

38. Calvin J. Swank and James A. Cosner, *The Police Personnel System* (New York: Wiley, 1983).

39. Robbins, *Organizational Behavior*, p. 44.

40. Whisenand, *Supervising Police Personnel*, p. 137.

41. Nathan F. Iannone, Marvin P. Iannone, and Jeff Berstein, *Supervision of Police Personnel*, 7th ed. (Upper Saddle River, NJ: Prentice Hall, 2008), p. 16.

42. Robert B. Denhardt, Janet Vinzant Denhardt, and Maria P. Aristigueta, *Managing Human Behavior in Public & Nonprofit Organizations* (Thousand Oaks, CA: Sage, 2008), p. 157.

43. Ibid., p. 159.

44. Whisenand, *Supervising Police Personnel*, p. 136.

45. Ibid., p. 137.

46. Ramon J. Aldag and Loren W. Kuzuhara, *Organizational Behavior and Management: An Integrated Skills Approach* (Cincinnati, OH: Thomson, 2002), p. 233.

47. Bowditch and Buono, *Primer*, p. 73.

48. Aldag and Kuzuhara, *Organizational Behavior and Management*, p. 274.

49. Bowditch and Buono, *Primer*, p. 65.

50. Abraham H. Maslow, *Motivation and Personality* (New York: Harper & Row, 1970).

51. Lynch, *The Police Manager*, p. 66.

52. Frank G. Goble, *The Third Force* (New York: Pocket Books, 1970).

53. Whisenand, *Supervising Police Personnel*, p. 70.

54. Denhardt, Denhardt, and Aristigueta, *Managing Human Behavior*, p. 152.

55. Dressler, *Management*, p. 289.

56. Aldag and Kuzuhara, *Organizational Behavior and Management*, p. 235.

57. Ibid., p. 236.

58. Lynch, *The Police Manager*, p. 68.

59. Thomas J. Peters and Robert H. Waterman, *In Search of Excellence* (New York: Collins, 2004).

60. Aldag and Kuzuhara, *Organizational Behavior and Management*, p. 236.

61. Clayton P. Alderfer, *Existence, Relatedness, and Growth* (Homewood, IL: Richard D. Irwin, 1981).

62. Aldag and Kuzuhara, *Organizational Behavior and Management*, p. 237.

63. Linda K. Stroh, Gregory B. Northcraft, Margaret A. Neale, Mar Kern, and Chr Langlands, *Organizational Behavior: A Management Challenge*, 3rd ed. (Mahwah, NJ: Lawrence Erlbaum Associates, 2001), p. 66.

64. Aldag and Kuzuhara, *Organizational Behavior and Management*, pp. 237–238.

65. H. A. Murray, W. G. Barrett, W. C. Langer, C. D. Morgan, E. Homburger, and H. S. MeKell, *Explorations in Personality: A Clinical and Experimental Study* (New York: Oxford University Press, 1938), p. 164.

66. Ruth Kanfer and Phillip L. Ackerman, "Work Competence—A Person-Oriented Perspective," in Andrew J. Elliot and Carol S. Dweck, eds. *Handbook of Competence and Motivation* (New York: The Guilford Press, 2007), pp. 339–340.

67. David McClelland, *The Achieving Society* (Princeton, NJ: Van Nostrand, 1961).

68. Robbins, *Organizational Behavior*, p. 50.
69. Stroh, Northcraft, Neale, Kern, and Langlands, *Organizational Behavior*, p. 54.
70. Douglas M. McGregor, *The Human Side of Enterprise* (New York: McGraw-Hill, 1960).
71. Lynch, *The Police Manager*, p. 72.
72. McGregor, *Enterprise*.
73. Denhardt, Denhardt, and Aristigueta, *Managing Human Behavior*, p. 160.
74. Aldag and Kuzuhara, *Organizational Behavior and Management*, p. 99.
75. Frederick Herzberg, "One More Time: How Do You Motivate Employees?" in Walter E. Natemeyer, ed. *Classics of Organizational Behavior* (Oak Park, IL: Moore, 1978).
76. Ibid.
77. Whisenand, *Supervising Police Personnel*, p. 143.
78. Herzberg, "One More Time."
79. Lyman W. Porter and Raymond E. Miles, "Motivation and Management," in Joseph W. McGuire, ed. *Contemporary Management: Issues and Viewpoints* (Englewood Cliffs, NJ: Prentice Hall, 1974).
80. Whisenand, *Supervising Police Personnel*, pp. 144–148.
81. Aldag and Kuzuhara, *Organizational Behavior and Management*, p. 240.
82. Porter and Miles, "Motivation."
83. Dressler, *Management*, p. 300.
84. J. A. Wagner and J. R. Hollenbeck, *Management of Organizational Behavior*, 2nd ed. (Upper Saddle River, NJ: Prentice Hall, 1995).
85. Richard R. Johnson, "Patrol Officer Perceptions of Agency Rewards and Punishments: A Research Note," *Police Criminal Psychology*, Vol. 24 (2009), pp. 126–133.
86. Ibid.
87. Ibid.
88. Victor H. Vroom, *Work and Motivation* (New York: Wiley, 1964).
89. Aldag and Kuzuhara, *Organizational Behavior and Management*, p. 261.
90. Ibid., pp. 262–263.
91. J. Stacy Adams, "Inequity in Social Exchange," in L. Berkowicz, ed. *Advances in Experimental Social Psychology*, Vol. 2 (New York: Academic Press, 1982).
92. Aldag and Kuzuhara, *Organizational Behavior and Management*, p. 266.
93. Dressler, *Management*, p. 294.
94. Stroh, Northcraft, Neale, Kern, and Langlands, *Organizational Behavior*, p. 80.
95. Aldag and Kuzuhara, *Organizational Behavior and Management*.
96. Whisenand, *Supervising Police Personnel*, pp. 144–145.
97. Dressler, *Management*, p. 305.
98. Ibid., p. 308.
99. Stroh, Northcraft, Neale, Kern, and Langlands, *Organizational Behavior*, p. 314.
100. Dressler, *Management*, pp. 306–307.
101. Herzberg, "One More Time."
102. Stroh, Northcraft, Neale, Kern, and Langlands, *Organizational Behavior*, p. 312.
103. V. E. Frankl, *Man's Search for Meaning* (Boston: Beacon Press, 1959).
104. W. F. Cascio, "Changes in Workers, Work, and Organizations," in W. Borman, R. Klimoski, and D. Ilgen, eds. *Handbook of Psychology*, Vol. 12, Industrial and Organizational Psychology (New York: Wiley, 2003), pp. 401–422.
105. Catherine Bailey and Adrian Madden, "What Makes Work Meaningful—or Meaningless?" *MIT Sloan Management Review*, Vol. 57, No. 4 (2016). Retrieved from http://sro.sussex.ac.uk/61282/.
106. Ibid., p. 56.
107. Ibid.
108. Ibid.

6

STRESS IN ORGANIZATIONAL LIFE

Its Nature, Causes, and Control

Learning Objectives

1. Identify the types of stress unique to law enforcement.
2. List the types of psychological reactions possibly caused by stress.
3. Explain the relationship between stress and job performance.
4. Describe three elements of a stress reduction program.
5. Describe program services that an Employee Assistance Program can offer.
6. Explain how you can take charge of your life.

Key Terms

alarm stage	organizational stress
ambivalent	physiological symptoms
ascendant	psychological symptoms
behavioral	qualitative
behavioral symptoms	quantitative
disenchantment stage	role ambiguity
EAP	role conflict
eustress	role pressures
indifferent	stress reduction
malstress	stressor(s)
organizational	Type A

A significant part of the 20th century was designated by some as "the age of stress." In earlier days, stress was induced by catastrophes, beasts of prey, or attacks by hostile tribe, but more recently, there has been a shift to stress and angst resulting from personal conflict, events, and environmental situations.[1] Today, job insecurity, societal conflicts, and the dangers of working the street that were unknown a few years ago confront police officers. Additionally, the demands of just existing in our dynamic and changing society coupled with the anxiety generated by conflict contribute significantly to a modification of our way of life. Repentant and reoccurring demands placed on us, and the generalized expectations from our complex lifestyle, have placed unprecedented psychological pressures on many of us. Law enforcement is no exception. Depression, alcoholism, and escapist behavior are becoming more prevalent.[2] In recent decades, police organizations have become increasingly concerned with the need for greater flexibility, responsibility, and learning opportunities in the workplace. Dramatic changes have occurred, and those changes have far outpaced our understanding of their implications for work life quality. One result of those changes has been increased stress among both managerial leaders and operational employees. Even though stress has been of concern to progressive administrators, it is becoming increasingly accepted that there is a gap in knowledge between what we know about stress and what we should know. It is difficult to imagine a society without stress. It can have both positive and harmful effects. In fact, normal stress is always present. Individuals who are well adjusted seem to have no difficulty in handling the everyday stresses of life. In recent years, however, those everyday stresses have come to concern those who study its impact on organizational behavior.[3]

Stress is a part of organizational life and an inevitable consequence of the relationships between individuals, groups, and the organization as a whole. Stress is a part not only of work but also of life itself. It can contribute to the personal growth and development of each officer, as well as to his or her good mental health. In the police context, an officer who works at peak efficiency because of stress will be satisfied, have a feeling of well-being, and accept stress as part of the working environment. On the other hand, excessive and prolonged stress in the same situation can cause an officer to perform inadequately because of its negative impact on the body.[4]

CASE STUDY   Lieutenant Mark Catlett

The county of Symphony has 326,567 residents and is situated in the mountains of Southern Colorado. It is an area that is widely known for outdoor recreation and a lot of visitors are attracted to the area during the four seasons. Fishing, hunting, and cross-country skiing are the main attractions. The state has 38,987 acres of park in the county, and the two major lakes in the area and outdoor camping during the summer are a special enticement.

The sheriff's office is located in the town of Rapid, which is the county seat. It has a population of 41,249. The town is the commercial center for the county, and the state police have a local barracks. There are 165 deputy positions in the department and 48 percent are assigned to patrol, 16 percent to investigations, and the remainder perform jail and court functions. Currently, the department has 12 vacant deputy positions, and the department works diligently to recruit new personnel but has been unable to fill the allocation.

Lt. Catlett supervises the investigative bureau that investigates violent crimes such as homicides, armed robberies, rapes, and aggravated assaults. More recently, the unit has assumed primary responsibility for domestic violence cases and juvenile cases. During the last reportable year, the department investigated 6 murders, 32 rapes, and 39 robberies. It also investigated 203 aggravated assaults, and 213 domestic violence incidents. Additionally, there were 91 automobile theft cases and 31 incidents of arson. The investigative bureau is shorthanded, and many cases do not receive the attention they deserve. Catlett is 43 years of age and has spent the last six years in the investigative bureau. Until recently, he has thoroughly enjoyed his work, as reflected in his semiannual performance evaluations, which have always been excellent. He has always been able to roll with the punch, but in the current year, he has found himself becoming increasingly tense and out of sorts.

Police work is Lt. Parson's life, and prior to the last year, he had no difficulty confronting difficult situations, but recently a number of the domestic violence cases were exceptionally horrendous. Five of the cases involved the use of knifes, and the women involved were mutilated. In two other cases, children were involved, and they suffered serious injury from the father or a male companion. In every instance, alcohol or drugs were involved and precipitated the mayhem. The crime scenes were unnerving even to veteran investigators, and officers confided that they were having headaches, experienced sleep disorders, and had difficulty in concentrating. The lieutenant felt that if the early warnings of stress continued, it could lead to a level that could have a negative influence on job performance. Also, with the shortage of personnel, investigators were starting to react negatively to quantitative overload. Some of the officers pointed out that they just did not have the time to adequately investigate cases that had been assigned to them.

The sheriff's office does not have a viable **stress reduction** program and had never made an effort to set up an Employee Assistance Program (**EAP**). Lt. Catlett had received approval from his supervisor to consult with the sheriff regarding this problem.

What responsibility does the lieutenant have for reducing job stress? Explain. List a number of items that you want to discuss when you see the sheriff. Would you recommend a solution for the problem? Why or why not? What should the department have done when the deputies began to show signs of stress impairment? Take the position that law enforcement is unique and that job stress is inevitable? Explain in detail.

It is clear, then, that certain stresses are normal in life. What we have to do is learn how to live with stress. A leading expert suggests three realistic antidotes to the stress problem:[5]

1. Decide what your personal stress levels are.
2. Determine your life goals.
3. Learn how to be needed by others.

This chapter explores some of the ways managers can identify stress, determine its causes, and relieve it in the working environment. We will begin by defining stress, both as a general term and as it applies to organizations.

Definitions of Stress

Stress creates different problems for each manager. Some handle it very well; others have a great deal of difficulty coping with its effects. If a manager understands stress, he or she will have a better chance of handling it quickly and effectively. Stress in general is defined as *the physical and psychological condition that results from attempting to adapt to one's environment.*[6] This definition makes it clear that stress is partly a function of personality and partly a function of the environment. In order for any environmental **stressor** to become important to us, it must cause a feeling of uncertainty concerning its potential negative impact. If the uncertainty caused by a **stressor** inhibits our ability to do something, stress will be rather high. If the uncertainty is insignificant and winning is not in doubt, then we will feel little stress and will view the **stressor** as inconsequential. Another factor to consider is *how* important the **stressor** is. If the situation created by the **stressor** is not very important, then even if it creates uncertainty, there is little stress. In other situations, some officers cannot cope with constraints that can prevent them from goal achievement.[7] Stress does not need to have such negative results; looking at it from a positive viewpoint, we can speak of "good stress," or **eustress**.[8] The environmental **stressor** itself is neither good nor bad—all that matters is the importance of the constraints it imposes and how the individual responds to them. Whether that response to stress is positive or negative may depend on the view the individual takes toward various life events.

Our attitude is what determines whether a specific **stressor**, such as poorly defined departmental policies, is perceived as pleasant or unpleasant, as a challenge or a constraint. By taking a positive view of a **stressor**, we can convert negative stress into **eustress**.[9]

This positive approach to stress, if fostered and developed by management, can serve to integrate officers into the department. A certain degree of stress, resulting from the differing value systems of individuals and the organization, can serve, in most instances, as the basis for creating a goal-oriented organizational culture. Managers must accept the fact that different individuals respond to stress differently, so it is important to foster eustress and strive to eliminate those aspects of the work environment that create negative stress.

Organizational stress is defined as *the general, unconscious, and patterned mobilization of an individual's energy when confronted with any organizational or work demand.*[10] Officers experience stress when they are confronted with difficulties that are perceived as exceeding a response capacity, and consequences can be detrimental. When an officer is disciplined for violating a regulation (e.g., firing a weapon at a moving vehicle in violation of departmental policy) and is suspended for five days without pay, he or she will react to this **stressor** either positively or negatively, depending partly on departmental opinion. In some police organizations, the suspension could be a badge of honor for vigorously enforcing the law, while in others, it could be seen as the action of a potential troublemaker. Conversely, there is evidence showing that when an officer is promoted, he or she is likely to experience stress even though it is a positive event.[11]

Organizational stress can have effects both on individuals and on the organization itself. For the individual, organizational stress can result in problems such as alcohol or drug abuse, psychosomatic disorders, or rigidity of behavior. A person under constant and continual stress may exhibit anger, thoughtlessness, defensiveness, or irritability.[12] At the organizational level, stress effects that managers can see include dropping productivity, declining morale, late completion of tasks, an increase in sick leave, or other signs of employee discontent.

Stress Unique to Police Work

Behavioral scientists in recent years have expressed a special concern about the number and types of stressors unique to law enforcement. Emotionally unbalanced people must be dealt with, street people must be confronted every day, alcoholics must be handled repeatedly, domestic disputes must be settled, and child abusers must be arrested. On the other hand, there are positive aspects of the job (such as giving first aid or finding a lost child), but unfortunately, they do not occur as often as the negative encounters. Other negative stressors include boredom, danger, shift work, lack of public support, unfavorable court decisions, unfair administrative policies, and poor supervision. Such stressors impede the police task and present a very strong challenge to police managers.

Altogether, research to date supports the following conclusions. First, stress can be extremely costly to a police department. In many states, a police officer's heart attack will result in early disability retirement. For example, courts in the state of California have repeatedly upheld compensation claims regarding coronary heart disease as occupationally related. Second, stress is cumulative.[13] A single negative **stressor** may or may not have serious effects on health, but with each additional **stressor**, such consequences become more likely.[14]

Police departments have struggled for years with the problem of how to treat officers who have become stress victims. A logical first step toward developing an appropriate department policy would be to identify officers vulnerable to stress symptoms and job situations likely to generate stress. An assessment tool that has been used for such early-warning purposes for more than 40 years is the life stress inventory devised by T. H. Holmes and R. H. Rahe.[15] This instrument was based on a large number of medical case histories in which specific life experiences were correlated with adjustments required.

The Holmes–Rahe inventory assigns to each of 43 potentially stressful life events a number of points that measure roughly how much adjustment the event is likely to require of a person. Some of these events are positive (marriage, for example, rates 50 points), others negative (death of a spouse rates 100 points). Based on the case histories, Holmes and Rahe estimated that a person who "earns" 200 or more points during a single year has a 50 percent chance of a serious breakdown in health within two years. The risk increases dramatically when the points exceed 300: The potential for serious illness reaches 75–80 percent.

Of the 43 life events identified in the scale, six are job related.[16] They are shown in the following list:

Item	Points
Being fired	47
Retirement	45
Major readjustments such as reorganization	39
Major changes in responsibility such as promotions, demotions, or lateral transfer	29
Trouble with the boss	23
Major changes in working hours or conditions	20

Not everyone has supported the use of the standardized weights used in the Holmes–Rahe scale. One expert has suggested that life events should be classified as good or bad and rated on how much effect they had on the individual's life (none to great) and how much control the individual had over them (none to complete).

A police-specific stress inventory was devised by James D. Sewell, who constructed a questionnaire of 144 events experienced by police officers and then had officers rate each event on a stressfulness scale of 1–100.[17] The highest rating (88) was assigned to violent death of a partner in the line of duty, the lowest (13), to completion of a routine report.

Of the officers who participated in the development of the law enforcement critical life events scale, slightly over half (52.1%) said they had experienced at least one of eight stress-related illnesses. The ailment most frequently cited was digestive disturbances (25.4%); second most frequent was an increased use of alcohol (19.9%). The top 25 critical life events are listed hereafter:

1. Violent death of a partner in the line of duty
2. Dismissal
3. Taking a life in the line of duty
4. Shooting someone in the line of duty
5. Suicide of an officer who is a close friend

6. Violent death of another officer in the line of duty
7. Murder committed by a police officer
8. Duty-related violent injury (shooting)
9. Violent job-related injury of another officer
10. Suspension
11. Passed over for promotion
12. Pursuit of an armed suspect
13. Answering a call to a scene involving nonaccidental death of a child
14. Assignment away from home for a long period of time
15. Personal involvement in a shooting situation
16. Reduction in pay
17. Observing an act of police corruption
18. Accepting a bribe
19. Participating in an act of police corruption
20. Hostage situation resulting from aborted criminal activity
21. Response to a scene involving the accidental death of a child
22. Promotion of inexperienced/incompetent officer over you
23. Internal affairs investigation against self
24. Barricaded suspect
25. Hostage situation resulting from a domestic disturbance

While the Sewell instrument has received limited testing, it can help managers keep track of critical events in the professional lives of subordinates. When a subordinate experiences events from the Sewell and the Holmes and Rahe lists (such as divorce, marital separation, or the death of a spouse), a police manager should react by personally providing appropriate support or by seeing that a professional counselor gives support. As an example of the kinds of situations that can arise, Table 6–1 presents a number of critical life events with a combined stress score exceeding 300.

If all these events happened to an employee during one year, the employee's likelihood of having serious **psychological** or **physiological symptoms** within the next two years would increase dramatically.

Other studies have compared how male and female officers in a large law enforcement agency rated a number of potentially stressful events. Both sexes identified, as the most significant **stressors**, events that highlighted how important it is for managers to focus on human resources, equipment, and supervision. Interestingly, male officers expressed a greater concern about career issues, whereas female officers had their

Table 6–1
COMBINED STRESSFUL LIFE EVENTS OCCURRING IN ONE YEAR THAT REQUIRE A MANAGERIAL RESPONSE

Event	Value of Life Change Units
Divorce	73
Oral promotion review	57
Written promotional review	55
Changing work shifts	50
Reassignment/transfer	46
Unfair administrative policy	46
Total	**327**

Table 6–2
LAW ENFORCEMENT OFFICERS KILLED AND ASSAULTED

Year	Assaulted	Killed
1997	52,149	132
1998	60,673	142
1999	55,026	107
2000	58,398	135

Source: Bureau of the Census, *Statistical Abstracts of the United States, 2002*, 121st ed. (Washington, D.C.: USGPO, 2003), p. 323.

greatest concern with personal safety issues.[18] In another study, which looked at officers in two states, a researcher found that female officers did not generally experience any more work-related stress than white male officers in the same departments. At the same time, the study showed that women police officers' felt danger was an important **stressor**, in contrast to male officers who gave it a low rating.[19]

Danger in police work is real. Every year a sizeable number of law enforcement officers are victims of felonious assault or murder. Table 6–2 shows the number of officers assaulted and killed in five different years. Since 2000, there has been a significant decrease in the number of officers killed annually, and the numbers of assaults have remained about the same. Of special concern is the number of officers killed annually from accidents. Many of these officers are killed in automobile and motorcycle incidents followed by deaths from such things as cleaning a weapon, training exercises, or being accidentally shot in a cross-fire incident during police operations. Since the 1990s, there has been an increase in the accidentally killed category, but this may just be a reflection of the increased number of officers performing law enforcement activities.

Francis A. Graf presented some interesting observations in his study of a Canadian police department. Two-thirds of the officers he surveyed felt stressed by "never" or "almost never," having successfully handled problems created by work, by feeling that change was not conducted effectively, and by their lack of confidence in their ability to deal with work hassles.[20]

Transitory Stages of Life

Another police-focused stress study was carried out in 21 police organizations in western New York State during the early 1980s by John M. Violanti and James R. Marshall. They found that officers' perception of stress typically went through four stages in the course of a career set forth in Table 6–3. This result is different from those of earlier studies.[21]

Alarm Stage (0–5 Years).

The early period of an officer's career involves adjusting to the reality of the street. Life is usually entirely different from circumstances the officer experienced while attending the police academy. Actual police work is also entirely different from what is depicted by police shows on television. Faced with the demands of the job, the new officer has the tendency to question his or her personal ability to handle police work. All these factors cause stress, and stress increases over the five-year period. This is a normal pattern and reflects the adjustment that occurs when confronted with new and varying situations.

Disenchantment Stage (6–13 Years).

Stress increases further during this stage, as officers learn that not all crimes can be solved—that there is a limit to what can be done. Officers continue to question their ability to do good police work and control their personal destinies.

Personalization Stage (14–19 Years).

In this stage, there is a dramatic decrease in stress. An officer who has been working long enough does not find the demands of police work so great. There is also a lessening of

Table 6–3	
TRANSITORY STAGES OF A POLICE CAREER	
Alarm	(0–5 years)
Disenchantment	(6–13 years)
Personalization	(14–19 years)
Introspection	(20 years and over)

concern because the fear of failure loses its importance. This is a period when an officer becomes more concerned with personal goals.

Introspection Stage (20 Years and Over).

With the exception of concern for retirement, stress continues to decrease during this stage, which might even be described as a coasting period. An officer is usually more secure in the job by this time, and failure is of limited concern.

If the longitudinal model just described remains constant under additional scrutiny and replication in other departments, it will prove that police managers should focus **stress reduction** programs on officers in the early stages of their careers. If a department has a *field training officer* (FTO) program, it is an excellent place to educate new officers about the nature and types of stress they are likely to encounter during a career.

Stressors at Work

It is very important for police managers to recognize the varying sources of stress because the impact of stress on an officer can lead to poor health and even injury.[22] Increasingly, managers are becoming interested in stress and its potential impact on job behavior. Given our present level of knowledge, though, it is not yet possible to develop a comprehensive list of **stressors** and their possible consequences.

It is essential to remember that stress comes in two forms: *malstress* (bad or negative stress) and *eustress* (good or positive stress). One officer can view a specific stressor as being inimical, while another finds it rewarding and enjoyable. In law enforcement, some **stressors** are easily identified, but others are subtle, emerging only after careful consideration. The first thing for a manager to do in combating **malstress** is to identify the stressors peculiar to a specific task or assignment and work out a way of modifying the stressful working environment.[23] When one of the stressors identified is found to be of concern to managerial and operational personnel, it should be carefully analyzed to see if it is actually causing stress in the organization.[24]

The Job

The following sections address many of the work-related stressors peculiar to law enforcement. We will not attempt to discuss all potential **stressors**, but only those that are significant to police management.

Role Conflict and Ambiguity

Role conflict and ambiguity represent quite significant sources of stress for law enforcement personnel and problems for their agencies. *Role conflict* occurs when an officer is simultaneously subject to two (or more) sets of pressures, compliance with one of which would hinder or prevent compliance with the other.[25] The roles to be performed by a contemporary police department are certainly not cut-and-dried. Police officers have many responsibilities besides enforcing laws.

If we suggest that the primary function of law enforcement in a democracy is the prevention of crime, we need to define carefully whether we mean keeping crime from happening or merely keeping it from getting out of control. Typically, police are under pressure to do everything at once, and they have to balance roles like maintaining the peace with competing roles like identifying criminals and bringing them to justice. What is an officer to do when an immediate supervisor pushes him or her to spend more time handling inebriated individuals on the beat but higher-level management at the same time pushes him or her to provide more comprehensive documentation of daily events (a time-consuming process), and there is not enough time to do both?

These competing expectations of an officer are experienced by him or her as **role pressures**; significant, continuing **role pressures** constitute **role conflict**, which is generally recognized as a **stressor**.[26] The more conflict an officer is subjected to by inconsistent demands, the greater the potential for him or her to be affected by negative stress.[27]

Another type of role conflict occurs when a supervisor communicates incompatible or conflicting expectations. For example, a lieutenant in charge of a burglary unit expected an improvement in the conviction rate but found it difficult to accept investigators' needs to spend a great deal of time developing informants. The investigators viewed the lieutenant's two demands (more convictions, less developmental time) as diametrically opposed.

Personal role conflict occurs when there is a perceived incompatibility between the expectations of one individual and those of others in the organization. This is especially apparent in police work when an officer is pressured by other officers to conform to informal production standards (e.g., he or she may be urged not to disturb the status quo by writing more tickets than other officers or conducting more field interrogations during a shift).

All these forms of **role conflict** contribute to increased stress levels, greater levels of interpersonal tension, a lowering of job satisfaction, and decreased confidence in the organization. Interestingly, research has found that the higher up the chain of command conflicting messages originate, the greater is the job dissatisfaction among employees.[28]

Role ambiguity is the uncertainty resulting from a lack of clarity about tasks and the way the individual can perform them. Such a situation can be stressful for an officer, especially if a structured environment is very important for him or her. On the other hand, some officers readily accept and actually thrive on ambiguity. Managerial jobs in law enforcement are prone to ambiguity by virtue of the way law enforcement is organized. Line officers control information needed for decision-making, but police managers also need such information to perform their jobs. In an effort to control the discretion of officers, police organizations constantly generate rules and regulations aimed at making outcomes predictable and reducing ambiguity in the working relationships between leaders and officers.[29]

Such efforts to reduce role ambiguity can lead to significant problems at the operational level. In one department, for example, police administrators have forbidden use of the chokehold as a means of restraining someone but have never authorized an alternative means of restraint, telling line personnel only to "use restraint appropriate for the situation." Officers at the operational level consider this policy inadequate because it is open to conflicting interpretations, and the burden of interpreting it is left to them. **Role ambiguity** has been found to decrease satisfaction in general life as well as on the job. It lowers individual self-esteem and can lead to anxiety and feelings of resentment.

Work Overload and Underload

From time to time almost everyone has experienced work overload, but it is of special concern when it becomes chronic. It can cause an employee to feel helpless. Time constraints or deadlines can become such a burden to managers that the job seems to be out of control. Almost everyone has felt the stress caused by having too much to do, whether his or her job is dispatcher, sworn officer, clerk, or supervisor. Work overload can be **quantitative** or **qualitative**.[30] More familiar to most of us is *quantitative overload*. There is just too much to do. It is difficult for an investigator to handle a caseload of 123 residential burglaries. Even when cases are prioritized in terms of solvability, there is only so much time that can be devoted to investigating each case.

Qualitative *overload* is best described as a situation in which employees feel they are not competent enough to perform certain tasks or that performance standards are unrealistic and too high.[31] For example, this type of overload can appear when a highly qualified line officer is promoted to a supervisory management position. Though operationally competent, this person does not have the capacity to shift gears and accomplish tasks through the efforts of others.

Finally, work overload can be a **stressor** when a manager has too many distinct types of tasks to perform. If one must constantly shift from one type of task to the next, the adjustment can be frustrating, and this at some point becomes a **stressor**. Such overloads occur quite often at the middle-management level when the incumbent of a position has no sense of the real responsibilities of the job or when he or she fails to delegate tasks to subordinates.[32]

The other side of the coin is seen when there is too little work to do and boredom sets in, especially when the work underload occurs over an extended period.[33] In many police departments, officers working the midnight shift find that the infrequency of calls for service can make the hours drag on endlessly.

Either work overload or work underload can make employees feel frustrated and anxious about the working environment. Work can become a burden rather than a rewarding experience. This detracts from the quality of working life, a concept which, as one expert has pointed out, has received increasing attention in recent years.[34]

Use of Deadly Force

In an earlier part of this chapter, danger as a component of police work was discussed. We now consider the *use of deadly force*. Our knowledge of shootings by police officers is irregular and sporadic. Killings and assaults *against* police officers in the United States are documented annually in the Uniform Crime Reports, but it is another story when one attempts to determine how many civilian deaths result from legal intervention. The U.S. Public Health Service is the only agency that addresses this matter. They take their data from Standard Death Certificates, but some researchers feel that this source is suspect because of uneven quality in the medical reports and errors in recording the information. Some experts have concluded that civilian deaths by legal intervention are underreported by 50 percent. In 2013, 516 "deaths by legal intervention" were recorded; if the estimate of the experts is correct, the police actually killed some 1030 civilians, as compared to 27 officers being feloniously killed while on-duty during the same year.[35]. This is a ratio of about 1:38.[36]

There are approximately 17,876 state, county, and local police agencies in the United States, with some 836,787 full-time sworn police personnel who are confronted with an untold number of violent situations every day. When these statistics are compared to the estimates of killings by police officers, it is evident that very few police officers are involved in civilian deaths by legal intervention. The evidence also suggests that the majority of police shootings occur in large cities; hence, the vast majority of officers, especially in smaller communities, are never involved in a police shooting.[37]

When a police shooting does occur, there are serious legal and psychological implications. In addition to it being stressful for officers to be ever vigilant and be anticipatory of potential deadly force situations, at no time in our history has there been as much scrutiny related to police use of force and deadly force encounters as there is today. Not only are there comprehensive examinations by administrators, but also citizens, media outlets, advocacy groups, and professional organizations. These increases in analyses have been prompted by questionable use of force incidents and technological advances such as body worn cameras. There are also proposed changes for increasing standards relating to deadly force encounters. For example, the Police Executive Research Forum is currently urging policing agencies to augment current reasonableness standards established by the Supreme Court in the case of *Graham v. Conner*[38] and go beyond to implement best policies, practices, and training which provide more specific advice to officers on how to carry out the legal standard.[39]

After a deadly force encounter, the officer can suffer from post-shooting trauma, be sanctioned by the department, and/or be subjected to legal consequences and spend an inordinate amount of time before a grand jury or in court defending the action. Police leaders should be fully aware of the need to give officers who have been involved in a shooting the opportunity to deal with the emotional consequences of their actions. It is in the best interests of the department, the community, and the officer to have a psychological debriefing, allowing an officer to express feelings about the incident, to become involved in peer counseling, and counseling from a departmental psychologist. Without question every officer should receive maximum support from EAPs. Such measures have proven successful in reducing malstress.

Physical and Environmental Factors

Police officers can suffer from stress when their working environment extends beyond a reasonable comfort zone. Potential stress factors include temperature, humidity, sunlight, weather, noise, air pollution, carbon monoxide from vehicles, electromagnetic sources, lead from firearms, drug contamination, HIV, radiation, biological, and chemical. For example, a reasonable temperature comfort zone ranges from 65° to 80°F. In one police department in the central valley of California, the police cars were not air-conditioned, even though summer temperatures often exceeded 100°F.

The chief of police in this valley town had a vehicular temperature study conducted. On an average summer day, in a vehicle without air-conditioning, the temperature was 135°F. The city manager refused to purchase air-conditioned vehicles for the department until it was pointed out to him that once resale prices were taken into account, the cost difference between air-conditioned cars and non-air-conditioned ones was negligible. In another community, three-fourths of the patrol vehicles had been driven more than 100,000 miles and were in a general state of disrepair. Only through political pressure generated by the police union did the governing body establish a replacement and repair policy for police vehicles. In both instances, morale improved dramatically.

Shift Work

Law enforcement agencies are in business around the clock and expected to be available every day. The public demands unlimited availability of their unique services. As a result, officers work all hours of the day and night, every day including holidays. This work schedule is a significant source of occupational stress.

Shift work is not normal. The "rotating shift" schedule is very taxing on an officer's life. Our bodies are adjusted on what is called "circadian schedules," that is, repetitive daily cycles. Our bodies like to have a regular eating time, sleeping time, waking time, and so forth. An officer doing shift work never gets a chance to stay on a schedule. This upsets his or her physical and mental balance in life. The changing work schedule also upsets the routine patterns that are needed in healthy marriage and family development. Strong marital and family development is based on rituals, such as dinners together, "inside jokes," and repeated activities. The rotating shift worker has less chance to develop such rituals, and his relationships suffer. This predisposes the officer's family to potential problems ranging from children acting out to divorces.[40]

Police shift work has an especially adverse impact on families. Mothers and fathers may not be available during school hours and often miss important family functions (birthdays, holidays, and graduations) due to their work schedules.[41] Night and rotating shift schedules also raise health and safety issues. They can lead to sleep disorders and gastrointestinal ailments and are related to emotional disturbances and increased risk of occupational injury.[42] Research evidence indicates that the stressful impact of shift work equally affects both male and female officers.[43] In an effort to reduce officer stress and improve officer wellness, many agencies have assessed flexible hours or alternate shift schedules such as 12-hour, 10-hour, or hybrid shifts.

Management Practices

Police leaders at every level may create situations leading to stress for themselves as well as for their employees.[44] A leader in an organization is in a position to exert a tremendous amount of influence on how tasks are accomplished and the methods used to attain goals.[45] Employee stress and well-being are integrally tied to the conduct and practices of police leaders. It is unfortunate but true that some management practices create stress for police employees. An example is micro-management wherein an unbelievable amount of

> **Table 6–4**
> **TWELVE TIPS FOR REDUCING EMPLOYEE STRESS**
>
> 1. Ensure effective two-way communications with employees.
>
> 2. Be fair and honest in communications with personnel and confirm that they understand your expectations.
>
> 3. Act as a safety valve to allow employees to vent and protect them from others in the chain of command.
>
> 4. Be involved in employee assignments and be available for guidance.
>
> 5. Project a positive attitude.
>
> 6. Lighten up.
>
> 7. Accept the responsibility of both leadership and management.
>
> 8. Learn to balance home, office, and personal stress.
>
> 9. Foster a healthy working environment.
>
> 10. Learn to build and encourage employee's self-esteem.
>
> 11. Plan effectively.
>
> 12. Display organizational loyalty and maintain your own counsel.
>
> *Source:* James D. Sewell, "Dealing with Employee Stress: How Managers Can Help—or Hinder—Their Personnel," *FBI Law Enforcement Bulletin*, Vol. 75, No. 7 (2006), pp. 1–6.

stress is placed on structuring and controlling to such an extent that operational efforts are stymied and officers are never allowed to develop the skills needed to work independently and grow professionally. Effective leaders soon learn that there must be a balance between professional demands, family responsibilities, and personal issues. To be truly effective as a leader, James D. Swell has created 12 tips for managers that can be used to reduce employee stress (see Table 6–4).

Leadership problems occur at every level in organizations, and one of these—dealing with supervisors who have authoritarian leadership styles—is difficult for many people. It generally causes tensions and pressures beyond the control of the individual. Some subordinates respond by accepting this type of supervision and suppressing the resulting stress and hostility. Others object to such arbitrary leadership behavior by becoming hostile. The former responses, over a period of time, will (in all probability) result in undesirable physiological changes; the latter responses will serve to release some tension but at the same time create a stressful environment.[46]

Certainly, some employees function effectively under an authoritarian leadership style, but today most officers respond more readily to expert and referent power than to legitimate and positional power (see Chapter 10 for an extended discussion of power).

CASE STUDY Chief Wesley Howard

Chief Howard is in his third term in his elected position in the City of Hollow. His predecessor supported him when he ran for the position of chief of police, and this was a major factor in his election that had light-hearted opposition. This police department is one of the few where the head of the department is an elected position. His entire career had been with the police department, and in those 28 years, he worked in every division. Howard is 51 years old, and the father of three grown children and has been married since he was 19. Two of his boys are currently attending college, and the third will graduate from high school next year. Howard entered the police department as soon as he was eligible, and it fulfilled a desire to work in law enforcement. It was the only career he ever wanted. His initial assignment was to work undercover in the narcotics detail, and he earned a reputation as a skilled investigator. Additionally, he has previous experience in patrol and support services. He had also been the head of the departmental SWAT team, and he was supported by numerous members of the department when he ran for office.

The city of Hollow is a community with a population of 395,671 and has a police force with 723 sworn positions. The city's major population groups consist of Asians, 15.2; black, 35.7; white, 31.8; and Hispanic, 21.6 percent. A number of residential buildings in the community are marginal, and 19.1 percent of its residents are

(continued)

below the poverty level, and just under one-third of the residents earn less than $24,999 annually. The crime rate for a city its size is higher than one would hope, and in the last reportable year, there were 127 homicides, which had increased from 83 some four years earlier. The homicide unit of the Investigative Division was staffed by a lieutenant and 11 investigators, and the workload was overwhelming. In the last year, this unit handled not only homicides but also 744 unexplained/suspicious death cases, 11 officer-involved shootings, and 2 in-custody deaths. In addition, the unit investigated 17 attempted murder cases and, in its efforts, solved 47 homicides. The police department is understaffed by 37 positions, and a statewide recruiting effort has proven to be less than successful. The overtime budget for the Homicide Unit has proven to be almost unmanageable. Up to now, the city has been able to fund overtime for the investigator, but with revenue down, it is becoming apparent that the budgetary shortcoming will cause the department to become more selective in what cases will be fully investigated. The rest of the department is hamstrung, because of the lack of funds, and Uniformed Services

officers are working 12-hour shifts in an effort to meet the demands for police services. Morale is low, and fewer arrests are being made for serious crimes. At the same time, officers are seizing fewer weapons and frisking fewer gang members. The officers are putting forth a strong performance effort, but there is just too much to do with too few people. Longer shifts and overtime are starting to take their toll. A number of officers are exhibiting signs of stress, and the departmental psychologist is inundated with requests for service. At the same time, the city manager is calling for a significant cut in the police department's budget, with one specific recommendation—the elimination of the department's psychological support contract.

If you were Chief Howard, how would you deal with this issue? In other words, is there a real justification for employing a psychologist to provide counseling services, or should officers be expected to handle their own personal problems? Discuss in detail. If you support the need for psychological service, how would you justify this position? Why or why not? Outline a paper supporting your position.

Leadership studies to date have not supported any one style as being best in terms of creating the least amount of stress. Therefore, we must assume that a style of leadership which might be stressful for one officer to work under might not be stressful for another.[47]

There is some indication that some present-day police leaders are not effective at providing performance feedback (see Chapter 14). This is especially true when it is presented in a highly authoritarian manner: Employees tend to respond negatively regardless of the content. For the most part, this type of feedback emphasizes one-way communication and is stress inducing. The manager has a far better chance of reducing stress if he or she creates an atmosphere that fosters two-way communication.[48]

If there is anything characteristic of American law enforcement, it is its bureaucratic nature and its extreme reliance on rules and regulations. Carefully delineated policies are a standard feature of police departments. Rules and regulations outline the authority, responsibility, and duties of every individual in a department. In many instances, it seems there is a policy on everything. If something occurs that puts a department in a bad light, the immediate response, in many agencies, is to create a rule that will deal with the situation. One police department has six manuals covering everything from how to operate a radio to how to give an informant a control number. In another instance, the New York City Police Department in its effort to deal with officer misbehavior has 370 classifications for misconduct by officers that range from food stamp fraud to frequenting an illegal operation.

Some policies are just restatements of state law; others are precise and technical, while still others prove to be moral statements. Some policies are only a few sentences long; others ramble on for pages. Of the many police departments in the United States, one can find some agencies with carefully delineated policies and others where it is almost impossible to find written policies.

Agency policies, when they exist, should be written so that they become firm commitments between the agency and its personnel. If correctly written, policies promote uniformity and continuity. A good policy is one that includes enough detail to ensure that desired results are attained but at the same time does not unnecessarily restrict the exercise of discretion.

Rules, regulations, and policies should be developed jointly between management and agency personnel through formal and informal meetings. Guidance documents created with the participation of those who will be responsible for following them have a much better chance of successful implementation. Jointly developed policy can serve as a stress reducer. It also fosters creative decision-making because it acknowledges the need for discretion. Rules and regulations can become **stressors** when they are exceedingly detailed and circumscribe discretion to the extent that agency personnel feel stifled and suppressed. A leader should monitor supervised employees in order to identify potential sources of stressors and then work to minimize them.[49]

Change is another **organizational** stressor. In recent years, police have been asked to implement new philosophies and programs such as community policing, problem-solving policing, and Compstat.[50] The aftermath of 9/11 has put police in America on the front lines in the battle against terrorism and the effort to provide homeland security.[51]

Consequences of Workplace Stressors

The President's Task Force on 21st Century Policing identified officer wellness and safety as being a critical concern for police organizations, leaders, managers, and officers. The task force focused on many issues that affect officers' physical, mental, and emotional health.[52]

The quest for officers' physical, mental, and emotional health should permeate the culture of law enforcement and, more specifically, its practices, procedures, requirements, attitudes, and behaviors.[53] A work environment that is void of respect, support, and fair treatment causes stressors for officers. Of special concern is the lack of respect by leaders, managers, and supervisors.

Studies indicate that workplace stressors are associated with increased psychological problems for police officers such as conflict with co-workers and romantic partners, in addition to issues related to self-esteem.[54] Methods police officers utilize to cope with stress are usually unhealthy and may lead to actions linked with increased risks of negative outcomes.[55] A study examining police stress and the management of it was conducted with 201 officers from agencies with under 100 sworn personnel. Officers who worked many hours per week reported stress and, most often, a resulting deep-seated anger that they utilized as a way to deal with the stress.[56]

Another study of 232 officers utilized four types of stressors: (1) Critical Incidents, (2) Department Politics, (3) Daily Hassles, and (4) Work–Home Conflicts.[57] Strong family support was found to be associated with weaker political stressors and stronger police support with weaker Work–Home conflict. Again, officers who worked many weekly hours reported stronger Work–Home conflicts. Also, of interest is that married officers absorbed more stress from critical incidents than did unmarried officers.[58] Finally, Daily Hassles were found to be the police stressor most often accompanied by negative psychological outcomes such as anger, diminished self-esteem, and more romantic partner aggression.

EAPs (discussed later in this chapter) could be employed to identify and mitigate some of the officer stressors in the workplace. By addressing this complex body of issues, EAPs can prevent and reduce police officer stressors and thereby improve officers' mental and emotional health.

External Factors

In recent years, increasing attention has been given to the relationship between law enforcement and the community. The police leaders of tomorrow will have to meet the challenges of unprecedented societal transformations. Numerous communities are changing rapidly because of urbanization, technological advancement, population explosion, changing morality, and transient lifestyles. Approximately 18 percent of the populations are between 5 and 17 years of age, and the vast majority of people live in metropolitan areas. At the same time, the nation is graying in as much some 12.6 percent are 65 or older. These factors will place increasing demands on the police, and their role will have to be increasingly flexible. Laws will have to be enforced in such a way as to ensure that a reasonable balance is maintained between collective needs and individual rights.[59]

Community relations have been a continuing problem in many police departments. For example, in one large agency study, community relations was ranked fourth as an external stress inducer. Slightly more than one-third of the officers studied cited community conflict as contributing to stress.[60] In a more recent study of women police officers, a negative public attitude was cited as a source of stress. As the police are called on to perform different and more numerous tasks and the public increase its scrutiny of police activities, we can speculate that a negative community attitude will continue to prevail in many towns and cities. However, it can be speculated that police departments that adopt a community problem-solving orientation may find negative relations with citizens reduced considerably.

The criminal justice system (especially the courts) is a significant **stressor** for police officers. Many officers feel that courts are too lenient and that judges show a greater consideration toward the defendant than the community does. They also see the courts demonstrating a lack of regard and interest when court appearances are scheduled. Consideration is never given to the shift an officer works in or an officer's days off that can conflict with a court appearance.

The police express a similar concern for defense attorneys, public defenders, and the tactics used in court. These concerns are well demonstrated when a defense attorney diligently shops around in order to find a "lenient" judge or plays the postponement game to the hilt in an effort to delay the trial as much as possible. Another tactic of many public defenders is to attempt to discredit officers' testimony and actually do everything possible to put the officers on trial rather than the defendant.[61]

Recent research supports the proposition that the impact of stress on an employee's behavior definitely reflects that person's personality traits, such as tolerance for ambiguity, extroversion, dogmatism, and rigidity.[62] Every person has distinct personality and **behavioral** traits that are modified and influenced by such variables as gender, age, ethnic origin, and family. The overall life expectancy for women is almost eight years longer than men. Some of this difference might be explained genetically, but researchers believe that much is attributable to men smoking more, consuming more alcohol, and being more apt to exhibit Type A behavior—all typical reactions to stress. As more women enter law enforcement, it seems likely that they will experience and react to stress much as their male counterparts do.[63] In one study, it was found that levels of work anxiety were the same for both sexes. However, as we mentioned, women found danger to be a more important **stressor** than did male police officers. On the other hand, female officers intervened more often when infractions occurred, possibly because they were more cynical about human behavior. Such interventions (in spite of their greater concern for danger and lesser degree of self-confidence) suggest that policewomen try harder than men.[64]

In another study, women present a different perspective. Out of 19 different **stressors**, the most common one centered on their status as women. Even after women were in the department for six years, male officers did not fully accept them. The actions of the male officers definitely increased the stress level of the female officers as they were ignored, harassed, watched, gossiped about, and viewed as sex objects.[65]

As women assume more managerial positions in law enforcement, their behavior seems likely to parallel that of women managers in business, that is, they will smoke more and increase their use of alcohol, tranquilizers, antidepressants, and sleeping pills—all in reaction to the new **stressors** they will be facing.

With affirmative action programs and a broadening recruitment base in many agencies, members of minority groups are entering the managerial ranks and being affected by occupational stress as a result. In some instances, stress is a reaction to racial prejudice. Carried to its extreme, a minority manager can begin to feel inadequate, develop a sense of inferiority, or experience a loss of self-esteem.[66] One study found that African American police officers tended to rely more on colleagues from other minorities than did Caucasian officers. They also expressed their feelings less often than whites did in an effort to get others to like them. Women officers, the study revealed, tended to cope with stress by using escape mechanisms such as exercise, social activities, peer groups, and written records.[67]

When minority managers are few in number, their access to the "informal organization" is difficult, which limits their ability to obtain information and contacts they may need in order to do their job effectively. In some agencies, even the formal organization does not provide them the support needed for success. This is currently the case in one large department, which is under court order to promote a certain percentage of minority officers to managerial positions. These managers are isolated from the formal organization and denied access to the informal organization. In some instances, their exclusion impairs their ability to perform at an acceptable level. Special training and support are needed if all new managers are to succeed. This is especially pertinent when the new manager is a member of a minority group.[68]

Many groups in an organization try to influence their members, using forms of pressure that can become sources of stress and tension. (For a detailed discussion of groups and their characteristics, see Chapter 12.) Members of a team or a work shift exert pressure on each other in order to bring about certain kinds of behavior. Informal groups can resist the attainment of departmental objectives, reduce individual freedom, and force members to conform to production standards. On the other hand, managers who are knowledgeable enough to understand thoroughly how a group behaves can use the group to build individual members' self-confidence, to provide a channel for self-expression, and to reduce tension within the organization.[69]

Stressors related to the availability or no availability of career development opportunities are common in local law enforcement agencies. One nationwide survey discovered that only 6 percent of all police personnel held administrative positions. This means that most police officers will be very fortunate to attain the rank of corporal or sergeant and that they have only an extremely limited chance of achieving a rank beyond the supervisory management level.[70] Career variables become **organizational stressors** to an individual when they cause frustration or anxiety. Just the process of pursuing a promotion can prove to be stressful. Officers have to compete for promotion by taking tests, written and/or oral; candidates can fail outright or pass but be ranked so low as not to be promoted. As officers grow older and remain un-promoted, dissatisfaction with the job increases.[71]

Management training is a necessary function of human resource management. Its lack of availability can contribute to stress felt by managers. When an organization promotes an officer to a managerial position, it has an obligation to provide the training, skill, and knowledge he or she needs in order to achieve organizational goals. Of special need is to provide training in stress management. The law enforcement profession is not uniquely subject to occupational stress, but the services it provides to the public are so important that any obstacles to effectiveness—such as stress among employees and managers— need to be dealt with promptly and energetically. As we have seen, one of the causes of stress is exclusion of employees from the decision-making process. Additional, negative impact on an organization can occur for a number of reasons to include the following:[72]

1. Stress caused by low job satisfaction
2. Not being allowed to utilize skills/knowledge
3. Poor working relationship with supervisors/managers
4. Conflicting relationship with peers
5. Few promotional opportunities
6. Low self-esteem

Community policing, which emphasizes problem solving by line officers, is one way management can actively solicit officer participation.[73]

A decentralization of tactical decision-making down to the beat level does not imply abdication of executive obligations and functions. It means that first-line supervisors assume greater managerial responsibilities and make every effort to tap the wisdom and experience of line officers. The chief executive, too, must become personally involved in the participative management process from its inception through implementation and subsequent assessment.

Symptoms of Stress

Organizationally induced malstress (bad stress) can be tremendously important to both the individual and the organization. Reactions to stress can be divided into three categories—physiological, **behavioral**, and psychological—which will be discussed later in this chapter. Reactions to stress also vary from individual to individual; as a way of understanding these differences, we will divide the employees of a typical police department into three types based on their career attitudes ("**ascendant**," "**indifferent**," or "**ambivalent**") and look at how stress affects each type.

Ascendant

The term *ascendant* describes employees who are "on the fast track"; their sole purpose is to move through the ranks as fast as possible. Even if it takes playing musical chairs to accomplish it, ascendant individuals will strive to attain as much rank as soon as possible and then apply for every vacancy occurring in other agencies, with the goal of attaining the rank of chief (generally in a small department) and then moving up to a larger agency.

Ascendant managers relate positively to the job and the department, react favorably to feedback from superiors, and above all are goal oriented. Such individuals are generally known as **Type A** persons. Work is more important than anything else to them; social and family matters generally take second or third place. Ascendant managers vigorously pursue advanced academic degrees and, in order to become as eligible as possible for promotion to the top, seek to attend the Administrative Officers Course of the Southern Police Institute at the University of Louisville.

Stress is of little consequence to ascendant individuals. In fact, they accept it as an important part of their managerial aspirations—something to thrive on. However, not everyone can make it to the top; those who fall by the wayside suffer extensively from job stress.[74]

Indifferent

The **indifferent** individual typifies most of the regular members of a police organization. Indifferent individuals do not actively seek to attain rank in the organization, and they view power as an interest of others. They perceive change as threatening; their real goal is to maintain the status quo. In some instances, **indifferent** officers react to malstress by leaving the organization, either actually or symbolically. Even if they do not actually leave, they escape mentally by daydreaming or just putting in their time as indicated in Table 6–5.

Table 6–5
ATTITUDES TOWARD WORK

Ascendant

Feels strong task orientation

Identifies with the department

Treats work as primary

Thrives on stress

Readily accepts feedback from superiors

Problems can be solved by working harder

Indifferent

Never seeks power

Identifies with the informal organization

Obtains support from work groups

Is active in police unions

Accepts change with reluctance

Gravitates toward off-the-job satisfaction

Feels an inability to control own destiny

Ambivalent

Resists new rules and regulations

Avoids commitment to the department

Does not like to make decisions

Is frustrated by the inability to do the job well

Eventually develops lessened commitment to the department

Indifferent officers are apt to seek protection from management decisions by joining and becoming active in a police association or union. They view peers as a primary support group, and the department's informal organization is strengthened by their participation. Both peers and the informal organization help **indifferent** officers deal with **organizational** stressors.

Ambivalent

The third type of officers is appropriately described as **ambivalent**. These individuals take the **alarm stage** of police service (0–5 years) in stride, but when **the disenchantment stage** (6–13 years) starts, they become very frustrated with their jobs. As they begin to feel they cannot control their destiny, they become anxious about work. Things are not as clear cut as they once were—the shadow of doubt enters the picture. Over a period, such individuals become out of step with the organization, and if they attain the level of first-line supervisor, it is usually their highest rank. These individuals find it increasingly difficult to make any decision other than routine ones, and they eventually become less committed to the department. Anxiety about their jobs can create stress that results in one or more **behavioral** changes.

Physiological Symptoms

A great deal of the early research on stress concentrated on physiological symptoms; as noted by two experts, Leonard Territo and James D. Sewell,[75] they are still of importance. A pioneer in stress research, Hans Selye, set forth a three-stage process of stress damage, which he called the *general adaptation syndrome (GAS)*:[76]

1. Alarm reaction
2. Resistance
3. Exhaustion

The initial stage is one of mobilization, as the body responds to a stress-inducing situation. As that first stage subsides, the resistance stage begins, and the body increases its reaction to the threat. The battle for survival begins. When resistance becomes ineffective, the final stage, exhaustion, takes over; adaptive energy lessens and lessens. Eventually the individual dies.

Studies of physiological reactions to stress have centered on the cardiovascular system, with a special emphasis on heart attacks. This is especially applicable in law enforcement. Many cardiovascular irregularities have been determined by several different state court systems to be job related and a reason for retiring on disability. In some police departments, retirement on disability (with various medical reasons) appears to be quite easy for officers to be granted; in others, it is very difficult. In one department with more than 1,000 employees, 91 percent of officers retiring were granted a disability retirement. This seems to make a mockery of the intent and purpose of the disability retirement system. One police executive was given a disability retirement because of a bad back, but in fact he was an avid hunter who had no difficulty carrying deer carcasses great distances or performing house remodeling activities requiring him to lift very heavy objects.

By way of contrast, another police chief was in his attic moving some items and thought his wife had turned the lights off by accident. He soon discovered, however, that he was blind from a stroke. Even though he later recovered part of his eyesight, he was unable to continue work. The city vigorously fought his efforts to receive disability retirement, but a court eventually ruled in his favor.

Stress-induced **physiological symptoms** vary considerably. Some of them appear in Table 6–6 as early warning signs of job stress; they also include such maladies as ulcers, backaches, and changes in metabolism.[77] The link between any specific **stressor** and particular **physiological symptoms** is not clear. Various studies have correlated the incidence of certain risk factors with specific occupations but such statistical correlations have been unable to establish causation for specific symptoms. In time, researchers may be able to measure causal relationships in more detail.[78] Particularly important for police leaders to understand are the **behavioral** and psychological consequences of stress, which we discuss next.

Table 6–6
EARLY WARNING SIGNS OF JOB STRESS

Headaches	Upset stomach
Sleep disorders	Job dissatisfaction
Difficulty in concentrating	Low morale
Short temper	

Source: NIOSH Publication No. 99–101, *Stress at Work* (Cincinnati: National Institute for Occupational Safety and Health, Work Group, 1999), p. 8.

Behavioral Symptoms

An individual who is experiencing a high level of stress (too intense and too frequent) and is unable to find a suitable outlet may respond by exhibiting behavioral symptoms that can affect performance on the job.[79] Further research is needed in this area. It seems reasonable to assume that stress (with its impact on performance) results from an interaction between the individual's personality, the task being performed, and the working environment.

The relationship between stress and performance has been clearly identified by those researching stress. In this relationship, it can readily be seen that as one moves from a low to a moderate level of stress, productivity increases. At a very low level of stress, employees may not be challenged to perform effectively. As stress increases, most employees are stimulated to perform better and more rapidly. An optimal level of stress exists for each situation and for each individual. Poor performance is the result either when excessive stress drives individuals to the point of agitation or when demands are unrealistic.[80]

Even moderate levels of stress can have a negative influence on employee performance if the stress is so persistent and constant that it reduces the employee's ability to deal with it constructively. Such cumulative effects are especially noticeable in the case of officers assigned to vice or narcotics work, so police administrators have learned to rotate personnel assigned to such units after two or three years.

Behavioral symptoms related to rising levels of stress include an increased use of tobacco products, alcohol abuse, drug abuse, appetite disorders, and (possibly) involvement in accidents. Of special interest are research indications that patrol officers suffer from a higher level of fatigue impairment than the general population and that this fatigue can be controlled administratively, using measures such as shift assignment policies, shift rotation, and shift differential pay.[81] The excessive consumption of alcohol or the use of other drugs can have severe consequences for both the individual and the organization. Alcohol abuse has always been recognized as a problem. One expert estimated that 25 percent of police officers in the United States were dependent on alcohol.[82] A study of 500 police officers in 21 police departments determined that police officers used alcohol as a socially acceptable stress reliever.[83] In a recent study, officers anonymously reported that their vulnerability to alcohol abuse had increased during their first five years of police employment. They also reported experiencing emotional effects and stress when they attended a police funeral, were the subject of an internal affairs investigation, experienced a needle prick or exposure to body fluids, made a violent arrest, or personally knew victims.[84]

Managerial leaders should be on the lookout for early signs of employee stress and should watch for deterioration of work performance as shown in such behaviors as the following:

1. Excessive absenteeism
2. Unreported absences
3. Late arriving and leaving early

4. Poor quality of work
5. Erratic work performance
6. Failure to meet work standards
7. Friction with co-workers
8. Increased accident rates

Not all these behaviors mean that an officer is under **malstress**, but they are indications that this possibility should be considered. Managerial leaders should of course not limit their monitoring of employee performance to negative indicators; to be fair to employees, managers should also keep track of signs of excellence like high energy levels, alertness, strong motivation, calmness under pressure, thorough problem analysis, sound decision-making, and positive attitudes toward work.

Psychological Symptoms

Dissatisfaction with one's job is the most obvious psychological manifestation of **malstress**. Psychological reactions to stress generally are emotion laden and involve thought processes rather than some overt behavior. Psychologically based stress is usually characterized by increased tension, irritability, anxiety, procrastination, or becoming bored with the job.

Psychologically, officers usually react to **malstress** by turning to defense mechanisms in an attempt to reduce the associated anxiety. Officers can engage in such activities as not answering calls rapidly or submitting incomplete reports. They never deal directly with the **malstress**, and they might not even be aware they are suffering from it.

Psychological problems that can result from **malstress** include marital discord, family conflict, sleep disturbances, sexual dysfunction, depression, and job burnout.[85]

Additionally, **organizational stress** can, in some instances, lead to sleep disturbances. Many officers suffer from insomnia caused by a very common **stressor**—shift work. Other typical work-related problems in law enforcement—such as worries about being promoted, about conflict with a fellow employee, or about testifying in court—can also lead to debilitating sleep disturbances. Excessive use of caffeine and/or alcohol can disrupt sleep patterns. When sleep deprivation becomes chronic, it can have a negative impact on an individual's mood that in turn can affect job performance.[86]

Stress Programs for Family Members

Depending upon available time and expertise, many departmental stress programs and mental health practitioners offer the same services to family members as they furnish to officers: assessment and referral, crisis intervention, **critical incident** debriefing, and short- and long-term counseling. In many departments, the most common problem for which officers seek treatment is marital or other relationship difficulties.

Family members can be a major source of support for officers. A good marriage can serve to sustain a police officer when he or she is dealing with job-related stress and can contribute to a successful police career. In this respect, law enforcement is no different from other occupational areas. Some relationships end in divorce, but evidence shows that police divorce rates are similar to other professional groups.

Critical incidents can traumatize the relatives of officers just as severely as the officers themselves. Family members' fear and shock can be compounded by ignorance of an event. Experts recommend that critical incident debriefing for officers involved in the incident should include family members. It is also recommended that family members be given a separate debriefing, and peer support should be offered by spouses of officers.

When departmental policy encourages sound family relationships, training programs can provide extra support for spouses. Such programs emphasize teaching coping techniques, improving communications, and working out problems. A number of agencies conduct seminars for couples, and some offer the services of a police psychologist.[87] One observer pointed out that although implementing a **stress reduction** program would initially consume departmental resources, the program would lead to better morale and improved productivity.[88]

Stress Reduction

Employees and managers are the most important components of police organizations, and they consume the largest portion of an organization's budget. Their physical and mental well-being contributes directly to the effectiveness of the organization. Having become aware of the impact eustress and **malstress** can have, both on the individual and on the organization, police organizations are giving increased consideration to developing programs aimed at fostering greater production with less stress and more enthusiasm for work.[89]

Individual Response to Stress

Various techniques have been developed that individuals can use to cope with stress effectively. They include exercise, planning, proper nutrition, and mental relaxation. In many instances, stress begins to be recognized by individuals only when things seem to be out of control. Many of us work from day to day and give little consideration to planning. Not only do we fail to consider our life goals realistically, we fail to spend any time contemplating how to deal with job demands, changes in society, and all the other pressures we feel when encountering issues and heading off crisis situations.[90]

Take Charge of Your Own Life.

One way individuals can defend against **malstress** is to review job expectations realistically, comparing them to what is currently happening in the organization. This may, in some cases, enable them to identify and change some counterproductive behavior of their own that is holding them back. In other instances, the process might persuade them to accept the reality of the working environment and quit "fighting the organization." The important thing is for individuals to take charge of their own lives, without waiting for the organization to solve problems they might be able to solve themselves.

Managers may be able to reduce their own exposure to stress by delegating part of their workload to qualified subordinates. Alternatively, they may be able to devise better time management plans. For example, a manager might prepare a schedule at the beginning of each day and follow it as closely as possible. If individuals really take control of their own lives, work can become enjoyable and rewarding. This is a far better response to the **malstress** problem than relying on addictive substances.[91]

Relaxation.

Job-related stressors cannot be avoided. Deadlines, interpersonal conflicts, and incidents requiring disciplinary measures—there are any number of potentially stressful events. When individuals begin to feel tense or anxious, it should be a signal to employ some type of stress reliever as soon as an opportunity can be found.

Most experts agree that relaxation techniques can play a key role in the control and reduction of stress. In the early 1970s, Herbert Benson and his colleagues discovered what they called "the relaxation response"—a decrease in heart rate, metabolic rate, respiratory rate, and eventually blood pressure that can be brought about by using any of a variety of techniques.[92] Benson and Klipper found that techniques successful in eliciting the relaxation response included four common elements:[93]

1. A place free of distraction, noise, and interruptions
2. A mental device to help focus thoughts and prevent the mind from wandering (This mental device can be a word or phrase—even as simple as the number one, monosyllabic and emotion free—or something in the environment—some people fix their gaze on an object or concentrate on the rhythm of breathing.)
3. A passive attitude (distractions should be countered by refocusing on the mental device being used)
4. A comfortable and relaxed position (not necessarily the classical lotus position; an ordinary sitting position is adequate, but lying down is not recommended because falling asleep is to be avoided)

The authors provided the following instructions for individuals to use in bringing about the relaxation response:[94]

1. Remain in a comfortable position. Sit quietly and refrain from moving or fidgeting.
2. Prevent visual distractions by closing your eyes.
3. Relax all your muscles by starting at the feet and working upward. With practice, total relaxation can be accomplished in one minute or less.
4. Breathe through your nose and concentrate on the breathing activity. When exhaling, repeat the mental device we discussed.
5. Engage in this activity for 10–20 minutes once or twice a day. Upon completion, sit quietly for a few minutes before opening your eyes; stay in the same position, with your eyes open, for a few minutes.
6. Do not be anxious about achieving a deep relaxation. Permit relaxation to occur at its own pace.

A real advantage of the Benson relaxation response is that it does not require any formal training. There is clear evidence for the benefits it provides, which have a practical and realistic application to the workplace. A number of other relaxation techniques, ranging from muscular relaxation to biofeedback, are listed in Table 6–7. Police managers may find any or all of these techniques useful, either in dealing with their own stress or as part of a program aimed at reducing and controlling **malstress** within the organization.

Breathing Exercises.
Breathing is so much a part of our life that we seldom take note of it. When an insufficient amount of oxygen reaches the lungs, the flow of carbon dioxide (a waste product) out of the body is diminished; the retention of carbon dioxide can lead over time to the deterioration of body organs and tissues, potentially resulting in headaches, panic attacks, depression, exhaustion, nervousness, and muscle tension. Any of these conditions can intensify stress and make it harder to cope with.[95] Good breathing habits can help counter all these bad effects. Breathing techniques can be easily learned and practiced almost anywhere, by themselves or in combination with other relaxation processes. (Please note that although the techniques can be learned quickly, it may take several months for their full benefit to be felt.)[96]

Table 6–7
MENTAL RELAXATION

Relaxation response

Meditation

Dynamic breathing

Relaxing by exhaling

Alternative nostril breathing

Complete breathing standing

Muscular relaxation

Progressive muscle relaxation

Imagery

Hypnosis

Centering

Prayer

Biofeedback

Physical Exercise.

It is generally agreed that exercise is one of the best and most helpful means of reducing stress. Individuals committed to reducing stress in their lives should consider participating in an exercise program, which promotes not only physical well-being but peace of mind. It is increasingly common for law enforcement agencies to support physical conditioning programs, including such activities as 10-km runs, the Police Olympics, and the "Pig Bowl" (football).

Numerous agencies now provide their officers with exercise facilities, including bicycles, free weights, weight machines, and treadmills. All this has been in response to an increased awareness of the many values of vigorous exercise:[97]

1. Improves the performance of the circulatory system
2. Delays degeneration of the body
3. Reduces the pulse rate
4. Tones muscles
5. Improves posture
6. Increases endurance
7. Burns calories
8. Strengthens the heart muscles
9. Decreases low-density lipoproteins (harmful cholesterol)

There are three categories of exercise: aerobics, stretching, and toning. Aerobic exercises, which include such activities as running, jogging, brisk walking, swimming, and martial arts, are the most familiar and popular. Performed regularly (three to five times per week) and for a reasonable period of time at each session (30 minutes to an hour), these exercises will increase stamina and strengthen the cardiovascular system. A truly balanced exercise program should include all three categories of exercise.[98]

Different kinds of exercise provide different benefits. For example, individuals who need to lose weight would be well advised to jog, whereas individuals concerned about flexibility would be better off doing calisthenics, yoga, tai chi, or playing handball or squash.

Numerous professional organizations have cautioned that before beginning an exercise program, a medical evaluation is in order. In police departments requiring an annual physical examination, the physician should screen each officer before allowing him or her to engage in vigorous exercise. Aerobics, in the view of some, is almost synonymous with jogging, but there are many other options, and experts encourage individuals to select an exercise they enjoy. Other aerobic exercises include pedaling a stationary bike, jumping rope, running in place, swimming, or playing organized sports such as basketball, water polo, tennis, or racquetball.

The ultimate goal of aerobics is to improve endurance and cardiovascular conditioning (activities like weight lifting bring about excellent benefits of their own, such as building up skeletal muscles, but they have limited aerobic effect). Aerobics is an integral and essential part of a **stress reduction** program. Whatever aerobic exercise is selected, it must be vigorous enough to raise the heart rate to approximately 80 percent of what has been established as the maximum heart rate. The target rate is easily calculated by subtracting the exerciser's age from 220 and multiplying the result (the maximum heart rate) by 0.8. For example, the target heart rate for someone 25 years of age would be 156 (220 minus 25 equals 195, times 0.8). During workouts, the heart rate should be within 10 beats of the target rate. An exercise program should be designed to ensure what is described as functional fitness. It consists of cardio-respiratory endurance, muscular strength, body composition, and muscular flexibility.

Physical Conditioning of Employees

The Albuquerque Police Department provides for physical conditioning of all department personnel. The program is designed to keep officers motivated to maintain their fitness level. The goal is to develop greater awareness and emphasize the importance of staying fit. The department conducts annual physical fitness testing, for its 900 officers, including leg press, chest press, sit-ups, sit and reach, a 1.5-mile run, and body composition evaluation. Body fat is measured and included in each officer's health status evaluation but is not used as part of the overall fitness score.

The officers are evaluated utilizing fitness categories and rankings established by the Cooper Institute based on data from over 100,000 individuals considered representative of the U.S. population. The institute's ranking system identifies specific levels of fitness for men and women broken down into 10-year age increments.

The department conducts annual physical assessments during a three-month period. The incentive program provides compensatory time and T-shirts for the officers as awards. Officers receive specific amounts of compensatory time off depending on how well they perform on the assessment. This has proven to be an effective method of promoting total fitness within the department.

Officers and civilian staff have 24-hour access to two gyms that are equipped with state-of-the-art exercise equipment including treadmills, life cycles, free weights, machines, and an aerobics room. The department has five substations throughout the city and a communications center, each of which is also furnished with basic fitness equipment. The department recently completed an all-weather 400-meter running track.

Having a complete, ongoing physical conditioning program in place ensures that department personnel will be more productive while reducing complaints, injuries, and absenteeism. It is the responsibility of administrators that officers have every advantage possible, including the best training, equipment, and physical conditioning.[99]

Employee Assistance Programs

The **EAP** concept is new to law enforcement, but it has been a part of many businesses for more than 40 years. Initially these programs concentrated on alcoholism, but in the 1970s, consideration widened to emotional and stress-related problems. Today, some **EAP**s offer a broad range of services to help employees deal with issues like the family and, more recently, retirement.

A significant guideline that addresses this issue is Standard 22.2.10 promulgated by the Commission on Accreditation for Law Enforcement Agencies. It recommends that an agency make available to employees an EAP designed to assist in the identification and resolution of concerns or problems (personal or job related), which may adversely affect an employee's personal or professional well-being or job performance. These personal concerns may include, but are not limited to, health, marital status, family, financial, substance abuse, emotional/stress, and other personal matters. The Commission specifies that the EAP shall include, at a minimum[100]

1. A written directive describing program services;
2. Procedures for obtaining program services;
3. Confidential, appropriate, and timely problem assessment services;
4. Referrals to services, either workplace or community resources for appropriate diagnosis, treatment, and follow-up;
5. Written procedures and guidelines for referral to and/or mandatory participation; and
6. Training of designated supervisory personnel in the program services, supervisor's role and responsibility, and identification of employees' behaviors that would indicate the existence of employee concerns, problems, and/or issues that could impact employee job performance.

As more and more agencies comply with this standard, viable **EAP**s will positively impact on law enforcement personnel to the benefit of the public, the agency, and all personnel.

A comprehensive program can address many problems (see Table 6–8). When planning for the implementation of an EAP in a law enforcement agency, a manager should first determine the current conditions in the department. Such a survey should include an analysis of the organization, a detailed study of the need for such a program, and a survey of community resources.

Table 6–8

PROBLEMS THAT CAN BE ADDRESSED BY AN EMPLOYEE ASSISTANCE PROGRAM

Alcoholism	Substance abuse
Job stress	Job burnout
Anxiety	Depression
Parent–child conflict	Single parenting
Grief	Smoking
Nutrition	Exercise
Weight control	Divorce
Marital separation	Police shootings
Family	Health
Financial	Critical incident
Gambling	Retirement

Source: Adapted from John G. Stratton, "Employee Assistance Programs: A Profitable Approach for Employees and Organizations," in Harry W. More and Peter C. Unsinger, eds. *Police Managerial Use of Psychology and Psychologists* (Springfield, IL: Charles C Thomas, 1987); Commission on Accreditation for Law Enforcement Agencies, *Standards for Law Enforcement Agencies*, 4th ed. (Fairfax, VA: Commission on Accreditation for Law Enforcement Agencies, 2001).

An effective EAP can be of benefit not only to the organization but also to the individual. As organizations become increasingly concerned about the quality of working life, **EAP**s appear likely to play a very important part in reducing organizational stress and helping officers deal with **malstress**. This is especially true when officers respond to a critical incident that involves a tremendous loss of life, such as the terrorist attack against the twin towers in New York City—an unbelievable disaster and a very traumatic experience for the responding officers. Today there is a critical need for law enforcement agencies to provide counseling, rehabilitative, and health promotion services for all personnel.

In one instance, the U.S. Department of Justice and the City of Steubenville, Ohio, entered into a consent decree (CD) after their investigation determined that the city manager caused and condoned a pattern of abuse of police authority because of inadequate policies, a failure to train, monitor, supervise, and discipline officers. The CD provided the following:[101]

The City shall contract for or provide an **EAP**. This program was at a minimum to provide counseling and stress management to officers. The program was required to be staffed by sufficient licensed and decertified counselors who are trained and experienced in addressing psychological and emotional problems common for officers. Except when the City imposed mandatory counseling as a supervisory tool, officers shall be free to attend counseling confidentially and without any adverse actions taken against them.

This remedy reflects the serious need for police departments to provide a variety of services in personnel matters. A significant component of the CD is that of confidentiality. There seems to be a continuing pattern in many law enforcement agencies of mistrust between line officers and the "brass." Mutual trust is missing in many agencies, and the managers of the organization are viewed as lacking in positive leadership qualities, perpetuators of bureaucratic rules and regulations, inadequate information providers, and masters of deceit and strong supporters of negative internal politics. In a few agencies, the departments are run by "juice" and "rabbis" rule the roost. Some of those who work the street feel that confidentiality never prevails in any counseling situation, leaks are inevitable, and there is a fear that after asking for help that one would be labeled as "crazy" or an employee that should not be in the agency. In one instance, a sergeant who was depressed never considered going to the departmental psychologist because he truly believed that he would no longer be considered for promotion and would eventually be terminated. He felt that counseling was indicative of personal weakness and reflected on his persona.

Peer Counseling

Peer counseling has become a part of law enforcement during the last few decades. The first such program, directed by two recovering alcoholics, was offered by the Boston Police Department. The concept spread to other departments and has been successful because of the general hesitancy of police officers to seek professional assistance. A fellow officer is cut from the same cloth and can be highly successful when counseling colleagues because he or she shares common experiences and special training. In 2006, the International Association of Chiefs of Police (IACP) ratified Peer Support Guidelines in order to provide a frame of reference wherein officers and civilian employees are given needed psychological support. It is an indication that someone at the operational level and still working the streets is well qualified to provide needed assistance in some instances of personal or professional crisis. In viable programs, where such programs have been implemented, a peer is specially trained to intercede in a time of need. This is the fulfillment of a special need after a critical incident, a shooting incident, or the death/injury of a public safety officer. Officers working as a peer support person along with licensed mental health professionals have been very successful as dealing with crises of varying types.[102]

CASE STUDY   Captain Deborah Pike

Captain Pike is in charge of the northern district in a rapidly growing police department. There are 1451 sworn officers assigned to the district. They are divided into three shifts, with the largest number assigned to the swing shift. Detectives are in the process of being decentralized, and it is anticipated that a number of detectives will be transferred to the district at the beginning of the next fiscal year. Captain Pike's primary concern is administering the station house in such a way that called-for services are answered rapidly and adequate public safety services are provided. The area patrolled is primarily commercial, containing warehouses and some manufacturing units. Additionally, there are some residential sections that were initially large homes that have been converted into apartments. There is some sign that the district is revitalizing, but it will take a number of years. Some of the lofts of warehouses are being converted into condos and residents are returning to this area. The crime rate is high (when compared to other parts of the city); armed robberies, home invasions, and aggravated assaults led the way. Besides violent crimes in the district, property crimes are increasing, and lately, there has been a surge of auto thefts.

Even with laptop computers, a state-of-the-art dispatching system, and a large number of civilian support personnel, the station house's workload is excessive. Priority calls become backed up, and the paperwork is overwhelming; the officers feel as though they are drowning in reams of paper and entangled in red tape. It seems to be almost a circus, and the officers complain that all they do is go from one call to the next. There even is inconsistency between the shifts on supervisors' instructions on how to respond to the backed up calls for service.

Captain Pike's predecessor has requested additional personnel for the last five years. Even though his requests have been thoroughly justified, additional officers were never assigned. The city just does not have the resources to support the police department. The mayor and the city administrator have made it clear that the police department will not get additional funding. Federal grants are drying up, and the near future looks quite bleak economically. "Status quo" or even worse seems to be the byword of the day.

Since her arrival nine months ago, Captain Pike has been shocked by how fast morale is deteriorating. Some of the officers have "bitched" in the past but now complaining seems to be pervasive. Seldom does one hear truly positive statements. In the past, the locker room was a place for jokes and free interchange between officers, but for the most part, it is now quiet and subdued. The primary focus of discussion usually revolves around officers' inability to keep up with the demands of the job.

The captain has noticed that a number of officers are late in attending roll call, that sick leave is being used more frequently, and that there is a tremendous increase in what can only be termed "sloppy police work." First-line supervisors and watch commanders are spending a great deal of time dealing with the line officers' increasingly poor performance. All these problems seem to be mushrooming.

Captain Pike has consulted with all the managers under her command, police union representatives, and other key officers, including staff personnel in headquarters, and finds that there is a consensus—something has to be done to improve working conditions and reduce the stress created by the job.

With this in mind, the captain decided to appear at each roll call to discuss the problem and let everyone know that she is concerned and everyone is working diligently on the problem. If you were Captain Pike, what would you do next? List three alternative solutions. If malstress is the real problem, what should be done before things get worst? Discuss in detail how would you deal with increasing "sloppy police work"? Would you address the supervisors? If so, how and on what issues would you address them? If you wouldn't address the supervisors, why not?

SUMMARY

Stress is unique not only to each situation but to each individual. Some handle stress very well; others have a great deal of difficulty coping with it. Outlook on life is important. A specific **stressor**, such as a poorly defined policy, can be viewed either as greatly significant or of little importance. If viewed positively, a negative **stressor** can be converted into eustress (positive stress).

Stress is not unique to law enforcement, but there are certain stressful events and situations especially prevalent in police agencies, such as danger, boredom, lack of public support, unfavorable court decisions, and unfair administrative policies.

An assessment tool used by psychologists for a number of years is the Holmes–Rahe life stress inventory. It provides a rough measure, in points, of how great an adjustment various life events require of an individual over a specified period (e.g., the death of a spouse "costs" the individual 100 points). A somewhat similar scale has been developed that rates 144 critical life events that may be experienced by police officers during their careers. This scale has not been extensively tested but can be used by police managers evaluating the impact of stressful events on their subordinates.

One expert has found there are several transitory stages affecting stress perception: alarm, disenchantment, personalization, and introspection. These stages can be used as benchmarks for the initiation of stress reduction programs. **Stressors** in law enforcement vary but generally can be categorized as job and organizational characteristics, external factors, personal variables, group characteristics, and resource management issues.

Responses to organizational stress will vary from individual to individual, but they are usually described as taking **behavioral**, psychological, or physiological forms. Dealing with employee stress is clearly tied to managerial practices, and 12 tips are identified that a leader can utilize to confront organizational issues. Most studies of **physiological symptoms** have centered on the cardiovascular system, but stress-induced symptoms such as headaches, chronic fatigue, stomach pain, backaches, and chest pains are also widely recognized. **Behavioral symptoms** are what usually come to the attention of police managers first, because of their impact on job performance. Symptoms related to rising levels of stress include an increased use of tobacco products, alcohol abuse, drug abuse, appetite disorders, and accidents. Managers on the lookout for early signs of employee stress should watch for deterioration of work performance as shown in such behaviors as excessive absenteeism, poor quality of work, erratic work performance, failure to meet work standards, friction with co-workers, and any other type of behavior that seems unusual.

Psychologically, officers usually react to **malstress** (bad or negative stress) by turning to defense mechanisms in an attempt to reduce the associated anxiety. They may become tense, irritated, anxious, and even bored with the job. When such behavior continues over an extended period of time, it can result in marital discord, family conflict, sleep disturbances, sexual dysfunction, depression, and job burnout. Having become aware of the impact eustress and **malstress** can have, both on the individual and on the organization, police organizations are giving increasing consideration to developing programs aimed at fostering greater production with less stress and more enthusiasm for work.

The Albuquerque Police Department has been very successful with its physical conditioning of all personnel annually, and a very important process is the annual testing of the physical well-being of officers and civilians. All personnel have access to two gyms that are equipped with state-of-the-art exercise equipment including treadmills, life cycles, free weights, machines, and an aerobic room.

Employee assistance programs and their possible implementation should include a detailed analysis of the organization, a detailed study of the need for such program, and a survey of community resources. If it is determined there is a need for such a program, it can be designed to address a range of problems ranging from anxiety to family problems. The Commission on Accreditation for Law Enforcement Agencies has created specific minimal standards for EAPs.

Of special importance is the continuing focus on peer counseling, and to support this trend, the International Association of Chiefs of Police has ratified Peer Support Guidelines that set forth a frame of reference that allows a peer support individual to work with mental health professionals when dealing with varying types of crises. This is an acknowledgment of the value of using peers in the counseling process.

DISCUSSION TOPICS AND QUESTIONS

1. Compare eustress and malstress.
2. What are some of the consequences of organizational stress?
3. What can a manager do to reduce the organizational stress felt by women police officers?
4. What are some of the behavioral symptoms a manager should look for that might indicate the presence of malstress?
5. What are some of the things a police manager can do to reduce stress?
6. How do role conflict, ambiguity, and work overload create stress?
7. Describe the characteristics of each of the following types of officers: ambivalent, indifferent, and ascendant.
8. Describe stress-induced physiological symptoms.
9. What problems should an employee assistance program address?
10. Contrast the alarm, personalization, and disenchantment stages.

FOR FURTHER READING

Heith Copes, ed., *Policing and Stress* (Upper Saddle River, NJ: Pearson-Prentice Hall, 2005).

This text is a collection of writings created by leading police researchers. It examines the sources and consequences of stress and presents specific coping techniques. Consideration is given to the sources of stress and then turns to an examination of critical incident stressors. The writings are cross-cultural and represent the United States, Australia, Canada, and New Zealand. Some of the articles take the position that law enforcement is no more stressful than other occupations, and other articles point out that it is a stressful occupation. The second part of the collection focuses on what can happen when stress occurs and exemplifies the need for additional research in this area. The last chapter focuses on police suicide.

James D. Sewell, "Dealing with Employee Stress: How Managers Can Help—or Hinder—Their Personnel," *FBI Law Enforcement Bulletin*, Vol. 75, No. 7 (2006), pp. 1–6.

The author recommends that law enforcement management must have a flexible approach and focus on a positive and healthy working environment. There is a description of ineffective and inappropriate management styles and techniques. Several steps are presented to help managers reduce employee stress and improve work conditions. These steps include establishing effective communications between managers and employees, fostering a positive work environment and focusing on the health of employees. The author provides 12 tips for reducing employee stress that include the need for managers to lighten up and project a positive attitude.

Rebecca M. Pasillas, Victoria M. Follette, and Suzanne E. Persmean-Chaney, "Occupational Stress and Psychological Functioning in Law Enforcement Officer," *Journal of Police and Criminal Psychology*, Vol. 21, No. 1 (2007), pp. 1–13.

This study evaluated avoidance coping, occupational stress, and distress in a sample of 48 officers in a community of 75,000. The researchers concluded that police officers reported higher levels of psychological distress than the general population. If officers used avoidant coping strategies, they experienced a higher level of occupational stress and psychological distress. The authors suggested that departments should create intervention strategies that focused on decreasing occupational stress that they anticipated would decrease avoidance behavior and improve the psychological health of officers.

Richard Clark and Michael Haley, "Crisis Response Tools for Law Enforcement," *The Police Chief*, Vol. LLX, No. 8 (2007), pp. 94–101.

This article describes Critical Incident Stress Management (CISM) that is defined as a multicomponent system. It is a structured, small-group crisis intervention that occurs from 2 to 14 days after an incident. The process focuses on a broad range of incident to include death in the line of duty, serious injury, mass causalities, terrorism, officer-involved shootings, motor vehicle accidents, and the death of children. Incidents are responded to by a team of mental health expert and at least one trained peer supporter. It is a group support process that is designed to the impact of traumatic incidents on police personnel and other emergency responders. It intervenes when there is an obvious need to provide psychological services.

ENDNOTES

1. Moshe Zeidner and Gerald Matthews, "Evaluation Anxiety—Current Theory and Research," in Andrew J. Elliot and Carol S. Dweck, eds. *Handbook of Competence and Motivation* (New York: The Guilford Press, 2007), p. 141.

2. J. Barton Cunningham, *The Stress Management Sourcebook*, 2nd ed. (Lincolnwood, IL: Lowell House, 2000), pp. 4–6.

3. Karl Albrecht, *Stress and the Manager* (New York: Touchstone, 1986), pp. 7–10.

4. Donald Hellriegel, John W. Slocum, Jr., and Richard W. Woodman, *Organizational Behavior*, 7th ed. (St. Paul, MN: West, 1996), p. 568.

5. Hans Selye, *Stress without Distress* (New York: New American Library, 1975).

6. Lawrence A. Murphy and Theodore F. Schoenborn, *Stress Management in Work Settings* (Washington, D.C.: National Institute for Occupational Safety and Health, USGPO, 1987), pp. 15–25.

7. Ibid., p. 48.

8. Albrecht, *Stress and the Manager*, pp. 61–63.

9. V. A. Leonard and Harry W. More, *Police Organization and Management*, 9th ed. (New York: Foundation Press, 2000), p. 168.

10. James C. Quick and Jonathan D. Quick, *Organizational Stress and Preventative Management* (New York: McGraw-Hill, 1984).

11. Gregory Moorhead and Ricky W. Griffin, *Organizational Behavior*, 8th ed. (Boston, MA: Houghton Mifflin, 2006), p. 198.

12. James D. Higgins, *Human Relations* (New York: Random House, 1982); Vivian B. Lord, "The Stress of Change: The Impact of Changing a Traditional Police Department to a Community-Oriented, Problem-Solving Department," in Heith Copes, ed. *Policing and Stress* (Upper Saddle River, NJ: Pearson Prentice Hall, 2005), pp. 55–72.

13. Stephen P. Robbins, *Organizational Behavior: Concepts, Controversies, and Application*, 11th ed. (Englewood Cliffs, NJ: Prentice Hall, 2004), pp. 91–110.

14. Richard S. Lazarus, *Stress and Emotion: A New Synthesis*, 2nd ed. (New York: Springer, 2006), p. 49.

15. T. H. Holmes and R. H. Rahe, "The Social Readjustment Rating Scale," *Journal of Psychosomatic Research*, Vol. 11 (1969), pp. 213–218.

16. Lazarus, *Stress and Emotion*, pp. 51–52.

17. James D. Sewell, "The Development of a Critical Life Events Scale for Law Enforcement," *Journal of Police Science and Administration*, Vol. 11 (1983), p. 1 and a copy of the instrument was obtained from the author.

18. Virginia E. Pendergrass and Nancy M. Ostrove, "Survey of Stress in Women in Policing." Unpublished paper presented at the American Psychological Association (1984).

19. Richard M. Davis, ed., *Stress and the Organization* (Los Angeles, CA: University of Southern California Press, 1979).

20. Francis A. Graf, "Police Stress and Social Support," *Journal of Police Science and Administration*, Vol. 14, No. 3 (1986), p. 41.

21. John M. Violanti and James R. Marshall, "The Police Stress Process," *Journal of Police Science and Administration*, Vol. 11, No. 4 (1983), p. 4.

22. NIOSH Working Group, *Stress at Work* (Cincinnati, OH: National Institute for Occupational Safety and Health, 1999), p. 5.

23. Kenneth R. Pelletier, *Healthy People in Unhealthy Places* (New York: Delacorte/Seymour Lawrence, 1984), pp. 63–75.

24. J. J. Hurrell, Jr., D. L. Nelson, and B. L. Simmons, "Measuring Job Stressors and Strains: Where We Have Been, Where We Are and Where We Need to Go," *Journal of Occupational Health Psychology*, Vol. 4, No. 3 (1998), pp. 368–390.

25. Dennis W. Organ and W. Clay Hamner, *Organizational Behavior: An Applied Psychological Approach* (Plano, TX: Business Publications, 1982).

26. Peter Finn and Julie Esselman Tomz, *Developing a Law Enforcement Stress Program for Officers and Their Families* (Washington, D.C.: Office of Justice Programs, National Institute of Justice, 1997), pp. 6–7.

27. Ellen Kirschman, "Organizational Stress: Looking for Love in All of the Wrong Places," *The Police Chief*, Vol. LXV, No. 10 (1998), pp. 127–135.

28. Dennis J. Stevens, "Police Officer Stress," *Law and Order*, Vol. 47, No. 9 (1999), pp. 77–81.

29. Gary Johns, *Organizational Behavior: Understanding Life at Work* (Glenview, IL: Scott Foresman, 1988), pp. 235–241.

30. J. J. Hurrell, Jr., and L. R. Murphy, "Occupational Stress," in W. M. Rom, ed. *Occupational and Environmental Medicine*, 3rd ed. (New York: Little, Brown, 2001), pp. 36–42.

31. NIOSH Working Group, *Stress at Work*, p. 7.

32. Organ and Hamner, *Organizational Behavior*.

33. Katherine Ellison and John L. Genz, *Stress and the Police Officer* (Springfield, IL: Charles C Thomas, 1983), p. 17.

34. Albrecht, *Stress and the Manager*, p. 135.

35. Centers for Disease Control and Prevention. (2013). *Deaths: Final data for 2013–Detailed tables for the National Vital Statistics Report (NVSR)*. Atlanta, GA: Author. Retrieved from: http://www.cdc.gov/nchs/data/nvsr/nvsr64/nvsr64_02.pdf

36. Federal Bureau of Investigation. (2012). *About Law Enforcement Officers Killed and Assaulted, 2012*. Washington, D.C.: Criminal Justice Information Services Division. Retrieved from https://www.fbi.gov/about-us/cjis/ucr/leoka/2012

37. Dennis J. Stevens, "Police Officer Stress and Occupational Stressors: Before and after 9/11," in H. Copes, ed. *Policing and Stress* (Upper Saddle River, NJ: Pearson–Prentice Hall, 2005), pp. 103–105.

38. *Graham v. Connor*, 490 U.S. 386 (1989).

39. Police Executive Research Forum, *Guiding Principle on Use of Force* (Washington D.C., 2016).

40. Harry W. More, *Current Issues in American Law Enforcement—Controversies and Solutions* (Springfield, IL: Charles C Thomas, 2008), pp. 82–84.

41. James J. Fyfe, ed., *Readings on Police Use of Deadly Force* (Washington, D.C.: Police Foundation, 1982).

42. Dan Goldberg, "10 Reasons Cops Are Different," http://www.heavybadge.com/10reason.htm. See also, John M. Violanti, "Dying for the Job: Psychological Stress, Disease, and Mortality in Police Work," in H. Copes, ed. *Policing and Stress* (Upper Saddle River, NJ: Pearson–Prentice Hall, 2005).

43. David A. Alexander and Leslie G. Walker, "The Perceived Impact of Police Work on Police Officers' Spouses and Families," *Stress Medicine*, Vol. 12 (1996), pp. 239–246; John M. Violanti and Fred Aron, "Police Stressors: Variations in Perception among Police Personnel," *Journal of Criminal Justice*, Vol. 23 (1995), pp. 287–294.

44. More, *Current Issues in American Law Enforcement*, pp. 91–103.

45. He Ni Zhao and Carol Archibald, "Gender and Police Stress: The Convergent and Divergent Impact of Work Environment, Work-Family Conflict, and Stress Coping Mechanisms of Female and Male Police Officers," *Policing*, Vol. 25, No. 4 (2002), pp. 687–708.

46. Finn and Tomz, *Developing a Law Enforcement Stress Program for Officers and Their Families*, pp. 126–127.

47. Tony L. Jones, "Autocratic vs. People-Minded Supervisors," *Law and Order*, Vol. 46, No. 5 (1998), pp. 32–36.

48. L. R. Murphy, "Stress Management in Work Settings: A Critical Review of the Research Literature," *American Journal of Health Promotion*, Vol. 11 (1996), pp. 112–135.

49. Harry More and O. R. Shipley, *Police Policy Manual—Personnel* (Springfield, IL: Charles C Thomas, 1987), pp. 47–91.

50. Lord, "The Stress of Change."

51. Stevens, "Police Officer Stress and Occupational Stressors."

52. President's Task Force on 21st Century Policing, *Final Report of the President's Task Force on 21st Century Policing* (Washington, D.C.: Office of Community Oriented Policing Services, 2015).

53. Ibid.

54. S. Hakan Can, Helen M. Hendy, and Turgay Karagoz, "Law Enforcement Officer Stress Survey-Revised (LEOSS-R): Four Types of Police Stressors and Negative Psychological Outcomes Associated with Them," *Policing: Journal of Policy and Practice*, Vol. 9, No. 4 (2015), pp. 144–176.

55. Robyn R. M. Gershon, Briana Barocas, Allison N. Canton, Xianbin Li, and David Viahov, "Mental, Physical, and Behavioral Outcomes Associated with Perceived Work Stress in Police Officers," *Criminal Justice and Behavior*, Vol. 36 (2009), pp. 275–289.

56. S. Hakan Can and Helen M. Hendy, "Police Stressors: Negative Outcomes Associated with Them and Coping Mechanisms That May Reduce These Associations," *Police Journal: Theory, Practice, and Principles*, Vol. 87 (2014), pp. 167–177.

57. Can, Hendy, and Karagoz, "Law Enforcement Officer Stress Survey-Revised (LEOSS-R)."

58. Ibid.

59. Bureau of the Census, *Statistical Abstract of the United States*, 127th ed. (Washington, D.C.: USGPO, 2008), p. 327.

60. W. H. Kroes, Joseph Hurrell, and Bruce Margolis, "Job Stress in Policemen," *Journal of Police Science and Administration*, Vol. 11, No. 1 (1974), pp. 97–102.

61. Ellison and Genz, *Stress and the Police Officer*, p. 49.

62. A. P. Brief, R. S. Schuler, and M. Van Sell, *Managing Job Stress* (Boston, MA: Little, Brown, 1987).

63. Leonard and More, *Police Organization and Management*, p. 166.

64. Finn and Tomz, *Developing a Law Enforcement Stress Program for Officers and Their Families*, p. 10.

65. Judie W. Wexler and Deana Logan, "Sources of Stress Among Women Police Officers," *Journal of Police Science and Administration*, Vol. 11, No. 1 (1983), pp. 46–53.

66. Thomas D. Kirkpatrick, *Supervision* (Boston, MA: Kent, 1987).

67. Robin N. Harrick and Merry Morash, "Gender, Race and Strategies of Coping with Occupational Stress in Policing," *Justice Quarterly*, Vol. 16, No. 2 (1999), pp. 303–328. See also, Robin Harrick and Merry Morash, "Police Coping with Emotions, Gender, and Minority Status," in H. Copes and M. L. Dantzker, eds. *Policing and Stress* (Upper Saddle River, NJ: Pearson–Prentice Hall, 2005).

68. Michael T. Matteson and John M. Ivancevich, *Controlling Work Stress: Effective Human Resources and Management Strategies* (San Francisco, CA: Jossey-Bass, 1987), pp. 129–142.

69. Kirkpatrick, *Supervision*.

70. Brian A. Reaves and Timothy C. Hart, *Law Enforcement Management and Administrative Statistics, 1999: Data for Individual State and Local Agencies with 100 or More Officers* (Washington, D.C.: Bureau of Justice Statistics, 2000), p. xi.

71. George L. Kelling and Mark H. Moore, *The Evolving Strategy of Policing* (Washington, D.C.: National Institute of Justice, 1987), pp. 21–32.

72. Jerrod S. Greenberg, *Comprehensive Stress Management* (Dubuque, IA: William C. Brown, 1983), p. 87.

73. Kelling and Moore, *The Evolving Strategy of Police*, p. 48.

74. Robbins, *Organizational Behavior*, 6th ed., p. 271.

75. Leonard Territo and James D. Sewell, eds., *Stress Management in Law Enforcement* (Durham, NC: Carolina Academic Press, 1999), pp. 210–239.

76. Albrecht, *Stress and the Manager*, pp. 67–68.

77. James Campbell Quick, Lawrence R. Murphy, and Joseph J. Hurrell, Jr., *Stress and Well-Being at Work: Assessments and Interventions for Occupational Mental Health* (Washington, D.C.: American Psychological Association, 1992), pp. 252–291.

78. Albrecht, *Stress and the Manager*, pp. 67–68.

79. Robbins, *Organizational Behavior*, pp. 91–110.

80. Quick and Quick, *Organizational Stress and Preventative Management*.

81. Hellriegel, Slocum, and Woodman, *Organizational Behavior*.

82. Bryan Vila, *Tired Cops: The Importance of Managing Police Fatigue* (Washington, D.C.: PERF, 2000), p. 31.

83. W. Kroes, *Society's Victim: The Policeman: An Analysis of Job Stress in Policing* (Springfield, IL: Charles C Thomas, 1976), pp. 29–47.

84. John M. Violanti, James R. Marshall, and Barbara Howe, "Stress, Coping, and Alcohol Use: The Police Connection," *Journal of Police Science and Administration*, Vol. 13, No. 2 (1985), pp. 99–104.

85. Joseph A. Harpold and Samuel L. Feemster, "Negative Influences of Police Stress," *FBI Law Enforcement Bulletin*, Vol. 71, No. 9 (2002), p. 3.

86. Quick and Quick, *Organizational Stress and Preventative Management*.

87. Grace Kannady, "Developing Stress-Resistant Police Families," *The Police Chief*, Vol. LX, No. 8 (1993), pp. 92–99.

88. Sam Torres, David L. Maggard, Jr., and Christine Torres, "Preparing Families for the Hazards of Police Work," *The Police Chief*, Vol. LXX, No. 10 (2003), pp. 108–114.

89. Quick and Quick, *Organizational Stress and Preventative Management*.

90. Albrecht, *Stress and the Manager*, pp. 173–184.

91. Barry L. Reece and Rhonda Brandt, *Effective Human Relations in Organizations*, 10th ed. (Boston, MA: Houghton Mifflin, 2008), pp. 382–389.

92. Quick and Quick, *Organizational Stress and Preventative Management*.

93. Herbert Benson and Miriam Z. Klipper, *The Relaxation Response*, 2nd ed. (New York: Harper Torch, 2000), pp. 159–160.

94. Ibid., p. 163.

95. Martha Davis, Elizabeth Robbins Eshelman, and Matthew McKay, *The Relaxation & Stress Reduction Workbook*, 6th ed. (Oakland, CA: New Harbinger, 2008), pp. 19–25.

96. Cunningham, *The Stress Management Sourcebook*, pp. 247–255.

97. George B. Dintiman and Jerrold S. Greenberg, *Health through Discovery* (Reading, MA: Addison-Wesley, 1980).

98. Peter D. Bullard, *Coping with Stress: A Psychological Survival Manual* (Portland, OR: ProSeminar Press, 1980).

99. Ray Schultz and Art Acevedo, "Ensuring the Physical Success of the Department," *Law and Order*, Vol. 48, No. 5 (2000), pp. 34–37.

100. Commission on Accreditation for Law Enforcement Agencies, *Standards for Law Enforcement Agencies*, 5th ed. (Fairfax, VA: Commission on Accreditation for Law Enforcement Agencies, November 2006), p. 22.2.

101. U.S. Department of Justice, Civil Rights Division, Special Litigations Section, *Misconduct Pattern or Practice Program* (Washington, D.C.: U.S. Department of Justice, 2007), pp. 1–5.

102. International Association of Chiefs of Police, "Peer Support Guidelines," *The Police Chief*, Vol. LXXIV, No. 10 (2006), pp. 89–92.

7

CONFLICT

Nature, Causes, and Management

Learning Objectives

1. List and discuss the recognizable steps involved in the conflict-development cycle.
2. Distinguish the historical phases of management thinking as it relates to organizational conflict.
3. Identify and discuss the most common causes of conflict in complex organizations.
4. Differentiate between functional conflict and dysfunctional conflict.
5. Describe the conflict-management strategies and techniques that apply to police work.
6. Describe the structure and function of employee assistance programs (EAPs).
7. Describe the process of principled negotiation.

Key Terms

aggression
behavioralists
collaboration
competition
conflict
cooperation
dysfunctional conflict

employee assistance programs (EAPs)
functional conflict
interactionists
principled negotiation
problem employees
traditionalists

Human behavior is diverse and varies tremendously regarding its interpersonal dimensions. Modes of interpersonal behavior lie along a continuum from collaboration at one end to overt **aggression** at the other (see Figure 7–1). **Collaboration** exists to help members of a group accomplish their collective goals, provide mutual assistance, and minimize personal antagonisms. **Cooperation** is a basic form of interaction in which two or more individuals coordinate their behavior to achieve a particular objective. **Competition** emerges when individuals attempt to maximize their advantage while disadvantaging others. Mutual assistance and personal antagonism are both low in healthy competitive situations. **Conflict** arises in those situations where someone or something has thwarted or is about to thwart someone else's goals. **Aggression** arises as the result of the conflict. It is intentional or unintentional behavior designed to injure the people or things perceived to be the source of the conflict.[1] This chapter examines the nature, causes, and management of conflict in complex criminal justice organizations.

Figure 7–1
*Collaboration–Aggression
Continuum.*

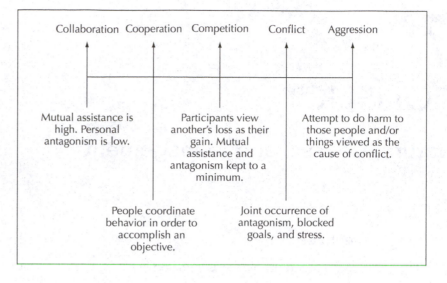

Anson Weller is 54 years old. He is a high school graduate who worked his way up through the ranks at the Harmerville Police Department. Weller has been the chief of police since 1975.

Harmerville is a relatively small, economically depressed town in what is known as the "rust bucket" area of the northeastern United States. The department's authorized strength is 15 FTE (full-time-equivalent) police officers. Most of the officers are part-time. The department's only sergeant, Nick Pason, is in charge of the night shift.

Chief Weller is and always has been an autocratic Theory X manager. He runs an incredibly tight ship and has been dubbed "Captain Hook" because of his propensity to fire people. The city council has always acquiesced and rubber-stamped these personnel actions, even though some of them were of questionable legality.

While there has always been an undercurrent of discontent within the department, most officers kept their complaints to themselves for fear of being fired. Some officers have become much more vocal over the last couple of years.

Some newly hired part-time officers openly criticized the chief's methods and—as a group—urged their colleagues to unionize under the State Labor Relations Act. They also discussed the situation with the executive director of the Fraternal Order of Police (FOP). The FOP expressed an interest in organizing the workforce in the department. To focus public attention on the issue, the FOP leaked the story to a friendly reporter. The banner headline said it all: *Police Morale Plummets, Officers Want Union Protection.*

The chief was livid and denounced the unionists as radicals who were trying to destroy the police department. After an internal investigation, Chief Weller fired two of the part-time officers for "conduct unbecoming an officer" and "actions detrimental to the welfare of the department." After a rancorous public hearing in which each side impugned the motives of the other, the tame city council upheld the dismissals. The conflict between the chief and his subordinates continued unabated and got progressively worse.

The FOP filed an unfair labor practice charge with the State Labor Relations Board (SLRB). The SLRB ruled Chief Weller interfered with the lawful activities of his employees. It ordered its staff to determine if there was sufficient interest in holding an election to select a collective-bargaining agent. In an election, the employees voted unanimously to affiliate with the FOP. The city and the FOP are now in the process of negotiating the first collective-bargaining agreement (CBA). Chief Weller is not actively involved in the negotiating process.

Chief Weller and his employees are still at odds with each other. There is no end in sight as far as personal animosity goes. The chief has vowed, on some occasions, to "bust the union." Union members continue to attack the chief as a petty dictator who should be forced out of office. While much of this vitriolic rhetoric is designed to influence the ongoing negotiations, it is clear that the conflict is far from over.

What kind of social dynamics was involved in this conflict situation? How would you classify the chief's basic philosophy as it relates to his reaction to the conflict? Identify the different stages in the development of this conflict episode. What do you feel could have been done by the chief to deal with this conflict before it got out of hand?

Interpersonal Conflict

Conflict within an organization involves the breakdown or disruption of normal activities to a point where individuals or groups experience real difficulty in working with one another, and nobody is willing to compromise.[2] In a general sense, interpersonal conflict is a condition in which two or more people have a difference of opinion involving values, goals, perceptions, or scarce resources and one or more of them threaten or attempt to gain an advantage over the others by exercising power. Conflict can in some circumstances be positive because it offers individuals a chance to share information and shed new light on a situation. Conflict begins when one party (person or group) perceives that another party has frustrated or is about to frustrate them in an area they consider important.[3]

Conflict results from perceived incompatible differences resulting in some form of interference or opposition. If people perceive that the differences exist, then a conflict state exists. To be successful managers, police administrators must learn to understand conflict and develop the skills needed to manage it. Learning how to deal effectively with conflict is one of the most challenging aspects of any manager's job.

Conflict can spark creativity and innovation in the organization. People are often reluctant to raise questions due to the fear of retaliation. The stifling of dissent also stifles creativity. The first step to ensure the benefits of conflict is to limit it to issues with "game changing potential." Instead of assigning blame and going over past hurts, we should invest in the future, and ways to move the organization forward—what could happen, the benefits to achieve. Fights should not focus on individual self-interest, dropping agendas, and examining how to improve person's lives. The conflict must follow the rules and persons must be able to lose with dignity, accepting the bad news with grace.[4]

Types of Interpersonal Conflict

Behavioral scientists who specialize in the study of social interaction have identified the following three distinct types of interpersonal conflict: conflict between individuals, conflict between individuals and groups, and conflict between groups.

1. *Conflict between individuals.* Probably the most common type of conflict is a conflict between individuals. Some people dislike one another—their personalities clash. Two people in conflict tend to disagree with each other concerning role expectations and appropriate performance. The intensity of the conflict will depend on issues, personalities of people involved (regarding intellect, problem-solving skills, mental health, and so forth), internal inhibitions, external constraints, and situational variables.

2. *Conflict between individuals and groups.* Conflicts can also occur between individuals and groups. These clashes arise from differences in opinion concerning appropriate norms, values, ethical orientations, and behaviors. Individuals who violate group-shared expectations are usually isolated, punished, and labeled as "deviant." Conflict over work norms creates special problems. Most work groups establish informal yet binding norms that prescribe certain behaviors and prohibit others. When a person falls short of or exceeds the norms established by the group, social distance increases. Offenders may be excluded from group-related social activities or cut off from the informal communication process (known as the grapevine), eliminating them from a very important source of job satisfaction. If there is a serious conflict between individual behavior and group norms, the group will do everything within its power to change the individual's "deviant" behavior. Here again, the intensity of the conflict will depend on a wide variety of different factors.

3. *Conflict between groups.* American society can be seen as a collage of social groups, formal and informal, interacting with each other as they pursue their own goals and objectives. Each social group develops an identity reflecting its specialized task, function, structural configuration, location, size, and degree of cohesion. As indicated in Chapter 3, all social groups develop unique personalities based on racial, ethnic, and cultural considerations. Task-oriented work groups generate their own distinct cultures based on their shared beliefs, values, attitudes, interests, and behavioral norms. As group cohesion increases, the differences between it and other social groups accentuates, leading to polarization between competing groups. The polarization of competing groups in the same sociocultural milieu (an organization, a society, or a nation) almost always sets the stage for destructive intergroup conflict. The nature, extent, and intensity of the conflict will depend on the specific issue in dispute, relative group strengths, collective rationality, internal control mechanisms, leadership, external constraints, and situational variables.[5]

Figure 7–2
Types of Interpersonal/Intergroup Conflict.

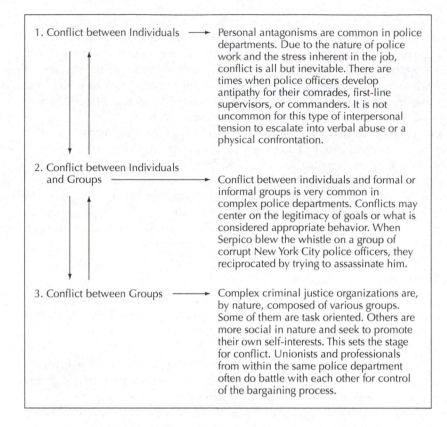

1. Conflict between Individuals → Personal antagonisms are common in police departments. Due to the nature of police work and the stress inherent in the job, conflict is all but inevitable. There are times when police officers develop antipathy for their comrades, first-line supervisors, or commanders. It is not uncommon for this type of interpersonal tension to escalate into verbal abuse or a physical confrontation.

2. Conflict between Individuals and Groups → Conflict between individuals and formal or informal groups is very common in complex police departments. Conflicts may center on the legitimacy of goals or what is considered appropriate behavior. When Serpico blew the whistle on a group of corrupt New York City police officers, they reciprocated by trying to assassinate him.

3. Conflict between Groups → Complex criminal justice organizations are, by nature, composed of various groups. Some of them are task oriented. Others are more social in nature and seek to promote their own self-interests. This sets the stage for conflict. Unionists and professionals from within the same police department often do battle with each other for control of the bargaining process.

Police work is an extraordinarily complex goal-oriented human activity and, as such, provides a natural habitat for all three types of interpersonal/intergroup conflict (see Figure 7–2).

As we noted, conflict is a disruptive situation between two or more individuals (or groups of people) stemming from substantive disagreements over beliefs, values, attitudes, goals, scarce resources, or normative behavioral expectations. Conflict is ubiquitous. It is also endemic to human nature. From an organizational point of view, conflict is antithetical to the development of the collaboration needed to achieve collective goals and objectives.

Conflict-Development Cycle

It is important that police administrators learn to understand the dynamics of conflict. Conflict does not normally appear suddenly out of the blue. In fact, it passes through a cycle of progressive stages as tension builds. The stages or steps in the conflict-development cycle are as follows:

1. *Latent conflict.* At the latent stage, all of the basic conditions for future conflict exist but have not been recognized as a problem by potential adversaries. The most likely sources of substantive disagreement in an organizational setting are competition for scarce resources, role conflicts, and incompatible expectations.

2. *Perceived conflict.* Here, one or both of the parties recognize the causes of the conflict. Some latent conflicts are never perceived as conflicts per se and do not cross the threshold of awareness.

3. *Felt conflict.* At this point, tension starts to build between the participants. Felt conflict differs from the perceived conflict in that at least one of the parties begins to experience discomfort, stress, or anxiety.

4. *Manifest conflict.* The struggle begins in earnest, and the behavior of the participants makes the existence of the conflict obvious to others who are not directly involved in the dispute. Manifest conflict takes the form of overt behavior such as apathy, withdrawal, minimum job performance, sabotage, and open aggression.

5. *Conflict resolution.* Attempts to resolve the conflict can range from approaches that ignore it to strategies designed to confront it head-on and resolve it in such a way that all parties can achieve their goals.[6]

6. *Conflict aftermath.* Resolution or suppression ends the conflict, establishing new conditions, leading to effective cooperation or a new conflict, much worse than the previous one.[7]

From this perspective, conflict is as an unfolding process rather than a discrete event that occurs at one moment in time. The process consists of a series of episodes. Each episode involves an escalation in tension corresponding to the stages of the conflict-development cycle. The resolution of conflict sets the stage—in a dialectical sense—for new life experiences. While this process is fairly simple to understand, it is much more complicated than it might appear, since not all conflict passes through every stage in the cycle. Also, the participants in the conflict may not be at the same stage. One party might be at the manifest stage (ready to launch an attack), while the other is at the latent stage and unaware that a confrontation is brewing.[8]

Conflict theorists also use the cyclical approach to illustrate how participants process events in the conflict-development cycle. In destructive conflict situations, for example, winning becomes the object and is considered far more important than coming up with mutually acceptable solutions to substantive disagreements. The antagonists begin to conceal relevant information or pass on distorted information to mislead their opponents. Based on psychosocial dynamics, individuals become more committed—at an emotional level—to their original positions. Groups, on the other hand, become more cohesive and may substitute groupthink for rational analysis. Any deviation from the party line results in the imposition of immediate and severe sanctions. Contact with adversaries is discouraged except under controlled circumstances. Contrasting conceptions are formed and projected on opponents through the use of negative stereotypes. These stereotypes fuel the fire of discontent and are used to justify escalation in the level of conflict. Inherently aggressive people, who can turn others on and the tactical skill needed to exploit conflict, tend to emerge as strategists or group leaders. Aggression intensifies hostility and perpetuates the struggle until someone wins.[9] Destructive conflict is almost always a zero-sum equation. "To the victor go the spoils."

Edmonson and Smith break down interpersonal conflict into two parts and then discuss how to deal with it. *Task conflict* focuses upon substance—differences in opinion on how to do the work or conduct the enterprise. It should focus on a careful analysis of the facts of the situation. Personality differences fuel *relationship conflict* and lead to personal attacks and tensions.[10] "Hot topics" often degenerate into negative interpersonal emotions where people disagree on the relevance and interpretation of the data. To prevent such problems, Edmonson and Smith (2006, pp. 12–25) recommend three methods to resolve interpersonal conflict. First, "manage yourself"—reflect on your reaction, reframe the situation, and reflect on the issue at hand. Second, "manage conversations" and address issues directly, avoiding personal attacks. Third, "manage relationships" to build trust and clarify positions. The task is to address relationship conflicts directly and cool them down, rather than heat them up.

Similarly, Patterson, Grenny, McMillan, and Switzler recommend a "free flow of information" to bring controversies out into the open. Focus on what you want—for yourself, for others, and for the organization.[11] They urge us to avoid the "Sucker's Choice" of wanting to win the argument at any cost and justifying personal attacks. Instead, question your motives, control your emotions, and search for healthy options to conduct a dialogue.[12] Avoid telling "victim stories" ("It's not my fault!"), "villain stories" ("It's all your fault!"), and "helpless stories" ("There's nothing else I can do!"). Turn victims into actors, villains into humans, and the helpless into the able.[13] Police supervisors should attempt to mediate conflict by exposing personal struggles between officers that spark defensive reactions and help the parties examine their true motives.[14]

Conflict in Formal Organizations

Management theorists often disagree with one another when it comes to defining conflict and assessing its role in organizations. The literature suggests that there have been three relatively distinct phases in the development of thinking about conflict in organizational settings: (1) the traditional phase, (2) the human relations phase, and (3) the interactionist phase. **Traditionalists** viewed conflict as pathological and something to avoid at all costs. Behavioralists perceived conflict as a natural yet resolvable disturbance in the balance or equilibrium of an organization. Modern interactionists contend that a certain amount of conflict is necessary if goal-oriented groups are to perform effectively.

The Traditionalists

This early approach to conflict assumed that all interpersonal/intergroup conflict was bad. Traditional theorists believed, for example, that in well-managed organizations there would always be positive cooperation between labor and management. The conflict is a dysfunctional outcome caused by factors such as poor communication, lack of openness and trust between people, and failure of management personnel to respond to the needs or aspirations of their subordinates. If conflict reared its ugly head, it was management's job—through the use of logic and rational analysis—to determine the cause of the malfunction and to correct it on management's terms. The traditionalists subscribed to a Theory X perspective. Anyone who created conflict within the organization was considered persona non grata. In the past, departments fired disruptive police officers for the good of the service.

The Behavioralists

During the late 1940s, the human relations approach displaced traditionalism as the dominant view of conflict in formal organizations. **Behavioralists** accepted conflict as an inevitable fact of life whenever people were required to work together. Conflict was as a natural yet resolvable disturbance in the balance or equilibrium of an organization. Personal idiosyncrasies caused conflict. Human relations theorists focused their attention on the use of group dynamics (through such mechanisms as encounter groups, T-groups, and guided group interaction) to resolve disruptive interpersonal and intergroup conflict. A modified behavioral approach emerged during the late 1960s. Its proponents maintained that conflict created a paradox in complex organizations. While it often led to serious problems and dysfunctional behavior, it could also be beneficial if it evoked enough anxiety to motivate the parties to resolve their substantive differences through cooperative problem solving and participative management. Emphasis began to shift to the positive aspects of conflict management.

The Interactionists

A refinement of the human relations approach is to assimilate conflict when it is beneficial and discourage it only when it becomes harmful. **Interactionists** encourage some forms of conflict because harmonious, peaceful, tranquil, cooperative, and collaborative work groups tend to become static, apathetic, and openly resistant to innovation or change. They believe in introducing and maintaining a minimum level of conflict to keep the group viable, self-critical, and creative. Conflict can be constructive (or "functional") if it heightens anxiety to the point where the organization is forced to take proactive steps toward a realistic solution to the problem. Dysfunctional conflict, on the other hand, always has a negative influence on group performance and is detrimental to the welfare of all group members. The actual demarcation between functional and dysfunctional conflict is neither clear nor precise; it depends on the situation, the players involved, and the dynamics between the two. However, although some conflict is healthy and contributes to overall group performance, most groups and formal organizations try to eliminate it whenever possible.[15]

Organizational politics is often the basis of conflict, reflecting the absence of trust. Secrecy allows conflict-based politics to thrive and prosper. Openness is the antidote to the problem—let people know the basis for decisions. To do otherwise gives every rumor credibility. People must examine and admit their motives—*What do I want?* All members of the organization must engage in openness to alleviate the problems raised by politics.[16] Manage conflict to reveal and sponsor its benefits. Methods must be developed to promote discussion but prevent character assassination. Conflict is an opportunity for coaching, getting people across the organization to collaborate to benefit the entire organization. People must not expect bosses to settle conflicts without their participation. Instead, the parties must work together to jointly identify the issues and address how to solve them constructively. The resolution of the conflict must be transparent.[17]

A police department is not one of Max Weber's ideal organizational types. It is a microcosm of the society at large. Consequently, conflict within departments is the rule rather than the exception. As public officials who are responsible for getting things done through others and managing conflict, police administrators have an affirmative duty to study the causes of conflict and develop strategies designed to control them.

Causes of Organizational Conflict

Although it is possible to identify a great number of factors that can lead to conflict, much of the conflict in organizations appears to come from one of six sources:

1. Interdependence
2. Differences in power, status, and culture
3. Organizational ambiguity
4. Competition for scarce resources
5. Drive for autonomy
6. Bifurcation of subunit interests

Interdependence

Conflict always occurs within a context of mutual interdependence. There is a potential for conflict whenever people or organizational groups are dependent on each other to achieve their own particular goals. Pooling interdependence combines the output of two relatively independent groups to help the organization achieve its goals. Problems of sequencing occur when one group depends on another for input (such as raw materials or clientele). The dependency is either one way or reciprocal (where groups exchange inputs as well as outputs). Interdependence sets the stage for conflict in that the participants are required to interact with one another and exercise some power over each other. Large police departments are composed of many specialized work groups that interact to varying degrees in a coordinated effort to accomplish specific goals and objectives.[18]

Differences in Power, Status, and Culture

Intergroup conflict is very likely to erupt when there are significant disparities in power, status, and culture in a particular organization. Because of the complexity of police work, the following factors are important:

1. The real power to influence outcomes for individuals, groups, and the organization as a whole is seldom, if ever, distributed in the manner depicted by the chain of command on the organization chart. There is a very natural tendency for people or groups to acquire disproportionate amounts of power and to use that power to their advantage. Conflict is inevitable whenever there is a struggle for power.
2. Status, like power, is not shared equally among all persons or groups within a complex organization. In fact, differential status is the rule rather than the exception. Status (the value conferred on someone by significant others) is often related to education, training, assignment, rank, and political influence. Status differences normally do not create interpersonal or intergroup conflict when those with lower status are dependent on those of higher status. Most formal organizations work this way. Group members are socialized to expect and accept this kind of order

in work-oriented relationships. Because of the great complexity of modern police work, though, there are times when individuals or groups with technically lower status find themselves in a position to control the action and give orders to persons with higher status. There is, for example, a great potential for status-based conflict in situations where detectives—the so-called prima donnas of the police profession—find themselves under the functional supervision of uniformed patrol personnel. Also, unbridled competition for status can, in and of itself, degenerate into debilitating conflict in complex criminal justice organizations.

3. An organization's culture, or way of life (see Chapter 4), consists of shared beliefs, values, motives, norms, and behaviors exhibited by members of a group as they pursue their collective interests, goals, and objectives. Since complex organizations are composed of many work groups, some cultural diversity is normal. When two or more distinct cultures develop within the same organization, the clash in beliefs, values, motives, and behavioral expectations almost always leads to some overt conflict. The nature and extent of this conflict will depend on the issue, the emotional responses generated, the resources available, the tactical skills of the combatants, the importance of winning or losing to the various subcultures, and the overall level of reinforcement derived from mindless groupthink. Broderick argues that there is and will continue to be a great deal of conflict between those police officers who subscribe to the due process model of American law enforcement (the idealists) and those for whom crime control is the sole objective of police work (the realists). One group emphasizes functioning within constitutional constraints. The other group is utilitarian and operates on the implicit assumption that the end justifies the means.[19]

It is the police administrator's responsibility to manage—not eliminate—the conflict caused by differences in power, status, and culture within complex criminal justice organizations.

Organizational Ambiguity

Task uncertainty in nonroutine situations, coupled with organizational ambiguity, tends to create a sense of anomie (or normlessness) that exacerbates the potential for serious interpersonal/intergroup conflict. If such things as jurisdictions, goals, behavioral expectations, and performance criteria are not clear and specific, truly spontaneous conflict becomes possible. Under such circumstances, both the formal and the informal rules that govern task-oriented interaction break down. The lack of purposeful interaction makes organizations less efficient, effective, and productive. It also leads to the formation of factions. Once factions (cohesive subgroups) form and develop distinct cultural orientations of their own, they begin to pursue their interests as opposed to those outlined in the organization's mission statement. Organizational ambiguity of one kind or another is the most frequent cause of substantive conflict between managers and their subordinates. The emphasis on collective bargaining in law enforcement can be traced to the human need to minimize conflict-causing ambiguity in the workplace. Collective bargaining follows the assumption that a certain amount of controlled conflict (via negotiation) is healthy and represents an appropriate alternative to the spontaneous, often destructive, conflict that is generated by organizational ambiguity.[20]

Competition for Scarce Resources

Every organization operates on a finite budget, personnel, equipment, and other resources. What resources one component (or subunit) gets, other subunits do not get. As dependence on the same resource increases, so does the likelihood that competition will degenerate into open conflict. The chances that conflict will occur increase in direct proportion to the degree of scarcity.

Battle lines are drawn, and people or groups jockey for the power to capture the resources needed to achieve their own goals. Scarcity has a way of converting dormant or latent hostility into overt conflict—between individuals, between individuals and groups, or between groups.[21] Overt conflict can range all the way from an episodic show of disrespect to intentional sabotage. It is not uncommon for specialized units to siphon resources away from the patrol division, reducing the patrol division's ability to protect life and property, preserve the peace, prevent crime, and apprehend criminals.[22] Patrol officers feel exploited and become very cynical when denied the resources required to do their job. Cynicism creates and then perpetuates conflict in complex criminal justice organizations.[23]

Drive for Autonomy

Complex organizations are created, structured, and maintained to coordinate the activities of people in the workforce as they pursue mutually acceptable goals and objectives. As a rule, most newly hired employees enter the organization with a fairly broad zone of indifference. In other words, they are willing to accept direction from significant others in the organization who have either the legitimate authority or the power to issue orders and expect compliance.[24] This willingness helps to stabilize interaction patterns within the group. When superiors and subordinates do not agree with each other on the boundaries of the zone, however, the result is often conflict. Conflict erupts when subordinates resist direction and assert their autonomy. Most managers do not fully appreciate the fact that human beings perceive themselves as having certain freedoms (a "set of free behaviors") and that they are—over time—motivated to resist threats to, or abridgment of, those freedoms.[25] The possessor of freedom will try to reestablish it. The most direct way of reestablishing freedom is to challenge the authority of the manager as a representative of the status quo. Facing such challenges, managers may feel threatened and respond by invoking policies, procedures, rules, and regulations—with the aim of regaining control of the recalcitrant employee's on-the-job behavior. While this response may ensure minimum conformity, it can have dysfunctional consequences. It allows the problem to fester as a continuous source of conflict and perpetuates minimally acceptable performance on the part of the employee.[26] The rigid paramilitary structure in most police departments tends to exacerbate the psychological reactance syndrome that we just outlined.

Bifurcation of Subunit Interests

The bifurcation of subunit interests is a natural source of conflict in complex organizations. Subgoals of the organization delegated as a task to an organization subunit may become the subunit's major or exclusive goal, creating the potential for conflict. In the worst case, there can be a head-to-head competition between subunit goals and the overall goals of the organization. The potential for conflict increases dramatically when two or more specialized work groups with differing goals are functionally dependent on one another. This consideration is particularly important when one group's success at reaching its goals or accomplishing its tasks depends not only on what it does but on the behavior of other people or groups as well.[27] The desire of a special investigative team to "apprehend dopers and put them behind bars" might become intense and cloud their judgment. They might even make a deal to help get a potentially violent burglar (who terrorized a particular neighborhood) out of jail in exchange for information. The detectives in a situation like this would have allowed their own goals to supersede those of the police department, the legislature, and the community at large.

Dysfunctional Conflict

Interpersonal or intergroup conflict is dysfunctional when it creates intolerable anxiety, disrupts healthy relationships, wastes excessive amounts of time or energy, keeps an organization from accomplishing its lawfully prescribed mission (goals and objectives), or leads to destructive behavior. It is the manager's job to neutralize debilitating conflict and reward those who make positive contributions to the work group. Police administrators must do everything in their power to foster loyalty, cooperation, and a sense of teamwork. They have an affirmative duty to deal with the troublemakers who thrive on creating unnecessary conflict. If large-scale antagonism continues to exist, the reward system probably encourages confrontation and conflict instead of teamwork.[28]

O'Hara offers suggestions on dealing with people who are not "team players." First, do not jump to conclusions. Try to determine the source of the person's lack of participation. It may be due to a personal problem rather than their lack of enthusiasm or effort. Instead, begin a dialogue aimed at determining the source of the problem rather than making accusations. Accordingly, make sure the group does not ostracize the person. Get the group involved in the issue, and identify new ways to motivate everyone by recognizing and building upon individual skills and expertise.[29]

Functional Conflict

While the destructive effects of dysfunctional conflict are obvious and fairly easy to articulate, the positive effects of functional conflict are far subtler. Good managers have learned to recognize the dual nature of conflict and evaluate it regarding cost versus benefit. Some of the useful aspects of conflict are as follows:[30]

- It can act as a major stimulant for change.
- It can foster creativity and innovation.
- It can clarify issues and goals.
- It can encourage individuality.
- It can enhance communication.
- It can increase energy within a unit.
- It can promote cohesiveness.
- It is psychologically healthy.

The positive value of any conflict episode will depend, to a great degree, on the problem-solving skills of the manager who is responsible for resolving it. Effective police administrators are utilitarian in that they are willing to use any conflict-management strategy they feel is appropriate given the particular conflict situation. Table 7–1 contrasts functional with dysfunctional conflict.

Table 7–1
FUNCTIONAL AND DYSFUNCTIONAL CONFLICT

Conflict is functional when:

1. It turns on and energizes people.

2. It leads to goal-oriented interaction.

3. It helps people sharpen their goals, methods, and procedures.

4. It moves individuals or groups to higher levels of achievement.

5. It opens up channels for more communication.

6. It helps to release pent-up frustration and acts as a healthy catharsis.

7. It leads to more awareness and greater understanding.

Conflict is dysfunctional when:

1. It creates unhealthy and debilitating anxiety.

2. It siphons off energies that could otherwise be spent on productive activities.

3. It disrupts or destroys normal interpersonal or intergroup relationships.

4. It creates a situation in which "might" is used to conquer what is "right."

5. It keeps the organization from accomplishing its assigned mission, goals, and objectives.

6. It focuses on personalities rather than issues.

7. It leads to abnormal frustration, unhealthy anxiety, withdrawal, obstructionism, aggression, and other forms of destructive group behavior such as slowdowns, strikes, and "jungle warfare."

Reacting to and Managing Conflict

Conflict, like all other elements in the administrative process, must be managed so that it is not allowed to run amok. It is the job of managers to keep conflict functional and within the parameters of organizational necessity.[31] To motivate their personnel and increase the overall productivity of the workforce, they must try to stimulate healthy competition while minimizing the negative influence of dysfunctional conflict in the organization. Police administrators react to conflict issues, episodes, and situations in a variety of ways; depending on the circumstances and their managerial skills, they may either resolve the conflict or make it worse. Conflict resolution techniques run the gamut from cosmetic to functional.

Based on a review of the literature, it is clear that there are many strategies for dealing with conflict in complex organizations. While each may be effective under certain circumstances or in certain situations, some are of limited value because they fail to get at the sources of the conflict. Others have the potential to be effective but may be very difficult to implement. It is the manager's job to sort through the alternatives and choose the conflict-resolution strategy or technique most likely to succeed, given existing constraints.[32]

CASE STUDY   Lieutenant Michael Parks

Lt. Michael "Micky" Parks is a 19-year veteran of the Sparta Police Department. He is a fatherly college-educated man with the demeanor of an empathetic elementary-school teacher. The lieutenant has an easy-going personality and a unique ability to establish almost instantaneous rapport with other police officers. Under normal circumstances, he is an ideal mentor and coach.

Raymond Perkowski, a newly promoted sergeant, was initially assigned to the patrol division. He reported directly to Lt. Parks. They bonded spontaneously and became very good friends. Lt. Parks was the teacher, and Sgt. Perkowski was an eager student. He was a protégé who enjoyed picking the brain of his mentor. Sgt. Perkowski did not object to the fact that the lieutenant called most of the shots and made nearly all of the important decisions. After all, it eased his (Perkowski's) anxiety and made him look good to the brass.

As the sergeant became more comfortable with his role as a supervisor and started to believe in himself as a professional, he began to question his relationship with Lt. Parks. He felt a need to distance himself from the lieutenant.

Since Sgt. Perkowski liked Lt. Parks as a person, he did not want to hurt his feelings. He sent subtle messages designed to tell the lieutenant to back off. When the subtle approach failed, and the lieutenant kept interfering in his professional life, Sgt. Perkowski got angry. Since he was unable to vent his frustration, the anger turned to resentment. Sgt. Perkowski began to avoid the lieutenant whenever possible. He cooled their relationship as much as he could.

One night Lt. Parks—without Sgt. Perkowski's knowledge—took disciplinary action against one of Sgt. Perkowski's patrol officers. When Sgt. Perkowski heard about the incident, he got so angry that he initiated a confrontation with the lieutenant. He burst into the lieutenant's office and challenged his authority. After a heated exchange, Sgt. Perkowski told Lt. Parks that he was "sick and tired of being mothered" and that he wanted to be left alone to do his job. He told the lieutenant to "butt out" of his life.

Lt. Parks was mystified by what he saw as Sgt. Perkowski's bizarre behavior and vowed never to talk to the "ungrateful S.O.B." again.

What would you, as a conflict-management theorist, tell the lieutenant about the cause of his conflict episode? What can he do to ensure that it does not happen again? Be very specific.

Techniques

Management theorists have identified, described, and analyzed the conflict-management techniques most often used by practitioners. The most common ones are as follows:

1. Avoidance
2. Dominance
3. Soothing
4. Compromise
5. Resource acquisition
6. Superordinate goals
7. Structural change
8. Behavioral change
9. Use of principled negotiation

Avoidance.

Rather than dealing with conflict, many managers choose to close their eyes and pretend that it does not exist. Avoidance may be the most common method of addressing conflict, although what it does is ignore it. Stalling while studying a problem is the administrative equivalent of turning a blind eye to the conflict situation in hopes that things will sort themselves out and the problem will resolve itself. While this does not happen often, it does happen. Avoidance may be reasonable if the perceived consequences of the conflict are inconsequential, there is little chance of winning, or the costs far outweigh the benefits. However, a pattern of avoidance can lead to crisis management. Crisis management often occurs when conflict situations are ignored, thus causing more problems. They then must be resolved immediately without regard to cost. The most effective managers are inclined to confront conflict head-on; they are least likely to ignore it.[33]

Dominance.

The autocratic response to conflict is to rely on one's formal authority (i.e., position power) to force others to cease. The hierarchical structure of complex organizations builds on superior–subordinate relationships. Managers occupy strategic positions and are responsible for resolving dysfunctional conflicts. In effect, the manager can force compliance.[34] Due to the paramilitary nature of police work, many police administrators have learned to rely almost exclusively on their formal authority to force decisions on their subordinates. They wield this authority by their position in the chain of command. This type of autocratic command can be useful in making quick decisions designed to achieve short-term results, but it seems to be a misguided response in most situations. Coercing a cessation of conflict treats only the symptoms, not the cause or causes of the problem. As a result, the unresolved conflict is almost certain to erupt again. It may be even more destructive the second time around.

Soothing.

Soothing, or smoothing things over, is not much more than a diplomatic plea for more sensitivity or understanding. It is designed to defuse dysfunctional conflict by calming things down and straightening out ruffled feathers. If there are no substantive conflict issues involved, soothing may be the appropriate managerial response. By applying salve to the egos of those who conflict with one another, the manager helps eliminate much of the friction. Both sides can focus on points of agreement and downplay differences. The risk in this strategy is that real conflict may go unresolved. It may be pushed under the rug and allowed to fester. Under these circumstances, the conflict may become much worse.[35]

Compromise.

Compromise is a practical and popular approach to conflict management because it fits in with the realities of life in complex organizations. It consists of the mutual trading of offers, counteroffers, and concessions between those involved or their representatives.[36] The distinguishing feature of compromise is that each party is required to give something up to come to a mutually acceptable middle ground. There are no clear winners or losers. Everybody gets a little piece of the action. Compromise is one of the principal techniques used to resolve conflict in police departments throughout the United States. In some ways, though, it is the worst. Compromise puts expediency ahead of principle. Ignoring causes allows them to fester. Also, compromise decreases accountability and ensures that mediocrity prevails. If two competing, good ideas merge into one mediocre or bad idea, everybody loses. Holden argues organizations are better off avoiding compromise. He believes that everyone should be allowed to win or lose on occasion. Such action bolsters morale and generates better ideas designed to resolve interpersonal or intergroup conflict.[37]

Resource Acquisition.

A very important source of conflict in complex task-oriented organizations is unhealthy competition for scarce resources. The best way for managers to defuse this conflict is to acquire additional resources and to distribute them equitably. While this sounds fairly simple, it is often difficult to achieve.[38] Legislative bodies fund police departments from a finite and exhaustible tax base. Additional resources may not be available. This financial reality confronts police departments every day. Management by retrenchment and cut-back is here to stay. The rank structure in police departments may turn healthy competition into a form of dysfunctional conflict. When the chances for promotion are scarce, competition for it is certain to develop into intense conflict competing for that particular resource. One strategy for managing this kind of conflict is to diversify the rank structure and increase the total number of administrative positions. While the addition of managerial positions may increase morale, job satisfaction is usually temporary because the level of expectation also increases. Top-heavy organizations are seldom, if ever, efficient, effective, or productive.

Superordinate Goals.

A superordinate goal is a highly valued state of affairs where two or more conflicting parties cannot reach the cooperation of both or all of them. A manager using this conflict-management technique arranges conditions in such a way that people or groups are compelled to work together to overcome a common threat or achieve shared goals. The creation of superordinate goals is a functional strategy designed to transform "them" (out-group members) into "us" (in-group members). This strategy has the potential to reduce the level of destructive conflict.[39] Labor and management may put aside their deep-seated differences and work together when convinced survival of the organization is contingent on collaboration. Concession and take-back contracts are very common in the hostile world of shrinking resources. The use of superordinate goals should not be viewed as a panacea, however. Since they do not deal with the causes of conflict, superordinate goals may only delay the conflict. Most police administrators may find that there are real limitations on their ability to generate tailor-made superordinate goals.

Structural Change.

Reorganization is a common conflict-management strategy. Making transfers, developing new organizational relationships (setting up new departments, creating new coordinator positions, or uncoupling conflicting units), enlarging administrative areas to accommodate different units, and realigning managerial responsibilities reduce conflict. Transfer is one of the most popular methods used to manage dysfunctional conflict in complex organizations. Organizations reassign difficult employees to positions limiting the potential for destructive behavior. Police administrators often find that it is much easier to isolate recalcitrant personnel in relatively innocuous positions than it is to terminate their employment. Every police department can place troublemakers in very low status positions, minimizing their negative influence on work-group dynamics. There are two basic problems with this strategy, however. Even these low-status positions require personnel who are interested in the work and competent enough to do it. Positions as an undesirable disciplinary assignment will cause good people to avoid it out of fear that it will destroy their career. Such perception debilitates the entire organization. Transfers do not necessarily resolve conflicts. They may just move them from one location to another within the police department.[40]

Behavioral Change.

Inducing specific changes in behavior is one of the most difficult conflict-management techniques. One approach involves the use of *planned interventions* to change the beliefs, values, attitudes, and motives of one or more of the antagonists. Managers often try to help those in conflict understand and empathize with one another as they come to grips with personal emotions, values, and behaviors in conflict situations. Quite different from this is the *social learning* approach. The concept of psychosocial motivation is discarded in an attempt to understand and change the behavior that produces conflict. Managers identify the kind, category, or class of behavior (such as verbal, nonverbal, or emotional response) that must be changed. They try to determine what counterproductive "stuff" the persons involved have learned that now controls their behavior. They then factor these bits and pieces of information into a comprehensive diagnosis of the conflict situation and apply techniques (like modeling, direct reinforcement, or persuasive communication) that are likely to produce the desired change in behavior. In other words, by changing the consequences their subordinates expect from their behavior, managers can alter and direct that behavior.[41] However, changing behavior is not nearly as simple as it might appear. Resocialization and behavior modification techniques may produce harmful results in the hands of amateurs. They are also costly and time consuming. Consequently, resocialization and behavior modification have not been used extensively in law enforcement.

Principled Negotiation.

One way to prevent dysfunctional conflict is to encapsulate through the formulation of reasonable policies, procedures, rules, and regulations. They specify how group members are to interact with each other. Principled negotiation confronts issues directly. It focuses on identifying and clarifying the cause or causes of the conflict and moving systematically toward its resolution. Emphasize issues rather than personalities. The objective is to identify mutually acceptable ways of dealing with problems.[42]

> Principled negotiation shows you and your opponent how to obtain what you are entitled to and still be civil. It enables you to be equitable while protecting both of you against being taken advantage of.[43]

Again, principled negotiation aims to decide issues on their merits rather than resort to a haggling process.

Whisenand outlines six steps involved in "Getting to Yes":[44]

1. *Don't bargain over positions.* Avoid getting locked into a position, forcing defense of it.
2. *Being nice is not the answer.* Establish a collaborative context.
3. *Separate the people from the conflict.* Build trust and understanding.
4. *Concentrate on interests, not positions.* Identify where interests overlap and are compatible.
5. *Generate a number of options.* Review the possibilities before deciding what to do.
6. *Adopt objective criteria.* The use of an objective standard will help you to deal with the problem rationally.

If you must yield in the negotiation process, then choose to yield to principle, not to pressure.

Managerial Styles and Conflict Management

Police administrators, like all other managers, eventually settle into patterns, methods of operation (MO), or styles of conflict management that reflect their personalities and meet their own unique needs. Based on differing characteristic approaches to conflict resolution, researchers have identified five basic types of managers:

1. *Competitors ("Sharks").* Competitive managers are self-confident, assertive, and aggressive. They use power, intimidation, and domination to achieve their own goals in a win–lose environment. They are driven to win in a zero-sum game.
2. *Avoiders ("Turtles").* Avoiders are "lose–lose" managers who choose to remain neutral and duck dysfunctional conflict at all costs. They fear the potential damage

of confrontation and are willing to limp along within the constraints imposed by the status quo.

3. *Accommodators ("Teddy bears").* These managers formulate and live by a utilitarian lose–win philosophy designed to ensure their survival. Accommodators are not assertive or aggressive; they usually give way to conflict by folding under pressure. They go along to get along.

4. *Compromisers ("Foxes").* Compromise-oriented managers put expediency before principle as they seek short-term solutions to long-term problems. Compromise is a "lose–lose" strategy deifying the middle ground. Compromisers are always willing to make concessions to achieve consensus.

5. *Collaborators ("Owls").* These are "win–win" managers who accept the premise that conflict is inevitable and—depending on its nature and extent—a potentially positive aspect of life. They look for creative solutions to problems through the purposeful integration of divergent perspectives.[45]

Each style has both positive and negative features. As a result, good managers tend to favor a contingency approach. The contingency view of conflict resolution views the fundamental assumption that an effective managerial response is dependent on the synergistic interaction between the manager, the antagonists, and the totality of circumstances inherent in the situation.[46] In other words, they pick and choose the style they feel is most likely to produce the desired result.

The Problem Employee as a Source of Conflict

Most police officers are intelligent, hardworking, and helpful human beings. They usually exhibit positive mental attitudes, and they work in concert with their colleagues and managers to accomplish the police department's mission, goals, and objectives. Unfortunately, most work groups have at least one or two members who are continuous sources of dysfunctional conflict. It is the manager's job to either transform these recalcitrant troublemakers into productive human resources or—as a last resort—purge them from the organization.

Problem employees are usually honest people who—for one reason or another—simply do not fit into the organization and, as a result, engage in disruptive behaviors. They may be suffering from health problems, stress-induced burnout, mental illness, or social malfunctions related to such things as unhealthy romantic relationships, marital discord, drug abuse, and alcoholism. These personal problems can lead to apathy, absenteeism, interpersonal conflict, intergroup antagonisms, overt aggression, and other destructive and dysfunctional forms of behavior.[47]

There is absolutely no doubt that an employee's personal, medical, and emotional problems may seriously affect job performance and can generate a considerable amount of internal organizational conflict. In a police department with 100 or fewer employees, a single employee can create significant problems for the entire organization. A few unhappy, dissatisfied, conflict-oriented workers can—and often do—consume more of a police administrator's time and energy than do the hardworking, productive employees who make up the great majority of the staff.[48]

In the past, troublesome employees were considered to be throwaways. People perceived as the cause of organizational conflict were warned, disciplined, or transferred, depending on their willingness to conform to the expectations of management. Those who could not or would not change their behavior were terminated for the good of the service.[49] Things have changed rather dramatically, however. The human, financial, and organizational costs associated with firing experienced personnel have become prohibitive. Police administrators are now expected, where it is possible and when it is in the best interest of the department, to salvage rather than to fire people.[50] Managers coach and counsel problem employees to contain dysfunctional conflict and improve performance. This kind of *economic humanism* is on its way to becoming the norm in police administration.

Officer Jake Evans is a member of a large metropolitan police department on the west coast. He has been with department for approximately 14 years, and during that time has been an exemplary officer with numerous commendations and no disciplinary issues of note. Because of his solid service record and work ethic, Officer Evans applied for, and was selected to, an assignment with the Department's elite Metropolitan Division. Since his assignment to Metro, Evans had done a great job, and was considered a thoughtful and intellectual individual.

After having served in Metro for over four years, an incident occurred, which compelled Evans to write to the Police Protective League in the form of a "letter to the editor." The Protective League is not a true union; however, it is an extremely powerful organization with much bargaining power in terms of contracts and policy. Additionally, the League publishes a newsletter once a month, which is widely read by the entire department and retirees. To put it in perspective, membership in the League is not mandatory; however, about 98 percent of officers and middle supervisors are members. All of those members receive the paper at their homes.

Evan's letter dealt with the Chief of Police participating in a "Gay Pride" parade in one of the city's largely homosexual communities. He stated he was against the Chief participating, and that officers—specifically the Chief's security detail, which consisted of three uniformed personnel—should not be forced to work during the event. He took issue with the expense, which comes from taxpayers, and any advocacy toward the gay community. There was mention of recruiting efforts in the gay community being misplaced. Additionally, he went on to say that because he is a Christian, he felt homosexuals were morally corrupted, not children of god, and he opined gays were basically evil and lesser humans.

Members who read the letter made no less than 20 complaints against Officer Evans. Evans was immediately pulled from the field and placed on desk duty. Ultimately, none of the complaints were pursued because it was determined, with city attorney advice, that despite the fact the paper was a publication associated with the Department, it was not an official Department publication, and Evan's right to free speech could not be usurped.

Evans was eventually returned to the field and he retained his assignment in Metro.

Officer Evans was clearly expressing personal beliefs, based on his personal value system. How can managers deal with these types expressions when they are inappropriate for the workplace? What can be done to express the Department's regrets to those who were offended by Evan's words? Do you agree with not imposing discipline?

Employee Assistance Programs (EAPs)

Most managers do not have the clinical training or expertise needed to deal with all of the personal, physical, and emotional problems of their subordinates. Consequently, more and more police departments are establishing Employee Assistance Programs (EAPs). These EAPs are designed to improve personal and organizational performance by making prevention, diagnostic, and treatment services available to ill or troubled personnel.[51]

The majority of law enforcement agencies with 100 or more officers now have employee assistance programs.[52] They vary tremendously in size, scope, and overall level of sophistication. Comprehensive EAPs usually provide prevention, intervention, and treatment services to those who are at risk or in need:

1. *Prevention.* Prevention (intended to educate employees) is designed to keep potential problems from becoming real problems.
2. *Intervention.* Intervention (stepping into a situation) is a proactive attempt on the part of management to influence the course of events.
3. *Treatment.* Treatment (the application of remedies) represents a concerted effort by a professional staff to cure problems.

Thus, EAPs are designed to help employees cope with their personal and work-related problems, such as alcoholism and drug abuse, sexual harassment, financial planning, child and elder care, depression, and domestic violence.[53]

Police administrators play a dual role in an EAP. First, they monitor on-the-job behavior and evaluate actual job performance. If an employee's behavior becomes unacceptable or job performance is below par, the administrator must determine if organizational or personal problems cause the problem. Second, if the unacceptable behavior or poor performance is due to personal factors, it is the administrator's job to confront the employee constructively. As part of this confrontational process, the problem employee should be encouraged to seek help through the EAP.

EAPs establish a clear division of labor. Managers detect problems, confront employees, make necessary referrals, and perform a follow-up function. Prevention, intervention, and treatment services are provided by a professional staff with the training and

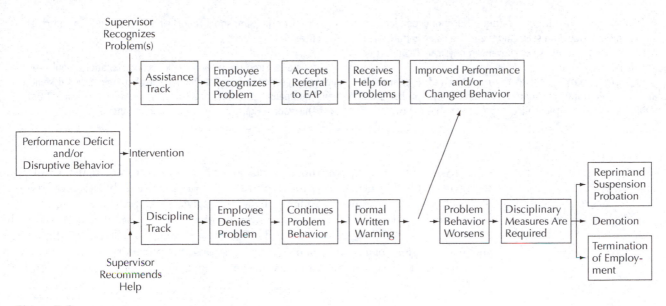

Figure 7–3
Dealing with Performance Deficits and Disruptive Job-Related Behavior.

expertise needed to help troubled employees cope with personal problems that cause disruptive behavior or performance deficits. If problem employees elect not to participate in an EAP or if they fail to benefit from participation in a program, they must—under normal circumstances—be dealt with through the formal disciplinary process. Figure 7–3 illustrates these options.

While EAPs may not be the panacea some claim them to be, they are tools that police administrators can use to help troubled employees overcome personal, physical, emotional, and social problems that have a negative impact on job performance. The benefits EAPs offer to the employee, and the organization, include the following:[54]

1. Increased probability of success
2. Increased referrals
3. Joint training sessions
4. Increased morale
5. Real help in response to one's "cry for help"
6. Stigma reduction
7. Feeling of being cared for as a person
8. Affordable access to help

CASE STUDY   Lieutenant Barry Simpson

Barry Simpson is a bright, streetwise police officer with a degree in human resources management. He was just promoted and assigned to the research and planning unit of a fairly large municipal police department. The department has been plagued by personnel problems and has lost a great deal of its credibility. Lt. Simpson's job, as a human resources development specialist, is to pinpoint the cause or causes of the problem and recommend managerial strategies designed to remedy the situation.

Based on an in-depth analysis of over 90 cases that resulted in severe disciplinary action, Lt. Simpson concluded that interpersonal conflict between police officers and civilians was a significant precipitating factor. He also found that much of this dysfunctional conflict was rooted in the physical, emotional, and social problems of troubled employees. It became obvious to him that these personal problems were exacerbated by the stress inherent in police work and the inhospitable psychosocial environment within which police officers ply their trade.

Lt. Simpson's research helped him to understand that interpersonal conflict (induced by unresolved personal problems) exacts an incalculable toll on any complex organization regarding poor performance, lost productivity, absenteeism, disciplinary action, and turnover. He concluded that the traditional response—to terminate problem employees—may be "penny wise and pound foolish"—a short-run solution to a long-range problem. The cost of replacing otherwise competent employees for drug or alcohol dependency is often much more costly than salvaging them. The same is true when it comes to dealing with those employees in physical discomfort or emotional distress.

In a preliminary report to the deputy chief in charge of research and planning, Lt. Simpson called for an emphasis on economic humanism in the police department. The deputy chief signed off on Lt. Simpson's report and forwarded it to the chief of police.

If you were Lt. Simpson, what specific recommendations would you give to your superiors? How should they go about minimizing dysfunctional interpersonal conflict and salvaging troubled employees? Use the framework in Figure 7–3 to frame your response.

Every police department should establish, or have access to, an independent EAP that works with management and for employees. The program must be designed to protect each employee's rights (including the right to privacy) yet provide managers with the information necessary to protect the health and welfare of the citizens served and of the employees seeking help. Once an EAP is up and running, self-referral should be encouraged. Also, management should adopt a strong disciplinary policy that incorporates mandatory participation in the EAP as an alternative to punitive action in conflict situations.[55]

CASE STUDY   Assistant Chief Roland Larson

The Chief of the Demopolis Police Department has been asked by the city manager to prepare a strategic, five-year plan that will address the numerous issues that will confront the department in the future. The agency is in its second year of a community policing program that has been less than successful. The latest community assessment report indicates that there is still need to improve communications with the community, that police personnel feel that they need more training in problem solving, that the public is becoming increasingly concerned with public safety issues, and calls for service are not answered as rapidly as desired.

The Chief has assigned Assistant Chief Roland Larson to set up a task force to prepare the five-year plan. The department serves an urban community and has 274 sworn personnel and 42 civilians. Fifty-two percent of the personnel are uniformed and their regularly assigned duties include responding calls for service. The department has specialized units including bias-related crimes, community crime prevention, drunk driving enforcement, environmental crimes, repeat offenders, and victim assistance.

Patrol personnel, in numerous instances, have offered resistance to the new policing approach with its emphasis upon improving the quality of life in the community. They express the belief that community policing was instituted by executive fiat. There is a general feeling that the needs of the officers have been ignored. Line officers feel that they have been told to solve neighborhood problems but not given the time or tools to be effective. Conflict varies within the department and seems to be concentrated in the line unit. This is in contrast to the investigative division and staff units that have readily accepted the change, but feel that there is a lack of coordination with the line unit. The police union that represents the majority of personnel in the department has remained neutral over the issue of community policing, but is becoming increasingly restless as the patrol units continues to express grave concerns about training and implementation of community policing.

Given your knowledge of group behavior, how would you go about creating this task force? What personnel would you ask to become members of the task force? How would you deal with the conflict in the department? How would you deal with the specialized units in the department? What conflict resolution technique would you think would be the most promising? Why?

SUMMARY

Interpersonal and intergroup conflict is a ubiquitous and a normal fact of life in complex criminal justice organizations. Conflict arises in situations where someone or something thwarts or is about to thwart someone else's goals. It is an unfolding process rather than a discrete event.

Many police administrators harbor traditionalist views about conflict. They view all conflict as dysfunctional and bad. Their goal is to eliminate it at any cost. Modern-thinking police administrators, on the other hand, view conflict somewhat differently. They accept constructive conflict and try to neutralize destructive conflict. The interactionist school of organizational thought believes conflict is beneficial when it forces the parties to reevaluate situations and to take proactive steps toward realistic solutions to divisive problems.

The common sources of conflict in complex criminal justice organizations are (1) interdependence; (2) differences in power, status, and culture; (3) organizational ambiguity; (4) unbridled competition for scarce resources; (5) drive for autonomy; and (6) bifurcation of subunit interests. Conflict is dysfunctional when it creates too much anxiety, disrupts healthy relationships, consumes an excessive amount of time and energy, keeps the organization from accomplishing its mission, or leads to destructive behavior. Functional conflict, on the other hand, energizes people, enhances communication, provides an outlet for pent-up frustration, and becomes an educational experience.

This chapter outlined some potentially effective conflict-management strategies for police departments. One of the most promising is the use of principled negotiation. Principled negotiation seeks to prevent hardening of attitudes and issues so that the parties involved will work toward true compromise and conciliation.

Problem employees are often a source of dysfunctional conflict in complex criminal justice organizations. Under these conditions, it is management's responsibility to neutralize the conflict or reduce it to an acceptable level. Based on the emerging philosophy of economic humanism, many police departments have established employee assistance programs. These EAPs are designed to improve organizational as well as a personal performance by making prevention, intervention, and treatment services available to ill, troubled, or disruptive personnel. Competent police administrators learn how to develop and manage all kinds of human resources rather than waste them.

DISCUSSION TOPICS AND QUESTIONS

1. What are the basic behavior modes shown in the collaboration–aggression continuum? Describe them, and give an example of each one.

2. Define *interpersonal conflict*. How does it differ from intergroup conflict in an organizational context?

3. List the stages or steps in the conflict-development cycle. Explain how they fit together as a part of a dynamic, unfolding process.

4. Identify the three distinct phases of management thinking as it relates to organizational conflict. How do the interactionists differ from the traditionalists?

5. What are the six primary causes of conflict in complex criminal justice organizations? Give examples.

6. Contrast functional with dysfunctional conflict. Discuss the most useful aspects of organizational conflict.

7. Identify the most common conflict-management techniques used by police administrators. What is the premise of principled negotiation?

8. What are the basic managerial types of police administrators regarding their approach to resolving interpersonal and intergroup conflict?

9. What is the basis of the employee assistance program movement? What is the role of the manager in the EAP process?

FOR FURTHER READING

Robert B. Denhardt, Janet V. Denhardt, and Maria P. Aristigueta, *Managing Human Behavior in Public and Nonprofit Organizations* **(Thousand Oaks, CA: Sage, 2015).**

These authors offer a detailed explanation of the causes and results of conflict in public and nonprofit agencies. They cover conflict-resolution strategies in detail and offer their recommendations.

Kerry Patterson, Joseph Grenny, Ron McMillan, and Al Switzer, *Crucial Conversations: Tools for Talking when Stakes are High* **(New York: McGraw-Hill, 2002).**

The authors present methods for conducting productive negotiations to resolve conflicts.

Paul M. Whisenand, *Supervising Police Personnel: The Fifteen Responsibilities* **(Upper Saddle River, NJ: Prentice Hall, 2007).**

Whisenand analyzes conflict and its consequences in law enforcement agencies and what administrators can do to address them. He strongly recommends principled negotiation as a method of conflict resolution.

ENDNOTES

1. Stephen P. Robbins and Timothy A. Judge, *Organizational Behavior* (Upper Saddle River, NJ: Pearson Prentice Hall, 2013), p. 119.

2. Eric J. Van Sylke, *Listening to Conflict* (New York: AMACOM, 1999).

3. Kenneth W. Thomas, "Conflict and Negotiation Processes in Organizations," in Marvin D. Dunnette and L. M. Hough, eds. *Handbook of Industrial and Organizational Psychology* (Palo Alto, CA: Consulting Psychologists Press, 1992), pp. 651–717.

4. S. N. Joni, and Damon Beyer "How to Pick a Good Fight," *Harvard Business Review* (2009, December), pp. 2–11.

5. Robbins and Judge, *Organizational Behavior*, pp. 143–144.

6. Elliot M. Fox and Lyndall Urwick, *Dynamic Administration: The Collected Papers of Mary Parker Follett* (New York: Hippocrene Books, 1973).

7. Louis Pondy, "Organizational Conflict: Concepts and Models," *Administrative Science Quarterly*, Vol. 12 (1967), pp. 296–320.

8. Hal G. Rainey, *Understanding and Managing Public Organizations* (San Francisco, CA: Jossey-Bass, 2014), p. 411.

9. Robbins & Judge, *Organizational Behavior*, pp. 143–144.

10. Amy C. Edmonson and Diana M. Smith, "Too Hot to Handle? How to Manage Relationship Conflict," *California Management Review*, Vol. 49, No. 1 (2006), p. 6.

11. K. Patterson, J. Grenny, R. McMillan, and A. Switzler, *Crucial Conversations: Tools for Talking When Stakes Are High* (New York: McGraw-Hill, 2002), p. 20.

12. Ibid., pp. 37–41.

13. Ibid., pp. 106–114.

14. D. Corcoran, "How Useful Is a Problem-Solving Approach to Police Station Conflict Management: Keeping the Peace among Police Officers," *International Journal of Police Management*, Vol. 16, No. 2 (2014), pp. 113–123.

15. Robbins & Judge, *Organizational Behavior*, pp. 143–144.

16. J. Grenny, "Yes, You Can Make Office Politics Less Toxic," *Harvard Business Review* (November 2017), pp. 2–5.

17. J. Weiss and J. Hughes, "Want Collaboration? Accept, and Actively Manage, Conflict," *Harvard Business Review* (March 2005), pp. 1–10.

18. John R. Schermerhorn, James G. Hunt, Richard N. Osborn, and M. Uhl-Bien, *Organizational Behavior* (Hoboken, NJ: John Wiley & Sons, 2010), p. 237.

19. John J. Broderick, *Police in a Time of Change* (Prospect Heights, IL: Waveland Press, 1987).

20. L. S. Miller, H. W. More, and M. C. Braswell, *Effective Police Supervision* (New York: Routledge, 2017), pp. 537–540.

21. Schermerhorn, Hunt, Osborn, and Uhl-Bien, *Organizational Behavior*, p. 237.

22. V. A. Leonard and Harry W. More, *Police Organization and Management* (New York: Foundation Press, 2000), p. 330.

23. G. Cordner, *Police Administration* (New York: Routledge, 2016), p. 235.

24. C. Barnard, *The Functions of the Executive* (Cambridge, MA: Harvard University Press, 1976).

25. Jack W. Brehm, *A Theory of Psychological Resistance* (New York: Academic Press, 1966).

26. Schermerhorn, Hunt, Osborn, and Uhl-Bien, *Organizational Behavior*, pp. 234–235.

27. Ibid.

28. Robbins and Judge, *Organizational Behavior*, p. 485.

29. C. O'Hara, How to Work with Someone Who Isn't a Team Player. *Harvard Business Review* (April 21, 2017), pp. 2–5.

30. P. Whisenand, *Supervising Police Personnel: The Fifteen Responsibilities* (Upper Saddle River, NJ: Prentice Hall, 2007), p. 245.

31. Whisenand, *Supervising Police Personnel*, p. 245.

32. Robbins & Judge, *Organizational Behavior*, p. 450.

33. Whisenand, *Supervising Police Personnel*, p. 245.

34. Schermerhorn, Hunt, Osborn, and Uhl-Bien, *Organizational Behavior*, p. 245.

35. Ibid.

36. Schermerhorn, Hunt, Osborn, and Uhl-Bien, *Organizational Behavior*, p. 241.

37. Ibid.

38. Robbins & Judge, *Organizational Behavior*, p. 458.

39. Ibid., pp. 377–378.

40. Miller, More, and Braswell, *Effective Police Supervision*, p. 382.

41. Ibid., p. 436.

42. Robert B. Denhardt, Janet V. Denhardt, and Maria P. Aristigueta, *Managing Human Behavior in Public and Nonprofit Organizations* (Thousand Oaks, CA: Sage, 2015), p. 340.

43. Whisenand, *Supervising Police Personnel*, p. 280. Roger Fisher, William Ury, and Bruce Patton, *Getting to Yes: Negotiating Agreements without Giving in* (New York: Penguin, 1991).

44. Ibid., pp. 280–282.

45. Thomas, Conflict and negotiation processes.

46. Miller, More, and Braswell, *Effective Police Supervision*, pp. 174–177.

47. Ibid., p. 441.

48. Ibid., pp. 442–445.

49. Leonard and More, *Police Organization and Management*, p. 48.

50. Whisenand, *Supervising Police Personnel*, p. 250.

51. D. B. Goldstein, "Employee Assistance for Law Enforcement: A Brief Review," *Journal of Police and Criminal Psychology*, Vol. 21 (2006), pp. 31–40.

52. Ibid.

53. G. Shawn Reynolds and Wayne E. K. Lehman, "Levels of Substance Use and Willingness to Use the Employee Assistance Program," *The Journal of Behavioral Health Services and Research*, Vol. 30 (2006), pp. 238–248.

54. Goldstein, Employee Assistance.

55. Miller, More, and Braswell, *Effective Police Supervision*, p. 297.

8

DECISION-MAKING

The Essential Element in Applied Management

Learning Objectives

1. Identify key elements in the definition of a managerial decision.
2. Demonstrate the steps involved in the rational decision-making process.
3. Define the terms *bounded rationality* and *satisficing*.
4. Identify the differences between Systems 1 and 2.
5. Consider the nature and effects of biases leading to irrational decision-making.
6. Consider the advantages and disadvantages often associated with group decision-making.

Key Terms

anchoring
attribution errors
bounded rationality
brainstorming
comparative analysis
confirmation bias
decision
decision-making
Delphi technique
emotional tagging
group decision-making

intuitive decision-making
loss aversion
managerial decisions
nominal group technique
nonprogrammed decisions
pattern recognition
programmed decisions
rational decision-making
reflective urgency
satisficing
Systems 1 and 2

In the most general sense, to decide is to make up one's mind. A **decision** is a choice from among a set of available alternatives. **Managerial decisions** are choices made between alternative courses of action and translated into administrative behavior that is designed to achieve an organization's mission through the accomplishment of specifically targeted goals and objectives. The key elements in this definition of a managerial decision are (1) choices, (2) alternatives, (3) targets, and (4) purposeful behavior.

CASE STUDY   Chief Gary Pirsig

Lyndora is a small, relatively affluent community adjacent to a major industrial city in the Midwest. It appeared until quite recently that Lyndora would escape the drug epidemic. The crack cocaine death of a very popular local high school basketball player shattered this illusion, however. The coroner's inquiry into the young man's death concluded that teenage drug abuse was common and represented a serious health problem. Based on the coroner's report, the news media demanded more drug enforcement activity by the police.

Gary Pirsig, the new chief of police who came from outside the department and serves at the pleasure of the city council, was reluctant to act. The chief was, by his admission, uncomfortable making unanticipated decisions in unsettled circumstances. He was sensitive to the political liabilities inherent in making a "wrong" decision, and he wanted to avoid criticism at all costs. After a particularly nasty editorial in the local newspaper, Pirsig's anxiety level skyrocketed to the point where he became physically ill and had to take three days off from work.

The chief refused all requests for interviews and issued a news release saying that his department's drug enforcement policy was under review. He admitted to a close friend that he was using this stalling announcement to avoid making hasty decisions.

The ploy did not work. The media continued to press its demands for action. The chief prepared and circulated the rough draft of a new drug enforcement policy emphasizing full enforcement and user accountability to get the media off his back. The draft policy called on police officers, in addition to arresting all drug pushers, to apprehend and prosecute everyone, regardless of age, who possessed illegal drugs or drug paraphernalia. The new "get tough" policy was scheduled to go into effect in 10 days.

After receiving some negative feedback on the policy from school administrators, elected officials, and concerned parents, the chief had second thoughts and put the drug enforcement policy on hold for further study. Chief Gary Pirsig's indecisiveness has caused a morale problem in the police department and has strained his relations with members of the city council. In fact, there have been calls for his resignation.

Chief Pirsig has a big problem. He violated some very basic principles and committed the two cardinal sins associated with decision-making. How should this situation have been handled? Based on the information in this chapter, what process would you have used to decide how to deal with this particular problem? Be specific.

1. *Choices.* If a police administrator does not have the opportunity or ability to make a choice, there is no real decision. Following rules, obeying orders, or being coerced to act in certain ways cannot—without a great deal of distortion—be construed as making decisions.

2. *Alternatives.* There must be more than one possible course of action available in order for the police administrator to have a choice. Effective managers look for and/or try to create realistic options for resolving problems.

3. *Targets.* To inform the decision-making process, goals should be written, measurable, both challenging and attainable, and communicated to organizational members.[1]

4. *Behavior.* Making decisions is irrelevant unless they are translated into action. To quote General George S. Patton, "When a decision has to be made, make it. There is no totally right time for anything."[2]

Decision-making is the complex process of generating and evaluating alternatives and making choices based on relevant knowledge, beliefs, and judgments. Whisenand notes, "Decision making is the centerpiece of police leadership and management. It serves as a start and end point. It is the driving force of self-efficacy and organizational results. It is the life blood of all ideas, practices, and challenges that follow. Our ability to choose—to make decisions—is to be forever prized and always appreciated."[3]

Decision-making is a natural and ubiquitous human activity. It is, in terms of modern organization and management, one of the most important, if not the most important, of all managerial activities. Virtually every management action is contingent, to one degree or another, on decision-making. Chester I. Barnard[4] identified decision-making as one of the "functions of the executive." Two other management theorists, Claude George[5] and Herbert Simon,[6] go so far as to say that management is, in fact, synonymous with decision-making. While this may be an overstatement, it helps to explain why so much attention is being focused on decision theory and its application in complex criminal justice organizations.

Problem Solving and Decision-Making

The terms *problem solving* and *decision-making* are used interchangeably in the context of management because managers spend most of their time making decisions to resolve problems. Allison[7] defines the decision-making process as rational, consisting of four steps:

1. Translate goals into objectives, and then translate objectives into payoffs and utility.
2. Choose among alternatives.
3. Consider the consequences.
4. Select the alternative whose consequences have the greatest utility.

Based on these concepts, decision-making is a multistep process through which problems are recognized, diagnosed, and defined. Alternative solutions are generated, selected, and implemented. This process helps produce a personal commitment to a given course of action and is manifest in one's willingness to invest energy, effort, expertise, and other resources to achieve a desired end state of existence.

All managers are obligated to make decisions designed to resolve problems that fall within the scope of their authority. These decisions can be broken down into two categories: (1) personal decisions and (2) organizational decisions. Personal decisions are those that, due to their nature and complexity, cannot ordinarily be delegated to others. Making a major decision (e.g., to terminate the employment of a high-ranking exempt manager) may require several subsidiary judgment-based decisions that can only be made by the chief executive. In other situations, a major decision (like where to build a new jail) may be announced by the chief of police even though different people acting in their organizational capacity made many subsidiary decisions. Allison calls this the organizational process model.[8] While chief executives do not make all decisions personally, they are ultimately responsible for all of the decisions made by their subordinates.

Organizational Decision-Making

While all of us make a wide variety of personal decisions, only certain members of any organized work group have the ability and the desire to exercise formal decision-making authority. Even when people have the ability and desire to make decisions, they are not, under normal circumstances, empowered to make them unless they have been granted specific authority to do so. There must be some rationale to stipulate who within a particular organization has the responsibility for which decisions. The lack of specificity in this area produces ambiguity, anxiety, and a sense of anomie.

One generally accepted rationale comes from two factors: (1) the scope of the decision and (2) the designated level of management. The scope of the decision is the proportion of the total organization it is likely to affect—the greater the proportion, the broader the scope of the decision. The levels of management in a hierarchical order indicate formal authority and position power.

1. *Upper-level managers* are the appointed or elected top executives who serve as agency administrators, department heads, and program directors. Executive work is not that of the organization per se, but the specialized work of maintaining the organization in operation. These top executives are expected to establish a sense of purpose, formulate overall policy, and make those decisions that affect the organization as a whole.

2. *Middle-level managers* come between the top and lower levels of the organization. They are the bureau chiefs and division heads who act on behalf of their superiors to interpret department policies, coordinate the activities of work units, motivate employees, and maintain discipline. Middle-level managers make decisions designed to achieve results. Their decision-making authority is limited and always constrained by preexisting policy.

3. *Lower-level (supervisory) managers* are responsible for the job-related activities of others. They are the work-group leaders charged with getting subordinates to carry out specific tasks as set down by middle managers. Lower-level managers are expected to motivate workers to perform these tasks within a framework of established policies, procedures, rules, and regulations. Consequently, for these managers decision-making is highly structured and related almost exclusively to operational considerations. The rationale is fairly simple: the broader the scope of a particular decision, the higher the level of the manager who is likely to make it.

Nothing just stated precludes any manager who has the primary responsibility for deciding against seeking the advice of other management personnel or subordinates. Only fools try to make decisions in a vacuum. Top-notch police managers tap every available resource. They also know that it might be desirable to allow members of the work group to make certain decisions. We discuss group decision-making later in this chapter.

Influences on Decision-Making

As we noted, no decisions are made in a vacuum. Decisions are made by people at different levels in the organization, and every decision is influenced to one degree or another by the environment, the dynamics of the decision situation, and the personal characteristics of the decision-maker. These factors are not independent variables. They work in conjunction with one another to produce idiosyncratic decisions. We discuss each of the factors to gain insight into the decision-making process.

Decision theorists frequently discuss what is called the state of nature. State of nature refers to those aspects of a decision-maker's environment that affect choice. Environmental factors can be grouped into two basic categories: (1) the internal environment and (2) the external environment. Some of the internal factors that affect choice are as follows:

1. The specificity of the organization's mission, goals, and objectives.
2. The delegation of sufficient authority to enable managers to carry out their assigned duties.
3. The degree of autonomy given to management personnel at different levels in the organization.
4. The leeway granted to managers by departmental policies, procedures, rules, and regulations.
5. The availability of valid, reliable, and objective information on which to base decisions.
6. The time and energy used to select, train, and retain well-qualified managers.
7. The nature, extent, and effect of intra-organizational conflict.
8. The restrictions imposed on management via the collective-bargaining process.
9. The adequacy of the reward system in promoting timely and effective decision-making.

The external factors that affect choice include, but are not limited to, the following:

1. Social instability
2. Rising expectations
3. Professional ethics
4. Legal constraints
5. Dwindling resources
6. Political conflict
7. Technological change

Internal and external environmental factors are never under the direct control of the decision-maker. Effective decision-makers learn to accept and cope with this uncertainty, complexity, volatility, and risk. Good managers are willing to take a calculated risk. Since they see decision-making as a challenge, they are seldom immobilized by fear of the unknown in a systematic way.

Situational Variables

No two decision situations are exactly the same. There are simply too many variables. Every problem that elicits a decision is unique in terms of the following:

1. Nature
2. Extent
3. Difficulty
4. Urgency
5. Seriousness
6. Complexity
7. Solution

Each decision is a unique product of the dynamic interaction between the decision-maker, environmental factors, and situational variables. No one makes correct decisions all the time. Good managers are usually decisive and process information in such a way that they make right decisions more often than wrong decisions. Effective decision-makers dare to be different. They unshackle themselves from the past and use creative problem solving as a ticket to success.

Personal Variables

There is a personal dimension to managerial decision-making in all complex criminal justice organizations. Even in the most favorable environment and in relatively stable situations, the personal characteristics of managers have a great influence on the quality of their decisions. Two police administrators evaluating identical data, related to the same problem, based on identical criteria, may reach different conclusions. Decision theorists account for such disparities in terms of unique personal factors such as the following:

1. *Mental health.* While they do not always make the right choice, emotionally healthy managers tend to be adequate decision-makers. Managers with strong self-concepts know themselves and are inner directed. Those who see themselves as problem solvers are unlikely to avoid or to postpone decisions. They do not fear that decisions will lead to failure or personal loss. Emotionally unhealthy managers, on the other hand, usually have difficulty in processing information and making decisions. Psychotics are out of touch with reality, and neurotics distort it. Impulsive managers become anxious and irritable over delays. They take action without adequate fact-finding or analysis. Compulsive managers are just the opposite. They are detail minded, cautious people who seek refuge in procrastination. Compulsive managers are very insecure. They allow decision situations to deteriorate due to their emotional need to minimize risks. Understanding the role of the personality in making decisions is important. It has practical value in improving the overall quality of managerial decision-making.

2. *Intellectual capacity.* Because of the formal education usually required of personnel who enter management in the private sector, people with average or below-average intelligence seldom get the chance to test their abilities. Most of the middle- and top-level managers in the private sector are in the upper 10 percent of the general population in terms of intelligence. There is little doubt that this intelligence contributes to their ability to make decisions. Due to the nature of the promotion process in most police departments, police administrators exhibit

a much wider range of intelligence. Within this range, the qualitative aspects of a police administrator's intelligence may exert more influence on decisions than his or her intelligence quotient (IQ). A division chief with an IQ of 120 and a great deal of common sense is in a better position to make good decisions than another upper-level manager with an IQ of 130 and little or no common sense. It is likely that the division chief will make even better decisions if he or she is knowledgeable, competent, mature, and emotionally healthy. While intelligence is positively correlated with managerial performance, the relationship is extremely complex.

3. *Education and experience.* The more complex, technical, or global a decision is, the more important it is for the decision-maker to have access to a broad reservoir of related information. Consequently, education and experience can make a significant contribution to the overall quality of managerial decisions. Decision theorists are quick to point out that the level of relevant knowledge is not necessarily correlated with the years of education or experience, however. It is dependent on the strength of the individual's motivation as well as the nature, extent, and quality of his or her learning experience. In some cases, too much experience can have a negative influence on decision-making. Some managers become experience bound and make major decisions based on past successes even if the current situation calls for creative problem solving and a break with tradition. The effect is also negative when a police administrator's education and experience have led to the development of undesirable managerial practices.[9]

4. *Values, attitudes, and perceptions.* As discussed in Chapter 4, managers bring their beliefs, values, attitudes, and perceptions with them to the workplace. Values are expressions of what a person considers to be worthy and to have a potential for need satisfaction. Attitudes are predispositions to evaluate and act in some favorable or unfavorable way. Values and attitudes are factored into our perception and help to shape it. Perception is a process used to give meaning to our environment by organizing sensory impressions. Colored by our values and attitudes, perception can short-circuit **rational decision-making**.[10] Under these circumstances, a manager's values and attitudes have a direct influence on the identification of problems, alternatives, and choice criteria in decision-making. Good police administrators strive diligently to overcome the negative aspects of selective perception. While there is no such thing as objective reality, history is replete with examples of value systems getting in the way of sound decision-making.

5. *Motivation to act.* Managers are unique individuals who are different from one another in terms of their motivation to act. Identifying problems, evaluating data, and searching for solutions require analytical ability as well as creativity. They do not require courage. Making a decision to act based on these processes is another matter altogether. Taking action, which is the essence of decision-making, requires managers to risk their reputations, their positions, and sometimes even their careers.[11] Good managers have confidence in themselves and are motivated to take risks. Police managers who have a healthy need to acquire power usually feel comfortable making tough decisions. They find decision-making pleasurable and self-affirming. Making decisions is an expression of power and a symbol of their value to the organization. Managers with a strong need for affiliation often have a very hard time making organizational decisions. An unhealthy dependence on others detracts from the decision-making task, distorts perception, and lowers their resolve to take unpopular actions. The excessive need for safety or security almost always has the same effect because decision-making involves risk taking. Managers who are offended by constructive criticism, who feel threatened when their subordinates make suggestions, and who fear change frequently make decisions that meet their emotional needs but that fail to solve organizational problems.[12] It is essential for departments to recruit, screen, select, and train managers who have the ability to make correct decisions and to link those decisions with action.

Types of Organizational Decisions

Management personnel at all levels make many kinds of decisions. Some are fairly simple; others are very complex. Top executives make strategic decisions that affect and guide the total organization. Lower-level managers spend most of their time making operational decisions involving limited actions designed to achieve a work unit's goals and objectives. Middle-level managers play a dual role: They (1) help executives develop long-range strategies and (2) see to it that line managers convert available resources into valuable goods or services.

Another way to categorize organizational decisions is regarding how routine or well-structured they are as opposed to how novel or unstructured they happen to be. Routine decisions include those that recur frequently, involve standardized decision-making procedures, and entail a minimum of uncertainty. Decision-makers rely on policies, procedures, and past precedents. In this simple context, the solution is self-evident, and the leader can make sense of the situation easily. The "command and control" style typical of police departments works best here. Directives are straightforward, and decisions can be delegated. Still, leaders must guard against oversimplification. The situation can be incorrectly classified, and problems can result.[13]

Some theorists conceptualize managerial decisions on a continuum from the well structured to the very poorly structured. Partially structured decisions fall somewhere between the two endpoints. Herbert Simon viewed these endpoints as "programmed" and "nonprogrammed." **Programmed decisions** are repeatedly made, on a routine basis and in concert with preestablished alternatives. **Nonprogrammed decisions**, on the other hand, are elicited by new and unique problems.[14] They are normally made in poorly structured situations where there are no preexisting or readymade courses of action. Programmed and nonprogrammed decisions can ordinarily be distinguished from one another by (1) how unique the problem is, (2) to what degree one solution is specified, (3) who is responsible for making the decision, and (4) in what organizational setting the decision is made. It is clear that deciding how to schedule police personnel is much easier than deciding what to do in a union-initiated work stoppage. Figure 8–1 illustrates graphically the difference between programmed and nonprogrammed organizational decisions.

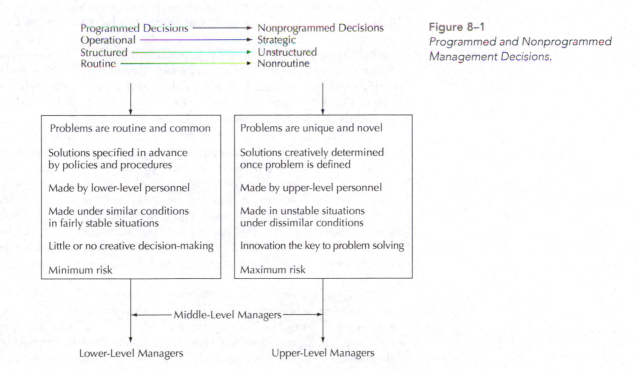

Figure 8–1
Programmed and Nonprogrammed Management Decisions.

Heuristic versus Objective Decisions

Managerial decisions can also be classified in terms of the processes used to make them. *Heuristic decisions* are gut-level choices based on intuition and personal judgment. The most common heuristic approaches to problem solving are rules of thumb and trial and error. Decisions are made on the basis of similar past experiences or the advice of significant others. The essence of the heuristic model is that the criteria used to validate a decision are internal to the personality of the decision-maker, not external to it.[15] Consequently, heuristic decisions—while they may be perfectly rational—are subjective and uniquely personal. Whisenand contends that situations do not always lend themselves to rationality and leaders must often rely on their good sense and instinctive feelings.[16]

Objective decisions are logical, fact-based choices that are expected (in terms of probability) to solve problems.[17] Reaching objective decisions is much more difficult than using one's sixth sense. Objective decision-making involves the following:

1. Scanning for problems
2. Identifying problems
3. Listing probable causes
4. Designing solutions
5. Evaluating solutions
6. Choosing an alternative
7. Implementing a decision
8. Analyzing feedback
9. Making adjustments

Here again, organizational decisions are on a continuum, with most decisions falling somewhere between the two endpoints (heuristic and objective).

Reactive versus Proactive Decisions

Organizational decisions reflect the motivation to act. *Reactive decisions* respond to a perceived problem the decision-maker needs to resolve. The nature of the stimulus and strength of the drive to resolve the problem help establish the urgency of the response. Crisis decisions at either the strategic or the operational level are always made under pressure. Crisis situations are characterized by surprise, urgency, stress, anxiety. They threaten high-priority goals. These situations must be stabilized so that patterns can be identified to prevent future crises. The leader must take decisive action. Crisis decisions are often made heuristically, based on intuition, experience, instantaneous analysis, and emotional considerations rather than objective rationality. Even though a crisis decision may lack scientific objectivity and can be very difficult to justify on a logical basis, it may solve the problem. The danger here is that leaders can become overconfident and overcommitted to an effective decision that does not fit future circumstances.[18]

Proactive decisions focus on the future. They are a by-product of the planning process, and they prepare police managers to deal with the problems they could face down the road. Proactive decision-making involves predetermining future courses of action by deciding when, where, how, and by whom a task or set of tasks will be accomplished. Proactive decisions are preparatory and normally made in an orderly manner, under calm conditions, without the pressure generated by time constraints. Contingency plans (products of proactive decision-making) are designed to counteract the chaos generated by fear of the unknown. While a good tactical plan for dealing with hostage situations cannot guarantee successful negotiations, it sets the stage for coordinated response during a crisis.

Authority for organizational decisions is distributed according to institutional norms. Managers in bureaucratic organizations normally exercise what Max Weber called rational–legal authority.[19] While they may seek advice, bureaucratic managers view themselves as single rational actors when it comes to making decisions that fall within the scope of their authority. Consequently, individual decisions are the rule rather than the exception.

Bureaucratic managers equate decision-making with power and resist any encroachment on that power. Under these circumstances, they control the speed of the decision-making process and the content of the decisions. As the humanistic philosophy of management has displaced traditional bureaucratic thinking, the emphasis has shifted away from exercising power over subordinates to sharing power with them. As a result, group decisions are much more common. Teams, committees, task forces, and review panels have become well-established aspects of organizational life. Group decision-making helps satisfy workers' need to participate in making those decisions that affect them. While there are some disadvantages, there is evidence that in complex situations—where there is no clear-cut solution—groups using a consensus approach tend to be more effective than individuals. Where problems are less complex, and special skill is required, individual managers with proper education and training tend to excel. Group decision-making is explored in more detail later in this chapter.

Whisenand[20] offers the following decision-making rules for police managers:

1. **Never make a decision that should be delegated.** Some police managers believe that since they have the authority to decide an issue and the responsibility for the decision, they must make it themselves.

2. **Never make a decision today that can be reasonably delayed.** Take advantage of the time available, and do not make a decision in haste. Timing is as important as the decision itself. For example, Abraham Lincoln's Cabinet advised him to wait for a Union victory before announcing the Emancipation Proclamation. As a result, his decision was made from strength rather than desperation.[21]

3. **Decide if the decision is yours to make.**

4. **Take extra care with "Big Ticket" decisions.**

5. **Enforce the rules.** The failure of a leader to enforce the rules due to a desire to remain popular or to avoid criticism can lead to ruin.

Problem Solving through Rational Decision-Making

Given the complexity of modern police work and the crucial need for effective decision-making in the administration of justice, decisions can no longer be relegated to seat-of-the-pants, best guessing. **Intuitive decision-making** is an unconscious process created out of the distilled experience. "Police managers must select choices that are sometimes based as much on intuition (gut feelings) as on precise analysis and objective logic."[22]

Intuition is the basis for courageous decision-making in a time of crisis. Typically, decisions from the gut are made in situations where there is no precedent and a paucity of evidence.[23] There is also urgency—time pressure to make the decision quickly. Sostrin recommends practicing **reflective urgency**—the ability to bringing conscious, rapid reflection to the current priorities to align thinking with a swift course of action. To avoid hasty decision-making, identify what is limiting the time to think. Make careful use of the time available to make the decision. Focus on difficult tasks and avoid the temptation to do less tedious things.[24]

Rational decision-making refers to a sensible, logical, and objective approach based on investigation rather than heuristic intuition. Rational decision-making is a process involving several very distinct steps designed to help managers discover optimal solutions. It is a structured approach that allows them to identify opportunities and zero in on the real problem to be solved. The problem-solving process we describe here is illustrated in Figure 8–2.

The best organizational decisions follow a series of steps leading to a particular conclusion. The steps in the decision-making process follow.

Step 1. Awareness of the need to make a decision. Opportunities and problems activate decision-making. A prerequisite for effective decision-making is the awareness that a decision is required. The most serious situation exists when dire consequences are possible, and the decision-maker is unaware that a problem even exists. When police managers are blindsided by an unanticipated problem, it is often very difficult for them to

Figure 8–2
Nine Steps in Rational Decision-Making.

Rational decision-making entails scanning the environment, identifying significant unresolved problems, designing alternative solutions to those problems, and choosing the one best solution in terms of situational constraints.

1. Awareness of the need to make a decision. Decision-making is activated by the recognition of opportunities as well as problems.

2. Identifying an existing problem. When feedback suggests there is a problem, it must be diagnosed and defined in explicit terms.

3. Listing possible and probable causes. Once the problem has been identified and articulated in succinct terms, all possible causes must be considered.

4. Designing alternative solutions. Good decision-makers are inclined to develop and test a fairly wide range of creative solutions.

5. Evaluating alternative solutions. All viable solutions must be evaluated in terms of probability, effect, importance, feasibility, sufficiency, and realism.

6. Choosing an alternative solution. All viable options must be analyzed and compared to one another in order to select objectively the one best alternative.

7. Implementing a decision. A decision is meaningless unless it is translated into effective action.

8. Analyzing feedback. Managers are obligated to gather and analyze feedback in order to assess the effectiveness of a given solution on a targeted problem.

9. Making necessary adjustments. Good managers are proactive and do not hesitate—based on the analysis of feedback—to make necessary midcourse corrections.

regain their equilibrium. According to an adage, "forewarned is forearmed." In the final analysis, problem awareness is a function of the manager's knowledge, perception, and motivation to know what is going on. Good police administrators have very sensitive antennae and relish the thought of resolving organizational problems through proactive decision-making.

Step 2. Identifying an existing problem. Clearly, describe the nature of the problem and all its attributes. This action avoids addressing the problem improperly. The two cardinal sins in decision-making are procrastination and vacillation. Often, they lead to "crisis management" decisions. Even if managers occasionally make wrong decisions, it is usually better for them to take action when action is needed than to take no action at all. Decisiveness has a stabilizing influence on subordinates. Indecisiveness is easily perceived and generates disrespect, destroys confidence, lowers morale, and adversely affects performance.

When feedback suggests there might be a problem, it is the manager's job to recognize it, examine it, and determine what caused it. A common mistake in organizational decision-making is concentrating on finding the right answer rather than identifying the right problem. Finding the real problem can be difficult. Good managers focus their attention on what is and compare it to what should be. Focusing on the real problem saves time, energy, and effort. It gives managers an opportunity to mobilize the resources needed to correct the problem. Managers often confuse symptoms (indications that there is a problem) with causes; as a result, they may spin their wheels or tilt at windmills.

Complex organizations and complicated environments require police administrators to gather and analyze information in a concerted effort to ensure an accurate diagnosis. Because of errors in conceptualization, managers more frequently fail to identify the right problem than they fail to solve the problem they eventually take up.

Step 3. Listing possible and probable causes. Once managers have identified and articulated the problem in very succinct terms, they are ready to look for the cause or causes of the problem. A cause may be a person, fact, or condition that is responsible for an effect. Good police administrators try to think of all possible reasons that help to explain the existing state of affairs. Depending on the importance of the decision, they may consider a few that seem impossible. Good managers are creative, imaginative, and resourceful. They have an innate or acquired need to recognize cause and effect, no matter how oblique the relationship might be. This ability is critical because it sets the stage for the development of alternative solutions. Causes range along a continuum from possible to probable. Those at the "probable" end of the continuum become the focus of further inquiry and the catalyst for decision-making.

Step 4. Designing alternative solutions. If there is only one solution to a particular problem, managers—no matter how competent they happen to be—are not in a position to devise alternatives, and no decision is required. In most situations, however, police administrators are called on to develop viable solutions. Formulating alternatives is more of an art than a science. The artistry comes from considering an appropriate range of solutions while reaching out for creative ideas not made obvious by scientific investigation. Poor decision-makers settle for the easiest and most available solutions and have little or no desire to find the best-possible solution. Poor decision-makers rely very heavily on intuition and similar past experiences to fashion alternative solutions to new problems. They lack both the imagination and the motivation to attempt creative problem solving. Poor decision-makers are victimized by perceptual predispositions (or mind-sets) that interfere with the free association of ideas. This prevents new and useful solutions from emerging. Breaking the mind-sets produced by experience, education, prejudice, and emotional conflict is the primary task of those who aspire to think creatively. Effective police administrators are aware of the organizational, biological, physical, technological, and economic constraints that limit their discretion in making decisions, and they learn to work creatively within them.[25]

Step 5. Evaluating alternative solutions. It is important to consider as many alternatives as time and other resources allow. Their goals should be carefully considered. These goals should be specific. Specificity not only clarifies but also makes it possible to measure and evaluate the extent to which they have been successfully attained. Alternatives should also be tested to determine their feasibility before they are fully implemented. Choices must not be restricted or limited. It takes a certain amount of imagination to develop alternative modes of action. The manager should make use of subordinates and their knowledge during this stage of the process. They can be a great source of imagination.

How alternative solutions are designed and expressed almost always depends on the manager's problem-solving skills, his or her perception of the problem to be solved, and the nature of the problem itself. It is at this stage that decision-makers attempt to assess the advantages (benefits) and disadvantages (costs) of each alternative. Evaluate solutions in terms of their probability, possible effects, and importance. Solutions are also evaluated in relation to sufficiency, feasibility, realism, and rationality. According to Simon, the psychological act of evaluating alternatives consists of measuring them vis-à-vis certain value indices that are associated with the realization of our values.[26] The correctness of a particular decision is a relative matter. It is correct if it selects appropriate means to achieve desired ends. Rational decision-making is concerned with selecting preferred alternatives based on some system of values whereby the consequences of the police administrator's behavior can be evaluated. There are several types of rationality. A decision is *objectively rational* if it is the correct behavior for achieving maximum results. It is *subjectively rational* if it achieves maximum results in relation to real knowledge of the subject. It is *consciously rational* to the degree that the adjustment of means to ends is an intellectual process. It is *deliberately rational* when the adjustment of means to ends is intentional. A decision is *ethically rational* when it conforms to the moral standards of the individual and is considered proper by those in the appropriate reference group. Decisions that appear to be irrational may be very rational in light of the decision-maker's goals or the dynamics of the situation.

Step 6. *Choosing an alternative solution.* Consensus requires that decision-makers consider all possible alternatives. Decision-makers must also be open-minded and willing to hear dissent in a most tolerant manner. Criticism is to be expected. Criticism is inevitable in complex organizations. Considered positively, criticism means that the manager is doing something worthy of attention. Competent police administrators know it is impossible meet the needs and/or expectations of everyone affiliated with their departments. As part of a management team, they are required to satisfy the expectations of their superiors while trying to earn the respect of their subordinates. Good managers do what they can under the circumstances and put up an umbrella to keep the rain of criticism from running down the back of their neck.[27]

It is a grievous error to make decisions based on inadequate data. Information is the raw material out of which effective decisions are made. Once the real problem is identified and realistic solutions have been designed, managers seek to find the alternative that will maximize results in terms of specific objectives. Good police administrators weigh, measure, or judge the various truly viable alternatives in terms of effort, cost, risk, or other criteria, in order to discriminate among them and rank them in terms of the probability that they will resolve the problem. **Comparative analysis** is the data-based comparison of viable alternatives, in light of explicit criteria, to select the optimum line of action. This type of analysis is not a substitute for managerial intuition or a denial of its worth. It is a technique for making decisions more effective by reducing imprecision and error. One of the most useful analytical techniques is known as the *decision matrix.* The matrix approach utilizes data, criteria, alternatives, and judgment as the basis for choosing a particular course of action. As illustrated in Figure 8–3, viable alternatives (solutions)

Figure 8–3
Decision Matrix.

Comparative analysis is the data-based comparison of viable alternatives, in light of explicit criteria, to choose an optimum line of action designed to solve a given organizational problem.

The problem: To determine which semiautomatic pistol will be purchased to replace department-issued service revolvers.

Criteria		Alternatives			
		Pistol A	Pistol B	Pistol C	Pistol D
1. Operation	(05)	5 [25]	4 [20]	4 [20]	4 [25]
2. Power	(08)	4 [36]	4 [36]	5 [40]	5 [40]
3. Capacity	(07)	4 [28]	4 [28]	5 [35]	5 [35]
4. Cost	(03)	3 [09]	3 [09]	3 [09]	2 [06]
5. Maintenance	(06)	4 [24]	3 [18]	5 [30]	2 [12]
6. Reliability	(10)	3 [30]	4 [40]	5 [50]	4 [40]
7. Safety	(09)	4 [36]	3 [27]	4 [36]	4 [36]
Total		188	178	220	194

Legend: The numbers in parentheses are weights indicating the importance of a criterion. Those in brackets are scores that reflect how well an alternative satisfies a criterion. Totals show how the alternatives compare to one another in terms of all the criteria. All other things being equal, the alternative with the highest total represents the best solution to a particular problem.

are listed horizontally, and the criteria by which alternatives will be judged are listed verti-cally. Managers assign a numerical weight to each criterion, from most important to least important. For each criterion, managers assign a numerical score to each alternative (from excellent to unsatisfactory) based on how well it satisfies the criterion. The alternative scores are then multiplied by the criterion weights to produce a numerical value for each alternative/criterion relationship, and those values are summed for each alternative. The optimal alternative is the one with the highest sum. If—after very careful analysis—there is no significant difference between the leading alternatives, personal preference becomes the most important factor in the decision.

Step 7. *Implementing a decision.* While analyzing data and making decisions based on the outcome of the analysis are inherent in the manager's role, deciding what to do is only part of the process. The next step is to translate the most beneficial alternative into action. Unless organizational decisions are supported by appropriate managerial action, there is little or no chance that they will be successful. Once the solution has been chosen, it is the police administrator's job to plan its implementation. The decision-maker must determine who will do what, where, when, and how to carry out the decision. In terms of percentage of time, decision-making takes up a relatively small portion of each manager's workday. Much of a manager's time is spent organizing the environment, mobilizing resources, and motivating others to implement his or her decisions. Emphasizing the decision-making activities of police administrators may produce a distorted view of their function. There are eight traps that can affect the way we make decisions:[28]

1. *The anchoring trap* leads us to treat the first information we receive as the best and most accurate.
2. *The status quo trap* causes us to wish to maintain the current situation when better alternatives exist.
3. *The sunk cost trap* makes us likely to perpetuate past mistakes due to unwillingness to change because we would abandon what we have expended in support of present conditions.
4. *The confirming-evidence trap* causes us to seek that information that supports our current position and to discount information that criticizes it.
5. *The framing trap* takes place when the problem is improperly defined.
6. *The overconfidence trap* occurs when we overestimate the accuracy and relevance of current forecasts.
7. *The prudence trap* causes us to be overcautious when we make estimates about uncertain events.
8. *The recallability trap* is sprung when we give undue emphasis to recent, dramatic events.

Every decision must have an implementation strategy. The best decision, left unimplemented, will have no more effect than if the problem was never recognized.

Step 8. *Analyzing feedback.* An evaluation must be made to assess the effectiveness of the decision. Managers must keep track of who is doing what and to gather feedback in a conscientious effort to assess the effect of that particular solution on the targeted problem. Managers need to know whether an action is accomplishing the intended results. While doing something separates dreamers from achievers, the action is only part of the equation. It is learning from experience that is important. Good police administrators keep their eyes and ears open. By understanding the dynamics that produce correct decisions, they can better assess environmental factors, problems, solutions, implementation strategies, and so on, as they prepare themselves to handle subsequent decision situations.

Step 9. *Making necessary adjustments.* The ability to make reasonable, correct, and timely decisions is an important skill in the repertoire of effective managers. Police administrators who know what is happening and what is to be accomplished garner respect from their peers as well as their subordinates. On the other side of the coin, police executives lose confidence in and respect for those lower-level managers who are plagued by indecision or who are unable to forge a link between decisions and actions.

Since decision-making goes with the territory, effective police administrators learn not to waste time or energy worrying about decisions made. They avoid anxiety by living in "day-tight compartments" and trying not to second-guess themselves.[29] The only time a manager should reconsider a decision is if it is wrong or if there is a genuine need to consider alternative courses of action.[30] Vacillation has often been the kiss of death for managers. While these principles cannot guarantee successful decision-making on the part of every police administrator, they provide guidelines for activating and managing the decision-making process.

The quality of a decision is determined by factors such as the following: (1) sufficiency of data, (2) accuracy of the database, (3) perceptual ability of the decision-maker, (4) problem-solving skill of the manager, (5) adequacy of the implementation strategy, and (6) nature of the follow-up. Proactive police administrators take decision-making in stride. They are not afraid to admit that they have made a mistake or that a solution they have chosen is inadequate to resolve a particular problem under a given set of circumstances. Good managers are eager to take action and do not hesitate—based on feedback discussed in step 8—to make rational midcourse corrections as environmental conditions change or as the unknowable future becomes the experience of the present. Effective decision-makers tend to be intelligent, perceptive, creative, and proactive. Getting the job done right is almost always more important to them than the ego trip associated with being right all of the time. Only fools make decisions and then dismiss them. Good managers track decisions and are prepared to make those adjustments that become necessary to ensure the efficiency, effectiveness, and productivity of the organization.

There is nothing magical about the nine-step decision-making process just discussed. When it comes to routine problems, most managers go through this thought process quickly and without much conscious effort. Unique organizational decisions require more action. Since relatively few organizational decisions require a split-second decision, it may be advisable to move in a deliberate, step-by-step fashion to arrive at the very best decision. Most administrative problems do not require immediate resolution. Consequently, managers have some flexibility in the timing of their decision-making. In most important decisions, this cushion is measured regarding hours, if not days. While a rush to judgment can have catastrophic effects, procrastination is an unacceptable alternative. Competent police administrators adapt their decision-making to the situation.

CASE STUDY   Captain Jayson Moore and Lieutenant Royce Strauss

Captain Jayson Moore, a 17-year veteran of the police department, is a colorful character who learned his trade in the "school of hard knocks." While he has had little or no formal training as a manager, he is acknowledged to be a good decision-maker. He uses his experiences as a guide to the future; he chooses among alternative courses of action based on hunches, gut-level feelings, and rules of thumb. He is right most of the time. Captain Moore and the heuristic tradition he represents are anathemas to the cadre of college-educated managers who control the department.

To become more systematic and objective in his decision-making, Captain Moore enrolled in a senior-level management course offered through the police academy. According to the syllabus, the course was to emphasize managerial problem solving based on rational decision-making and comparative analysis.

Concerned that his lack of formal education might put him at a disadvantage for mastering the material, Captain Moore set up an appointment with the instructor (Lt. Royce Strauss). He asked the lieutenant to explain the rational decision-making process and to illustrate it through the use of comparative analysis. Captain Moore also wanted to know at what point decision-making becomes a science rather than an art.

If you were the lieutenant, how would you explain the mechanics involved in the rational decision-making process to Captain Moore? What steps are required to identify, compare, and choose from among viable alternatives? Define comparative analysis, and give an example of how it might be used in police work. Would you argue that it is always the police administrator's duty to select the best alternative in every decision situation? If not, why not? Is there any need for judgment in objective decision-making?

Limitations on Rational Decision-Making

Decision-making lies at the center of the administrative process. Under ideal conditions, police managers are expected to make rational data-based decisions utilizing the model just described. Since organizational decisions are usually made in an environment of uncertainty and risk, by people who differ greatly in terms of their basic values, acumen, knowledge, and problem-solving skills, complete rationality is an unachievable goal. Neuroscientists have determined that our animal brains are not constrained by our cortexes when we make decisions. Our biological, emotional side finds pleasure in making money and seeking revenge. Thus, our higher cognitive functions are not always in control when we attempt to make rational decisions. Morse warns that we should ignore our gut at our peril. Our emotional side is often in control even when we do not desire it to be.[31]

Herbert Simon, one of the leading opponents of the economic-man model, argues that the model simply does not describe actual decision-making behavior in complex organizations. Simon contends that instead of searching for and choosing the best option, many managers settle for decisions that are only good enough to get by. Other decision scientists believe that since people are involved, the best possible decision is seldom made.[32]

Bounded Rationality

Responding to what he considered to be the unrealistic assumptions of the economic model, Simon developed an alternative set of assumptions. According to him, decision-makers are not guided by perfect rationality but by **bounded rationality**.[33] He argues that all administrators have limitations on their ability to process information and to make rational decisions. Their ability to reason is limited by constraints such as the following:

1. *Organizational anomie.* Conflicting and continually changing goals or objectives.
2. *Lack of relevant data.* Insufficient and often less-than-objective information.
3. *Physiological factors.* Energy levels, reflexes, habits, and physical skills.
4. *Psychological factors.* Beliefs, values, motives, experiences, and perceptions.
5. *Knowledge of the job.* Actual job-related knowledge of the decision-maker.

All organizational decisions are made within these boundaries.[34] Consequently, it is not unusual for police administrators to misread a decision situation, fail to see a problem, recognize only a limited number of alternatives, or miscalculate the consequences associated with a particular solution. When this happens, they are not irrational. They are simply making the most rational decision possible within a bounded information set. The goal of any organizational decision-maker is to expand these boundaries just as far as he or she can. While it is clear that there is a natural desire to make the best decision possible, the possible and the best are not always compatible concepts.

Bounded rationality recognizes that it is impossible to assimilate and understand all of the information necessary to optimize. So people **satisfice**—they seek solutions that are satisfactory and sufficient. A completely comprehensive and exhaustive review of all potential solutions is impossible. If it were made, we would likely be unable to absorb it. Therefore, we consider only those alternatives that differ only in a small way from one another. The resulting tendency is to pick the alternative that is "good enough" (the **satisficing** one) rather than the best available.[35]

Muddling Through

This pragmatic approach to decision-making is also discussed by Lindblom, who calls it "muddling through."[36] Lindblom examines how managers actually make decisions. He assumes that they adapt to each situation in a fragmented way that does not presume rationality. Values and feelings also play an important role in decision-making. Satisficing provides flexibility for those managers who want to avoid failure or mistakes that could jeopardize future promotions, pay raises, continued employment, and so forth. Satisficing is a strategy designed to lessen the danger associated with uncertainty and risk. Many management theorists believe that satisficing is necessary, even desirable, in some situations because of the following constraints:

1. Managers have limited time to devote to organizational decision-making.
2. Managers deal with many complex and competing problems simultaneously.
3. Managers have access to only a relatively small amount of the data concerning any given problem.
4. The cost of procuring and utilizing information to make a better decision may be prohibitive.
5. Some data may not be available to the decision-maker regardless of cost.
6. Bureaucratic managers are not necessarily well trained in using research, logic, or advanced reasoning.
7. Public problems are value-laden, and there is no real consensus about how to approach them.
8. Managers do not always have the independence necessary to make objective or impartial decisions.
9. Major decisions often require public funds controlled by independent legislative bodies.[37]

Satisficing occurs in all aspects of decision-making. During the problem identification stage of the process, for example, police managers ordinarily gather just enough data to give them an adequate picture of what is causing the increase in a particular type of crime. Then, based on their knowledge and problem-solving skills, they develop a short list of viable options that appear to be adequate to solve the problem. If the feasible alternatives all have unacceptable negative consequences, administrators will usually not pick the best of the negatives but will continue to search for another alternative with positive aspects.[38] It is better to compromise and make a less-than-optimal decision than to make no decision at all.

Biases distort decision-making. **Confirmation bias** leads people to ignore evidence contradicting preconceived notions. **Anchoring** occurs when one piece of evidence weighs more heavily than merited in the decision-making process. With **loss aversion**, the decision-maker worries about risk and fails to take action. Rational thought can limit the impact of such biases.

Decisions are often an unconscious process governed by nonrational processes. One problem is **pattern recognition**: assumptions based on familiar prior experiences and judgments including falling prey to inappropriate self-interest.[39] Another issue is **emotional tagging**: the emotion associated with our memories of thoughts and experiences—the presence of distorting judgments and misleading memories.[40] These problems are sources of bias causing us to leap to conclusions quickly without considering alternatives. To counter them, Campbell, Whitehead, and Finkelstein offer the following safeguards:[41]

- **Inject fresh experience or analysis.** Examine new information and get a different take on the problem. Lay out the range of options.
- **Introduce further debate and challenge.** Confront biases.
- **Impose stronger governance.** Require decision approval at a higher level. List the main decision-makers and focus on one.
- **Check for inappropriate self-interest or distorting attachments.**
- **Check for misleading memories.**
- **Repeat the analysis with the next most influential purpose.**

This list is a call for caution and questions our decision-making biases.

Ariely identifies other factors that make decisions "predictably irrational." One problem is relativity—we look at our decisions relatively, comparing them to the most available alternative. It is also difficult to make decisions effectively when we are in an emotional state. What needs to be recognized is that social norms build loyalty, and make people want to pitch in and extend their performance for the good of the organization.

This is especially true in policing where people respond to the social norms of the profession—saving lives and providing justice.[42] Our irrational behaviors are systematic and predictable. We make these mistakes over and over again.[43]

Similarly, Kahneman reveals the "biases of intuition." In decision-making, we tend to assume things carelessly, without close attention to them through "assumption heuristics" or mental shortcuts. His aim is how to recognize situations in which mistakes are likely and try harder to avoid significant mistakes when stakes are high. When we make decisions quickly, we are more likely to make mistakes. Kahneman posits that our brains operate under two systems: **System 1** thinks fast and features intuitive, automatic thinking. It is an intuitive response to your surroundings and sensory input based on mental conventions, both learned and natural, and cannot be turned off. "System 1 operates automatically and quickly, with little or no effort and no sense of voluntary control."[44] In contrast, **System 2** is slow, rational, and calculating. It does not jump to quick conclusions. It is a deliberate effortful thought process that normally runs in low priority mode, is able to make limited computations, and monitors your behavior. "System 2 allocates attention to the effortful mental activities that demand it, including complex computations."[45] These systems do not work in parallel and our tendency and preference are to work quickly and follow System 1.

Another decision-making bias identified by Kahneman is WYSATI—"What You See Is All There Is." WYSATI leads to three problems:[46]

1. **Overconfidence**: Neither the quantity or quality of the evidence counts for very much in subjective confidence.
2. **Framing Effects**: Different ways of presenting the same information evoke different emotions.
3. **Base-Rate Neglect**: Your conclusion is not affected by statistical fact.

The influence of WYSATI is that we ignore information questioning our predisposed decision.

Another cognitive bias is anchoring. It occurs naturally with the first draft of a plan. We accentuate the positive and become overly optimistic (Lovallo & Kahneman, 2003, p. 3).[47] Leaders also tend to overestimate their talents and make **attribution errors**—misperceiving conditions, exaggerating their ability to exert control over them, and discounting the role of luck. Also, organizations tend to discourage pessimism and stifle debate. They dismiss naysayers, branding them as disloyal and misguided, undermining critical thinking. The organization fails to examine the external environment for information. Insider views take precedence.[48]

Building Blocks for Effective Decision-Making

Robert B. Denhardt and his colleagues offer the following guidelines for effective decision-making:[49]

1. *What is or is not the problem?* What is, should be, or could be happening?
2. *State your purpose.*
3. *Set your criteria.* What do you want to achieve? What do you want to preserve? What do you want to avoid?
4. *Establish your priorities.*
5. *Search for solutions.* How can you meet your criteria? What are the possible courses of action?
6. *Test the alternatives.*
7. *Troubleshoot your decision.*

However, these guidelines only provide direction for the individual manager. What should the manager do to generate consensus and gain the support of his or her subordinates for the chosen decision?

1. Define and verify the problem fully and accurately.
2. Use the problem to generate solutions.
3. Prevent premature evaluation of solutions.
4. Provide a climate that values disagreement.
5. When possible, gain consensus from all of those affected.[50]

The best managerial decision-makers tend to be intelligent, knowledgeable, competent, collegial, decisive, and action-oriented. They respect subordinates and incorporate them into the organizational decision-making process.

Group Decision-Making

For all practical purposes, the unilateral decision-making associated with autocratic management in complex organizations is heading down the path toward extinction. As police departments move away from the quasi-military model to a more humanistic configuration, they emphasize delegating authority and nurturing participative decision-making. Many organization/management theorists contend that operational decisions should be made collectively at the "lowest level possible" by people who are directly affected by the decisions.[51] Modern organizations have become so complex that the single-rational-actor (one-person) model of decision-making is no longer appropriate.

Group decisions are collective decisions produced by specifically designated groups such as committees, study teams, task forces, and review panels. **Group decision-making** occurs when members of the group provide input and positively participate in the problem-solving process. Group decision-making is particularly appropriate for making important nonprogrammed decisions (like how to deal with a unique hostage situation or what to do about police corruption). Since these decisions are likely to be complex, few managers have all the intelligence, acumen, knowledge, skills, and temperament necessary to make the best decision possible. Good managers know their limitations. They are not afraid to share the power to make certain types of decisions with other people in the organization if it helps to produce better decisions.

Many organization/management theorists argue that groups are in a position to make better decisions than individuals. Harnessing the potential of group decision-making and avoiding its deficiencies provides a level of proficiency greater than that of solo decision-makers. The key to achieving a high level of performance in any group decision-making hinges on the availability of people-oriented managers who can maximize the group's assets and minimize its liabilities. With proper training, police administrators can learn to perform this function.

Advantages of Group Decision-Making

Group decision-making provides the following advantages:

1. *Pooling of information provides diversity and expansion of alternatives for consideration.* There is more knowledge and information in a group than in any one of its members. Consequently, decisions that require knowledge—internal and external to the police department—generally give groups an advantage over individual decision-makers. By pooling the resources of several people, there is much more information on which to base a sound decision.
2. *The social arousal of participants is greater.* Group membership can motivate and inspire individuals. American society values democratic methods. Group decision-making is consistent with democratic ideals. As a result, collective decisions are often perceived as being more legitimate than those made by a single person. When police administrators, as principal decision-makers, fail to consult with significant others before making important organizational decisions, the exercise of complete power may create the perception that decisions are made arbitrarily as well as autocratically. This perception can lead to intraorganizational conflict and poor morale.

3. *Social rewards for participation are provided.* Many decisions fail after the final choice is made simply because people do not accept the solution. As noted earlier, in the discussion of participative management, employees want to be involved in making organizational decisions that affect them. They become more committed to decisions in which they have invested their time, energy, effort, and expertise. This commitment translates into support for the decision and satisfaction among those required to implement it. When groups solve problems, more people accept and feel responsible for making the solution work. Members of a decision-making group understand the solution. They are aware of the alternatives and know why they were rejected. Communication is maximized when significant others are incorporated into the organizational decision-making process.

4. *Division of labor provides the development and the utilization of expertise present in all members of the group.* In addition to more input, groups tend to bring more heterogeneity into the organizational decision-making process. Since members of the group have different perceptions and unique approaches to problem solving, they contribute to the decision-making process by knocking each other out of old ruts in their thinking. Diversity in thinking gives police administrators the opportunity to choose from an array of creative approaches and innovative solutions.

5. *Solutions tend to be of higher quality.* Groups outperform individuals working in isolation.[52]

Whether group decisions are, in fact, better than those made by a single rational actor depends on personal as well as situational factors. Good managers are flexible. They use the decision-making model that is most likely to produce the best result under the circumstances.

Drawbacks of Group Decision-Making

There are drawbacks to group decision-making. They include the following five factors:

1. *Social pressure.* The desire to be a good group member and to be accepted by one's peers tends to squelch disagreement and promote consensus.[53] Psychosocial factors may become more important than objective decision-making. Reaching agreement in the group is often confused with finding the right solution and making the correct decision (see Chapter 7 for a more detailed discussion of group dynamics).

2. *Valence of solutions.* Possible solutions (alternatives or options) elicit critical and supportive comments from members of the group. When one proposed solution receives considerably more positive than negative reaction, it may—based on its relative strength, or valence—be acted on regardless of its actual capacity to solve the problem. This is the transition point where idea getting is turned into decision-making via intuition rather than through objective analysis.

3. *Domination by a few.* In most groups, a few dominant individuals emerge and capture more than their fair share of influence on outcomes. They achieve this power through a greater degree of participation, persuasive ability, and/or stubborn tenacity. This has been called the iron law of oligarchy. If the dominant coalition is composed of those members with low to medium ability, the group's overall effectiveness tends to suffer. The quality of every group decision is influenced to one degree or another by the knowledge, abilities, and interpersonal skills of its (formal and informal) leaders.

4. *Conflicting secondary goal: winning the argument.* When a decision-making group is confronted with a problem, the initial goal is to resolve it, but the formulation of several competing alternatives or options causes another problem. Members have a natural inclination to adopt and support a particular position. They take it upon themselves to sell the favored solution. Converting those with neutral viewpoints and refuting those with opposing views become part of the decision-making process. The goal shifts to having one's own solution chosen rather than finding the best solution possible under the circumstances. This new goal is totally

unrelated to objective analysis or the quality of the decision. Ego-centered decisions of this kind can result in lowering the overall quality of managerial decisions in complex criminal justice organizations.

5. *Consumption of time.* It takes time to assemble and lead a productive decision-making group. The dynamic interaction that occurs once the group has been formed is often inefficient. As a result, groups almost always take more time to reach a decision than would be the case if a single rational actor were making the final choice. Unskilled managers may be so concerned with finding a solution that they terminate the discussion before consensus is achieved, or they may be so interested in getting input that they allow the discussion to become redundant and boring. Both of these conditions limit management's ability to act quickly and decisively when the need arises.[54]

Group decision-making, with its assets and liabilities, has become a permanent feature of the landscape of contemporary organization management. Among other potential applications for police management, the Delphi method can be a powerful tool to help police organizations forecast the future for the purposes of strategic management, and facilitate policy and program development.[55] Group consensus will become the dominant characteristic of police administration. As the shared decision model evolves, the distinction between supervisors and subordinates will become much less significant.[56] Police managers will serve as group facilitators who share decision-making power with others.

Humanistic Approach

Interest in group decision-making originated with the human relations school of management and theorists like Mary Parker Follett, Elton Mayo, Abraham Maslow, Keith Davis, Douglas McGregor, and Warren Bennis. Humanism stresses the importance of group dynamics and participative management in achieving an organization's mission, goals, and objectives. They see participation in decision-making as democracy in action, a way of opening communications, diffusing authority, and motivating people to make a greater commitment to the organization.[57] Humanistic managers in America, like their Japanese counterparts, believe that people—not capital spending or automation—are the primary source of productive gain. They see their employees as their most important asset and treat them as partners, with dignity and respect.[58] They strive to achieve genuine consensus, collaboration, and collegiality. Humanists believe that group decisions are far superior to those made by a single decision-maker exercising formal authority.

Current research tends to support the humanistic approach when it comes to nonprogrammed organizational decisions. Researchers have found that groups make more and better decisions than individuals working alone.[59] Some management theorists argue that controlled conflict between members helps to stimulate better quality in a group's decisions. Skillful police administrators try to create a climate of disagreement (without causing hard feelings) because they know that properly managed disagreement can be a source of creativity and innovation. They adopt a Hegelian perspective and view disagreement as producing ideas rather than generating difficulty or trouble. Managers who perceive those who disagree with them as troublemakers obtain fewer innovative solutions and achieve far less acceptance of group decisions than do managers who see such people as having valuable ideas.[60] Good managers can differentiate between the decisions they must make and those that should be made by the group.

Evidence suggests that there are some important differences between group decisions and decisions that might be made by individuals within the group. What appears to happen in group discussions is that members who were leaning in one direction before the discussion began to shift further in that direction, toward more extreme positions. In some cases, group decisions are more conservative than individual decisions, but more often than not the shift is toward greater risk taking.[61] It is important to "spread the risk" and "defuse responsibility." If a risky nonprogrammed decision turns out poorly, all members of the group share the negative consequences, and no individual is likely to be singled out for punishment. Laboratory experiments show that unanimous group

Table 8–1
BENEFITS OF GROUP DECISION-MAKING

1. Broad knowledge base	10. Synergistic disagreement
2. Access to more information	11. Generally better decisions
3. Accuracy in diagnosis	12. More comprehensive decisions
4. Multidimensional analysis	13. The inclination to take risks
5. Multiple alternatives	14. Greater creativity
6. Collaborative problem solving	15. Increased job satisfaction
7. Ease of acceptance	16. Sense of self-fulfillment
8. Accuracy in communication	17. Greater unity of purpose
9. Inherent legitimacy	

decisions are consistently more risky than the average of the individual decisions. If a group endorses a riskier position than its members, a "risky shift" occurs. Table 8–1 summarizes the positive aspects of group decisions.

Improving Group Decision-Making

The most common form of collective decision-making takes place in goal-oriented groups where members interact with each other face to face. However, as our prior discussion of the drawbacks of group decision-making demonstrated (see Table 8–2), interacting groups often censor themselves and pressure individual members to discard their thoughts and to adopt the group's perspective. This phenomenon is known as "groupthink."[62]

Groupthink, in this context, is the natural tendency for members of a cohesive decision-making group to become emotionally bound to suboptimal decisions, without analyzing them individually or critically.[63] Measures like leader training, brainstorming, nominal group, and Delphi techniques can overcome such problems.

Leader Training

Group decision-making has the potential to become the dominant approach to solving organizational problems. Police administrators must now be trained not only as rational decision-makers but also as work-group facilitators. They will be expected to convene the group and guide the discussion. Since this is a new role for most police administrators, they must be trained to facilitate group discussions without trying to manipulate them. As group leaders, they can make or break the decision-making process. If managers act like autocrats and try to sell preconceived decisions, they lose the advantages of participative management—reducing the acceptance of them. If managers abdicate their duty to

Table 8–2
NEGATIVE ASPECTS OF GROUP DECISION-MAKING

1. More time consuming	6. Emphasis on winning
2. Less consistent	7. Illusion of valence
3. Pressure to conform	8. Groupthink
4. Domination by a few	9. Escalation of risk*
5. Interpersonal games	

*While risk taking can be a very positive attribute, extreme group-generated and reinforced risk is antithetical to rational decision-making. A lynch mob is a group in which the risk shift takes the concept of law and order to an illogical extreme.

provide adequate guidance for the group, the group may produce low-quality decisions that are ineffective in meeting the needs of the organization. Managers should follow the following guidelines to lead decision group meetings:[64]

- Inform people about necessary preparations for a meeting.
- Share essential information with group members.
- Describe the problem without implying the cause or solution.
- Allow ample time for idea generation and evaluation.
- Separate idea generation from idea evaluation.
- Encourage and facilitate participation.
- Encourage positive restatement and idea building.
- Use systematic procedures for solution evaluation.
- Encourage members to look for an integrative solution.
- Encourage consensus, but don't insist on it.
- Clarify responsibilities for implementation.

These skills are not abstract concepts, but specific behaviors. They can be learned through training and tested in practical situations through the use of simulation and role playing. Leader training improves the overall quality of group decisions and helps to ensure their acceptance by others in the organization.

Brainstorming

Brainstorming is a special type of group decision-making process that was initially developed in the advertising industry to help trigger creativity and promote innovation. It is an idea-generating technique that encourages consideration of any ideas and prohibits criticism of those ideas. Managers who use brainstorming in problem solving have identified several factors that tend to improve the overall effectiveness of brainstorming sessions:[65]

- *No criticism!* Adverse judgments about your own or others' ideas are to be withheld.
- *"Freewheeling"* is invited. No idea is too wild or crazy. The more creative or unusual the idea is, the better it is.
- *Quantity is desired.* Generate as many ideas as possible. The greater the number of ideas, the greater is the likelihood that one will work.
- *"Piggybacking"* is encouraged. Participants should build on the ideas and suggestions of others. Combining and extending others' ideas is a critical aspect of successful brainstorming.
- *Brainstorming sessions* are structured to maximize the group's creativity.

In the typical brainstorming session, 6–12 people sit around a table. The manager or designated group leader states the problem in clear and concise terms so that all participants understand it. Members of the group are allowed to "freewheel," generating as many solutions as they can within the allotted time. All of the proposed alternatives are recorded for subsequent discussion and analysis. Once the analysis has been completed and the options have been narrowed down to a reasonable number, the group or an authorized decision-maker selects the option that appears most appropriate given the circumstances. This approach—while it is not always effective—can be useful in dealing with public policy and administrative problems. It is particularly valuable when the problem necessitates trying to find new ways of dealing with a situation.

Nominal Group Technique

The **nominal group technique** (NGT) for decision-making represents a refinement of the brainstorming approach. It follows many of the guidelines used in brainstorming but differs in that members of the group function independently. Unlike traditional brainstorming, NGT generates ideas and evaluates them continuously throughout the entire decision-making process. Ideas are generated nominally (e.g., without group interaction) to prevent inhibition and conformity. Interaction and discussion take place during the evaluation phase. It is structured in such a way as to make sure that every idea gets adequate attention. True collaboration occurs when group members consider the merit of each fully articulated alternative collectively. NGT attempts to minimize the biases that arise and that are reinforced in group dynamics.[66] Once the problem has been presented to the decision-making group for resolution, the following steps take place:

- Individuals silently and independently write down their ideas and alternative solutions to a stated problem.
- All members take turns presenting their ideas, and these ideas are recorded on a chart or chalkboard.
- The ideas are discussed only to clarify them. Evaluative comments are not allowed.
- A written voting procedure is used to rank the alternatives.

An effective variation in the NGT process is to go back and repeat the first three steps. The group fleshes out new ideas or amplifies recommendations before taking the final vote. If there is no clear consensus, the entire process can be repeated until the group reaches a mutually acceptable compromise. Figure 8–4 illustrates this process.

Delphi Technique

The **Delphi technique** used in group decision-making was originally developed by the prestigious Rand Corporation (a think tank) to make technological predictions. This process is similar to the NGT just discussed except that it does not require the physical presence of the participants. There is, in fact, no face-to-face interaction. Consequently, it is possible to poll a group of experts without bringing them together in the same place at the same time. The people who are selected to serve as members of the group do not actually make final decisions. Their job is to generate conceptually sound alternatives for consideration by organizational decision-makers.[67] The heart of the Delphi approach is to determine expert opinion through a series of questionnaires. This process typically involves the following four sequential steps:[68]

1. The first questionnaire distributed to members of the Delphi group identifies the problem and asks for alternative solutions to it.
2. The Delphi coordinator summarizes the solutions, and the summary is returned to participants along with a second questionnaire specifically designed to identify areas requiring further clarification and consideration.

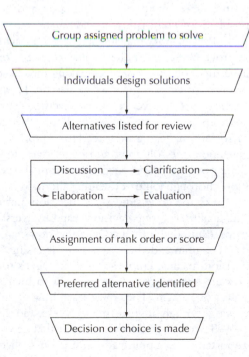

Figure 8–4
The Nominal Group Technique.

Figure 8–5
The Delphi Approach to Decision-Making.

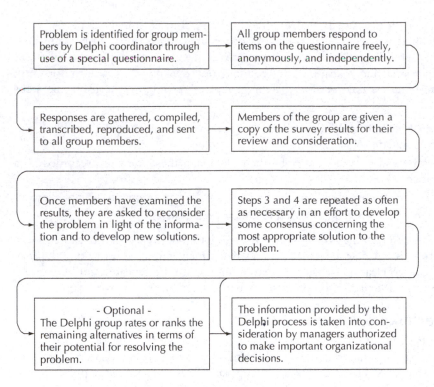

3. The results of the second questionnaire are presented to the participants, who rate the various alternatives presented.
4. Members' ratings are tabulated, and a summary of the data and resulting decision are returned to the participants.

Figure 8–5 presents the Delphi technique. Like the NGT, the Delphi approach insulates group members from the undue influence of others. It gives police administrators the opportunity to explore complex issues without unwieldy analysis. Respected experts are kept on tap to share their personal beliefs, values, and accumulated knowledge. One drawback to the Delphi method is the lengthy time frame involved in the questionnaire phases. Quick decisions are the exception rather than the rule. Another problem is achieving consensus through compromise. The best solution may be ignored if group opinion shifts toward a compromise decision. Despite these disadvantages, the Delphi technique is an efficient method of drawing on and pooling expert judgment while avoiding the problems of conformity and domination that often occur in interacting groups.

Participatory management and formal group decision-making have the potential to improve complex criminal justice organizations. Many police management theorists believe that collective decision-making may become the dominant form of organizational problem solving during the next decade. They support this trend and argue that meaningful employee involvement in the decision-making process will increase job satisfaction as well as produce better decisions. Research indicates that because of the synergistic effect of social dynamics, groups tend to be more vigilant than individual decision-makers. They generate more solutions, and better ones, to organizational problems. When employees share power with management and are allowed to make meaningful decisions, they do a more thorough job of evaluating alternatives than do individuals acting alone.

On the downside, group decision-making is complex, time consuming, and slow. The quality of group decisions can be adversely affected by (1) inherent pressure to conform, (2) undue influence by a few dominant individuals, (3) conflicting personal goals, or (4) an unintended escalation in risk taking. To overcome the negative aspects of group decision-making, emphasize the manager's role as a group facilitator. Train managers to become leaders who share power with their subordinates rather than merely exercising power over them. They must learn how to enhance the effectiveness of group decision-making through brainstorming, NGTs, and the Delphi method.

There is absolutely no doubt that group decision-making will play an increasingly important role in police administration. Collective decision-making is here to stay.

CASE STUDY   Lieutenant Coleman J. Karras

Lieutenant Karras earned a BA in sociology before he joined the police department in 1969. He continued his education and was awarded an MBA several years later. Lieutenant Karras is an intelligent, caring, and committed person who puts the welfare of the organization ahead of his interests. During his 20 years with the Metropolitan Police Department, he has served in various capacities. The lieutenant is viewed as a hard-working and self-disciplined professional.

The lieutenant, who until recently was commander of an intensive patrol unit assigned to an inner-city precinct, was reassigned and designated as director of the department's graphic arts bureau. It is a staff position and considered a stop on the fast track to a higher rank.

The previous director, an alcoholic, had given bureau personnel little or no direction. Because of the lack of management, the unit was in chaos. It had become the laughingstock of the police department. Lieutenant Karras's job was to clean up the mess. Since he was not familiar with the work of the bureau and had never been in a staff position before, he realized that he was not, by himself, prepared to manage the unit in an efficient, effective, and productive manner.

After seeking advice from other administrators and doing a great deal of introspection, Lieutenant Karras concluded that to succeed in the new assignment, he needed to share some decision-making authority with his subordinates. He was convinced that, except in a limited number of situations, the single-rational-actor model would not work. He viewed participative management and group decision-making as the most realistic approach. Based on his education and training, he was willing to share power with subordinates rather than exercise power over them. Lieutenant Karras was glad to play the role of group coordinator and facilitator.

If you were Lieutenant Karras's adviser, which of the three group decision-making techniques would you recommend he use to identify problems and generate creative solutions to those problems? Explain to the lieutenant how the process works and the results that you would expect him to achieve.

CASE STUDY   Lieutenant James Perkins

Lt. James Perkins has been a member of the Sparksville County Police Department for 11 years. There are 354 sworn officers and 72 civilians in his agency. The city has a population of 213,000 with a diverse constituency: 62 percent white, 21 percent Mexican American, 11 percent African American, and remainder are Orientals and Native Americans. The city has a strong manufacturing base, including an automobile assembly plant. Additionally, the city is in a major metropolitan area in an agricultural state located in the central part of the United States.

While serving in the department, Perkins was in patrol for seven years and in investigations for three years. His current assignment is in the Technical Services Bureau where he works in the training unit. Currently, the department has its own police academy that prepares recruits and trains first-line supervisors. Managerial training is conducted by the local university under Peace Officer Standards and Training (POST) guidelines.

Within a 75-mile radius, there are currently three different basic police academies. There has been a recent push to consider the possibility of consolidating these training entities. Sparksville county has never allowed other agencies to send personnel to its academy. The other two academies function on a part-time basis, depending upon hiring practices. Sparksville has a new chief, Sara Stewart, who has expressed an interest in establishing a consolidated academy. The state training commission has long been an advocate of centralized training and will support a feasibility study to consolidate training.

Chief Stewart has given Lt. Perkins the responsibility of serving on a study committee to investigate the implications of consolidated training for recruits and supervisors. She has asked Perkins to prepare a position paper supporting consolidation and describing its implications. The local community college has indicated an interest in locating the new academy on its campus and creating a board of directors to supervise its operation. In addition, POST has volunteered to monitor and fund the feasibility study.

What decision-making model would you use to address this problem? If you were Lt. Perkins, what factors would you consider when preparing the report? Who would you interview in the department? Why? What outside members would you want to interview? Why? List the advantages and disadvantages of consolidated training. What position would you take regarding affiliation with the community college?

SUMMARY

A decision is a choice from among a set of alternatives and is intended to accomplish a goal or resolve a problem. The key elements in decision-making are targets, alternatives, choices, and behaviors. Managers continually (1) monitor the environment for problems—conditions that require a decision, (2) design appropriate alternative courses of action for solving the problems, and (3) select the alternatives that they—based on their knowledge, expertise, and experience—believe will work in given situations. In short, managers make the calls and see to their execution: "They manage relationships with key constituencies. They align and mobilize team members for support."[69]Tichy and Bennis found that the judgment of leaders is the result of a process that resides in three domains: people, strategy, and crisis. The decision itself is made in three phases. In the preparation phase, leaders frame the issue to be addressed and mobilize key stakeholders. The second phase is the decision itself. The third is acting on the call itself–learning and adjusting as needed. Effective leaders also make use of "redo loops" in the process. They reconsider the parameters of the decision, relabel the problem, and redefine the goal that increases its acceptance among followers.[70]

Good managers avoid procrastination and vacillation. They are decision-makers who expect criticism and refuse to worry about it. They know that external constraints and personal limitations have an influence on the quality of their decisions.

The most challenging part of any police administrator's job is to make proactive, nonprogrammed decisions. For all practical purposes, modern management has abandoned the heuristic model and embraced the scientific approach, which emphasizes fact-based, objective, and rational decision-making and involves the following:

- Perceiving the need to make a decision.
- Identifying the specific problem.
- Listing all possible and probable causes.
- Designing viable options or alternatives.
- Evaluating alternatives in light of specific and detailed criteria.
- Choosing the most appropriate alternative.
- Implementing the decision in a timely way.
- Analyzing feedback to assess effectiveness.
- Making necessary midcourse corrections.

Since external and personal constraints make absolute rationality impossible, good managers learn how to compromise and are often willing to settle for less-than-optimal decisions. These satisficing decisions are considered to be adequate, not the best.

Some organizational decisions are made by single rational actors in positions of authority. To do a good job, they need to know the institutional constraints imposed on their decision-making power. They must also perform the following:

- Distinguish between personal and organizational decisions.
- Minimize the number of decisions made in crisis situations.
- Let subordinates make decisions they are capable of making.
- Anticipate the political fallout that might be generated.
- Realize that beliefs and values influence decision-making.
- Approach decision-making from a problem-solving perspective.
- Assess problems regarding importance, priority, and status.
- Formulate viable and creative solutions for major problems.
- Select the most appropriate alternative given the situation.
- Monitor their decisions and make all necessary corrections.

Good managers see decision-making as a challenge rather than a chore. They rely on existing policies, procedures, rules, and regulations to solve problems whenever possible. Also, they make it a policy to consult with significant others before making major nonprogrammed decisions. The best decision-makers do not attempt to anticipate every eventuality associated with the choice of a particular alternative, nor do they expect to make the right decision all of the time. Managers should abandon their reliance upon obsolete knowledge, traditions that are unsupported by fact, patterns based upon their experience, and methods that they can skillfully apply when making decisions. Instead, they should tap into research evidence that is valid and reliable. Decisions should be firmly grounded in the latest and best knowledge of what works.[71]

DISCUSSION TOPICS AND QUESTIONS

1. What are the four elements in the operational definition of a managerial decision?

2. Why are the terms *problem solving* and *decision-making* used as synonyms in management? Identify the three stages in the problem-solving (or decision-making) process.

3. Discuss the cardinal sins in decision-making. Give an example of how one of these sins has affected you personally.

4. How does a police administrator's level in the managerial hierarchy affect the scope of his or her decision-making authority?

5. Discuss the influence of internal, external, and personal constraints on managerial decision-making. Which do you feel are the most important? Justify your answer.

6. What is the difference between a programmed and a nonprogrammed organizational decision? Give at least three examples to illustrate the point.

7. Why are objective decisions perceived as better than heuristic decisions even when heuristic problem-solving techniques work?

8. What series of steps should a single rational actor follow while making important nonprogrammed decisions? Discuss each of these steps in light of a problem with which you are familiar.

9. Discuss the biases complicating rational decision-making. How can they be dealt with?

10. Define *comparative analysis*. Explain how it can be used by police administrators.

11. What did Herbert Simon mean by the term *bounded rationality*? How is this term related to the concept of *satisficing*?

12. Discuss the advantages and disadvantages of group decision-making. How does it fit into the humanistic philosophy of management? What role does the manager play in the group decision-making process?

13. Discuss four ways to improve group decision-making. Which one do you think is best? Why? Give an example of how it might be used in a police department.

FOR FURTHER READING

Dan Ariely, *Predictably Irrational: The Hidden Forces that Shape Our Decisions* (New York: Harper Collins, 2008).

Ariely reviews research on how our brains affect decision-making in irrational ways that are predictable. His purpose is to expose them and make us aware of them.

William Bratton with Peter Knobler, *Turnaround—How America's Top Cop Reversed the Crime Epidemic* (New York: Random House, 1998) and Rudolph W. Giuliani, *Leadership* (New York: Hyperion, 2002).

The two prime movers in the implementation of the Compstat paradigm, Bratton and Giuliani, offer their views

on decision-making. Bratton's candid analysis of his management style and Giuliani's views on September 11th are the crucial attributes of these works.

Boris Johnson, *The Churchill Factor: How One Man Made History* (New York: Riverhead Books, 2014).

Johnson reviews major decisions made by Churchill and how they changed the course of history.

Daniel Kahneman, *Thinking, Fast and Slow* (New York: Ferrar, Straus & Giroux, 2011).

Nobel Prize winner Kahneman reviews our thought processes, and explains the mechanisms of Systems 1 and 2, outlining their impact on decision-making.

ENDNOTES

1. S. Robbins and M. Coulter, *Management* (Upper Saddle River, NJ: Pearson Prentice Hall, 2018), p. 252.
2. Alan Axelrod, *Patton on Leadership: Strategic Lessons for Corporate Warfare* (Paramus, NJ: Prentice Hall Press, 1999), p. 129.
3. Paul M. Whisenand, *Managing Police Organizations* (Upper Saddle River, NJ: Pearson Prentice Hall, 2014), p. 17.
4. C. Barnard, *The Functions of the Executive* (Cambridge, MA: Harvard University Press, 1976).
5. Claude George, *Management in Industry* (Englewood Cliffs, NJ: Prentice Hall, 1964).
6. Herbert Simon, *The New Science of Management Decisions* (Englewood Cliffs, NJ: Prentice Hall, 1977).
7. Graham T. Allison, *The Essence of Decision: Explaining the Cuban Missile Crisis* (Boston, MA: Little, Brown, 1971). pp. 29–30.
8. Ibid.
9. Peter Drucker, "On the Profession of Management" *Harvard Business Review* (April 1998), p. 32.
10. Robbins and Coulter, *Management*, p. 50.
11. Allison, *The Essence of Decision*, pp. 29–30.
12. Whisenand, *Managing Police Organizations*, p. 56

13. David J. Snowden and Mary E. Boone, "A Leader's Framework for Decision Making," *Harvard Business Review* (November 2007), pp. 68–76.

14. Simon, *The New Science of Management Decisions*.

15. W. Gore, *Administrative Decision Making: A Heuristic Model* (New York: Wiley, 1964).

16. Whisenand, *Managing Police Organizations*, p. 15.

17. Irving L. Janis and Leon Mann, *Decision Making: A Psychological Analysis of Conflict, Choice, and Commitment* (New York: The Free Press, 1971), pp. 11–15.

18. Snowden and Boone, A leader's Framework.

19. H. H. Gerth and C. Wright Mills, *From Max Weber: Essays in Sociology* (New York: Oxford University Press, 1946).

20. Whisenand, *Managing Police Organizations*, pp. 12–13.

21. Doris K. Goodwin, *A Team of Rivals: The Political Genius of Abraham Lincoln* (New York: Simon and Schuster, 2005).

22. Whisenand, *Managing Police Organizations*, p. 15.

23. L. Buchanan and A. O'Connell, "A Brief History of Decision Making," *Harvard Business Review* (January 2006), pp. 1–7.

24. J. Sostrin, "Strategic Thinking: How to Act Quickly without Sacrificing Critical Thinking," *Harvard Business Review* (April 2017), pp. 1–3.

25. S. Robbins and T. Judge, *Organizational Behavior* (Upper Saddle River, NJ: Pearson Prentice Hall, 2013), p. 8.

26. Robert B. Denhardt, Janet V. Denhardt, and M. Aristigueta, *Managing Human Behavior in Public and Nonprofit Organizations* (Thousand Oaks, CA: Sage, 2015), p. 129.

27. Herbert Simon, *Administrative Behavior: A Study of Decision-Making Processes in Administrative Organizations* (New York: Free Press, 1976).

28. John S. Hammond, Ralph L. Keeney, and Howard Raffa, "The Hidden Traps of Decision Making," *Harvard Business Review* (January 2006), pp. 52–61.

29. Allison, *The Essence of Decision*.

30. Larry Bossidy and Ram Charan, *Execution: The Discipline of Getting Things Done* (New York: Crown Business, 2002).

31. Gardiner Morse, "Decisions and Desire," *Harvard Business Review* (January 2006), pp. 42–61.

32. Herbert Simon, *Models of Man* (New York: Wiley and Sons, 1957).

33. Ibid.

34. Ibid.

35. Robbins and Judge, *Organizational Behavior*, p. 176.

36. Ibid.

37. Charles E. Lindblom, "The Science of Muddling Through," *Public Administration Review*, Vol. 19 (1959), pp. 79–88.

38. Ibid.

39. Andrew Campbell, Jo Whitehead, and Sydney Finkelstein, "Why Good Leaders Make Bad Decisions," *Harvard Business Review* (February 2009), pp. 1–7.

40. Ibid., p. 3.

41. Ibid., pp. 3–5.

42. D. Ariely, *Predictably Irrational: The Hidden Forces that Shape Our Decisions* (New York: Harper Collins, 2008), p. 91.

43. Ibid., p. 317.

44. D. Kahneman, *Thinking, Fast and Slow* (New York: Ferrar, Strauss & Giroux, 2011), p. 20.

45. Ibid., p. 21.

46. Ibid., pp. 87–88.

47. Dan Lovallo and Daniel Kahneman, "Delusions of Success: How Optimism Undermines Decisions," *Harvard Business Review* (July 2003), pp. 1–9.

48. Ibid., pp. 4–6.

49. Denhardt, Denhardt, and Aristigueta, *Managing Human Behavior*, pp. 142–144.

50. Ibid., pp. 144–145.

51. Robbins, and Judge, *Organizational Behavior*, p. 188.

52. Ibid., p. 290.

53. Ibid., p. 291.

54. Ibid.

55. Robert Loo, "The Delphi Method: A Powerful Tool for Strategic Management," *Policing: An International Journal of Police Strategies & Management*, Vol. 25, No. 4 (2002), pp. 762–769.

56. L. Miller, H. More, and M. Braswell, *Effective Police Supervision* (New York: Routledge, 2017), pp. 180–181.

57. Robbins and Coulter, *Management*, pp. 33–34.

58. Thomas J. Peters, and Obert H. Waterman, *In search of Excellence: Lessons from America's Best-Run Companies* (New York: Warner Books, 1982).

59. Robbins and Coulter, *Management*, p. 91.

60. Ibid., p. 92.

61. Ibid.

62. Irving L. Janis, *Victims of Groupthink* (Boston, MA: Houghton Mifflin, 1972).

63. Miller, More, and Braswell, *Effective Police Supervision*, pp. 231–232.

64. Gary Yukl, *Leadership in Organizations* (Upper Saddle River, NJ: Prentice-Hall, 2006), p. 343.

65. John R. Schermerhorn, James G. Hunt, Richard N. Osborn, and M. Uhl-Bien, *Organizational Behavior* (Hoboken, NJ: John Wiley & Sons, 2010), p. 199.

66. Ibid., p. 200.

67. Ibid.

68. Linda K. Stroh, Gregory B. Northcraft, and Margaret A. Neale, *Organizational Behavior* (Mahwah, NJ: Lawrence Erlbaum and Associates, 2002), p. 242.

69. Noel M. Tichy and Warren G. Bennis, *Judgment: How Winning Leaders Make Great Calls* (New York: Portfolio, 2007), p. 1.

70. Noel M. Tichy and Warren G. Bennis, "Making Judgment Calls," *Harvard Business Review* (October 2007), pp. 94–107.

71. Jeffrey Pfeffer, and Robert I. Sutton, "Evidence-Based Management," *Harvard Business Review* (January 2006), pp. 62–75.

9

POWER

Its Nature and Use

Learning Objectives

1. Define *power*.
2. Distinguish between power and politics.
3. Identify the types of power.
4. Describe how power is acquired.
5. Distinguish between referent and expert power.

Key Terms

avoidance
buffing
charisma
coalition power
coalition tactics
coercive power
commitment
compassion
compliance
decision premise
depersonalization
dominating power
ecological power
empowering power
empowerment
expert power
hubris syndrome
illegitimate
information power

legitimate
legitimate power
legitimating tactics
organizational politics
personal power
political intelligence
political power
position power
positional power
pressure tactics
process power
redirecting responsibility
referent power
representative power
resistance
reward power
scapegoating
working the rules

A sentence quoted extensively in newspapers, magazines, journals, and police training programs is *Power corrupts, and absolute power corrupts absolutely.* The implication is that a person who has an excess of power will use it unwisely.[1] The concern that police managers have too much power is definitely invalid, at least in today's organizations, where in many instances they do not have the power they need in order to function effectively.

Legal and social constraints circumscribe the power of managers. Laws and regulations such as the Civil Rights Act, the Age Discrimination in Employment Act, the Equal Employment Opportunity Act, and rulings by federal courts have resulted in restrictions and limited the power base of police managers.[2]

The pressure exerted by interest groups, citizens, city managers or mayors, city councils or boards of supervisors, state legislatures, civic groups, and unions also reduce power.[3] All these elements combine at different times to limit or restrict the power exercised by police managers. An illustration of this is officer membership in unions or associations, coupled with collective bargaining with police unions.[4]

Also, the personality of the manager and the characteristics of the organization itself act as modifiers of power. Some organizational members view police managers as power hungry; the behavior of others suggests that they do not like to exercise power. This dichotomy is especially apparent in matters involving discipline. Some managers will go out of their way to avoid confronting deviant organizational behavior, while others relish the prospects of conflict.

CASE STUDY   Lieutenant Fred Weaver

Lt. Fred Weaver currently commands the Youth Services Bureau in a medium-sized police department in a city that is primarily a bedroom community, with a large commercial section and no industry. There are a large number of young citizens in the community; thus, it is especially important for the police department to emphasize the prevention of crime—for example, sponsoring Police Athletic League with various sports activities held throughout the year.

Lt. Weaver attended the local university, earning a degree in psychology. He was very active in campus activities and earned letters in both baseball and track. As a high school student, he joined a police-sponsored Explorer Scout unit and played baseball in the Police Athletic League. He continued these activities as a college student. He joined the police department after graduation.

He then attended the regional police academy and graduated first in his class. Weaver's first assignment was to patrol, where he served for three years with distinction. In his fourth year of service, he was promoted to sergeant and assigned to the Youth Services Bureau, where he supervised the Explorer Scout unit and coached the baseball team.

In Weaver's seventh year of service, he was promoted to lieutenant and became the commander of the Youth Services Bureau. During his three years assigned to the bureau, he has become indispensable as a fund-raiser. He is an excellent speaker and appears before community groups frequently. Under his leadership, the bureau's influence has extended greatly, and many public officials as well as important citizens in the community view Lt. Weaver as the real spokesperson of the department.

During the last three years, Lt. Weaver has quadrupled the unit's income from outside sources and has introduced an annual circus and a youth Olympics program. Both these programs were instant successes and clearly enhanced the reputation of the bureau.

The chief of police is beginning to sense that he has lost control of the bureau and that it is almost becoming an independent police unit. It is a tenuous situation. The chief feels that Lt. Weaver is becoming a threat to his position and is attempting to gain all the power he can.

Lt. Weaver's point of view is that he is only trying to do his job, not searching for power, and that he makes decisions to ensure that the bureau stays the primary crime-prevention unit in the community.

If you were the chief, how would you deal with the potential problem? Could Lt. Weaver have done things differently to avoid being perceived as a power threat? What types of power do both leaders have?

Structurally, the bureaucratic nature of a police organization distributes power from top to bottom. Power follows the hierarchy of the police organizational structure—the higher the rank, the greater the amount of power.[5]

Definitions of Power

Power is a concept with negative connotations. Managers who have power deny it. Power seekers do everything possible to camouflage their efforts. Lastly, those who are adept at securing power are reluctant to discuss how they acquired it. It is the ability to influence others to carry out your will despite resistance.[6] From a negative perspective, power implies a master–slave relationship or at the very least, a superior–subordinate relationship. McClelland defines two types of power—dominating and empowering.[7]

1. **Dominating power** seeks to keep individuals weak and dependent on the leader.
2. **Empowering power** aims to promote individuals and build commitment to the organization and its goals.

Empowering power is used for positive ends and is developed through group decision-making. Managers thus face the difficult job of balancing these conflicting types of power in the pursuit of organizational goals.

Researchers who have analyzed the concept of power have defined it in different ways. The following definitions demonstrate the variability:

1. Power is the capacity to translate intention into reality and sustain it. Leadership is the wise use of this power. Vision is the commodity of leaders, and power is their currency.[8]
2. Power is the absolute capacity of an individual agent to influence the behavior or attitudes of one or more designated target persons at a given point in time.[9]
3. Power refers to a capacity that the leader has to influence the behavior of a follower so that the subordinate follows the leader's wishes. The greater the dependency, the more power one person has over another. The perception of the person determines who is the target of the power relationship.[10]

Each of these definitions describes either the ability or the capacity to control the behavior of an individual or a group to attain some goal. Effective leaders utilize power to achieve organizational goals and build upon the belief that leaders and followers share the belief in the legitimacy of such goals.[11] These definitions accept the premise that everyone in an organization possesses some power, giving him or her the capacity to choose between alternatives. Not everyone in an organization has equal power, and certainly, not everyone controls his or her future. Implicit in the definitions is a degree of dependency between members of an organization, as well as some discretion for the individual when responding to efforts to influence his or her behavior.

It is clear that managerial power, when used correctly, generally involves bringing together resources to accomplish something. Effective managers understand the uses, limitations, sources, and characteristics of power. If power is used to make employees totally dependent, then it is being used ineffectively. If it is used sparingly or in a helping mode, it is more apt to be effective.

Managers exercise power to influence subordinates in a certain way:

1. **Commitment**: An outcome in which the follower agrees with the leader's decision and make the required effort see it effectively implemented.
2. **Compliance**: The follower does what the leader asks in an apathetic and unenthusiastic manner with only a minimal effort.
3. **Resistance**: The follower openly opposes the leader's decision and actively avoids ways to carry it out. It includes the following: (a) refusal to implement the decision, (b) make excuses about why it cannot be carried out, (c) try to persuade the leader to retract or change the decision, (d) ask higher authorities to overrule the decision, (e) delay acting in the hope that it will be forgotten, and (f) make a pretense of compliance but then sabotaging implementation.[12]

Different types of managers, then, use power for different reasons, but to some degree, managers are continually using power as a means of influencing others. Influence is the behavioral response to the application of power.[13] When people are convinced to change their behavior, to change their opinion, to complete a certain act or activity, or to support a different position, then a manager can be said to have exerted influence over a follower, a peer, or a superior.

Prince illustrates how power is exercised in meetings, often in a dysfunctional way. Meeting participants are always aware of the manager's power. The manager exercises authority over the administration of punishments and rewards. This fact stifles the conduct and content of meeting discussions. Participants typically seek the approval of the manager and do not speak their mind. Most managers exercise a judgmental style in meetings, reflecting their power. Rejection is one judgmental attribute. The participant feels put-down if the rejection is punishing and negative. Prince recommends managers assume a judicious style in meetings, relying on experience and the wisdom not to judge and reject suggestions but to teach, guide, and capitalize on the experience of subordinates to ensure the success of the organization.[14]

The Power Base

Power has meaning not only to the individual but also to groups and organizations. At some time or another, everyone has heard an individual referred to as powerful, and it is always someone who can influence behavior. Decisions are made, goals attained, or changes instituted. Power involves the interaction between two individuals. This personal interaction is described as consisting of five types of power: reward power, coercive power, legitimate power, referent power, and expert power (see Figure 9–1).[15]

Reward Power

Rewarding an employee for performance is one of the best ways a manager can influence behavior. **Reward power** reflects the manager's formal authority to extend both rewards and punishment to subordinates.[16] The manager controls these items, has the capacity to deliver them, and will do so if the targeted person performs in the desired fashion. Some elements of reward power are financial. Within the limits of their organizational structure, managers can threaten job transfer, withholding pay raises, demotion, and even firing of underperforming subordinates via their control over the performance appraisal system. In terms of financial rewards, they may have the power to authorize promotions, pay increases, bonuses, and the size of a unit's budget.[17] Nonfinancial rewards include better job assignments and work conditions—such as a larger office or a reserved parking spot.[18]

Most police officers pursue promotions actively and find them to be one of the best ways, if not the best way, to obtain status and receive recognition, both within the organization and in the greater community. Normally, a sergeant can recommend someone for promotion, but the chief takes the action.

In recent years, the reward power of police chief executive officers has extended as typical promotion lists have expanded, and chiefs have greater latitude in the selection process. For many years, a chief was required to select from the top three candidates for promotion, but in recent years, many agencies review the top eight candidates.

The increasing size of police departments dilutes the reward power of the chief executive officer. It has become increasingly necessary for the chief to rely on recommendations from others. In smaller police departments, every officer considered for promotion may be personally acquainted with the police chief—except for instances where lateral transfers from other organizations are considered.

In law enforcement, intrinsic rewards such as special assignments, praise, and awards have a great deal of importance. One source of motivation is that some officers desire to be recognized and accepted as productive members of the organization. Managers at various levels within the organization can satisfy such desires by assigning officers to special units such as K-9 or SWAT. In most instances, officers find an assignment to these units desirable. In some departments, the same holds true for assignment to crime prevention, traffic (motorcycle), and investigations. There are some other intrinsic rewards of importance to officers, including a wide range of managerial actions. Managers should strive to encourage participation whenever possible.

Figure 9–1
The Power Base of the Manager.

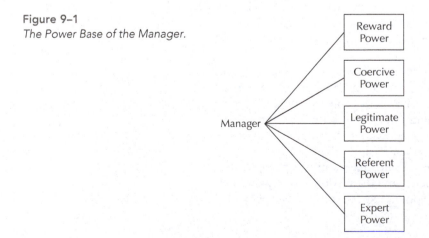

Thus, it is important to share power. Ways to share power include delegating authority commensurate with responsibility. It is important to remember that some officers are not ready to exercise additional organizational power because they cannot accept the responsibility. Managers are advised to limit delegations to those who potentially can benefit, then monitor their performance, and, when necessary, teach the employee how to exercise the newly acquired power to support departmental goals.

Whenever possible, a manager should strive for consensus during the decision-making process as a means of increasing mutual trust. The goal is to create an atmosphere whereby subordinates respond to this type of reward by becoming more creative, demonstrating a higher degree of initiative, and exhibiting a greater dedication to the department; this dedication makes for a better operating department. Police managers should adopt a facilitative leadership style and avoid repression. When the situation demands, a police manager must still respond to the situation (especially during emergencies), issuing orders followed without any thought of participation or consensus.

Exercising Reward Power

Most employees respond positively to reward power, and the same holds true for managers. If subordinates need rewards from the organization, the result will be a commitment to the department. If the perception is that organizational rewards exploit employees or given to employees who do not deserve them, the reward power has little meaning. Measurable performance criteria promotions, not subjective evaluations, determine promotions. The specific reason or reasons for the promotion should be made known to everyone.[19]

The same principle holds for rewards such as being given a desirable assignment or being assigned to a critical investigative team: When making assignments, inform people why, and do it publicly at roll call, in a department bulletin, or via a special memorandum.

Other rewards a manager can give a range from the acknowledgment of a job well done to officially commending an officer. Use public recognition whenever the situation allows. The problem is that it takes time. A manager must make an effort if the officers in the organization feel publicity is important.

The giving of rewards is a pleasurable experience for both the recipient and the manager. One useful technique is to acknowledge police officers' accomplishments publicly every spring during a "Police Week" ceremony.

Coercive Power

Coercive power is at the other end of the continuum from reward power—as we have just discussed, it involves administering punishments or withholding rewards. It uses fear of punishment and sanctions to control the behavior of subordinates. Punishment can take many forms, including suspension, demotion, official reprimand, and more subtle sanctions such as giving an officer an undesirable assignment.

The extreme sanction is termination. Even for a first offense, many departments will dismiss an officer for the following:

1. Soliciting, accepting, or offering a bribe
2. Being involved in the theft of cash or city property
3. Falsifying city records
4. Destroying city records
5. Falsifying time reports, mileage reports, or expense accounts
6. Deliberately withholding information (relating to work) from supervisors

In many police departments (because of the 24-hour orientation), the night shift is imposed on officers to punish them or to put them where they are out of sight and mind. The same strategy transfers employees to undesirable locations. For example, the discipline can be the assignment of an officer to a station that is many miles from his or her home, requiring a long commute.

Table 9–1
MANAGER'S COERCIVE POWERS

Termination	Transfer
Suspension	Relocation
Official reprimand	Strict supervision
Undesirable job assignment	Enforcement of rules and regulations

Officers differ in their preferences for assignments. Some officers like to work traffic and others do not. Others enjoy the action of working a crime beat, whereas still others would rather do anything but this task. In most instances, a police manager, especially the supervisory manager, will know what an officer likes and dislikes and can use this knowledge for punishment.

Overly strict supervision is another way to administer punishment. A recalcitrant officer can have incident reports repeatedly returned for rewriting. Rules and regulations can be enforced down to the crossed *t* or dotted *i*. Every deviation can be written up and documented. First-line supervisors can punish subordinates by monitoring of the procedures and techniques used to stop someone for a traffic violation. In most instances, the supervisor can find reasons to write a report—for example, the improperly parked police vehicle, the officer's approach to the car was wrong, improper radio use, or the officer detained the offender too long (see Table 9–1).

All this harassment can result in a punishing working environment. The repeated application of negative sanctions can result (at its extreme) in a decision by an officer to quit—or in some instances, to file a grievance against the supervisor. In other cases, an officer can respond to the sanctions by treading water—doing just what is acceptable. The influence of police unions reduces the coercive power of police managers.

Exercising Coercive Power

The best exercise of coercive power is never to exercise it at all. Unfortunately, situations do occur in which it becomes necessary for a police manager to discipline an officer. Instead of using their power to dictate methods, effective executives empower members of the organization to discover and implement new and better ways of doing things.[20] Few managers enjoy exercising coercive power. It is usually a time-consuming process and can be emotionally exhausting. Disciplined officers can become resentful, and minimal performers at the extreme can become so negative that they are just not pleasant to be around.

Managers are striving to get officers to comply with official procedures or rules and regulations. The use of coercive power seldom results in commitment. Compliance, resentment, or obstructionism may result.

Most police departments use numerous rules and regulations to spell out task performance and implementation. They identify infractions and punishments. For example, police managers can use progressive discipline ranging from informal discussion to discharge.[21]

It is imperative for the manager to make sure all employees are aware of policies, procedures, and regulations, especially when procedures are changed or modified. As the old saying goes, *Ignorance is no excuse, nor is the failure to advise.* The key is to communicate—often and effectively.

There is clear-cut logic requiring a manager not only to inform those supervised of the punishment but also (when a violation occurs) to warn them about the sanction. When targeting an employee for possible punishment, a paper trail serves as a basis for later disciplinary action if needed. It is much more effective to tell an officer, "You were warned of the failure to comply with the departmental procedure on July 1, August 5, and August 15," than it is to say, "Well, I warned you."

The same idea applies to performance reviews. The process should be a real dialogue between the employee and the manager, in other words, two-way communication. At the time of a performance evaluation, the boss should never inform employees for the first time of their inability to perform their job properly.

The use of coercive power should follow an investigation to determine that a violation occurred. Also, if there is latitude as to the exact nature or type of punishment, every effort should be made to ensure that it is appropriate to the situation and commensurate with the seriousness of the infraction or offense. Effectiveness requires the perception that credible punishment is undesirable. Coercion can arouse anger and resentment and may result in retaliation. It is not likely to sponsor commitment by subordinates but should result in compliance.[22]

Lastly, every employee has the right to be warned or reprimanded privately. The manager has this obligation. Punishing in public has the potential of permanently straining a manager's relationship with employees. Punishment is a no-win situation for everyone involved.

Kramer[23] discusses how "great intimidators" use fear to realize their vision for the organization. They are not simply bullies. They possess **political intelligence** and use intimidation and power to exploit the anxieties and vulnerabilities detected. They impatiently eliminate obstacles to change and do not suffer from doubt or timidity. They dispassionately view individuals as instruments to get things done. They confront people through tough questioning about their purpose and motives. They coerce them to gain an edge and achieve results once thought impossible. The use of confrontation forces people to reveal how they feel about an issue. Great intimidators perform (like General George S. Patton's "game face" scowl) to transmit menace and terror, often using abusive language. They know how to use anger and rage to get their way. While they master facts, they also keep their aims private to keep people off balance regarding a final decision. Surprisingly, they attract the "best and brightest" to work for them, sponsoring respect and a desire to perform well to please the intimidator.

While their tactics are often successful, the great intimidators also fall prey to their dysfunctions. Because people are unwilling to confront them, debate is stifled, allowing them to win arguments they should lose and depriving them of the "checks and balances" needed to reach good decisions. They stop listening to others, believing they are infallible. They also fail to keep track of the enemies they create and the power of their opposition.

Legitimate Power

Legitimate power considers one's position, role, and status in the organization. The incumbent possesses legitimate power as long as assigned to an office or position. The power remains when another individual assumes the position. In law enforcement, rank is closely associated with legitimate power. Power generally increases with each higher rank. It includes the formal authority to control and use organizational resources including assignment to work activities. The Chief of Police is the chief executive officer of the department and the departmental authority on all matters of policy, operations, and discipline to assure the effective performance of the department. This power results from the fact that the chief is a legitimate occupant of that position—**position power**.[24]

In law enforcement, the boss has the right to command. The authority identifying that right is usually quite specific, as the following police directive shows:[25]

> *Compliance with Lawful Orders.* The department is an organization with a clearly defined hierarchy of authority. It is necessary because unquestioned obedience of a superior's lawful command is essential for the safe and prompt performance of law enforcement operations. The most desirable means of obtained compliance are recognition and reward of proper performance and the encouragement of a willingness to serve. However, negative discipline is necessary where there is a willful disregard of lawful orders, commands, or directives.

This directive clearly illustrates that a superior has accompanying reward and coercive powers. Unity of command is also stressed, and there is a finite chain of command.

All employees are aware of their relative positions in the organization, what tasks they are immediately responsible for, and to whom they are accountable.

In law enforcement, departmental directives will also spell out command responsibilities for handling unusual occurrences. A field commander or the senior assistant officer will have the authority to direct the operation and will be held responsible. A senior commanding officer may make suggestions, but supervision is left up to the field commander. Unless properly relieved, senior command officers will assume command of an unusual occurrence; it is normal for a police department to have a policy holding the officer accountable for unfavorable developments even if he or she has chosen not to take command. For example, at a bombing scene, the departmental policy will specifically state the responsibilities of the first officer at the scene and the responding field commander. At the crime scene, specifications exist for evidence collection procedures and who will collect.

Legitimate power is also known as **positional power**. The formal position held in an organization provides positional power. In police organizations, positional power is a matter of the hierarchical relationships identified by the organizational chart. There is a definite division of labor identifying lines of control.

The departmental manual specifically identifies the duties of members of the organization and spells out the legal basis by citing statutes and ordinances. Police departments are especially concerned with command responsibility and specify that police managers will be responsible and accountable for each aspect of their command. A commanding officer is required to work within policy guidelines and legal constraints when coordinating and directing subordinates.

Policies require police managers to enforce department rules and regulations and ensure compliance with department policies and procedures. Because of the potential negative impact of certain situations or unusual occurrences, most police departments have policies carefully spelling out when the watch commander will notify the chief of police that such a situation is in progress.

Exercising Legitimate Power

Legitimate power represents a type of power a police manager possesses because subordinates believe that he or she has the right to command. It is the same as formal authority. Police organizations outline managerial duties in legal documents and legitimate them.

Most officers readily accept legitimate power. It is a natural phenomenon to follow the dictates of someone of higher rank when the request is reasonable and authorized by policy or rules and regulations. The forceful use of legitimate power is unreasonable. Forcefulness should be limited to those situations in which it is obvious that it is the only way to obtain compliance.

When sending a formal request to subordinates, the manager should adopt a solicitous manner with a concern for them. Sending the request through the chain of command reinforces its legitimacy. Whenever possible, a formal request should include a reason or reasons for its transmittal to set a positive frame of reference for the request.

In every instance, a request should be followed up as a means of ensuring that the recipient understands the request and realizes that the request is not only legitimate but also necessary.

Referent Power

Referent power is difficult to define because it is intangible. It is related to the ability of a manager to influence the behavior of subordinates because they identify with him or her. It can be the result of the manager's intelligence or some aspect of his or her personality that subordinates like or admire. When a leader's characteristics are exceptional in the eyes of followers, the leader is charismatic.

Charisma is the personal magic of leadership arousing special loyalty or enthusiasm for a public figure. It is usually used to describe a political leader such as John Kennedy or a military commander such as George Patton. In law enforcement, William Bratton and August Vollmer are examples of charismatic leaders who had large numbers of supporters.

Charismatic leaders benefit from the perceptions of their subordinates. Charisma helps everything fall nicely into place. Followers desire to please leaders for whom they have strong feelings of affection, admiration, and loyalty. Such personal identification is the basis for the sponsorship of approval and acceptance—with loyalty as its base. It is also increased by showing concern for the needs and feelings of others, demonstrating trust and respect, and treating people fairly. It is dependent upon the integrity and character of the leader.[26]

A manager with whom employees identify easily has referent power. A key element of this type of power is trust. When an officer trusts a police manager, it enhances the working relationship. Honesty and dependability are elements of trust. If followers discover that a leader has exploited or manipulated them in pursuit of self-interest, the leader loses trust. Trust is a positive variable engendering acceptance and a real desire to follow. When trust is present, the manager is in a position to influence outcomes.

Exercising Referent Power

The key element of the effective utilization of referent power is subordinate compliance because the subordinate does not want to disturb the working relationship. Requests are complied with because subordinates like their manager and they identify with him or her. It develops out of admiration of another and a desire to be like that person.[27]

To enhance referent power, the manager should do everything possible to create a working relationship based on mutual respect. Fairness and equity are essential when dealing with subordinates, showing a genuine concern for the interests and needs of subordinates. Finally, whenever the opportunity presents itself, managers should identify individuals who would be most desirable to have in their unit and then actively recruit them.

Follower loyalty and responsiveness allow a manager to get things accomplished easily. The manager's desire can be a simple request—the response to which is usually positive. The key is that the followers respond because they want to, not because it is required. A police manager can enhance and reinforce personal power by becoming an astute observer and participant in the decision-making process whenever possible. Being asked for information provides an opportunity for face-to-face interaction and the potential to influence the ultimate decision.

It is difficult to imagine any manager (other than the most charismatic) being able to rely solely on personal power, without the support of other power bases. Regarding command responsibility, a police manager is obligated to perform a full range of administrative functions, relying on a personal initiative to ensure the highest level of performance possible.

One can have both positional and personal power. When combined, a police manager will have the highest possible level of influence over subordinates, superiors, and peers.

Expert Power

When managers control the behavior of others due to their knowledge, experience, or judgment, they have **expert power**. This special information might have been acquired over an extended period or as a consequence of special training, but in every instance, such expertise provides a base for obtaining subordinate compliance. It is relevant when others are in need of the expertise and advice of the leader. It increases when competence is demonstrated—solving problems, making good decisions, providing valuable opinions, and completing projects.[28]

When managers have relevant, useful, and important information, they are in a position to exert influence extending beyond their other powers. In recent years, law enforcement agencies have increasingly relied on the expertise of professionals, especially in the areas of law and psychology. It is quite common to find police departments employing police legal advisers and police psychologists.

Also, as police departments have grown in size, supervisors have developed expertise in numerous areas, including the investigation of auto theft, bunco, forgery, sex crimes, and computer crimes. In other instances, managers developed unique skills in planning, budgeting, or doing other administrative tasks, giving them additional power.

Expert power (if it is to be of benefit to a department) should not be autocratic, but a process of balancing technical competence and allowing subordinates, superiors, and peers to achieve goals and objectives. We anticipate that technical knowledge will become increasingly important. Experts will have to learn how to manage the complexities of interdependent relationships they encounter if the organization is to be responsive and adapt to changing conditions.[29]

Exercising Expert Power

Managers should make every effort to become knowledgeable in special areas. When they develop special skills needed by others within the organization, they have an expert power base.

Managers should work diligently at attaining and maintaining a specialized skill because it adds to credibility. At the same time, managers should readily admit any lack of knowledge and never try to bluff their way through. In almost every instance, bluffing will catch up with them and jeopardize their reputation. The best position to take is "I will find the answer to the question."

Managers can reinforce **personal power** by expanding their expert power as much as possible. They should take advantage of every opportunity to attend special training programs. Police managers with computer and information management expertise are influential.[30] Specialization reinforces personal power, as can be seen when one develops expertise as, for example, a computer specialist, labor negotiator, or polygraph examiner.

Presenting an image of being an expert can reinforce expert power. When making presentations or discussing issues related to expertise, it is essential to be direct, decisive, and above all, believable. When explaining things to those less knowledgeable in a specific area, do not use jargon or attempt to impress them with complicated examples. Present material at the lowest possible level and make sure everyone understands it. If there is any doubt about understanding the material, go over it again; make a point of singling out those who appear puzzled, and provide them with the help they need to understand the topic or issue under discussion. Above all, never do anything that would threaten a subordinate's self-esteem.

Additional Sources of Power

There are a number of power sources that go beyond the original list compiled by French and Raven. Yet, these forms of power are related to the ones that we have discussed. For example, several forms of power emerge from legitimate (positional) power. **Process power** is control over methods of production and analysis.[31] In policing, control over the crime analysis unit would represent this type of power. **Information power** is exercised when the manager controls the access to and flow of information vital to organizational operations. Managers guard the "right to know" because it puts them in a position to control events, not just respond to them.[32] Another form of legitimate power is **representative power**—a formal right conferred by the organization that allows the manager to speak on behalf of the organization. Also related to legitimate power is **ecological power**. This form of power is based upon control over the physical environment, technology, and organization of the work. It is also related to influence over the culture of the organization—its shared norms, values, and beliefs of its members.[33]

Managers can extend their personal power by increasing the visibility of their job performance by

1. Expanding the number of contacts that they have with senior people.
2. Making oral presentations of work.
3. Participating in problem-solving task forces.
4. Sending out notices of accomplishment.
5. Generally seeking additional opportunities to increase personal name recognition.[34] Managers can also attempt to influence decision premises in the organization. A **decision premise** is a basis for defining a problem and selecting among alternative potential solutions to it. If you define the problem in a manner that fits your expertise, you set yourself up as the person charged with solving it.[35]

Other forms are tied to the ability to influence groups within the organization. **Coalition power** is the ability to control another's behavior indirectly because the individual owes an obligation to you or to another as a part of a larger collective interest. To build a coalition, individuals negotiate trade-offs to arrive at a common position.[36] **Empowerment** is the process by which managers help others acquire and use the power needed to make decisions affecting themselves and their work. Empowerment inspires followers to overcome their limitations. It emphasizes the ability to make things happen.[37]

Negative Aspects of Power

Some leaders use power for their own aggrandizement. They fail to realize they are dependent upon the performance of others and the availability of resources. Therefore, they need to promote cooperation. This dependency increases as one gains more formal authority in an organization. For these reasons, the command of power is an overrated method of insuring performance through giving orders. Kotter offers more effective ways of generating power. One is to create a sense of obligation among subordinates so they will do things on their own. Another is to become recognized as an expert in a certain area through visible achievement. A final method is to create a perceived dependence upon the leader by finding and acquiring resources and exerting influence. The leader can also use persuasion, the formal evaluation system, and other available rewards.[38]

Similarly, McClelland and Burnham determined that managers fall into three groups. Affiliative managers have a need to be liked rather than a desire to get things done. They make decisions to increase their popularity, but not to achieve the goals of the organization. The second group of managers are motivated by the need to achieve and could care less about what people think of them. They are more concerned with personal recognition. However, institutional managers are interested in building power influence rather than personal achievement. Their subordinates have a greater sense of responsibility, promote organizational goals, and have more team spirit.[39]

Power causes leaders to lose compassion for their charges. It impairs our neurological ability to connect with others. The **hubris syndrome** is a disorder of power associated with overwhelming success over a period of years. The answer is to practice **compassion**—the intent to contribute to the happiness and well-being of others. Leaders can make a habit of it by applying it intentionally to any engagement and at every opportunity.[40]

Results from an experiment showed that on days the participants felt powerful, they reported more negative interactions with others—engaging in abusive behaviors (yelling, swearing, rudeness, belittling co-workers). They also perceived co-workers treated them poorly (addressing them unprofessionally, speaking in a condescending tone, paying little or no attention to their opinions). They reported a "power hangover" when they went home perhaps due to their guilt over how they conducted themselves at work. However, leaders rated as "agreeable" abused co-workers less because they prioritized maintaining positive relations with them.[41]

Power: A Summary

An effective manager influences the behavior of others in the work environment. There are distinctions in the five bases of power listed earlier. Expert and referent power bases are more informal in nature. Legitimate, reward, and coercive power bases are more formal. The extent to which a manager uses one power base can definitely modify power from another base. Unquestionably, when a manager is adept at rewarding, employees respond to a greater extent and prove to be more supportive. On the other hand, when a manager uses coercive power as a consistent managerial style, it can create resentment among subordinates.[42]

The interaction between power sources varies considerably and is modified by how subordinates perceive a manager, whether or not the unit is important to the organization, and whether subordinates are dependent. Legitimate power provides a manager with a supporting base for the utilization of reward or coercive power. This supporting base can be altered. For example, in a large police department, the chief of police could transfer a deputy chief from a position as head of investigations to an administrative position. This is really a disciplinary transfer: By changing the deputy chief's functional location, the chief would be reducing the deputy chief's legitimate power, reward power, and coercive power.

CASE STUDY   Lieutenant Luis Gonzales

Lt. Luis Gonzales has been a member of the Crater Police Department for 11 years and a lieutenant for two years. Crater has a population of 83,000 and is part of a metropolitan area in the northwestern United States. When still a sergeant, Gonzales was assigned to the Support Services Bureau and became involved in the electronic automation of the department.

Lt. Gonzales attended City University where he majored in business administration and minored in computer sciences. This academic preparation, coupled with his intense interest in computers, served as a base of knowledge when the department decided to automate its communications and records center.

Gonzales first surveyed other police departments to determine what computer-aided dispatching systems they used. Also, he visited state and federal agencies to obtain the latest information on computer applications to law enforcement. Then he wrote a proposal, obtained internal approval for it, and submitted it to various computer vendors.

Once the city selected a vendor, Lt. Gonzales was assigned to work full-time monitoring the installation of the computer-aided dispatch system. This process took nine months. The system was proved effective. It solved problems with dispatch. The chief of police then assigned Lt. Gonzales to head a team to computerize the records system.

With this new assignment, Lt. Gonzales became a real expert in the application of computers to law enforcement. Other departments seek his advice because he has proven to be very skillful. He runs hands-on training programs for the department, receiving enthusiastic acclaim from all the attendees.

The investigative unit is now capable of accessing computerized criminal records, case files, and field interrogation reports. The system drastically reduced response time for service calls. Immediate access to department records enhances the ability of units to respond.

Lt. Gonzales is the leading department expert on computers. Other managers in the department have limited computer experience, so they have had to turn to Lt. Gonzales for help, enhancing his reputation. As a result, he spends more time away from the department. In every instance, the other departments reimburse the city for Lt. Gonzales's expenses.

During the last two years, Lt. Gonzales has become a real power within the department. It seems that everyone relies on him. Since Lt. Gonzales has unique expertise, there is a great deal of resentment. Part of it can be attributed to a forthcoming promotional examination for captain at the end of the year. Four other eligible lieutenants feel Lt. Gonzales has the inside track because of his expert power.

The conflict is apparent and known to everyone in the department. Lt. Gonzales is at a loss about what to do. He is perplexed by the whole problem and is considering discussing it with the chief. If you were Lt. Gonzales, how would you deal with this problem? What would you tell the chief? Would you ask to be assigned to another position?

Knowledge is power. The higher the position in the department, the greater the amount of information one can process. When we are in the know, we are more apt to be involved in the decision-making process, and when we can make or have decision-making input, there is an acquisition of power.[43]

Another symbol of power is the ability to obtain resources such as personnel, equipment, and supplies. Resources are important to success, and a manager who obtains the resources needed to accomplish tasks and achieve department goals adds to his or her positional power.

Influence

Influence determines the exercise of power and the effectiveness of goal accomplishment. As Theodore Roosevelt said: "You are probably acquainted with the old proverb: 'Speak softly and carry a big stick—you will go far.' If a man continually blusters, if he lacks civility, a big stick will not save him from trouble; and neither will speaking softly avail, if back of the softness there does not lie strength, power."[44] The exercise of power involves the use of influence. Without it, managers would never get their work done. There are nine distinct influence tactics:[45]

1. *Legitimacy:* builds upon organizational authority. The tactic used is aligned with organizational rules, regulations, and policies.
2. *Rational persuasion:* presentation of rational arguments and facts that the tactic proposed is logical and has the potential to be effective.

3. *Inspirational appeals:* emotional appeal to the follower's values, needs, hopes, and aspirations. They are designed to stir strong emotions to enlist the support of followers by arousing ideals that promise to make things better—freedom, justice, liberty, fairness, and equality.

4. *Consultation:* collaborating with followers and recognizing their expertise to develop effective plans, objectives, and goals. Consultation increases the follower's support and motivation for accomplishment by facilitating their support for the proposal.

5. *Exchange:* rewarding followers for their performance and compliance.

6. *Personal appeals:* asking for help based upon personal loyalty and friendship.

7. *Ingratiation:* the use of flattery and praise before seeking compliance.

8. *Pressure:* the use of threats, warnings, and repeated demands to insure compliance.

9. *Coalitions:* seeking the help of others to persuade followers to join in the proposed effort. This tactic can also help you to overcome resistance to change because you have already sought and obtained the support of others.

Legitimating tactics aim to establish authority and right to seek certain things. **Pressure tactics** include threats, warnings, and demands. They include attempts to establish firm control over an individual's performance at work. **Coalition tactics** attempt to enlist the support of others to ensure the completion of a task. Tactics are more likely to be accepted when viewed as legitimate. Overall, the exercise of power influences the success of a leader.[46]

Goldsmith offers suggestions on how to "manage up"—to influence decision-makers in your organization and make your presence felt. First, you must sell your position to management. They are under no obligation to "buy" your position. Second, emphasize how your suggestion will serve the entire organization, not just your unit. Leaders usually focus on the larger whole than on specific sections of the organization. Finally, present a realistic cost-benefit of your position, not just its supposed benefits. You must show how the benefits of your suggestion outweigh organizational costs.[47]

The "softer" tactics tend to be most effective. Coercion leads to resentment and opposition. Offering them in combination may achieve the best result. Nye reminds us that power is the ability to get what you want, and it requires tools—coercion (hard power) or attraction (emotional appeals—soft power). Hard power alone cannot solve complex problems. Smart power involves the combination of both. It is preferable to use persuasion as a motivator rather than rely upon coercion.[48]

The preferred power tactic used most often when dealing with either superiors or subordinates is reason. Circumscribed by the need to comply and exist in a legal environment, law enforcement officers are prone to utilize rules, regulations, and policies when reasoning with others in the organization. When managers have an abundance of power, they are more apt to use a variety of power techniques than do those who have a limited amount of power.

Assertiveness is a backup strategy that powerful managers use when the situation dictates or when other techniques have proven to be ineffective. A manager can start with a simple request or an effort to reason with someone and then shift to a more forceful, assertive approach to obtain compliance. If a manager encounters resistance from a subordinate, the technique utilized can indicate the point where sanctions come into play.

When managers attempt to influence subordinates as a means of obtaining compliance and ensuring the attainment of goals, the techniques most frequently used are reason, assertiveness, and friendliness. As managers exert both positional and personal power when attempting to influence subordinates, there is a greater reliance on personal power.

When managers have had a favorable experience utilizing a power strategy (such as reason), they are more apt to rely on that method in the future. If reason proves to be ineffective, a manager will then try to obtain compliance by using other techniques such as assertiveness or friendliness.

Effective managers are those who utilize power with restraint tailored to the specific situation. They are fully aware of both the positive and negative consequences of power. They apply power with care and concern for personnel as well as for the organization.

An interesting approach to power is to turn it into influence by specifically utilizing power bases. However it is done, it is an effort to obtain true commitment, and not just mere compliance. A manager wants employees to work diligently at a task accomplishment. It is not a question of just doing one's job, but doing it with dispatch and effectiveness. Workers who plod along and perform work at a barely acceptable level are responding to power with compliance, but not commitment. Commitment reflects an effective use of power.

Politics

Politics is power in action[49]—the "allocation of power."[50] **Political power** includes activities that influence or attempt to influence the distribution of advantages and hindrances within an organization by an individual. It can be **legitimate** (complaining to a supervisor, bypassing the chain of command, forming coalitions, obstructing organizational policies or decisions through inaction or excessive adherence to rules, and developing contacts and allies outside the organization) or **illegitimate** (sabotage, whistle blowing, or symbolic protests, like the "blue flu"—where police officers simultaneously call in sick to object to enforcement of an organizational policy). Personality influences the ability of followers to use such means ("high Mach" individuals who seek power for its own sake to advance their desires and ambition), their identification with and investment in organizational goals and their stake in conformity to them.[51] Politicking is also more common in organization cultures that feature the following: low trust, role ambiguity (uncertainty of one's place in the organization), unclear performance evaluations and criteria for promotion, zero-sum allocation of rewards (the only way to get a reward is to take it from someone else), authoritarian decision-making, high pressure for performance, and self-serving superiors.[52]

Organizational politics is the management of influence to obtain ends not sanctioned by the organization or to obtain sanctioned ends through non-sanctioned means. It is also the art of creative compromise among competing interests. Managers are often considered political when they seek their own goals, or when they use means that are not currently authorized by the organization or that push legal limits.[53] Political power is a necessary function resulting from differences in the self-interests of individuals—to develop socially acceptable ends and means that balance individual and collective interests.

Jarrett defines organizational politics as a variety of activities associated with the use of influence tactics to improve personal or organizational interests. He outlines four levels of organizational politics in the form of terrain:[54]

1. *The weeds:* The influence of informal networks can block the long-term interests of the organization. Identify and deal with informal brokers to isolate their possible deleterious impact.
2. *The rocks:* This is the stabilizing foundation of the organization built upon its formal sources of authority—positional with defined authority and access to resources. However, when a leader is dysfunctional, it may be necessary to redirect their energy to positive outcomes by providing reasoned arguments to protect their "legacy."
3. *The high ground:* This combines formal authority with organizational systems such as rules, structures, and policy guidelines. While they protect subordinates from the whims of individuals, they may also lead the organization to become overly bureaucratic. To combat this problem, work outside the mainstream to provide some measure of independence, flexibility, and an alternative source of power.
4. *The woods:* This is the implicit norms of the organization—hidden assumptions and unspoken routines. Exposing them removes hidden barriers to the execution of strategy.

Understanding this political terrain will help leaders combat the impact of organizational politics.

Subordinates will engage in politics in their fashion. **Avoidance** is common where the employee must risk being wrong or where actions may yield a sanction. **Working the rules** ensures employee protection if they strictly adhere to all the rules, policies, and procedures and do not allow deviations or exceptions. **Depersonalization** involves treating individuals as numbers, things or objects. **Redirecting responsibility** is a form of "passing the buck," that is, one form is closely following organizational rules. Here, employees will strictly limit their effort to the limits of their official job description ("It's not my job!"). With "**buffing**," individuals only take action when all the paperwork is in place, and it is clear that they are merely following procedure. **Scapegoating** involves blaming the problem on someone or some group that has difficulty defending itself or blaming the problem on uncontrollable events.[55]

Whisenand reminds police managers that they must deal with overlapping stakeholders in the police organization—mayors, city council members, civil service commissions, and the media. He emphasizes "the necessity of participating in the external, political environment" that is a "painful and distasteful part of the job."[56]

Bolman and Deal state that leaders must be involved in politics. They offer four key skills to manage an environment of scarcity, diversity, and conflict—the conditions that managers face every day:

1. *Agenda setting:* This involves imparting direction and addressing the concerns of major stakeholders in the organization.
2. *Mapping the political terrain:* You should develop a political map that illustrates the power held by each of the key stakeholders and the interests that they seek. It will help reveal potential sources of resistance.
3. *Networking and building coalitions:* Determine whose help you will need and develop relationships so that people will be there when you need them. Engage in "horse trading"—promising rewards in exchange for resources and support. The basic point is simple: As a leader, you need friends and allies to get things done. To get their support, you need to cultivate relationships.
4. *Bargaining and negotiation:* Determine the motives of all persons involved. Bargaining involves the judicious use of threats rather than sanctions. Threats must be credible. They are effective only if your opponent believes you will carry it out. They must also be made at the appropriate level.

Leaders who get a reputation for being unethical, manipulative, and self-interested will have difficulty building the coalitions that they need to get things done. The dilemma is deciding when to adopt an open, collaborative strategy or when to choose a tougher, more adversarial approach.[57]

CASE STUDY   Chief George Green

Metropolis mayor Amos Johnson announced that the city was facing a $20 million budget shortfall. One of the proposals to address it was to charge police officers more money for their take-home cars. Officers with take-home cars currently pay $30 a month, but they pay $60 a month if they use it for off-duty work. The city wants to charge $100 a month and $160 if used for off-duty work. The mayor also considered selling one of the police department's helicopters, laying off some civilian police employees to help balance the budget, before ultimately deciding to start charging police officers for the take-home cruisers. The increased fees are expected to save the city about $110,000 a month.

Officers received a memo that they have a week to decide if they will pay the higher fee for their take-home cars or give them up. "Take-home cars are a privilege, not an entitlement," said Police Chief George Green. "Officers don't pay gas, don't pay insurance or maintenance." The city originally wanted the increased fees to take effect at the beginning of the fiscal year. However, the Police Union took the issue to court, and an injunction was granted. However,

earlier this week, the Court of Appeals threw out that injunction, clearing the way for the higher fees.

Chief Green asserted that the deadline for officer participation was still in place. The Police Union also took the issue to the State Labor Cabinet for a ruling, where it will take three months to reach a decision that could then be appealed to the courts. Ultimately, it could take years for the issue to reach a final decision.

Police Union president Bill Yates denounced Chief Green's decision. "This is an issue that affects wages and hours and working conditions," said President Yates. "It is something that should be negotiated, and city government is refusing to do that." Yates also asserted that the city should have waited until after the Labor Cabinet hearing was conducted before making a final decision. The Labor Cabinet will decide if the city is entitled to raise the fees without first negotiating with the union. "We, of course, were hoping they would wait until after our hearing," Yates said. "This is still an issue that should be bargained with the bargaining unit."

Chief Green replied that the city is not in a position to wait until the Labor Cabinet hearing is conducted because their decision would not be final. It could take months or even years before a final decision is reached. If the Labor Cabinet rules against the city, the higher fees will have to be refunded.

At the end of December, Metro County Circuit Court Judge John Ryan issued an injunction keeping city government from charging officers more money for their take-home cars. The following week,

the State Court of Appeals threw out Judge Ryan's injunction. Thus, the city has won the first two rounds. "We will meet with the Mayor, and he will make a decision shortly on how he wants to proceed from here," said Chief Green.

Discuss the power and political methods used by each of the actors in this case: Mayor Johnson, Chief Green, and the Police Union. Can this issue be resolved to the satisfaction of all parties?

SUMMARY

Power is the ability, the vigor, and the strength to influence others and to control one's own destiny. Correct use of power by a manager involves bringing together resources to accomplish something. Effective managers are those who understand the uses, limitations, sources, and characteristics of power.

Power affects individuals, groups, and organizations. When considering power and its implications, we can identify five types of power: reward, coercive, legitimate, referent, and expert. Within police departments, managers will have greater control over reward power in direct proportion to their higher position in the organization. Some common reward powers are praise, commendations, special assignments, additional responsibility, and two-way communication.

Coercive power uses the fear of punishment and the sanctions a manager avails to control the behavior of subordinates. Punishment may take many forms, including suspension, demotion, and official reprimand as well as more subtle sanctions such as giving an officer an undesirable assignment.

Legitimate power flows from the position, role, and status held within the organization. In law enforcement, rank reflects legitimate power. Power generally increases along with rank. All employees in a police organization are aware of their relative positions in it, which employees they are immediately responsible for, and to which managers they are accountable.

Managers are said to have referent power when their employees can easily identify with them. A key element of this type of power is trust. When an officer trusts a manager, it enhances the working relationship.

The last power base is expertise. It involves the skill a manager possesses because of knowledge, experience, or judgment. Organization-relevant information gained by an employee increases the power base used to deal with an increasingly complex society and the accompanying social problems.

An effective manager is one who influences the behavior of others in the work environment by using either positional or personal sources of power. Positional power is the power gained from the actual formal position a manager holds in the organization. Personal power is something entirely different. It comes from the personal characteristics and traits a manager possesses.

How police managers use power sources and bases is important if they are to be truly effective. There are times when one technique can be used effectively to influence subordinate or peer behavior, while at other times, the choice of a different tactic will be needed. Power must be exercised with honesty and integrity for all parties to be satisfied.

DISCUSSION TOPICS AND QUESTIONS

1. What sources of power are available to police managers? Which is the most effective?

2. What are the specific rewards police managers can use?

3. What specific methods are available to a police manager using coercive power when strictly supervising an officer?

4. Compare and contrast personal and positional power.

5. What techniques can a manager use to influence others?

6. What can a police manager do to apply expert power?

7. Differentiate between legitimate and reward power.

8. How can a manager utilize referent power?

9. How can politics affect an organization?

10. How should politics be managed?

FOR FURTHER READING

Stanley Bing, *What Would Machiavelli Do?—The Ends Justify and Meanness* (New York: HarperCollins, 2000); V, *The Mafia Manager—A Guide to the Corporate Machiavelli* (New York: Thomas Dunne, 1991).

These authors offer a tongue-in-cheek view of how Machiavelli would advise corporate managers to succeed in business.

Deborah Himsel, *Leadership—Sopranos Style* (Chicago, IL: Dearborn Trade Publishing, 2004); Anthony Schneider, *Tony Soprano on Management* (New York: Berkley, 2004).

Using examples from America's favorite fictional mobster, these authors analyze the leadership style of Tony Soprano. They do not suggest the "whacking" of adversaries or problem employees, but they do provide lessons on how Soprano exercises power.

Anthony Jay, *Management and Machiavelli—Discovering a New Science of Management in the Timeless Principles of Statecraft* (San Diego, CA: Pfeiffer, 1994).

Jay offers a slightly more serious analysis of how the principles of power developed by Niccolo Machiavelli apply to management and leadership of today's organizations.

Robert I. Sutton, *The No Asshole Rule* (New York: Warner Business Books, 2007).

The object of Sutton's treatise is the high performer who abuses their expert power by attacking the powerless within the organization. The organizational climate suffers by tolerating such behavior. The gains generated by the abusive talent are outweighed by the damage to the organization.

ENDNOTES

1. John P. Kotter, *Power and Influence* (New York: Free Press, 1985); Rosabeth M. Kanter, "Power Failure in Management Circuits," *Harvard Business Review*, (July–August 1979), p. 65.
2. S. Robbins and M. Coulter, *Management* (Upper Saddle River, NJ: Pearson Prentice Hall, 2018), p. 160.
3. Jeffrey Pfeffer, "Understanding Power in Organizations," *California Management Review*, (Winter 1992), pp. 29–50.
4. G. Cordner, *Police Administration* (New York: Routledge, 2016), pp. 202–204.
5. Max Weber, "Bureaucracy," in W. E. Natermeyer and J. T. McMahon, eds., *Classics of Organizational Behavior* (Prospect Heights, IL: Waveland, 2001), pp. 351–357.
6. A. DuBrin, *Political Behavior in Organizations* (Thousand Oaks, CA: Sage, 2009), p. 60.
7. David McClelland, "The Two Faces of Power," *Journal of International Affairs*, Vol. 24 (1970), pp. 36, 41.
8. W. Bennis, and B. Nanus, *Leaders: The Strategies for Taking Charge* (New York: Harper & Row, 1985), pp. 17–18.
9. Gary Yukl, *Leadership in Organizations* (Upper Saddle River, NJ: Prentice-Hall, 2013), p. 186.
10. Stephen P. Robbins and Timothy A. Judge, *Organizational Behavior* (Upper Saddle River, NJ: Pearson Prentice Hall, 2103), p. 412.
11. Ibid.
12. Yukl, *Leadership*, p. 187.
13. Ibid.
14. G. Prince, "Creative Meetings Through Power Sharing," *Harvard Business Review*, (July–August 1972), pp. 47–53.
15. J. French and B. Raven, "The Bases of Social Power," in D. Cartwright, ed., *Studies in Social Power* (Ann Arbor, MI: University of Michigan Press, 1959), pp. 150–165.
16. J. Schermerhorn, J. Hunt, R. Osborn, and M. Uhl-Bien, *Organizational Behavior* (Hoboken, NJ: John Wiley & Sons, 2010), p. 283.
17. Robbins and Judge, *Organizational Behavior*, p. 414.
18. Yukl, *Leadership*, p. 189.
19. Ibid.
20. Ibid., p. 190.
21. L. Miller, H. More and M. Braswell, *Effective Police Supervision* (New York: Routledge, 2017), p. 384.
22. Yukl, *Leadership*, pp. 199–200.
23. R. Kramer, "The Great Intimidators," *Harvard Business Review*, (February 2006), pp. 1–9.
24. Robbins and Judge, *Organizational Behavior*, p. 375.
25. Harry W. More and O. R. Shipley, *Police Policy Manual—Personnel* (Springfield, IL: Charles C Thomas, 1987), p. 98.
26. Yukl, *Leadership*, p. 318.
27. Robbins and Judge, *Organizational Behavior*, p. 415.
28. Ibid.
29. Miller, More, and Braswell, *Effective Police Supervision*, p. 171.
30. Yukl, *Leadership*, p. 193.
31. Schermerhorn, Hunt, Osborn, and Uhl-Bien, *Organizational Behavior*, p. 284.
32. Ibid.
33. Yukl, *Leadership*, pp. 192–193.
34. Schermerhorn, Hunt, Osborn, and Uhl-Bien, *Organizational Behavior*, p. 287.
35. Ibid., p. 288.
36. Ibid., p. 285.
37. Ibid., p. 289.
38. John P. Kotter, "Power, Dependence and Effective Management," *Harvard Business Review*, (July–August 1977), pp. 1–11.
39. David C. McClelland and David H. Burnham, "Power Is the Great Motivator," *Harvard Business Review*, (January 2003), pp. 1–10.
40. R. Hougaard, J. Carter, and L. Chester, "Power Can Corrupt Leaders. Compassion Can Save Them," *Harvard Business Review*, (February 2018), pp. 2–5.

41. T. Foulk and K. Lanaj, "Feeling Powerful at Work Makes Us Feel Worse When We Get Home," *Harvard Business Review*, (July 2017), pp. 2–4.

42. Schermerhorn, Hunt, Osborn, and Uhl-Bien, *Organizational Behavior*, p. 283.

43. P. Northouse, *Leadership: Theory and Practice* (Thousand Oaks, CA: Sage, 2004), p. 6.

44. J. Strock, *Theodore Roosevelt on Leadership: Executive Lessons from the Bully Pulpit* (Roseville, CA: Prima Publishing, 2001), p. 94.

45. Robbins and Judge, *Organizational Behavior*, p. 418.

46. Yukl, *Leadership*, pp. 202–203.

47. M. Goldsmith, "How Can I Do a Better Job of Managing Up?" *Harvard Management Update Newsletter*, (2008), p. 1.

48. Different Voice: A conversation with leadership expert Joseph S. Nye, Jr.—"Smart Power," *Harvard Business Review*, (November 2008), pp. 55–59.

49. Robbins and Judge, *Organizational Behavior*, p. 424.

50. Whisenand, *Managing Police Organizations*, p. 190.

51. Robbins and Judge, *Organizational Behavior*, pp. 414–415.

52. Ibid.

53. Schermerhorn, Hunt, Osborn, and Uhl-Bien, *Organizational Behavior*, p. 292.

54. M. Jarrett, "The 4 Types of Organizational Politics," *Harvard Business Review*, (April 2017), pp. 2–8.

55. Schermerhorn, Hunt, Osborn, and Uhl-Bien, *Organizational Behavior*, pp. 295–296.

56. P. Whisenand, *Managing Police Organizations* (Upper Saddle River, NJ: Pearson Prentice Hall, 2014), p. 191.

57. Lee G. Bolman and Terrence E. Deal, "The Leader as Politician: Navigating the Political Terrain," in J. Gallos, ed., *Business Leadership* (San Francisco, CA: Jossey-Bass, 2008), pp. 336–348.

10
COMMUNICATION

The Vital Process

Learning Objectives

1. Describe why it is important for a manager to become a skillful communicator.
2. Identify the nature and extent of informal communication.
3. Describe the critical features of the grapevine.
4. Describe the importance of body language.
5. Compare and contrast survey and feedback techniques used to improve communication.

Key Terms

channels	informal communication
decoding	listening
diagonal communication	noise
downward communication	organizational communication
dual reporting	receiver
encoding	sender
feedback	span of control
grapevine	survey feedback
horizontal communication	upward communication

Effective communication is vital. As Paul Whisenand notes, "Communication is information that flows throughout a police organization to bind it together. It directs the organization as to where and when to go, and it measures the progress of the organization. Communication makes it possible to have all of the organization's various parts moving toward its mission."[1]

One of the major figures in public administration, Chester Barnard, listed several features of communication in his classic work *The Functions of the Executive*.[2]

1. The channels of communication should be definitely known.
2. There should be a definite formal channel of communication to every member of an organization.
3. The line of communication should be as direct and short as possible.
4. The complete formal line of communication should normally be used.
5. The persons serving as communication centers should be competent.
6. The line of communication should not be interrupted while the organization is functioning.

Barnard's basic concepts outline the need for clear communication in organizations.

CASE STUDY   Lieutenant Donald Bear

Donald Bear has just been promoted to lieutenant and assigned to field operations. In this position, he reports directly to the assistant chief of the department and serves as watch commander on the swing shift.

Lt. Bear has been a member of the department for nine years and before his promotion served as a first-line supervisor for three years. His appearance fits the stereotype of a manager. He is 6 feet 4 inches tall, weighs 210 pounds, and keeps himself in top physical shape. He has taken numerous courses at the local university and is currently working on an MBA.

All of Bear's time as a first-line supervisor was in records and planning. He gained a world of experience in preparing operational plans and the annual departmental budget. In this capacity, he functioned primarily as a numbers cruncher, so his relationship to line personnel was limited.

Immediately upon promotion, he was fortunate enough to attend an 80-hour seminar offered by the Southern Police Institute at the University of Louisville. Armed with theory, he has now reached the time for application. After a "honeymoon" of five and a half months, he has just encountered the first major issue needing his administrative expertise; it involves communication.

Lt. Bear has verbally disciplined Officer George Mandering for engaging in horseplay on two separate occasions over a three-week period. In each instance, Officer Mandering left a typewritten note in the mailbox of another officer, purportedly an order from the assistant chief transferring the officer to the midnight shift. Both officers who received the notes became very upset because the change conflicted with prescheduled vacations.

The lieutenant was caught in the middle in both instances because he was unaware of the incidents until the officers came to him and complained. Lt. Bear identified the perpetrator and felt an oral reprimand is sufficient under the circumstances. However, when the assistant chief heard about the incidents, he became very upset and expressed the opinion that Officer Mandering should receive formal punishment for unduly harassing other employees.

This is a problem of communication that can be listed under the heading, *Why didn't he or she tell me?* It is a question often asked in organizations. Lt. Bear thought he was doing what was right, but his superior disagreed.

In your judgment, what action should Lt. Bear have taken, or do you agree that oral reprimand was enough? How much and what things should he communicate to the assistant chief? Should all instances of discipline be communicated to one's superior?

Communication is the process whereby the organization and its managers translate policy and procedures into agreed-on day-to-day decisions and acceptable operational activities. A manager uses communication as a vehicle for motivating, disciplining, and training officers to achieve organizational goals. Also, a police manager plans and organizes work, issues directives, give orders, and evaluates employees' unit and departmental performance, all to attain objectives and create a safe community.

Defining Managerial Communication

What is an acceptable definition of managerial communication? The problem is the extensive number of definitions of just the word *communication*, let alone the term *managerial communication*. Communication serves four major functions within a group or organization: control (of workplace behavior and performance), motivation (clarifying what is to be done), emotional expression (of feelings), and information (needed to make decisions).[3]

Thus, managerial communication involves two entirely different and distinct functions (see Figure 10–1). The first aspect is **organizational communication** and includes standard operating procedures, rules, regulations, memoranda, and policy statements. The other element is interpersonal communication, in which a great deal more is communicated than specific messages. It includes emotions, needs, and feelings modifying and conditioning verbal messages.[4]

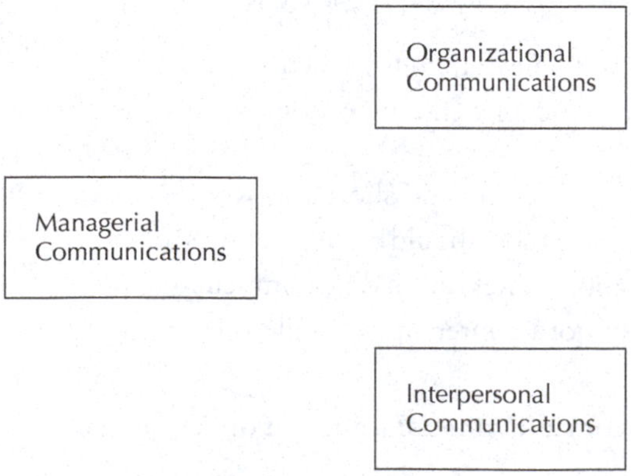

Figure 10–1
Components of Communication.
Kentucky State Police, General Duties, Responsibilities and Guidelines: Chapter 16, OM-B-7

Organizational Communications

Managerial Communications

Interpersonal Communications

There is a critical need for managers to understand the complexity of the communication process and to strive for enhancement and improvement until it is open, continuous, and related positively to goal attainment. Communication among members of an organization is extremely important. When communication is faulty, problems abound and resolving them consumes a major portion of managerial time.

Effective communication between individuals is problematic when one party assumes that everyone concerned is aware of all aspects of the issue, whereas, in fact, many are still uninformed. If the basic assumption is faulty, then (in all likelihood) the results will be defective. Interpersonal communication involves the exchange of information. Not only must information be transmitted, but it must also be understood.

There are some barriers to effective communication:[5]

1. *Failure to listen.* Listening inattentively, passively, or not at all.
2. *Noise in communication.* Interference with the message.
3. *Misuse of language.* Excessively vague, inaccurate, inflammatory, emotional, positive, or negative language.
4. *Lack of feedback.* One-way communication, in which the receiver provides no return of information about whether and with what effect the information came across. **Feedback** communicates how one feels about something another person has done or said.[6]

When communication is poor, it can be exceedingly costly and in some cases harmful. If organizations have a vital force, it is communication. It is the binding ingredient of an organization. When a message is not understood, the immediate reaction is to find fault. Generally, a communication gap or barrier is the problem.

Rainey lists even more particular communication barriers between groups:[7]

1. Definition of disagreement between groups as a "win or lose" conflict.
2. Attempts by a group to aggrandize its power and emphasize only its own goals and needs.
3. Use of threats.
4. Disguise of true positions and active distortion of information.
5. Attempt to exploit or isolate another group.
6. Emphasis by a group only of the differences and the superiority of its position.

Finally, Rainey notes seven specific communication distortions that plague public bureaus:[8]

1. *Distorted perceptions.* Inaccurate perceptions of information that result from preconceived ideas or priorities or from striving to maintain self-esteem or defend cognitive inconsistency.
2. *Erroneous translation.* Interpretation of information by receivers in ways not intended by the senders.
3. *Errors of abstraction and differentiation.* Transmission of excessively abstract or selective information. Underemphasis on differences in favor of similarities or excessive polarization of fairly similar positions.
4. *Lack of congruence.* Ambiguity or inconsistency between elements of a message or between one message and other sources of information.
5. *Distrust of source.* Failure to accept an accurate message because of suspicions about bias or lack of credibility of the source.
6. *Jargon.* Communication difficulties are resulting from highly specialized professional or technical language that confuses those outside the specialization (and often those within it).
7. *Manipulation and withholding of information.* Active distortion or withholding of information to support a group's interests and influence the receiver.

In many instances, a great deal of effort is expended to find a scapegoat to blame for inadequate communication. This choice proves to be a lot easier than dealing with the problem directly. While a common source of organizational problems is faulty communication, the mere act of improving communication will not make up for poor leadership or an inadequately structured organization. Good communication supports and reinforces the managerial processes of planning, organizing, directing, and controlling a law enforcement agency.

CASE STUDY   Jim Morton

Jim Morton has been a road patrol officer in a southeastern urban department for six years. The department employs approximately 80 sworn officers divided among various units, such as road patrol, criminal investigations, narcotics/vice, and a TACC (Targeting Area Community Concerns) squad. Officer Morton has attended college and received his bachelor's degree. He is a highly motivated officer and well-liked by his peers and most supervisors.

Officer Morton has always been dependable and made good decisions based on the relevant facts at the time. After two years with the department, Officer Morton was a member of the SWAT (Special Weapons and Tactics) team, where he was considered a valuable team member for several years. It was not long before Officer Morton was selected to be a field training officer, assisting with the training of new cadets from the academy. He was valued as a training officer and focused his training in several critical areas, such as officer safety, report writing, and ingraining the importance of integrity, as he was always considered to have high moral values. Officer Morton wrote excellent reports and worked his assigned cases to completion.

After three years with the department, Officer Morton made the TACC squad. The squad consisted of two officers who were assigned a variety of tasks depending on community needs. The officers worked with very little supervision and generally were selected for their self-motivation. Officer Morton was also sent to school to become a high liability trainer, where he instructed firearms for other department members.

Officer Morton became the subject of an internal affairs investigation regarding deception. He was dispatched to an alarm call and responded by radio that he was in route. A non-sworn employee said they observed Officer Morton at the police department and he could not have responded to the call. The investigation, which was conducted by Captain Smith, sustained the allegation and recommended termination for being untruthful. Officer Morton stood by his conviction that he was not lying. His Police Benevolent Association attorney was able to secure his job.

The full investigation was unavailable for other department members to view; however, it appeared to be a common consensus among line officers, that Officer Morton had been telling the truth. A halo effect appeared predominant with most employees. The perception was Officer Morton was a good officer with high morals and integrity.

Since that incident, Officer Morton's work quality and quantity began to spiral. He was often late for work, sometimes only a few minutes, and began using a large quantity of his sick leave, generally due to stomach ailments. Officer Morton's entire personality and behavior began to change. It seemed critical that he convince his peers he was telling the truth. The department's overall morale seemed to be declining.

Officer Morton's sergeant began documenting his tardiness, and again, he was disciplined. During this period, Officer Morton became a profound supporter for the union, which was not representing the department currently. Due to the low morale and lack of communication between command and line personnel, representation for the union was introduced, although implementation was unsuccessful by two votes. The chief and his command staff took the incident personally. It was suspected that Officer Morton played a key role in the attempted union representation.

A few months later, Officer Morton was disciplined again regarding the use of four-way restraints on a prisoner. Captain Smith, who was sporadically reviewing videotapes from patrol car cameras, discovered that he improperly restrained and carried a prisoner. Although there was no complaint from the defendant and the department had not trained its members in the use of four-way restraints, Captain Smith recommended suspension. Officer Morton's sergeant made it known that he disagreed with Captain Smith's decision and felt that it was a training issue; however, he was still suspended. Within a few weeks of the incident, the department began training its personnel in the use of four-way restraints.

Officer Morton returned to work but made it well known that it was only a matter of time before they (administration) found another reason to discipline him. Within six months, Officer Morton resigned, pending another internal investigation.

Which forms of communication could have been used to change the negative attitude of Officer Morton once he was reinstated? What steps could management have taken to change the perception, morale, and negative attitude of the group of officers who supported him? Did Captain Smith lack introspection? Were his decisions based on emotion or was discipline administered fairly in this case?

Managerial Functions

The role of communication is distinctly different for each of the major managerial functions. Effective management calls for a different application of communication skills, which vary from level to level within the organization. If communication is to be effective, all levels of management from the top down must nurture it. It is also essential for managers to recognize the human processes involved in communicating and utilize a variety of techniques when dealing with different managerial functions.[9]

Communication and Planning

Planning serves as the integrating function for a manager. It ties together separate entities as goals evolve, and the identification of objectives for each function. Plans must be developed in a positive and outgoing manner. A useful plan must be based on current information, and in many instances, officers at varying levels throughout the organization will have important information to contribute.

One of the problems in some agencies is that plans are developed in isolation, and those responsible for plan implementation are never consulted. It seems logical for the preparation of plans to involve the people who will have to implement them, especially when the plans affect the way they will have to do the work.

A police department should continually gather pertinent information, convert it to a usable format, and distribute it to all personnel. The police supervisor is responsible for communication with others in such a manner that employee understanding, trust, and mutual support are engendered.[10]

Good planning requires a manager to communicate continually with all information sources (including personnel in other organizations). All information received should be evaluated even if it is not received through the normal chain of command. Rejecting vital information could lead to the failure of a plan when the implementation phase is reached.[11]

An effective police manager should view planning as fulfilling the following communication criteria:[12]

1. Openness within the organization and encouraging communication
2. Organizational climate fostering communication
3. Suggestion system allowing for continuous input
4. Access outside the chain of command so input can be received from all personnel
5. Continuous and responsive feedback

Firm commitment by police managers to an interactive type of planning that involves (as frequently as possible) managers and agency personnel at all levels will lead to a greater degree of effectiveness as the agency deals with a dynamic and constantly changing society.

Communication and Organizing

The organizing function of police managers brings together various activities and groups and places them within a structure of authority so that agreed-upon objectives and goals can be attained. Organizational structure provides the framework for transmitting formal communication. The advantage of formal communication is its predictability—it follows the chain of command, which serves as a filtering system as messages are sent and modified at each level of the organization. In some instances, the filtering process can dilute a message to the point of distorting the original meaning. Usually, however, formal messages are given serious consideration because they come from known and reliable sources.

Span of Control.

Several factors must be taken into consideration in structuring an organization. One of these is the **span of control**—the number of subordinates reporting directly to a supervisor.[13] It includes such factors as the supervisor's capacity (taking into account his or her ability, experience, and level of energy) to oversee the activities of others directly.[14]

Managers must assess their ability. Those who delegate authority and practice a style of leadership emphasizing trust are capable of supervising more subordinates. Likewise, managers adept at effective communication can expand their span of control because they spend less time discussing trivia and clarifying distorted messages.[15]

It is also true that when employees are well trained and self-motivated, a manager can easily supervise a larger number of them. When a community problem-solving program is fully operational, for example, a police manager will find himself or herself able to supervise a greater number of subordinates. If the span is too broad, the following symptoms may occur: Communication between managers is poor, feedback fails to provide viable information needed to control operations, and performance standards prove to be unrealistic.[16]

Line and Staff.

Another organizational problem arises when a law enforcement agency becomes large enough for a distinction to be made between line and staff. Recognizing the line and staff distinction is the initial step to take when a department arranges related functions into specific units. The value of this distinction is that it provides for the proper location of the two major functions of police organizations: preparation for the delivery of police services and the actual delivery of those services.[17]

The key to determining what is line and what is staff is not what specific functions they perform but how directly they contribute to the attainment of departmental goals. The staff serves the line, supplying it with records, data, transportation, and material so that the line can discharge its functions, which are operational.

Smaller organizations do not have separate staff units, but as a department grows, specialization is necessary to provide support services. Initially, functions such as communications, records, and evidence control evolve. As the agency continues to grow, such units as psychological service, crime analysis, and research and development are added.

Ignoring line and staff conflicts and allowing poor conditions to continue thwart effective communication. When the chief supervises an excessive number of immediate subordinates, the office tends to become a bottleneck with effective communication decreased and work impeded. When a communication network functions at maximum effectiveness, it serves to unify the organization, reduce confusion, and improve efficiency. In this age of information technology, managers must communicate as directly as possible with all employees to access relevant information to the task at hand.[18]

Johnson provides advice on how leaders should communicate during times of change. Followers need clear signals about the need for change and what it means for them. First, leaders must tell followers exactly what they want—not only regarding tasks but also outcomes. They must explain why change is necessary, what the extent of it will be, what will improve as a result, and how to measure improvement. Measurement of outcomes is a tedious task requiring accuracy. Leaders must demonstrate their commitment to the change and act accordingly in a very visible manner.[19]

Dual Reporting.

Some police agencies have organized under a matrix system. This type of structure alters the traditional concept of unity of command and allows for multiple supervisors, making it essential for police managers to learn how to function under a dual-reporting system (see Figure 10–2). To make this kind of management work calls for the strengthening and formalization of secondary systems.

The problem-solving police department must learn to overcome the barriers to communication that arise under dual reporting. Formalizing frequent interaction between managers ensures sharing of power and decision-making. In other words, talk, but, above all, listen.

Figure 10–2
Dual-Reporting System in a Matrix Organization.

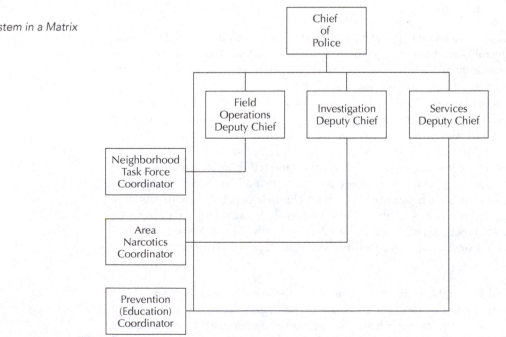

In a new unit, communication becomes increasingly complex. Both formal and informal lines of communication change. It usually takes a considerable period before units adapt to each other and communication becomes effective.[20]

Communicating with the Media.

Kingshott (p. 244) lists three objectives the police have when dealing with the media: (1) getting the facts about crime to the public, (2) making an appeal for witnesses to come forward, and (3) reducing the fear of the public concerning the crime incident. He recommends following a new paradigm of mutual respect, eliminating the old "us versus them" bias to establish cooperation between police and the media in the achievement of these objectives.[21]

Communication and Directing

A large part of a police manager's time is spent communicating. Their ability to send appropriate messages determines their managerial effectiveness. Communication will be more accurate, undistorted, and effective when it is properly filtered and routed within the organization. Communication is information that flows throughout a police organization to bind it together. It directs the organization as to where and when to go, and it informs the organization about whether or not progress is being made—making it possible to have all of the organization's various parts moving toward its mission.[22]

Establishing and utilizing communication networks in the organization can help bring about positive leadership. When managed effectively, communication networks ensure information is moved from one point to another within the organization for the greatest benefit of every member.

A positive leadership style can contribute directly to organizational effectiveness by creating an organizational climate that fosters real communication. A manager should view every employee as someone who can make a positive contribution to the department. A working relationship should be established, allowing for continuous employee input. If officers are considered genuine assets, communication can ensure their skills are utilized. If communication is to be effective, it must be nurtured at every management level—from the chief to the first-line supervisor.

Communication and Control

The controlling function is utilized extensively by law enforcement agencies to measure the performance of other managerial functions. Feedback provides a way of assessing the planning process, and (as just indicated) directing emphasizes the control of officer behavior. Finally, the organization is usually structured to place responsibility and authority in specific subunits of the department. Control, then, can certainly be viewed as an important ingredient and an integral part of the other managerial functions.

Control involves comparing the actual outcomes with planned outcomes. It can only be accomplished when communication is adequate and reliable. Controls are designed to provide a police manager with information regarding progress. Good communication serves the following four important functions:[23]

1. *Information function.* Communication provides information for decision-making. To make reasoned choices, managers require information concerning alternatives, future events, and potential outcomes of their decisions.
2. *Motivational function.* Communication encourages commitment to organizational objectives, thus enhancing motivation.
3. *Control function.* Communication clarifies duties, authority, and responsibilities, thereby permitting control. If there is ambiguity concerning such things, it is impossible to isolate the sources of problems and to take corrective actions.
4. *Emotive function.* Communication permits the expression of feelings and the satisfaction of social needs. It may also help people to vent frustrations.

Deciding what information is needed to have a positive process requires a manager to review the control system constantly and evaluate it regarding its impact on employees. Compliance with standards is higher when employees find them to be realistic.

Managerial Communication

Communication is important but it still confuses and confounds some managers. Every manager strives to communicate successfully. Communication must be carefully studied and continuously readjusted for proper clarity to avoid confusion. Unfortunately, a poorly written document or a misinterpreted oral message can create serious problems. Frequently, managers believe they are communicating when exactly the opposite is true.

Police officers, as they enforce the law, constantly make decisions that deny citizens their freedom. Likewise, law enforcement managers make innumerable daily decisions that have positive and negative impacts on officers as well as citizens. Police managers cannot perform any of the four phases of the managerial process—planning, organizing, directing, and controlling—without communicating either formally or informally.

Communicating with any degree of effectiveness is demanding and time consuming. It is not easy, nor does it just happen. The process of communicating requires the attention of everyone in the organization. It cannot be turned off and on based on the whim of a manager. It must constantly be refined and adjusted to the current situation.

CASE STUDY   J. Fred Sullivan

The chief executive officer of a county law enforcement agency was recently the subject of controversy when a full-page ad publicizing a shopping center appeared in a local newspaper. The heading for the ad read "Crimes of Fashion" and featured a young handcuffed model attired in a tight-fitting black evening gown, leaning forward, with her eyes closed and lips pouting. Off to one side of the ad was a shadowy male figure wearing dark glasses, and a police vehicle was identifiable in the background.

The male figure in the ad was the sheriff, J. Fred Sullivan, who was running for reelection. Two other candidates for the position lost little time in criticizing the sheriff. The opposing candidates depicted the ad as antifeminist and as a vivid expression of sexual bondage.

The sheriff posed for the ad at the request of the shopping center, which contacted him through his campaign manager, Virginia Marsh. Sheriff Sullivan was not compensated for appearing in the ad, but $200 was donated to two different charitable organizations.

Women's organizations are expressing shock over the incident, claiming that the ad is negative toward women and condones violence.

Their concern is that the ad damages their years of effort to change the attitudes of the public and law enforcement toward women.

Both the sheriff and his campaign manager say that the ad was done for charity, without intent to insult or demean anyone.

The women's groups find the ad to be so offensive they are considering picketing the sheriff's home and office, as well as the shopping center. The sheriff and his campaign manager have apologized. The shopping center claims the ad will not be used again, and an apology appeared in the following issue of the newspaper. Also, the shopping center donated money to a women's organization.

In this instance, the message the sheriff and the shopping center wanted to convey was interpreted by the women's groups as supporting violence against women. Why did the women's groups view the message negatively? Would the ad have had the same negative response if the young model had not been handcuffed? Could the ad have been designed in a way that would have been less controversial? Should a public figure appear in an ad to promote specific business interests?

Generally speaking, the police chief executive officer serves as the spokesperson for the agency as well as its leader and figurehead. The other two managerial levels focus more on internal communication and subordinate interaction. All managerial levels have a reasonable amount of contact with citizens and citizens groups, but such contact is least for the supervisory manager. Here is a listing of the communication tasks performed by first-line supervisors in descending order of importance:[24]

1. Provide feedback to subordinates regarding their job performance. It should include such things as identifying strengths and weaknesses as well as calling attention to exceptional or inadequate performance.

2. Prepare written employee performance evaluations.

3. Respond to subordinates' inquiries regarding departmental policy, legal questions, and discretionary decision-making.

4. Meet with and provide direction to subordinates regarding particular violations, investigative techniques, and case processing.

5. Brief subordinates on new or revised policies and procedures.

6. Communicate subordinates' concerns, desires, and suggestions to management.

Communication defines the nature of a law enforcement agency and is a time-consuming process. Communicating is exceedingly complex, and managerial effectiveness depends on identifying and overcoming communication barriers.

Realistic Communication Process

Effective communication requires a free and open exchange among all levels of management. Typical of the communication dilemma is the feeling seemingly shared by supervisors at every level of the organization that the administration gives subordinates everything they need to know but could do a much better job of passing information down to the supervisory level.[25]

Communication in organizations involves three major actors: individuals, groups, and the organization itself.[26] Communicating is a mental maze to be mastered. If it is to be improved, we must become aware of what constitutes effective communication and use it. Poor communication is a waste of time and energy—so the goal is to avoid inadequate communication at all costs. The **sender** of a message is responsible for transmitting with clarity and ensuring the message is not only received but also understood.[27]

An individual sending a message must do everything possible to affect the behavior of the recipient. One person's communication with another can be effective only if (1) the message is encoded, (2) the message is transmitted, (3) the message is decoded, and (4) the **receiver** of the message interprets and understands it correctly.[28]

The communication process provides a means of viewing the complexity of making oneself understood in an organizational context. One model of the process involves six stages and two modifiers (see Figure 10–3).

Sender

The source of a message can be anyone in or outside the organization. It is important to note when someone is trying to function as the sender of a formal or informal message. If the sender has a great deal of expertise and is knowledgeable, the communication is received. The rank of the sender is another crucial factor. Certainly, when the sender is the chief, the message receives immediate attention.

Gatekeeping occurs when the sender of a message determines the importance and relevance of the message. When a police manager is a sender, the chain of command serves as a vehicle of transmission, and decisions are constantly made about what messages should be sent.

Encoding

When the message is converted into a readily understandable form, it is **encoded**. A message can either be verbal or nonverbal. It is desirable to choose symbols (e.g., read the *Miranda* warning) that everyone can understand. Many things influence the encoding process. One of the major variables is the personality of the sender (or organizational members) who encodes the message. Every member of an organization has his or her perception of what a message should accomplish and how it should be encoded.[29]

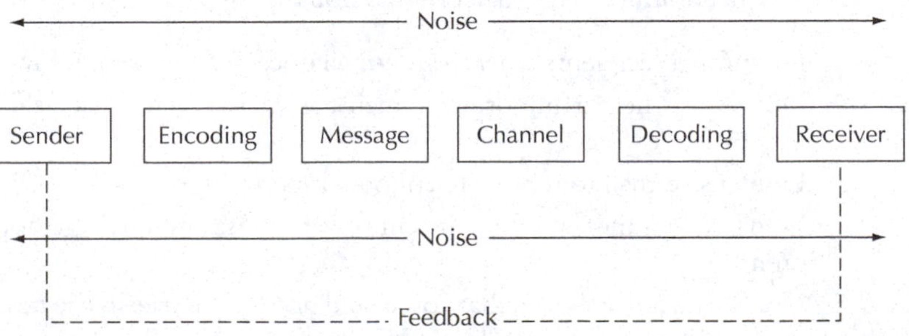

Figure 10–3
Realistic Communication Process.

Vocabulary and expertise can play major roles in the sender's ability to encode data, ideas, or the interpretation of information. Encoding is not easy. It requires a manager to select a symbol representing what is communicated.

Message

The specific information transmitted constitutes the message. It might be some symbol creating an awareness of need, pointing out a problem, or expressing an opinion about a matter of concern to the department. Whatever the intent of the message, it is in the sender's best interest to be sure it gets through loud and clear. There is no guarantee that the message as understood by the receiver will be the same as the message intended by the sender. **Noise** can always confound the meaning of the message.[30]

One of the most difficult tasks for police managers is to write standard operating procedures, rules, regulations, or departmental policies. It seems that such documents have to be written and rewritten several times before every level in the organization places a stamp of approval on them; employees may need the training to interpret and use them.

Written formal communications are tangible and verifiable. Rules are printed, stored for an indefinite period, and can be consulted in the future.[31]

Each police manager who prepares a message should seek to answer the following questions:

1. What is the real message I want to send?
2. Is there sufficient information to support the message?
3. Does any word or phrase imply something not intended?
4. Is there any possibility the message can be misinterpreted?
5. What will be the reaction to the message?
6. Will the message produce the intended results?

However, there are several drawbacks to formal, written communication. First of all, they take time and must be responded to formally. If a manager relies on the rules too often, it could create morale problems and create distance from subordinates. They can frustrate feedback and slow down both decisions and actions.[32]

Channel

In law enforcement agencies, some communications **channels** are available for transmitting messages, including radio, teletype, computer, teleconferencing devices, telephone, electronic mail, and voice mail. Other potential channels include bulletin boards, departmental newsletters, or, when appropriate, verbal and nonverbal communication. In general, the supervisory police manager spends more time communicating verbally than managers at higher levels in the chain of command.

As police departments grow and become more decentralized, there is a tendency for communication to become depersonalized. The terminal on the desk or in the police vehicle becomes the major channel for transmitting messages. The screen and the keyboard increasingly dominate the communication process—the in-basket and the mailbox are slowly being replaced. Messages can be sent and received, police records checked, license numbers processed, case files reviewed, and bookings checked without leaving one's vehicle or desk. E-mail and the Internet are enhancing such tasks as recruiting as well as providing yet another form of organizational communication.

Whisenand offers five e-mail dos and don'ts:

1. Do inform recipients when your e-mail does not require a reply.
2. Do verify whether important e-mail has been received by asking the person to acknowledge it.
3. Don't use e-mail to replace telephone or personal contacts.
4. Don't send a message to your entire list unless the message applies to everyone on it.
5. Don't send any message that you would not want to see in the newspaper or tacked to the front door of your home.[33]

Decoding

When a message is received, it undergoes **decoding**—it is interpreted and given meaning by the receiver. If the message is decoded improperly, it will not be understood.

A message becomes significant when meaning is given to symbols (e.g., "book the suspect"). When decoding, a receiver should try to ascertain the following:[34]

1. What the sender *intended* to say
2. What the sender *actually* said
3. What the receiver *heard*
4. What the receiver *thinks* he or she heard
5. What the receiver *said*
6. What the sender *thinks* the receiver said

Each of these factors serves to modify the decoding process, and the accuracy of the receiver's interpretation will depend on his or her ability to respond adequately to each factor.

Receiver

The receiver is the person or persons to whom the message is sent. Like the sender, the receiver can inadvertently distort or misinterpret the message in any of several ways. Motives, emotions, and how one perceives a message all tend to impair effective communication. Selective perception will cause the receiver to distort a message in many instances. This filtering system prevents messages from being completely understood. The message must have meaning before someone can react to it.

Selective perception is more apt to occur with oral messages. Personality, previous experience, and some stimulus modify the perception of the received information. Different people will react to messages differently.[35]

Miscommunication can also occur because some words allow for different interpretations, some receivers are poor listeners, feedback is inadequate, and nonverbal communication can be interpreted differently.

Feedback

Until feedback occurs, communication is not a two-way process. Feedback only occurs when a receiver responds to the sender, with something as simple as a nod of the head or as complex as the preparation of a detailed report.

Without feedback, the sender will never know whether a message has been received. Feedback in the performance evaluation process has the following characteristics:[36]

1. *Intention.* Effective feedback is directed toward improving job performance and making the employee a more valuable asset. It is not a personal attack and should not compromise the individual's feeling of self-worth or image. Rather, effective feedback is directed toward aspects of the job.

2. *Specificity.* Effective feedback is designed to provide recipients with specific information so that they know what must be done to correct the situation. Ineffective feedback is general and leaves questions in the recipients' minds; it may leave the recipients frustrated in seeking ways to correct the problem.

3. *Description.* Effective feedback is also descriptive rather than evaluative. It tells the employee what he or she has done in objective terms rather than presenting a value judgment.

4. *Usefulness.* Effective feedback is information that an employee can use to improve performance. It serves no purpose to berate employees for their lack of skill if they do not have the ability or training to perform properly. Thus, the guideline is that if it is not something the employee can correct, it is not worth mentioning.

5. *Timeliness.* There are also considerations in timing feedback properly. As a rule, the more immediate the feedback is, the better. This way the employee has a better chance of knowing what the supervisor is talking about and can take corrective action.

6. *Readiness.* For feedback to be effective, employees must be ready to receive it. When feedback is imposed or forced on employees, it is much less effective.

7. *Clarity.* The recipient must clearly understand the feedback. A good way of checking this is to ask the recipient to restate the major points of the discussion. Also, supervisors can observe facial expressions as indicators of understanding and acceptance.

8. *Validity.* For feedback to be effective, it must be reliable and valid. Of course, when the information is incorrect, the employee will feel that the supervisor is unnecessarily biased or the employee may take corrective action that is inappropriate and only compounds the problem.

When used properly, feedback will not only improve the communication process, but it will provide a foundation for better departmental morale and heighten the potential for attaining objectives and goals.

Noise

The last feature of the communication process is noise—defined as anything disrupting communication. It includes not only physical noise but also attitudes and emotions interfering with either interpreting the message or providing adequate feedback. In recent years, substantial job stress is a type of noise that makes it difficult for some individuals to concentrate on a message.[37]

At the beginning of the communication process, noise can interfere with the conceptualization of the message, making it unclear. When a message is encoded, the wrong symbol may be selected. The use of slang, jargon, or unknown technical terms contributes to this problem. When the message is transmitted, it can be garbled—especially when it is oral rather than written. Decoding can be the next stage at which noise appears when perceptions are different. The message can be misunderstood due to the recipient's attitude and values.

Finally, emotional bias plays a very important part in communication noise. The receiver's attitudes, values, and experiences all serve as a filter within the communication process and can cause a message to be altered or misinterpreted. Filtering, whether intentional or unintentional, can result in only part of the message being transmitted or interpreted. An awareness of emotional bias is the first step in working to reduce noise in the communication process.[38]

Silence

Perlow and Williams examine how remaining silent is detrimental to organizational progress. Subordinates often feel pressure to refrain from raising questions or objections due to fear of retaliation. Such reluctance has a high cost, generating anxiety, anger, and resentment, and shutting down creativity or innovation. Individuals also keep quiet for social reasons—to maintain good relationships with bosses and co-workers. They perceive their silence is a method to advance in the organization. Often, when differences in operational methods are small, it is best to remain silent and avoid conflict over unimportant issues. Bosses also feel the virtues of silence when it is necessary to confront an employee over poor performance. If left uncorrected, such errors damage the organization. To alleviate these problems, people must recognize their power. Both leaders and followers depend upon one another for good performance. It is necessary to raise issues as an individual or form a coalition to bring them to the forefront to handle them effectively.[39]

Formal Organizational Communication

Effective communication within a police organization becomes increasingly difficult as the agency becomes larger and decentralized. Many police organizations have formalized communication channels based on military models—as we have noted, a strict chain of command best describes the typical police organization.

Communication networks within a department reflect both its hierarchical nature and the differentiation of functions within it: Communication flows horizontally as well as vertically. The functions performed by police departments require extensive communication. Decisions by managers are generally dependent on information received from operational personnel in various departmental units.

Police bureaucracies are unique in that line personnel are usually the ones at the focal point of activities generating an organizational response to an incident. Consequently, the information line officers feed into the communication network is crucial to the department's operations.[40]

Downward Communication

Downward communication involves messages from senders relatively high in the organizational structure to receivers in lower-level positions (supervisor to subordinate). There are five types of downward messages:[41]

1. *Job instructions*. Directions for doing specific tasks. This type of message is most often given priority in police organizations. Police officers receive direct orders from their supervisors, training sessions, training manuals, and written directives. The objective is to ensure the reliable performance of every police officer in the organization.

2. *Job rationale*. Information about how one task relates to other tasks in the organization. Job rationales provide police officers with a full understanding of their positions and how they are related to other positions in the same organization. Many police officers know what they are to do but not why. Withholding information on the rationale of the job not only reduces the loyalty of the member to the organization but also means that the organization must rely heavily on job instructions. If officers do not understand why they should do something or how their jobs relate to the organization, then there must be sufficient repetition in the task instructions so that individuals behave automatically.

3. *Procedures and practices*. Messages indicate the "rules of the game" in the organization—the role requirements for its members. In addition to receiving instructions about the job, police officers receive information about other duties and privileges they have as members of the police organization.

4. *Feedback*. Messages can tell individuals about their performance on the job. These are necessary to ensure that the organization is operating properly, and they serve as a means to motivate individual performers. Feedback must be given properly.

5. *Indoctrination*. Messages provide information about overall organizational goals and the relationship of individual goals to organizational goals. The purpose is to implant organizational goals for personal ones.

Unlike many business managers, who rely on a constant upward flow of information from the bottom of their organizations, police managers devote a great deal of their time to downward communication, with the aim of controlling the discretion of line officers. They do this by issuing orders and developing standard operating procedures.

The chain of command determines the usual flow of messages. It gives priority to information that starts at the top and filters down through the organization (see Table 10–1). Except in critical situations, managers give responding to memos from the chief priority over responding to memos from subordinates or other managers.[42]

Generally, in addition to the five types of downward messages listed earlier, downward communication concerns itself with the following types of messages:

1. Policies
2. Procedures
3. Rules and regulations
4. Performance feedback
5. Schedules

Table 10–1

SAMPLE DEPARTMENTAL POLICY

Officer Duties and Responsibilities at Scene of Air Ambulance Usage

Officers at the scene of an air ambulance usage should ensure the following:

1. Clear an area of at least 100 × 100 feet for a helicopter landing pad.

2. Park cruiser in such a manner that the headlights indicate the direction in which the helicopter will come in over the top of the cruiser.

3. Advise the air medical team if the patient received any prior medical treatment at the scene of an emergency.

4. Keep spectators away from the aircraft.

5. Not approach the aircraft from the rear under any circumstances.

6. Not allow a vehicle to be driven closer than 50 feet to the aircraft.

7. Not carry any item in the vicinity of the aircraft that will extend above the height of the individual, such as portable radios with an extended antenna.

8. Not assist the aircraft crew with the patient unless requested to do so.

9. Advise post of the departure of the aircraft.

Source: Kentucky State Police, *General Duties, Responsibilities and Guidelines: Chapter 16,* OM-B-7.

---

6. Operational plans
7. Training bulletins
8. Informational memoranda
9. Legal decisions

Even though downward communication has the cloak of power backed by organizational authority, a police executive manager should create an environment that allows for two-way communication. If communication flows only in one direction, then those at lower levels in the organization will resort to modifying or filtering the messages as they come down the chain of command.

Managers must try to avoid the following mistakes when conducting downward communication:[43]

- Pronouncements from "on high"
- Frequent dramatic changes in direction
- Reliance on formal communication
- Policies without explanations
- Ambiguous "bureaucratese"
- Silence

If managers can understand the impact of communication on subordinates and do something about it, communication can become more effective. If employees get the information they need, they perform better as individuals and in groups. Policies and procedures are necessary to guide the downward communication process.[44]

Upward Communication

Upward communication involves communication from sources in lower-level positions to receivers in relatively higher positions. It starts with the line officer. As each message goes up through each level of the organization, it is filtered and distorted more than messages are in downward communication. Upward communication is vital because it provides managers with a means of evaluating the messages they have sent down the chain of command. It is a way of identifying problems, and in many instances, it is the quickest way of really finding out what is going on in the organization.

Upward communication from subordinates includes the following:

1. Information about their performance or grievances
2. Information about the performance and grievances of others
3. Feedback regarding organizational practices and policies
4. Feedback concerning what needs to be done and how to do it
5. Requests for clarification of the goals and specific activities

Great barriers to upward communication exist. Because of bureaucratic structuring, a tremendous amount of important information never reaches the upper-level decision-makers. Managers are unlikely to be in the habit of listening to their staffs rather than talking to them. Staff members are also reticent to give negative feedback to their superiors because it may adversely affect them. They tell the manager not only what they think the manager wants to hear but also what they want the manager to know.[45]

It is very important for managers to determine whether the information received from subordinates is accurate. Subordinates must trust a boss and be willing to forward negative information when necessary. Upward communication of a negative type should not place the originator at risk—it should be accepted as a challenge to management to change or fix something that has gone wrong.

The upward flow of communication in police organizations is not noted for spontaneous and objective expression, despite attempts to formalize the process of feedback up the line. As an example of how one can be placed at risk, a deputy chief of police in a medium-sized city publicly criticized how the department handled a situation involving a police officer barricaded in a motel room. The officer was finally talked out of the room without anyone being injured, and after the departmental investigation, he was allowed to resign from the department. The deputy chief who voiced his displeasure with the handling of the case was placed on administrative leave, and he retired in short order.

Horizontal Communication

Horizontal communication is part of the normal working conditions within a department. For example, two officers talk with each other about a common problem, or an officer discusses a case with a detective or a criminalist, or a records supervisor is consulted about information on a suspect or a defendant. Such communication is initiated to coordinate tasks, solve problems, share information, and resolve conflict.[46]

Communicating horizontally, across unit boundary lines, is fraught with difficulty. There are a number of reasons why peers may not communicate. For example, rivalry for recognition and promotion may cause reluctance. Subordinates may also have difficulty communicating with highly specialized peers in other divisions.[47]

Whisenand states that "communicating across and diagonally in a police organization assures it of seamless operations" and offers the following reasons for encouraging such communication:[48]

1. *Teamwork.* Confusion, conflict, and frustration result from a lack of coordination between work units. In the absence of teamwork, detectives and the narcotics unit could be investigating the same crime; one patrol unit could be messing up the operations of another, and so on. By helping to coordinate tasks, informal communication contributes to the fulfillment of organizational goals.
2. *Common problems.* Weakness in horizontal and diagonal communication nearly guarantees that the root causes of a police problem will go undetected. Techniques such as brainstorming can help a department engage in problem-oriented policing.
3. *Feedback needed by individuals.* Most of us want to know what others think about our efforts. Some of this feedback occurs within the work unit and meets our ego and esteem needs, which are feelings of value to the organization.

4. *Professional guidance.* The sharing of information among work units increases the probability that the various groups are acting in concert with approved service values and quality standards.

5. *Conflict resolution.* The members of one department may meet to discuss a conflict inherent in the department or between units.

Also, horizontal communication can improve service delivery to clients by cutting red tape and going directly to the heart of a problem. Such flexibility empowers individuals both inside and outside the organization. As horizontal communication assumes an increasingly important place in the overall communication process, it will bring greater balance to organizations and serve as a major vehicle in improving the delivery of police services.

Another form of communication is diagonal. **Diagonal communication** sets up a gangplank across the organizational boundaries between persons at different levels—both upward and downward. It guarantees the following:[49]

1. Enhanced teamwork
2. Promotion of improvement
3. Immediate feedback
4. Speed in operations
5. Agility in changing tasks and goals

It is clear that the type of communication method used is dependent upon both its purpose and the place of the desired target in the organizational structure.

Holding Meetings

Prewitt lists points on when to conduct and how to communicate in meetings:[50]

1. **Be clear about the purpose of the meeting.** What is the purpose of the meeting? It is important to establish the purpose of a meeting at the outset. Meetings should be results-oriented.

2. **Is the meeting necessary?** Clarifying what the meeting will accomplish answers this question. Perhaps an e-mail message or memo could also communicate information.

3. **Prepare for the meeting.** Establish the time, place, and duration of the meeting. Distribute a four- or five-point agenda before the meeting. Brief participants on the importance of attendance, what they should be prepared to present, and the anticipated outcome.

4. **Avoid haphazard decision-making.** Decide who will chair the meeting and who should participate. The discussion builds consensus.

5. **Establish criteria to evaluate proposed solutions.** Provide sufficient time for follow-up.

Following these suggestions can make meetings more productive and valuable.

Communication in the Informal Organization

As we have observed, a vast majority of the problems in organizations result from faulty communication. Effective police managers become adept at solving such problems by becoming sensitive to one additional communication system—the informal system.

The bureaucratic organization sets forth the communication relations between members of an organization in explicit detail; the informal organization identifies, in most instances, the individuals with whom organizational members prefer to communicate. Whisenand contends that most initial developments of ideas in police departments originate in **informal communication** channels. The main advantage of developing ideas in this fashion is twofold: They can be withdrawn or changed without fear of official disapproval.[51] When allowed to choose for themselves, people carry on a great deal of communication within informal channels.

In police departments, these informal channels become necessary under certain conditions. Whisenand offers five conditions for their development:[52]

1. The greater the degree of interdependence among activities within the department is, the greater the number and use of subformal channels.

2. The more uncertainty there is about the objectives of the department, the greater the number and use of subformal channels. When the environment is relatively unpredictable, people cannot easily determine what they should be doing by referring to that environment. Consequently, they tend to talk to each other more to gain an improved understanding of their situation.

3. When a police organization is operating under the pressure of time, it tends to use the subformal channels extensively because there is often no time to use the formal channels. Thus, police administrators reach out for information whenever they can get it, from whatever channel is necessary.

4. If the divisions of a police organization are in strong competition, they tend to avoid subformal channels and communicate only formally. Conversely, closely cooperating sections rely primarily on subformal communication.

5. Subformal communication channels are used more frequently if department members have stable relationships with each other than if their relationships are constantly changing.

A word of caution is necessary when considering the informal aspects of organizations because one individual can belong to more than one group. The membership of any single group is constantly changing. Nonetheless, the informal organization is a vital part of the communication process.

The Grapevine

A unique form of informal communication within an organization is the **grapevine**. In fact, it is an inevitable part of human behavior and an important element of a communication system. It cannot be eliminated, even though it can be harmful as well as helpful.[53] The grapevine never appears on the department's organizational chart, but it carries a number of messages and often works rapidly.

For the most part, the messages are oral, although in some instances written messages are sent through this informal communication system. Examples include the selective circulation of a proposal to reorganize the department or an internal affairs investigative report. The grapevine in an organization has no respect for rank or authority and can link members in any combination of directions.

The grapevine functions constantly. Sometimes it transmits a great deal of information; in other instances, the messages (of any reasonable importance) are few, and the grapevine performs a more social function. One characteristic of the grapevine is that it usually operates faster than the formal communication system. Another characteristic is distortion. Messages can easily become garbled and ambiguous as they move through the grapevine at a rapid pace.[54]

The grapevine generates rumors. A rumor is an unverified belief flowing freely through the grapevine. A rumor is seldom factual but cannot be refuted easily. As a message moves through the grapevine, the gaps are filled in, and embellishment can become significant. If the message is exceedingly complex, the rumor mill will simplify it.

A police manager should tap into the grapevine by making a sincere effort to learn its messages. The best plan of action is to make relevant inquiries of those who are part of the informal communication network. It is always amazing what different people in an organization know. Ask the secretaries, clerks, janitors, or active members of employee groups. Any or all of them can help identify current areas of concern.

The grapevine can be an important addition to the formal communication process. It can give a manager insight into employee emotions, attitudes, and concerns. It can also be used to monitor the overall morale of organizational personnel.

August Vollmer, the father of American policing, combined formal and informal communication in his "crab sessions." As Chief of the Berkeley CA police department,

Vollmer used these sessions to examine issues officers had with him, their fellow officers, or city government openly and without repercussions. Vollmer also used them to introduce training topics to his officers.[55]

Improving Communication

Several techniques are helpful in improving communication. Each of the techniques we describe has both advantages and disadvantages, so a manager should select the technique or techniques appropriate for use within his or her particular organization.

Listening

Managers need to develop listening skills. The key is to be sensitive to the purpose of **listening**. Empathetic listening is called active listening. It encourages people to say what they mean.[56]

Listening is a skill necessary for communication. It must be developed and put into practice.

Survey Feedback

Surveys can be useful to managers because they provide information about employee perceptions. Surveys may be conducted by personally interviewing officers and other employees or by using the telephone. Face-to-face interviewing is time consuming, but it allows the interviewer to ask a large number of probing questions. A telephone survey allows the interviewer to talk to more agency personnel.

It is not necessary to contact every member of the department when conducting a survey. That is why the sampling technique is recommended. A survey can be conducted by dividing the sample by rank, gender, age, ethnic origin, or any other compelling critical element. A random sample results when the manager or a researcher selects each participant in such a way that everyone has an equal chance of being selected.

An employee survey can provide management with information about the communication process as well as serve as an excellent vehicle for improving and increasing the flow of information upward. This information cannot be easily obtained in other ways. Surveys allow employees to express their attitudes about such issues as[57]

- Communication
- Motivational factors
- Coordination
- Control
- Planning
- Directing
- Satisfaction

This information (obtained by questionnaire) can serve as the basis for a follow-up study and changes in the communication system. The survey-feedback instrument can be used to change and improve the department's communication process. It can prove useful in revealing problems and clarifying issues. However, if superiors ignore the results of an employee survey, the survey project can backfire and result in increased employee frustration, turnover, absenteeism, job apathy, cynicism, and even sabotage.[58]

Emotions

Gallo offers five methods to control emotions during difficult conversations. To close down the natural "fight or flight" response to conflict, try breathing. Focus on your breath by inhaling, counting to six and exhaling. You could also anchor your body by getting up and walking around or placing your feet firmly on the floor. Saying a mantra (like "It's only business, not personal") can remind you to stay calm and focused. If you acknowledge and label your feelings, it is easier to let them go and prevent their damaging influence. Finally, you could take a break for a while when things get heated.[59]

CASE STUDY Jerry Olsen

Jerry Olsen has been with the Seaville Police Department for the last nine years. He is currently assigned to the patrol division and is on the swing shift. He is regarded as an excellent officer and during his service with the department has received 12 commendations for outstanding performance.

Officer Olsen is extremely well liked by his peers and is respected as a real street cop. He attended college for two years and made the decision not to pursue any additional formal education. He enjoys his job and has no desire to achieve a higher rank. In fact, he has been eligible to take the sergeant's examination twice but refused both times.

Recently, the department adopted rewards, gifts, and gratuities policy, which states in part, "Officers shall not solicit, directly or indirectly, any person, firm, or organization for any reward, gratuity, contribution, or gift." This new policy was discussed at length at roll call, and its intent and implications seemed to be understood by everyone.

The officers on Officer Olsen's team always have a coffee break at Lillie's Grill, and they do not pay for their coffee. The manager of the café strongly supports the practice, and it is clear to the staff that the presence of the officers provides added security. The café is located in a high-crime area and is unquestionably an oasis in the desert. Even the patrons like to see the officers come into the café because their presence is calming.

Lt. Cal Germann, watch commander, advised the officers that free coffee violates the new department policy. The officers feel very strongly that a couple of cups of coffee cannot be considered a gratuity or gift. Officer Olsen, serving as the spokesperson for the team, points out that although the officers do not pay for the coffee, they actually leave tips exceeding its price.

Lt. Germann is adamant. He claims that the free coffee is a violation of policy. On the other hand, the officers feel strongly that the policy is not intended to cover such a minor thing as a cup of coffee. All parties involved heard about the policy at roll call, but there is a misunderstanding about its intent.

How might communication be improved at the roll call meeting other than reading the policy and limiting the discussion to answering questions? The question of a cup of coffee never came up during the original discussion. How can the roll call session be conducted? How should the policy be rewritten to cover Lt. Germann's concern (which is interpreted as prohibiting such things as free coffee)?

SUMMARY

Communication is the vehicle that police managers use to translate policy and procedures into day-to-day decisions and acceptable operational activities. Managers utilize communication to motivate, discipline, and train officers and civilian employees to achieve organizational goals.

Managerial communication involves two entirely different and distinct types of communication—organizational and interpersonal. Organizational communication concerns itself with standard operating procedures. Interpersonal communication deals with emotions and feelings modifying and conditioning messages.

The role that communication plays is distinct for each of the major managerial functions: planning, organizing, directing, and controlling. The manager must nurture communication at all levels of the organization, learn to recognize the human processes involved in communicating, and utilize a variety of techniques for each of the managerial functions.

There are three major actors involved in organizational communications: individuals, groups, and the organization itself. According to one model, each act of communication can be broken down into six elements (sender, encoding, message, channel, decoding, and receiver) and two modifiers (feedback and noise).

Formal organizational communication systems include three types of communication: downward, upward, and horizontal. Each influences the agency differently and places unique demands on police managers at different levels in the organization.

The informal organization identifies the individuals and groups with which members communicate. The informal groups include task groups, friendship groups, and other special-interest groups. The grapevine is another supplement to the formal system of communication, making the communication process even more complex.

Finally, a police manager can use several different techniques to improve organizational communication. Survey interviews can be used to determine employee perceptions. If the survey responses indicate problems, police managers should develop a plan to improve the communication process.

The following guidelines are helpful in the improvement of communication skills:[60]

1. Remember that effective communication involves creating meaning, transmitting meaning, and deciphering meaning. The communication process can break down at any of these stages.

2. Recognize the many barriers that inhibit effective communication.

3. Practice supportive communication.

4. When speaking, consider your audience and make sure that your content, tone, and approach fit the situation.

5. When you wish to persuade someone to your position, consider your credibility and work to improve it.

6. Listen, listen, and listen!

7. Remember that body language communicates as much as, or more than, what you say.

8. Take advantage of electronic communication, but use electronic channels only when they are appropriate.

9. In specialized forms of communication, always consider the receiver or audience and the norms and expectations embedded in the situation.

10. Remember to consider the ethics of communication. Your ethics and integrity are most clearly on display when you communicate with others.

Finally, it is important to consider the value of face-to-face communication. Clarification can be asked for and received.[61]

DISCUSSION TOPICS AND QUESTIONS

1. Compare and contrast organizational communication and interpersonal communication.

2. When a police department operates with a dual reporting–type structure, what are the communication problems?

3. What can a manager do to create an organizational climate fostering *real* communication?

4. Do supervisory managers and middle managers have the same types of communication problems?

5. Differentiate between feedback and noise as parts of the communication process.

6. Is under-communicating more serious than over-communicating?

7. Describe how a manager can deal with a rumor.

8. What is the difference between service and functional authority?

9. What are the functions of listening?

FOR FURTHER READING

Arthur Bell and Dayle Smith, *Management Communication* (New York: John Wiley, 1999).

Written by leading experts in the field, this text provides valuable suggestions on how to improve communication within organizations.

Ellen Hochstedler and Christine M. Dunning, "Communication and Motivation in Police Departments," *Criminal Justice and Behavior*, Vol. 10 (1983), pp. 47–69.

This study reports the results of a survey completed by 1,000 police officers in a large southwestern police department. The satisfaction indicators used in the study showed that the most important kind of communication was vertical.

ENDNOTES

1. Paul M. Whisenand, *Managing Police Organizations* (Upper Saddle River, NJ: Pearson Prentice Hall, 2014), p. 70.
2. Chester I. Barnard, *The Functions of the Executive* (Cambridge, MA: Harvard University Press, 1938), pp. 175–181.
3. Stephen P. Robbins and Timothy A. Judge, *Organizational Behavior* (Upper Saddle River, NJ: Pearson Prentice Hall, 2013), p. 336.
4. L. Miller, H. More and M. Braswell, *Effective Police Supervision* (New York: Routledge, 2017), p. 92
5. Hal Rainey, *Understanding and Managing Public Organizations* (San Francisco, CA: Josey Bass, 2014), p. 393.
6. John R. Schermerhorn, James G. Hunt, Richard N. Osborn and M. Uhl-Bien, *Organizational Behavior* (Hoboken, NJ: John Wiley & Sons, 2010), p. 257.
7. Rainey, *Managing Public Organizations*, p. 393.
8. Ibid.
9. G. Cordner, *Police Administration* (New York: Routledge, 2016), pp. 312–313.
10. Whisenand, *Managing Police Organizations*, p. 77.
11. Harry W. More and Michael O'Neill, *Contemporary Criminal Justice Planning* (Springfield, IL: Charles C Thomas, 1987), p. 113.
12. V.A. Leonard and Harry W. More, *Police Organization and Management* (New York: Foundation Press, 2000), pp. 469–471.
13. Stephen P. Robbins and Mary Coulter, *Management* (Upper Saddle River, NJ: Pearson Prentice Hall, 2018), p. 329.
14. Ibid., p. 330.
15. Leonard and More, *Police Organization and Management*, p. 188.
16. Ibid., pp. 187–188.
17. Ibid., pp. 190–191.
18. Robbins and Coulter, *Management*, p. 56.
19. Elsbeth Johnson, "How to Communicate Clearly during Organizational Change," *Harvard Business Review* (June 13, 2017), pp. 2–6.
20. Edward R. Maguire, *Organizational Structure in American Police Agencies: Context, Complexity and Control* (Albany, NY: State University of New York, 2001), p. 108.
21. Brian F. Kingshott, "Effective Police Management of the Media," *Criminal Justice Studies*, Vol. 24, No. 3 (2011), pp. 241–253.
22. Whisenand, *Managing Police Organizations*, p. 75.
23. Ramon J. Aldag and Loren W. Kuzuhara, *Organizational Behavior and Management* (Cincinnati, OH: South-Western, 2002), p. 189.
24. Miller, More, and Braswell, *Effective Police Supervision*, pp. 101–109.
25. James L. Lundy, *Lead, Follow, or Get Out of the Way* (San Diego, CA: Avant Books, 1986).
26. Schermerhorn, Hunt, Osborn, and Uhl-Bien, *Organizational Behavior*, p. 256.
27. Robbins and Judge, *Organizational Behavior*, p. 338.
28. Ibid.
29. Ibid.
30. Schermerhorn, Hunt, Osborne, and Uhl-Bien, *Organizational Behavior*, p. 257.
31. Robbins and Judge, *Organizational Behavior*, p. 358.
32. Whisenand, *Managing Police Organizations*, pp. 73–74.
33. Ibid., p. 80.
34. Robbins and Coulter, *Management*, p. 438
35. Robbins and Judge, *Organizational Behavior*, p. 353.
36. Fred Luthans, *Organizational Behavior* (New York: McGraw-Hill, 2002), pp. 343–344.
37. Schermerhorn, Hunt, Osborne, and Uhl-Bien, *Organizational Behavior*, p. 257.
38. Robert B. Denhardt, Janet V. Denhardt, and Maria P. Aristigueta, *Managing Human Behavior in Public and Nonprofit Organizations* (Thousand Oaks, CA: Sage, 2015), p. 256.
39. Leslie Perlow and Stephanie Williams, "Is Silence Killing Your Company?" *Harvard Business Review* (May 2003), pp. 3–8.
40. Ellen Hochstedler and Christine M. Dunning, "Communication and Motivation in a Police Department," *Criminal Justice and Behavior*, Vol. 10 (1983), pp 47–69.
41. Whisenand, *Managing Police Organizations*, p. 75.
42. Luthans, *Organizational Behavior*, p. 346.
43. Steven Cohen and William Eimicke, *The New Effective Public Manager* (San Francisco, CA: Jossey-Bass, 1995), p. 90.
44. Whisenand, *Managing Police Organizations*, p. 75.
45. Ibid., p. 76.
46. Robbins and Coulter, *Management*, p. 445.
47. Ibid.
48. Whisenand, *Managing Police Organizations*, p. 76.
49. Ibid.
50. E. Prewitt, "Pitfalls in Meetings and How to Avoid Them," *Harvard Management Update Newsletter* (1998), pp. 3–5.
51. Ibid.
52. Ibid.
53. Robbins and Judge, *Organizational Behavior*, pp. 344–345.
54. Ibid.
55. Willard M. Oliver, *August Vollmer, the Father of American Policing* (Durham, NC: Carolina Academic Press, 2017), pp. 230–232.
56. Schermerhorn, Hunt, Osborne, and Uhl-Bien, *Organizational Behavior*, p. 261.
57. Leonard and More, *Police Organization and Management*, pp. 234–235.
58. Ibid.
59. Amy Gallo, "How to Control Your Emotions during a Difficult Conversation," *Harvard Business Review* (December 1 2017), pp. 2–4.
60. Denhardt, Denhardt, and Aristigueta, *Managing Human Behavior*, pp. 283–284.
61. Ibid., p. 268.

11
GROUPS AND TEAMWORK
Human Dynamics at Work

Learning Objectives

1. Differentiate between formal groups and informal groups.
2. Compare leadership in formal and informal work groups.
3. Describe the concept of group culture and the mechanisms used to instill self-control.
4. Identify the elements of the interactionist perspective.
5. Assess the role of the police administrator in managing group dynamics.
6. Evaluate the impact of group dynamics on organizational productivity.

Key Terms

affiliation
attitudes
behaviors
closed groups
cohesiveness
collective behavior
command group
complexity
composition
conformity
cross-functional
culture
ethical orientation
group structure
groupthink
imprinting

informal groups
linking-pin
need orientation
norms
peer leadership group (PLG)
roles
role set
self-directed
size
subculture
taboos
task groups
teams
values
work group

Working collectively seems, at first view, to be a natural and effective way to solve problems, but putting the concept into practice poses continuing challenges to law enforcement managers. A thorough understanding of groups and group dynamics is needed, but in the police world in particular, some administrators have been reluctant to accept the group dynamics approach to management; they have gone to great lengths to maintain the illusion that an organization is little more than an aggregate of individuals performing a common function. There are several reasons why they prefer to deal with their subordinates individually rather than collectively:

1. Their training and experience have accustomed them to handling problems on a person-to-person basis; they are not conditioned to look for systemic variables or interaction patterns that might have contributed to a problem.

2. The individual approach to resolving personnel problems is quicker and easier than identifying and analyzing systemic and group factors. Learning to understand and deal with groups requires more time, energy, effort, and expertise than many managers are willing to give.

3. Dealing with individuals rather than groups helps managers retain control over the flow of authority within their organizations. This approach justifies department rules, managerial prerogatives, and limitations on interaction with employees.

CASE STUDY   Chief David Salee

Salee is the chief of police of Reidsville, a city with a population of 151,459 located in the North West. The department has a total of 151 sworn officers; 60 percent of those officers respond to calls for service and 9 percent are assigned to investigations. Five percent of the officers are female, and 67 percent of the sworn officers are white, 23 percent are Hispanic, and 5 percent are Asian. The minimum educational requirement for entry is an HS diploma, and officers receive educational incentive pay and tuition reimbursement. New officers are required to complete an 880-hour academy and then supervised in the field for an additional 400 hours. There is a police union that is very strong and has the support of the majority of the members of the city council as well as the city manager. Over the years, the union has developed a strong position in the politics of the city, and it makes a sizeable contribution to candidates each election year. The union has been instrumental in obtaining collective bargaining and exerts a strong influence in the community.

The city has a gang problem that has grown substantially over the last five years, and there is general unrest in the community, which feels the police department is not doing enough. One Citizen—a large group—has demanded action, and the city council is finally starting to realize that the city has a grave problem that is not being dealt with any degree of effectiveness. This group has a wide constituency with the goal of working for better government.

Salee was appointed to the position by the mayor with the approval of the city council, and he decided to move slowly within the department and build support from the community and work at developing his own power base within political circles. He also had a plan to sell his strategy for change to civic and religious groups. He felt that just to deal with the department was a no-win situation.

He was brought in from the outside, and prior to that time, every chief had spent his or her career in the Reidsville Police Department. Chief Salee, a college-educated realist, served in every rank up to assistant chief in a department that had 1,100 sworn officers and was a well-rounded administrator, having served in numerous positions over his 24-year career. He came to the job knowing that he would have a difficult time because of the opposition to outsiders. Historically, the department did not allow lateral transfers, and it was generally known that the selection board favored local talent at the entry level. In fact, this caused numerous out of towners to move to the community as a means of enhancing their employability. He has been in office for only nine months, and the honeymoon was definitely over. He had been ordered by the mayor to streamline the department and make it more efficient, effective, and productive.

While the new chief has good intentions, he is having a difficult time overcoming institutional inertia. After a very careful analysis of the situation, he has concluded that his managerial options are limited by organizational and cultural constraints that have to be confronted if a positive change is to occur. Chief Salee cites the following limitations:

1. All classified positions (including detective) up to the rank of division chief have civil service status.
2. Permanent duty assignments are awarded based on seniority among those officers bidding for them.
3. The department is characterized by a rigid chain of command with an emphasis on control through executive decision-making.
4. The delegation of authority within the department is subject to "traditional" limitations.
5. The police union opposes major changes in police operations.

The chief feels that he has little leeway to allocate financial resources or make temporary reassignments of police personnel. Before he could confront internal problems, external problems dominated the news and internal problems took a backseat. Prior to his arrival, gang activity had been a continuing problem. What brought it to a head was a series of obviously related and particularly brazen gang activities including drive-by shootings that are causing panic in the city, and citizens are afraid to go out after dark. After the traditional methods and procedures failed to produce results, the city's leading newspaper decried what it called "police bungling" and demanded immediate "action." The chief is convinced that inappropriate personnel assignments, organizational rigidity, bureaucratic infighting, and a battle over turf are hindering departmental response to gang activity. He feels that his job is on the line and the reputation of the department is at stake.

Although the constraints he identified are real, Chief Salee does have options. What are they? What would someone with knowledge of groups and group dynamics do in this particular situation? How would you deal with the citizen group? How would you deal with the gang problem? Explain. What would you do to enhance your power as the chief?

According to one police management theorist, it is far less threatening for a manager to condemn individual police officers as lazy, inept, or corrupt than it is to raise substantive questions about the department's structure, operating procedures, and goals.[1] Some police administrators do not have the knowledge, technical expertise, conceptual ability, or human skills needed to understand and deal effectively with group dynamics in the workplace, but this is changing rapidly as managerial leaders are becoming more aware of the importance of organizational behavior. Competent police managers have a knack for resolving problems and handling personnel. They have learned to appreciate the importance of groups and the group process. They know that people and groups are the human resources on which all social organization is built.[2]

The Group Phenomenon

Effective police managerial leaders never forget that human beings are social animals.[3] They know that we all need to have interpersonal relationships with other people. Meaningful social interaction is essential for human development and is a very important source of personal fulfillment. Virtually everything we do is in conjunction with or through others. Our unique personality (**attitudes**, **values**, and **behaviors**) evolved in response to the interaction we had with other people in a variety of very different situations.[4] In terms that are more succinct, people do not exist apart from social groups. All people are born into them, transformed through them, and eventually buried by them.

Based on the idea that each person exists and develops a sense of self largely in response to meaningful interaction with important others, many social scientists believe groups are the basic unit of social organization. Groups perform a wide variety of functions, including providing their members with companionship, emotional support, a normative perspective, and a frame of reference for **collective behavior**. People behave based on how they perceive themselves and how they feel they are perceived by important others within their groups.[5] The interpersonal relationships that police administrators are most concerned with are those found in the work environment, which are normally started and maintained to facilitate the accomplishment of work. In the workplace context, group-based interpersonal relationships are good if they help get tasks accomplished and meet the work-related needs of group members.[6]

Definition of a Group and/or Team

A group is more than a mere collection of human beings who happen to be in physical proximity to one another or who share a common interest or characteristic. According to Ronald Smith and Frederick Preston, a group consists of a number of persons who interact with each other in an organized way. They share common traits, views, **values**, circumstances, and a sense of togetherness.[7] More specifically, a group is defined as being composed of (1) two or more people, (2) who are consciously aware of one another, (3) who consider themselves to be a functional unit, and (4) who share in the quest to achieve one or more goals or other common benefit.[8]

A team is defined as a number of persons associated in some joint effort. A second definition states it is a number of persons associated together in any work. Interestingly, there are numbers of definitions that allude to sports and games. In any event, the definition of a group is more comprehensive than the definition of a team. One can instantly see the similarities in the differing definitions. In fact, the group definition could just as easily define a team in many instances. At the same time, it is appropriate to acknowledge that a team is a group of people who have a high degree on interdependence as they strive to attain a goal or complete a task. Additionally, teams are best described by what they actually do and are led by one supervisor/leader. Interestingly, enough teams have an exceptional degree of self-management; they share responsibility and assess their own performance. In this chapter, the reader should keep this in mind when considering the issues and complexities when dealing with groups/teams.

Two basic requirements must be met before an aggregate (a number of people who happen to be clustered in one place) qualifies as a work group. First, the individuals must interact with each other in some organized manner. Members share **norms**, role expectations, and social status. Second, there must be "consciousness of kind"—that is, members must recognize themselves as bound together by common traits, perspectives, and circumstances. The combination of these two elements creates a single, dynamic, and goal-oriented social entity.

Groups and teams differ tremendously in **size**, function, structure, and sophistication. Some groups are one-dimensional, in that they exist for a single purpose. Others have one dominant purpose and various ancillary purposes. Some very complex groups juggle a number of coordinated purposes simultaneously. Without question, groups exhibit their own unique personalities. They can carry on their activities with great vigor and enthusiasm or they may be laid-back, even lackadaisical. They can be as small as just two people or as large as the NYPD, the federal government, or the entire United States. Groups also differ with respect to their activity levels and the nature of the interpersonal transactions among their members:

1. *Primary groups.* Primary groups are those in which members develop personal, intimate, and enduring relationships based on frequent and meaningful interaction.
2. *Secondary groups.* Secondary groups are less intense and more segmented than primary groups because the occasional interaction between members is shallow, impersonal, and practical in nature.

Membership in certain social groups (such as families, nations, and sometimes churches) starts at birth. Membership in other groups (such as schools, military services, or juries) comes later in life and may be voluntary or involuntary. The groups that people join voluntarily may be (1) open to everyone, (2) limited to certain categories of people in the population, or (3) open only to those who are willing to go through some type of screening or initiation. Groups can be deliberately organized or may evolve slowly and without conscious intent, through a process of natural selection. Social scientists often describe groups in terms of their positions along various kinds of continuums.

Groups run the gambit in terms of their placement on a continuum as indicated in Table 11–1. Their position is clearly not in concrete and highly variable. They can be formal and part of the organizational structure or informal (ad hoc). Additionally, in some departments they can be highly functional or in other instances clearly dysfunctional and prove to be detrimental. They can be positively related to other groups or in some other instances operate as a detached entity to the primary organization. Other police organizations range from directive to participative; some can be found to be proactive and others reactive.

Of special concern to the police manager is whether the group is receptive to change or resistant. Regardless of their characteristics, it is clear that groups provide the context within which almost all human behavior occurs.[9]

Definition of a Work Group

It is the police administrator's job to maximize employee productivity within the context of the work group. For our purposes, a **work group** is a task-oriented group that has been created by formal authority of an organization to transform resource inputs (such as

---

Table 11–1
THE NATURE OF GROUPS CONTINUUM

Highly structured	Unstructured
Formal	Informal
Functional	Dysfunctional
Related	Unattached
Segmented	Unified
Autocratic	Democratic
Reactive	Proactive
Resistance to change	Receptive to change
Task oriented	Human relations oriented

money, material, equipment, ideas, and personnel) into product outputs (such as reports, decisions, services, and law enforcement activities). A police department, like all other very complex and task-oriented organizations, is composed of an interlocking network of work groups. Police administrators and first-line supervisors perform what Rensis Likert described as the **linking-pin** function in the network.[10] Through the activities of these officers, each of whom is a senior member of one or more groups and a subordinate member of one or more others, multiple work groups are interconnected in such a way as to create a sense of totality for the organization.[11]

Work Groups

All formal work groups are created as the result of the organizing function inherent in management and through which police officers are assigned to different tasks and task groups by some higher authority (chief executive officer) or the head of a particular sub-group (unit commander). The productivity of any work group depends on how managers handle the division of labor and delegation of authority within the group.

Formal work groups can be temporary or permanent. In either case, they are created by management to contribute to the organization's productive purpose as articulated in its mission, goals, and objectives. Permanent work groups are relatively stable and usually appear on organizational charts as departments, divisions, bureaus, or other units. The generic organizational chart presented in Figure 11–1 displays an inverted hierarchy of function based on work-group membership, component interaction, and formal structure. Temporary work groups such as task forces, on the other hand, are normally created by managers to perform special tasks that existing permanent groups are, for whatever reason, not equipped to deal with efficiently or effectively.

Ad hoc committees, project teams, and task forces are typical temporary work groups designed to accomplish specific objectives, and they are quite common in law enforcement. Once a temporary work group achieves its objective, it is dissolved, and officers detailed to it are returned to their permanent duty assignments.[12] Typical of these types of temporary work groups are those that have dealt with specific issues such as the color of the patrol vehicles or whether officers should be restricted from being tattooed.

At the same time, many law enforcement agencies have developed a wide range of teams to include SWAT, search and rescue, drugs, tactical, and hostage rescue. Many of these started as temporary teams and have evolved into a permanent organizational fixture. When a group becomes a formal entity within an organization, a leader is designated. The leaders of groups obtain the power and legitimate authority needed to coordinate the work of subordinates from top management.[13] Whether they succeed or not, however, depends in large measure on their knowledge, expertise, and leadership skills. The officially designated manager of a work group or team is not necessarily the group member who exerts the most influence over the job-related behavior of fellow employees. He or

Figure 11–1
Formal Work Groups.

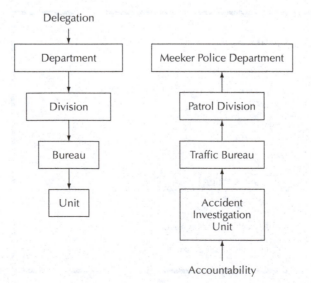

she is typically task oriented and eager to get the job done as quickly and effectively as possible even if that means using his or her official position, power, and authority coercively. According to Robert Fulmer, formal leaders—who usually have the institutionalized power and authority to direct, discipline, or fire members of their own particular work group—tend to use negative motivation. They rely on the use of differential status, discipline, and punishment to accomplish their objectives.[14]

Recently, a number of agencies have created a Peer Leadership Group **(PLG)** that serves as a means to allow employees to "buy" into the organization and allowing them to become a "stakeholder." The goal is to have officers become involved in the future of the department and to make them realize that their opinions are valued. The employees choose a minimum of three officers, and they set on the group for a designated period of time. Supervisory and police managers are not allowed to be members. Any member of the agency can bring a problem to the group. It is believed that officers will respond openly to a peer. Also, the **PLG** does not bypass departmental general orders or directives. Every effort possible has to be made to ensure that meetings do not become gripe sessions. Members of the group decide how often they need to meet and create their own rules.

Members of the group strive to address and resolve problems and open communications within the agency. In larger agencies, it might be necessary to have more than one group and the **size** of the group should be such that it is manageable. If necessary, members of the group can request a meeting with the chief to discuss issues that the committee cannot resolve. This process opens up lines of communications and is geared to tap the ideas and concepts of departmental employees.[15] In one department using the peer group, an officer described the need for dealing with seven abandoned homes with absentee owners that were a constant police problem. The officer recommended that the city attorney draft a letter that the owners could sign and allow the police to have access to the property. The proposal was reviewed and submitted to the chief, and in every instance, the absentee landowners consented to the access, and the beat officers in the affected areas made numerous arrests and recovered stolen property in four of the homes. For the last six months, the consent letters have proven invaluable, and the program has been expanded to other parts of the city.

Cliques

Natural subgroups, or cliques, can be found within nearly all formally designated work groups. When two or more employees come together in an effort to satisfy mutual needs or share common interests, an informal group comes into being. These **informal groups** evolve from spontaneous interactions among compatible individuals who are looking for validation as human beings and social reinforcement for appropriate behavior. **Informal groups** help satisfy member needs for companionship, security, belonging, and self-esteem. Although they are not created by those in authority, seldom have defined goals, and are usually transitory, **informal groups** are influential in police organizations. They provide their members with social acceptance, friendship, and an opportunity to develop meaningful interpersonal relationships.[16] They also provide satisfactions that are often denied or thwarted by formal group **affiliations**.[17] These groups are formed to fulfill very important psychosocial needs for security and camaraderie among members. A formal group can also function as an informal group if members freely choose to associate with each other on and off the job.[18]

Informal groups (or cliques) are shadow organizations; they do not exist officially. They arise out of the interactions, attractions, and needs of individuals. Members are not assigned to these groups. Membership is voluntary and dependent on the mutual attraction the individual and the group have for each other. **Informal groups** create intricate patterns of influence that extend far beyond the mechanical representations drawn on an organizational chart. **Informal groups** provide their members with a human infrastructure. They can concern themselves with a broad range of issues ranging from working conditions to policy interpretation.[19] Members identify with one another and share common perspectives, and this generates a sense of solidarity. They are often able to manipulate the work environment for their own purposes by redefining responsibilities and work relationships within the organization.[20] This may result in the flow of the organization's legitimate authority being altered or circumvented altogether.[21] In other situations,

informal groups can be supportive of an organization. One officer might, for example, show a fellow member of his or her group how to perform a specific task in a more productive way; this could simultaneously benefit the trained officer, the group the two officers belong to, and the formal organization.[22] Effective administrators know how to recognize and deal with **informal groups**. Dalton Melville, in his classic study of industrial organizations, identified three basic types of **informal groups**, or cliques, that tend to develop within the social environments created by complex organizations: horizontal, vertical, and random (or mixed).[23]

Horizontal Cliques.

This type of clique is composed of two or more people from the same functional area and the same level (or rank) in the hierarchy. Two or more patrol officers in a department's SWAT (Special Weapons and Tactics) team might become a small informal group because of their shared concern about the team's safety, given their commander's lack of field experience or reluctance to incorporate their ideas into the decision-making process. In another instance with a motorcycle unit, every motor officer worked to have the department purchase dual sport motorcycles that had both on and off road capabilities. This was eventually accomplished, and the new motorcycles allowed officers to work in undeveloped areas within the city limits and patrol a river trail. Due to the nature and complexity of police work, almost all police officers belong to one or more horizontal cliques.

Vertical Cliques.

These cliques consist of two or more people from the same functional area (or department) who are at different levels in the hierarchy. Police officers at various ranks often socialize with each other. These **informal groups** are formed and maintained based on similarity of interests and common needs for acceptance, security, self-esteem, and a genuine sense of accomplishment. Many police officers are members of vertical subgroups within their department. An example would be officers who have a special interest in developing self-defense skills and band together to improve their skills.

Random Cliques.

These random or mixed cliques involve two or more people who come from various departments, ranks, and locations. This type of informal network is often made up of individuals who want to get things done and who share a common desire to avoid the red tape normally associated with bureaucracy. Formation of random cliques is often stimulated by a common membership in organizations like the Masons, the Knights of Columbus, or the Southern Police Institute Alumni Association. Many officers become involved in random or mixed cliques in an effort to maximize their overall influence as law enforcers.

Because of the nature of their work, police managers should expect to interact with virtually every type of informal group just described. It must be acknowledged that the activities of influential cliques can lead to disagreement, antagonism, and even challenges to organizational structure and management.[24] Managers must learn to identify informal leaders and help them (and their groups) achieve personal goals and objectives that are consistent with those of the organization as a whole.

Every informal group has at least one leader. Informal leaders, unlike formal authority figures, are not appointed; they derive power from their followers. Group members voluntarily accept suggestions, instructions, and even direct orders from the informal leader because of their respect for his or her personality, knowledge, abilities, and skills. Since informal leadership is both dynamic and situational, it can almost never be delegated. Formally appointed leaders are seldom, if ever, able to function simultaneously as informal leaders of cliques.[25] The two roles are usually mutually exclusive.

Membership

Groups, whether they are formal (created by authority) or informal (spontaneous and goal oriented), can also be classified, based on their criteria for membership, as "open" or "closed."

An *open group* is one that has relatively few restrictions on who is allowed to join. There are few specific requirements. Open groups are constantly adding and losing members.

New members can bring enthusiasm, creativity, and eagerness for change. Maintaining a healthy balance between change and stability requires group leaders to spend considerable time and effort socializing new members. Open groups are future oriented, energetic, unpredictable, and usually hard to manage.

A *closed group* restricts its membership to a selected few by imposing stringent requirements. Membership is relatively stable. Power and status relationships are well established and fixed. "**Groupthink**," which will be discussed later in this chapter, is a common characteristic of closed and highly cohesive groups. They tend to lose their flexibility and adopt a single perspective. Elitism tends to mask the absence of critical thinking. Tightly **closed groups** quickly become "self-perpetuating" cliques.[26]

Open and *closed* are maximum terms and represent opposite ends of a continuum. Most groups fall somewhere in between the two extremes. All police organizations are composed of relatively open and relatively **closed groups**. Once again, it is the manager's job to coordinate the activities of these groups in such a way that they all make positive contributions to the organization.

Groups as Functional Units

The group phenomenon needs to be understood in terms of action as well as structure. From this perspective, a group consists of people acting together as a functional unit. The interaction process allows for a number of officers to coordinate action that is directed, consciously or unconsciously, toward some common objective in anticipation of receiving some type of gratification. Some theorists (known as "social interactionists") place primary emphasis on participation in collective activity rather than on group membership per se. They are not concerned with individuals as total organisms but with those aspects of their behavior that contribute to the collective enterprise. Group action is regarded as something that is constructed out of the diverse efforts of independently motivated human beings moving together toward some shared goal or objective. According to Robert Albanese, this particular concept of group implies some degree of interdependence, mutual influence, and interaction among those people seeking to accomplish a common purpose.[27]

Social interactionists explore group-based human behavior from the interaction/influence perspective we discussed in Chapter 3. They contend that a group does not really exist until its members are involved in *doing* something together (see Table 11–2).

Groups that become functional entities are defined, as viewed by social interactionist, when two or more officers interacting with other members. Another prerequisite is to share one or more goals. Involvement in this definition is the key, and members allow themselves to be governed by a normative system of **attitudes, values**, and behavior; that lead to a stable relationship. Additionally, it is found that officers will form subgroups based on interpersonal attraction or rejection. Interactionists view groups as synergistic, meaning that people working together within a group are able to produce a greater total effect than would be possible if they worked independently; they form a whole that can be greater than the sum of its parts.[28]

Table 11–2
GROUP-BASED HUMAN BEHAVIOR—AN INTERACTIVE/INFLUENCE VIEW

1. A group does not exist until its members are involved in doing something.

2. Members must share one or more goals.

3. Members must allow themselves to be governed by a normative system of **attitudes**.

4. The group must have stable relationships.

5. Members will form subgroups based on interpersonal attraction or rejection.

People join and remain in formal and **informal groups** for a variety of reasons. As noted earlier, human beings are social animals with an innate need to interact with others. In addition, most people—as a condition of employment—are assigned to work with other people in groups. From a utilitarian point of view, people who join groups remain active in them because they have expectations that membership will benefit them in some way. They associate groups with positive outcomes and have formed positive **attitudes** about group participation. Social scientists argue that most people continue to join and remain in groups because they receive positive reinforcement from group behavior.

Police officers join formal and **informal groups** within their organizations for exactly the same reasons. They are looking for ways to fulfill their occupational roles while trying to meet personal needs. These personal needs fall into two broad categories: (1) psychosocial and (2) economic. While both of these needs promote purposeful interaction among employees, psychosocial factors (some of which will be discussed in succeeding sections) are the more influential.

Affiliation

One reason police officers join subgroups (formal and informal) is their need to interact with other people and enjoy the companionship of those with whom they have something in common. These subgroups provide structured environments in which police personnel pursue collective interests and establish lasting friendships. Due to the clannish nature of police work and the 24-hour-a-day rotational scheduling, the requirement for **affiliation** is often met on the job or not at all.

Security

All human beings have a basic need for safety and security. People want protection from real as well as imagined external threats. Many police officers experience feelings of insecurity that can only be alleviated through interaction with supportive group members. Probationary police officers sense that there is safety in numbers. By joining a group whose members have already experienced and survived the probationary period, they are able to reduce their anxiety. Rookie police officers can learn the ropes faster and become part of the grapevine information network much more quickly by joining a group than by going it alone. The capacity for **informal groups** to indoctrinate and socialize new members into the organizational routine gives these groups a great deal of power.

Self-Esteem

Membership in groups, particularly high-status in-groups, can help police officers develop a sense of worth and self-esteem. In addition to gaining internal satisfaction, they develop close interpersonal relationships that provide them with great opportunities for recognition and praise usually unavailable to those outside the group. Groups provide acceptance, perspective, support, and a milieu in which members feel safe and secure. It should be kept in mind that self-esteem is a natural by-product of subgroup affiliation.

Power

Group membership can serve as a source of power in two very different ways. First, subgroup solidarity contributes to an employee's sense of safety and security. Police officers believe in the old adage, "United we stand, Divided we fall." There can be little doubt that workers organized into cohesive groups enjoy far greater power than they do as individuals. This is the principle on which the labor union movement was built. Second, subgroup membership gives members the opportunity to become leaders. They can exert influence over others in the group even though they do not occupy formal positions of authority within the police department. Informal group leaders normally avoid all the responsibilities that come with positions of formal authority.

Self-Concept

Subgroup membership helps individual police officers deal with the introspective question "Who am I?" People have a need to establish an identity and locate themselves as objects in their symbolic environment. According to Charles H. Cooley's concept of the "looking-glass self," people do not see themselves directly but only as reflected in the behavior of others toward them.[29] In other words, our conception of self is essentially based on what aspects of ourselves we see mirrored in the groups to which we belong. Self-conceptions develop through social interaction in groups. Groups are a very good source of evaluative feedback. Continuous interaction provides a good basis for a collective assessment of each member's personality and behavior, and each member's experience with other members helps him or her measure the credibility of their assessments. Important members of a group may well be willing to give colleagues candid positive and negative feedback that police managers often try to avoid giving. Coming from a member of the subgroup, the feedback is more readily accepted.

Accomplishment

Some groups form simply because it takes more than one person to complete a task or because the task is made easier through cooperative effort. Other groups come into being for more complicated reasons. Human beings are social animals who have an innate need to collaborate with one another in order to achieve their individual and collective goals. Police officers join groups to pursue mutual interests. They pool their knowledge, energy, expertise, talent, and tools to accomplish certain tasks. They derive natural satisfaction from achievement, and voluntary interaction with their peers gives them a sense of fulfillment.

Economics

Police officers may join groups to pursue their own economic self-interests. They often become members of labor unions, fraternal organizations, professional associations, and (promotion examination) study groups with a utilitarian expectation that they will benefit financially from membership. While economic security can be seen simply as part of a police officer's basic need for safety and security, it also represents a pathway to self-actualization. Driven by years of financial deprivation, police officers' quest for economic security has become one of the most inflammatory issues in American law enforcement. Police officers are now one of the most unionized categories of public employees in the United States.[30]

One of the most important factors leading to interpersonal attraction and group formation in law enforcement organizations is the opportunity to interact. Paul Whisenand contends that proximity is a critical variable. Many subgroups form simply because police officers are assigned near one another. All other things being equal, those police officers who live near each other or who work closely together have far greater opportunities for interaction than those officers who are physically separated.[31] This is especially true in urban areas where officers can reside in varying communities, and their only contact may be at work. This explains, in part, why officers on adjoining beats gather at the same restaurant—to socialize.

Group Survival

Whether or not a particular formal or informal subgroup survives and makes a substantive contribution to the organization depends on its success in (1) achieving goals and objectives, (2) meeting the psychosocial and economic needs of group members, and (3) facilitating smooth, meaningful interaction between those members involved in goal-oriented transactions. The long-term survival of a group is usually contingent on bringing these three factors into a state of dynamic equilibrium.

Groups overlap one another in all complex police departments. As a result, police officers are normally active participants in several subgroups, informal and formal, simultaneously. A police captain, for example, might belong to the chief's staff, the Command Officers' Association (union), the department's precision shooting team, the Black caucus, the Police Athletic League, and the Blue Knights Motorcycle Club all at the same time. Under normal circumstances, the captain plays a variety of different roles (leader, follower, technician, facilitator, counselor, teacher, and so forth) in these groups. Versatility is a key ingredient in successful role playing within an organization.

Types of Groups

As noted earlier, groups can be described in terms of their positions along various kinds of continuums:

1. Primary/secondary
2. Formal/informal
3. Voluntary/involuntary
4. Horizontal/vertical
5. Open/closed
6. Esoteric/utilitarian
7. In-group/out-group

Groups can also be categorized in terms of their principal function. Leonard Sayles has suggested the following four fundamental working categories that in actual operation overlap and can complement each other: (1) command, (2) task, (3) interest, and (4) friendship. In some instances, all of the categories listed in Table 11–3 in an organization and in other instances any single category can prove to be dominant and exert a great deal of influence on the organization.[32]

Command Groups (Top Management)

Command groups are vertical groups in complex organizations in which orders are given. A group's structure is determined by a formal organizational chart and chain of command, and it is composed of all subordinates who report to one particular police manager. A captain, a lieutenant, a sergeant, and the sergeant's immediate subordinates form a command group. Activities normally take place on orders from a superior. Even if these orders are phrased as requests, the group is still a command group because of the rank relationships between group members.

Task Groups (Project)

A task group is a temporary unit created by formal authority to deal with a specific project or task. Police administrators are finding that task forces, being smaller and less formal than most traditional command groups, are also faster and more productive. Task boundaries are not limited to those in the immediate chain of command. In fact, they often cross command boundaries. The activities of task groups and project staffs create situations in which members are able to communicate and coordinate with each other to determine the best way to achieve a goal. If a police officer is suspected of being an alcoholic, for example, communication and coordination among the sergeant, the shift commander, the employee assistance program manager, the personnel director, and the chief may be necessary to resolve the problem. In a command group, emphasis is on following directions. In a task group, on the other hand, emphasis is placed on defining the task and getting it done.

Interest Groups

In interest groups, the focus is on the group itself. While they may have a chain of command and assigned tasks, they exist because of the mutual interests of all their members. Police personnel, for example, might band together to have their work schedule changed,

Table 11–3
FUNCTIONAL CATEGORIES OF GROUPS

1. Command

2. Task

3. Interest

4. Friendship

to support a colleague who has been disciplined, to protest the establishment of a civilian review board, or to seek improvements in wages, hours, and working conditions; they would be choosing to engage in collective action in order to advance their common interests. Interest groups usually exist for a shorter period than other groups because the objectives that bring them together are likely achieved or abandoned.

Friendship Groups

Friendship groups exist primarily because members like being together. Members normally have one or more characteristics in common. Their interaction, which frequently goes beyond work, may be based on sports, hobbies, religious **affiliations**, interest group activities, professional memberships, or fraternal associations. While members of groups may have met at work or through other groups, real friendship sustains their interpersonal relationships.[33]

These categories are not mutually exclusive. While they often overlap and intertwine, they still provide police administrators with a frame of reference for understanding the structure and function of groups.[34] Every organization has its own constellation of informal as well as formal groups that creates a unique personality or climate that differentiates it from all organizations.

Anatomy of a Group

Diversity within Groups

Today, more and more work in organizations is conducted in groups. These groups may be utilized to work on small tasks or large projects. When groups of different people convene, two results may occur. First, the differences in people belonging to the group may cause dissention. The propensity for the existence of diversity among group members making it more difficult for them to work together is called diversity-consensus dilemma.[35] This may occur due to obstacles related to communication and/or the expectations of individuals belonging to the group. Conversely, when groups are comprised of like individuals, it may be easier for them to bond and thereby work together.

However, this lack of diversity can restrict viewpoints and in turn, stifle ideas, viewpoints, and innovation. Diversity based upon varied values, personalities, experiences, demographics, and cultures among the members, is an important group input.[36] Research indicates the most creative teams include a mix of experienced people and others whom they haven't worked with before.[37] Four important reasons for organizations to ensure group diversity include the following:[38]

1. *Resource imperative.* The workforce of today is comprised of people from varied backgrounds with different life experiences.
2. *Capacity-building strategy.* Organizations are always changing. Successful organizations quickly adapt to new situations, proactively identifying new opportunities and capitalizing on them.
3. *Marketing strategy.* To ensure services are designed and appeal to diverse customer bases, organizations are utilizing people from diverse backgrounds for their specialized insights and knowledge.
4. *Business communications strategy.* The world is constantly changing. As it does, other organizations are utilizing diversity groups of people to excel. Organizations that choose like-minded individuals to solve problems will be ineffective in their external interactions and communications.

Other benefits of diversity include gains in worker effectiveness and efficiency, minimal disputes and grievances, improved services to the community, increased productivity and innovation, greater flexibility and adaptability in systems-oriented or global environments, minimization of isolation and exclusion of different categories of workers, and improved social connectivity.

Organizations are more likely to reap these benefits when they go beyond meeting the minimum requirements for legal compliance. Police organizations should strive to understand both the social and cultural complexities inherent in embracing diversity and strive to be frontrunners in promoting not only diversity, but inclusiveness.

While some take a broader view of diversity in groups moving well beyond gender, race, and ethnicity, to include group member age, backgrounds, experiences, training, etc., the focus here will pertain to the proceeding.

Race and Ethnicity

Race is a controversial issue. Few topics evoke more feeling or passion. *Race* denotes a category of people perceived as distinctive based upon certain biologically inherited traits such as skin color.[39] *Ethnicity* is an additional set of cultural characteristics often corresponding with race.[40] In the past, many organizations concentrated on race and ethnicity from a compliance perspective, that is, equal equity, affirmative action, etc. Over time, diversity has shifted to a focus on inclusion. This change in organizations occurred primarily because of retention issues. While it was easy to hire diverse individuals, it was difficult to retain them.

The belief that racial and ethnic diversity holds a potential to help groups accomplish their intent has spurred research to determine associations between diversity and group performance. Racial and ethnic diversity is more likely to enhance group effectiveness when group members work collectively rather than individually.[41] Additionally, these diverse groups have the potential to thrive based upon an integration-and-learning perspective (vs. one concentrating on equality or fairness).[42] Diverse groups also have the potential to excel if there is a high level of psychological safety,[43] past experience of working together for a long period of time,[44] high levels of interpersonal similarity,[45] or when the task is complex and non-routine.[46]

Gender

To begin with, there is little difference between men and women when it comes to work performance. There are no disparities in relation to problem-solving ability, analytical skills, critical thinking, competitive drive, motivation, sociability, or learning ability.[47] While gender diversity is still a work in progress, women are more and more part of the workplace at every level, in every occupation. Over the past few decades, organizations have redefined the roles of men and women in the workplace.[48] Even so, no differences are displayed between men and women related to job performance.

Groups of employees make organizational decisions every day and are integral to operations. As groups and teams are a foundation in organizations, many have studied what elements make a group/team successful. Gender diversity is one potential determinant of a group/team's effectiveness. This diversity affords the group/team a variety of knowledge and skills. Gender diverse groups/teams are more generous, and groups/teams with a larger percentage of women excel by building meaningful relationships and creating successful work processes.[49]

Diverse groups/teams lead to scrutiny of other members' actions. Such examinations by members can allow individuals to become more aware of their personal biases, biases that can obstruct their view to key information, lead to errors, and hamper innovation. Diversity is not only based on race, ethnicity, and gender, it encompasses informational differences, reflecting a person's education and experience, as well as values or goals that can influence the perception of individual regarding the mission or goals of the group or organization.

Groups

No two groups are the same, and individual groups are never the same over time. They are distinct and evolving entities within an environmental setting. While each group develops a unique personality, all groups have certain structural components that differentiate them from aggregates. Researchers have identified five primary structural components that are common in formal as well as **informal groups**. These are listed in Table 11–4. Every police administrator needs to understand these basic sociological concepts because they are often used to analyze group behavior and it enhances their ability to manage the organization.

One way to analyze groups is to look at the various *roles* played by group members. A role is a set of expectations and behaviors associated with a given position in a social

> **Table 11–4**
> **STRUCTURAL COMPONENTS OF FORMAL AND INFORMAL GROUPS**
>
> 1. Role
> 2. Norms
> 3. Values
> 4. Status
> 5. Culture

unit (e.g., a group, organization, or institution). The sociological use of this term is similar to its theatrical use. For every function that is performed in a group, there is a role. Most groups, for example, have roles labeled "leader" and "follower." The group also has expectations about how these roles should be performed. As in a drama, a role makes sense only if there is a supporting cast interaction based on a pattern of reciprocal *claims* and *obligations*. A claim consists of those things we expect others to do by virtue of their role; an obligation is what we feel bound to do by virtue of our role. What constitutes a claim by one party to the transaction is an obligation for another member of the group. Without socially defined roles and the regularized behavior these roles produce, collaborative, goal-oriented human behavior would be impossible.

Police personnel play multiple roles within police departments and adjust their roles to the expectations of the group they are part of at a given time. Role playing involves living up to the obligations of the role that has been assumed and insisting that other players do the same. Role behavior can be classified into three categories: (1) task related, (2) maintenance related, and (3) individual related. (These categories were developed more than 50 years ago, but they are still relevant today.)[50] Task-related roles require behavior directly related to establishing and achieving the mission, goals, and objectives of the group. Maintenance-related roles call for those behaviors directly related to the well-being, continuity, and development of a particular group. Individual-related roles—the "joker," "chronic complainer," "hedonist," "opponent," and "troublemaker," for example—are scripted to meet the needs of individual members rather than those of the group. Even though such individual roles can be functional under certain circumstances, they are usually dysfunctional and have a negative effect on the group as a whole.

Roles within Groups

Researchers have identified an almost endless array of different roles that can be found in organizations. Whether or not one of these roles emerges will depend on the nature of the group, its task, and the situation involved. Here are some of the most common social roles:

1. The *leader* influences, motivates, and coordinates the goal-oriented activities of other group members.
2. The *follower* does willingly those things the leader asks in order to accomplish the organization's goals and objectives.
3. The *expert* provides technical information and practitioner skills relevant to achievement of the group's task.
4. The *enforcer* sees to it that group **norms** and **values** are understood and adhered to and that violations result in appropriate sanctions.
5. The *facilitator* works to avoid destructive intragroup conflict through consensus building and compromise.[51]
6. The *devil's advocate* questions virtually every suggestion or managerial decision affecting the group.
7. The *scapegoat*, for a variety of social and psychological reasons, gets blame for group failures.

Figure 11–2
The Role Set of the Patrol Officer.
Based on John J. Broderick, Police in
a Time of Change (Prospect Heights,
IL: Waveland Press, 1987).

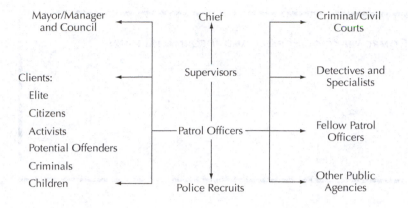

As noted earlier, most people occupy several roles simultaneously. Each of these roles belongs to a *role set*, which can be thought of as a theatrical "cast of characters"—all those group members (in other **roles**) who interact with a given role in some way and have legitimate expectations concerning the behavior of the person playing that role. Role sets are important because they pressure individuals to conform to role-related expectations.[52] The **role set** of a patrol officer is depicted in Figure 11–2.

At the same time, one should be mindful of *role conflict*, which happens when a person tries to perform two roles that impose contradictory or incompatible demands on him or her. Since most people play a variety of very different roles, and since there will always be varying expectations about how a person should behave in a given set of circumstances, role conflict is inevitable. According to Dean Champion,[53] there are several kinds of role conflicts that managers must learn to deal with. These conflicts arise from (1) the dissimilar demands of two different **roles**, (2) the simultaneous playing of numerous roles, (3) internal stressors like the time or skill required to play roles properly, and (4) different expectations about how a particular role should be carried out. Clearly, role conflict is inherent in group dynamics.[54]

CASE STUDY   Chief Pat Murphy

The city of Parker is located in the northeast United States. The city was founded in 1764, and the police department can trace its history back to the early 1800s. The department is proud that it has employed individuals from the same families from one generation to the next with the dominant group being of Irish origin. The current chief of police, Pat Murphy, has spent his whole career in the department and has served in numerous administrative positions. All of the administrative positions above captain are filled by the chief and, needless to say, they are all of Irish descent. Some 30 years ago, a considerable number of newly hired were of Italian origin. During the last 10 years, there has been an influx of other ethnic groups that has included a sizable number of Hispanics. Top management in the department is primarily filled by the Irish, and more and more Italians are assuming positions of advanced responsibility up to the position of captain, followed by Hispanics, who are assuming first-line supervisory and middle-management positions. As a relatively homogeneous group, until recent years, members of the workforce shared similar **values, attitudes, norms,** and social perspectives. Consensus was the rule rather than the exception, but this has changed, and officers are divided into three large ethnic groups. There is quite a bit of competition between the groups especially on promotional examinations and even intramural sports. A highly sought-after position is that of the departmental pistol team, and for the first time in history, some of the Irish members are being replaced. Also, each ethnic group has study groups to prepare officers for promotion. If there is a common denominator between the groups, it is in the pursuit of higher education, and there is a mind-set that a degree enhances one's ability to be looked upon

favorably. For the most part, most officers socialize with members of their own background and hold annual picnics, engage in athletic activities, and celebrate holidays together. With few exceptions, they are best described as closed groups. This ethnic divide has started to surface in the department, and many officers are becoming discontented and vocal about favoritism in assignment and the need for a change. In actuality, there has been an undercurrent of discontent for some time that has been focused on the Irish leadership.

Most police officers, unless they have achieved higher ranks that were made through promotions, strive to become a detective. Within the department, some 18 percent of the sworn officers are assigned to the Investigative Division out of 463 positions. Once an individual becomes an investigator, he or she usually remains in that division until retirement. It is a coveted position, and every one of the incumbents feels that they are the elite component of the department. The division receives considerable funding for external training in specialties ranging from the polygraph to managing informants. More recently, a number of the officers have received special training on homeland security and/or dealing with gangs. Most of the officers in this division are of Irish ancestry, in fact, 62 percent, followed by 28 percent who are Italian, and the remainders are Hispanic and a number of smaller ethnic groups.

The spotlight in the community is on crime and what is perceived as a general inability of the police department to handle the situation. Three recent incidents where innocent bystanders were shot because they were in the wrong place at the wrong time have caused segments of the community to focus on the police department, and this has resurrected a concern about ethnic relations in the department.

While there seems to be a minor gang problem, it has not focused on violence by weapons.

The compositions of the gangs in the community represent all three ethnic groups, and there has been an informal agreement between them to divide up the city and engage in activities that do not compete with each other. For the most part, the gangs function within their own neighborhoods, but conflict occurs when turf comes into question. If altercations occur between gangs, the conflict has been physical rather than the use of deadly force. So far most of the violence has been between gangs.

Based on the concept of groups and group dynamics, how would the chief explain this situation? How can one deal with groups? What could and should be done to make sure that any type of change is not just cosmetic? What specific things should be done to reduce the tensions in the department? Can this problem be addressed through additional training? Can assimilation be mandated? Why or why not?

Group-Shared Norms and Values

Based on meaningful interaction among members, groups formulate definitions of appropriate and inappropriate behavior. These definitions become normative standards by which all members of the group are judged. Social norms are group-generated, accepted, reinforced, and internalized expectations that are translated into informal as well as formal rules of conduct that guide human behavior in a given situation. **Norms** require (prescribe) or prohibit (proscribe) certain types of conduct, depending on the circumstances. Members of the group are rewarded if they conform to group-shared expectations and punished if they deviate from the group's **norms**. Virtually all of our actions are influenced by the **norms** of one group or another. Most of these have been internalized so thoroughly that people conform to them without being consciously aware that they are conforming. *Norms* are internalized in the subconscious and become part of our very existence.[55] **Norms** can ordinarily be categorized in terms of the intensity of the feeling, the extent of the social reaction, and the consequences (in terms of sanctions) generated when a group-shared expectation is violated. There are four basic types of social **norms**: (1) folkways, (2) mores, (3) **taboos**, and (4) laws.

Folkways

Folkways are customs, conventions, or traditions of **informal groups** that members tend to follow almost automatically. Police officers, for example, learn to use a unique job-related vocabulary. They are also expected to remain calm and collected even in highly stressful situations. Violation of a folkway normally elicits a relatively mild negative reaction from other members of the group.

Mores

Mores are the morally binding customs of a group. They are among the strongest norms and comprise the basic ethical behavioral judgments of a particular group. Mores represent those standards of behavior the violation of which elicits intense feelings and very serious consequences. Some mores are considered more important than others and are condemned much more strongly. While "blue coat" crime violates the mores of the average police officer, turning in the officer may be even more repugnant to a loyal group member who has been socialized to believe that maintaining "the code of silence" and supporting "the officers in blue" are more important than eliminating crime or corruption within the police department.

Taboos

Taboos represent an absolute prohibition against behavior so atrocious as to be almost unthinkable. **Taboos** are the strongest **norms**, and they elicit maximum consequences. Police work has its taboos—lack of courage, for example, or failure to back up an officer who is in danger and needs assistance. Those who break **taboos** may face ostracism by their group or their society; in extreme cases, they may be subject to criminal sanctions.

Laws

Laws have been defined as "customs in decay." They represent group-shared expectations that have been translated, for reasons that may or may not be evident, into state demands. The severity of group reaction is measured in terms of the behavior's classification as a summary offense, misdemeanor, felony, or capital crime. Within an organization, policies, procedures, rules, and regulations function as laws do in the world at large. The failure to abide by departmental policies, procedures, rules, and regulations elicits the imposition of sanctions ranging from an oral reprimand to involuntary termination of employment. Legitimate **norms** are also articulated in civil service legislation, police department accreditation standards, and the Law Enforcement Code of Ethics.

Although we have drawn distinctions among folkways, mores, **taboos**, and laws, it is important to note that the boundaries between these categories are somewhat arbitrary and often based on selective perception. In reality, **norms** fall on a continuum in terms of importance and social significance. They do not apply equally to every individual or group. **Norms** are produced through a dynamic interactive process and continue to change over time. They are best viewed as fluid, shifting guidelines for thinking and behavior.[56]

Group-generated shared **values** play a crucial role in the personal and professional lives of police personnel. **Values** are abstract and general beliefs about what is right, good, and desirable. **Values** are the heart and soul of a group; they provide the philosophical glue that holds the group together. **Values** are not specific rules for action, but general precepts to which people give allegiance and about which they have strong feelings. **Values** constitute a general guidance system for thinking and behaving. Interests, **attitudes, norms**, and behaviors originate in and are reflected by some value or set of **values**. The word "values" has a variety of meanings. In the most general sense, **values** are global beliefs concerning what is good (e.g., freedom, justice, the "American way") and what is bad (e.g., war, poverty, dishonesty). These **values** provide a cultural base for determining the appropriateness of our behavior (see Chapter 5 for an extended discussion of values).

From a managerial point of view, a value is an enduring belief that a specific mode of conduct or goal is preferable to others in a given set of circumstances. Paul Whisenand defines a value as a fairly stable yet changeable belief that a particular means to a particular end is preferred over the alternatives.[57] Since police officers have more than one value, managers must learn to think and to judge on-the-job behavior in terms of a *value system*.

A value system is a set of beliefs concerning preferred modes of conduct and goals in a hierarchical ranking of relative importance. A value system is a relatively permanent perceptual framework that influences and shapes the general character of each individual's behavior. People are what they value. They discipline themselves and interact with important others according to their personal value system. **Values** produce **attitudes** that generate and shape all purposeful human behavior. An attitude represents a state of mind that is focused on an object or event in an individual's psychological world. **Attitudes**, for police officers as well as other people, are a concrete manifestation of a person's basic **values**.[58] Fair treatment of a very unpopular minority-group subordinate, for example, is indicative of a commitment to administrative due process and fundamental fairness in the workplace. **Values** cut across specific situations to which **attitudes** are tied.

The Learning Process

While genetics shape broad patterns of human behavior, most value-related behavior is learned. People are exposed to and internalize **values** throughout life. The most intense learning takes place during the first 20 years and normally consists of three very distinct phases: (1) imprinting, (2) modeling, and (3) socialization.

Imprinting.

From a sociological point of view, the mind of each baby at birth is a tabula rasa, a blank slate. Through interaction with important others during the first six or seven years of life, babies learn by osmosis to react to and cope with the exigencies of life. Their personality is formed, setting the stage for virtually all their future mental, emotional, and social development. The principal actors in the **imprinting** process are parents and other members of the primary group who have a responsibility to nurture children so they can survive, thrive, and move toward far greater autonomy. The infrastructure of a person is the child as formed during these very critical years.

Modeling.

During the modeling phase (between ages 7 and 14), children begin to identify with, and pattern their behavior after, an expanding number of family members, peers, and heroes in the outside world. Group membership also begins to play a much more prominent role in their life; they identify with their group as a whole and with significant others within the group. As a result, new **values** and patterns of behavior are integrated with behavior learned through earlier **imprinting**. Children construct ego (based on information from a variety of sources) and try to measure the ideal. A child's value system is a composite produced by **imprinting** and modeling.

Socialization.

Between ages 14 and 20, social life is organized primarily in terms of friends. Peer influence reaches its zenith and meaningful interpersonal relationships center on common interests or activities. These young men and women spend a great deal of time defining and integrating the beliefs, standards, and **values** of peers into their own unique personalities. It is during this particular phase of the developmental process that young people achieve physical maturity and adopt a dominant value system. This value system is a guide for internal self-control and molds the individual's personality. Adolescence usually involves experimentation, verification, clarification, and validation of group-shared **values**.[59] Once a value system is in place, it serves as an internalized set of standards designed to guide human behavior in ambiguous situations.

The fourth phase is from about age 20 on and is identified as the paradigm. The value system that was developed during childhood and adolescence locks in and becomes the standard by which people determine what is good and what is bad in a given set of circumstances. While much of the socialization we experience occurs during childhood and adolescence, the inculcation of **norms, values**, and ethics continues throughout life. New police recruits are taught the **values** of the police profession and are expected to perform their duties in certain ways. Police officers are rewarded when they conform to group-shared expectations and exhibit appropriate **values**. They are punished when they fail to do so. **Values** activate, sustain, and legitimize human conduct.

Status in Groups

Social status is a very important concept in the study of group dynamics. Behavioral scientists point out that each person is involved in a complex web of social relationships. We all interact with other human beings in a variety of group settings. Social groups consist of a number of people whose relationships are based on a set of interrelated roles and statuses. They interact with each other in more or less standardized ways based on the **norms** and **values** they accept. They are united by a consciousness of kind and a similarity of interests that enable them to differentiate fellow group members from nonmembers.

In a very general sense, status refers to any position that is held within a group. It also refers to a person's position or rank in relation to other members of the work group. Status is a measure of worth (in terms of prestige or esteem) conferred on a person or position by a social group. Persons or positions with high status in a group are considered more valuable in certain respects than most of those to whom they are compared. Many have legitimate authority and real power in the organization of which the group is a part. They also have corresponding duties and responsibilities. This ranking is important because it contributes to the ordering of social interaction and structuring of social relationships. The complex array of roles and statuses that defines the behavior of individuals and specifies their relations with one another constitutes what social scientists call social organization and/or social structure.[60] A police department is a formal organization built on patterned regularity in behavior and interaction.

Few people or positions have universally high status in all situations. In fact, a high-status person or position in one group may have no status at all in another group setting. It is complicated because human beings belong to many groups and occupy different statuses simultaneously. According to behavioral scientists, much of our group-oriented behavior consists of acquiring, enhancing, and preserving social status.

Statuses are designations assigned to individuals and/or positions by the group. They emerge from the process of collective living and are normally broken down into two basic categories: (1) *ascribed status* and (2) *achieved status*. An ascribed status is derived from attributes over which individuals have no control (age, gender, and race) or from membership in groups to which they are assigned by others (family, religion, and nationality). Based on this ascribed status, the person is expected to acquire and perform certain socially defined roles. Achieved status, on the other hand, is the result of action taken by the individual. Achieved status is earned status. Candidates compete for status and are required to demonstrate that they have the ability to fulfill a particular role. Officially designated leaders, for example, are usually given the respect and esteem due a superior based on the authority inherent in their formal positions within their organizations. Natural leaders, regardless of their rank, earn the respect and esteem of their colleagues—often informally. They share power with followers as well as exercising power over them. Followers do willingly what their leaders ask of them. Ideally—but rarely—formal authority and real leadership come together in the police department's official chain of command. Behavioral scientists refer to this state of affairs as "status congruence."[61]

Group Culture

Social groups—including work groups—are produced by and reflect certain aspects of the culture in which they exist. Groups also create subcultural milieus of their own. **Culture** consists of all the knowledge, **values, attitudes, norms**, behavioral patterns, language, and artifacts that are passed from one generation to the next and form a way of life for those within the group. In the most general sense, culture is a way of life that defines appropriate modes of thinking, acting, and feeling. It exists because human beings are able to share their creations and pass knowledge on to subsequent generations. A common culture is the glue that holds any group together.

Culture is often referred to as the collective personality of the group. Work groups—like the police—develop a distinctive, at times unique, orientation. In fact, the police are frequently described as a culture within a culture.[62] Policing is a vocation somewhat isolated from the rest of American culture. The common knowledge, **values, attitudes, norms**, and behavioral patterns police officers share may help explain why efforts to reform police departments can arouse extensive opposition from the rank and file.

Police officers also share a common language or argot. There are strong bonds of loyalty and secrecy and a feeling of "us against them" among police personnel. Officers see themselves as "the thin blue line" or "the blue minority." The police academy is the first formal step in the socialization process and is designed to influence the police recruit's **values, attitudes**, and behaviors. Socialization is the process through which individuals learn proper ways of thinking, acting, and feeling in a particular **culture**. Academy training serves to separate trainees even further from the society. In addition, various on-the-job experiences provide for continued socialization that draws police officers more deeply into the police **subculture**.[63] The pillars on which that **subculture** is built are loyalty, solidarity, esprit de corps, and secrecy. While they do not seem to produce either job satisfaction or equitable law enforcement, they become an integral part of each police officer's working personality.[64]

Most police administrators have been promoted through the ranks. Their friends, colleagues, and on-the-job experiences have shaped their management styles and their approach to discipline, training, and supervision. Knowledge of **informal groups** and subcultural values, **norms**, and group dynamics will help ensure the success of contemporary police management. According to Edward Thibault and his colleagues, understanding the subcultural context within which police work takes place may be more important than all other knowledge and administrative skills combined.[65]

Group Dynamics

Group dynamics are those forces within the group that affect task performance and member satisfaction.[66] These dynamics are the same that occur during team development. The group process transforms resource inputs into group outputs. Effective police managers learn to harness and deploy the energy created as the result of positive group interaction. Work groups grow and mature just as individuals do. As groups begin to mature, members learn to understand and trust each other. They are better able to work together in making decisions and solving problems. There are six recognizable stages in the group (team) development process: orientation, conflict and challenge, cohesion, delusion, disillusion, and acceptance.[67]

Orientation (Stage 1)

This is a crucial stage if the group is to become a viable entity. The group formation begins with a consciousness of kind and/or recognition of common interests. Prospective members tentatively identify with a group and cautiously enter into a give-and-take relationship with incumbent members. They seek mutual acceptance and focus their attention on the tasks performed, the ways the group can satisfy their psychosocial needs, the ground rules for behavior, and the status a particular group or task has within the larger organization. They derive much of their initial impression of the group through subjective evaluation of the characteristics and behaviors of incumbent members.

Conflicts and Challenge (Stage 2)

Conflict and challenge can in some instances occur at the initial organizational meeting and as group development involves the process of getting a better feel for the **composition** of the group and for its assigned tasks.[68] New members learn how to do the job and what to expect in terms of need satisfaction. It is not uncommon for competition and conflict to emerge. Coalitions are often formed to work out strategies for doing the job or to enhance the chances for need satisfaction.[69] As members work together, they learn each other's strengths and weaknesses. Joint problem solving and group decision-making reinforce the team concept. In most cases, meaningful participation cements relationships and promotes efficiency, effectiveness, and participation. As a result, individual members are much more likely to invest their time, energy, effort, and expertise in psychologically satisfying and rewarding group-oriented activities.

Cohesion (Stage 3)

The cohesion stage of group development is the point at which everything comes together. Member motivation changes from primarily hedonistic (attempting to satisfy their own needs) to much more altruistic (internalizing the group's goals). There is a realization that the group can accomplish more as a unit than can individuals acting on their own. Consequently, there is an incentive for members to channel their individual efforts into group solidarity and teamwork. Members receive a psychological as well as a social payoff when they cooperate with each other, encourage others within the group to achieve their full potential, and create an environment in which goal achievement becomes a form of need satisfaction. Under these conditions, the group becomes a goal-oriented and cohesive social entity in which common **values, norms**, and ethical orientations regulate individual as well as **collective behavior**. At this stage, the individual member and the group find themselves in a state of dynamic equilibrium.[70]

Delusion (Stage 4)

The delusion stage of group development is the point where some degree of uncertainty occurs. It dawns on some members that things are not going the way they should as interpersonal problems arise. In some situations, some members will go along with an agenda just to get something done. Others will question what is being done and will disagree with the way things are being handled. Still others will decide that they cannot do anything about how things are being done and become passive. It is a stage when everything possible should be done to get through swiftly with a minimum of turmoil and disruption.

Disillusion (Stage 5)

At this point, members of a group become out of sort and begin to express that the group is going nowhere and faltering. In this stage, a member or two will become disruptive if things are not being done the way that they think they should be done.

Conflict occurs as members become polarized as some resist the group process, and there is a tendency for some to deal with personalities, not issues. It is a make it or break it point, and the leader of the group must become forceful in resolving conflict and not letting things get out of hand.

Acceptance (Stage 6)

In the last stage, the group matures and assumes the control function from other organizational entities and sets standards for regulating member behavior. Members seek to avoid anomie[71] (a sense of normlessness) and willingly submit to the will of the group as embodied in its **values, norms**, standards, and other mechanisms designed to guide behavior or ensure **conformity**. They tacitly agree to abide by informal rules and regulations designed to keep them performing successfully without surrendering their individual autonomy. The group controls itself, and individual members control themselves in an effort to benefit the rest of the group. According to Robert Fulmer, mature work groups tend to be self-regulating, self-motivating, and self-directing.[72] They take care of their own needs and are able to solve problems arising within the group. At the same time, mature groups seek to avoid **groupthink** and try to remain flexible enough to adapt to changing tasks and environmental factors.[73]

Work groups go through life cycles just like all other living organisms. At any given time, some new groups are just forming, while others are beginning to come together as distinct and identifiable entities. Some become fully integrated and reach the stage of dynamic equilibrium. While some groups achieve a degree of stability and permanence based on their maturity, others lose their capacity to change and they move toward extinction. Police administrators need to understand the life cycle of groups so they can harness a group's energy and make the adjustments necessary to increase its efficiency, effectiveness, and productivity.

Within a group goal-oriented human beings learn relevant knowledge, job skills, and appropriate behaviors. Members interact with one another and communicate their mutual expectations concerning exactly how work is to be performed. Membership in the work group gives participants the opportunity to model correct behaviors, provide instruction or technical assistance to neophytes, and exchange evaluative feedback about job performance. Group members are in a position to exert a direct influence on each other's beliefs and/or predispositions concerning work and how it is to be done. They are in a unique position to encourage interdependence and accomplish work.[74] Functional work groups also provide members with security, emotional support, and an in-group perspective. They give members a sense of identity (vis-à-vis their work) and the opportunity for ego involvement in mutually satisfying activities. An effective work group is multidimensional in that it achieves high levels of task performance and human resource maintenance over a protracted period of time.[75]

Human Relations and Management

The human relations school of management and the organizational humanists (discussed in Chapters 3 and 5) emphasize the importance of group dynamics in task performance and human resource maintenance. The human relations movement can be traced back to two pioneering studies that were conducted during the mid-1920s at the Hawthorne Works of the Western Electric Company. The study produced concrete evidence that work groups and work-group participation have a direct influence on individual productivity. Elton Mayo and his colleagues discovered that social variables—like interaction patterns, supervisory styles, and work-group pressure to raise or lower production—played a key role in determining how much effort employees within a particular work group were willing to expend. In one case, these factors operated to increase overall productivity; in the other, they acted to restrain it. In both instances, however, the research team concluded that insight into job performance could be obtained by paying attention to important aspects of human behavior.[76]

Some theorists have a totally negative view of the human relations approach to management. They base this attitude on one or the other of two basic assumptions: (1) social groups do not really exist or (2) groups exist but are a bad thing. Others, such as orga-nizational humanists and group dynamists, take an exactly opposite view. Social groups exist in all complex goal-oriented organizations, theorists say; their reality is demonstrated by the difference it makes to individuals whether they are accepted or rejected by social groups and whether their work groups are healthy or unhealthy. The pro-group theorists also argue that groups are good, because they satisfy deep-seated needs of employees for **affiliation**, affection, recognition, and self-esteem. Group membership promotes al-truism, loyalty, and a sense of belonging; cooperative interaction enables human beings to achieve objectives they could not accomplish by themselves. One researcher found that the theory of cooperation and competition can be useful for identifying the social processes that help **teams** grapple with problems and work effectively.[77] There are even some pro-group extremists who believe that everything can and should be done by and in groups. They contend that individual responsibility, person-to-person supervision, and even individual problem solving are bad.

Dorwin Cartwright and Ronald Lippit reject the assumption that individual and group interests are incompatible and have challenged it with five assertions about indi-viduals, groups, and group dynamics:[78]

1. *Work groups are real.* They are a natural part of the social backdrop. There is dramatic evidence—from a wide variety of different sources—to show that work-group decisions are often more successful in producing substantive and durable changes in human behavior than are methods dealing with people as isolated individuals.

2. *Work groups are omnipresent and inevitable.* Human beings are animals with an instinc-tive need to interact with one another in a group-generated milieu built around communication and supportive interpersonal relationships. People are incapable of living in geographical proximity without forming groups and/or rewarding group participation in one way or another.

3. *Work groups mobilize powerful synergistic forces that produce effects most important to people.* Members' roles in groups affect how others behave toward them and how they feel about themselves. Group membership can be a blessing or a curse. People have been traumatized both by exclusion from work groups and by enforced membership in work groups. It is also clear that events within a group can have repercussions on others—members and nonmembers—not directly involved in the events.

4. *Work groups may produce both good and bad consequences.* The assumption that groups are completely good or bad is likely to lead to selective perception, tunnel vision, and research that tend to be ideological rather than scientific. Groups are multidi-mensional, and their value always depends on the situation.

5. *The desirable consequences resulting from work-group interaction can be deliberately enhanced.* Through knowledge gained by researchers into group dynamics theory, managers—including police administrators—can help make work groups more efficient, effective, and productive. (It should be noted that some behavioral scien-tists find this a cause for ethical concern; they are reminded of the kinds of social manipulation explored in George Orwell's chilling novel *1984*.)

Work groups play a critically important role in attitude formation and provide mem-bers with a repertoire of appropriate skills to do the job. Work-group standards (based on shared values) become the gauge by which to measure individual performance. While standards may be articulated by management, they are normally internalized by employees via the socialization process. Socialization is designed to promote overall uniformity in thought and action based on the group's **values, norms,** and **ethical orientation**. This emphasis on the work group—as opposed to the individual—leads to a tendency on the part of work-group members to change their opinions to conform with significant oth-ers in the group, to change the opinions of others, and to redefine the boundaries of the group to exclude those individuals holding deviant points of view. The collective suc-cess of any work group will have a direct impact on the job performance of individual members.

Collaboration

There is ample evidence to demonstrate that when individuals work cooperatively rather than competitively, the work group's **cohesiveness** increases, and the work itself better meets employee needs. Research suggests that both cooperation and group cohesion have a positive influence on an individual's productivity. D. W. Johnson and his colleagues examined the findings of 120 studies designed to evaluate individual productivity in terms of three prevailing reward structures:[79]

1. *Cooperative reward structure.* Goal attainment by each member facilitates goal attainment by others within the work group.
2. *Competitive reward structure.* Goal attainment by one member blocks the attainment of goals by other work-group members.
3. *Individual reward structure.* Goal attainment by one member is unrelated to the activities of other members.

In most cases, cooperation yielded higher levels of work-group productivity than competition or individual efforts. This is a much more important factor in small work groups than in large work groups and when members work interdependently rather than independently.

Creating a Winning Team

A working definition of a team has to be expanded beyond that provided earlier in the chapter, and it suggests a high degree of interdependence wherein members focus on achievement of a goal/objective, and this is usually accomplished through the completion of a task. At the same time, there is an overlapping between a group and a team depending upon the situational factors that are present.

Work Groups versus Teams

A significant difference from a group is that a team had a considerable degree of self-management and autonomy, and normally they have the authority to assess progress and actual performance. The end result is what counts. The leadership in a work group is resilient and clearly focused in contrast to a team that has a tendency to function with a shared leadership role. In terms of accountability, the work group emphasizes individual accountability, while the team stresses mutual accountability as well as individual accountability. Also, the work group deals with individual work units, while the team produces a collective work product. A group leader has the tendency to run a very efficient meeting with a timetable and an agenda, while the true team leader functions best in an open-ended discussion and an active problem-solving process. Additionally, the group leader discusses, renders a decision, and, if needed, delegates in contrast to a team leader who works with members in an effort to arrive at a workable decision. Finally, the team leader measures performance based on a collective work product, and the group leader is seen as measuring effectiveness based on the degree of influence over others. Effective team leaders have proven to be those who can recognize and contribute to a decisive group process.

Types of Teams

Within law enforcement there are various types of teams, and some of them bear a great deal of similarity to varying types of groups. At the pinnacle of the organizational pyramid is the **command group** that is responsible for the development of the mission of the organization as well as vision and core value statements. Each of these is discussed in detail in Chapter 14. Their overview of an agency is to look at the "big picture." There are also **task groups** (project teams) that are created by management, and such a team is given a specific assignment such as determining the type of firearm that should be used by sworn officers. Membership in such a project team is based on expertise and experience, and generally such an entity is given a specific date, within which time a complete report has to be submitted to management. The role of a project team is to recommend and serve in an advisory capacity. A third type of team is **cross-functional**, and it has been found to be useful in breaking down barriers in hierarchical agencies that have existed for an extended period of time. For the most part, these agencies have a long history of division of labor, and in some instances, mayor divisions function independently. With the creation of such a team with representatives from different divisions, the team is charged with working to improve operations. The final team is **self-directed**. It can apply to any of the earlier named teams. It is a self-starting team and given a great deal of discretion, and it determines its own time schedule and reporting requirements. In some instances, it will require special training in order to enhance its potential for achievement. Training could include such topics as team problem solving, goal setting, conflict resolution, measurement tools, or other topics that will facilitate accomplishment.

Research suggests that a team leader is an individual who has developed the capacity to persuade and motivate others to achieve objectives and goals. This type of team leader is easily identifiable because they have demonstrated the capacity to work with a group of officers and transform them into a cohesive, dynamic, and hard-charging productive work group. A positive team climate comes into existence because the leader demonstrates clear-cut skills, presents a convincing attitude, provides guidance in establishing priorities, and achieves goal attainment. Officers readily respond to explicit and persuasive communications, positive directions, specific directed coaching, and empowerment as needed. A successful team leader gains cooperation and commitment from others, excels at building consensus, shares power and responsibility, and maintains rapport with team members.

This suggests that a team leader has to perform in many different ways. This includes being a mentor, counselor, and, above all, a trainer. At the same time, one cannot ignore being a constructive facilitator and working diligently at developing team members. This is a tall order and most demanding, but the rewards are many as the team leader sees members develop and grown into decisive contributors. As much energy as possible should be directed to creating a team that has the attributes of being viable, focused, and cohesive. When this happens, team members will value their membership in the team and become advocates. As a consequence, team objectives are more easily attained. With cohesive enhancement, members become more open in their communication as well as more receptive to team needs and the group process, and they rely less on their own personal status within the group.

With the emergence of trust and a shift to empowerment, the foundation is laid for realistic teamwork. This becomes evident as there is a creation of a working environment that as a minimum supports diverse perspectives, approaches and opinion, fairness, self-esteem, empathy, and creativeness. The process of building a team involves a great deal more than just applying a few chosen techniques. It is a complex process and requires the dual efforts of the team leader and its members. It is a learning course of action, and members must become skilled at how to become a viable team member, and early on it should be acknowledged that it is an ongoing process, not just a one-shot occurrence. An effective team leader is one who influences and persuades by communication, directing, coaching, and delegating, as the situation dictates. It is no longer just giving orders but providing direction and guidance. It is a time for coaching, sharing, and training and actually leading team members and moving away from micro-management. Today's team leaders will become successful if they consider and respond to member's needs, feeling, and capabilities.

Team building involves recognizing and contributing to group processes and working to establish group identity, foster team spirit, and create a healthy environment that allows for the eventual development of shared decision-making. Experience has shown us that effective team leaders exhibit a number of readily identifiable behaviors that are set forth in Table 11–5.

A team leader who exhibits the aforementioned characteristics will be well on the way to supervising an effective team. If any of these characteristics are missing, it can result in a less-than-adequate team performance. Over time, officers working as a team will begin to exhibit shared **values** based on trust that is the cornerstone of a positively functioning team. Slowly and surely, members of a team will begin to value cooperation, become committed, and realize the importance of collaboration. As a group of officers

> **Table 11–5**
> **CHARACTERISTICS OF AN EFFECTIVE TEAM LEADER**
>
> 1. Creates a shared vision of the team.
> 2. Creates a working environment that encourages creative thinking and innovation.
> 3. Facilitates open communications.
> 4. Actively participates but does not dominate team meetings.
> 5. Assists team members in developing themselves.
> 6. Recognizes efforts of team members.
> 7. Demonstrates sensitivity to cultural differences.
> 8. Constantly focuses on team objectives.
> 9. Interrelates with other departmental units and reports the results to team members.
> 10. Projects high expectation.

grow, they will accept divergent opinions and become more risk prone. Once officers feel they are part of the team and have developed a feeling that they really belong and can make a difference and growth opportunities are evident, the maturity of the team will reach a level where team members will feel empowered. Unfortunately, some teams do not reach this level because they have not been given the tools of shared power and responsibility or the means to achieve task assignments. When team members are given the opportunity to influence the work environment, astonishing things can happen. They suddenly realize that they are no longer just a cog in a wheel. Given the chance, a dedicated officer will accept a working environment that allows for commitment to the work team and will eventually exercise self-management and self-control.[80]

Interesting things occur when a team becomes fully functional. One can see that authority emanates from knowledge rather than rank or position. Decision-making and participation become localized and based on enhanced knowledge and the skills of individual members, and the working environment becomes results oriented. Observers of such a team immediately see the commitment and loyalty of the members and the resulting trust. Team vitality is clearly evident, and team members are given an opportunity to achieve and develop. Contributions are acknowledged, and rewards extended for teamwork and collaboration. Finally, there is a focus on performance that allows team members to commit to each other, and the team development process becomes ongoing.[81]

Teamwork that will result in a winning team comes to pass because of the hard work involved in understanding the behavior of team members and the leader. The team leader must strive to create a team wherein each officer accepts and promotes the four Cs of team membership that are as follows:[82]

1. Collaborate
2. Conform
3. Contribute
4. Cooperate

First, there must be a motivation to collaborate with another team member on a creative concept and not consider who receives recognition for the idea. In a truly functioning team effort, it is immaterial who receives accolades, no matter the type, because the real reward is in the accomplishment.

Next, it is essential that each member of a team have the willingness to conform and work toward the achievement of each and every team decision. This means that every team member must carry his or her own weight, the team leader must work diligently to ensure **conformity**, recalcitrant members must be dealt with, and a truly nonconformist should be removed from the team. It is also essential that team members contribute skills to problem solving and not hold back for personal or self-interest reasons. Lastly, cooperation is essential. The interests of the team are more important that individual interest. When the four Cs are fulfilled, tasks are completed with enthusiasm, self-discipline, and minimal supervision.

The concept of community policing adds a new dimension that challenges the leadership style and management in law enforcement agencies because the group concept has been expanded to encompass members of the community. It is necessary to include civic officials or their representatives, businesses, members of the public, and providers of social services. Officers who are engaged in community-oriented policing and problem solving must work with those who are affected by problems as a means of problem resolution. With citizen input concerning the needs of the community, a new role was created for residents as well as police officers. When the City of Chicago implemented its Chicago Alternative Policing Strategy (CAPS), it started with several police districts before expanding its program to the entire patrol division. Then as the result of reorganizations, the city was divided into 279 beats. Each beat had nine or ten officers and they were supervised by a sergeant. Each supervisor was charged with leading quarterly team meetings that involved officers from every shift. This territorial orientation provided for the following:

1. The assignment of an officer to beat where a partnership could develop with community residents and problems could be addressed.
2. Officers were allowed to work with the community and reduce the time they spent on answering service calls.
3. Officers were given an opportunity to know their beat to include hot spots, crime trends, and community resources.[83]

The implementation of this program was not without difficulty because of the high percentage of 911 calls. Efforts to resolve this problem resulted in shifting calls to free-roving rapid-response teams, but that never really solved the problem. Over the years, there have been several efforts to revitalize the program, but there are still difficulties such as allowing officers to spend more than 30 percent of their time in preventive activities. Supervisors are responsible for correct mistaken assignments and allowing officers to remain in a community-policing mode, but that is still a goal that has not been attained. Change is difficult, and Chicago should be commended for their past and current efforts to deal with a difficult problem.

Influences on Work-Group Behavior

Clearly, people's performance in work group or team settings is influenced by a number of factors. These include the task, the work environment, the maturity level, ambient stimuli (related to membership), and discretionary stimuli (such as social acceptance, rejection, and communication). Other relevant variables include **complexity**, **need orientation**, **size**, **composition**, **norms**, **cohesiveness**, and **groupthink**.

Complexity

Simple tasks ordinarily place fewer demands on the work-group process than tasks that require greater knowledge (technical and other) or social skills. As the overall complexity of tasks increases, it usually becomes more difficult for members of a work group to achieve a productive balance between quantity and quality. Members must distribute their efforts more broadly on increasingly complex tasks that require greater interdependence, cooperation, and coordination. If the work-group process does not adjust to these demands, individual performance will begin to suffer, with a concomitant reduction in job satisfaction. Conversely, if work-group members are competent, have needs that are in sync with those of the organization, and can work collaboratively with each other, job satisfaction and performance will tend to increase as the complexity of the task increases. Whether complexity has a negative or a positive effect on the job performance of individual officers will depend on the situation as well as the collective attributes of those involved.

Need Orientation

Work group members with conflicting needs march to different drummers. The willingness of one individual to exert an effort voluntarily on behalf of the group is always contingent on a variety of factors. A key element in the functioning of a work group is the degree to which there is interpersonal compatibility—based on needs—among its members. William C. Schutz developed his "fundamental interpersonal orientation" theory of behavior more than 40 years ago.[84] It is designed to help explain how people orient themselves to each other based on how strongly they need to express and receive feelings of inclusion, affection, and control. Those with a need for inclusion strive for prominence, recognition, and prestige. People with a need for affection manifest it in friendliness and the desire to seek emotional bonding with others in the group. Members with a need to control have a tendency to rebel against those with authority; they resist being controlled by others and refuse to be compliant or submissive. Work groups in which members have reciprocal and compatible needs are usually more efficient, effective, and productive than those that are plagued by incompatibilities. Work-group members who are motivated by very different or conflicting needs are much less likely to work well together.

Antagonistic needs, drives, aspirations, and goals hinder collaboration and have a negative influence on the performance of the work group itself and the individuals within it. Symptoms of these debilitating incompatibilities include widespread apathy, open hostility, struggles for control, poor job performance, lowered productivity, and domination of the group by a few powerful and politically adroit members who operate on the "divide and conquer" principle.

Size

Formal and informal work groups vary greatly in **size**, as we have seen, but most that maximize interaction have fewer than ten members. One approach to the analysis and understanding of behavior in work groups focuses on activities (what each member does), interactions (communication between members individually or between members and the group as a collective entity), and sentiments (personal and group shared and reinforced **values, attitudes**, beliefs, and feelings).[85]

As the **size** of a particular work group increases, competing forces are unleashed and the number of potential relationships increases geometrically. These changes may foster better performance or make things worse. On the positive side, an increase in work-group **size** increases the human resources available. It may also bring in additional skills that can help accomplish assigned tasks more efficiently and effectively. Finally, expanding the work group may make it more representative of the department and thus could offer greater opportunities for **affiliation** and meaningful participation. On the downside, any real growth in **size** increases the potential for problems in communication, coordination, and quality control. Expansion may require the imposition of a more formal work-**group structure** (well-defined tasks, roles, and statuses), which may in turn make individual members more inhibited and less productive. If the work group gets so large that its internal interactions can no longer be conducted primarily face-to-face, some of its (human and financial) resources will have to be shifted from task achievement to maintenance functions. The complexity of the coordination problems that must be resolved before a work group can achieve its full potential tends to increase faster than **size**. It is very difficult to attain and maintain optimum motivation, morale, performance, and productivity as more and more people join the work group. According to John Schermerhorn and his colleagues, larger work groups suffer some real disadvantages in terms of individual performance and group effectiveness.[86] Many of these problems can be overcome in law enforcement through proactive management of the process.

Composition

Job performance, effectiveness, and group dynamics are all influenced to one degree or another by the demographic, professional, and psychosocial characteristics of individual members. In order to fulfill their roles and take advantage of their competencies (such as intelligence, maturity, motivation, personality, technical skill, and physical ability), individuals must be capable of functioning in a work-group setting. This is extremely important because the performance of an individual member can be greatly enhanced or restricted—deliberately or unintentionally—by other members.

Homogeneous work groups are composed of members who have similar backgrounds, **interests**, **values**, **attitudes**, and other traits. Successful heterogeneous groups, on the other hand, tend to accept and thrive on diversity. Open work groups tend by nature to be heterogeneous. They bring a wide variety of skills and perspectives to bear on problems. This diversity can, at times, lead to competition, conflict, and a lack of direction. Closed work groups are much more homogeneous. Homogeneity produces common goals and increases the likelihood that there will be relatively harmonious working relationships among group members. Due to their innate similarities, it is easy for individual members to buy into the group's culture. **Conformity** to work group–shared **values**, **norms**, and **ethical orientations** becomes the rule rather than the exception.

In spite of government-mandated equal employment opportunity and affirmative action hiring programs, the police profession usually functions near the closed-group end of the continuum. The selection process is designed to identify men and women who possess an affinity for membership in the informal culture as well as the formal organization. According to Jerome Skolnick and Thomas Gray, affinity represents a predisposition to adhere to a distinctive set of sentiments that can be expanded and reinforced through training and socialization.[87] Affinity is the operative concept used to separate those who are technically qualified to become police officers from those who will probably be able to absorb the requirements of the legal system, the formal police organization, and the police subculture.

Managers must exercise judgment in selecting human resources in order to create a healthy balance between homogeneity and heterogeneity. Individual performance and work-group productivity are directly related to the degree of fit experienced by those involved in a collective enterprise. Police work is undergoing a fundamental transition. It is in the process of moving away from resisting and fearing individual differences and moving toward accepting and utilizing them. The more diverse the membership, the more skilled an administrator must be in reconciling individual differences and managing group dynamics.

Norms

As defined earlier, **norms** are guidelines for accepted and expected social behavior that are inculcated in an individual's subconscious mind through the socialization process. They reflect work group–shared ideas about how individual members are supposed to behave inside and outside the group. Work-group **norms** not only regulate formal and informal relationships between members of the workforce but also control the overall quantity and quality of the work itself. Socialization is a dynamic process whereby the culture of the group is transmitted from one generation of workers to another through the socialization process. New members learn to identify with, model, internalize, and derive intrinsic social satisfaction from **conformity** with the **values**, **norms**, and ethical standards of the group.

As the result of socialization, the police officer develops a distinct consciousness of kind, a self-concept, and a reaffirmation of personal worth expressed in terms of approval and support.[88] Work groups exert a strong influence on the behavior of their members by providing them with security, support, encouragement, and positive reinforcement for appropriate behavior. Work groups also punish those members who deviate from their group-shared expectations. They use ridicule, shame, and the threat of expulsion to elicit **conformity**.[89]

Virtually every aspect of a police officer's behavior is regulated by **norms**. As a result, the **norms** of the work group determine what is to be done, how it is to be accomplished, who is to do it, and how much value it has to the group as a whole.

Cohesiveness

Some work groups are much more cohesive than others. Used in this context, **cohesiveness** is regarded as a characteristic of a group in which all of the forces acting on members to remain in the group are greater than those forces acting on them to leave it. According to Robert Albanese, cohesive forces—those holding a work group together and strengthening interpersonal relationships among members—can be grouped into two very basic categories: (1) those that positively influence the achievement of personal goals and (2) those that satisfy group members' needs for meaningful and supportive interaction with important others in the group.[90] In a best-case scenario, there will be congruence between organizational needs (for efficiency, effectiveness, and productivity) and members' needs (for belongingness, achievement, meaningful participation, and recognition) within a dynamic, synergistic, and hospitable social milieu.

Police officers find themselves in closed and relatively cohesive work groups. They work under hazardous and stressful conditions that draw them into a kind of brotherhood.[91] Confronted with the demands of the public, expectations of administrators, and pressures from their peers, police officers find themselves caught up in a web of insecurity, confusion, and frustration. Since it is almost impossible to resolve these personal dilemmas on their own, they identify with the group and cultivate its support by strengthening interpersonal relationships with other officers. As the police have become more occupationally cohesive, their bonds with the public have grown weaker. In some instances, these two groups have polarized and treat each other as adversaries.[92]

Most police officers have now adopted the attitude that "No one can understand me but another cop." Recruits are screened and selected based on how well they will fit the police mold. They are then very carefully socialized to internalize the **values, norms**, and **ethical orientations** of the work group. At this point, they become full-fledged members of the police subculture. They think, behave, and operate by the same rationale as their colleagues. **Cohesiveness** and performance are directly related in several ways: (1) the successful performance of group tasks can increase cohesiveness, (2) even failure can lead to **cohesiveness** in a threatening or win–lose situation, and (3) **cohesiveness** can produce an increase in individual and/or group performance. The highest levels of performance are normally found in highly cohesive groups that value productivity and have established uniformly high-performance **norms**.[93] On the other side of the coin, **cohesiveness** can have a negative effect on performance if there is a conflict between organizational objectives and group members' needs. A high level of **cohesiveness** coupled with low-performance goals promotes low performance. Under these circumstances, both individuality and innovation are discouraged.[94]

The police **subculture** is viable and has a strong influence on police agencies. These **norms** exert a strong influence over the individual conduct of officers, and it does not take long for a new officer to learn what acceptable behavior is. **Norms** come into existence as the result of group interaction. It is readily apparent that police departments meticulously demand a strong degree of loyalty. Rigid departmental rules and regulations reinforce the institutionalization of loyalty, and any nonconformist will be treated as a nonentity formally as well as informally.

Interaction between officers conveys the need to reinforce the "code of silence," and it is always a reality and pervasive. When the "code of secrecy" is coupled with "the code of silence," an officer should not inform on another officer even in cases of corruption. In some instances, this will lead to falsify records or perjury themselves. A fellow officer is never turned in to the administration for sloppy police work, not performing duties, or failing to respond to a call for services. When a group is exceptionally cohesive, it is possible for tolerance levels to control productivity. In many instances, the police **subculture** is out of step with the **norms** of society. Such variables as solidarity, esprit de corps, and isolation tend to socialize police officers and reinforce the police subculture. It is clear that the culture of law enforcement is deep seeded and can control every aspect of police work. Other reinforcers include a common argot of the field as well as a legalistic language. **Taboos**, while not extensive, include the absolute necessity of never being allowed to show fear and above all one should be courageous no matter how dangerous the situation.[95]

Groupthink

Groupthink has become one of the most influential concepts in the behavioral sciences.[96] As just described, group **cohesiveness** is the degree to which individuals desire and are motivated to maintain their affiliation with a group. **Cohesiveness** can be a double-edged sword. Although it can have a very positive effect on performance, too much cohesiveness can become pathological. It discourages individuality, critical thinking, and innovation. **Groupthink** is a common characteristic of excessively cohesive groups. Loyalty to the group (in terms of its **values, norms**, and subcultural perspectives) becomes the most powerful group-shared expectation. Any behavior—from the inside or the outside—that harms the group or diminishes its solidarity is viewed as divisive, illegitimate, and very unacceptable. It can reach the point where the members' strivings for unanimity override a realistic appraisal of other courses of action.[97] **Conformity** and consensus replace analysis. It becomes "us" versus "them." "Them" refers to anyone outside of the group, even if that person has legitimate authority and administrative responsibility related to the group's function. **Groupthink** can foster the belief of invulnerability.

Groupthink is a real hazard in police work. It is nourished by an obsession with loyalty, solidarity, esprit de corps, dependability, and secrecy. Many police officers are willing to tolerate incompetence, corruption, brutality, and "bluecoat" crime rather than to "blow the whistle" or "hang dirty linen in public." They openly resist civilian control and have deep-seated antipathy for whistle-blowers, internal affairs personnel, civilian review boards, and those officers who are induced to break "the code." Police managers must be alert to the following symptoms of groupthink:[98]

1. A false impression of invulnerability.
2. Pressure against those who deviate from the majority viewpoint.
3. Fear of being penalized for deviating from the majority viewpoint.
4. A shared false impression of unanimity and consensus.
5. A perception of outsiders as wicked, unintelligent, or feeble.
6. An unquestioned belief in the principles of the in-group.
7. The presence of self-appointed "mind guards" who shield the leader and other group members from information contrary to the party line.
8. The screening of negative feedback to the group.

There are a number of classic cases of **groupthink** that clearly illustrate the pitfalls in the process. Sociologists and psychologists studied the NASA space shuttle challenger disaster that exploded shortly after takeoff in 1986, and there was a tragic loss of several astronauts including the initial "Teacher in Space." The launch date for the satellite was delayed because of engineering problems, but agency scientists were adamant about launching. A number of misjudgments and an inadequate evaluation of the risks coupled with the fact that Congress was considering funding NASA led to the disaster. The scientists viewed themselves as invulnerable and ignored warnings from some scientists. Without question, this is an established case of **groupthink**.[99]

A more recent case occurred in the last Iraq War. Data from the Clinton administration were used by the Bush administration on what proved to be false grounds that Saddam Hussein was reconstituting nuclear weapons, had biological weapons and mobile biological weapon production facilities, and had stockpiled and was producing chemical weapons. The prevailing view of things was accepted, decisions were rationalized, and there was a completed belief in the in-group. Outside information was ignored and unanimity prevailed. The weapons did not exist.[100]

Conformity is a natural and normal aspect of group dynamics. Conformity becomes pathological when it manifests itself in **groupthink** and has a negative effect on individual performance as well as work-group productivity.

Accepting and Managing Work Groups

The traditional Theory X (autocratic) approach to management is slowly but surely giving way to the kind of participative self-management that McGregor called Theory Y.[101] Experienced administrators understand that groups and the group process are a new part of the landscape in police work. They know that without the group's energy, effort, expertise, and support, the chances of achieving the organization's mission, goals, and objectives are slim. The division of labor and task specialization associated with work in law enforcement organizations places a premium on cooperation, collaboration, and coordination in the workplace. Purposeful interaction and synergy provide an impetus for productivity. A lack of healthy group involvement and support is a kiss of death in those situations requiring **collective behavior**. Successful administrators see the management of group dynamics as a critical variable in effective task accomplishment. Consequently, they spend a great deal of their time in group development and maintenance. They seek to identify and resolve those problems that make the work group dysfunctional. It is their job to dismantle the barriers that obstruct intergroup as well as intra-group communication, neutralize destructive conflict, and encourage all members to become active participants in the group process.

Participatory management evolved from the concept of organizational humanism espoused by some members of the human relations school of management. It consists of a proactive and integrated strategy designed to increase organizational productivity, as well as individual satisfaction, by giving members of the workforce a substantive role in the decision-making process. Members of the work group are permitted (within the parameters established by management) to establish their own goals and to achieve these goals through a collaborative effort. Once this participatory group process is set in motion, administrators can garner much-needed support by allowing work groups to function with minimum intervention. Under these circumstances, managers assume a different role. They do less directing and more coordinating. They help guide and give substance to the group process by serving as resource persons, role models, teachers, and coaches. Modern police administrators are expected to convert the work group's synergistic effort into productive outputs.[102]

Skillful police administrators utilize their knowledge of groups and group dynamics to meet human needs as well as to motivate their immediate subordinates. They know that membership in a goal-oriented group tends to enhance the satisfaction, performance, and productivity of its members in relatively ambiguous and unstructured situations where they exercise a great deal of discretion. Ethical managers avoid using the group process to manipulate police personnel. They view employees as good and are committed to confirming them as whole persons. Ethical police administrators oppose game playing and cultivate genuine collaboration. They build supportive relationships with individuals and groups based on mutual respect and trust. Mutual respect and trust are part of the glue that holds any productive enterprise together.

Managerial Strategies

Richard W. Plunkett has identified seven basic principles he believes managers should follow in order to minimize a work group's tensions and conflicts.[103] He felt this would maximize the group's performance, cooperation, collaboration, coordination, and contribution to the organization:

1. Accept the existence of groups, subgroups, and cliques as a fact of organizational life. These **informal groups** are allies to be won over and brought to bear on common problems. A manager must work with these groups, not oppose them.

2. Identify informal leaders and seek their cooperation. They have to be reckoned with. The power they possess can be valuable when resolving organizational problems. Informal leaders often recognize the advantage of cooperation and try to avoid conflict. Informal leaders have a strong influence with followers and other informal leaders. They know the opinions and **attitudes** of their group and represent them when communicating with management.

3. Thwart intergroup rivalry and win–lose situations. Establish achievable standards. Stress—through word and deed—the importance of cooperation and teamwork. Treat all subordinates fairly, without regard to their group, subgroup, or clique affiliation. Ask for input from all groups and, when appropriate, integrate it into the decision-making process.

4. Do not compel people to choose between you and their group. If a manager backs them into a corner, demanding an "either/or" choice, they will usually pick the group. Loyalty to and membership in a subgroup or clique is not necessarily a negative. Members can serve both the organization and the group if their goals are harmonious. People can be loyal and unopposed to a manager as long as that manager is fair, predictable, and loyal.

5. Adopt a mentor's mind-set toward all groups, subgroups, and cliques. Team spirit and camaraderie are the trademarks of **informal groups** that must be cultivated. Be firm, play fair, and demand that subordinates reciprocate. Team players know the value of rules and fair play. Enlist meaningful participation from the groups and allow them to enhance their sense of worth.

6. Appeal to individual group members and to each group's sense of capability. All members have a need to be good at what they do and to know how they are viewed by others. Give people objectives that, when met, will instill a sense of accomplishment, confidence, and pride. By setting organizational objectives and helping subordinates set their own goals, administrators motivate employees to excel and find ways in which to build confidence and self-respect. Point out how poor performance hurts others and makes everyone's job much more difficult.

7. Use the traditional and not-so-traditional levers to encourage cooperation. Levers are tools used to influence people in specific situations. Management levers such as job assignments, overtime, primary action, merit pay, and sincere praise may be effective. Most of them are effective if they are used when subordinates trust and respect the manager. Trust and respect are by-products of the manager's knowledge, ability (technical, interpersonal, and group), skills, and demonstrated concern for the group and its members.

This is a tall order to fill. While it is very difficult to deal effectively with groups, subgroups, and cliques in the workplace, managing groups and group processes now consumes a lion's share of the police administrator's time.

CASE STUDY   Officer Robert Gonzalez

Officer Gonzalez joined a big city police department six years ago. He was a high school graduate from a middle-class family in a small town. His parents spoke Spanish, English, and French, and he was fluent in all three languages. His first six months in the department (after the academy) was an eye-opener and somewhat of a cultural shock. At first he was lost, and he had some difficulty in adjusting to the lifestyles of a big city. It soon became apparent that the police had bonds of loyalty and secrecy and that there was a general feeling of "us against them." He found that he was part of a subculture that demanded a high level of esprit de corps and solidarity. It was soon apparent that the officers he worked with viewed themselves as the "thin blue line." His fellow officers that were in his academy class came from varying backgrounds, and most of them had lived in metropolitan areas all of their lives. They shared diverse values, attitudes, and perspectives. Slowly but surely the officers felt the need to belong and assimilated the new subculture, and in relatively short time, they became comfortable interacting with one another. They became a source of mutual support to each other.

Robert Gonzalez, like most of his peers, started out slowly and was somewhat overawed by the total process, but in time he began to think, act, and feel like a cop. He wanted to be a good cop. His goals were to preserve the peace and to protect people and society from criminals. Gonzalez placed a relatively high value on individual rights and due process of law. He really wanted to protect and serve, but with the reality of the street and the social status that he sought, within the group, he quickly accepted the norms and values of his peers and of his field training officers (FTO). Gonzalez was a good candidate for the socialization process and quickly learned the importance of going along with the flow. The taboos were readily apparent such as failure to back up an officer who is in danger and above all exhibit bravery in the face of danger or suffer the consequences and be ostracized by the group. Gonzalez also learned that his immediate sergeant would be the most important in his life while working. This proved to be especially true during the two-year probationary period.

After three years in the patrol division, Officer Gonzalez was reassigned. He was placed in a Joint Gang Task Force, which consisted of 26 investigators and 1 supervisor from 6 jurisdictions who formed a tightly knit work group. This was a group that was just organized, and he wanted to become a full-fledged member of the group.

It consisted of a homogeneous and cohesive group of bilingual people who identified with each other and shared a unique set of values, attitudes, and beliefs related to their job. Based on continual face-to-face interaction among themselves and with gang members, they soon became a viable component in the effort to control gang activities. It was immediately apparent that the task force rewarded loyalty, secrecy, and conformity to group-shared expectations. Their highest priority was to suppress gang activity to reduce the occurrence of gang-related crimes. Some of the activities the task force performed skirted the law, and it was not uncommon that they conducted illegal searches and stopped many individuals who were not known to have a gang affiliation. In other instances, arrests were made without probable cause, and many suspected gang members were booked and then released. In other words, get them off of the street. Although Bob Gonzalez tried to remain neutral and adhere to his set of personal values, he needed recognition, support, and approval from the group. Subconsciously, he wanted to be a "stand-up guy," and he felt compelled to sacrifice his standards to achieve acceptance and status from the work group. Membership in the group became an end in itself. Abstract notions of right and wrong became irrelevant to him. Integrity consisted of loyalty to and protection of the group. The rationalization was that no one really got hurt, and there was a real need to preserve peace in the communities.

Using concepts related to groups and group dynamics, explain what happened in this situation. When does group cohesiveness cease to be positive and become pathological? Are subcultures in police work inevitable? Explain. What steps might you take, as a police administrator, to prevent this from occurring?

SUMMARY

Human beings are social animals that live, work, and find varying degrees of psychosocial validation in groups. Groups, as the basic unit of social organization, provide people with a cultural milieu in which to satisfy their personality needs as well as their social need for interaction with significant others. Each person develops a social identity, a unique sense of self, and an internalized set of normative controls through meaningful interaction with other people during the socialization process.

Most people belong to and participate in a wide variety of formal organizations and informal cliques. Some groups are task oriented and highly structured. Other groups are much more casual and coalesce around vague (loosely defined) common interests. These groups tend to emphasize the importance of meaningful interpersonal relationships as opposed to the task itself.

Each group develops a distinctive social orientation, or collective persona. New members are socialized to behave in certain ways. They are expected to learn and internalize appropriate roles, **norms**, values, and cultural perspectives. All members are rewarded for **conformity** to group-shared expectations and punished if they deviate. Consciousness of kind and internalized self-control reduce conflict and promote collaboration.

Groups that become functional entities are defined, as viewed by social interactionist, when two or more officers interact with other members. Another prerequisite is to share one or more goals. Involvement in this definition is the key, and members allow themselves to be governed by a normative system of **attitudes**, values, and behavior that lead to a stable relationship. Additionally, it is found that officers will form subgroups based on interpersonal attraction or rejection.

Work groups are mechanisms through which goal-oriented human beings learn relevant knowledge, technical skills, and job-related behaviors. Groups have life cycles just like all other living organisms. Group dynamics have an effect on individual performance. Group dynamics also influence the efficiency, effectiveness, and productivity of the organization. Whether these effects are good or bad will depend on member needs and the complexity of the task; the **size, composition, norms**, and **cohesiveness** of the group; and the prevailing reward structure.

Stages in the group developmental process include the following steps: orientation, conflict and challenge, cohesion, delusion, disillusion, and acceptance. Teamwork that will result in a winning team comes to pass because of the hard work involved in understanding the behavior of team members and the leader. The team leader must strive to create a team wherein each officer accepts and promotes the four Cs of team membership: collaboration, conform, contribute, and cooperate.

Experienced police administrators accept that groups, subgroups, and cliques exist within the police department. They understand that groups are inevitable and ubiquitous. They also know that groups unleash powerful synergistic forces that can have either good or bad consequences, depending on the situation. The police administrator's principal job is to manage the department's human resources in such a way as to increase its overall efficiency, effectiveness, and productivity. In order to accomplish this objective, he or she must do the following: (1) accept the group phenomenon as a fact of organizational life; (2) identify and seek cooperation from informal group leaders; (3) prevent dysfunctional competition and the development of win–lose situations; (4) avoid forcing members to choose between allegiance to management and to their group; (5) adopt a coach's attitude toward groups, subgroups, and cliques within the organization; (6) motivate work groups by appealing to their sense of competence; and (7) utilize traditional and nontraditional methods to encourage individual effort as well as group collaboration.

The police **subculture** is viable and has a strong influence on police agencies. These **norms** exert a strong influence over the individual conduct of officers, and it does not take long for a new officer to learn what acceptable behavior is. Norms come into existence as the result of group interaction. It is readily apparent that police departments meticulously demand a strong degree of loyalty.

Effective team leaders have proven to be those who can recognize and contribute to a decisive group process. Research suggests that a team leader is an individual who has developed the capacity to persuade and motivate others to achieve objectives and goals. This type of team leader is easily identifiable because they have demonstrated the capacity to work with a group of officers and transform them into a cohesive, dynamic, and hard-charging productive work group. A positive team climate comes into existence because the leader demonstrates clear-cut skills, presents a convincing attitude, provides guidance in establishing priorities, and secures goal attainment.

In order to be successful in working with groups, police administrators must have knowledge, good interpersonal skills, and a positive attitude concerning subgroup participation in the organization's decision-making process. This will enable them to channel the energy, effort, and expertise of group members in such a way as to achieve the mission, goals, and objectives of the police department. Truly, knowledge is power, and skill is the ability to translate knowledge into action.

DISCUSSION TOPICS AND QUESTIONS

1. List and discuss the distinct social functions that groups perform for their members.

2. What are the characteristics of formal work groups, and how do they differ from informal groups within law enforcement agencies?

3. How do social interactionists define a group, and why do they place such an emphasis on action?

4. What are the principal psychosocial needs that motivate human beings to join and remain active in informal as well as formal groups?

5. Name and discuss four categories commonly used to classify groups in terms of their function. Which are most often associated with the division of labor?

6. Identify and describe the primary structural components that are common to both formal and informal groups.

7. The police are referred to as a subculture. What is a subculture? What are values and norms, and how are they passed on to new members?

8. How does the prevailing reward structure influence individual performance and work-group productivity?

9. Identify, list, and discuss the characteristics of work groups that have a direct effect on individual performance and organizational productivity.

FOR FURTHER READING

Leigh Thompson, *Making the Team: A Guide for Managers*, 3rd ed. (Upper Saddle River, NJ: Prentice Hall, 2008).

The author sets forth numerous real-world examples and illustrations of effective and ineffective teamwork. The text includes 95 new case studies and reviews 194 new research studies. It includes a review of how to accurately improve team performance as well as how one can manage the internal dynamics of teams including diversity, conflict, and creativity. Such things as decision-making are reviewed in detail with an emphasis on groupthink and unethical decision-making. The author also includes a review of such features as team identity, emotion, and development. The text explores networking, leadership styles, coaching, and inter-team relations.

Gregory P. Rothans, "Six Strategies for Successful Team-Building Workshops," *The Police Chief*, Vol. LXXIII, No. 6 (2006), pp. 48–52.

The Team-Building Workshops (TBW) can be an important part of an organizational development process.

It is recommended for use when engaging in strategic planning, working through organizational dilemmas, developing a new program, or facilitating a management transition. The six strategies for success include the following:

1. Begin with the end in mind.

2. Plan early.

3. Select the right facilitator.

4. Effectively manage the facilitator.

5. Follow the rule of three.

6. Follow through and follow up.

The rule of three strategies suggests that a leader should spend one-third of the time working on goals, one-third of the time working in small groups, and one-third of the time socializing. A significant key to the process is to spend time selecting a capable facilitator in order to maximize the potential of the process.

John C. Maxwell, *The 17 Indisputable Laws of Teamwork: Embrace Them and Empower Your Team* **(New York: Thomas Nelson, 2001).**

Written in a popular style, this book addresses the vital topic of teamwork and how one can empower members of a team. The author presents a number of guidelines that he has chosen to call laws. This includes such elements as the law of the edge, the law of high morale, the law of the big picture and the law of the bench. Additional consideration is given to the law of the bad apple, law of the chain, law of the compass, law of identity, and the law of significance. These and other laws cover a wide range of organizational behavior, and the text includes illustrations of team leaders from history, business, the church, and sports.

Fran Rees, *How to Lead Work Teams: Facilitation Skills,* **2nd ed. (San Francisco, CA: Jossey-Bass, 2001), pp. 1–240.**

The author takes the reader, step by step, through an L.E.A.D. model, showing how one can develop facilitation skills that will help make one an outstanding leader, motivator, and facilitator.

This innovative model (L.E.A.D.) includes the following:

1. Leads with a clear purpose.
2. Empowers to participate.
3. Aims for consensus.
4. Directs the process.

The model shows step by step how to develop facilitation skills that will help one to become a better leader. The author presents methods of articulating group goals and purposes and talks about how to encourage thoughtful discussion (including disagreement), brainstorming, and active listening. She recommends techniques for encouraging team members to communicate in ways that enhance teamwork and achieve results. She reviews means of obtaining consensus by such techniques as summarizing and documenting.

ENDNOTES

1. Jim L. Munro, *Administrative Behavior and Police Organization* (Cincinnati, OH: Anderson, 1997), pp. 89–93.
2. John R. Schermerhorn, James G. Hunt, and Richard N. Osborn, *Managing Organizational Behavior*, 9th ed. (New York: Wiley, 2005), pp. 199–204.
3. Elliott Aronson, *The Social Animal* (San Francisco, CA: Freeman, 1976), pp. 165–166.
4. Herbert J. Chruden and Arthur W. Sherman, Jr., *Personnel Management*, 6th ed. (Cincinnati, OH: South-Western, 1980), pp. 8–20.
5. Richard N. Holden, *Modern Police Management*, 3rd ed. (Englewood Cliffs, NJ: Prentice Hall, 2000), pp. 37–47.
6. Robert Albanese, *Management* (Cincinnati, OH: South-Western, 1999), pp. 518–530.
7. Ronald W. Smith and Frederick W. Preston, *Sociology: An Introduction* (New York: St. Martin's, 1982).
8. Richard W. Plunkett, *Supervision: The Direction of People at Work*, 9th ed. (Boston, MA: Allyn & Bacon, 2000), pp. 321–333.
9. Peter I. Rose, *The Study of Society: An Integrated Anthology*, 4th ed. (New York: Random House, 1980).
10. Rensis Likert, *Organizational Theory* (New York: McGraw-Hill, 1961), pp. 21–24.
11. Schermerhorn, Hunt, and Osborn, *Managing Organizational Behavior*, pp. 213–214.
12. David H. Holt, *Management: Principles and Practices*, 3rd ed. (Englewood Cliffs, NJ: Prentice Hall, 1993), p. 69.
13. Plunkett, *Supervision*.
14. Robert M. Fulmer, *Supervision: Principles of Professional Management* (New York: Macmillan, 1982), pp. 338–341.
15. Jay Burch, "Peer Leadership Group for Employees—Management Communications," *Law and Order*, Vol. 56, No. 10 (2008), pp. 130–134.
16. Holt, *Management*.
17. Schermerhorn, Hunt, and Osborn, *Managing Organizational Behavior*.
18. Plunkett, *Supervision*, pp. 213–214.
19. Darrel Ray and Howard Bronstein, *Teaming Up: Making the Transition to a Self-Directed, Team Based Organization* (New York: McGraw-Hill, 1994), p. 88.
20. Thomas A. Kayser, *Mining Group Gold: How to Cash in on the Collaborative Brain Power of a Group* (El Segundo, CA: Serif Publishing, 2001), p. 1.
21. H. Joseph Reitz and Linda N. Jewell, *Managing* (Glenview, IL: Scott Foresman, 1985).
22. Harry W. More and Larry Miller, *Effective Police Supervision*, 5th ed. (Cincinnati, OH: Anderson, 2007), p. 212.
23. Dalton Melville, *Men Who Manage: Fusions of Feelings and Theory in Administration* (Cincinnati, OH: Anderson, 1959), pp. 3–12.
24. John Gastil, *Democracy in Small Groups: Participation, Decision Making, and Communications* (Philadelphia, PA: New Society Publishers, 1998), pp. 222–234.
25. Plunkett, *Supervision*, p. 309.
26. Reitz, *Managing*.
27. Robert Albanese, *Managing: Toward Accountability for Performance* (New York: Macmillan, Richard D. Irwin, 1978), pp. 520–522.
28. Robert M. Fulmer, *The New Management* (New York: Macmillan, 1987), pp. 322–323.
29. Smith and Preston, *Sociology*.
30. H. Joseph Reitz, *Behavior in Organizations* (Homewood, IL: Richard D. Irwin, 1987).
31. Paul Whisenand, *Supervising Police Personnel: Back to Basics* (Englewood Cliffs, NJ: Prentice Hall, 2003), p. 258.
32. Leonard R. Sayles, *Research in Industrial Human Relations* (New York: Harper & Row, 1957).
33. Whisenand, *Supervising Police Personnel*.
34. Fulmer, *Supervision*, p. 93.
35. L. Argote and J. E. McGrath, "Group Processes in Organizations: Continuity and Change," in C. L. Cooper and I. T. Robertson, eds., *International Review of Industrial and Organizational Psychology* (New York: Wiley, 1993), pp. 333–389.

36. Daniel R. Ilgen, Jeffrey A. LePine, and John R. Hollenbeck, "Effective Decision Making in Multinational Teams," in P. Christopher Earley and Miriam Erez, eds., *New Perspectives on International Industrial/Organizational Psychology* (San Francisco: New Lexington Press, 1997); Warren Watson, "Cultural Diversity's Impact on Interaction Process and Performance," *Academy of Management Journal*, Vol. 16 (1993).

37. "Dream Teams," *Northwestern* (Winter 2005), p. 10; Matt Golosinski, "Teamwork Takes Center Stage," *Northwestern* (Winter 2005), p. 39.

38. Adapted from Rob McInnes, Diversity World, www.diversityworld.com.

39. C. Calhoun, D. Light, and S. Keller, *Sociology*, 6th ed. (New York: McGraw-Hill, 1994), p. 24.

40. Ibid.

41. Jennifer A. Chatman, Jeffrey T. Polzer, Sigal G. Barsade, and Margaret A. Neale, "Being Different Yet Feeling Similar: The Influence of Demographic Composition and Organizational Culture on Work Processes and Outcomes" (1998). Retrieved from https://eds.a.ebscohost.com/eds/pdfviewer/pdfviewer?vid=0&sid=f4e164f4-831f-45eb-971a-5d0ff6d97565%40sessionmgr4007. Accessed on August 15, 2018.

42. Robin J. Ely and D. A. Thomas, "Cultural Diversity at Work: The Effects of Diversity Perspectives on Work Group Processes and Outcomes," *Administrative Science Quarterly*, Vol. 46, No. 2 (2001), pp. 229–273.

43. Cristina B. Gibson, and Jennifer L. Gibbs, "Unpacking the Concept of Virtuality: The Effects of Geographic Dispersion, Electronic Dependence, Dynamic Structure, and National Diversity on Team Innovation," *Administrative Science Quarterly*, Vol. 51, No. 3 (2006), pp. 451–495.

44. David A. Harrison, Kenneth H. Price, and Myrtle P. Bell, "Beyond Relational Demography: Time and the Effects of Surface- and Deep-Level Diversity on Work Group Cohesion," *Academy of Management Journal*, Vol. 41, No. 1 (1998), pp. 94–107.

45. Jeffrey T. Polzer, Laurie P. Milton, and William B. Swann, "Capitalizing on Diversity: Inter-Personal Congruence in Small Work Groups," *Administrative Science Quarterly*, Vol. 47, No. 2 (2002), pp. 296–324.

46. Clint A. Bowers, James A. Pharmer, and Eduardo Salas, "When Member Homogeneity Is Needed in Work Teams: A Meta-Analysis," *Small Group Research*, Vol. 31, No. 3 (2000), pp. 305–327.

47. W. W. Fleischhacker and M. Delazer, "Sex Differences in Cognitive Functions," *Personality and Individual Differences*, Vol. 35, No. 4 (September 2003), pp. 863–875; Anthony F. Jorm, Kaarin J. Anstey, Helen Christensen, and Bryan Rodgers, "Gender Differences in Cognitive Abilities: The Mediating Role of Health State and Health Habits," *Intelligence*, Vol. 32, No. 1 (January 2004), pp. 7–23.

48. See Maureen M. Black and E. Wayne Holden, "The Impact of Gender on Productivity and Satisfaction Among Medical School Psychologists," *Journal of Clinical Psychology in Medical Settings*, Vol. 5. No. 1 (March 1998), pp. 117–131.

49. S. Hoogendoorn, H. Oosterbeek, and M. van Praag, "The Impact of Gender Diversity on the Performance of Business Teams: Evidence from a Field Experiment," *Harvard Business Review: Women and Public Policy Program*, (2013). Retrieved from http://gap.hks.harvard.edu/impact-gender-diversity-performance-business-teams-evidence-field-experiment.

50. Kenneth J. Benne and Paul Sheats, "Functional Roles of Group Members," *Journal of Social Issues*, Vol. 4 (1959), pp. 41–49.

51. Fran Rees, *How to Lead Work Teams: Facilitation Skills* (San Francisco, CA: Jossey-Bass, 2001), pp. 13–87.

52. Reitz, *Behavior in Organizations*.

53. Dean J. Champion, *The Sociology of Organizations* (New York: McGraw-Hill, 1975), pp. 119–120.

54. Ely Chinoy and John P. Hewitt, *Sociological Perspective* (New York: Random House, 2000), pp. 23–31.

55. Smith and Preston, *Sociology*.

56. Charles Zastrow, *Social Problems: Issues and Solutions* (Florence, KY: Wadsworth Publishing 1999), pp. 59–62.

57. Whisenand, *Supervising Police Personnel*, p. 93.

58. Albanese, *Managing: Toward Accountability for Performance*, pp. 520–521.

59. Morris Massey, *The People Puzzle: Understanding Yourself and Others* (Reston, VA: Reston Publishing, 1979), pp. 168–187.

60. Chinoy and Hewitt, *Sociological Perspective*.

61. Schermerhorn, Hunt, and Osborn, *Managing Organizational Behavior*, pp. 444–446.

62. Smith and Preston, *Sociology*.

63. Jerome H. Skolnick and Thomas J. Gray, eds., *Police in America* (New York: Educational Associates, 1975), pp. 121–125.

64. Steve Herbert, "Police Subculture Reconsidered," *Criminology*, Vol. 36 (1998), pp. 343–369.

65. Edward A. Thibault, Lawrence M. Lynch, and R. Bruce McBride, *Proactive Police Management*, 7th ed. (Upper Saddle River, NJ: Prentice Hall, 2006), p. 244.

66. Geoffrey P. Alpert and Rodger G. Dunham, *Policing Urban America* (Prospect Heights, IL: Waveland Press, 1996).

67. Linda N. Jewell and H. Joseph Reitz, *Group Effectiveness in Organizations* (Glenview, IL: Scott Foresman, 1981).

68. Ibid., p. 45.

69. Thibault, Lynch, and McBride, *Proactive Police Management*.

70. Muzafer Sheriff and Carolyn W. Sheriff, *An Outline of Social Psychology* (New York: Harper & Row, 1956).

71. Emile Durkheim, *Suicide* (New York: The Free Press, 1951).

72. Fulmer, *The New Management*.

73. J. Stephen Heinen and Eugene Jacobsen, "A Model of Task Group Development in Complex Organizations and a Strategy for Implementation," *Academy of Management Review*, Vol. 1 (1976), pp. 98–111.

74. Andrew J. Dubrin, *The Complete Idiot's Guide to Leadership*, 2nd ed. (New York: Alpha Books, 2000), p. 152.

75. Robert A. Sutermeister, *People and Productivity*, 3rd ed. (New York: McGraw-Hill, 1976), p. 243.

76. Jerald Greenberg and Robert A. Baron, *Behavior in Organizations: Understanding and Managing the Human Side of Work*, 7th ed. (Boston, MA: Allyn & Bacon, 1999), pp. 260–267.

77. Steve Alper, "Interdependence and Controversy in Group Decision Making: Antecedents to Effective Self-Managing Teams," *Organizational Behavior and Human Decision Processes*, Vol. 74, No. 1 (1989), pp. 33–52.

78. Dorwin Cartwright and Ronald Lippit, "Group Dynamics and the Individual," in Robert A. Sutermeister, ed., *People and Productivity* (New York: McGraw-Hill, 1976), pp. 215–217.

79. David W. Johnson, Geoffrey Maruyama, Roger T. Johnson, Deborah Nelson, and Linda Skon, "Effects of Co-Operative, Competitive and Individualistic Goal Structure of Achievement," *Psychological Bulletin*, Vol. 89 (1981), pp. 47–62.

80. Ray and Bronstein, *Teaming Up*, p. 81.

81. John R. Katzenbach and Douglas K. Smith, *The Wisdom of Teams: Creating the High Performance Organization* (Boston, MA: Harvard Business School Press, 1993), pp. 16–18.

82. Ken H. White and Elwood N. Chapman, *Organizational Communications—An Introduction to Communications and Human Relations* (Upper Saddle River, NJ: Prentice Hall, 1979), pp. 89–91.

83. Wesley G. Skogan, Lynn Steiner, Jill DuBois, J. Erik Gudell, and Aimee Fagan, *Taking Stock: Community Policing in Chicago* (Chicago, IL: Institute for Police Research, Northwestern University, 2002), pp. 1, 4–5.

84. William C. Schultz, *FIRO: A Three-Dimensional Theory of Interpersonal Behavior* (New York: Rinehart, 1958).

85. Gary Dessler, *Management Fundamentals: Modern Principles and Practices*, 4th ed. (Reston, VA: Reston Publishing, 1985), pp. 264–266.

86. Schermerhorn, Hunt, and Osborn, *Managing Organizational Behavior*, pp. 215–216.

87. Skolnick and Gray, *Police in America*, pp. 12–13.

88. Sam S. Souryal, *Police Administration and Management* (St. Paul, MN: West, 1997), pp. 39–51.

89. Munro, *Administrative Behavior and Police Organization*, pp. 92–101.

90. Albanese, *Managing: Toward Accountability for Performance*.

91. Mark Baker, *Cops* (New York: Pocket Books, 1989), pp. 3–31.

92. Harry W. More, *Current Issues in American Law Enforcement – Controversies and Solutions,* 1st ed. (Springfield, IL: Charles C Thomas, 2008), pp. 103–108.

93. John M. Ivancevich, Andrew D. Szilagyi, and Marc J. Wallace, *Organizational Behavior and Performance* (Santa Monica, CA: Goodyear, 1977).

94. Whisenand, *Supervising Police Personnel*, p. 105.

95. More, *Current Issues in American Law Enforcement*, p. 46.

96. Marlene E. Turner and Anthony R. Pratkanis, "Twenty-Five Years of Groupthink Theory and Research: Lessons from the Evaluation of a Theory," *Organizational Behavior and Human Decision Processes*, Vol. 73, No. 2/3 (1998), pp. 105–115.

97. Gregory Moorhead, Christopher P. Neck, and Mindy S. West, "The Tendency Toward Defective Decision Making within Self-Managing Teams: The Relevance of Groupthink for the 21st Century," *Organizational Behavior and Human Decision Processes*, Vol. 73, No. 2/3 (1998), pp. 327–351.

98. Anthony R. Pratkanis, "Twenty-Five Years of Groupthink Theory and Research" and I. L. Janis, "Groupthink among Policy Makers," in G. M. Kern and L. H. Rappoport, eds., *Varieties of Psych-History* (New York: Springer, 1976).

99. Richard P. Feynman, *Appendix to the Rogers Commission Report on the Space Shuttle Challenger Accident: Personal Observations on the Reliability of the Shuttle* (Washington, D.C.: USGPO, 1992), pp. 1–9.

100. Lawrence H. Silberman and Charles S. Robb, *Report to the President, Commission on the Intelligence Capabilities of the United States Regarding Weapons of Mass Destruction* (Washington, D.C.: USGPO, 2005), p. 3.

101. Vivian A. Leonard and Harry W. More, *Police Organization and Management*, 9th ed. (New York: Foundation Press, 2000), pp. 307–308.

102. Holt, *Management*.

103. Plunkett, *Supervision*, pp. 329–330.

12

CHANGE

Coping with Organizational Life

Learning Objectives

1. Define and explore *change* as a natural phenomenon in complex criminal justice organizations.
2. Differentiate between planned and unplanned change.
3. List and discuss the most frequent targets of planned-change efforts in complex organizations.
4. Identify and explore issues related to diagnosis, resistance, implementation, evaluation, institutionalization, and diffusion.
5. List the factors that can aid the planned change process in public agencies.

Key Terms

change agents
diagnosis
external forces
planned change
reactive change

refreezing
SARA model
technological change
unfreezing
vision statement

We live in a world of kaleidoscopic change—change that is remarkable for its breadth, depth, and accelerating pace. The term *change* refers to any alteration that occurs in the organization of the total environment.[1] According to Alvin Toffler, change is the process by which the future invades our lives and shapes our behaviors. He argues that change is not merely a necessary aspect of life. It is life.[2]

Change is a natural and inevitable manifestation of organizational life. However, the success of any change initiative will ultimately depend on the ability of the executive team to properly implement change and the willingness of employees to alter their behaviors.

Bill Orion is a traditional Theory X manager who has ruled the Smithton Police Department with an iron fist for the last two years. The department has an authorized strength of 17 sworn personnel and three civilians. A very weak and easily manipulated civil service system has produced a staffing pattern based on political patronage and nepotism rather than merit. Under the existing circumstances, loyalty to the chief is considered more important than developing professional competence in police work. As a result, routine departmental decision-making has been centralized to the point where the police chief executive makes virtually all decisions. Subservience is rewarded, not creative problem solving.

Several incidents have served to focus media attention on problems within the police department. The most recent incident, involving the suicide of a prisoner, has become something of a cause célébre.

The prisoner, a young man, arrested for a relatively minor crime, was placed in a holding cell pending completion of the booking process. The arresting officer observed the prisoner trying to hang himself with a noose made from his shirt. The officer intervened, took the shirt away, and reported the incident to his immediate supervisor.

Sgt. John Caperton talked with the prisoner and concluded that he was emotionally disturbed. Since he did not want to decide on how to handle the situation, Sgt. Caperton spent 10 minutes on the phone discussing the matter with Chief Orion. When he returned to the holding cell, he found the young man's body. He had hanged himself using a tube stocking attached to a bar in a window opening. It was the second suicide in the holding cell in three months.

According to one political insider, "All hell broke loose!" The dead man's family excoriated the police for failing to provide the proper supervision or care for mentally ill offenders, the media clamored for an objective investigation by a neutral third party, and the Smithton City Council called on Mayor Yarnell to fire Chief Orion.

If you were the mayor, what would you do in this situation? Why does it often take an incident of this magnitude to precipitate a substantive change in complex bureaucratic organizations? What are the most common indicators of the need for planned organizational change? Why is it better to be proactive rather than reactive in circumstances like these?

Unlike the private sector, government agencies face several unique hurdles to organizational change. First, agency leaders are chosen on such factors as their command of policy, technical expertise, or political connections, not their track record as an agent of change. Second, the window of opportunity to make change for government officials is much shorter. Third, the rules and regulations to prevent misuse of power and resources in the government workplace impede change efforts. Finally, democratic decision-makers include external constituencies who must be heard (Ostroff, 2006, pp. 1–2).[3] For these reasons, governmental change efforts should emphasize improving agency performance by identifying measurable objectives and setting priorities and make an effort to engage external stakeholders.

Police departments continuously change because they are organic and relatively open social systems. They exchange information, energy, and material in various environments. Police departments are not static structures. They consist of dynamic interrelationships between people performing those functions necessary to achieve the mission, goals, and objectives of the organization. Managers must make their employees understand that there is no penalty for taking risks so long as they are taken for the right reasons.[4]

One of the most important measures of an organization's strength is its ability to adapt to and incorporate change. Aldag and Kuzuhara divide organizational change into two basic categories: (1) **planned change** and (2) **reactive change**.

1. *Planned change* occurs when managers develop and install a program that serves to alter organizational activities in a timely and orderly way.
2. *Reactive change* occurs when managers simply respond to the pressure for change when that pressure comes to their attention. Usually, this is a piecemeal approach because managers are facing problems that need immediate resolution.[5]

Change agents are individuals and groups that act as catalysts and assume responsibility for managing the change process. The change agent is someone responsible for coordinating the planning and development of a new program or the revision of an old one. Such an individual will guide the analysis of the problem to be solved, search for causes of the problem and review similar interventions in use elsewhere, and facilitate the collaboration of clients, staff, and consumers involved in the planning process.[6]

A change intervention is an intentional action on the part of someone to make things different. Most planned changes are problem-solving efforts initiated by managers acting in their capacity as change agents. For all practical purposes, initiating and coping with change is the essence of the modern police administrator's job.

Unfortunately, most substantive organizational change occurs only when managers find themselves under intense pressure to act. The hard fact is that most individuals and organizations resist change. *Reactive* police administrators try to keep their departments on a fairly steady course. They are wedded to the past and glorify the status quo. They rely on cosmetic changes as they attempt to adjust to new conditions. The problem is that change is synergistic and cumulative. A series of small incremental changes can accumulate to cause a significant alteration in the operation of the organization.[7]

Proactive managers, in contrast to their reactive counterparts, are future-oriented and much more inclined to embark on a program of planned change. They believe in the systematic approach to initiating and managing organizational change. Planned change involves deliberate actions to alter the status quo. Proactive police administrators set out to change things, to chart new courses rather than maintain the current ones. They want to anticipate changes in the environment and to develop ways of dealing with predicted conditions.

There is absolutely no doubt that the rapidity, intensity, and complexity of change facing law enforcement in contemporary American society require police administrators to learn both to use and to understand planned-change strategies. Learning how to initiate and manage planned change is one of the most important functions of a manager. Part of a manager's job is to manage change—to lead the organization through it productively. Managers in complex criminal justice organizations are no exception. They do not, as a rule, have the option of not initiating and managing substantive change—those organizations that fail to adapt to the changes in their environment almost always fail to accomplish their mission, goals, and objectives. While they may not disappear, these organizations tend to wither away and die on the vine. Police administrators face a somewhat paradoxical situation. They must respond both to the need for organizational stability and to the need for change. Good managers create and maintain environments that balance the demands for stability and change.

Whether the change is good or bad depends on how it affects the organization. The pace and scope of change are important. There can be too much change or too little. From an organizational perspective, change for the sake of change is not a good thing. A police department that is in a constant state of flux will ordinarily be unable to establish and maintain the regularized patterns of collaborative behavior needed to ensure effectiveness.

Forces Influencing Organizational Change

Police administrators face a variety of factors that dictate the necessity for changes in structural relationships and organizational behavior. The most important dimension of each factor is the degree to which it can be influenced or resolved by the intervention of management. Some problems are easily resolved because the solution is apparent. Others are much more complicated and may well be beyond the control of a particular manager. Good managers concentrate their efforts on making needed changes in areas where they have responsibility and in which there is a reasonable expectation of success. Rationality and judgment are critical components in creative problem solving. Creative problem solving is a key to the successful implementation of a planned change.

Sources of Change

Two basic sources pressure all organizations for change. These sources are either external or internal to the organization. While this distinction is somewhat arbitrary, it provides a fairly convenient basis for discussing forces for change.

External Sources.

Modern police departments are open systems that take inputs from the environment, transform some of them into public services, and send those services back into the environment as outputs.[8] Like other organisms, police departments consume external resources to survive. They must be able to attract resources—such as capital, personnel, equipment, and knowledge—and must be able to market what they produce in the way of services. External sources of change are those factors outside an organization that modify the organization's ability to attract resources or market its services. These factors include competition and changes in economic conditions, the labor force, public expectations, the physical environment, social norms and values, and legal constraints. It usually forces outside the organization that trigger strategic changes. Changes are also often required for survival, but strategic changes implemented under crisis conditions are highly risky. Police agencies have consistently demonstrated their ability to change when driven to it by such **external forces** as legislation, court opinion, media pressure, political figures, commissions of inquiry, the federal government, pressure groups, and high-profile incidents.[9] Often, police departments have had change imposed on them from the outside because their leadership failed to recognize environmental conditions that demanded it.

Internal Sources.

The internal sources of pressure to change include conflict, administrative changes, technical changes, declining productivity, changes in key agency personnel, and interpersonal issues such as shifts in workers' attitudes toward their supervisor or their benefits package.[10] A certain amount of intra-organizational conflict is normal and healthy. Under the right conditions, it leads to creative problem solving and produces adaptive change. Administrative changes involve restructuring the organization or revising policies, procedures, rules, and regulations. Technological changes include new paradigms, methods, tools, equipment, and so forth. People changes are concerned primarily with changes in values, attitudes, motivation, skills, and on-the-job behavior. Since change is both synergistic and cumulative, a change in one area leads to changes in others. Problems occur in police organizations because many administrators do not recognize the interdependencies of these internal change areas.[11]

Technological, Sociocultural, and Organizational Factors

A few of the factors encouraging change warrant special consideration because they have had a major impact on police organizations and management. They are as follows: (1) technological factors, (2) sociocultural factors, and (3) organizational factors.

Technological Factors.

Technological change occurs when a new method—such as new machinery, knowledge, tools, or techniques—is used to transform resources into a service.[12] **Technological change** has had an enormous impact on American law enforcement. The ongoing knowledge explosion has revolutionized modern police work and created a legion of specialists to deal with crime in an enormously complex society. The development and deployment of technology—in such forms as handheld radios, computers, computer-assisted fingerprint identification, offender profiling, infrared surveillance, field drug testing, electronic eavesdropping, voiceprint analysis, thermo-tracking, genetic (DNA) fingerprinting, forensic odontology, operations research, mechanical speed detection, and so on—have changed policing forever. If the recent past is indicative of the future, today's mind-boggling technology will become obsolete tomorrow. With our entry into the 21st century, new police administrators must acquire the skills required to keep up with and manage rapidly escalating technological change.

Sociocultural Factors.

Profound social and cultural changes are taking place in American society as it moves toward a rendezvous with its future. These changes reflect our changing values concerning life, human existence, social equity, productive work, and the government's role in dealing with the revolution in rising expectations. As the population has expanded, it has become more diverse. It is aging, becoming more ethnically diverse, and becoming much more litigious in pursuit of social justice. Police departments are beginning to mirror the society at large. Based on changing demographics and Equal Employment Opportunity/Affirmative Action programs, more women and minorities have joined police forces. More and more nontraditional employees are moving into supervisory positions.

More women occupy police executive positions. Organizations are now aiming less for diversity and more for inclusion—a shift in emphasis from employees' differences to their similarities.[13]

Organizational Factors.

Administrative pressures come from intentional managerially induced chains of goals, practices, procedures, policies, deadlines, and reward systems. Newly appointed police chief executives are likely to be enthusiastic, energetic, and proactive. They are often eager to change things they perceive as creating problems within the organization. They see themselves as change agents.

One of the crucial tasks facing a manager as a change agent is to develop and communicate his or her vision for the organization. This vision should meet several criteria:

1. It should be simple and idealistic, a picture of a desirable future rather than a complex plan with quantitative objectives and detailed action schedules.
2. It should appeal to the values, hopes, and ideals of organizational members and its external stakeholders, to obtain their support.
3. It should address basic assumptions about what is important to the organization, how it should relate to its environment, and how people (both employees and clients) should be treated.
4. It should present an attainable future grounded in present reality.
5. It should be focused enough to guide decisions and actions but general enough to allow initiative and creativity.

In sum, the **vision statement** should convey an image of what is important to the organization, what can be achieved, why it is worthwhile, and how it can be done.[14]

Typically, leaders face the difficult task of changing the culture of their organizations. Organizational culture is made up of the characteristic values, traditions, and behaviors an organization's employees share. A value is a basic belief about what is right or wrong, or what one should or shouldn't do.[15] If the culture promotes divisive values and resists change, there are a number of steps that a manager can take to initiate change:

1. *Clarify expectations.* Make it clear what values you expect your subordinates to follow.
2. *Use signs, symbols, stories, rites, and ceremonies.* They can serve as powerful vehicles to illustrate the values that you wish to inspire and establish.
3. *Deliberately teach, coach, and be a role model for the values you want to emphasize.* "Talk the talk *and* walk the walk." What the manager does sends the real signals and ultimately does the most to create and sustain the organizational culture. People will take note of what things the leader attends to and handles them. The leader who institutes a policy or procedure and then fails to act on is demonstrating that it is not important or necessary.
4. *Communicate priorities by how you allocate rewards.* Leaders communicate their priorities by how they link raises and promotions (and other nonmonetary rewards) to performance. Those employees who "walk the walk" must be rewarded. Failure to recognize contributions and achievements sends a message that they are not important. The rewards should also be differentially allocated to affirm the importance of some performances over others. Failure to perform requires disciplinary action.
5. *React vigorously to crises.* A leader's response to a crisis sends a strong message about values and assumptions. Where was Winston Churchill before World War II? Rudolph Guiliani before 9/11? The leader who supports and communicates values when under pressure communicates that those values are important.[16]

Successful change management requires clear and open communication between the leader/manager, subordinates, and stakeholders.[17]

Changes in values, interests, attitudes, skills, motivation, and job performance generate interorganizational pressure. Some of these changes are elicited and reinforced by managers. They are achieved and nurtured through a strong personnel selection procedure, specialized training, and continuous review in the form of performance appraisals. Other changes occur because of changes in the overall composition of the workforce. New and nontraditional employees bring new values, aspirations, and goals with them into the workplace. While hierarchical bureaucracies require individual employees to accept subordinate status within the organization, people today are less willing to serve as subordinates. Whether managers are ready for it or not, the ethic of participation has spread across America, bottom-up, and is having a radical impact on the way employees expect to be treated by their employers. People whose lives are affected by managerial decisions are demanding a meaningful role in making those decisions. Empowering people by reducing bureaucratic restraints and providing the resources needed to make change successful.[18]

Police officers are the avant-garde of the participatory democracy movement because they have more education than the population at large, place far greater emphasis on achieving self-fulfillment, and exhibit an instinctive need to redesign their jobs or reconfigure organizational relationships regarding their values, interests, motives, and abilities. The process of implementing change also involves motivating, supporting, and guiding people. Yukl offers the following guidelines for implementing people-oriented change:[19]

1. Create a sense of urgency about the need for change.
2. Prepare people to adjust to change.
3. Help people to deal with the pain of change.
4. Provide opportunities for early successes.
5. Keep people informed about the progress of change.
6. Demonstrate continued commitment to the change.
7. Empower people to implement the change.

These suggestions may ease the pain and uncertainty of dealing with change at a personal level and thus ensure success.

Internal factors are a powerful force for change in complex criminal justice organizations. These factors are significant. Most organizational management theorists subscribe to a synergistic point of view. They contend that a change in any one of the areas just discussed leads to changes in the others. The dynamics that produce change are the same as those in the fabled perpetual-motion machine, and an absence of change is abnormal under any circumstances. The realization that change is a natural and inevitable aspect of organizational life has led to a resurgence of interest in initiating and managing planned change (see Figure 12–1).

CASE STUDY   Body-Worn Camera Policy

The Cooperstown Police Department issued body-worn cameras (BWCs) to its officers. The policy of the department allows the release of BWC footage to the public—in response to citizen concerns raised at City Council meetings. Citizens felt that the department had previously restricted the release of BWC videos while permitting officers to review footage before making statements about police shootings. Opposition to the review policy was strong during the meetings.

Chief Boone stated that the policy change was appropriate. He said most police departments permit officers to watch BWC videos while drafting their reports or before speaking to investigators following a shooting. BWC footage will not be classified as "investigative material" and thus will no longer exempt the city from releasing videos as required under the Public Records Act of the state. Now, BWC videos will be released "to the greatest extent possible."

The department can still restrict the release of BWC footage if it would harm an investigation, and violate the law, or if the case involves "potential civil litigation."

The policy also states that the department will not use BWCs to record people engaged in protests or other First Amendment activities or as a surveillance tool of the general public. BWCs will be turned on by officers when they believe a criminal law violation occurs. Chief Boone assured the public that the BWC policy would be reviewed and revised as the cameras are used and when "best practices" emerge across the country. The Cooperstown Fraternal Order of Police agreed with the BWC policies as stated. Chief Boone hopes that the use of BWCs by officers will reduce citizen complaints, illuminate police–citizen encounters, and increase perceptions of police legitimacy among the public.

How should this policy change be handled?

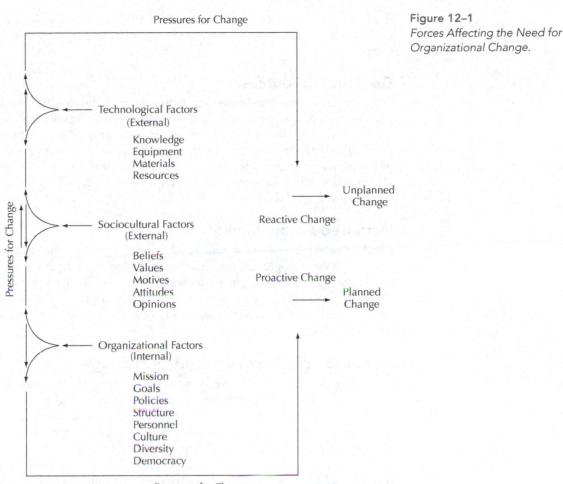

Figure 12–1
Forces Affecting the Need for Organizational Change.

Recognizing the Need for Planned Change

Good police administrators are good because they are multidimensional human beings. They can process large amounts of abstract information and to learn from their own experiences. Competent managers possess better-than-average problem-solving skills. They also exhibit a great deal of flexibility in adjusting their managerial style to cope with changing conditions. Proactive managers continuously scan the internal as well as the external environment for symptoms of organizational change. The remainder of this chapter is designed to create a paradigm that will help police administrators do the following:

1. Recognize the internal indicators that signal the need for some planned change.
2. Implement the required change via a planned intervention strategy.
3. Regulate change by monitoring, evaluating, and managing the process.

Decision-making is a form of problem solving and is, in fact, the essence of management. Police organizations are not static structures. They are organic in the sense that they are entities composed of dynamic interrelationships among people performing those functions necessary to achieve the organization's mission, goals, and objectives. As people or goals change, a need arises for some modification in the organization's structure or functions. For police managers to function effectively in their role as problem solvers, decision-makers, and organization change agents, they must perceive problems that exist and can create solutions to resolve them. Wayne Welsh and Phillip Harris have identified three trends that have increased the need for planned change in police organizations. They are (1) declining resources, (2) increased accountability, and (3) expansion of knowledge and technology.[20]

Declining Resources

Declining tax revenues and reductions in funding periodically affect the delivery of public services. Part of the problem resides with increased public concern over high taxes and the resultant reluctance of legislators to increase them even when revenues are insufficient. Partly as a consequence of declining public resources, groups have organized to promote change via advocacy. Inspired by organizations such as Mothers Against Drunk Driving (MADD), groups have arisen in response to such problems as domestic violence, homelessness, and HIV/AIDS.

Increased Accountability

Lessened availability of public resources has led to a push for increased accountability. As a result, public managers are now required to demonstrate the cost-effectiveness of their operations. Typically, public managers seek grants to fund new initiatives and operations. Government funding agencies require them to submit plans including evaluations of the anticipated effectiveness of the programs to be funded. Managers must be able to present such evaluations and use their results.

Expansion of Knowledge and Technology

Justice information systems have expanded in recent years. Programs such as Compstat are based on and make direct use of, information generated by statistical information systems. Compstat is a clear example of how computers can help generate information to be used to guide program operations. On the downside, the spread of computers has also made possible new forms of crime, especially identity theft.

These trends indicate the need for planned change. Sometimes a crisis, negative feedback about an organization's effectiveness, or routine organizational analysis makes it clear that immediate intervention is required. Structural change implemented in a short period is emphasized. At other times, change is the result of a long-range plan of organizational development designed to strengthen the organization by altering certain aspects of its internal environment.

Targeting Change

Managers can, at least in theory, change just about any aspect of their organizations they wish to change. Since change is such a broad concept, however, it is useful to identify those areas in which planned change has been most common.

Goals and Strategies

Organizations are often compelled by major changes in their external environments to change their goals and the strategies used to reach them. Many police departments, for example, are moving away from the law enforcement model and are placing more emphasis on crime prevention through community-oriented policing.

Technology

The organizational effect of technological change can be minor or major, depending on the applicability of the innovation. DNA fingerprinting has the potential to revolutionize modern law enforcement when it comes to identifying, apprehending, and successfully prosecuting criminals.

Job Design

Jobs can be redesigned and enriched to offer more variety, autonomy, identity, significance, feedback, and self-fulfillment. The police agent concept focuses on the development and deployment of generalists instead of specialists.

Structure

The structure may be modified to enhance efficiency, effectiveness, and productivity. Many police departments are revising their policies, procedures, rules, and regulations to broaden spans of control and decentralize decision-making.

People

The membership of an organization can be changed regarding its (1) composition (through hiring and firing) and (2) skills and attitudes (through training). Professional police departments, like almost all other successful organizations, have developed sophisticated personnel systems and emphasized the importance of training.[21] Nearly every state has enacted comprehensive legislation establishing minimum qualifications for police personnel and mandating extensive job-related training. The choice of what to change and how to change it is up to management and depends, in large measure, on management's analysis of what internal and external factors are signalling that change is needed.

The Winds of Change

Because of their paramilitary nature, police departments have usually imposed change unilaterally (and in all probability will continue to do so). Top police administrators, because they are accountable for the efficient and effective operation of their departments, still insist on playing a key role in defining, determining the need for, and directing planned change. Even so, it is now clear that more and more police administrators are beginning to recognize the value and appropriateness of the shared-power approach. Police officers are certainly adaptable to change, and they accept it readily when they become actively involved in the decision-making process.[22]

The Process of Planned Change

Change involves a sequence of psychological adjustments, behavioral alterations, or organizational transformations that occur over time. Most views concerning planned change involving individuals in organizations can be traced back to the work of Kurt Lewin[23] and Edgar H. Schein.[24] They both see all planned change as the result of a very basic three-stage process: (1) unfreezing the status quo, (2) moving to a new state, and (3) **refreezing** the new state to make it permanent (see Figure 12–2).

The process begins with **diagnosis**. The accurate diagnosis of organizational problems serves two crucial functions. First of all, it contributes to unfreezing by showing everyone concerned that the problem does, in fact, exist. Second, once the unfreezing takes place, further diagnosis helps clarify the problem and suggests what type of change is required. It is one thing to feel that police officer morale has fallen dramatically but quite another to be sure that this is the case and to develop an effective intervention strategy to resolve the problem. Accurate diagnosis ensures that managers have the opportunity to deal with causes rather than mere symptoms.

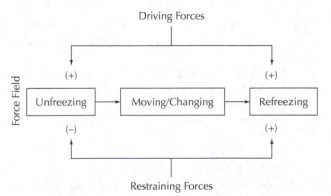

Figure 12–2
Planned-Change Process.

"J.C." Holleran is administrative captain in a large municipal police department. The department is heading into a budget deficit and must reduce costs or cut services. Capt. Holleran has been ordered by the deputy chief of police to find ways to reduce the amount currently being spent on personnel. They have tentatively agreed to seek a 10–15 percent across-the-board reduction in personnel costs.

Captain Holleran adopted the shared-power perspective inherent in participatory management. He formed a deficit-reduction task force to analyze the available data, determine the cause or causes of the problem, and recommend appropriate solutions. The task force consisted of managers and rank-and-file police officers appointed by the collective-bargaining agent (the union). The task force was authorized to access all of the department's financial data. After excessive deliberations, the task force formulated a cost-containment plan instead of recommending cuts in service.

The task force's cost-containment plan called for a temporary freeze on all hiring, restrictions on overtime, a minimal reduction in court-time reimbursement, and an expansion of the telephonic complaint reception/screening program. Following the announcement of the plan, Captain Holleran and Deputy Chief Ray Runion met with union leaders as well as the chief to elicit support for the proposal.

During the briefing, Chief Holleran asked the following series of questions:

1. Who is most likely to be affected by the proposed changes?
2. How will employees, the department, and the public be affected by the proposed changes?
3. What kind of resistance can be expected if the proposed changes are put into effect?
4. What strategies can be used to minimize resistance to the proposed changes?
5. What are the odds of achieving the projected savings in personnel costs?

He asked Capt. Holleran to prepare a position paper outlining answers to these questions.

Assume that you are Capt. Holleran. Prepare a position paper for submission to Chief Holleran. Address each of his concerns to the best of your ability. Use the information presented in this chapter as the basis for your narrative.

Diagnosis takes various forms and can be performed by a variety of individuals. If the problems requiring change are routine, they are best diagnosed by those in the existing chain of command. If the problems are nonroutine or complex, police administrators may be well advised to seek specialized diagnostic help from a change agent. Change agents, whether they are on staff or come from outside the organization, bring an independent, objective perspective to the diagnosis while working with those who are to change. Diagnosis involves analyzing the organization, recognizing performance deficits, and identifying problems. Diagnosticians acquire their information from a variety of sources: (1) observations, (2) interviews, (3) questionnaires, and (4) record reviews. Careful diagnosis is critically important to the success or failure of any planned-change effort. Proper diagnosis clarifies the problem, indicates what needs to be changed (regarding technology, structure, or people), and suggests the appropriate strategy for implementing the change with a minimum of resistance. There are three stages to diagnosis:

1. Problem identification
2. Isolation of primary causes of the problem
3. Development of an appropriate and effective solution to the problem

These three stages can be made more specific as follows:

a. Researching each problem
b. Documenting the nature of the current police response
c. Assessing its adequacy and the adequacy of existing authority and resources
d. Engaging in a broad exploration of alternatives to present responses
e. Weighing the merits of these alternatives and choosing from among them[25]

Problem-oriented policing (POP) is a clear example of how to conduct a diagnosis. POP requires police organizations to develop systematic processes for examining and addressing problems. The POP approach to diagnosing and correcting problems uses a four-stage process called SARA (Scanning, Analysis, Response, and Assessment):

1. *Scanning.* Identifying the problem.
2. *Analysis.* Learning the problem's causes, scope, and effects.

3. *Response.* Acting to alleviate the problem and developing an appropriate and effective solution to the problem.

4. *Assessment.* Determining the effectiveness of the response.[26]

Research on police initiatives that won the annual Goldstein award for problem-oriented policing has revealed that the **SARA model** is having an impact on organizations.[27] **Unfreezing** is the process of getting an organization ready for change—recognizing the need for change and overcoming resistance to it. Unfreezing occurs when there is dissatisfaction with the status quo, and someone feels the need to alter it. Unfreezing realizes existing technology, job design, or structure is ineffective or that the attitudes or skills of employees are no longer appropriate. Support for current values and behavior disappears, and old ways are seen as no longer desirable or acceptable. Unfreezing is often precipitated by a crisis of some kind or produced as the result of routine organizational analysis. Good managers utilize organizational analysis to scan the internal and external environments for potential problems and initiate planned change before a crisis occurs.[28]

Moving

Moving occurs when driving forces overcome restraining forces, and a change plan is implemented. The change plan is developed by the change agent to introduce different attitudes and behaviors into the vacuum created during the unfreezing of the status quo. These change efforts range from minor to major. Significant change takes place only when members of the workforce identify with and accept new ideas, approaches, and relationships. The mere introduction of change does not ensure permanent elimination of the previous condition.[29]

Refreezing

Change requires internalization. Internalization is the social/psychological process of trying, adopting, and becoming committed to new attitudes or behaviors. Without positive reinforcement, newly acquired attitudes and behaviors cannot become a permanent part of an individual's normal repertoire. Refreezing is the process of institutionalization— making the change an organizational habit. It stabilizes the change by balancing both driving and restraining forces.[30]

The mechanics of planned change are the same for organizations as for people because changing people is the critical variable in changing the structure or function of any complex criminal justice organization. Police management training is a very good example of the planned change process. Trainers (on behalf of the police chief executive) facilitate the unfreezing process by inducing a certain amount of stress in trainees, to make them recognize a need for change. Exposing trainees to new ideas, values, and skills to achieve the goal. Moving begins when the trainees give credence to these ideas, values, and skills and translate them into new forms of behavior. Once new ideas, values, skills, and behaviors elicit appropriate reinforcements (internal or external rewards and punishments), the refreezing process takes over. Trainees accept, identify with, and internalize the change, incorporating it into their personality structure. It also becomes a recurrent, predictable, and intrinsically rewarding aspect of their job behavior.

While there is great value in being aware of unfreezing-moving-refreezing theory and understanding the dynamics involved in it, good administrators know that using this knowledge effectively requires a tremendous amount of skill. It is difficult to accomplish. The manager/change agent concept applies to small and medium-sized departments as well as to large urban law enforcement agencies.

Dynamics of Planned Organizational Change

Based on a study of successful planned change in some complex organizations, Larry E. Greiner developed a comprehensive model to explain the dynamics involved in the process.[31] Greiner's model consists of six phases or steps.

Phase 1

Phase 1 is pressure on, and arousal of, upper-level management to take action. Top management perceives a need or pressure to change something. One or more significant problems, such as corruption, labor unrest, a sharp decline in performance, or deteriorating community relations cause pressure. Such crises create a sense of urgency—a need to correct a wrong and to view the problem as a priority.[32]

Phase 2

Phase 2 is intervention by a respected person (acting as a change agent) and focus on the internal problem. In some cases, a new person enters as a change agent. This person leads a reexamination of past practices and current problems.[33] Outside consultants are often brought in to define the problem and help members of the organization focus on it. In other situations, internal staff members who are trusted and considered to be experts may be assigned responsibility for attacking a particular problem. Such a "guiding coalition" of influential people can mobilize commitment. The change agent must be careful to "choose the right lieutenants." "Idea champions" will mobilize political support and ensure success.[34]

Phase 3

Phase 3 is a diagnosis of the data and identification of the problem. Information comes from a variety of sources. The change agent and others analyze the information in light of their responsibility for initiating and managing planned change in the organization. The process defines the problem in concrete terms.

Phase 4

Phase 4 is the development of some creative alternatives and an organizational commitment to action. Successful change agents stimulate thought and avoid using the same old methods. Participatory problem solving is encouraged. Subordinates who are allowed to participate in making decisions that affect them will probably be much more committed to the course of action that is finally selected. The change agent must have the active assistance of the employees to implement the change. However, subordinates may not have the tools, authority, or freedom to implement the change. They must be empowered—must believe in the change and must believe that they can make it happen.[35]

Phase 5

Phase 5 is experimentation with various alternatives and analysis of results. Before the creative solutions developed during the previous phase are implemented organization-wide, they are pilot tested on a limited scale and evaluated regarding their effectiveness. The structure of large police departments lends itself to this type of exploration.

Phase 6

Phase 6 is reinforcement from results and acceptance of the planned change. If the course of action has been tested and found to be valid, it is likely to be more willingly accepted by those who will be affected. As an organization improves, the improvement itself functions as a reinforcement and fosters a continuing commitment to planned change.

Figure 12–3 outlines the process. Greiner's model provides police administrators with a convenient list approach to planned change.

Too many managers are inept when it comes to dealing with planned change. They venerate the status quo and actively resist change. Because of personal biases, inexperience, and lack of managerial skill, they fall back on comfortable courses of action fitted to the past. Preexisting solutions seek problems irrespective of the real problem. This type of tunnel vision creates and exacerbates organizational problems. Poor police administrators are part of the problem instead of being part of the solution.

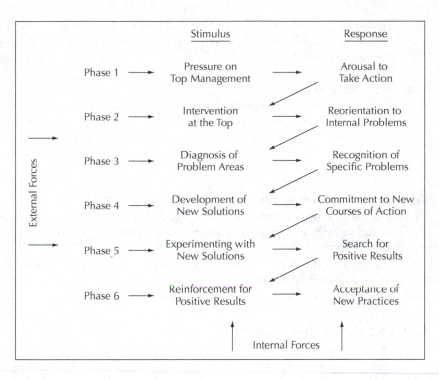

Figure 12–3
Dynamics of Planned Change.
Based on Larry E. Greiner, "Patterns of Organizational Change," Harvard Business Review, Vol.45 (1967), pp. 119–130.

Resistance to Change

Resistance to change is ingrained in organizations and the individuals who make them up. Police officers resist change when they fear that its costs outweigh its benefits to them. This resistance takes many forms and ranges from simply ignoring something to open rebellion. There are two sources of resistance to change: individual and organizational.

Individual Resistance

Managers should not simply assume that individual resistance to change is the result of stupidity, sloth, arrogance, or ignorance. Rainey asserts that people may have well-justified reasons to resist: "Some ideas are bad ideas. They deserve to be resisted."[36] Also, some government officials or leaders may become too personally invested in the new programs. They cannot rationally judge the potential for success. Whatever the source, implementation of change requires overcoming individual resistance.

Habit.

Habit often captures workers—they do the same things over and over again because these ways are familiar and comfortable.[37] In a complex world, habit reduces the need to make more decisions.[38] People have "sunk cost"—past investments of time, energy, and experience—in their job routines. If there is no obvious need for a change in operations, resistance will result. Support for change requires evidence of serious problems in the current mode of operations.

Security.

People feel threatened by change. If they have a high need for safety, they will resist it. Change can be personally inconvenient. The nature of the change and the reasons for it require explanation.

Fear of the Unknown.

Change typically introduces ambiguity and uncertainty. Workers often expect the worst. They wonder how the change will affect them in the future and what further changes may result. Such fears are not unfounded. Workers will feel threatened by the proposed change if they think it will render their expertise obsolete. Such fears may apply to certain entire groups or divisions within the organization. This fear extends to the belief that the proposed change is not feasible and is unlikely to succeed. The failure of previous reform efforts breeds cynicism.[39]

Loss of Status and Power.

Change often threatens the balance of power in an organization. Changes threatening the autonomy, authority, power, or status of a group or subunit will encounter resistance, regardless of their merit. A reduction in status caused by the change is threatening. People may also resent interference from others or be reluctant to take orders from others.[40]

Threat to Values and Ideals.

Change that is inconsistent with strong values and ideals will be opposed. For this reason, changes that threaten the organizational culture are difficult to implement, even if they are needed.

These events threaten to individual self-interest. If proposed changes do not benefit individuals directly, they are likely to be strongly opposed. They threaten changes in skills, power, relationships with others, social status, and self-esteem.

Organizational Resistance

As goals, relationships, and people change, the need for modification of organizational structure and function increases. The organization itself often resists change. Dorothy Guyot once likened attempts at police organizational reform as "bending granite."[41]

Inertia.

Like individuals, organizations have inertia—they tend to continue in the same direction at the same rate. Denhardt and colleagues assert that public agencies are particularly "risk averse"—they place a high value on not "rocking the boat."[42] The source of inertia may be the *structure*. Some organizations have built-in mechanisms to ensure stability. The hiring process defines selection criteria for new employees through job descriptions, rules, and operational procedures. Yet, the organizational culture may shape their job behavior in different ways. History and tradition can also serve as impediments to change.[43] *Groups* can also generate inertia through the enforcement of group norms on individuals who may wish to support change. Union opposition to changes is a good example of this form of inertia.[44]

Limited Focus of Change.

Organizational units are dependent on one another. Changes can thus affect more than one unit. The larger structure may nullify or blunt changes aimed at a lower level.

Threat to Expertise.

Organizational change can threaten specialized units. For example, decentralization (a key feature of community policing) allows beat officers to become generalists and assume some investigatory functions, undermining the need for specialized units (such as detectives).

Threat to Established Power Relationships and Resource Allocations.

If a proposed change threatens the decision-making authority of the organization, resistance will result. Resources are a source of power, so any change in budget allocations or other resources will cause resistance.[45]

Beer asserts the fears described earlier cause resistance to change. The organization must make strong efforts to qualify employees in newly required skills. Training, counseling, and coaching from human resource professionals as well as supervisors are required. Input to the planning process will also help to alleviate employee fears and make change less of a threat.[46]

CASE STUDY   Chief Charles S. Ahern

Charles Ahern, a veteran law enforcement officer, has been chief of the Johnson County Police Department (JCPD) for a little over three years. This county is a border state and part of a major metropolitan area. With an authorized strength of 272 sworn officers and 37 civilians, it is one of the largest law enforcement agencies in a six-county megalopolis.

The JCPD has long been considered to be one of the most professional police organizations in the state. It has an excellent pay scale and attracts top-notch personnel. As a result, the department has been able to avoid most of the problems, and almost all of the criticism leveled at other large police departments in the area. In fact, Chief Ahern was recently elected to serve as the third vice president of the nation's most prestigious professional law enforcement association.

Since personnel complaints were few and far between and the JCPD had never experienced a bona fide case of corruption, management adopted a fairly casual attitude concerning internal discipline. Although it violated generally accepted standards, supervisors in the normal chain of command were assigned to investigate personnel complaints lodged against their subordinates.

When a high-ranking police official was indicted on a RICO (racketeer-influenced corrupt organization) charge related to drug trafficking, it became obvious that there was a glitch in the system. It was clear there was no objective mechanism to investigate and resolve allegations of corruption. Because of the magnitude of the case and the heat it generated, Chief Ahern realized that corrective action (in the form of a planned change) was required.

Chief Ahern contacted the executive director of the International Association of Chiefs of Police (IACP) and arranged for its consultants to come in. Their job was to define the problem and help members of the department focus their attention on it. After reviewing the available data, analyzing the organization, and comparing the JCPD with departments of similar size, the consultants recommended the creation of an internal affairs unit.

A representative task force was formed and assigned to work with the IACP consultants to develop structural models congruent with the department's culture. After exploring several different configurations, the task force constructed a model similar in both its structure and its function to the one recommended by the National Advisory Commission on Criminal Justice Standards and Goals. The commander of the internal affairs unit was to report directly to the chief, and unit personnel would remain outside of the normal chain of command. According to the model, the internal affairs unit would investigate all personnel complaints (including corruption) and make recommendations concerning disciplinary action to the chief police executive.

The internal affairs unit became an operational component of the JCPD per Executive Order 6734. It was later upgraded to division status.

Identify the six phases in the dynamics of a successful organizational change. Are they all accounted for in the case study? If not, which are missing?

Implementing Planned Change

Managing change through shared responsibilities is a comprehensive approach that combines the best aspects of both top-down and bottom-up processes. Top management provides leadership, support, and coordination; lower-level managers and nonmanagement personnel, working in diagnostic problem-solving groups, make and implement operational change decisions.

A climate for planned change occurs when recognition of the need for it is coupled with a heightened sense of dissatisfaction and a genuine desire to alter the status quo. Since even the slightest change can be frightening, painful, or disruptive to the employees involved, changes must be initiated carefully and managed with sensitivity. Many well-meaning and necessary changes in criminal justice organizations fail to get off the ground or to achieve what they are expected to achieve, simply because police administrators are unable to create a win–win atmosphere that is conducive to substantive change.

To become successful change agents, managers must learn to make their subordinates psychologically willing to make an effort to change. One of the key elements of leadership is to establish guidelines for how to implement change.

Fernandez and Rainey (2006) list eight factors to guide change in public organizations.[47]

- **Factor 1—Ensure the Need:** Leaders must verify and persuasively communicate the need for change. Individuals will be convinced of the need and an effective planning process will result.
- **Factor 2—Provide a Plan:** This will convince organizational members of the urgency for change.
- **Factor 3—Build Internal Support for Change and Overcome Resistance:** Cite the successful experience of the organization and how the change will promote it in the future. It is also important to create psychological ownership by disseminating critical information and providing meaningful employee feedback during implementation.

- **Factor 4—Ensure Top Management Support and Commitment:** Leaders must champion the need for change and take risks to achieve change.
- **Factor 5—Build External Support:** Leaders must seek and develop support from powerful external stakeholders.
- **Factor 6—Provide Resources:** They must be provided to avoid stress and facilitate implementation of the change as well as the continued effective operation of the organization.
- **Factor 7—Institutionalize Change:** Make the change enduring by embedding innovations into daily institutional routines.
- **Factor 8—Pursue Comprehensive Change:** The process must be tied to the desired end state and subsystems of the organization. It should not be isolated and solitary.

These factors can act as a compass, guiding the change process and the organization itself.

Due to civil service regulations, politics, legal constraints, and the limited terms of agency heads, few public administrators have experience as change agents. Ostroff (2006) lists five principles that have guided successful public agency change efforts:[48]

1. Improve Performance against Agency Mission: Employees must rediscover the reason why the agency was created—to promote the public welfare.
2. Win over Stakeholders: Both internal (public employees typically are in for the long term) and external (who benefit from the agency's services).
3. Create a Road Map: Identify performance objectives, set priorities, and "roll out the program."
4. Take a Comprehensive Approach: Demonstrate what the change program means for the entire organization.
5. Be a Leader, Not a Bureaucrat: Barriers to change must be overcome rather than respected.

Together, these principles demonstrate how public managers can successfully implement change.

It is the police administrator's job to create a positive atmosphere for change by demonstrating that the rational planning of change is superior to seat-of-the-pants decision-making—and far less risky. Police officers will be more inclined to take in stride the ambiguity, confusion, and fear associated with change if they are allowed to participate in the process and to perceive change as an opportunity rather than a threat. Whisenand recommends that managers share with employees both the decision-making responsibility that leads to change and the credit for the eventual success in achieving change.[49]

Ferrazzi draws parallels to organizational change and therapeutic objectives of 12-step programs like Alcoholics Anonymous. Common attributes include:[50]

- **Nothing happens without a readiness to change.** You cannot force people to change, but you can help them do so.
- **Replace old habits with new ones.** The goal is to replace negative habits with positive ones.
- **Sponsorship deepens commitment and sparks results.** Role models within the organization are more effective than external experts.
- **Community without hierarchy is a catalyst for change.** The change effort should be self-directed.
- **You are the company you keep.** As positive role models, informal leaders are a good source of leverage for change.
- **Continuous introspection is key.** Followers should examine and question their past performance and motivations.
- **The goal is progress, not perfection.** People must be coached to overcome setbacks and reverse poor performance.

Breaking old habits is difficult, but new working methods can be established.

Battilana and Casciaro concluded that change agents were more successful when they used the informal network to promote change, matched the organizational network to the type of change pursued, and had close relationships with "fence-sitters" (persons ambivalent to the change effort). Change resisters were handled on a case-by-case basis, watching closely to ascertain their motives.[51]

There are several ways to sponsor continuous change. Organizations must provide training to sell new ideas and note that they support the proposed change. Authority may be required to overcome organizational resistance. New behaviors must become deeply entrenched, so they are routine but not taken for granted by internal and external stakeholders. Innovation and strategic thinking must be fostered and promoted. Four organizational pathologies must be avoided: (1) creativity without learning, (2) institutionalization without creativity, (3) ideas without implementation, and (4) change without a strategy.[52]

Tools are available to facilitate organizational change. Their use depends upon the extent of what people agree on what they want, the results they seek from the change, and the sacrifices they are willing to make to achieve desired results. When consensus is absent, leaders must use "power tools" (fiat, force, coercion, and threats) to gain cooperation. When cooperation is present, training, and establishing operating procedures and measurement systems are in order.[53]

The success or failure of a planned change effort can usually be traced back to the attitudes of those to be affected by the change. Police officers must be convinced they will benefit from any proposed change or at least not be adversely affected by it. A history of fair, honest, and competent management lays a foundation for trust and the acceptance of change. The police manager must also present a sense of what the change involves and what employees should do—he or she should provide direction and be patient.[54]

Evaluation

Evaluation must not be the "missing link" in planned-change efforts. Ideally, plans for the evaluation of the change effort should be built into the planning process from the beginning. Typically, the following evaluation tasks must be conducted to provide information that will guide the entire planned-change effort:[55]

1. Verify that resources are devoted to meeting previously unmet needs.
2. Verify that planned programs provide services.
3. Examine (monitor) the results.
4. Determine which services provide the best results.
5. Select the programs that offer the most-needed types of services.
6. Provide information needed to maintain and improve quality.
7. Watch for unplanned side effects.

The evaluation must be designed to provide feedback from program activities. This feedback forms part of an information loop to improve service delivery and performance. The feedback portion of the loop begins with the monitoring function, which determines whether the service has been delivered as designed. It will also determine whether the program has been effective and whether it should be continued, expanded, or terminated.

CASE STUDY   Commander Jerry Spore

Jerry Spore was disgusted. As commander of the 10th Division of the Metropolitan Police Department (MPD), he had just issued an ultimatum to Deputy Chief Robert Powell. All officers not in compliance with the new uniform standards within two weeks' time would be issued official reprimands that carry time-off-without-pay sanctions. He just couldn't understand what the problem was.

It all began two years ago, when a group of city officials responded to complaints from citizens about the military design of MPD officers' uniforms. Until that time, officers still donned the old-fashioned eight-pointed hat. Their other accessories were also traditional in style. Leather Sam Browne belts were worn over leather pant belts. Gun holsters, cuffs, and other equipment pertinent to the job were attached to the Sam Browne belts. City officials perceived citizens' comments to be reflective of the total MPD image, and they prompted Spore to work on improving that image by modifying the uniforms.

Continued

Spore took the task seriously. He formed a committee of local citizens and business people to research and evaluate possible uniform modifications. Uniform suppliers called on the committee and encouraged them to adopt coordinated uniforms and accessories designed to maximize utility. The committee's conclusions were that they could get a lot of "bang for their buck" by simply changing key accessories in the uniform. They recommended that the city purchase new Sam Browne belts, new pant belts, and new rounded-top hats for the officers. The committee recommended that the uniforms be introduced in the police academy, and then adopted by the entire force over a period of six months, allowing for ample acquisition and distribution time.

All new recruits, therefore, were issued new belts and hats, as were all experienced officers. The hats were accepted almost without comment, but the belts met with resistance. The outside of the pant's belt was Velcro, as was the inside of the Sam Browne belt, thus allowing them to be conveniently attached. Belt closures were also Velcro. The belts required less maintenance and were slightly less expensive than the former standard belts.

Officers claimed that the rigid Velcro backing cut the pant's loops. They also said that the belts were uncomfortable to wear. Spore observed that the problem probably related more to obesity than to the belt design. The more portly officers were accustomed to wearing their belts low, under their abdomens, and the backing material on

the new belts did not cooperate. A few of the older officers also complained that the new belts were dangerous. They argued that each officer placed tools necessary for protection in a slightly different spot on the belts, and that this change could actually cost an officer's life in an emergency situation.

Officers fresh out of the academy discarded the new Velcro-style belts and replaced them with leather versions. Anyone seen with a Velcro belt was labeled as "green," or "nerdy." The change had been completely ignored by the other officers, and apparently Powell had been reprimanded by the now-disbanded committee about the waste of its time and money.

Meanwhile, Powell had been given the task to shape up these officers. Powell sensed that there was a lot more than logic behind the officers' resistance. Powell judged that Spore had made one key mistake in handling this whole uniform business, and that mistake was affecting the entire change process. He didn't blame the officers for their gripes, but he knew that his own neck was on the line. Powell was only one year from retirement, and didn't want to blow things now.

Using change methods in this chapter, what do you think Spore's key mistake was? What were the forces for change behind the uniform use? Use a change model to recommend an ideal plan for making the transition to the new uniform.

SUMMARY

Change is a natural and inevitable aspect of organizational life. Police administrators are expected to cope with spontaneous change as well as to initiate, implement, manage, and evaluate planned change in their departments. Proactive managers are future-oriented. They are inclined to change things and chart new courses of action. Proactive managers anticipate change and are prepared to adapt to it. To be successful as change agents, managers must understand the internal (organizational) as well as external (environmental) factors pushing for change. Good administrators pay special attention to technological, sociocultural, and organizational factors.

Managers must know how to recognize the need for change. Faulty decision-making, functional failure, poor communication, and lack of innovation should be considered red flags. It is up to management to determine who or what to target for change. They also choose how to effect the change. The shared-power approach to organizational problem solving is gaining in popularity.

No matter which approach is used, the basic change process is the same. Successful change requires unfreezing the target organization, moving it to a new state, and refreezing the change to make it permanent. The dynamics of planned change involve pressure on, and arousal of, top management to take action; intervention by a respected person; diagnosis of the data and identification of the real problem; development of creative alternatives; experiments with the alternatives; and reinforcement of the results.

To be effective change agents, police administrators must work on their diagnostic skills. Identifying the right problem is half the battle won. Good managers reduce resistance to change by incorporating subordinates into the problem-solving process whenever it is feasible. The unilateral imposition of planned change is being abandoned by some police departments in favor of a combined top-down/bottom-up approach. Participatory management has become one of the most influential concepts in contemporary management theory.

Police administrators have a responsibility to assess the impact of a planned change regarding member behavior and organizational outcomes. If changes in behavior or outcomes are beneficial, they should be institutionalized through positive reinforcement techniques. Once refreezing has taken place, all changes must be passed on to others through the organization's socialization process. Modern police managers need to acquire an understanding of, and appreciation for, their role in the change process. One thing is certain: Police administrators will be spending more of their time initiating, implementing, and managing planned change during the next decade.

DISCUSSION TOPICS AND QUESTIONS

1. Define *change*. Explore the difference between spontaneous change and planned change. Which occurs more often?

2. What is a change agent? Why are proactive managers considered to be change agents? Explain your reasoning.

3. List and discuss the forces or pressures that precipitate the need for planned change in complex criminal justice organizations. Identify those that warrant special consideration.

4. When does a positive climate for planned change exist? What does willingness have to do with it? How would you hedge your bet to ensure that the planned change takes root and is institutionalized?

5. Identify the target areas in which planned change has been the most common. Describe each of these areas. Who is ultimately responsible for determining what is to be changed and how it is to be changed?

6. Describe the unfreezing, moving, and refreezing process as it relates to organizational change as well as personal behavior. Illustrate this process through the use of examples.

7. What are the six phases normally associated with any successful organizational change? Elaborate on each one, and show their dynamic relationship to one another.

8. Why do so many people resist substantive change in the workplace? If resistance is not all bad, what purpose does it serve?

9. What are the elements of the SARA model? How can it help guide the planned-change process?

10. Analyze a change that has occurred in your organization. Consider the following questions:

    a. How did the change come about?

    b. How did the change agent trigger the change? How was it brought forward? What was done and said? Was it implemented in a participatory or an authoritarian fashion?

    c. How did others in the organization react to the change? What was the nature of the resistance? How was it overcome?

    d. What was your initial reaction to the change? Did you support it initially, or were you won over?

    e. How is the change working out? Looking back, what would you have done differently if you were the change agent?

FOR FURTHER READING

Dorothy Guyot, "Bending Granite: Attempts to Change the Rank Structure of American Police Departments," *Journal of Police Science and Administration*, Vol. 7 (1979), pp. 253–284.

A classic article on the difficulties of establishing reform and change in police agencies.

Wayne N. Welsh and Phillip W. Harris, *Criminal Justice Policy and Planning* (Cincinnati, OH: Anderson, 2013).

This entire text is based on the planned-change model. It provides key examples of how criminal justice planning can benefit the entire system.

ENDNOTES

1. Douglas C. Eadie, "Leading and Managing Strategic Change," in J. L. Perry ed. *Handbook of Public Administration* (San Francisco, CA: Jossey-Bass, 1996), p. 499.

2. Alvin Toffler, *Future Shock* (New York: Bantom Books, 1972).

3. F. Ostroff, "Change Management in Government," *Harvard Business Review* (May 2006), pp. 1–8.

4. Robert B. Denhardt, Janet V. Denhardt, and Maria P. Aristigueta, *Managing Human Behavior in Public and Nonprofit Organizations* (Thousand Oaks, CA: Sage, 2015), p. 379.

5. Ramon J. Aldag and Loren W. Kuzuhara, *Organizational Behavior and Management* (Cincinnati, OH: South-Western, 2002), p. 479.

6. Wayne N. Welsh and Phillip W. Harris *Criminal Justice Policy and Planning* (Cincinnati, OH: Anderson, 2013), p. 9.

7. Stephen P. Robbins and Mary Coulter, *Management* (Upper Saddle River, NJ: Pearson Prentice Hall, 2018), p. 219.

8. Daniel Katz and Robert L. Kahn, *The Social Psychology of Organizations* (New York: Wiley, 1978).

9. Sheldon Greenberg and Edward A. Flynn, "Leadership and Managing Change," in W. A. Geller and D. W. Stephens eds. *Local Government Police Management* (Washington, D.C.: International City/County Management Association, 2004), p. 67.

10. Robbins and Coulter, *Management*, p. 215.

11. Gary Cordner, *Police Administration* (New York: Routledge, 2016), p. 148.

12. Robbins and Coulter, *Management*, p. 209.

13. Ibid., p. 210.

14. Gary Yukl, *Leadership in Organizations* (Upper Saddle River, NJ: Prentice Hall, 2013), p. 89.

15. Ibid., p. 90.

16. Ibid., pp. 84–88.

17. Alan W. Steiss, *Strategic Management for Public and Nonprofit Organizations* (New York: Marcel Dekker, 2003), pp. 278–279.

18. Yukl, *Leadership*, p. 84.

19. Ibid., pp. 84–88.

20. Welsh and Harris, *Criminal Justice Policy and Planning*, pp. 6–8.

21. Robbins and Coulter, *Management*, p. 210.

22. L. Miller, H. More, and M. Braswell, *Effective Police Supervision* (New York: Routledge, 2017), pp. 248–249.

23. Kurt Lewin, *Field Theory in Social Science* (New York: Harper & Row, 1951).

24. Edgar H. Schein, *Organizational Psychology* (Engelwood Cliffs, NJ: Prentice Hall, 1980).

25. Herman Goldstein, *Problem-Oriented Policing* (New York: McGraw-Hill, 1990).

26. John C. Eck and William Spelman, *Problem Solving: Problem-Oriented Policing in Newport News* (Washington, D.C.: Police Executive Research Forum, 1987).

27. Jeff Rojek, "A Decade of Excellence in Problem-Oriented Policing: Characteristics of the Goldstein Award Winners," *Police Quarterly*, Vol. 6, pp. 492–515.

28. Yukl, *Leadership*, pp. 82–83.

29. S. Robbins and T. Judge, *Organizational Behavior* (Upper Saddle River, NJ: Pearson Prentice Hall, 2013), p. 284.

30. Ibid., p. 285.

31. Larry E. Greiner, "Patterns of Organizational Change," *Harvard Business Review*, pp. 119–130.

32. Robbins and Judge, *Organizational Behavior*, p. 593.

33. H. G. Rainey, *Understanding and Managing Public Organizations* (San Francisco, CA: Jossey-Bass, 2014), p. 435.

34. Robbins and Judge, *Organizational Behavior*, p. 593.

35. Ibid.

36. Rainey, *Managing Public Organizations*, p. 423.

37. Robbins and Judge, *Organizational Behavior*, p. 582.

38. J. Schermerhorn, J. Hunt, R. Osborn, and M. Uhl-Bien, *Organizational Behavior* (Hoboken, NJ: John Wiley & Sons, 2010), p. 357.

39. Denhardt, Denhardt, and Aristigueta, *Managing Human Behavior*, p. 351.

40. Ibid., p. 352.

41. Dorothy Guyot, "Bending Granite: Attempts to Change the Rank Structure of American Police Departments," *Journal of Police Science and Administration*, Vol. 7 (1979), pp. 253–284.

42. Denhardt, Denhardt, and Aristigueta, *Managing Human Behavior*, p. 379.

43. Greenberg and Flynn, *Leadership and Change*, p. 73.

44. Robbins and Judge, *Organizational Behavior*, p. 255.

45. Ibid., p. 288.

46. Michael Beer, "Leading Change," *Harvard Business School*, No. 9–488–037, pp. 5–6.

47. Sergio Fernandez and Hal G. Rainey, "Managing Successful Organizational Change in the Public Sector," *Public Administration Review*, Vol. 66 (March/April 2006), pp. 169–173.

48. Frank Ostroff, "Change Management in Government," *Harvard Business Review*, Vol. 84 (May 2006), pp. 142–151.

49. Paul M. Whisenand, *Supervising Police Personnel: The Fifteen Responsibilities* (Upper Saddle River, NJ: Prentice Hall, 2007), p. 134.

50. Keith Ferrazzi, "Managing Change, One Day at a Time," *Harvard Business Review* (July–August 2014), pp. 2–4.

51. Julie Battilana and Tiziana Casciaro, "The Network Secrets of Great Change Agents," *Harvard Business Review* (July–August 2013), pp. 2–8.

52. Thomas B. Lawrence, Bruno Dyck, Sally Maitlis, and Michael K. Mauws, "The Underlying Structure of Continuous Change," *MIT Sloan Management Review*, Vol. 47, No. 4 (2006), pp. 59–66.

53. Clayton M. Christensen, Matt Marx, and Howard H. Stevenson, "The Tools of Cooperation and Change," *Harvard Business Review* (October 2006), pp. 1–9.

54. E. J. Posevac and R. G. Carey, *Program Evaluation: Methods and Case Studies* (Upper Saddle River, NJ: Prentice Hall, 2003), pp. 3–6.

55. Whisenand, *Supervising Police Personnel*, pp. 126–127.

Index